Handbook on International Trade Policy

Edited by

William A. Kerr
University of Saskatchewan, Canada

James D. Gaisford
University of Calgary, Canada

IN ASSOCIATION WITH THE ESTEY CENTRE FOR LAW AND ECONOMICS
IN INTERNATIONAL TRADE

Edward Elgar
Cheltenham, UK • Northampton, MA, USA

Published by
Edward Elgar Publishing Limited
Glensanda House
Montpellier Parade
Cheltenham
Glos GL50 1UA
UK

Edward Elgar Publishing, Inc.
William Pratt House
9 Dewey Court
Northampton
Massachusetts 01060
USA

A catalogue record for this book
is available from the British Library

Library of Congress Cataloguing in Publication Data

Handbook on international trade policy / edited by William A. Kerr, James D. Gaisford.
    p.   cm. — (Elgar original reference)
  Includes bibliographical references and index.
  1. Commercial policy. 2. International trade. 3. Commercial treaties.
  I. Kerr, William A. (William Alexander) II. Gaisford, James D.
  HF1411.H2575   2006
  382′.3—dc22   2006023684

ISBN 978 1 84376 939 2 (cased)

Printed and bound in Great Britain by MPG Books Ltd, Bodmin, Cornwall

Contents

Contributors

Arashiro, Zuleika
Senior Researcher, Brazilian Institute for International Trade Negotiations (ICONE), São Paulo, Brazil

Barichello, Richard
Associate Professor, Faculty of Land and Food Systems, University of British Colombia, Canada

Baylis, Katherine
Assistant Professor, Faculty of Land and Food Systems, University of British Columbia, Canada

Beaulieu, Eugene
Associate Professor, Department of Economics, University of Calgary, Canada

Belcher, Ken
Associate Professor, Department of Agricultural Economics, University of Saskatchewan, Canada

Benarroch, Michael
Professor, Department of Econonomics, University of Winnipeg, Canada

Copeland, Brian R.
Professor, Department of Economics, University of British Columbia, Canada

Cranfield, John
Associate Professor, Department of Food, Agricultural and Resource Economics, University of Guelph, Canada

Gaisford, James
Professor, Department of Economics, University of Calgary, Canada

Gerber, James B.
Professor of Economics and Director, Center for Latin American Studies, San Diego State University, USA

Gervais, Jean-Philippe
Canada Research Chair in Agro-Industry and International Trade, Centre for Research on the Economics of Agri-Food (CREA), University of Laval, Canada

Gilbert, Christopher L.
Professor, Interdepartmental Centre for Research in Economics and Management, University of Trento, Italy

Hester, Annette
Special Research Fellow, Centre for International Governance Innovation, Waterloo, Canada

Hobbs, Jill E.
Professor, Department of Agricultural Economics, University of Saskatchewan, Canada

Hufbauer, Gary
Reginald Jones Senior Fellow, Institute for International Economics, Washington, DC, USA

Isaac, Grant E.
Dean and Professor, College of Commerce, University of Saskatchewan, Canada

Ivus, Olena
Doctoral Student, University of Calgary, Canada

Jank, Marcos S.
President, Brazilian Institute for International Trade Negotiations (ICONE), São Paulo, Brazil

Josling, Tim
Senior Fellow, Freeman-Spogli Institute for International Studies, Stanford University, USA

Kendall, Lindsay
Graduate Student, University of Calgary, Canada

Kerr, William A.
Van Vliet Professor, University of Saskatchewan, Canada and Senior Associate, Estey Centre for Law and Economics in International Trade, Saskatoon, Canada

Lang, Sarah
Graduate Student, University of Calgary, Canada

Larue, Bruno
Canada Research Chair in International Agri-Food Trade, Centre for Research on the Economics of Agri-Food (CREA), University of Laval, Canada

Lau, Carol Chui-Ha
Lecturer, Concordia University, Montreal, QC, Canada

Leger, Lawrence
Senior Lecturer, Department of Economics, Loughborough University, United Kingdom

Loppacher, Laura J.
Research Associate, Estey Centre for Law and Economics in International Trade, Saskatoon, Canada

Lutz, Stefan
Lecturer, University of Manchester, School of Economic Studies, United Kingdom and Senior Fellow, Center for European Integration Studies (ZEI), Bonn, Germany

Maneschi, Andrea
Professor of Economics, Vanderbilt University, Nashville, USA

Meilke, Karl D.
Professor, Department of Food, Agricultural and Resource Economics, University of Guelph, Canada

Miner, William M.
Research Associate, Centre for Trade Policy and Law, Ottawa, Canada

Nassar, André M.
General Manager, Brazilian Institute for International Trade Negotiations (ICONE), São Paulo, Brazil

Oegg, Barbara
Consultant, Institute for International Economics, Washington, DC, USA

Perdikis, Nicholas
Senior Lecturer, School of Management and Business, University of Wales – Aberystwyth, UK

Phillips, Peter W. B.
Professor, Political Studies, University of Saskatchewan, Canada

Read, Robert
Senior Lecturer, Department of Economics, Lancaster University Management School, UK

Rude, James
Assistant Professor, Agribusiness and Agricultural Economics, University of Manitoba, Canada

Scholefield, Ryan
Graduate Student, University of Calgary, Canada

Skully, David
Professor, Department of Economics and Social Science, BRAC University, Dhaka, Bangladesh

Strong, Aaron
Post Doctoral Research Fellow, University of Calgary, Canada

Weintraub, Sidney
Dean Rusk Professor Emeritus, Lyndon B. Johnson School of Public Affairs, University of Texas at Austin and William E. Simon Chair in Political Economy, Center for Strategic and International Studies, Washington, D.C.

Whalley, John
University of Western Ontario, Canada and NBER, USA

Young, Linda M.
Assistant Professor, Department of Political Science, Montana State University, USA

Abbreviations

AARQ	Association for the Administration of Rice Quotas, Inc
ACM	Arable Common Market
ACP	African, Caribbean and Pacific countries
AD	anti-dumping
AIDS	Acquired Immune Deficiency Syndrome
ANZFTA	Australia–New Zealand Free Trade Area
APEC	Asia-Pacific Economic Cooperation
ASCM	Agreement on Subsidies and Countervailing Measures
ASEAN	Association of South East Asian Nations
AVE	*ad valorem* equivalent
BDH	Bhagwati–Dehejia hypothesis
BPTs	British Preferential Tariffs
CAC	Codex Alimentarius Commission
CACM	Central American Common Market
CAP	Common Agricultural Policy
CARICOM	Caribbean Community and Common Market
CBSA	Canada Border Services Agency
CCC	Commodity Credit Corporation
CEFTA	Central European Free Trade Agreement
CES	constant elasticity of substitution
CET	Common External Tariff
CGE	computable general equilibrium
CIF	Cost, Insurance and Freight
CIS	Commonwealth of Independent States
CITES	Convention on International Trade in Endangered Species
CITT	Canadian International Trade Tribunal
CM	Common Market
CODEX	Codex Alimentarius Commission
CP	Contracting Parties
CRS	constant returns to scale
CRTA	Committee on Regional Trade Agreements
CSCE	Coffee, Sugar and Cocoa Exchange
CU	Customs Union
CUSTA	Canada–US Free Trade Agreement
CVD	countervailing duty
DDA	Doha Development Agenda
DOC	Department of Commerce
DSB	Dispute Settlement Body

DSM	Dispute Settlement Mechanism
DSU	Dispute Settlement Understanding
EAC	East African Community
EC	European Community
ECLA	Economic Commission for Latin America
ECLAC	Economic Commission for Latin America and the Caribbean
ECOWAS	Economic Community of West African States
EEA	European Economic Area
EEC	European Economic Community
EFTA	European Free Trade Area
EMAA	Euro-Mediterranean Association Agreements
EPZ	export processing zone
ERP	effective rate of protection
EU	European Union
EV	equivalent variations
FAO	Food and Agriculture Organization
FCFS	first-come-first-served
FDI	foreign direct investment
FOB	free on board
FSU	Former Soviet Union
FTA	Free Trade Area
FTAA	Free Trade Area of the Americas
GATS	General Agreement on Trade in Services
GATT	General Agreement on Tariffs and Trade
GCC	Gulf Cooperation Council
GDP	gross domestic product
GHG	greenhouse gas
GM	genetically modified
GMO	genetically modified organism
GNP	Gross National Product
GPA	Government Procurement Agreement
GSP	General(ized) System(s) of Preferences
GTAP	Global Trade Analysis Project
HIV	Human Immunodeficiency Virus
HOS	Heckscher–Ohlin–Samuelson Model
IBC	Instituto Brasiliero do Cafe
IBRD	International Bank for Reconstruction and Development (World Bank)
ICA	International Commodity Agreement
ICCA	International Cocoa Agreement
ICO	International Coffee Organization

ICOA	International Coffee Agreement
ICTSD	International Centre for Trade and Sustainable Development
IEC	International Electrotechnical Commission
IIE	Institute for International Economics
IISD	International Institute for Sustainable Development
IIT	intra-industry trade
IIWD	inter-industry wage differentials
IMF	International Monetary Fund
INRA	International Natural Rubber Agreement
IPC	Integrated Programme for Commodities
IPPC	International Plant Protection Convention
IPRs	Intellectual Property Rights
IRS	increasing returns to scale
ISA	International Sugar Agreement
ISI	import substitution industrialization
ISO	International Organization for Standardization
ITA	International Tin Agreement
ITA	International Trade Authority
ITC	International Trade Commission
ITO	International Trade Organization
ITU	International Telecommunication Union
IWA	International Wheat Agreement
LAFTA	Latin American Free Trade Area
LCE	London Commodity Exchange
LDCs	Least Developed Countries
MC	marginal cost
MC	Monopolistic Competition
MEA	Multilateral Environmental Agreement
MERCOSUR	Southern Common Market (Brazil, Argentina, Paraguay, Uruguay)
MFA	Multifibres Arrangement (Agreement)
MFN	Most Favored Nation
MITI	Japanese Ministry of International Trade and Industry
MOU	Memorandum of Understanding
NAFTA	North American Free Trade Agreement
NAMA	non-agricultural goods market access
NEP	National Energy Program
NIC	newly industrializing country
NIEO	New International Economic Order
NRP	national rate tariff
NTBs	non-tariff barriers
OECD	Organisation for Economic Co-operation and Development
OFAC	US Treasury Department Office of Foreign Assets Control

OIE	International Office of Epizootics (World Animal Health Organization)
OPEC	Organization of the Petroleum Exporting Countries
PDO	Protected Designation of Origin
PGI	Protected Geographical Indication
PND	principle of non-discrimination
PPM	process and production methods
	nprPPM non-product-related PPM
	prPPM product-related PPM
PTAs	Preferential Trade Agreements
R&D	Research and Development
REPA	regional economic partnership arrangement
RFA	Risk Analysis Framework
ROO	rules of origin
ROW	Rest of World
RTA	Reciprocal Trade Agreements Act
RTA	Regional Trade Agreement
S&D	Special and Differential
SAM	social accounting matrix
SCM	Subsidies and Countervailing Measures
SDNT	Specially Designated Narcotics Traffickers
SDR	Special Drawing Rights
SDT	special and differential treatment
SLA	Softwood Lumber Agreement
SPS	Sanitary and Phytosanitary Measures
SST	Stolper–Samuelson Theorem
STE	State Trading Enterprise
TBT	Technical Barriers to Trade
TBT Agreement	Agreement on Technical Barriers to Trade
TRIMs	Trade Related Investment Measures
TRIPS	Agreement on Trade Related Aspects of Intellectual Property
TRQ	Tariff Rate Quota
UHT	ultra high temperature
UK	United Kingdom
UN	United Nations
UNCITRAL	United Nations Commission on International Trade Law
UNCTAD	UN Conference on Trade and Development
UNESCO	UN Economic and Social Council
UNITA	National Union for the Total Independence of Angola
URA	Uruguay Round Agreement
URAA	Uruguay Round Agreement on Agriculture

US	United States
USD	US dollars
USITC	US International Trade Commission
VERs	Voluntary Export Restraints
WIPO	World Intellectual Property Organization
WTO	World Trade Organization
WVS	World Values Survey
WWII	Second World War

Preface

Controversy over the conduct and coordination of international trade policy has become a politically charged issue in current times. At the World Trade Organization Ministerial Conference in Seattle in 1999, groups from civil society went to the barricades to protest various facets of 'globalization'. Similar spectacles have been repeated around the world frequently since that time. The debates over international trade policy are no longer the exclusive purview of academic economists, trade lawyers, bureaucrats and politicians. Suddenly, discussion concerning trade policy and trade agreements has burst out of the back rooms and into the limelight.

This handbook on international trade policy includes a comprehensive spectrum of trade-policy topics that should be attractive to both practitioners and interested observers alike. The coverage ranges from very general issues, such as why trade agreements exist, to highly specific issues, such as how politics affects the administration tariff-rate quotas. The contributors bring considerable expertise and insight to their topics, and they have set themselves an ambitious agenda that goes far beyond a simple review of academic literature. The intention throughout the volume has been to analyze how trade policy works and to assess the issues and controversies that have arisen in practice. Further, the volume is addressed to a broad policy audience. It has been designed to be accessible to those who have only an introductory knowledge of economics, and come to trade policy from a wide variety of occupational and academic backgrounds. The emphasis has been on readability. While diagrammatic methods of analysis are used to help systematically present some topics, the authors have avoided resorting to mathematical arguments in the text of their chapters. Where useful, appendixes have been provided.

The editors would like to thank the management and staff at Edward Elgar for their interest and assistance with this project. We also gratefully acknowledge the organizational support of the Estey Centre for Law and Economics in International Trade in Saskatoon, Saskatchewan. Laura Loppacher at the Estey Centre and Francine O'Sullivan and Suzanne Mursell at Edward Elgar deserve special recognition for their efforts behind the scenes, which have brought this project to fruition. Finally, we are very appreciative of the cooperation and enthusiasm of the contributing authors who have made the assembly of this volume a very pleasant task.

James Gaisford, Calgary, Canada
William Kerr, Saskatoon, Canada

1   Introduction to trade policy
William A. Kerr

The study of international trade by economists can be roughly divided into three general areas of inquiry: (a) trade theory; (b) empirical studies of trade; and (c) trade policy. The former seeks fundamental insights through the rigorous application of structural formalism and tightly specified assumptions. Empirical studies test the propositions of trade theory (Perdikis and Kerr, 1998) or attempt to garner insights from the statistical evidence pertaining to trade flows and related economic indicators. Trade policy deals with the economic effects of direct or indirect government intervention that alters the environment under which international transactions take place. Work in trade theory is most often undertaken within a *general equilibrium* context while trade policy, for the most part, is accomplished using *partial equilibrium* analysis. Trade policy deals with the winners and losers that arise from government intervention in markets. Vested interests are at the heart of trade policy, with government actions viewed as redistributive and open to influence. It has been the subject of many of the great economic debates of the last two and a half centuries and still provides topics that are hotly contested in the academic, political and civil society arenas.

Trade policy has been around since the dawning of economic science. While Adam Smith (1776)[1] may have had a number of motivations for writing *The Wealth of Nations*, there can be little doubt that a central task was to debunk the intellectual respectability of mercantilism – a trade policy prescription that favoured exports and eschewed imports. It can be argued that the development of trade policy since Smith's time has consisted of the gradual stripping away of the intellectual legitimacy of various protectionist theories that have attempted to identify narrow vested interests with the general good. Trade theory evolved from this process as economists sought ever greater intellectual rigour in trying to understand the underlying welfare implications of an economy choosing (or not) to engage in international trade. As trade theory fundamentally came down on the side of trade liberalization it was enlisted in the service of trade policy. The result of these endeavours has been to raise the cost of obtaining protection from those involved in the political process. Protectionists, however, have proved to be both formidable and tenacious – as one would expect as there is often much at stake.

The analysis undertaken in trade policy has, over time, had to deal with increasingly complex issues. In part this is a result of the expanding set of constraints that have been imposed on trade policy makers as trade liberalization has become a generally accepted goal of governments. This has often meant that governments have agreed to constraints on the use of direct trade policy instruments such as border taxes. Faced with these constraints, less straightforward and transparent trade policy measures may have to be devised when the politicians need to respond to protectionists' requests that arise.

In addition, the Great Depression of the 1930s which induced an era of high trade barriers – particularly tariffs – overlapped, to a considerable degree, with the Keynesian revolution that brought a general expansion in the role of government in the economy.

A myriad of subsidies, redistributive policies and regulations were put in place behind high tariff walls and without any regard for their potential effects on international commerce.

Over the long process of liberalization, particularly in developed countries, that began with the coming into force of the General Agreement on Tariffs and Trade (GATT) in 1947, tariffs were progressively removed and firms engaging in international trade increasingly found domestic policies in importing countries acting to inhibit the opportunities they could identify. As a result, trade policy analysis has had to examine questions that were long considered in the purview of domestic policy. Determining the trade effects of domestic policies is often much more complex than that associated with border measures. Further, as most domestic policies that inhibit trade have a domestic policy objective, questions of legitimacy often arise. This is particularly important given the temptation to respond to protectionist requests by imposing nefarious policies or regulations justified on the basis of some supposed domestic imperative. Trade policy interfaces increasingly with science (for example food safety, the environment), with analysis of consumer preferences (for example animal welfare, child labour) and social policy (for example sustainable development, labour standards). As a result, trade policy analysis has been broadened to include questions such as: What is the appropriate degree of caution in the face of scientific uncertainty?; Can the regulation of imports be enlisted to foster dolphin-friendly fishing methods?; or Is the regulation of the trade in rhinoceros horns likely to aid in the preservation of the species? These are competencies that have not been typically expected from trade economists.

Trade policy also deals with institutions and questions relating to the efficacy of those institutions. Governments have concluded a host of multilateral, regional and bilateral agreements and arrangements to manage trade. These agreements cover a host of topics from rules for trade in goods, to rules for trade in services, the international protection of intellectual property, what constitutes unfair trade, the regulation of international investment, when sanctions can be applied and what forms of subsidies are allowed, to name only a few. In some cases these rules have a sound economic underpinning such as the official preference for tariffs relative to other border measures while others, such as those pertaining to dumping, have only the most tenuous grounding in economic theory. Their application, however, will have economic consequences that can be illuminated through economic analysis.

The relative merit of various institutional arrangements, whether they are multilateral, plurilateral, regional, bilateral, unilateral or autarkic are also active topics of research interest in the trade policy area. There are literally thousands of agreements among countries that regulate trade in some fashion from the 140 member plus World Trade Organization to bilateral arrangements on the appropriate forms veterinarians can use to certify meat fit for export. There are agreements dealing with the classification of goods for tariff purposes, on how to value goods for the collection of tariffs and on how new products will be incorporated into the trade nomenclature. Even such apparently innocuous topics as tariff classification can have considerable economic ramifications and become contentious trade policy questions.

The development of trade policy is almost always contentious. At its most basic, this is because any change to trading arrangements among countries will lead to winners and losers. Of course, winners and losers will arise from a change in any government policy. The interesting question is why trade policy changes are consistently the subject of acrimonious debate. Part of the reason is that there is an expectation that governments should have as their primary concern the welfare of their own citizens. In many cases, changes in trade policy may be to the detriment of domestic vested interests and to the benefit of foreign competitors. For example, the removal of a tariff will be to the detriment of domestic firms whose markets have been protected and to the benefit of foreign competitors. From the perspective of the firms that lose from this trade policy change, their government is acting contrary to their expectations. Of course, this perspective fails to acknowledge the larger benefit domestic consumers reap from lower prices. Further, the losers are often confined to a few firms, which suffer commensurately larger losses. The consumers who benefit from the change in trade policy, on the other hand, each receive only a small benefit, and hence may not have a strong incentive to actively engage in activities that influence trade policy makers. The result is that public disagreements over trade policy are seldom undertaken in the context of dispassionate academic debate. They are full of rhetoric against 'cheap foreign goods ruining the market' and 'low paid foreigners stealing our jobs'. If protectionists win their arguments and liberalization does not take place there is no way to establish if their claims are true while if they lose the argument and liberalization takes place, the winners have no incentive to investigate the protectionists claims (Kerr and Foregrave 2002). As a result, there is an incentive to exaggerate claims regarding the expected losses from trade liberalization. Further, those who expect to lose from a change in trade policy have an incentive to attempt to associate their cause with the 'general good' so that their rent seeking activities have a cloak of legitimacy. Latterly, traditional commercial protectionist interests have been joined by civil society activists who are often characterized as being 'anti-globalization' and see the loss of 'local control' that arises from trade liberalization commitments as a major and visible manifestation of globalization. Their concerns have attracted a considerable constituency and resources and have brought new issues that have had to be accommodated in trade policy analysis. As a result, public debates pertaining to trade policy are often joined by well financed advocates. Their arguments are sophisticated and well targeted to sway policy makers and garner valuable support from the broad civil society. Given the degree of protection manifest in the trade policies of all but a handful of countries, these advocates and the interests they represent have enjoyed considerable success. The existence and ongoing development of trade policies that fly in the face of social welfare maximization suggests that trade policy analysis must extend beyond neoclassical-based welfare analysis and incorporate political economy elements such as rent seeking behaviour, political decision making and game theory.

Game theory also has a role in explaining the actions of states both in their trade strategies and the strategies employed during negotiations pertaining to the institutional rules under which trade can be conducted. Game theory and other aspects of modern industrial organization theory including transaction costs and New Institutional Economics have been adapted for, and harnessed to, the analysis of trade policy.

The workhorse of trade policy analysis, however, remains partial equilibrium, comparative static analysis. With all its shortcomings – inability to encompass general equilibrium interactions or to provide dynamic paths of adjustment – it provides the flexibility needed to handle complex markets and a wide variety of institutional arrangements that act to inhibit or enhance international trade. It also has the advantage of generally being accessible to a broad audience without advanced training in economics and its usefulness in undertaking analysis is not restricted to a relatively narrow group of academics. Further, its data requirements tend to be relatively modest thus allowing analysts to investigate topical questions. Of course, many trade policy practitioners use the most up-to-date empirical techniques and data intensive methods.

Trade policy is often undertaken at the interface of economics and law. International trade law is largely the outgrowth of international treaties although it has aspects that are rooted in the domestic trade laws of individual nation states and the conventions of international commerce that preceded more formal international institutions. The causality runs both ways. Economic (and commercial) considerations often drive the interest in codifying the ways in which government policy is allowed to interfere with the flow of goods and services across national boundaries. Firms that invest in international commercial activities generally want strong restrictions on the ability of governments to alter the commercial environment after their investments are made. Weak rules increase the risks associated with investing in international commerce and lead to opportunities forgone. Politicians, on the other hand, while generally understanding the benefits of liberal trade, want to be able to respond to requests for protection (or other trade distorting requests such as for the subsidization of exports) from their domestic constituents. Their political survival may well depend on being able to acquiesce to these requests. The constitution of international trade law at any point in time tends to reflect a compromise between these two forces. Thus, business people and other members of civil society often find international trade law frustrating because it does not provide the predictability that one generally expects from domestic legal systems, at least those in modern market economies. The compromise between the two forces tends to ebb and flow depending on the general state of the world economy. When the international economy is performing robustly, and hence it is easier to find new opportunities or otherwise accommodate through social policy those who would be losers from changes in trade policy, trade liberalization through greater restrictions on the trade inhibiting activities of governments tends to strengthen. Conversely, when global economic activity slows, politicians are faced with rising unemployment and fewer new opportunities for trade displaced workers and less tax resources with which to fund social policies. Requests for protection tend to rise and become more strident. As a result, trade liberalization tends to be officially put on hold and trade more restricted in fact.

Given the interplay of these two forces, it is probably not surprising that the codification of the economics of trade policy into international trade law requires long and difficult negotiations and precise but not necessarily predictable language. Trade policy analysis is required to understand the effects of governments' intervention in markets and to assist in the construction of the formal legal texts that constitute trade agreements.

Once the formal legal texts come into force, however, the causality begins to run the other way. As governments put in place policies within the constraints imposed by their formal international obligations, their effect on individual markets and trade patterns becomes the subject of economic analysis. In some international trade agreements there is an obligation to use the policy to achieve the domestic goal that distorts trade the least. Thus, a range of trade policy measures may have to be evaluated either by the imposing country to ensure that it is living up to its international obligations or by trading partners to ensure that the imposing country is not violating its obligations to their detriment.

If the application and legal interpretation of currently agreed international law proves too lax or too strict to achieve economic goals, then economic analysis is applied to formulating new negotiating positions and the causality is again reversed. Of course, proposals by individual countries or groups of countries need to be evaluated as to their economic effect by trade partners that will also be engaged in the negotiations and other interested groups in civil society. Thus, international trade policy is developed through the interaction of economic analysis and law formulation. Of course, trade law and economic analysis do not always develop in lock-step and trade law can, at times, be at odds with sound economic analysis (for example as is currently the case with anti-dumping (Kerr 2006)). Large divergences between international law and economically justified trade policy tend to become points of international tension where the confrontation between liberalization and protectionism become highly visible and politicized. One example is the treatment of agricultural trade in the General Agreement on Tariffs and Trade (GATT) where waivers from general GATT disciplines had long been granted. The waivers allowed the international markets for agricultural products to become heavily distorted over time. The economic consequences of the absence of disciplines on the policy making activities of governments began to spill over into other aspects of international commercial relations and, indeed, broader aspects of states' international relations. The result was, after admittedly acrimonious and prolonged negotiations in the GATT's Uruguay Round (1986–1994), an agreement to move the rules of trade for agricultural commodities towards conformity with general GATT disciplines, albeit without a pre-specified timetable. Thus, it is important to understand the economic forces that underpin the transboundary movement of goods and services and their interaction with government policies because simply interpreting existing international trade law does not provide insights into the stresses that can arise from interference in international markets. As trade policy is highly interdependent with international trade law, it is also concerned with the evaluation of the institutions that are put in place to administer international trade law and to handle other facets of trade relations such as negotiations and trade capacity building in developing countries. In some cases formal dispute settlement mechanisms have been built into international trade law institutions so that trade law, and its economic analysis, evolve through quasi-judicial interpretation.

Although formal trade facilitation/regulation institutions have probably existed as long as firms in different countries have engaged in international trade and came into prominence during the nineteenth century (for example the Zollverein and Steuerverein among various German states), it was not until the formal restructuring and structuring of international institutions by the victors of the Second World War that the modern era of international trade institutions came into being. The late nineteenth and first half of the twentieth century was characterized by technological innovations that allowed for international commerce to be conducted on a grand scale for the first time. These innovations related primarily to cost reductions and reliability improvements in transportation but also included time reducing revolutions in communications and new forms of organization for the management and financing of commercial activities. International institutions, however, were largely absent and those that did exist were limited in scope and in the constraints their commitments imposed on sovereignty. The experience of the Great Depression of the 1930s and the subsequent hostilities, along with the increased acceptance of the role of government that arose in the wake of the application of Keynesian economics (broadly defined) suggested to the peacemakers that international co-ordinating institutions were required to reduce the tensions that arise in international relations. In particular, there was a perception that the risks associated with the ability of countries to restrict trading access to resources was responsible, in part, for the military-based expansionism of the defeated Axis powers. Absence of co-ordinating mechanisms and institutional avenues to air and settle grievances were seen as a major institutional failure that contributed to the outbreak of the two world wars that defined the first half of the twentieth century. New institutions were required.

Four major areas where international tensions could arise were identified: (a) political disputes between states; (b) the strategic use of currency devaluation to gain a trade advantage; (c) the use of trade distorting measures; and (d) differences in levels of average national income. Prior to the Second World War there had only been an attempt at institutional co-ordination in the area of political disputes between states – the ill-fated League of Nations. Learning from the League's deficiencies, a new institution to deal with political disputes between states was created, the United Nations. To deal with the problems created by the strategic use of currency devaluation, the International Monetary Fund was created at negotiations which took place in Bretton Woods, New Hampshire in the United States. At the same venue, the International Bank for Reconstruction and Development (IBRD) – which is more commonly referred to as the World Bank – with the objective of fostering first post-war economic recovery and, in the longer term, economic development was also put in place.

To provide rules for international commercial relations and a mechanism for dealing with trade disputes, a fourth institution, the International Trade Organization (ITO) was also negotiated. These four organizations were to be the basis of a new and peaceful ordering of international relations. The ITO, however, was stillborn. While it had been negotiated by the administrative arm of the US government, there was not sufficient support in the US Congress for its ratification and it was, in the end, never submitted for a Congressional vote. Given US hegemony in global economic affairs in the early years after the Second World War, the ITO made little sense without the participation of the US and it was abandoned.

The ITO was conceived as a comprehensive international trade organization. One of its agreements dealt with rules of trade for goods and provided a mechanism for the reduction of tariffs. This agreement – The General Agreement on Tariffs and Trade – was salvaged from the ashes of the ITO and became the *de facto* multilateral institution dealing with international trade issues. One of its primary purposes was to provide a venue for the negotiation of the reduction of the very high tariffs that had been put in place during the Great Depression and remained in place in the late 1940s. Given there had been no effective restrictions on a country's ability to unilaterally impose trade barriers prior to the GATT, tariffs were the primary trade restricting mechanism in use. Thus, the relatively narrow mandate of the GATT was sufficient to foster a considerable degree of trade liberalization in its early years. This was accomplished through a number of negotiating 'Rounds' that took place periodically. In all, between 1947 when the GATT came into being and 1994 there were six Rounds. All made significant cuts to industrial tariffs. The negotiating Rounds each took longer to accomplish and became increasingly complex. In part this was because the number of member states increased, particularly in the wake of the process of de-colonization, and as the organization gained in prestige and impact. Negotiations also increased in complexity as other trade distorting policies of governments were encountered once border measures were reduced or removed. Further, as the

GATT prohibited new tariffs and did not allow existing tariffs to be raised above agreed levels (their 'bound' rate) governments faced with the political need to placate protectionists had to find alternative means to deliver protection (for example technical requirements). The result was that new topics were added to the GATT negotiating agendas, particularly in the later Rounds. Over time, however, the GATT's narrow mandate and institutional limitations became increasingly out of step with the requirements of modern international commercial relations.

At the last GATT Round of negotiations, the Uruguay Round, a reconstitution of the organization took place with a new organization, the World Trade Organization (WTO) coming into being in 1995. The GATT as an organization ceased to exist and the WTO took over the administration of a revised GATT agreement. The old GATT had not dealt with trade in services, which had become the fastest growing sector in modern market economies. During the Uruguay Round a new General Agreement on Trade in Services (GATS) was negotiated to be administered by the new WTO. More contentious, the WTO was also given responsibility for administering the new Agreement on Trade Related Aspects of Intellectual Property (TRIPS). Thus, the trade policy envelope was increased significantly with the establishment of the WTO.

The GATT, and subsequently the WTO, allows for the creation of regional trade agreements as long as they do not contradict commitments agreed at the multilateral organization. As a result, there is a plethora of regional and bilateral trade agreements, all with their own sets of rules and whose rulemaking covers areas of trade policy where the WTO is silent. Hence, the analysis undertaken in trade policy extends to topics that are beyond the institutional reach of the WTO.

The operation of trade institutions themselves can have trade effects. For example, the dispute settlement process has lags that can be used as a strategic advantage; if countries refuse to comply with dispute panel rulings, the aggrieved country is allowed to choose the products it selects for retaliation; and the process of acceding to the WTO allows existing members to extract concessions from applicants. The opportunities for engaging in strategic behaviour that are created by the rules of the institutions are also analysed by trade policy practitioners. The negotiation process has tended to be opaque. This lack of transparency has been the source of considerable criticism from activist civil society groups in recent years. As a result, the WTO and other trade institutions have been trying to become more transparent but there is a trade off between transparency and negotiating efficiency that is a contentious issue and a subject for trade policy analysis.

The questions encompassed by trade policy are clearly wide ranging and multi-faceted. Its study draws upon a wide range of economic theories, approaches and analytical tools. The mechanisms used by trade policy makers are only constrained by the inventiveness of the bureaucrats and others who devise them. The set of measures is not static and is ever expanding. The focus of the study of trade policy changes as new issues and problems arise. Those who work in the area need to update their human capital on an ongoing basis.

While there are few constants in this dynamic area of economic inquiry, one stands out in its persistence. The desire for protection from deteriorating economic circumstances whether or not the source of declining competitiveness is of foreign origin. As long as declining economic fortunes can be altered by imposing costs on foreigners, one can expect requests for protectionist trade policies. Foreign firms are always softer targets than domestic competitors, it is the 'real politik' of trade. Without this constant, however, there would be little need for the study of trade policy.

Note

1.   There are many versions of Adam Smith's classic. One accessible version is Smith (1994).

References

Kerr, W. A. (2006), 'Dumping – Trade Policy in Need of a Theoretical Make Over', *Canadian Journal of Agricultural Economics*, **54** (1), 11–31

Kerr, W. A. and R. J. Foregrave (2002), 'The Prophecies of the Naysayers – Assessing the Vision of the Protectionists in the US–Canada Debate on Agricultural Reciprocity, 1846–1854', *The Estey Centre Journal of International Law and Trade Policy*, **3** (2), 357–408, www.esteyjournal.com.

Perdikis, N. and W. A. Kerr (1998), *Trade Theories and Empirical Evidence*, Manchester: Manchester University Press.

Smith, A. (1994), *An Inquiry into the Nature and Causes of the Wealth of Nations*, New York: The Modern Library.

PART I

EVOLUTION AND ECONOMIC CONTEXT

2 Theory and practice in the conduct of trade policy
Sidney Weintraub

Introduction

Trade practice draws its legitimacy from trade theory, but by no means does it mimic theory. There are legitimate reasons for this: theory changes and it takes time for practice to catch up (and sometimes practice does not catch up); policies of sovereign countries are rarely based on economic theory alone, but rather on political economy; governance, particularly in democratic societies, must reflect the diverse interests of different regions and sectors; countries do not rely solely on market signals in their trade policy, but also on state trading that is guided by its own objectives; trade practice is heavily determined by the extent of a country's economic development. (Rich developed countries do not seek 'special and differential treatment', but poor developing countries do.[1])

The authors of the General Agreement on Tariffs and Trade (GATT), which was written toward the end of World War II, were trade specialists from market economies and the agreement reflects their views.[2] There are important examples of trade theory that found their way into the GATT at that time but probably would not be written into trade agreements in the same way today. Dominant theory at that time was that direct taxes (income taxes) were not passed forward to the purchaser of goods, but rather absorbed by the seller, whereas indirect taxes (value added and sales taxes) were passed forward to consumers. Hence, the GATT rule was that the seller could obtain a drawback for indirect taxes paid before export because they ultimately would be paid in the destination country, but that a drawback for direct taxes paid was a subsidy, and hence impermissible. Theory is no longer so clear-cut on the pass-forward versus pass-back of indirect and direct taxes, but the rule remains unchanged.[3] It was expected in the 1940s that there would be few customs unions and free-trade areas, which by definition violate the most-favored-nation clause (MFN), perhaps the single most important principle of the GATT, but such economic integration agreements have mushroomed. There may, indeed, be more trade conducted today on a preferential basis than on the nondiscriminatory terms of the MFN principle. The member countries of the World Trade Organization (WTO), which has superceded the GATT, have not really figured out how to handle this problem.[4]

The next section will discuss many of the major differences between trade theory and trade practice, while at the same time seek to capture how theory has influenced practice. There will then be a brief discussion about what prompts departures from trade theory in the conduct of international trade. This will be followed by a brief conclusion.

Trade theory and trade conduct

The period between the first and second world wars was typified by 'beggar-thy-neighbor' policies of numerous countries. As one country sought to place the burden of adjustment from the great depression on others, the other countries responded in kind. High import tariffs, other import barriers, and deliberately undervalued exchange rates were common; they were based on the conviction that exports created jobs and imports impeded job growth in the affected sectors. The folly of this behavior was clearly understood by the framers of the GATT, and of the International Monetary Fund as well,[5] and one of the significant considerations in drafting the GATT was to deter mercantilism. Theory on the defects of mercantilism was well established beginning with Adam Smith's *Wealth of Nations*.

> Consumption is the sole end and purpose of all production . . . In the mercantile regulations . . . the interest of our manufacturers has been most peculiarly attended to; and the interest, not so much of the consumers, as that of some other sets of producers, has been sacrificed to it.[6]

'Mercantilism' has now become like a dirty four-letter word and it is not used even as it is practiced. One US think tank affiliated with the labor movement measured the job loss in the United States as a result of the enactment of the North American Free Trade Agreement (NAFTA) by ascribing a definite number of jobs gained by every billion dollars of exports and those lost from every billion dollars of imports, and declared at various times how many jobs would be lost because both Mexico and Canada had surpluses in their trade balances with the United States.[7] The reasoning was ultra-simplistic; like the mercantilists pre-Adam Smith, exports were good and imports were bad and consumers were ignored. Another theoretical question is ignored in this kind of analysis, namely, whether a country like the United States should seek to create jobs through export surpluses or macroeconomic policy. The economics profession almost unanimously would put the task of seeking full employment in developed countries on macroeconomic and structural policies, not on trade policy.[8]

Many countries in East Asia, including China, Japan, South Korea, Singapore, Taiwan, clearly aim to keep their exchange rates undervalued in order to promote exports and impede imports. These countries have accumulated large foreign reserves through intervention in money markets to accomplish this. Latin American countries, where high inflation prevailed for decades, tended to have overvalued exchange rates; their import substitution policies in the post-World War II period made many of these countries indifferent to exports. This has now changed; indeed, Argentina today is copying East Asia and intervening in markets to keep its peso slightly undervalued.

Are these beggar-thy-neighbor policies in a twenty-first century context? Yes, but never so described by the practitioners or their advocates. Mercantilism, despite being shunned as a theoretical conception, is alive and thriving in practice. The nod to theory today is to shun the use of the word. The motives are to have a trade surplus, which is believed to give the country greater power in trade bargaining, create jobs at home, and deter imports, especially from countries that do not have similarly undervalued exchange rates.

Unilateral versus reciprocal reduction of trade barriers
Trade theory posits that a country benefits by having higher economic growth and a more equal distribution of income between holders of capital versus consumers and workers by lowering its import barriers, even when this is done unilaterally. Yet, in practice, both in the GATT and the WTO, lowering an import tariff or reducing other import barriers, such as a quota, is called making a 'concession'. Hence, in practice, lowering import protection normally takes place only when 'reciprocity' is obtained. The language of trade negotiations, of concessions and reciprocity, obviously departs from trade theory.[9] Countries have sometimes acted in accordance with theory and unilaterally lowered

import barriers. Chile did so under the influence of the 'Chicago boys' in the 1970s and 1980s during the dictatorship of Augusto Pinochet.[10] Mexico did so under less authoritarian leadership following its debt crisis in 1982 and the realization that its highly protective import-substitution policy had run its course. The reasoning in those two cases seems to have been that when protectionist practices fail, it may be wise to give a try to theoretical arguments. In both cases, it is now more or less unthinkable to contemplate a return to high protectionist practices.

Yet, there is a limit to unilateral reduction of import barriers. Neither Chile nor Mexico reduced its tariffs or other import barriers to zero, but instead left room for reduction to zero in reciprocal negotiations. Each country later reduced import tariffs to zero in concluding free trade agreements (FTAs) and each country, in fact, has signed many FTAs. There has been little reluctance in either country to eliminate most import barriers, but reciprocity was considered necessary beyond a certain point in the barrier-reduction process.

It was noted earlier that an objective of the least developed countries is to secure special and differential treatment in trade negotiations. Some of this undoubtedly will be obtained, but the tension in the ongoing Doha Round of trade negotiations in the WTO is on the degree that this favored treatment will be granted by the high-income developed countries, as compared with the demands of the richer countries for some reciprocity. The argument of the developed countries is based in part on trade theory that import-barrier reduction will foster faster growth in the developing countries, and in part on the self-interest of wanting to export more to the developing countries. A salient aspect of special and differential treatment relates to infant-industry protection.[11]

The case for infant-industry protection is to give time for new industries to mature before they must face competition from outside. Theorists have disagreed about the validity of the infant-industry rationale. John Stuart Mill supported the idea, but many of his contemporaries did not. Such protection has been widely granted; for example, the import-substitution policy of Latin America after World War II was premised on the need for protection to develop an industrial base.[12] The countries in Latin America and the Caribbean in which infant-industry protection had some positive effect were Brazil and Mexico (until 1982 in Mexico, when the underlying import-substitution policy collapsed), both of which were large enough economically to have scope for reliance on the domestic market at least, for a time. Chile, under the Chicago Boys, argued that if industries could not survive without high import protection, they should be allowed to die. The objective, the Chicago Boys argued, was that new activities not only had to compete in their home markets, but also be able to compete in the global market. That policy has worked well, at least after 1985, in that Chile's economic growth and development of competitive activities consistently exceeded those of other countries in Latin America.

Uniform versus escalating tariffs

The Chicago Boys also introduced another feature in their import tariffs that trade theorists have long advocated but which were violated in just about every other country – namely, uniformity of tariff protection. The rationale behind the theory is not to favor one domestic activity over another in the tariff structure. Tariff practice, nevertheless, has generally followed a pattern of higher import duties for products with greater value added. The reason was to protect domestic labor in the production of products. Thus the typical tariff structure has been low tariffs for raw materials that entered into the production of more complex products, intermediate-level tariffs for intermediate imports, and the highest tariffs for finished products that incorporated both raw materials and intermediate inputs. Capital goods needed in production lines generally had low or nil tariffs if they were not produced domestically. Countries practicing import substitution often imposed domestic content requirements on final products in order to encourage the production of intermediate goods at home. This frequently imposed a burden on manufacturers of final goods by forcing them to use higher cost and lower quality intermediate products; and, in the process, destroyed much of their export competitiveness.

Chile broke this pattern under the Chicago Boys. Chile's uniform tariff today is 6 percent ad valorem. As tariff levels decline, especially in the industrial countries, the escalation by degree of value added is also diminishing.

Regionalism and globalism in trade practice

The MFN principle enshrined in article I of the GATT is an expression of the framers that nondiscrimination should prevail in trade among countries, that is, that all exporting countries should be treated alike with respect to imports in the member countries, or contracting parties as they were called. There were existing preferential arrangements dating from before World War II, and these had to be taken into account, although there was considerable opposition to some of them, such as US antipathy toward Commonwealth preferences. In any event, article XXIV was inserted in the GATT to permit preferential arrangements when they included substantially all trade and did not, on the whole, raise import protection above what had existed previously.[13] The concept of trade creation versus trade diversion for estimating whether trade integration agreements led to more trade or merely diverted trade away from exporters not part of the integration agreement was initially set forth by Jacob Viner and, with refinements, has been used ever since.[14]

Free trade agreements and customs unions have proliferated over the years. These include the formation of what is now the European Union (EU), its subsequent expansion to what are now 25 member countries, the creation of the European Free Trade Area, the Canada–US Free Trade Agreement, then NAFTA, plus a host of similar agreements throughout Latin America and Asia. Jeffrey Schott lists 284 regional trade agreements either notified to the GATT or WTO or under negotiation as of May 2003.[15] Schott also notes that of the agreements notified to the GATT or the WTO, only a few were deemed consistent with GATT obligations, but none was ruled inconsistent; hence most were put in what he calls 'obscure legal limbo'.[16]

This situation is not just inconsistent with what the framers had in mind when the GATT was written, but rather a significant departure from what was contemplated. Practice has supplanted theory and this requires new theory. Preferential agreements were expected to be few in number and be subjected to rigorous scrutiny by the contracting parties. The post-World War II conception was for an end, or close to that, of preferential agreements and, instead, a global structure of nondiscrimination in international trade. It is hard to use the word 'globalization' to describe what has happened to the trading structure; 'regionalization' may be closer to the truth, but many preferential trade agreements cut across regions, such as the US–Jordan agreement, or Mexico–EU. The Sutherland consultative group argued that the preferential agreements have weakened the multilateral WTO and concluded that a trading system dominated by the MFN principle, that is, by nondiscrimination, will probably not be restored until negotiations bring border barriers so low as to erase the significance of tariff preferences.

At the same time, we know that trade has become global despite the barrier of discrimination, namely, the massive growth in Chinese and other Asian exports to the United States and Europe even though few Asian countries enjoy preferences in the US or European markets[17] (the United States and Singapore have an FTA, as do the United States and Australia). Geography has always been an important factor in the intensity of trade flows, and the growing trade in intermediate or input products has made geography even more important because of the low transport costs when these products are shipped to neighboring states for insertion into final products. Regional agreements have intensified these exchanges because the intermediate goods can be shipped back and forth without tariffs.

This reality makes the growth in China's exports to the relatively distant US market all the more remarkable. The China experience is reinforcing the global nature of trade, just as regional preferential agreements are not. The explanatory variables are numerous and hard to sort out. On one hand there are regional preferences that violate the MFN principle; regional trade agreements (NAFTA and the EU, for example) that vitiate the global trade aspiration; and proximity in both Europe and North America that encourages regional trade. On the other hand, China is able to overcome these disadvantages, presumably because of the low wages, an undervalued exchange rate, and other organizational skills. There may have to be an updating of trade theory to explain what is happening with respect to regional and global trade.

Agricultural trade

Agriculture may be the extreme example of the differences between trade theory and trade conduct. From the beginning, trade in agricultural products was treated differently from trade in other primary products and manufactured goods. The reason was that the developed countries – the United States, the EU and some individual European countries before that, and Japan – had domestic price supports that augmented production; and, in Europe and the United States, export subsidies of various kinds to unload the surpluses that resulted. Protection had to be high under these circumstances to avoid imports from upsetting the internal price arrangements. As a result, GATT and WTO negotiations, which were dominated by the very countries that used these subsidies extensively, made little to modest progress in reducing barriers to trade in key agricultural products.[18]

The pressure for reducing, even eliminating, domestic and export subsidies in the developed countries has become more intense as developing countries and other non-subsidizing agricultural producers gained more power in the WTO and pressed vigorously for their elimination; and campaigned, as well, for reductions in other import barriers, such as quotas and tariffs. There has been some progress in making agricultural trade more amenable to market forces, but complete correctives to decades of non-market government intervention are unlikely to take place all at once. Land prices, to cite one issue, have risen to incorporate the existence of these subsidies; and landowners who purchased high-priced farms may need some government assistance as the domestic subsidies diminish. Rural areas have more representatives in legislatures than their numbers or economic significance would warrant, and this will be hard to change in the United States, the EU and Japan.

All the signs, however, are that those changes will take place in the treatment of agriculture in international trade. This not only would bring practice closer to theory in the sense that market forces would play a greater role than they have in the past 60 years since the GATT came into existence, and would also bring a greater sense of justice in the trade competition between rich and poor countries.

What prompts departures from trade theory
The opening paragraph notes in a general way why trade practice differs from what trade theory would call for. There remains, however, a question of choice. Many departures from theory are protectionist in nature and there are almost limitless efforts to obtain protectionist measures. Some efforts succeed, others fail? Are there any patterns that can be discerned when the efforts succeed? Perhaps a more pertinent question is why all such efforts don't succeed. The efforts for restriction are pinpointed and the pressure for restriction is usually intense and well organized, whereas the opponents of restrictive measures generally are dispersed and usually less able to bring organized pressure to bear for their position.

An *ex ante* analysis of public choice theory should lead one to believe that the protectionists should always prevail. They don't. Indeed, they fail most of the time in developed countries like the United States and Western Europe. The trade theorists have done a good job of education of the benefits of generally unfettered international trade.

Departures from what trade theory prescribes have the best chance of success when the number of domestic jobs involved in a particular sector is large. The apparel industry fits this description and is an activity in which just about all developed countries, and many developing countries as well, have succumbed to protectionism. Indeed, the detail involved in setting forth the specific apparel items that are restricted has been quite remarkable; and this protection received the sanction of the GATT and the WTO for many decades. The international quota system was disbanded only in 2005, but bilateral restrictions against imports from China were restored, at least temporarily, by the United States and the EU.

President John Kennedy used the apparel industry as a sacrificial pawn when he sought authority from the US congress to engage in trade negotiations, especially with the then newly formed European Economic Community. He pointedly accepted a quota system for textiles, which probably would have been imposed in any event, in order to get the larger negotiating go-ahead.

The electoral power of particular interests (or 'special' interests as their opponents prefer to label them) often play a decisive role in maintaining protectionist departures from theory. Neither the United States nor EC countries can compete successfully in price terms without subsidies and import protection with sugar producers in developing countries. The United States found it necessary in 2004 to remove sugar from the FTA negotiated with Australia in order to obtain congressional approval of the agreement. Cane sugar producers have much political influence in Florida and Louisiana and beet sugar producers are politically potent in the upper Midwest of the United States, and the cost of production is borne by consumers and producers who use much sugar in their manufacturing processes. The leading political party in Japan (the Liberal-Democrats) gets much of its support from rural areas and, in turn, is prepared to force rice consumers to foot the bill.

A technique to bridge this kind of negotiating difference between importing and exporting countries is the use of tariff-rate quotas, namely, lower tariffs for imports up to a determined level, and then higher, often prohibitive, tariffs for imports above the quota level. This was used for sugar imports from Central American countries in their FTA with the United States (CAFTA) that was approved by the US congress in 2005. Mexico used a similar technique to control many agricultural imports, such as corn, over a transition period in NAFTA. Another technique to get around prohibitive import protection is to have a low level of protection for seasonal products like fruits and vegetables when domestic production is low, and high protection during the harvesting season in the importing country. Theory in these cases is allowed to dominate when competitive pressures are low, and protection is used when competitive pressures are high.

Conclusions
GATT was intended to alter the beggar-thy-neighbor policies that flourished to the detriment of the international trading system and economic growth in the years between World Wars I and II. Both GATT and the IMF were written to eschew these practices; or, put differently, to give greater sway to what trade theory tells us about global welfare. And, to a great extent, the framers of the post-war international institutions accomplished this. Trade protection was lowered and trade rules were made more precise; and it can be argued persuasively that these actions contributed to the relatively high growth of the post-World War II period.

However, old practices were not fully eliminated. The language changed but much of the pre-GATT conduct continued, although under different names. The push for under-valued exchange rates, especially in Asia, is mercantilism under a different name. Infant industry protection in developing countries was broadened into what today is special and differential treatment. Despite the fact that theory tells us that unilateral opening of a country's market to imports improves its welfare, a tariff reduction is called a concession. Unilateral tariff reductions are sometimes made, but reciprocity remains the norm. The primary principle of the GATT and the WTO is nondiscrimination, namely, the MFN clause, but preferential agreements have exploded. Tariff schedules are rarely uniform, but instead escalate in order to protect domestic labor input as value is added. Rich countries still interfere heavily in agricultural production, thereby frustrating the workings of international markets.

Trade conduct and trade theory are less disparate today than they were, say, in the mid-1930s; but important differences remain between the two.

Departures from trade theory are generally protectionist in nature. These departures usually are based on such realities as the amount of domestic labor that would be adversely affected by open markets, and the political strength of those who seek to maintain or raise protection for their products or their region of the country. Protectionists do not always succeed; and this is testament to the fact that trade theory benefits have penetrated deeply into the consciousness of the publics in the developed countries. It is hard to predict whether the long-term trend will be toward more adherence to trade theory and open markets, or greater influence of protectionist arguments. This will probably depend on how well the world economy fares.

Notes
1. Special and differential treatment is the phrase used in the World Trade Organization for providing exceptions to the rules to benefit developing countries.

2. Steve Dryden (1995), *Trade Warriors: USTR and the American Crusade for Free Trade* (New York: Oxford University Press) is a valuable discussion of the original framers in the United States and of the persons who later led in the development of US trade policy.

3. An early discussion on the trade treatment of different kinds of taxes can be found in Organization for Economic Cooperation and Development (1968), 'Report on Tax Adjustments Applied to Exports and Imports in OECD Member Countries' (Paris: OECD).

4. See report of consultative board chaired by Peter Sutherland for the director-general of the WTO, 'The Future of the WTO: Addressing Institutional Challenges in the New Millennium', January, 2005.

5. An objective stated in the first article of the IMF is to promote international trade.

6. Adam Smith (1776), *An Inquiry into the Nature and Causes of the Wealth of Nations*. I am using a Modern Library version published in New York by Random House in 1937, and the quotation is on pp. 625–6.

7. Scott, Robert E. (2000), *The Facts about Trade and Job Creation*. Issue brief, Washington, DC: Economic Policy Institute. See also www.epinet.org/content.cfm/briefingpapers_nafta01_us by Robert Scott, *NAFTA's Hidden Costs*.

8. Sidney Weintraub (1997), *NAFTA at Three: A Progress Report* (Washington, DC: Center for Strategic and International Studies), 11–15.

9. There is a good discussion of these and related issues in Douglas A. Irwin (1996), *Against the Tide: An Intellectual History of Free Trade* (Princeton, NJ: Princeton University Press).

10. The 'Chicago Boys' because many of the economists appointed by Pinochet had obtained their advanced degrees in economics at the University of Chicago and were influenced by such professors as Milton Friedman and Arnold Harberger.

11. Irwin, *Against the Tide*, contains extensive discussion of the infant-industry argument, pp. 116–37.

12. The most influential protagonist of the import-substitution policy in Latin America was Raúl Prebisch, when he was executive secretary of the Economic Commission for Latin America. Some of his writings on this theme are gathered in *Capitalismo Periférico: Crisis y Transformación*, 1981 (Mexico City: Fondo de Cultura Económico). ECLA (or ECLAC as it was later called in order to reflect the membership of Caribbean countries) later published a study which focused on the need for Latin American insertion in the world economy, *Policies to Improve Linkages with the Global Economy*, 1994 (Santiago, Chile: ECLAC). This marked a shift away from the earlier policy recommendations.

13. The European Coal and Steel Community, which went into effect on 24 July 1952 was not consistent with the 'substantially all trade' criterion and thus required a waiver from article XXIV by the contracting parties.

14. Jacob Viner (1950), *The Customs Union Issue* (New York: Carnegie Endowment for International Peace). Many of the refinements are laid out in Jeffrey A. Frankel (1997), *Regional Trading Blocs in the World Economic System* (Washington, DC: Institute for International Economics).

15. Jeffrey Schott, ed. (2004), *Free Trade Agreements: US Strategies and Priority* (Washington, DC: Institute for International Economics, table p. 7). Many more negotiations have been launched since Schott compiled his table, including many bilateral FTAs by the United States within and outside the Western Hemisphere.

16. Ibid., 5.

17. Mexico, despite its preferential treatment, has been displaced by China as the second largest supplier to the US market. Most of China's export growth to the United States took place before textile and apparel quotas were eliminated at the start of 2005, but after that happened there was surge in these exports from China to the United States and Europe prompting restrictive import measures.

18. Tim Josling and Dale Hathaway, 'This Far and No Farther? Nudging Agricultural Reform Forward', International Economic Policy Brief, Institute for International Economics, March 2004, is a brief note on agricultural trade negotiations. More thorough discussions of trade in agriculture can be found in: P. Gibson, J. Wainio, D. Whitley and M. Bohman (2001), 'Profiles of Tariffs in Global Agricultural Markets,' *Agricultural Economic Report*, No. 796, Washington, DC Economic Research Service, US Department of Agriculture; Dale Hathaway (2003), 'The Impacts of US Agricultural and Trade Policy on Trade Liberalization and Integration via a US–Central American Free Trade Agreement,' April; Timothy Josling (2004), 'An Overview of the Current WTO Agricultural Negotiations', in *Handbook of Agricultural Trade Negotiations*, ed., John Nash and Alex McCalla, Washington, DC: World Bank; International Agricultural Trade Research Consortium (2001), *The Current WTO Agricultural Negotiations: Options for Progress*, IATRC Commissioned Paper 18, Minneapolis, MN: IATRC, May; Kym Anderson, Will Martin and Dominique van der Mensbrugghe (2005), *Distortions to World Trade: Impacts on Agricultural Markets and Farm Incomes*, Washington, DC: World Bank, Paper (#3736).

3   History of economic thought on trade policy
Andrea Maneschi

The theory of international trade is the oldest applied area of economics.[1] During the mercantilist period that preceded Adam Smith's *An Inquiry into the Nature and Causes of the Wealth of Nations* of 1776, pamphleteers and businessmen discussed the rationale for foreign trade and its policy implications, and concluded that it was vital to the health of an economy and the power of the nation state. Speculations on foreign trade continued to play a vital role in the evolution of economic thought and the conduct of economic policy during the classical and neoclassical periods that followed mercantilism. The theory of any branch of economics carries with it implications for economic policy, and trade policy has been the subject of much debate, advocacy and analysis since mercantilist times. International trade theory and policy have remained the object of active research and controversy to our day. Newspapers and magazines frequently report on trade negotiations and trade agreements, both multilateral and bilateral, that modify a country's trade policy by altering tariffs and other trade impediments. At times they announce the formation of preferential trading areas whose member countries eliminate trade restrictions among themselves, while retaining them against nonmember countries.

Trade policy instruments used since mercantilist times include: (a) import tariffs (or duties); (b) export taxes; (c) import quotas or prohibitions; (d) export quotas or prohibitions; (e) export bounties (or subsidies); and (f) treaties of commerce with other nations. Some of these instruments are substitutes for one another. An import duty can always be found that has the same restrictive effect on imports as a quota, and if raised sufficiently high can cut off all imports, thus amounting to an import prohibition. Many other policies that are not listed above, such as exchange rate policy, fiscal policy, wage policy, and production taxes or subsidies, can also affect trade flows. As shown below, it may be optimal to use policies other than trade policies to alleviate market failures or to achieve noneconomic objectives, even though trade policies have often been used in their place.

This chapter examines the evolution of international trade policies in the mercantilist period, and in the classical and neoclassical eras.[2] Because of the extensive time period under review and the space constraint of this chapter, this survey of trade policies is necessarily incomplete. Some arguments for protection proposed in the classical and neoclassical periods, and in recent decades, have been omitted. These include the so-called 'Australian case for protection', where tariffs are used to redistribute national income to labor and encourage the growth of population, and John Maynard Keynes's argument for protection in order to alleviate unemployment. The analysis developed in the past quarter century of strategic trade policies that allow oligopolistic industries to garner monopoly rents in world markets has also been omitted.[3]

The mercantilist period
Mercantilism represents the view of national wealth and the policies best suited to promote it that prevailed in Europe from the early sixteenth until the late eighteenth

century. It was not a coherent school of thought in the same sense as other schools referred to below, such as physiocracy or the Ricardian school, that flourished under the influence of recognized leaders (François Quesnay and David Ricardo) and shared a common set of beliefs on economic theory and policy. Its exponents lived in different countries in an era when economic theories were rudimentary, and often the expression of vested interests. The impartial and scientific study of the economic world gathered strength in Britain in the seventeenth and eighteenth centuries, as shown by books and pamphlets that clearly anticipated the laissez faire and free trade views that became common in the nineteenth century after the publication of Smith's *Wealth of Nations*.[4]

Jacob Viner (1968: 439) described mercantilism as 'a doctrine of extensive state regulation of economic activity in the interest of the national economy'. Heckscher (1930: 337) similarly stressed the policy side in his definition of mercantilism, which 'in the sense of a policy and doctrine of protection represents the most original contribution of the period in question to economic policy and the one which has retained more sway over men's minds than any other'. The goals of mercantile policymakers, both noneconomic (national power) and economic (wealth and economic development), were regarded by them as complementary. According to Viner (1948: 292–3), 'by the mercantilists power and plenty were regarded as coexisting ends of national policy which were fundamentally harmonious'. Because of the sweeping character of the economic policies that they proposed and implemented, it is impossible to separate mercantilist trade policy from other policies they used to affect trade flows. It is also difficult to detect any overarching logic in the patchwork of policies in effect, since they were devised at different times for different reasons without any thought given to their mutual compatibility, and were subsequently implemented with different degrees of enforcement, or simply allowed to lapse.

A common aim of mercantilist writers, and an apparent obsession for some, was the promotion of a favorable 'balance of trade', defined as the excess of exports over imports in value terms. Many commentators have maintained that mercantilists wished to promote exports and discourage imports in order to accumulate the difference in the form of bullion (precious metals). This aim is epitomized in the title of Thomas Mun's classic contribution to the mercantilist literature, *England's Treasure by Forraign Trade, or the Ballance of our Forraign Trade Is the Rule of our Treasure*, published in 1664 but written some 40 years earlier. According to Mun (1664: 5), 'The ordinary means . . . to increase our wealth and treasure is by foreign trade, wherein we must ever observe this rule; to sell more to strangers yearly than we consume of theirs in value'. This underlines the extreme importance for mercantilists of foreign trade as the key to wealth and prosperity. The reasons for this are not as simple (or simple-minded) as has been often assumed. Mercantilists have been accused of confusing wealth with money, despite the fact that some explicitly referred to the Midas fallacy. The accumulation of precious metals over an indefinite period of time seems indeed a peculiar national policy target. Whether such a goal is even feasible was questioned by some writers even before the Scottish philosopher David Hume formulated the price-specie-flow mechanism, and showed that goal to be illusory. Another interpretation of that goal assumed greater importance with the passage of time, that a positive balance of trade led to a positive 'balance of labor': commodity exports were associated with 'foreign paid incomes' or the 'export of work', that is, to greater employment and a higher level of ouput, whereas imports meant that any gain in employment went to foreigners.[5]

Mercantile states tended to tailor their trade policies to the type of commodity in question, with export bounties and import duties graduated according to certain criteria. Some countries forbad the export of bullion at certain times, under penalty of death or severe fines. This policy was eventually revoked in England when writers such as Mun pointed out that the export of bullion to buy foreign spices or other commodities would eventually bring back a larger amount of bullion once they were re-exported. Exports of manufactures – particularly those with a high labor content – were encouraged, those of agricultural goods and raw materials were discouraged, and the export of machinery was condemned since it allowed foreigners to become productive in lines of activity regarded as a domestic preserve. Imports were tolerated and even encouraged if they related to necessities domestically not available or to raw materials that could be worked up into wrought goods, or if they represented a *quid pro quo* from a country willing to allow entry to domestic exports. Imports of luxuries or of finished manufactures were discouraged. In England in 1689 a corn law ('corn' being the generic term for all grains) established a new export bounty that continued almost uninterruptedly until 1814. Other commodities such as beef, sailcloth, and silk and linen manufactures, also benefited from export bounties.[6] Trade incentives included allowing private companies to monopolize certain foreign (as well as domestic) markets, or even to administer colonies. Trade prohibitions were much less common than import duties, in part because they tended to encourage smuggling even more than duties, and duties had the advantage of securing revenue for the exchequer.

Protection was also achieved by other means than trade policies. Certain industries were discriminated against so as to protect an industry with which they were competing. Since the re-export trade was important to mercantilists such as Mun as an indirect source of bullion earnings, steps were taken to foster it via drawbacks of import duties. Excise taxes on domestic consumption at times replaced import duties. Increasingly trade policy aimed much less to achieve an overall target for the balance of trade than to protect or otherwise encourage specific industries regarded as strategically or economically important (Irwin 1996, chapter 2). Mercantilists can be regarded as the first development economists, since their foremost preoccupation during the last century of their influence was to bring about a pattern of economic development consistent with what they regarded as a nation's priorities. Although the means they adopted to achieve this were clumsy, often incoherent, and marked by hostility toward other countries, they shared with the classical school that followed them the aim to maximize a nation's wealth.

The classical period

Although the classical school of economics is often said to have begun with Adam Smith and his *Wealth of Nations*, several writers in mercantilist times, both in Britain and on the Continent, anticipated key elements of this school of thought such as the advocacy of free trade. In England Dudley North, Isaac Gervaise, Henry Martyn and others preceded Smith in this, but their writings, in the form of pamphlets rather than books, remained almost unknown until they were rediscovered in the nineteenth century. A much more significant precursor of Smith was the first cohesive school of economists now known as the physiocrats, who were staunch advocates of freedom in both domestic and foreign trade. They regarded freedom in foreign trade as part of the natural order, going hand in hand with the doctrine of laissez faire in domestic trade. They particularly supported the freedom to export grain. In France stringent regulations had prevented grain exports until 1764, and become the subject of heated debate. This export ban was one of the many mercantilist measures that the physiocrats sought to abolish as detrimental to the interests of the agricultural classes with which their primary sympathies lay. The free export of grain would allow its price to maintain a satisfactory level (*bon prix*) even at times of abundant harvests. At such times the prevailing ban on its export would instead cause its price to fall, damaging both the profitability of agriculture and the prosperity of the nation.

Smith has often been called the prophet of free trade. This reputation is well deserved since his promotion of free trade was an important part of his relentless attack on mercantilism throughout the *Wealth of Nations*, especially in Book IV (titled 'Of systems of political economy') of the five books into which it is divided. The first eight of the nine chapters of Book IV expound and criticize the tenets of what Smith called 'the commercial or mercantile system'. Chapter 2 titled 'Of restraints upon the importation from foreign countries of such goods as can be produced at home' outlines the advantages of free trade between nations, and the harm caused by the interferences with free trade characteristic of the mercantile system, such as the ones described above. Smith discussed duties and prohibitions on imports in Chapters 2 and 3, drawbacks in Chapter 4, bounties (on both production and exports) in Chapter 5, treaties of commerce in Chapter 6, policies toward colonies in Chapter 7, the trade policies adopted in Britain toward particular commodities such as wool in Chapter 8. Chapter 5 concludes with a 'digression concerning the corn trade and corn laws' because of the importance of this commodity to workers and the popular views that trade in it, both domestic and foreign, should be controlled by the government. Although in general Smith favored instead a free market for grains, he was not opposed to small states imposing restrictions on their export of them in times of dearth or famine.

Smith advocated the dismantling of mercantilist restrictions on economic freedom and on free trade so that they could be replaced by his 'natural system of perfect liberty', where the interest of the consumer takes precedence over that of the producer. At the same time, his support of free trade was not unqualified, since he made exceptions to it in order to promote noneconomic objectives such as national defense. Since 'defence . . . is of much more importance than opulence', Smith supported Britain's navigation acts, even if the provision of greater national security led to a loss of economic efficiency. By encouraging greater employment of British sailors and the growth of shipping, 'the act of navigation is, perhaps, the wisest of all the commercial regulations of England' (1776: 464–5). The same concern for national defense led Smith to advocate bounties for industries assumed to be of strategic importance, since 'it might not always be prudent to depend upon our neighbours' for the supply of commodities such as sailcloth and gunpowder (1776: 522–3).[7] Smith also favored a duty on foreign goods equal in size to an existing tax on similar domestic goods, so as not to discourage production of the latter. In Chapter 2 of Book IV Smith listed two other possible exceptions to free trade as 'a matter of deliberation'. The first is retaliation against a foreign country that imposes duties on the home country's exports, although Smith warns that the success of this policy leading to the mutual elimination of tariffs depends on 'the skill of that insidious and crafty animal, vulgarly called a statesman or politician'. The second exception applies if trade was interrupted for some time leading to imports being replaced by domestic production that employs a large number of workers: 'Humanity may in this case require that the freedom of trade should be restored only by slow gradations, and with a good deal of reserve and circumspection' (1776: 467–9). Smith was also not opposed to moderate import duties or export taxes whose purpose was to produce revenue for the exchequer.

Smith was not optimistic about the likelihood of free trade being adopted in his country: 'To expect, indeed, that the freedom of trade should ever be entirely restored in Great Britain, is as absurd as to expect that an Oceana or Utopia should ever be established in it. Not only the prejudices of the public, but what is much more unconquerable, the private interests of many individuals, irresistibly oppose it' (1776: 471). But his plea for free trade was enthusiastically supported in the nineteenth century by most economists of the classical school that followed him. The most eminent members of this school, David Ricardo and John Stuart Mill, investigated the basis for foreign trade and the gains that accrue from it. Ricardo (who formed a 'Ricardian school' around him) elaborated the principle of comparative advantage in Chapter 7 of his *Principles of Political Economy and Taxation* (1817), making international trade the first applied field of political economy. He never explained what determines the terms of trade between two trading countries, and Mill completed Ricardo's work by attributing them to the force of reciprocal demand, or the demand of each country for its trading partner's export commodity.[8] Both authors believed in free trade, and agreed with Adam Smith that Britain's trade policy should aim at removing the many impediments in its way.

Ricardo's main policy aim was the repeal of Britain's Corn Laws. By artificially raising the price of grains, they raised money wages and landlord rents, and lowered the profit rate. This in turn reduced the rate of capital accumulation on which the dynamism of the economy depended, and hastened its approach toward a stationary state. The Corn Laws became a cause célèbre pitting the majority of classical economists pushing for their repeal against a small minority, of whom T. Robert Malthus (who favored agriculture over manufacturing, and was partial to the landlord class) was the chief exponent. Ricardo's advocacy of repeal turned on the dynamic argument that it would raise the rates of profit and of capital accumulation, rather than on the static principle of comparative advantage. The latter is confined to a few paragraphs in Chapter 7 of his *Principles* and never referred to again in his book, but the detrimental effect of the Corn Laws on the profit rate is mentioned repeatedly throughout it (Maneschi 1992). Ricardo's pleas for repeal in his writings and his speeches in Parliament fell on deaf ears in his lifetime. He died in 1823, and the Corn Laws were finally repealed in 1846.

Whereas the classical economists were preponderantly in favor of free trade in grains, they engaged in acrimonious disputes over several other issues where some of their luminaries favored protection over free trade. The export of machinery that could erode Britain's comparative advantage in manufacturing became a contentious issue among economists and in Parliament, which permitted it only in 1843.[9] Arguments also arose over the use of tariffs to turn a country's terms of trade (defined as the ratio between its export and import prices) in its favor, and the protection of infant industries. Both Malthus and Robert Torrens had noted that a tariff, by reducing a country's demand for imports, can lower their price on the world market and thus improve its terms of trade. Torrens gradually converted from favoring unilateral free trade (as was true of nearly all British economists in the early 1820s) to becoming an increasingly ardent proponent in 1833, and more completely in Torrens (1844), of what he called 'the principle of reciprocity', whereby Britain should lower or eliminate its import tariffs only with respect to trading partners that reciprocated. He was opposed in this by John McCulloch and Nassau Senior, but backed by John Stuart Mill. With Mill's influential support, Torrens's argument has become generally accepted as a key result in trade theory and a valid justification for tariffs. Although a tariff can in theory improve a country's terms of trade and its welfare, the classical economists who appreciated its theoretical merit observed that it invites retaliation, which if followed could lead to an overall loss of welfare for both trading countries due to their diminished ability to exploit their comparative advantages in trade.

Mill was also instrumental in securing acceptance of the need to support infant industries as a second legitimate argument for protection in the classical canon. Infant industries had been claimed to deserve government assistance in numerous mercantilist pamphlets and books, but this in the main reflected special pleading by those with a stake in their support. Adam Smith rejected infant industry protection as a legitimate policy tool, on the ground that even if the industry in question eventually became competitive in world markets, the resources it absorbed in the interim lower the economy's revenue and rate of capital accumulation below their levels without protection (1776: 458). Protection for infant industries and infant economies was persuasively argued by statesmen and economists in the developing countries of that time on the ground that the built-in advantages favoring established producers were otherwise too difficult to overcome. Alexander Hamilton, Secretary of the Treasury to George Washington, promoted policies to encourage the growth of the nascent American industries in the *Report on the Subject of Manufactures* he submitted to Congress in 1791. He was followed in this by John Rae, a Scotsman who migrated to Canada and then to the US. In Rae (1834) he criticized Adam Smith for not sufficiently encouraging invention and innovation in the *Wealth of Nations*, and failing to appreciate the need for infant industry protection. Mill was so impressed by Rae's book that it convinced him of the merits of such protection 'especially in a young and rising nation': 'A country which has this skill and experience yet to acquire . . .' as compared to one where a branch of production is long established '. . . may in other respects be better adapted to the production than those which were earlier in the field' (Mill 1848: 922). To allow it to take root, Mill recommended a protective tariff for a limited period of time. The German economist Friedrich List also spent some years in the US where he came under the influence of Hamilton's *Report* and its policy recommendations. List's book of 1841, translated into English as *The National System of Political Economy* (1885), argued against free trade for a country like Germany. It became a handbook for nationalist economists in Europe and other parts of the world, and recommended protection for developing countries until they develop the 'productive forces' that allow them to compete with more developed economies.[10]

The neoclassical period

As the classical school of thought gradually gave way to the marginalist economics of W. Stanley Jevons in England, Carl Menger in Austria, and Léon Walras in France and Switzerland, and to the neoclassical school founded by Alfred Marshall in England, trade theory and the justifications for trade policies underwent significant changes and refinements. Marshall depicted J. S. Mill's reciprocal demand analysis by means of offer curves, and Francis Edgeworth used them to illustrate the effects of commercial policy on the terms of trade. A third British economist, Charles Bickerdike (1906), explored the determination of the optimal tariff rate that maximizes a country's gain from trade by using demand and supply curves, together with the Marshallian tools of consumer and producer surplus. Edgeworth and Bickerdike recognized that a tariff decreases the volume of trade and hence the potential gains from it, and that a country's welfare is maximized when it sets a tariff such that, at the margin, the gain from improved terms of trade is just offset by the loss from a lower volume of trade. The Austrian economist Gottfried Haberler (1936) recast the theory of comparative advantage in terms of opportunity costs, illustrating production possibilities by means of a transformation curve. Part II of his book was devoted to trade policy, and included a searching analysis of the arguments for free trade and protection. Such arguments going back to mercantilist times were also lucidly examined by Viner (1937), who voiced criticism of some neoclassical models and tools of analysis as compared to classical ones.

Free trade policies enjoyed increasing support from the British public and statesmen for about a quarter century after the repeal of the Corn Laws in 1846. Economic difficulties in the last quarter of the nineteenth century led to disenchantment with free trade, and calls by economists mostly from the historical school of thought to promote 'tariff reform' and a policy of 'fair trade' because of the protectionism practiced by Britain's trading partners.[11] Again the issue of 'reciprocity' that Torrens and Mill had highlighted, and whose roots go back to Adam Smith's consideration of possible retaliation for tariffs, occupied some of the best minds of economists and statesmen. Marshall and his neoclassical confrères stood fast by their free trade convictions, and appeared stuck in a dogmatic refusal to consider that new conditions, such as the deindustrialization and employment losses that Britain was undergoing, and the ascendancy of the German and American economies thriving under the mantle of protectionism, required a fresh look at its continued applicability.[12] The climate of opinion also turned against free trade in the US, where the revenue tariffs imposed during the Civil War were not lowered when it ended. The distinguished American economist Frank Taussig, in his Presidential Address before the American Economic Association in 1904, noted that 'so far as the doctrine of free trade is concerned, enthusiasm has been supplanted by cautious weighing or open doubt' (1920: 3). Given the American experience with the development of manufactures, the infant industry argument was deemed potentially valid by both Taussig and Alfred Marshall. In 1883 Taussig published his first book, *Protection to Young Industries as Applied to the United States*, based on his doctoral dissertation. In later writings, he observed that whether an industry is worth protecting, and whether the initial loss from doing so is worth the ultimate gain, 'are not questions to be answered through deductive reasoning in terms of yes or no; they are to be answered, if at all, through laborious research and in terms of probabilities'. Moreover, 'the length of time to be allowed for the experiment should not be too brief . . . a generation, more or less, may elapse before it is clear whether success has been really attained' (Taussig 1931: 28, 22–3).

An argument for the protection of decreasing cost (or increasing return) industries was advanced by another American economist, Frank Graham (1923). Graham, who studied at Harvard under Taussig, showed that a country with a comparative advantage in an increasing cost industry may be hurt by trade when it shifts its resources from a decreasing cost industry, whereas its trading partner that specializes in the latter undoubtedly gains. Graham's argument is distinct from the infant industry argument, since protection for the increasing return industry can never be revoked. Although at the time his article evoked critiques from economists such as Viner, it eventually became one of the catalysts for the 'new trade theory' elaborated by W. J. Ethier, P. R. Krugman, G. M. Grossman, E. Helpman, J. Brander, B. Spencer and others since the late 1970s.[13]

The Romanian economist Mihail Manoilescu (1931) justified protection for economies such as that of his own country where the wage rate in the manufacturing sector exceeded the opportunity cost of labor measured by the agricultural wage. He argued and proved with numerical examples that free trade militated against the creation of a manufacturing sector on which the country's prosperity depended, and advocated protection for that sector. The condition that Manoilescu described in his book was examined carefully by mainstream trade economists, who however rejected the protectionist solution that he proposed. In the second half of the twentieth century, the market failure that he analyzed was seen to be one of several types of distortion to which economies may be subject. They include monopoly power in trade (which rules out free trade as the optimal policy), production externalities that cause social costs or benefits to differ from their private counterparts, and wage differentials between industries such as those postulated by Manoilescu (Bhagwati 1971). Each type of distortion was shown to have a first best policy intervention to offset it, and other policies were ranked in terms of second best, third best, and so on. The first best policy is one that attacks the distortion directly, without imposing unintended side effects. Trade policy such as a tariff is the first best policy only when the distortion arises from foreign trade, such as monopoly or monopsony power in world markets. Economists now argue against the general validity of the infant industry argument for tariffs, since a new industry can most efficiently be promoted with a production subsidy (a departure from laissez faire) combined with free trade, whereas a tariff imposes a concomitant consumer loss. Free trade and laissez faire have thus been shown to be independent of each other. It is recognized that if the first best policy is not available, a second best one such as tariff is better than no policy at all. Welfare economics and the theory of the second best have provided invaluable tools for selecting the best policies to cure market failures or achieve noneconomic objectives, and hence to ascertain whether trade policy is or is not called for.

Conclusions

In this brief and necessarily incomplete survey of trade policies since mercantilist times, Adam Smith's name stands out as the founder of the classical school of economic thought and the proponent of free trade as part of his 'system of natural liberty'. Despite the title of his most famous book, the 'wealth of nations' was not Smith's sole objective. He was willing to use trade and other policies, even if they resulted in a loss of efficiency, in order to achieve a variety of economic and noneconomic objectives. Noneconomic objectives such as national defense and protection for the industries that support it were invoked by Smith. Although he was more tentative about the use of protection to alleviate unemployment when imports flow into a country after a suspension of trade, he made a good case for a gradual approach to free trade. Economists of the classical school such as Ricardo agreed with him that in such cases protection should be removed gradually to allow factors to make an orderly redeployment from import-competing industries. Nowadays governments recognize the existence of the adjustment costs faced by these industries, and often provide trade adjustment assistance to extend unemployment benefits and provide retraining for workers as a condition for further trade liberalization.

Smith also allowed for the possibility of retaliation against a foreign country that imposes duties on the home country's exports, in the hope that this would lead to a mutual lowering of trade barriers and thus yield freer trade between them. Robert Torrens approved of this call for reciprocity in trade relations, and the issue remained alive in Britain and inspired the tariff reform debate of 1903. Reciprocity in tariff reductions was enshrined in the Reciprocal Trade Agreements Act passed by the US Congress in 1934 after the disastrous Smoot-Hawley tariff of 1930, and retaliation by other countries, had decimated world trade. This Act served as a basis for the trade negotiations conducted under the aegis of the General Agreement on Tariffs and Trade signed in 1947 by 23 countries. The GATT was later joined by many more signatory countries, and transformed in 1995 into the World Trade Organization that is the present-day forum for multilateral trade negotiations.

Notes

1. Parts of this chapter are based on Maneschi (1998).
2. The classical era started with the publication of Smith's *Wealth of Nations* in 1776 and lasted until the early 1870s. Neoclassical economics, associated with the British economist Alfred Marshall and his *Principles of Economics* of 1890, is a synthesis of classical thought with the marginalist economics that revolutionized the field in the 1870s.
3. Strategic trade policy, and the Australian and Keynesian cases for protection, are admirably reviewed by Irwin (1996, chapters 11, 13 and 14), who also examines whether any of them invalidates the case for free trade.
4. On 'enlightened' mercantilist writers who anticipated key features of classical economics, see among others Johnson (1937), Viner (1937), Letwin (1963), Hutchison (1988) and Magnusson (1994).
5. Johnson (1937, chapter 15) discusses this interpretation of mercantilist policy.
6. Viner (1937, chapter 2) provides examples of specific trade and other policies employed or proposed in England in the mercantilist period, and quotes some of their advocates.
7. On the role played by noneconomic objectives in the history of economic thought, see Maneschi (2004).
8. Mill attributed the terms of trade to reciprocal demand in his essay 'Of the Laws of Interchange between Nations; and the Distribution of the Gains of Commerce among the Countries of the Commercial World' in Mill (1844) that he had written, according to him, in 1829 or 1830. The essence of Mill's argument was reproduced in his *Principles of Political Economy* (1848).
9. The ban on the emigration of skilled artisans imposed by acts of Parliament in the eighteenth century was lifted in 1824.
10. On the policies advocated by Hamilton, Rae, List and other 'creators of comparative advantage', and on the merits of their arguments, see Maneschi (1998, chapter 5).
11. Similar calls for a 'level playing field' in commercial relations were voiced by politicians and spokespersons for special interests in the US and other developed countries after World War II.
12. On the British tariff reform debate, see Gomes (2003, chapter 7).
13. Brander and Spencer's articles gave rise to strategic trade policy as a new argument for protection. The validity of this argument is examined by Irwin (1996, chapter 14).

References

Bhagwati, J. (1971), 'The Generalized Theory of Distortions and Welfare', in J. N. Bhagwati, R. Jones, R. Mundell and J. Vanek (eds), *Trade, Balance of Payments, and Growth: Papers in International Economics in Honor of Charles P. Kindleberger*, Amsterdam: North-Holland.

Bickerdike, C. F. (1906), 'The Theory of Incipient Taxes', *Economic Journal*, 16: 529–35.

Gomes, L. (2003), *The Economics and Ideology of Free Trade: A Historical Review*, Cheltenham, UK, and Northampton, MA, USA: Edward Elgar.

Graham, F. D. (1923), 'Some Aspects of Protection Further Considered', *Quarterly Journal of Economics*, 37: 199–227.

Haberler, G. (1936), *The Theory of International Trade with its Application to Commercial Policy* (originally published in German in 1933), Edinburgh: William Hodge.

Heckscher, E. F. (1930), 'Mercantilism', in E. R. A. Seligman and A. E. Johnson (eds), *Encyclopaedia of the Social Sciences*, New York: Macmillan.

Hutchison, T. W. (1988), *Before Adam Smith: The Emergence of Political Economy 1662–1776*, Oxford: Basil Blackwell.

Irwin, D. A. (1996), *Against the Tide: An Intellectual History of Free Trade*, Princeton, NJ: Princeton University Press.

Johnson, E. A. J. (1937), *Predecessors of Adam Smith: The Growth of British Economic Thought*, New York: Prentice-Hall.

Letwin, W. (1963), *The Origins of Scientific Economics*, London: Methuen.

List, F. (1885), *The National System of Political Economy*, trans. S. S. Lloyd, London: Longmans, Green, and Co.

Magnusson, L. (1994), *Mercantilism: The Shaping of an Economic Language*, London: Routledge.

Maneschi, A. (1992), 'Ricardo's International Trade Theory: Beyond the Comparative Cost Example', *Cambridge Journal of Economics*, **16**: 421–37.

Maneschi, A. (1998), *Comparative Advantage in International Trade: A Historical Perspective*, Cheltenham, UK and Lyme, USA: Edward Elgar.

Maneschi, A. (2004), 'Noneconomic Objectives in the History of Economic Thought', *American Journal of Economics and Sociology*, **63**: 911–20.

Manoilescu, M. (1931), *The Theory of Protection and International Trade*, London: P. S. King.

Mill, J. S. (1844), *Essays on Some Unsettled Questions of Political Economy*, London: London School of Economics and Political Science reprint, 1948.

Mill, J. S. (1848), *Principles of Political Economy*, London: Longman, Green, 1920.

Mun, T. (1664), *England's Treasure by Forraign Trade, or the Ballance of our Forraign Trade Is the Rule of our Treasure*, London: Thomas Clark.

Rae, J. (1834), *Statement of Some New Principles on the Subject of Political Economy, Exposing the Fallacies of the System of Free Trade, and of Some Other Doctrines Maintained in the 'Wealth of Nations'*, Boston: Hilliard, Gray, and Co.

Ricardo, D. (1817), *On the Principles of Political Economy and Taxation*, in P. Sraffa (ed.), *The Works and Correspondence of David Ricardo*, vol. I, Cambridge: Cambridge University Press, 1951.

Smith, A. (1776), *An Inquiry into the Nature and Causes of the Wealth of Nations*, Oxford: Clarendon Press, 1976.

Taussig, F. W. (1920), 'The Present Position of the Doctrine of Free Trade', in F. W. Taussig, *Free Trade, the Tariff and Reciprocity*, New York: Macmillan.

Taussig, F. W. (1931), *Some Aspects of the Tariff Question: An Examination of the Development of American Industries under Protection*, third edition, Cambridge, MA: Harvard University Press. First edition published in 1915.

Torrens, R. (1844), *The Budget: On Commercial and Colonial Policy*, London: Smith, Elder.

Viner, J. (1937), *Studies in the Theory of International Trade*, New York: Harper.

Viner, J. (1948), 'Power versus Plenty as Objectives of Foreign Policy in the Seventeenth and Eighteenth Centuries', reprinted in J. Viner, *The Long View and the Short: Studies in Economic Theory and Policy*, Glencoe: The Free Press, 1958.

Viner, J. (1968), 'Mercantilist Thought', in *International Encyclopedia of the Social Sciences*, New York: Macmillan and Free Press.

4 Modern history of trade policy
William. M. Miner

Introduction

The modern history of trade policy is the record of the development of the multilateral trade system. At the centre of the system is the World Trade Organization (WTO) which provides the common institutional framework for the conduct of trade relations among member governments. It is responsible for matters related to a series of agreements and legal undertakings, including the General Agreement on Tariffs and Trade (GATT), and provides a framework for the development of a wider range of agreements and institutions related to trade.

The GATT was established following the Second World War (WWII) by a group of industrial countries which agreed that their trade and economic relations 'should be conducted with a view to raising standards of living, ensuring full employment and a large and steadily growing volume of real income and effective demand, . . . the full use of resources, and expanding the production and exchange of goods'.[1] They also agreed this could best be achieved by substantially reducing tariffs and trade barriers and eliminating discriminatory treatment in international commerce. These objectives of the GATT, and its successor institution, the WTO, provided the guidance and framework for the trade policies of most nations and the many various agreements and institutions that comprise the multilateral trade system of the twenty-first century.

Trade policies and trade agreements reflect the events and trends in the history of their evolution. They also exert a general influence on the forms and directions of trade and economic development. Hence the modern history of trade policy is best displayed on a chronological basis beginning with the origins of the multilateral trading system and its emergence in the post-WWII era. Over the following decades, the system has been broadened and deepened through successive multilateral and regional negotiations and related institutional developments. This process is continuing as nations confront traditional barriers to trade, and new issues and strategic concerns further constrain the movement of goods and services across borders.

Origins of the multilateral trade system[2]

The liberal trend in trade and economic affairs accompanied by general prosperity in the 1920s came to an abrupt end with the stock market crash and the onset of the Great Depression. Commodity markets collapsed and nations adopted policies to protect domestic producers and manage trade. The infamous US Smoot Hawley Act severely limited access to that market in 1930, and other industrial countries significantly increased their trade barriers. Economic policies shifted further inward as the devastation of war disrupted production and shipping, and closed borders. Food and material shortages led to controls over prices and trade.

The United States (US) was the undisputed leader in trade policy over this period. As early as 1934, the US Congress passed the Reciprocal Trade Agreements Act, delegating authority to the President to negotiate tariffs. Reciprocal trade agreements were negotiated with many countries prior to US entry into WWII.[3] The agreements contained provisions for tariff bindings, non-discrimination in trade, national treatment of imports, and commitments to treat one trading party no less favorably than another, the most-favored nation (MFN) clause. These provisions were to form the basis for the multilateral trade system. The US Act was extended in 1945 to provide authority to continue to negotiate reductions in tariffs and other barriers to trade.

The influence of Britain on post-war trade policy was significant but less profound. Departing from its traditional free trade principles, Britain maintained a system of tariff protection with preferential treatment for Commonwealth countries. Canada had relatively high tariff protection, and in 1932 led its Commonwealth partners in negotiating preferential access to the British market. These British Preferential Tariffs (BPTs) were vigorously opposed by the US but left their mark on the post-war trading system. Although Canada had pursued reciprocal free trade with the US periodically, the BPT system provided a sheltered market for its emerging industries. But Canada also pursued open trading arrangements for its agriculture and resource sectors in a similar manner to Australia, New Zealand and Argentina. Faced with the challenge of rebuilding their war-torn economies, the countries of Western Europe and Japan became more protective and interventionist in their economic policies. Trade with the Soviet bloc and China (Mainland) was extremely limited by their state systems and by the strategic export controls maintained by Western countries.

During WWII, and in the early post-war period, the leading industrial nations began to shift their external commercial policies from the ad hoc, unilateral and mercantilist actions of the 1930s, toward a more cooperative, multilateral approach. Against the background of extreme trade protection, the severe crises of global warfare, and the serious challenges of reconstruction, the US and its Western allies worked to develop a framework of rules and institutions to bring greater order to external relations and to promote economic growth and trade. International economic cooperation was envisaged to include mechanisms to deal with monetary, financial and trade affairs.

An agreement reached at Bretton Woods[4] in 1944 provided the basis for global cooperation in monetary and financial policies through the Charters of the International Monetary Fund (IMF) and the International Bank for Reconstruction and Development (IBRD – World Bank). The complete framework for this ambitious plan was to include an organization for international trade.

Following the formation of the United Nations in 1945, its subordinate body, the UN Economic and Social Council (UNESCO) adopted a resolution to organize a conference on trade and employment. Based on discussions with its trading partners and experience with reciprocal trade agreements, the US prepared a draft charter for an international trade organization (ITO). The charter was negotiated at preparatory meetings in London and Geneva in 1947. In the context of these meetings the first multilateral trade negotiation was conducted, and the text of a General Agreement on Tariffs and Trade (GATT) was agreed in Geneva, as a central element of the proposed ITO. It was also agreed that the GATT would be implemented in the following year through a Protocol of Provisional Application by the 23 nations engaged in the negotiations, pending completion and eventual adoption of the ITO. The Havana Charter for an ITO was agreed in 1947 but was not accepted by the US Congress or other governments. Thus, on 1 January 1948, the

GATT entered into force and became the central element of the multilateral trade system.[5]

The first GATT contained schedules of each participating government's tariff concessions, and rules and commitments, to be applied on a most favored nation basis including national treatment of imports in relation to domestic production. The articles dealt with specific trade mechanisms such as prohibitions on quantitative restrictions and subsidy disciplines, and provided for emergency action on imports, consultations and the redress of impairment of benefits. Because of the GATT's provisional status, trade preferences in force at that time were allowed to continue and existing legislation that was inconsistent with GATT provisions could be grandfathered. Agriculture was covered by the general rules but special provisions gave exemptions from full disciplines such as the prohibitions on the use of quantitative import restrictions and subsidy disciplines. Restrictions were also allowed to relieve shortages of essential goods, for balance of payments reasons, to protect human, animal or plant health, and to implement commodity agreements.

Throughout the modern history of trade policy, an increasing number of nations have used the GATT, and its successor body, the WTO, as the centerpiece and framework for their trade and economic policies. Today most countries adhere to the view that every economy will gain through international trade, and the gains will be enhanced through more open markets and trading arrangements. Thus, the basic principles of the GATT, to promote market efficiency and non-discrimination, have shaped or influenced the many specific and regional trade agreements and related institutions that together comprise the modern multilateral trade system.

Developing the trade system
The national policies of the major industrial countries in the post-WWII period were directed to achieving strong economic growth, full employment and reconstruction. International monetary conditions and the macroeconomic environment encouraged Western governments to work together to facilitate trade and maximize economic benefits. The focus of cooperation was through international institutions and the GATT provided the framework for most trade policies. Its provisional status encouraged consultation and compromise leading to a pragmatic approach to policy decisions. Despite the GATT principles of pursuing market oriented and non-discriminatory policies, its many derogations and waivers left governments with considerable flexibility in their trade policies. From the outset the development of the multilateral trade system reflected compromises between the US-led emphasis on the role of private enterprise and the market to achieve economic growth and full employment in relation to greater use of government intervention and management as practiced in Western Europe and in some other regions.

Throughout the 1950s and early 1960s successive rounds of multilateral negotiations yielded reductions in tariffs and the clarification and elaboration of rules to discipline and reduce trade restrictions and resolve disputes. The initial rounds centered on the accession of new members including Germany. Early negotiations were conducted on an offer and request basis, item by item, with the principal supplier leading the process. Following the example of the 1933 International Wheat Agreement (IWA), the negotiations of the Havana Charter included provisions for international commodity agreements to stabilize markets through price provisions, export quotas or buffer stock arrangements.[6] But governments retained the right to restrict trade to reduce supply shortages, for balance of payments reasons, or to support specific sectors, particularly agriculture. The US obtained a GATT waiver in 1955 to allow quota restrictions to protect its farm programs. The newly formed European Economic Community (EEC) implemented a highly restrictive Common Agricultural Policy (CAP) to push toward food self-sufficiency, and negotiated its acceptance by GATT members. Many European and Asian countries blocked or limited imports on balance of payments grounds. These actions and other derogations severely limited market access despite reductions in tariffs.

Trade policy in this early period focused mainly on consolidating and expanding tariff reductions, particularly with acceding GATT members, and attempting to overcome the quantitative restrictions to trade being maintained for monetary reasons, or to protect agriculture. There were growing pressures to limit market disruption from imports, particularly in the textiles and clothing sector. Japan joined the GATT in 1955 as its labor intensive and high technology products captured a growing share of world markets. The trade rules were bent further to accommodate temporary import restraints. With rising agricultural productivity and continuing market access restrictions, the issues of surplus disposal appeared on the trade agenda.

By the early 1960s, the patterns of trade were shifting as Asian exports increased, China entered the market as an importer of food and raw materials, and Western Europe focused on economic integration and internal trade. Russia and other Soviet bloc countries began importing grain while seeking to export industrial products. With significant tariff escalation for finished goods, and related anti-dumping and valuation restrictions, industrial countries continued to limit imports. Distortion in agricultural trade was widespread, and developing country market shares were declining. Initially the IWA yielded some benefits as a mechanism to manage domestic regimes and stabilize grain markets, but the pressures of over-supply and competition caused it and most commodity agreements to fail. Increasingly, Canada turned to the US market for industrial trade expansion through bilateral arrangements such as the automotive agreement. As more of the trade and trade issues were outside the purview of GATT, trade policy became fragmented and less open. The US Congress was turning more protectionist due to rising competition from imports and balance of payments difficulties. Without American leadership, multilateral trade liberalization was stalled.

The US administration undertook a major overhaul of its trade negotiation authority with the 1962 Trade Expansion Act. It was aimed at a substantial increase in trade to stimulate the US economy and strengthen Atlantic ties in the face of the emerging threat of the Soviet bloc. This launched the Kennedy Round of multilateral trade negotiations which began in 1964. Responding to the broader trade policy agenda of the 1960s, the negotiation encompassed several non-tariff issues in addition to a substantial, linear reduction in tariffs. More than 50 countries took part, and since many were developing countries, including newly independent nations, an early effort was made to respond to their problems. The developing countries were increasingly critical of the GATT over its focus on industrial nation trade. A UN Conference on Trade and Development (UNCTAD) was formed as a permanent institution in 1964. In a special GATT session in the same year, specific provisions were agreed as Part IV of GATT to promote the trade and development of less-developed nations.

The outcome of the Kennedy Round represented an impressive step in the development of the multilateral trade system. A significant cut in tariffs was agreed on an across-the-board basis, with some exceptions. As a result, the average industrial tariffs in the leading trading nations were brought below 10 percent, allowing North American industry to compete with Japan and Western Europe on the same basis.[7] But once again, agriculture was largely excluded. New codes were established to discipline the use of anti-dumping duties and customs valuation procedures representing an important step in directly applying trade rules to internal policies. The price elements of a new International Grains Arrangement with provisions for sharing the burden of food aid formed a part of the result. But otherwise, for developing country issues, little concrete progress came from the general undertakings of the new Part IV. Indeed, the Cotton Textile Agreement, implemented in 1961 as a temporary measure to limit imports of textiles and clothing, was extended.

New strains and directions

A series of political and economic developments immediately following the Kennedy Round shifted the focus of trade policies from tariffs and opening markets toward managing trade problems through rules, codes and unilateral actions. The Vietnam War, the collapse of the gold standard, and instability in commodity markets fueled inflation and monetary pressures. Competition for markets intensified as exports from Japan and newly industrialized Asia-Pacific nations took a growing share of world markets. A north–south divide in trade relations emerged as developing countries turned to UNCTAD to pursue a New Economic Order. Despite a brief period of scarcity, resources moved back into surplus as labor intensive output in developed countries was being replaced by higher technology products from Asia. A number of industrial countries imposed 'voluntary' export restraints (VERs) to further limit low cost imports, and some introduced export promotion schemes of their own.

The US had turned increasingly protectionist by the 1970s as exports became more important to their economy while their trade deficit widened. The US Congress refused to implement new GATT rules on customs valuation and anti-dumping reflecting their resistance to subjecting domestic laws to international rules. Facing an exchange rate crisis, Congress imposed a surtax on imports and levied taxes on US foreign investment. They adopted new Trade Law provisions to enable unilateral action to redress their trade concerns. The European Community was preoccupied with enlargement negotiations on the entry of Britain, Denmark and Ireland. Canada introduced foreign investment regulations, and supply management for dairy and poultry, backed with quantitative import controls. An oil embargo led to the successful formation of an exporter's cartel which aggravated inflationary pressures and monetary problems. There was an increase in contingency protection actions and trade disputes in this period.

These policy issues pushed trade liberalization and GATT cooperation to the sidelines. Many of the developments involved non-GATT nations, and the issues extended beyond the disciplines and the purview of the multilateral trade system. They signaled the beginning of fundamental changes in economic and trading relationships.

Once again monetary and macro-economic impacts on the multilateral trading system convinced nations of the need to negotiate additional rules and commitments. The challenges facing the major industrial nations over the Bretton Woods and GATT systems had stimulated the organization of annual Economic Summits of Heads of State (G7 countries) which began in Paris in 1974. The OECD, UNCTAD and GATT established work programs to prepare the ground for a further round of multilateral trade negotiations. It was evident that trade policy issues had moved beyond borders to include a full range of non-tariff barriers (NTBs). Import safeguards and issues of agricultural trade and economic development were more pressing. There was also the question of how to integrate trade with state-controlled economies into the multilateral system. In 1971, GATT adopted a waiver to allow leading members to negotiate general systems of preferences (GSP) to provide preferential tariffs to benefit developing countries. By the mid-1970s, a broad multilateral trade negotiation, the Tokyo Round, was underway. Its ambitious agenda dealt with traditional border issues of tariffs, quantitative restrictions and subsidies, but also with many NTBs that would involve changes in internal laws and regulations at federal, provincial and state levels.

The Tokyo Round concluded in 1979 and represented a further important step in constructing an effective multilateral trade system. It resulted in five new codes covering subsidies and countervailing duties, customs valuation, import licensing, technical barriers to trade and government procurement. The results included revisions to the anti-dumping agreement and an accord on trade in civil aircraft. The codes were part of the GATT system but did not amend the General Agreement and were binding only on signatory countries. Custom tariffs were reduced significantly including some agricultural tariffs. But the Round failed in its attempt to address the market disruption from low-cost imports and the use of voluntary export restraints applied outside the non-discrimination principles. Although developing countries were able to block new safeguard measures, they were dissatisfied with the outcome. Negotiations to re-establish economic provisions in the wheat agreement based on grain reserves were not successful. The wheat agreement was extended as a consultative body, with separate food aid provisions. Consultative agreements were also reached covering bovine meats and dairy products.

These codes and consultation arrangements, with varying levels of rules, commitments and adherents, were useful in reducing trade problems and influencing related internal policies and regulations but represented a different level of commitment. They demonstrated the flexible nature of the provisional status of GATT but offered limited security of access to markets or certainty in settling trade disputes. Although an additional part was added to the General Agreement to respond to the special needs of developing countries, and the GSP was completed, they experienced little benefits. While protectionist pressures were largely reigned in as negotiations proceeded, the many waivers and derogations persisted. The multilateral trading system now comprised several levels of benefits and obligations. As international trade policy commitments penetrated borders and dealt directly with internal policies, new issues of sovereignty and federal-provincial-state jurisdiction emerged.

Regional accords and a world organization
The gradual integration of the economies of industrial countries that had been underway since WWII accelerated in the 1980s and became a global phenomenon. Stimulated by new technologies, and led by rising foreign investment and trade in goods and services, the effects of integration began to dominate the trade policy agenda. The role of trade in economic development had long been recognized and the focus of trade policy was access

to markets. As international competition intensified, governments attempted to manage trade and influence each other's domestic policies through rules and codes. But as the integration and restructuring of economies proceeded, with some regions and sectors moving much further and faster than others, monetary and trade problems multiplied. The decade of the 1980s was marked by a diversity of economic and social conflicts and actions on a national, regional and multilateral basis.

A major global recession in the early 1980s stimulated another phase of protectionist actions. The US experienced growing trade and budgetary deficits, aggravated by an overvalued dollar, strong export competition and rising imports. Again the US Congress turned to unilateral actions and greater use of their trade remedy measures. The 1984 US Trade and Tariff Act included authority to pursue bilateral as well as multilateral trade agreements, and additional actions to limit imports and force trade and monetary concessions. The European Community also launched unilateral trade actions while continuing to emphasize the integration of member economies. Developing countries faced additional restrictions against their low-cost exports and had few GATT obligations or benefits. Most experienced rising foreign debt as their import replacement policies and investment restrictions hampered economic growth. Trade disputes increased, particularly for agricultural products. Tensions widened with new concerns over trade in services, investment and the protection of intellectual property. The viability of the GATT itself was tested by its inability to resolve traditional problems and to deal with new issues.

The trade agenda was broadening and becoming more complex, and the multilateral trade system began to adjust to the new reality. On the monetary side, the leading nations moved to strengthen coordination in macroeconomic and monetary policies. World Bank loans to developing countries were made conditional on economic and trade reforms. Stimulated by fiscal and trade pressures, governments in most regions began to open their markets to international competition. Many countries adjusted their economic policies to reduce regulations, limit or privatize intervention mechanisms, and lower subsidies.

Canada negotiated a free trade agreement with the US in the mid-1980s. Argentina, Brazil, Paraguay and Uruguay established a free trade zone (MERCOSUR) and were working toward a customs union. In most other regions, groups of nations took formal steps toward economic integration. Many of these arrangements were sanctioned by GATT members. Although the North American Free Trade Agreement (NAFTA), MERCOSUR, and common market arrangements in Central America (CACM) and the Caribbean (CARICOM) were in place during this period, they did not deter multilateral negotiations, and in some cases, contributed to them.[8] In addition, Ministerial discussions at Economic Summits, in GATT, the OECD, UNCTAD and other institutions, demonstrated that the world had moved beyond the original framework of GATT. A new level of formal cooperation in trade matters was considered essential, including a further round of multilateral trade negotiations.

The Uruguay Round began in 1986 with a broad mandate reflecting not only US and EEC compromises but also the growing influence of new alliances such as the Cairns Group of agricultural exporters and developing countries led by India and Brazil. The areas identified for negotiation represented the full range of trade policy issues of the period. They covered traditional and new issues, the latter including services, trade aspects of investment, and intellectual property. In addition to strengthening the GATT system, the agenda identified articles for review dealing with balance of payments measures, state trading, dispute settlement, trade policy reviews and institutional arrangements. A stand-still and roll-back of GATT-illegal measures was agreed. Among traditional issues, it was considered essential to reduce the extreme distortions in agricultural production and trade, and to address the excessive fiscal costs of farm support programs. It was also recognized that developing countries required better access to industrial markets to encourage investment and adjustments to global competition. It was also evident that improvements were needed in the dispute resolutions mechanism of GATT, and in its overall institutional capabilities.

The Uruguay Round marked a new phase in trade policy. It took eight years to conclude, demonstrating the difficulties faced by governments in reforming policies and restructuring economies in an increasingly interdependent world. Many developments over the period influenced the multilateral negotiations and added to their complexity. Mexico implemented fundamental economic reforms to join GATT, and open its economy to competition. The US, Mexico and Canada negotiated the North American Free Trade Agreement (NAFTA) and some of its provisions, notably those dealing with health and sanitary measures, influenced the WTO Agreements. Side agreements dealing with labor and the environment were added to NAFTA.[9] Several complaints were taken to GATT by the US, EEC and others, to challenge import restrictions and export measures, particularly for agricultural products. The US Congress adopted another protectionist Trade Bill in 1988 to increase pressure on its commercial partners and reduce its growing trade deficit. The European Community (EC) took a significant step in reform of the CAP toward a market-based rather than administered agriculture. They also completed a Single Market project in 1992 to further integrate their economies at the regulatory level. The fall of the Berlin Wall reinforced the need to integrate East European nations into the multilateral trade system.

Strenuous efforts at Economic Summits and in other Ministerial meetings put great pressure on governments to complete GATT reforms. The OECD, GATT secretariat and other economic organizations were actively involved in technical work on alternative approaches to trade issues. Agriculture posed the greatest challenge, and preparatory work focused on developing methods of measuring and comparing levels of support and trade distortion from policies in industrial nations. In the final stages the key sticking points were overcome in negotiations between the US and EC, but taking into account the positions of key groups of countries. The basic trade deal was reached in December 1993. The conclusion of the Uruguay Round brought a new regime into force, the WTO, and incorporated 40 agreements and accords in a single undertaking. This integrated package, the largest and most comprehensive commercial agreement yet achieved on a multilateral basis, was signed in Marrakech, Morocco in April 1994. It was accepted by all 125 Contracting Parties to GATT, and 30 other nations indicated their intention to accede. The Uruguay Round Agreements were described by some as the most important event in recent economic history.[10]

The WTO framework covered three main agreements, the GATT 1994, a General Agreement on Trade in Services (GATS) and an Agreement on Trade-Related Aspects of Intellectual Property (TRIPS). It added two important new elements, significantly improved dispute settlement rules and procedures, and a trade policy review mechanism. The result included agreements on agriculture, sanitary and phytosanitary measures, textiles and clothing, technical barriers to trade, trade related investment measures

(TRIMs), subsidies and countervailing measures, safeguards and a range of other trade issues. Ministerial decisions and declarations reflected additional commitments on the interpretation or elaboration of agreements and articles. Apart from four plurilateral agreements on civil aviation, government procurement, dairy and bovine meats, the result represented a single set of trade disciplines for all members. The provisional status of GATT was removed and waivers and exceptions were eliminated, or reduced to a transitional period for developing countries. As a result, the WTO becomes the centerpiece of the multilateral trading system for the twenty-first century.

Many aspects of the Uruguay Round Final Act represented turning points in the history of trade policy. Not only was a permanent international trade organization established, it is responsible for common rules and obligations to apply virtually without exception to all member nations. This represents a powerful endorsement of the principle of non-discrimination, and combined with an effective dispute settlement system, will discourage unilateral trade behavior. In a separate declaration, Ministers directed the WTO to cooperate with the Bretton Woods institutions in developing 'coherent and complementary international economic policies', recognizing the linkages between exchange rate stability, orderly macroeconomic conditions and trade, in creating sustainable growth and development, and correcting external imbalances.[11] The addition to the trade system of multilateral agreements on intellectual property and services was an important beginning in broadening the coverage of the multilateral system to encompass the rapidly expanding international movement of investment and services.

The Agreement on Agriculture represented a fundamental turning point in the treatment of this sector under international trade rules. From the outset it was agreed that the long-term objective is to establish a fair and market oriented agricultural trade system through a reform process. For the first time nations accepted comprehensive commitments for agriculture that would limit their authorities to erect border restrictions to import, implement internal policies that distort trade, or apply direct subsidies and support measures contingent on export. The prohibition on the use of non-tariff barriers and the conversion of existing NTBs into tariff equivalents was unique in the history of GATT. As a result waivers, exceptions and grandfathered protective measures disappeared, including the US authority to limit imports to support farm programs. Similarly, the acceptance of direct multilateral constraints on domestic agricultural policies was an unprecedented step for any sector. However, tariff rate quotas were introduced, with high over-quota tariffs and domestic support commitments allow substantial levels of subsidy to continue. Consequently, the immediate commercial impact of this historic outcome was limited, indicating that the process of liberalizing agricultural trade had only begun.

The WTO Agreement on safeguards and textiles and clothing signaled an end to the 1970s drift in trade disciplines toward managed protectionism. The restrictive multifibers arrangement (MFA) was to be phased out, but over a ten year period. But the reforms to the antidumping and countervailing duties disciplines are weak, and these policies continue to be used excessively. The TRIMs Agreement is only a modest step toward an effective code on investment despite the enormous impact of foreign investment flows on trade, technology transfer and economic performance. While the average level of customs duties is low after eight rounds of multilateral negotiations, tariffs are still excessive for some sensitive products.

Entering the twenty-first century

Multilateral trade liberalization continued to dominate the policy agenda as GATT members celebrated its fiftieth anniversary in 1998 and the WTO pursued a new round of multilateral negotiations to be completed early in the twenty-first century. The dominant developments shaping the post-Uruguay Round environment were described at that time by Renato Ruggiero, Director-General of the WTO, as the 'end of the Cold War, the dramatic rise of many developing countries and the massive increase in trade and investment flows around the globe that have expanded the frontiers of the trading system, and tested its ability to manage an economy of global dimensions'.[12] Now trade liberalization is not only concerned with traditional barriers to the flow of goods across borders but also the effects of international trade regulation on a wide range of other policies and issues – investment and competition laws, labor and environmental standards, health, taxation and a host of non-traditional concerns.

This broad, additional agenda was dramatically demonstrated at the WTO Ministerial Meeting in Seattle in 1999 when a large spectrum of civil society and non-governmental groups congregated in an effort to block the launch of a new round of trade liberalization. In a similar manner, organized opposition confronted the IMF, World Bank and Economic Summits at their meetings to promote monetary stability and economic prosperity. In the growing interdependence among nations through investment, technology transfer and rapid communications and commercial interchange, trade was viewed as a common denominator. Despite the success of nations in freeing up the exchange of goods and services to stimulate economic growth and improve the general standards of living, the multilateral trading system was confronted by other social and political objectives.

Nonetheless governments continued to construct regional and multilateral agreements to deepen and broaden the trading system. Steps were taken by the WTO and other trade institutions to make their operations more transparent and to promote a better understanding of the benefits of a rules-based trade system. Additional WTO agreements were negotiated in the 1990s to free up trade in telecommunications, financial services and information technologies. The EU moved further in accomplishing their economic union with the introduction of the euro, and expanding to 25 members. New CAP reforms were adopted to limit expenditures and decouple farm support from production and markets. Economic integration proceeded in other regions as well. There are negotiations toward a Free Trade Agreement of the Americas, with similar initiatives underway elsewhere. Although the US Congress continued to resist fiscal and trade reforms, and increased domestic support for agriculture, the Administration pursued regional and bilateral trade arrangements with several nations. China acceded to the WTO, and Russia joined the list of other nations seeking admission. However, trade challenges persisted, in some cases to restrict imports for traditional complaints such as contingency protection actions, or over newer issues, including genetically modified foods, animal health or for environmental reasons. Stronger WTO rules and the more effective dispute settlement mechanisms were being used by governments from large and small nations, both developed and developing, to confront unilateral and restrictive actions. The trade system was becoming more legalistic and more litigious.

The difficulties in launching a further round of multilateral trade negotiations at the turn of the century were eventually overcome. Developing countries were now the majority of WTO members, and through various coalitions, exerted a strong influence from the outset. Although their positions varied with their levels of development, common objectives included eliminating trade distorting subsidies, particularly agricultural export subsidies and reducing access restrictions, including trade remedy measures. But financial crises in Japan and South-east Asia, and trade and fiscal imbalances in the US and elsewhere, retarded progress. The movement toward regional free trade arrangements slowed. Once again issues around agricultural trade presented serious obstacles although the Uruguay Round Agreement committed governments to continue negotiations to progressively reduce support and protection to the sector.[13]

The Doha Development Round was initiated in November 2001. Its work program reflected the broad range of issues that represented trade policy at the turn of the century. These included traditional issues in agriculture, services, industrial product access, intellectual property, investment, competition, government procurement, subsidies, antidumping, dispute settlement and special and differential treatment for developing countries. Newer trade issues identified included trade facilitation, regional agreements, environment, e-commerce, small economies, technology transfer, less developed countries and technical cooperation. The program would also cover issues of trade, debt and finance, intellectual property and public health, geographical indications for specific products and other matters.[14] However, the negotiations have proceeded slowly and deadlines have been missed. Although a framework agreement was reached in Geneva by mid-2004 to provide specific direction to the negotiations, the Round is likely to continue for at least two years. Nonetheless, the history of trade policy indicates that nations will succeed in deepening and extending the multilateral trade system.

Summary and conclusions

The central element of modern trade policy is the emergence of the multilateral trade system in the last half of the twentieth century. Beginning during WWII, the US, supported by Britain, Canada and their allies, launched a new phase in international cooperation based on collective action in both economic and political affairs. Against the recognition that national economic policies had contributed to global warfare and economic depression, and recognizing the gains that could arise from more open trade, these countries began to work on a post-war framework to bring order to monetary, financial and trade affairs. The Bretton Woods Agreements led to the establishment of the IMF and IBRD, and a third pillar in an international trade organization was envisaged.

The ITO was finalized by the Havana Charter but not implemented. What were to have been its trade provisions were incorporated in a General Agreement on Tariffs and Trade and given force through a Provisional Protocol of Application. This Provisional Protocol, including the results of the first multilateral trade round in Geneva, became the centerpiece of the emerging multilateral trade system. Through successive rounds of trade negotiations, the GATT provided the framework for the development of trade policies of most nations of the world over the last half century.

The architecture and agreements of the multilateral trade system reflect the events and trends of the period of their development. The protectionism and economic hardships of the 1930s, and the devastation of global conflict convinced governments that their economic behavior must be subjected to international disciplines. The experiences of bilateral and plurilateral trade agreements of that period, and wartime measures of controls, financial agreements and international collaboration, demonstrated the potential gain of orderly trade and commercial cooperation. The demands of reconstruction, the strains of foreign exchange shortages and balance of payments problems were catalysts in the formation of GATT.

Growing economic interdependence pushed economies closer together. Trade expanded more rapidly than domestic production, and with rising foreign investment, played an increasing role in economic development. These factors, combined with periodic economic downturns, trade and payments crises, and specific commercial disputes, continued to bring governments back to the negotiating table. Successive rounds of negotiations, involving increasing numbers of countries and issues, shaped the development of the multilateral trading system.

More open trade and commercial interchange exposed new and different barriers, and each round of trade negotiations became more ambitious. Some countries pressed for faster or deeper trade liberalization. Others demanded special exemptions or differential treatment to respond to their national circumstances, to deal with specific issues, or to protect politically sensitive sectors. Groups of countries sought preferential treatment to encourage their economic development while other nations, notably in Western Europe, pushed their trade arrangements further or faster on a regional basis. These developments led to many additional multilateral and plurilateral agreements and institutional arrangements both within the UN framework and outside it. Some organizations, such as the OECD and UNCTAD, were primarily consultative bodies to facilitate reaching agreements. Several commodity agreements with economic provisions were negotiated but eventually became consultative arrangements. These formed part of broader efforts through the UNCTAD to address the economic problems of developing countries.

The trade policies and GATT negotiations of the 1950s and 1960s focused on rebuilding economies and promoting economic growth, stimulated by tariff reductions and more open borders. The agreements were broadened to include more countries and commitments, and to deal with trade disputes. Monetary and macroeconomic developments were catalysts in the launching of each multilateral round. By the 1970s new pressures from low cost imports, trade with state controlled economies, and the oil embargo and perceived commodity shortages, shifted the focus of trade policies toward managing as well as liberalizing trade.

The economic policies of the 1980s reflected an accelerating trend toward global integration and policy convergence. A revolution in information technology led to a disaggregation of traditional industrial structures, thereby greatly increasing foreign investment, market integration and the exchange of services. The restructuring of economies introduced a new dimension to trade policy, new concepts of sovereignty and the role of national borders. Governments were challenged to deal with sharp differences over the impact of trade and economic activities on social, environmental and a myriad of modern consumer issues and concerns. While the traditional barriers to trade remained challenging, for those sectors left behind in earlier trade liberalization, such as agriculture and textiles, new issues were emerging, stimulated by accelerating economic and social integration. Many countries, both developing and developed, shifted or even reversed their trade policies away from protectionism and market interventions, to open their economies to international trade and competition. Beginning in Western Europe following WWII, groups of nations came together to form regional arrangements to accelerate industry restructuring, economic growth and commercial exchange.

This new phase in trade policy was marked by many regional trade agreements and the most comprehensive multilateral negotiation in the history of GATT, the Uruguay Round. Described by some trade experts as the most important event in recent economic history, its Final Act launched the World Trade Organization in 1995. As the permanent international trade institution, it completes the ambitious plan for global economic cooperation envisaged half a century before, and incorporates some 40 separate agreements, including the GATT 1994, in a single undertaking accepted by most of the trading nations of the world. It includes agreements on trade in goods, services and intellectual property rights. The agreements cover the traditional trade barriers, reductions in tariffs and removal of waivers, derogations and most non-tariff barriers to trade. A beginning is made on liberalizing trade in agriculture and textiles. The WTO has much stronger dispute resolution mechanisms and a permanent trade policy review mechanism.

The trade policies of the modern era continue to evolve within the WTO framework. The WTO membership is expanding, with many of its new members drawn from the developing countries and former state controlled countries which are becoming market economies. Regional integration with new bilateral and plurilateral trade agreements is ongoing. With stronger and more effective dispute settlement provisions in the WTO and in some regional accords, there is a trend toward stricter adherence to rules and commitments. Trade policy is becoming more comprehensive and more confrontational as new issues and advocacy groups challenge the impact of trade on their interests and concerns. There are numerous trade policy issues that remain outstanding or only partially resolved including the use of anti-dumping legislation, countervailing duties and rules of origin to limit or prevent trade. Emerging security concerns and tighter border supervision present new challenges to cross-border trade. Despite this, and persistent protectionist pressures over labor concerns, trade deficits and macroeconomic developments, governments are working to improve the multilateral trade system. In the first years of the new century, virtually all of the trading nations of the world are engaged in a further round of multilateral negotiations with a focus on international development.

The modern history of trade policy is a record of the efforts by nations to move from policies based on power and unilateral and nationalistic economic behavior toward a multilateral system of consultations, rules, and agreed dispute settlement procedures. It involves the acceptance of a degree of international discipline over internal policies in relation to retaining full sovereignty over them. The adherence to the principles of the WTO framework for trade policies, of non-discrimination and national treatment, also demonstrates the acceptance of market and price-based economies over those managed through government interventions. The emergence of the multilateral trade system represents recognition of the growing interdependence of nations and the fact that all countries are affected by events elsewhere, whether open conflicts, monetary or macroeconomic developments, environmental issues or social or political unrest.

Behind the evolving events of the last half century, and the on-going concerns – economic, social, political – of rapidly integrating world economies, is the continuing challenge for governments to manage the benefits of expanding trade and economic growth in an acceptable manner in the face of inevitable change. There are indications that governments, and those they represent, recognize that there is a cost to society of shielding sectors from global competition or of providing forms of assistance to weaker sectors. The gains from trade have been demonstrated by the history of liberalization over half a century, and the full costs of trade protection, subsidies and related disputes are becoming recognized. This augers well for future trade liberalization. What is apparent in the early years of the twenty-first century, and is reinforced by this review of the history of modern trade policy, is the potential benefit in economic and social terms from more open trading arrangements. In the future, as in the past, nations can be expected to find a path to improve the level of their prosperity through cooperation in economic affairs and expanding trade in goods and services.

Notes

1. The General Agreement on Tariffs and Trade, Geneva, 1986.
2. Numerous publications provide a detailed history of the early development of the multilateral trade system and the GATT – see references, particularly: Jackson, John. H., *World Trade and the Law of the GATT*, 1969; and *Restructuring the GATT System*, 1990; Hart, Michael, *Fifty Years of Canadian Tradecraft*, 1998, and editor of 'Also Present at the Creation, Dana Wilgress and the UN Conference on Trade and Employment at Havana', 1995; Stone, Frank, *Canada, the GATT and the International Trade System*, 1984.
3. By 1942 trade agreements with 28 countries had reduced the US tariff by nearly 50 percent (Hart).
4. Charters for the IMF and World Bank were negotiated at Bretton Woods, New Hampshire and are known as the Bretton Woods Financial Institutions.
5. Most provisions of the General Agreement were drawn from the commercial policy chapter of the draft ITO Charter. The text of the Charter, with an introduction and analysis, is included in Hart, M., 'Present at the Creation'.
6. Chapter VI of the Havana Charter contained provisions for commodity agreements among producer and consumer countries to stabilize markets. Six agreements with economic provisions were negotiated in the post-WWII period covering wheat, tin, sugar, coffee, cocoa and natural rubber, Stone, F.; *Canada, The GATT and the International Trade System.*
7. Hart, M., *Fifty Years of Canadian Tradecraft.*
8. Article XXIV of the GATT provides an exception for countries which form customs unions or free trade areas with specific rules and conditions subject to approval. Under Article XXV, a waiver may be granted for other preferential trade arrangements (Stone). Descriptions and assessments of the numerous regional trade arrangements are provided in several publications, including those noted in 2. above. See also; Serra Puche, J., 'Regionalism and the WTO', and Smith, M. G. and Stone, F., *Assessing the Canada–US Free Trade Agreement.*
9. Lipsey, R. *et al.*, *The NAFTA, What's In, What's Out, What's Next*, C. D. Howe Institute, 1994.
10. Jackson, J., 'Emerging Problems of the WTO Constitution: Dispute Settlement and Decision-Making in the Jurisprudence of the WTO'.
11. World Trade Organization, *Uruguay Round Agreements and Final Act*, Geneva, 1994.
12. Ruggiero, R., Fiftieth Anniversary Forum.
13. Ingco, M. D. and L. A. Winters (eds), *Agriculture and the New Trade Agenda.*
14. World Trade Organization, *Doha Ministerial Declaration*, 2001. Regarding negotiations on trade and competition policy, Chapter V of the Havana Charter contained proposed rules for restrictive business practices.

References

Anderson, K. (1998), 'The Future Agenda of the WTO', 50th Anniversary Symposium, WTO, Geneva.
General Agreement on Tariffs and Trade (1986), Geneva.
Hart, M. (ed.) (1995), 'Also Present at the Creation, Dana Wilgress and the United Nations Conference on Trade and Employment at Havana', Centre for Trade Policy and Law, Ottawa.
Hart, M. (1998), *Fifty Year of Canadian Tradecraft*, Ottawa: Centre for Trade Policy and Law.
Ingco, M. D. and C. A. Winters (eds) (2004), *Agriculture and the New Trade Agenda: Creating a Global Trading Environment for Development*, Washington, DC: World Bank.
Jackson, J. (1969), *World Trade and the Law of the GATT*, Indianapolis: Bobbs-Merril.
Jackson, J. (1990), *Restructuring the GATT System*, London: Royal Institute of International Affairs.
Jackson, J. (1999), 'Emerging Problems of the WTO Constitution: Dispute Settlement and Decision-Making in the Jurisprudence of the WTO', in P. Ruttley, I. MacVay and A. Masa'deh (eds), *Liberalisation and Protectionism in the World Trading System*, London: Cameron, pp. 25–38.
Lipsey, R., D. Schwanen and R. J. Wonnacott (1994), *The NAFTA, What's In, What's Out, What's Next*, Toronto: C.D. Howe Institute.

Michelmann, H., J. Rude, J. Stabler and G. Storey (eds) (2001), *Globalization and Agricultural Trade Policy*, London: L. Rienner.

Ruggiero, R. (1998), 'From Vision To Reality: The Multilateral Trading System At Fifty', Address to the Brookings Institution Forum 'The Global Trading System: A GATT 50th Anniversary Forum', Washingtonm, DC, 4 March.

Serra Puche, J. (1998), 'Regionalism and the WTO', 50th Anniversary Symposium, WTO, Geneva.

Smith, M. and F. Stone (eds) (1987), *Assessing the Canada–US Free Trade Agreement*, Montreal: The Institute for Research on Public Policy.

Stone, F. (1984), *Canada, The GATT and The International Trade System*, Montreal: The Institute for Research on Public Policy.

The Tokyo Round Agreements (1986), GATT, Geneva.

World Trade Organization (1994), *Uruguay Round Agreements and Final Act*, Geneva: WTO.

World Trade Organization (2001), *Doha Ministerial Declaration*, Geneva: WTO.

Recommended reading

Baldwin, R. (1998), 'Pragmatism vs. Principle in GATT Decision Making: A Brief Historical Perspective', 50th Anniversary Symposium, WTO, Geneva.

Messerlin, P. (1998), 'The WTO's New Horizons', 50th Anniversary Symposium, WTO, Geneva.

Michelmann, H. J., J Rude,. J. Stabler and G. Storey (eds) (2001), *Globalization and Agricultural Trade Policy*, London: L. Rienner.

Ostry, S. (1998), 'Looking Back to Look Forward, The Multilateral Trading System After 50 Years', 50th Anniversary Symposium, WTO, Geneva.

5 Modeling approaches to the analysis of trade policy: computable general equilibrium and gravity models
Olena Ivus and Aaron Strong

Introduction

Gravity models and computable general equilibrium (CGE) models are the most commonly used analytical techniques to perform a quantitative analysis in the area of trade policy. These models provide a consistent economy-wide picture that can be very beneficial to policy makers. Both CGE and gravity models have the advantages of general equilibrium approaches in examining a great variety of questions. In the partial equilibrium models of international trade the focus is on one sector of the economy with the cross-sector effects being disregarded. General equilibrium modeling, in turn, takes explicit account of the consequences that a policy change in one sector has on other sectors of the economy.

The gravity model is a popular empirical approach to trade that has been used widely for analyzing the impact of different trade policy issues on bilateral trade flows between different geographical entities. This model takes an *ex-post* approach to perform trade policy analysis. Gravity models measure the effect on trade flows of a past trade policy. By contrast, CGE modeling takes an *ex-ante* approach, which involves quantifying the future effects of a new policy. In addition, gravity models only explain the pattern of bilateral trade and do not provide direct estimates of welfare costs. CGE models, on the other hand, are generally used to quantify the impact of a change in trade policy on countries' welfare levels and the distribution of income across multi-country regions.

The main goal of this chapter is to provide an introduction to both CGE and gravity models. The next section discusses the gravity model. First, the basic gravity equation is introduced. Second, the theoretical foundations of gravity models are provided. Third, issues and caveats concerning the empirical estimation of gravity models are considered. The section concludes with a selective review of studies based on the gravity model. The third section presents the CGE model. First, the advantages and disadvantages of CGE modeling are discussed. Second, the basic structure of CGE models is presented. Third, the steps used to construct a CGE model are described. The section concludes with a discussion of the Harrison/Rutherford/Tarr Multi-Regional Global Trade Model.

Gravity models

Tinnbergen (1962) and Pöyhönen (1963) were the first economists to use a gravity-style equation to analyze international trade flows. Since these foundations were laid, the gravity model has become a popular empirical trade approach that has been used widely for analyzing the impact of different trade policy issues on bilateral trade flows between different geographical entities. It has also been applied to a wide range of other questions, such as foreign direct investment, tourism, migration, commuting, and so on.

The basic gravity equation

The name of gravity model was derived from Newton's 'law of universal gravitation'. In this version of 'gravity', the extent of a trade flow between two countries is equal to the product of their masses or economic sizes divided by a resistance or distance factor. A justification for the gravity models of Tinbergen (1962) and Pöyhönen (1963) can be based on Walrasian general equilibrium theory. The gravity equation is viewed as a representation of demand and supply forces. In this case, aggregate income of the importer proxies the level of demand in the destination region and aggregate income of the exporter proxies the level of its supply. Distance is used as a proxy for transport costs.

In greater detail, the general gravity model specifies that the bilateral trade between countries i and j in year t is positively related the economic sizes of the two countries, proxied by GDP, and negatively related to the trade costs, proxied by distance between the two countries' capital cities. The baseline specification of the gravity model with exports as a dependent variable is summarized in Table 5.1.

In the importing country, a higher level of income should imply greater imports. In the exporting country, a higher level of income will give rise to a greater level of overall production and this, in turn, will increase the availability of goods for export. Distance drives a wedge between demand and supply, resulting in a lower equilibrium export flows. The model may be estimated for a single year, as a so-called cross-section of trading countries, or pooled over several years.

In order to account for as many extraneous factors as possible, it is common to augment the basic gravity equation with a number of extra conditioning variables that affect trade. Many authors estimate gravity equations with the per capita incomes of the exporter and importer as an additional measure of country size. Some authors have included a country 'remoteness' variable in the gravity equation. The effect of this variable measured by its estimated coefficient is expected to be positive, since the less remote a country is, the more sources of imports it has and, as a result, the smaller share of its imports comes from each particular source. Anderson and van Wincoop (2003), in turn, stress the importance of introducing 'multilateral resistance' terms – measured by the average trade barriers of the exporting and importing countries – into the estimated equation. They argue that adding a remoteness index is in discordance with theory, because it is a function of distance and it does not capture any other barriers to trade. Anderson and van Wincoop (2004) note that a multilateral resistance index may be replaced with importer and exporter country-specific effects. Rose (2004) applies an empirical strategy to control for as many 'natural'

Table 5.1　The baseline specification of the gravity model[a]

X_{ijt}	exports from country i to country j in year t depend on:
Y_{it}	GDP of the exporter i at time t
Y_{jt}	GDP of the importer j at time t
D_{ij}	distance between the trading regions i and j

Note:
[a] In the estimation procedure a log-linear form (that is taking the natural logarithms of the variables) is often applied. In this case the specification will be the following:
$\log X_{ijt} = \alpha + \beta_1 \log Y_{it} + \beta_2 \log Y_{jt} + \beta_3 \log D_{ij} + \varepsilon_{ijt}$

causes of trade as possible. In this case, the gravity equation includes variables for sharing a common land border, speaking a common language, ever having been colonized, using the same currency at time t, and so on.

The theoretical foundations of gravity models
Despite the gravity model's considerable empirical success (for example, its high explanatory power), it was long criticized for lacking strong theoretical foundations. More recently, different theories have been developed to establish rigorous theoretical underpinnings of the gravity model. Anderson (1979), Bergstrand (1985, 1990), Deardorff (1998), and Eaton and Kortum (2002) have developed micro-foundations for the gravity model. Anderson (1979) provided a theoretical basis for the gravity model by assuming constant elasticity of substitution (CES) preferences and goods that are differentiated by country of origin. Bergstrand (1990) derived a gravity equation from a monopolistic competition trade model in which the countries are completely specialized in different product varieties. In this case, each country is exports one variety of a differentiated product to other countries. Deardorff (1998) has shown that the gravity model can arise from the Heckscher-Ohlin model, which explains trade based on relative differences in factor endowments across countries. Eaton and Kortum (2002) obtained a gravity equation from a Ricardian type of model, which explains trade based on relative differences in technology across countries.

Feenstra (2004) notes that the conventional gravity model assumes identical prices across countries. Therefore, price is not included in the gravity equation as a variable that affects bilateral trade flows. Under the micro-foundations approach this results in misspecification of the gravity model. It is important to allow for differing prices due to trade barriers between the countries. The gravity equation with so called 'price effects' was derived by Anderson (1979). Feenstra (2004) suggests three approaches to estimating this equation. First, the price effects may be measured by price indexes, as in Bergstrand (1985) and Baier and Bergstrand (2001). Second, estimated border effects may be used as an alternative measure, as in Anderson and van Wincoop (2003). Third, a fixed-effects approach, which allows each country to be different, may be applied as in Redding and Venables (2000) and Rose and van Wincoop (2001).

Estimation of gravity models
The gravity model is a conventional method used to estimate the impact of various types of trade-related policies on international trade flows. Many gravity-model papers, for example, examine the effect of the formation of regional trade areas (RTAs). In this case, the gravity equation is extended using regional dummy variables, which indicate whether or not a pair of countries is in the same region. However, one needs to be careful when the interpreting the estimated coefficient, which describes the empirical effect of this dummy variable. Ideally, the intent is to measure the impact of the RTA, but other effects may also inadvertently be captured due to measurement problems. For example, the true costs of bilateral trade may be partially subsumed by the variables related to trade agreements because the distance between capital cities does not fully reflect the trade costs. Of course, simple distance measures are flawed in many ways; most countries have multiple economic centers and other features matter such as infrastructure quality and border waiting times.

Regional dummy variables, which are intended to show the impact of RTAs, may also catch the effects of any variables that are not included in the gravity regression. The baseline gravity model approach makes an assumption that the level of bilateral trade depends only on the included economic features of a given pair of countries. However, the level of export from country i to countries j and k may be different even if countries j and k have the same GDP levels and they are equally distant from country i. These differences can be explained by political factors, historical links, cultural similarities, and so on, that are correlated with levels of bilateral trade and with the baseline gravity variables. Omission or misspecification of these variables will lead to omitted-variables bias or the so called heterogeneity bias.

As demonstrated by Cheng and Wall (2005), standard estimation methods overestimate trade between low-trade countries and underestimated trade between high-trade countries.[1] They argue that the inability of the standard cross-section estimation to account for the pairwise heterogeneity of bilateral trade relations is the principal cause of the bias. To eliminate the heterogeneity bias Cheng and Wall (2005) adopted a model which includes both the country-pair and year specific effects. The term which is common to all years, but specific to the country pairs is used to take into account the specific country-pair effects between the trading partners, such as distance, border, language, culture, and so on. The term, which is common to all pairs, but specific to each year, is included to capture the year-specific fixed effects. They will catch all the omitted factors that affect bilateral trade, are constant across trading pairs and vary over time. Alternatively, Mátyás (1997) has emphasized: 'Unfortunately, none of the applications of this model bothered to take into account the local, target and time effects, which means that all practitioners were imposing the unnecessary restrictions . . . These are unlikely to be correct.' In this way, Mátyás (1997) argues that the correct econometric specification of the gravity model should include the importer (target) country effects, the exporter (local) country effects, and the time effects.

In summary, the main benefit of both of the above extensions of the gravity model is that they help to control for omitted variables that are unobservable or difficult to quantify. Adopting either or both extensions will provide a robustness check, which will help avoid misinterpretation of empirical results from the simpler formulations of the model.

Applications: The impact of membership in the WTO and RTAs on trade
Several studies have applied gravity equations to provide an empirical examination of the impact of multilateral or regional trade agreements on international trade and, thus, have contributed to the refinement of the gravity model approach. This section provides a selective overview of some of these applications.

A recent study by Rose (2004) provides a comprehensive econometric study that analyzes the effect of the World Trade Organization (WTO), the Generalized Agreement on Tariffs and Trade (GATT), and the General System of Preferences (GSP). The augmented gravity model studied real bilateral trade flows between trading countries for the period from 1948 to 1999. The author concluded that membership in WTO/GATT did not imply an increase in trade intensities because the volume of bilateral trade between members and non-members was not significantly different.

The results of Rose (2004) have been strongly questioned by Subramanian and Wei (2003) who contend that the analysis needs to take into account liberalization asymmetries arising from the WTO: between developed and developing countries; between developing countries that joined the WTO before and after the Uruguay Round; and between trade sectors. Once the econometric specification incorporates these types of unevenness in the patterns of trade liberalization, the impact of the WTO on promoting world trade appears to be strong and positive, although uneven. On the other hand, the authors suggest that Rose's gravity model specification needs to include country fixed effects to capture the impact of multilateral resistance.[2]

The economic implications of RTA formation for international trade have been examined in many empirical papers. Bayoumi and Eichengreen (1995) make an important distinction between trade creation effects, leading to increases in the intensity of trade between members of RTAs, and trade diversion effects, leading to decreases in trade with third countries.[3] The authors apply the gravity model with the addition of specific dummy variables to capture the impact of participation in various RTAs. A positive coefficient on the dummy variable indicating both countries of a bilateral pair are the members of the RTA, suggests that they trade more with one another than is predicted by their incomes and distance, and, so, would provide evidence of a trade creation effect. A negative coefficient on a dummy variable indicating that one country in a bilateral pair is a member of an RTA but the other is not, would suggest trade diversion *vis-à-vis* the rest of the world. In order to identify differences over time in the trade creating and trade diverting effects of EU integration, successive cross-sections were analyzed for a sample of 21 industrial countries and a period of 1953–1992. The authors found that the European Free Trade Association (EFTA) resulted in trade creation, while the European Economic Community (EEC) promoted trade within the region through the combination of trade creation and trade diversion. It is also noted that the accession of Spain and Portugal resulted in almost no trade diversion.

Christie (2002) presents a classical approach to the problem of quantifying potential trade levels, with a specific emphasis on trade flows with and within southeast Europe. After applying the gravity model approach and using panel data from 1996 to 1999 the author found that EU members trade 122 percent more than non-member countries, however the cross-section estimation for 1999 indicated that this effect decreased to 98 percent. The author notes: 'Overall, regional variables appear as significant in the panel model, but on separate cross-sections regression their significance deteriorates with the years'.

Chang and Winters (1999) have shown that regional integration, on average, has significant adverse effect on non-member countries exporting to the integrated market. Even if regional integration does not increase external barriers to trade, the excluded countries may still be negatively affected. This, for example, could arise from excluded exporters decreasing their prices to meet the competition from suppliers within the RTA.

Gravity models have also been widely applied to examine the link between trade and exchange rate volatility, trade and currency unions, trade and environment, and trade and growth. However, it is important to be cautious about drawing inferences from the results of gravity model estimation, particularly if only one model is being considered. As Piermartini and Teh (2005) point out, gravity-model results generally depend on a number of estimation choices, such as the use of aggregated or disaggregated data, the sample of countries, the length of time period, the specification of a gravity model, the use of country-specific or country-pair-specific effects, and so on.

Computable general equilibrium models

Although the gravity model provides a nice framework for considering *ex-post* analyses of trade policy, it is also desirable to have a tool for examining changes in trade policy prior to implementation in so-called *ex-ante* analysis. Computable/calibrated general equilibrium (CGE) models provide one such framework. One of the main motivations underlying the use of CGE models is to be able to consider large scale policy changes using the present economy as a benchmark. This aspect of large scale policy changes separates the ability of the policy analyst to evaluate policies using a simple theoretical model or a back of the envelope calculation to gauge the impacts of policies. Trade policy is an inherently large scale problem. Even a scale change in a single industry has the potential to cause drastic and unexpected consequences given backward and forward linkages within the economy. These interdependencies between industries need to be considered in order to analyze the full impact of policy changes.

Quantifying the impact of policies had its beginnings with Leontief (1951, 1953) in which he developed the structure of input–output models for economies. These models, still popular today, tend to focus on inter-industry connections to meet final demand and not necessarily an integration of production with consumption along with factor ownership. The theoretical underpinnings for analyzing a general or economy-wide equilibrium lie first with Walras (1896) who represented the economy with a system of simultaneous equations that describe supply and demand equilibrium or market clearing through a set of prices for goods and factors. Nobel laureates Kenneth Arrow and Gerard Debreu (1954) and Debreu (1959) extended the ideas of Walras to incorporate the conditions for which a competitive equilibrium exists. Further, they established the link between a market equilibrium and welfare. The first real CGE model can probably be attributed to Johansen (1960) in which a linear model of the economy is used to identify the sources of economic growth in Norway. The first rigorous treatment of the numerical algorithms involved to compute non-linear models can be attributed to Scarf (1969). More recently with the advent of improved software and computational power, there has been a steady increase in the use of computational methods to explore issues of interest not only to academics but also policy makers at all levels.

Why use CGE models?

In considering questions of trade policy, at one level we care about the qualitative impact, or about which production sectors and consumer groups will be positively and negatively affected by the policy change. Economic theory can provide us with these results in a variety of circumstances. Potentially more interesting is the degree to which groups are affected. CGE and other quantitative methods allow us to estimate these effects. Through simulation of the economy we will not only be able to know who are the winners and losers but also how big these gains and losses are in order to have a better sense of the economic and social impact of policy change. In addition to being able to know how big the gains and losses are, in order to make theoretical analyses tractable, a certain level of aggregation is needed. This aggregation loses the detail that many policy makers would like to have in order to make better informed choices. Through the use of computational methods, this curse of dimensionality may be weakened. The limits to the dimension of the problem are no longer driven by tractability but by data availability.

Trade policy changes and trade negotiations are usually not single dimensional, and there is usually a 'give and take' in different sectors as well as by different parties involved. Additionally, a set of policy changes may have both positive and negative effects on the same sector or group. Theoretical considerations do not allow us to know the magnitude of these impacts and to be able to compare them in a meaningful manner. Through the use of computational methods multiple and/or ambiguous policy changes may be analyzed. Along these same lines, much of economics is concerned with efficiency whereas many policy makers may be additionally concerned with equity implications of policy changes. We know that different consumer groups will be affected differently by the same policy change. Just as we may disaggregate sectors fairly finely, we may also disaggregate consumer groups. Again, the limit to which we may disaggregate is driven by data availability and not the tractability of the problem.

Structure of CGE models
One of the main advantages of a modeling an economy and especially modeling a detailed economy is that we must truly understand the structure of the economy. In general, there are really five main aspects that need to be considered when trying to accomplish the goal of modeling an economy:

1. How do goods and factors flow through the economy?
2. In each sector, how does production take place?
3. In each industry, what does the market structure look like?
4. At the consumer level, how does consumption take place?
5. Finally, who owns which factors of production and firms?

In general, the structure of a CGE model may be described using an open economy circular flow model, which illustrates the linkages between different sectors of the economy. As illustrated in Figure 5.1, firms purchase (demand) intermediate goods from other domestic or foreign firms and primary factors from households. They produce final output and sell (supply) it to households, government and the investment sector or export it to the rest of the world (ROW). In addition, some final and intermediate products are purchased (demanded) from abroad. The aggregate output in the economy is distributed across households, governments and the investment sector. Households own factors of production, sell (supply) them to firms and get a reward for using these factors. Rent for land, wages for labour, interest for capital and profit for entrepreneurship are used as income to demand consumer goods. The role of a government sector is to collect taxes on domestic and imported goods, pay subsidies, buy goods and provide public goods and services. In summary, the circular flow diagram divides the economy into two sectors: one concerned with producing goods and services, and the other with consuming them.

Production in a CGE model takes place under the assumption of profit maximizing firms. These firms take prices of factors and goods as signals and make decision about output and input mixes. Recently there has been a move to incorporate not just production through factors but also through the use of intermediate inputs in the production technology. The production technology is usually modeled using a production function that is a second order approximation of the data. That is, the production

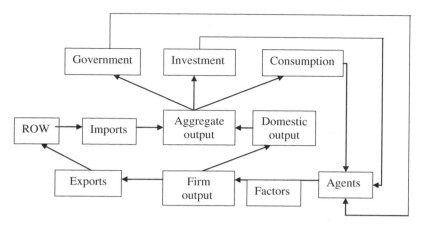

Note: [a] Firm output is divided into exports and domestically used output. Domestic output is combined with imports to create aggregate output. This allows domestic and foreign output to be imperfect substitutes as is common in many of the new trade models.

Figure 5.1   Circular flow of an economy[a]

technology will use a benchmark set of prices and quantities for a given year and then estimate the substitutability of the inputs from either the rest of the economic literature or through direct estimation using either time series or panel estimation. The other assumption that needs to be considered at the production level is that of market structure of the sector. Most commonly, models take perfect competition as the assumption. When considering trade policy, this may not be the case. Recently within the trade literature, both theoretically and numerically, there has been a move to imperfect competition either through an oligopoly or monopolistically competitive assumption.

Following the structure of the firms, consumer behavior has a similar structure. Analogous to firm behavior, consumers are assumed to maximize wellbeing, while taking good and factor prices as given. What distinguishes general equilibrium models from partial equilibrium is the ability to track the income of consumers. Consumers are assumed to own the factors of production as well as the firms. Many CGE models assume that there is a single representative economic agent that stands in for all economic agents. However, this need not be the case. If the focus of consideration for the policy change is on how different consumer groups are affected, this representative agent may be disaggregated to many such agents with different endowments of factors as well as firm ownership.

Finally, since firms are maximizing profit and consumers' wellbeing, we need to understand how these two sides of the economy interact. First, there is the assumption of full factor utilization. On the labor side, this means that there is full employment within the economy. Second, all markets, whether factor or good, must clear. Prices within the economy will adjust such that the supply of each good and factor will equal the demand. All of these assumptions come together into three types of conditions that will define a CGE model: market structure (zero profit) conditions, market clearing, and property rights (income balance) conditions.

Operationalizing CGE models
Following Markusen (2002), there are six steps to consider when constructing a CGE model of an economy. These are discussed in more detail below:

1. specify the dimension of the model;
2. choose functional forms for production, transformation and utility;
3. construct a micro-consistent dataset;
4. Calibrate the model to the data;
5. Replication of benchmark; and
6. run counter-factual experiments.

As a starting point to any modeling exercise, we must know the level of detail that the model must contain in order to analyze the economy at the appropriate scale. We must choose the dimension of the model or number of goods, factors, consumers, countries and active markets. Once the level of detail is chosen, the next set of assumptions that must be chosen is the structure or functional form of the production and consumption sectors. As discussed previously, this is usually chosen to allow the most flexibility to fit the data. Most commonly, a two level, nested constant elasticity of substitution is chosen. This allows the modeler to have the flexibility described above while not having to make too many additional assumptions regarding the parameters of the functions.

Once the structure of the model is chosen, data must be found to correctly calibrate the model to the appropriate level of detail. The data are usually constructed using two main types of data sources. First, a micro-consistent input–output matrix needs to be either constructed or obtained. Three common sources for this data are the Global Trade Analysis Project (GTAP), the Minnesota IMPLAN Group, Inc., and national level statistical agencies. Additionally, the International Food Policy Research Institute has a variety of input–output matrices for developing countries. If not already present in the data, the consumer side of the economy must be constructed. At the most basic level, this simply involves the final demand quantities, which are consumed and exported. In a more detailed model with heterogeneous consumer groups, consumer expenditure surveys may be used to obtain information on preferences and factor and firm ownership. From these data sources, a micro-consistent social accounting matrix (SAM) is constructed. The SAM is a generalization of the original work of Leontief (1951) that contains more detail about consumption and ownership and allows the modeler to have a benchmark equilibrium with which to calibrate the model. Combining the assumptions of the model with that of functional forms, the data are used to calibrate the parameters to replicate the benchmark equilibrium. Assuming that the economy presently satisfies the assumptions of market structure, market clearing and property rights in the economy, the model should reproduce the present economy. The ultimate goal of most CGE modeling exercises is to answer questions about how the economy responds to policy changes. Thus, the model should be able to replicate the present policy. Once a model is constructed to replicate the present economy, alternative counter-factual policies may be considered.

Application: the Harrison/Rutherford/Tarr Multi-Regional Global Trade Model
To measure the welfare benefits of the Uruguay Round of the GATT, Harrison *et al.* (1995, 1996, 1997) employ 'The Multi-Regional Global Trade Model'. The effects of the

Uruguay Round are quantified for 24 regions and 22 production sectors in each region in the four following areas: (a) tariff reductions in manufactured products; (b) replacement of non-tariff barriers in agriculture by the equivalent tariffs and obligatory commitments to decrease the level of agricultural protection; (c) the reduction of export and production subsidies in agriculture; (d) the removal of Voluntary Export Restraints (VERs) and Multi-Fibre Arrangements (MFAs). All distortions, such as taxes, tariffs, subsidies, VERs, and non-tariff barriers, are modeled as ad-valorem price wedges.[4] The data employed in the model come from the GTAP database for 1992 (Version 2). The results of the 'base' constant returns to scale and perfect competition static model suggest that the world welfare gains from the Uruguay Round would be $92.9 billion per year, out of which $18.8 billion are from manufacturing sector reforms, $58.3 billion are from agricultural reform, and $16 billion are from MFA reform.

Variations of the Multi-Regional Global Trade Model may be applied to analyze a wide range of trade issues. For example, it is possible to assess the impact of global free trade on the countries' welfare and the distribution of income across the regions. In addition, the impact of a county's accession to the WTO may be quantitatively assessed. Further, the model may be extended to analyze the effects of regional trade agreements on the member countries as well as on those excluded from membership regions. Incorporating the short-run effects of changes in the trade policy in addition to the long run effects will allow evaluation of the transaction costs associated with a policy change, which must be taken into account by policy-makers.

Conclusions

This chapter introduces the most commonly used analytical techniques for a quantitative analysis in the area of trade policy, namely computable general equilibrium and gravity models. Gravity models are popular empirical trade devices that have been used widely for analyzing the impact of different trade policy issues on bilateral trade flows between different geographical entities. CGE models are generally used to quantify the impact of a change in trade policy on the countries' welfare and the distribution of income across countries or multi-country regions. Through the use of computational methods, it is possible to analyze multiple policy changes and/or policy changes with ambiguous effects where theory is silent. Both types of models provide a consistent economy-wide picture that is beneficial to policy makers.

Notes

1.   The standard estimation method restricts the intercept of the gravity equation to be the same for all trading partners.
2.   This issue was discussed further in Anderson and van Wincoop (2003).
3.   Trade creation will occur if formation of a regional trade association results in the transfer of production from a high-cost source in a home country to the low-cost source in a partner country, because tariffs have been removed from the trade between these countries. Trade diversion, in contrast, will occur if production is transferred from a low-cost source in a third country to a higher-cost source in a partner country, because tariffs are no longer imposed on the goods from the latter.
4.   Important caveats concerning the conventional practice of *ad valorem* equivalent modeling are discussed in Chapter 18.

References

Anderson, J. (1979), 'A Theoretical Foundation for the Gravity Equation', *American Economic Review*, **69** (1), 106–16.

Anderson, J. and E. van Wincoop (2003), 'Gravity with Gravitas: A Solution to the Border Puzzle', *American Economic Review*, **93** (1), 70–92.

Anderson, J. and E. van Wincoop (2004), 'Trade Costs', *Journal of Economic Literature*, **42** (3), 691–751.

Arrow, K. and G. Debreu (1954), 'Existence of an Equilibrium for a Competitive Economy', *Econometrica*, **22** (July), 265–90.

Baier, S. and J.H. Bergstrand, (2001), 'The Growth of World Trade: Tariffs, Transport Costs and Income Similarity', *Journal of International Economics*, **53**, 1–27.

Bayoumi, T. and B. Eichengreen, (1995), 'Is Regionalism Simply a Diversion? Evidence from the Evolution of the EC and EFTA', NBER Working Paper #5283.

Bergstrand, J. H. (1985), 'The Gravity Equation in International Trade: Some Microeconomic Foundations and Empirical Evidence', *The Review of Economics and Statistics*, **67** (3), 474–81.

Bergstrand, J. H. (1990), 'The Heckscher–Ohlin–Samuelson Model, the Linder Hypothesis, and the Determinants of Bilateral Intra-Industry Trade', *Economic Journal*, **100** (4), 1216–29.

Chang, W. and A. Winters (1999), 'How Regional Blocks Affect Excluded Countries? The Price Effects of MERCOSUR', World Bank Working Paper #2157.

Cheng, I-H. and H. Wall (2005), 'Controlling for Heterogeneity in Gravity Models of Trade and Integration', *Federal Reserve Bank of St Louis Review*, **87** (1), 49–63.

Christie, E. (2002), 'Potential Trade in Southeast Europe: a Gravity Model Approach', Working Paper No. 21, The Vienna Institute for International Economic Studies, Vienna.

Deardorff, A. (1998), 'Determinants of Bilateral Trade: Does Gravity Work in a Neoclassical World?' in J. A. Frankel (ed.), *The Regionalization of the World Economy*, Chicago and London: The University of Chicago Press, pp. 7–22.

Debreu, G. (1959), *The Theory of Value: An Axiomatic Analysis of Economic Equilibrium*, Cowles Foundation Monograph No. 17, New York: John Wiley & Sons.

Eaton, J. and Kortum, S. (2002), 'Technology, Geography, and Trade', *Econometrica*, **70** (5), 1741–79.

Feenstra, R. (2004), *Advanced International Trade: Theory and Evidence*, Princeton and Oxford; Princeton University Press.

Harrison, G. W., D. Tarr and T. F. Rutherford (1995), 'Quantifying the Outcome of the Uruguay Round', *Finance & Development*, **32** (4), 38–41.

Harrison, G. W., D. Tarr and T. F. Rutherford (1996), 'Quantifying the Uruguay Round', in W. Martin and L. A. Winters (eds), *The Uruguay Round and the Developing Countries*, New York: Cambridge University Press.

Harrison, G. W., D. Tarr, and T. F. Rutherford (1997), 'Quantifying the Uruguay Round', *Economic Journal*, **107** 1405–30.

Johansen, L. (1960), *A Multi-Sectoral Study of Economic Growth*, Amsterdam: North-Holland.

Leontief, W. (1951), *The Structure of the American Economy 1919–1939*, New York: Oxford University Press.

Leontief, W. (1953), *Studies in the Structure of the American Economy*, New York: Oxford University Press.

Markusen J. R. (2002), *General-Equilibrium Modeling using GAMS and MPS/GE: Some Basics*, http://www.colorado.edu/Economics/courses/Markusen/GAMS/ch1.pdf.

Mátyás, L. (1997), 'Proper Econometric Specification of the Gravity Model', *The World Economy*, **20**, 363–8.

Piermartini, R. and R. Teh (2005), 'Demystifying Modelling Methods for Trade Policy', Geneva: WTO Discussion Paper no.10.

Pöyhönen, P. (1963), 'A Tentative Model for the Volume of Trade Between Countries', *Weltwirtschaftliches Archive*, **90**, 93–100.

Redding, S. and A. J. Venables (2000), 'Economic Geography and International Inequality', Center for Economic Policy Research, Discussion Paper no. 2568.

Rose, A. K. (2004), 'Do We Really Know that the WTO Increases Trade?' *American Economic Review*, **94** (1), 98–114.

Rose, A. K. and E. van Wincoop (2001), 'National Money as a Barrier to International Trade: The Real Case for Currency Union', *American Economic Review*, **91**, 386–90.

Scarf, H. (1969), 'An Example of an Algorithm for Calculating General Equilibrium Prices', *American Economic Review*, **59** (4), 669–77.

Subramanian, A. and S. J. Wei (2003), 'The WTO Promotes Trade: Strongly but Unevenly', NBER Working Paper No. 10024.

Tinbergen, J. (1962), *Shaping the World Economy – Suggestions for an International Economic Policy*, New York: The Twentieth Century Fund.

Walras, L. (1896), *Éléments d'économie politique pure; ou, Théorie de la richesse sociale*, Ed. 3, Lausanne: Rouge.

PART II

TRADE AGREEMENTS

6 Why are there trade agreements?
James Gaisford and Annette Hester

Introduction

Even the most cursory look at the conduct of trade policy suggests two predominant facts. On the one hand, countries rarely pursue free trade as a unilateral policy. On the other hand, countries frequently do pursue trade agreements on a multilateral or regional level. The purpose of this chapter is to shed light on these two central features concerning the conduct of trade policy. While most international trade textbooks provide reasonable explanations for unilateral trade policy interventions, their accounts of trade liberalization under the guise of trade agreements are frequently weaker, and their treatments of the connections between interventionism and liberalization are often lacking entirely. A cogent explanation of the relationship between trade policy interventionism and liberalization, however, can be gleaned from a strand of the literature addressing retaliatory tariffs, which was pioneered by Johnson (1953) and elaborated by Dixit (1987) and many others. This chapter draws heavily on Dixit in particular.

In the past 200 years, there have been few countries that have refrained from using trade-policy measures. Two examples of jurisdictions that have approximated a free-trade stance are Britain at the end of the nineteenth century and Hong Kong in the later twentieth century. At the other end of the spectrum, countries seldom cut off trade completely. The communist regime in Albania attempted to pursue a policy of economic isolation or autarky after World War II and China followed suit for a shorter time period during the Cultural Revolution. While these observations suggest that neither free trade nor autarky are policy equilibria, international trade theory is often misunderstood to imply that free trade is an equilibrium. As we will see, however, it is independently rational for any one country to impose trade policy measures, such as tariffs.

To avoid confusion, we hasten to observe that the legacy of economic thought with respect to international trade, which is discussed in Chapter 3, does demonstrate that, when markets are competitive, free trade allocates world resources efficiently and that free trade generates mutual gains for all countries relative to a state of no trade or autarky. Saying that free trade is better than no trade for any country, however, certainly does not imply that free-trade is a country's best policy. Similarly, to say that free trade allocates world resources efficiently does not imply that this, or any other, efficient allocation will be attained as a non-cooperative policy equilibrium when each country independently pursues it own trade policy.

As discussed in Chapter 2, there has been a proliferation of regional trade agreements, parallel to multilateral trade liberalization under the General Agreement on Tariffs and Trade (GATT) and the World Trade Organization (WTO). A key common element in the explanation of these divergent developments is that trade agreements appear to offer mutual benefits. The analysis in this chapter will confirm that cooperation between countries on at least partial trade liberalization is mutually beneficial. The overall implication that we will explore in this chapter is that precisely *because* free trade is not a robust policy equilibrium, there is a role for trade agreements. Moreover, in a multi-country world, the proliferation of regional trade agreements is a natural result.

To provide a systematic exploration of the nuances of the conduct of trade policy requires us to employ elements of game theory as well as international trade theory. In this context, a 'game' is a situation where the choices of any one player have a perceptible impact on the other players, and thus, indirectly affect their choices. In taking particular actions and pursuing an overall strategy, any one player must be cognizant of the impact on the actions and strategies adopted by all other players because these will in turn affect the first player's well being or payoff. While these strategic interactions among players add an unavoidable layer of complexity to the theory of international trade policy, we will endeavour, at every step of the analysis, to be clear and straightforward.

An initial trade policy game
To simplify the initial analysis of the trading game as much as possible, we make five important assumptions:

a1. Two countries, A and B, trade two goods.
a2. All markets are competitive.
a3. Each country sets its trade policy to maximize its national welfare.
a4. The countries are of equal size and the trading environment is symmetric.
a5. The trading game occurs only once.

Reality, of course, is much richer than the trading environment circumscribed by these assumptions. While the initial analysis is instructive, we will follow up with vital lessons that arise from relaxing each of these naïve assumptions.

In the initial scenario, Country A must import one good and Country B must import the other since there are just two goods. If neither country sets a tariff, of course, the result is free trade. Thus, in Figure 6.1, the free trade point is FT, where the tariff rate of Country A, t^A, and the tariff rate of B, t^B, are both equal to zero. Given that competitive conditions prevail in all markets, free trade is one position that is consistent with world efficiency, but it is not the only efficient point. If one country were to impede trade through a positive tax or tariff on its import, the other country could restore efficiency by expediting trade through an import subsidy or 'negative tariff' of appropriate size on its import. Although import subsidies are rare in practice, countries do occasionally impose such measures, especially on food products in times of shortage. In Figure 6.1, the WE curve is the locus of all tariff combinations for Countries A and B that are consistent with world efficiency.[1]

If the countries set tariffs that are sufficiently high, a state of no trade or autarky will result. For example, in Figure 6.1, if Country A sets a prohibitive tariff that is greater than or equal to t^A_{NT}, trade will be cut off even if B refrains from implementing a tariff.[2]

Further, all tariff combinations either on or above the no-trade curve, which is labeled NT, eliminate all trade between the countries. Between the WE and NT curves, trade volume are typically less than the efficient level, and below the WE curve, the trade volume is typically greater than the efficient level.

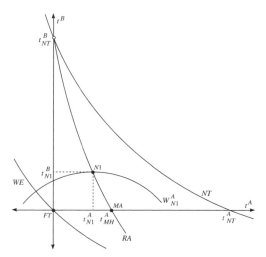

Figure 6.1   Autarky, world efficiency and Country A's trade-policy behavior

A country's optimum trade policy

It is reasonable to assume that each country controls its own trade policy, but not that of the other. Consequently, we can say Country A sets its trade conditional on the trade policy of Country B, and *vice versa*. For the moment we will naïvely assume that each country sets its trade policy to maximize its national welfare. In other words, we temporarily assume that trade policy is designed solely to benefit society as a whole, rather than favouring special (or vested) interest groups that have influence for one reason or another. We can use Figure 6.2 to show how national welfare is affected in both countries as A implements a tariff. We assume for simplicity that B does not tax or subsidize its imports or exports so that B's prices always reflect world prices. Given that DM^A is the demand for imports curve of A and SX^B is the supply of exports curve for B, under free trade, the trade volume is TV_{FT} and the world price is P^W_{FT}. A tariff imposed by Country A creates a wedge between A's domestic price, given by the import demand curve, and the world and Country-B price, given by the export supply curve. For example, if Country A's tariff rate rises from zero to t^A_{MA}, the trade volume will be reduced to TV_{MA}, the world and Country-B price will fall to P^B_{MA}, and the domestic price in Country A will rise to P^A_{MA}, which exceeds P^A_{MA} by t^A_{MA} percent. If Country A's tariff rate rises sufficiently, say to t^A_{NT}, it becomes prohibitive and trade is cut off entirely. The world price and Country-B price will fall to P^B_{NT} while the domestic price rises to P^A_{NT}, which exceeds P^B_{MA} by t^A_{NT} percent.[3]

Implementing a tariff generates a benefit as well as cost from a national welfare perspective. Moving from free trade to a tariff rate of t^A_{MA} imposed by Country A causes a loss of net consumer surplus equal to $A1 + A2$ dollars in Figure 6.2,[4] but government revenues rise by $A1 + B1$ dollars due to tariff collection. Consequently, the overall change in national welfare in Country A is equal to $B1 - A2$ dollars, which could be positive or negative. Equivalently, this overall change in A's welfare can be decomposed into a terms-of-trade gain of $B1 + B2$ and an efficiency loss of $B2 + A2$. The terms-of-trade gain is the result of Country A's market power; by restricting its imports, the world price declines. The efficiency loss arises because the tariff introduces a distortion into the world market.

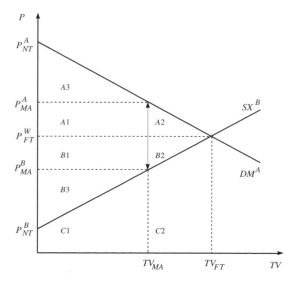

Figure 6.2   The impact of a tariff on national welfare

Since Country *A* experiences a terms-of-trade gain in addition to the efficiency loss, the overall effect on national welfare is ambiguous. Figure 6.2 shows a case where *A*'s national welfare increases with a tariff is equal to t^A_{MA} because $B1 > A2$, which implies that the terms of trade gain is greater than the efficiency loss.

If Country *A* imposes a tariff equal to t^A_{MA}, this causes a loss of net producer surplus equal to $B1 + B2$ dollars in Country *B*, as shown in Figure 6.2.[5] This terms-of-trade loss for Country *B* arises because of the adverse change in the world price. Whatever the impact on *A*'s domestic welfare, it can be concluded that its tariff always has a beggar-thy-neighbour effect on the rest of the world. Since the terms of trade effects in *A* and *B* cancel out when seen on a worldwide basis, only the efficiency loss remains. Consequently, a tariff always causes a misallocation of resources and an unambiguous overall loss to the world economy.[6]

It is useful to consider the impact of gradually increasing Country *A*'s tariff rate. When the tariff rate is equal to zero, the efficiency loss is equal to zero, but as the tariff increases the efficiency loss becomes positive and it gets larger at an ever-increasing rate. Ultimately, with a prohibitive tariff, which is greater than or equal to t^A_{NT}, the efficiency loss is equal to $A1 + A2 + A3 + B1 + B2 + B3$ dollars. Since the countries are temporarily assumed to be symmetric by assumption a4, each country exercises some market power over the world price and they do so to the same extent. Since Country *A* must then face an upward-sloping export supply curve from *B*, its terms-of-trade gain is initially positive as it raises its tariff rate above zero and its national welfare is necessarily higher than under free trade over a range of sufficiently small values of its tariff.[7] While the terms-of-trade gain becomes ever larger as the tariff increases, it increases at a decreasing rate. Finally, when the tariff is greater than or equal to t^A_{NT}, the terms of trade gain is equal to $B1 + B2 + B3$ dollars, which is necessarily smaller than the efficiency loss. Consequently, over a range of sufficiently large values of its tariff, national welfare in Country *A* is necessarily lower than under free trade.

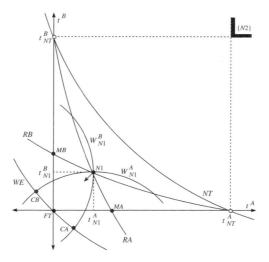

Figure 6.3   A trade policy game that is symmetric

In this scenario where small tariff rates bring higher welfare than free trade and, high tariffs yield lower welfare, there must be an optimum tariff at some intermediate value where Country *A* exercises its market power as a single buyer or monopsony to its best advantage.[8] Let us suppose that this optimum tariff happens to be equal to t_{MA}^A which leads to the trade volume of TV_{MA} in Figure 6.2. Returning to Figure 6.1, t_{MA}^A is then Country *A*'s best response to a zero tariff rate played by Country *B*. Since Country *B* is behaving competitively, while *A* is exercising its market power optimally, t_{MA}^A can be seen as *A*'s pure monopsony tariff.[9] In the analysis, thus far, Country *B*'s tariff rate has been set equal to zero, but there is nothing restrictive about this assumption. Given any non-prohibitive tariff rate played by Country *B* such as t_{N1}^B, Country *A*'s best response is an optimum tariff that is positive but not prohibitive such as t_{N1}^A because *A* has market power. In Figure 6.1, *RA* is country *A*'s best response curve. This best-response curve must lie between the no trade locus *NT* and the vertical axis where $t^A = 0$. Further, it will frequently have the steep negative slope shown in Figure 6.1 where a one percentage point increase in *B*'s tariff causes a less than a 1 percent decrease in Country *A*'s optimum tariff. We also note that Country *A* has dome-shaped welfare contours such as W_{N1}^A shown in Figure 6.1. At all points on a welfare contour, a country's national welfare is constant. Starting at *N1*, if Country *A* were to either raise or lower its tariff from the optimum rate, t_{N1}^A, its national welfare would fall. In the unlikely but fortuitous event that *B* then lowered its tariff below t_{N1}^B to a sufficient extent, Country *A*'s welfare could be restored to the original level that prevailed at *N1*. Thus, all points on the welfare contour W_{N1}^A yield the same national welfare for Country *A* as point *N1*, while all points inside this dome-shaped curve, yield higher national welfare for Country *A* because they imply an even lower tariff rate by *B*.

The key conclusion of our analysis of the optimum trade policy in this section is that it is individually rational for Country *A* to impose a tariff. Since the countries are symmetric, however, the analysis applies equally to Country *B*. Consequently, Figure 6.3 shows the best response curve of Country *B*, *RB*, in addition to that of *A*, *RA*.

Trade policy equilibrium

To begin with, suppose that the trade game is non-cooperative in the sense that each country chooses its tariff independently without coordinating with the other country. We can now search for possible Nash equilibria in a one-shot or static trade policy game. A non-cooperative Nash equilibrium is an outcome where neither player regrets its choice given the choice(s) of its opponent(s). In a one-shot trade policy game, it is immediately apparent that free trade is not a Nash equilibrium because neither country's tariff is an optimum or best response to the tariff set by its opponent. Conditional on B choosing a tariff rate equal to zero, Country A's best response would be to select outcome MA rather than FT in Figure 6.3 by playing its pure monopsony tariff. Similarly, if A were to choose a tariff rate equal to zero, then Country B's best response is to choose its pure monopsony outcome, MB, rather than FT. Consequently, both countries would have regrets if free trade were the outcome of the game. However, neither of the countries' pure monopsony outcomes are Nash equilibria. While Country A would have no regrets at MA, Country B would want to increase its tariff rate so as to move to its best response curve, RB.

Analogously, at MB Country B would have no regrets, but A would want to increase its tariff in order to reach the RA curve.

In Figure 6.3, there is a Nash equilibrium at $N1$ where the best-response functions of the two countries intersect. When B's tariff rate is set at t_{N1}^B, a tariff rate of t_{N1}^A is A's best response and *vice versa*. Since both countries set positive tariffs, we can describe the Nash equilibrium at $N1$ as a state of limited trade war. Moreover, in addition to satisfying the no-regrets criterion, there is good reason to expect that outcome at $N1$ may actually occur if the governments of the two countries understand the structure of the game. In deciding what tariff to play, the government of Country A reasons as follows: 'if we choose t_{N1}^A, then their best response is t_{N1}^B. Given that they do play t_{N1}^B, then our initial choice of t_{N1}^A is indeed optimal.' And, of course, with the government of B reasoning analogously, $N1$ is a natural outcome.[10]

Some, but not all, autarky outcomes are also Nash equilibria. In the subset of autarky outcomes given by $\{N2\}$, each country sets its own tariff at a prohibitive rate that would curtail trade even if its opponent set a tariff rate equal to zero. Since B's tariff rate has already cut off trade, A would not regret playing a prohibitive tariff and *vice versa*. Thus, the total trade war outcomes in $\{N2\}$ are also Nash equilibria. While the fact that free trade is not a Nash equilibrium appears to correspond nicely with the fact that in reality few countries unilaterally pursue free-trade policies, the fact that there are autarky equilibria at first appears at odds with reality. Closer inspection of the model, however, suggests that countries will tend to focus on the limited trade-war equilibrium at $N1$ because both countries are better off with some trade than with none (Dixit 1987: 335).

Further examination of Figure 6.3 reveals that the Nash equilibrium at $N1$ leaves untapped cooperative gains from mutual tariff reduction. Country A experiences higher national welfare inside (or below) its dome shaped welfare contour, W_{N1}^A, and similarly, B attains higher welfare inside (or to the left) of its welfare contour, W_{N1}^B. Consequently, mutual trade liberalization moving from $N1$ into the lens-shaped area between the two curves in the direction indicated by the arrow would raise welfare in both countries. Further, in the case of symmetric countries since point FT is in the lens, full liberalization to the free trade would be mutually beneficial. There are other points besides FT in the core of the trade policy game between CA and CB on the WE curve, which are both efficient and mutually beneficial.[11] While such points could be the target of cooperative trade liberalization, free trade is perhaps the most natural target for symmetric countries.

While the availability of gains from cooperation suggests a possible role for trade agreements, it is not possible to achieve such an agreement in a one-shot game specified by assumption a5. Suppose the two countries had an opportunity to collude prior to choosing their tariffs. In the absence of a world government that would allow countries to sue to recover damages, each country knows that it is in the interest of the other to renege on any commitments that are made and, thus, fully expects cheating. The limited trade war Nash equilibrium at $N1$, thus, remains the only plausible outcome in the context of the one-shot game. If the game is repeated, however, the possibility of future cooperation could conceivably provide sufficient incentive for a self-enforcing trade agreement.

Before turning to repeated games, it should be emphasized that fear of retaliation is not sufficient motivation for a rational country to unilaterally adhere to a zero-tariff strategy because it is in the other country's interest to implement a positive tariff regardless. Consequently, the virtual absence of unilateral free-trade strategies, which is observed in practice, is fully consistent with international trade theory.

Repeated trade policy games
We now relax assumption a5 by allowing the trade policy game to be infinitely repeated and we investigate whether free trade might arise, either spontaneously or through a trade agreement.[12] We immediately observe that the trade war outcome at $N1$ in Figure 6.3 remains a policy equilibrium. If each country adopts a static strategy where it always plays its $N1$ tariff rate, these strategies are mutual best responses. Neither country regrets its strategy, giving rise to a Nash equilibrium where the outcome is $N1$ in perpetuity. Further, this equilibrium passes the credibility tests that we invoke below. By analogous reasoning, perpetual outcomes in $\{N2\}$ can arise as credible policy equilibria supported by appropriate static strategies. Static free-trade strategies by both countries, however, do not constitute a Nash equilibrium since both countries would always regret playing a tariff rate equal to zero.

In addition to the outcomes at $N1$ and $N2$, there may be other pairs of strategies that constitute policy equilibria and for some free trade may be the observed outcome. Suppose that each country adopts a simple trigger strategy. With such a strategy, a country plays a cooperative tariff rate that is equal to zero in the first period. In subsequent periods, the country cooperates if its opponent has cooperated in all previous periods, but it plays a positive punishment tariff, say at its $N1$ level in Figure 6.3, if its opponent has ever deviated from cooperation. Such trigger strategies would clearly sustain free trade indefinitely. Further, these trigger strategies may be mutual best responses, and thus constitute a Nash equilibrium. For example, Country A will not regret its trigger strategy if the benefits from continuing cooperation are larger than the one period benefits from cheating.[13]

If neither country regrets its trigger strategy, the resulting Nash equilibrium will also be a perfect equilibrium where the punishments are credible threats. This is because the possible sub-game where both countries impose punishment tariffs at the $N1$ level forever is itself a Nash equilibrium; neither country regrets its strategy of perpetual punishment given the strategy of its opponent. On the one hand, the simplicity of trigger strategies appears to be attractive because it suggests that free trade might arise spontaneously in a repeated game. On the other hand, trigger strategies are completely unforgiving in the sense that the punishments go on forever, which makes them more problematic.[14] Further, the perfect equilibrium resulting from trigger strategies is not renegotiation proof. If a country did cheat and then tried to renegotiate to return to free trade rather than going through perpetual punishment, there would be an incentive for the other country to agree since it is worse off implementing the punishment than reverting to free trade. Since the threat of punishment is supposed to prevent cheating, this susceptibility to renegotiation undermines the initial logic of self-enforcing tariff cooperation through trigger strategies.

As discussed in Gravelle and Rees (2004), some pairs of carrot-and-stick strategies may result in equilibria that are renegotiation-proof and forgiving in addition to being credible. With such a carrot-and-stick strategy, a country cooperates with a tariff rate equal to zero: (a) in the first period; (b) when both countries have cooperated in the previous period; and (c) when punishment of either country has taken place in the previous period. The country imposes a one-period punishment if its opponent has played non-cooperatively in the previous period and it submits to a one-period punishment whenever it has played non-cooperatively in the previous period. The renegotiation-proof criterion implies that the country must be better off than at free trade when it is in the position of implementing a punishment, as well as worse off when it receives a punishment. If both countries adopt compatible carrot-and-stick strategies, free trade will be sustained indefinitely. Further, if the net benefits from cheating on both cooperation and punishments are negative, neither country will regret its strategy.

Given an infinitely repeated trade policy game, it is theoretically possible, but not empirically plausible, for free trade to emerge spontaneously as an observed outcome. For example, the complexity of the strategies and the need to coordinate on tariff levels for imposing and receiving punishments makes it highly improbable that the two countries would independently adopt mutually consistent carrot-and-stick strategies. It is attractive, however, to think of such strategy pairs in the context of a self-enforcing contract or trade agreement. In addition to rules defining cooperative trade liberalization, the analysis suggests that trade agreements should also be expected to include rules that apply when parties do not fulfill their obligations. Pervasive rules concerning unfair trade practices, which allow countervailing duties and antidumping duties, can be usefully understood in this context.[15] Consequently, trade agreements, which were impossible in one-shot games, become a much more likely development to sustain cooperation in repeated games.[16]

Unequal countries

We now relax assumption a4 by moving from a fully symmetric trading environment to one where Country B is larger than A. Since this typically gives more market power to B and less to A, the best response curve of B, RB, tends to shift to up while that of A, RA, shifts to the left in Figure 6.3. Consequently, the limited trade war equilibrium at $N1$ typically moves up and to the left leading to a higher tariff rate for the large country and a smaller rate for the smaller one as shown in Figure 6.4. In the limit in the archetypal small country case where Country A is sufficiently small (possibly infinitesimally small) relative to B, A's best response function coincides with the vertical axis and its optimum tariff is always equal to zero.[17] In the limit as we approach this small country case, the limited trade war Nash equilibrium at $N1$ coincides with B's pure monopsony point at MB because Country A no longer has any influence over world prices.

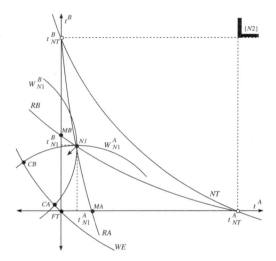

Figure 6.4   A trade policy game that is asymmetric

Regardless of the relative size of the two counties, limited trade liberalization by both countries remains mutually beneficial. The configuration of the welfare contours, W_{N1}^A and W_{N1}^B, in the neigborhood of $N1$ in Figure 6.4 remains the same as in Figure 6.3. Starting at $N1$ and reducing tariffs so as to move into the lens shaped area in the direction shown by the arrow continues to be mutually beneficial. Moving all the way to free trade, however, may not be mutually beneficial with asymmetric countries and it is not mutually beneficial in Figure 6.4. As we depart from the symmetric situation depicted in Figure 6.3 and increase the size of Country B relative to A, we have seen that the limited trade war Nash equilibrium moves up and to the left. Since the welfare contours associated with $N1$ are also displaced, points CB and CA also move up and to the left along the world efficiency locus, WE. Eventually, as shown in Figure 6.4, the free trade point, FT, will lie below and to the left of the lens enclosed by the welfare contours, W_{N1}^A and W_{N1}^B. In such an asymmetric situation, the large country, B, would experience an absolute gain from a move from free trade to the limited trade war equilibrium at $N1$. Consequently, pure free trade is not necessarily in the national interest of a larger country because it has the preponderance of market power.

While the mutual gains from limited trade liberalization suggests that cooperation through trade agreements remains a sensible objective, asymmetries between countries suggest that these agreements may be much more about managing trade than achieving pure free trade. For example, Markusen and Wigle (1989) showed that US welfare would only be slightly higher at free trade than in a Nash equilibrium whereas Canada would gain more, especially relative to its smaller GDP and population. How, then, can one understand US participation in the Canada–US Free Trade Agreement? Some have argued that the agreement really was about 'free trade' and that there were political grounds for US participation, possibly linked to encouraging the Uruguay Round of multilateral trade talks where success was in the US's interest. Others have argued that the US was interested in a set of rules that would manage trade such that, as the larger player, it would experience gains that were at least similar in magnitude to those of Canada. Overall, it appears that both the trade-politics and managed-trade theses are likely to be important in explaining US participation in trade agreements with smaller countries such as Canada, Mexico and Israel. Of course, granting some truth to both the trade-politics and managed-trade theses, still suggests that it would be naïve to believe that trade agreements lead to free trade.

Vested interests versus the national interest
While assumption a3 that each country maximizes its national welfare is an analytically simple political objective, it is not realistic. In reality, political processes are complex and countries rarely single-mindedly act in their broad national interest. When the political focus is on the next election, lobbying by interest groups typically has a strong influence on policy outcomes. Consequently, trade policy is almost inevitably skewed in the sense that it favours certain vested or special interests over others and over the national interest. In the past, various producer interests have tended to predominate in the determination of trade policy. Currently, however, activists from civil society have become increasingly involved. For example, environmental and consumer groups have gained prominence with respect to new trade issues concerning genetically modified food products, environmental and labour standards, and so on (see Gaisford *et al.* 2001; Beaulieu and Gaisford 2002). The chapters in Part III of this volume discuss the impact of a wide variety of trade policy instruments on the national interest and various special interests.

Note that the interests of producer groups have tended to have more political resonance when a group has been under pressure due to declining demand, technological change and/or increasing foreign competition. While lower-income groups have often had political *caché* in sectors such as textiles and agriculture in developed countries, labour unions and other powerful well-organized groups have also made a profound mark in areas such as steel and autos. Of course, politically motivated trade taxes are extremely unlikely to be equal to zero. With political realism, even the smallest countries with virtually no power in international markets will no longer adhere to a zero-tariff regime. Moreover, for governments in poor countries, import tariffs are frequently a budgetary necessity. In general, trade taxes will be either larger or smaller than the national optimum, and they could even be negative. Gaisford and Kerr (2003) show that when producer interests in agriculture are given extra weight, trade wars involving export subsidies may arise such as the grain wars between the US and the EU in the 1980s.

Imperfect competition
Assumption a2 concerning market structure is also highly problematic. Imperfect rather than perfect competition is the norm in most markets. Market power causes distortions in international markets such that free trade is no longer consistent with world efficiency. Nevertheless, when trade is liberalized and global markets become more integrated, there are frequently, but not always, mutual gains from greater competition, greater product variety and larger economies of scale. Such gains are particularly likely when firms face low barriers to entry into the sector (see Krugman 1979). As discussed in Chapter 13, the larger market size available with trade agreements tends to be very important for small and medium sized countries where the small domestic market, in isolation, would lead to high average costs and/or fewer product varieties for consumers.

Even when barriers to entry into a sector are low, governments continue to have a role in coordinating the market power of their firms. Consequently, it remains individually rational to intervene with tariffs to secure beneficial terms of trade effects of the type discussed above. When there are significant barriers to entry and few firms, persistent windfall profits are likely to arise. Such an oligopoly setting provides an additional profit-shifting rationale for trade policy intervention. Depending on the details of oligopolistic rivalry either export taxes or subsidies may be warranted to give domestic firms an edge in the international market place. For example, Brander and Spencer (1985) examine a simple Cournot duopoly where two firms engage in output or quantity rivalry. In this setting, it is individually rational for a country to impose export subsidies to allow its domestic firm to credibly commit to greater output and to force the foreign firm to cut back its output. With the export subsidy set at or near the optimum, the additional profits obtained by the domestic firm exceed the subsidy costs and make the country better off. Such strategic trade policy is discussed further in Chapter 28. This analysis sheds important light on the dispute between Canada and Brazil over control of the regional jet market by Bombardier and Embraer. Likewise, it is important for understanding disputes between the US and the EU in relation to Boeing and Airbus.

Additional countries
Of course, assumption a1, which specifies that there are only two countries in this model, is also highly restrictive. To take the opposite extreme, if there were infinitely many infinitesimally small countries, free trade would be a trade-policy equilibrium. This result, however, is not very interesting. There are a finite number of countries. More to the point, most countries have at least limited influence over some world prices and some countries have significant influence over many. Further, even those with negligible influence are likely to impose politically motivated trade measures. Consequently, it remains politically rational for each individual country to implement tariffs but it remains mutually beneficial for all countries to engage in at least partial trade liberalization. This provides a solid foundation for understanding the multilateral trade liberalization process that has taken place through sequential rounds of GATT negotiations and is now spearheaded by the WTO. Full multilateral trade liberalization is discussed further in Chapter 7.

Introducing additional countries to the model, however, does introduce a critical new dimension into the analysis. With as few as three countries, two countries could form a regional trade agreement (RTA) that liberalizes internal trade but leaves the third country out. Since each member country within an RTA provides preferential access to its domestic market to other member countries and applies trade measures, which discriminate against outsiders, RTAs are frequently called preferential trade agreements. While the GATT and the newer General Agreement on Trade in Services (GATS) generally frown on trade policy discrimination, both explicitly allow for RTAs provided that the member countries eliminate internal trade barriers on most goods and services and do so within a reasonable time frame.

Regional trade agreements generally create some new trade amongst member countries, but also divert trade away from low-cost outside countries. At constant world prices, member countries generally gain from trade creation and lose from trade diversion. However, both trade diversion and trade creation involve member countries trading more with themselves and less with the rest of the world. This trade restriction leads to world price changes that generally are beneficial for the member countries as a group but harmful to outsiders. Consequently, RTAs are at best a mixed blessing for the global trading system. While a new RTA may frequently but not always be beneficial to member countries, outside countries are typically hurt. A world where each country is a member of some RTA may still be superior for all countries to a world with no RTAs. This will be the case if the RTAs group natural trading partners that have low transport and transaction costs since trade diversion will be minimal (see Krugman 1991). Nonetheless, countries such as Japan, China and Taiwan may find it difficult to enter into a natural regionalization process with each other in spite of geographic proximity. Consequently, such countries tend to be more vulnerable as RTAs proliferate. Issues concerning RTAs are discussed further in Chapters 8–12. Since a world with many countries and many goods makes it difficult to negotiate significant trade-liberalizing steps on a global basis, the proliferation of regional trade agreements is easily understood within the game-theoretic analysis in this chapter.

Conclusion

This chapter has attempted to shed light on why countries frequently engage in negotiating trade agreements on a multilateral and regional level even though they almost never pursue free trade as a unilateral policy. This in itself is interesting. However, it is important to go a step further to acknowledge that, while free trade would allocate world resources efficiently, at least in a competitive market setting, it is seldom a reasonable policy objective for a country. Moreover, in a world of imperfect competition, where countries are asymmetric in size and power, and governments must be cognizant of a variety of conflicting interests, achieving free trade is a virtual impossibility.

Clearly, there is a disconnect between most governments' rhetoric on trade agreements – that free trade is the best policy – and what these agreements are able to deliver. Given our analysis, it is not surprising to find that citizens, worldwide, are increasingly disenchanted with these so-called free-trade policies. More troublesome, mistrust of governments and the multilateral system that supports the world-trading regime appears to be widespread and rising. In the face of this awkward conjuncture, we believe it would be more constructive for governments to match their rhetoric with their true interests and what they can reasonably expect to accomplish.

Notes

1. World efficiency requires that one country cannot be made better off without making the other(s) worse off. At any inefficient point not on the WE curve both countries could be made better off. At any efficient point on the WE curve one country cannot be made better off by hurting the other. Comparing points on the WE curve, national welfare is higher in A and lower in B than at free trade at any point below and to the right of FT where A's tariff is positive and B's tariff is negative because the net effect of the trade policies is to shift purchasing power from B to A. Given that each country is a competitive economy, world efficiency will arise if and only if each country has the same domestic price ratios for every pair of tradable goods.
2. A simple mathematical argument can be used to show that the independently prohibitive tariff of country B, t_{NT}^B, is equal to that of A, t_{NT}^A (see Dixit 1987).
3. When the tariff is t_{MA}^A, $P_{MA}^A = (1 + t_{MA}^A)P_{MA}^B$ and that when it is t_{NT}^A, $P_{NT}^A = (1 + t_{NT}^A)P_{NT}^B$.
4. For each successive increase in the trade volume, the height of the import demand curve measures the additional or marginal benefit of imports for Country A. Thus, when the import volume is TV_{MA}, the total benefit from trade for Country A is $A1 + A3 + B1 + B3 + C1$ dollars and when the import volume is TV_{FT}, its total benefit is $A1 + A2 + A3 + B1 + B2 + B3 + C1 + C2$ dollars. In the two respective scenarios, A's total

expenditures by the private sector on imports are $A3 + B1 + B3 + C1$ and $B1 + B2 + B3 + C1 + C2$ dollars. Consequently, when imports are TV_{MA}, A's net benefit to the private sector from imports is $A1$ dollars and when imports are TV_{FT} its net benefit is $A1 + A2 + A3$ dollars. Since we are examining an import or net demand curve, this net benefit can be called an *importer surplus* or net consumer surplus. Moving from TV_{FT} to TV_{MA} is associated with an increase in the domestic price in country A from P_{FT}^W to P_{MA}^A, which reduces net consumer surplus by $A1 + A2$. Notice that this reduction in importer surplus represents the area inside the import demand curve and between the two price lines. The price increase hurts consumers and leads to a reduction in gross consumer surplus, but it is beneficial to producers and leads to an increase in gross producer surplus. Nevertheless, there is an unambiguous loss in net consumer surplus from the increase in the domestic price because the quantity consumed exceeds the quantity produced for an importing country.

5. For each successive increase in the trade volume, the height of the export supply curve measures the additional opportunity cost or marginal cost of exports for Country B. Thus, when the import volume is TV_{MA}, the total opportunity cost of exports for Country B is $C1$ dollars and when the import volume is TV_{FT}, its total cost is $C1 + C2$ dollars. In the two scenarios, B's total revenues from exports are $B3 + C1$ and $B1 + B2 + B3 + C1 + C2$ dollars respectively. Consequently, when exports are TV_{MA}, B's net benefit to the private sector from exports is $B3$ dollars and when imports are TV_{FT} the net benefit is $B1 + B2 + B3$ dollars. Since we are examining an export or net supply curve, this net benefit can be called an exporter surplus or net producer surplus. Moving from TV_{FT} to TV_{MA} is associated with a reduction in the domestic price in country B from P_{FT}^W to P_{MA}^B, which reduces net producer surplus by $B1 + B2$. This reduction in exporter surplus represents the area inside the export supply curve and between the two price lines. The price reduction is beneficial to consumers and leads to an increase in gross consumer surplus, but it hurts producers and leads to a decrease in gross producer surplus. Overall, there is an unambiguous loss in net producer surplus from the reduction in the domestic price because the quantity produced exceeds the quantity consumed for an exporting country.

6. Note that Figure 6.2 does show that Country A, as well as B, is better off under free trade than with no trade. Country A gains an importer surplus equal to $A1 + A2 + A3$ dollars while B gains an exporter surplus equal to $B1 + B2 + B3$ dollars. Thus, there are mutual gains from trade! This of course does not change the fact that A is better off still when it has a tariff equal to t_{MA}^A and B has a tariff equal to zero.

7. Later we discuss asymmetric countries including the archetypal small country case where country A has no market power and faces a horizontal export supply curve.

8. The optimum tariff occurs where the marginal cost of an extra unit of imports is equal to the marginal benefit. While the marginal benefit of imports is equal to the domestic price given by the import demand curve, the marginal cost of imports exceeds the world price of an additional unit purchased given by the export supply curve. This is because in addition the world price paid for all the previous or *intra-marginal* units is bid up moving outward on the export supply curve.

9. To summarize, over a range of small tariffs between zero and t_{MA}^A, national welfare increases as the tariff rate increases. At the optimum tariff, t_{MA}^A, national welfare reaches its peak. Over a range of excessive tariffs between t_{MA}^A and t_{NT}^A national welfare declines as the tariff rate increases. For prohibitive tariffs greater than or equal to t_{NT}^A, national welfare remains constant at its autarky or no-trade level, which is lower than with a tariff equal to zero.

10. Multiple Nash equilibria resembling $N1$ are possible because the best response functions, RA and RB, may intersect more than once. While this leaves our conclusion that free trade is not a Nash equilibrium unaltered, the presence of multiple pure-strategy equilibria makes it problematic to expect that any single equilibrium will arise. A mixed-strategy equilibrium where neither player regrets the probabilities that it assigns to playing each possible equilibrium tariff becomes more likely.

11. Country A is equally well off at $N1$ and CB, but it is better off at FT and better off still at CA. This ordering is reversed for Country B.

12. Our discussion of repeated trade policy games runs parallel to the more detailed discussion of repeated oligopoly games in Gravelle and Rees (2004, 417–32).

13. More formally, A does not have regrets if the present value of the gains from mutual cooperation at FT rather than $N1$ exceed the one-period benefits from deviating with a pure monopsony tariff, which leads to MA rather than FT. This criterion must hold if the interest rate at which Country A discounts the future is sufficiently low.

14. If both countries adopted equally simple tit-for-tat strategies, there would be immediate but limited punishments followed a quick return to free trade. With a 'tit-for-tat' strategy a country plays a cooperative tariff rate equal to zero in the first period and in each period where its opponent cooperated in the previous period, but it plays a positive punishment tariff if the other country deviated in the previous period. While the tit-for-tat strategies are simple and forgiving, the sub-game of perpetually oscillating punishments does not pass the no-regrets test for credible punishments.

15. Contingency measures that are applicable in the case of unfair trading practices are discussed in Part IV of this volume. The political policy objectives that underlie such measures are, not surprisingly, more

complex than the national welfare maximization that drives our simple model.

16. This analysis of infinitely repeated games could be readily extended to games that always continue to a subsequent period with a positive probability. Further, similar results could be obtained in a finitely repeated game with a definite endpoint in period T. This latter feature is somewhat unusual. Suppose that $N1$ were the only Nash equilibrium. Since there is a one-shot game in the last period, $N1$ will be the outcome in period T. This means that there would be no possibility of future cooperation in the second-to-last period, implying an outcome of $N1$ in period $T - 1$ and, by extension, all earlier periods. Trade agreements as well as spontaneous free trade, thus, would be ruled out. As Dixit (1987) points out, the presence of autarky Nash equilibria in $\{N2\}$ in the trade policy game does rescue the possibility of cooperation in the second to last period, because non-cooperative behaviour in period $T - 1$ can be punished with autarky in period T. Consequently, cooperation in period $T - 1$ and all earlier periods remains possible even though $N1$ would still be the outcome in period T.

17. The defining feature of the small country case is that B would face a horizontal or perfectly elastic export supply curve from A in Figure 6.2. Since areas $B1$, $B2$ and $B3$ would disappear there would be no terms of trade gain, only an efficiency loss, when A imposes a tariff. Consequently, in the limit as we approach the small country case, A's optimum tariff goes to zero.

References

Beaulieu, E. and J. D. Gaisford (2002), 'Labour and Environmental Standards: the "Lemons Problem" in International Trade,' *World Economy*, **25**(1), 59–78.

Brander, J. A. and B. J. Spencer (1985), 'Export Subsidies and International Market-Share Rivalry,' *Journal of International Economics*, **18**, 227–42.

Dixit, A. K. (1987), 'Strategic Aspects of Trade Policy,' in T. Bewley (ed.), *Advances in Economic Theory, Proceedings of the 5th World Congress of the Econometrics Society*, Cambridge: Cambridge University Press.

Gaisford, J. D., J. E. Hobbs, W. A. Kerr, N. Perdikis and M. D. Plunkett (2001), *The Economics of Biotechnology*, Cheltenham, UK and Northampton, MA, USA: Edward Elgar Publishing.

Gaisford, J. D. and W. A. Kerr (2003), 'Deadlock in Geneva: the Battle over Agricultural Export Subsidies,' *International Economic Journal*, **17**(2), 1–18.

Gravelle, H. and R. Rees (2004), *Microeconomics*, third edition, Upper Saddle River, NJ: Prentice Hall.

Johnson, H. G. (1953), 'Optimum Tariffs and Retaliation,' *Review of Economic Studies*, **21**, 142–53. Revised and enlarged version in H. G. Johnson, *International Trade and Growth*, Harvard, MA: Harvard University Press, 1958.

Krugman, P. (1979), 'Increasing Returns, Monopolistic Competition and International Trade,' *Journal of International Economics*, **9**, 469–79.

Krugman, P. R. (1991), 'The Move Toward Free Trade Zones,' in P. King (ed.), *International Economics and International Economic Policy*, Second ed., New York: McGraw Hill, 1995, Ch. 8.

Markusen, J. R. and R. M. Wigle (1989), 'Nash Equilibrium Tariffs for the United States and Canada,' *Journal of Political Economy*, **97**, 368–86.

7   Overview of trade agreements: the multilateral system
Tim Josling

The logic of a multilateral trade system

The development of a multilateral trade system is a project that requires political, economic and legal support. Political support has traditionally been provided by hegemonic powers encouraged by a mixture of self-interest and altruism and backed up by political elites in those countries.[1] Other countries add their support out of a mix of unwillingness to be sidelined and awareness that the system itself helps to restrain hegemony. Over time the strength of political support can wax and wane, and the composition of the hegemonic alliance can change. The multilateral system can break down if there is critical disillusionment in the hegemonic powers with its value and performance. Alternative systems, including that based on regional trade agreements, tend to be encouraged by weakness at the multilateral level, though in reality these two systems appear to co-exist fairly well.[2]

Economic support comes from two sources. One is the notion that the provision of rules that reduce transactions cost in international trade is a global public good, that would be underprovided by governments in the absence of multilateral pacts.[3] Such global good provision does not require an assumption of altruism, as all can potentially gain, but it does require some leadership and cooperation, to avoid the pitfalls of the prisoners' dilemma. And the economic benefits are not equally distributed, which may lead to problems of equity. The second economic motive is that of quasi-mercantilist expansion of trade driven by exporters and potential exporters seeking new markets. This trade expansion is encouraged by those politicians that regard exports as creating jobs and improving trade balances. Alternative trade systems can also provide public goods, at least at the regional level, and can satisfy some of the mercantilist desires, but they are likely to be less efficient to the extent that they discriminate against excluded countries, reward regionally competitive exporters and protect industries within the region from outside competition. And, if rivalry breaks out among regional groups, the costs of trade can increase and the economic advantages diminish.

Legal support emanates from the benefits of developing international law covering commercial transactions across borders and inter-state relations in the economic sphere.[4] But the nature of the legal construction is itself unclear, with some trade lawyers arguing that the trade structure constitutes a constitution enforceable by whatever sanctions governments wish to bestow and others preferring to view it as an intergovernmental agreement deriving its legitimacy from domestic legal processes. Whether one views the legal structures of the multilateral trade system as an extension of national law or a form of transnational constitution by which countries agree to be bound, the existence of a multilateral trade system impinges on domestic legal processes. Unlike the political support, one would not expect continuous change in the legal basis for multilateral rules, though these are certainly capable of substantial innovation when the politics is right.

The interaction of the political, economic and legal rationales for a multilateral trade system give the system itself a degree of complexity and apparent confusion. There are times when politics rules and leads to sub-optimal economic outcomes, and there are times when a legal imperative clashes with political reality. But to be successful, the system has to satisfy broad economic objectives of supporting growth and reducing transactions cost, have enough of a legal character to give credibility to its rules, and enjoy political acquiescence if not enthusiasm from the major sponsors.

This chapter takes a pragmatic stance with an economist's bias. What exists in the way of a multilateral trade system has practical importance to actors, primarily those in the private sector and others whose livelihood is impacted by trade. Those actors participate in the process of defining the trade stance of a country and hence indirectly help to establish the rules for the multilateral system. Governments both act as agents for these actors and have their own strategic interests less closely related to the traders and multinational enterprises. Consumers gain from trade but are relatively silent when it comes to making trade policy, and when they speak they often voice arguments that are more protectionist than liberal. Sometimes strategic interest, as well as the general economic good, requires the governments to bind their own hands, in a way that leads to the rather convoluted rhetoric of trade policy. But nevertheless, regardless of the difficulty of explaining the actions of governments, the establishment of a functioning multilateral trade system in the 50 years after the Second World War represents one of the finest achievements of intergovernmental cooperation.

The remainder of this chapter discusses the development of the multilateral trade system over the post-war period; the rules of the system, as embodied in the General Agreement on Tariffs and Trade (GATT) and subsequently the World Trade Organization (WTO); the scope of the system as it reacted to (and facilitated) the development of global markets and spread to include important new aspects of trade; the structure of the system and its governance; and the current state of the system as it adjusts to tensions arising from the broadening of its mandate and the increasing inclusion of developing countries.

The development of the multilateral trade system

The current multilateral system is based on the post-war construction of the GATT, with the US and the UK taking the leading roles in its design. The procedures and rules of the GATT in turn owe much to the post-depression trade policy of the US as manifest in the Reciprocal Trade Agreements Act (RTA) of 1934. Both the political support for the con- clusion of trade agreements in the US and the legal framework provided by the RTA (giving the President more authority for negotiating with other countries, so long as it was on a reciprocal basis) made it possible to construct a system in the post-war era to guide the reconstruction of the world economy.[5]

As joint hegemons, the US and the UK attempted to design this new multilateral system to fit in with both post-war geopolitics and geoeconomics. A rules-based liberal trade system would help to prevent another collapse of the world economy and halt the drift towards communism. However, there were some fundamental differences between the views of the two industrial powers, on the continuation of preferences and on the use of trade instruments for support of macro-economic policy, and the plans for the multilat- eral trade system lagged behind those for the monetary and financial institutions agreed at Bretton Woods. This lack of unity resulted in the still-born International Trade

Organization and left the trade system without a formal institutional structure. The informality of the trade system, however, proved advantageous in allowing for constructive ambiguity in trade rules. The major powers were able to make use of the 'space' for accommodating interest groups that might have derailed a more legally binding system.[6]

The GATT system proved its resilience and usefulness over 50 years of expanding trade. The system became a useful way to encompass the newly independent countries that resulted from the breakup of the European empires. Though still connected to their previous colonial power by trade agreements, these countries benefited from a simplified accession process into the GATT that helped to broaden their trading horizon. Another success of the system was its ability to control the protectionist tendencies of the emerging European trade bloc. Many of the GATT negotiating rounds were a more or less direct consequence of the widening and deepening of the European Community. As the EC became an economic power, it proved mutually convenient for the US and the European powers to use the GATT mechanism to develop a relatively liberal multilateral trade regime to avoid the fragmentation of the trade system into competing protectionist blocs.[7]

In spite of the convenience of the system for the major industrial powers, the GATT went through major crises in the 1950s and again in the 1970s. By the 1980s, its institutional weakness had become a liability rather than an asset. The Uruguay Round, initiated in 1986, became the locus of discussion about the institutions and rules needed to guide the expansion of world trade. And the outcome was a stronger and more coherent set of rules, together with the setting up of the World Trade Organization as a full-fledged multilateral institution in 1994.[8] After nearly 50 years, the multilateral trade system had reached maturity.

The rules of the multilateral trade system
The central pillar of the multilateral trade system, as embedded in the GATT/WTO, is the principle of non-discrimination, both among members (most-favored nation treatment) and between domestic and foreign sources (national treatment).[9] The justification for non-discrimination is broadly that this limits the power of large trading countries to pick and choose trade partners, and it lessens the scope for domestic customs and regulatory bodies to protect domestic industry by setting higher standards for imports. But discrimination is not in fact outlawed: it might be more accurate to call the principle 'mutually-agreed discrimination', where granting preferences to other members of customs unions and free trade areas is accepted and where developing countries (and in particular the least developed countries) obtain as a matter of course special and differential treatment (SDT).[10] In the case of national treatment, national laws and practices regularly discriminate among sources of goods, but again the basis for such discrimination has to be agreed. Thus health and safety regulations use more-or-less objective criteria to guard against the import of pathogens. Unjustified and unsanctioned discrimination is however condemned, and many of the cases before the dispute settlement panels have revolved around this principle.

The multilateral rules also direct how a government should institute its trade policy. First, the use of tariffs is enshrined as the preferred means of controlling imports. This instrument is seen to be both transparent and easily negotiable downwards.[11] And the notion of banning quotas and other import schemes that invite discrimination fits well with the concept of a trade system that applies in the same way to all. In addition to limits on trade policy, the multilateral trade rules of the WTO ban most export subsidies and any domestic subsidies that are specific to particular group of producers and that cause harm to the interests of others. Over time, the reach of trade rules expanded into areas traditionally thought of as the province of domestic policy. Thus the boundary between trade policy and domestic policy has become increasingly blurred.

To keep a balance between export and import-competing interests, countries insist that the multilateral trade system has adequate safeguards against market disruption and predation by overseas firms. Over time, the GATT and the WTO have developed a set of such safeguards that may be taken by countries in cases of injury to import-competing sectors or surges in import levels. The rules governing trade remedies evolved slowly from the somewhat weak provisions in the GATT through the attempt in the Kennedy Round to control anti-dumping actions to the optional Codes on subsidies and on anti-dumping measures of the Tokyo Round until finally being negotiated in the UR as Agreements integral to the system.[12] General safeguard provisions under the GATT have also been elaborated, and individual agreements (on Agriculture and on Textiles) have their own safeguards. Though the popularity of these various trade remedies changes over time, their role in the trade system seems assured.

Central to the operation of the GATT/WTO as an institution is the idea that each country has to contribute in order to make use of the services of the system. Thus the *modus operandi* of the WTO is built around the notion of reciprocal obligations by all parties to the agreement. By extension, reciprocity also guides the form of negotiations, with countries obliged to agree to sometimes painful tariff cuts in exchange for better access to other members' markets.[13] As with non-discrimination, this principle of reciprocity is modified in practice, as least developed countries are not expected to grant reciprocity in trade negotiations, and are relieved of some of the general obligations. Developing countries also grant less than full reciprocity as an aspect of SDT.

The intended outcome of reciprocity is that obligations are entered into freely by member governments in negotiated agreements and are assumed to reflect a balance that is acceptable to all. As a consequence, changes in the rules or procedures can only be made with unanimity and actions that threaten the balance of advantages can be challenged on the grounds of 'nullification or impairment' of expected benefits. All this requires the setting up of an institution to facilitate exchanges among governments and to resolve disputes arising from ambiguities or deliberate violations. So one important function of the dispute settlement process is to preserve the balance generated by reciprocal obligations and negotiated trade concessions.

The scope of the multilateral trade system
The Uruguay Round of trade negotiations brought about a major expansion of the scope of the multilateral trade system.[14] The GATT was limited to trade in goods. But other types of trade, particularly trade in services, had been growing rapidly as a manifestation of the trend towards global business models. The negotiations on bringing service trade under multilateral rules were contentious, with developing countries fearing that the industrial countries dominated the service sectors. Even more problematic was the suggestion by the developed countries that trade-related aspects of intellectual property protection be included in the talks, along with some aspects of investment that impinged directly on trade. Many developing countries did not have intellectual property protection

laws, and considered that introducing such protection would mainly favor the industrial world. Likewise, rules on trade-linked investment policies seemed to limit the scope for developing countries to guide their economies.

Eventually a deal was struck by which two areas of trade that particularly interested developing countries, greater market access for agricultural goods along with a reduction of subsidies paid to farmers in industrial countries, and an end to the quota system for controlling textile trade, were included along with services and intellectual property.[15] This significant increase in scope for the multilateral trade system was introduced along with the institutional and legal developments mentioned above. The result was a structure that more closely mirrored the realities of globalization, albeit reflecting the asymmetries of economic power that seemed to many to be exacerbated by the global marketplace.

Just as increasing depth of regional integration tends to attract new members (Baldwin 1996) so the increased scope of the multilateral trade system made it more essential for countries once excluded to join the multilateral trade system. This was made dramatically more easy in the course of the 1990s by the collapse of the alternative political model, that of state socialism in the former Soviet bloc and in China, and the adoption of trade and economic reforms in much of the developing world, particularly in Latin America. The WTO became a vital support for the transition economies and those embracing the 'Washington Consensus' of economic liberalism. Emerging economies found the environment of trade liberalization supportive of their domestic economic strategies. Thus expanding membership seemed to be good for both current and new members, and the WTO welcomed all comers with open arms.

By the time of the Singapore Ministerial in 1996 the expansion of the scope of the WTO began to clash with the expanded membership. The expanding functions suggested by the developed countries included aspects of investment and competition policy as well as trade facilitation and government procurement (the so-called Singapore Issues).[16] In addition, many developed countries sought to add trade rules to support labor standards and address environmental issues. In this they were supported by civil society groups that had begun to question the desirability of further expansion of trade and the impacts of globalization on jobs and the environment. The developing countries, still struggling to adopt the obligations inherited in the Uruguay Round and concerned that the benefits that they thought that they had won during those negotiations were slow in materializing, were less than enthusiastic about expanding the scope of the multilateral trade system.[17] And they particularly mistrusted the motives of those who argued for the adoption of tougher labor and environmental standards, which they feared would rob them of their competitiveness.

All these issues converged at the Seattle Ministerial, in late 1999, which was intended to launch a new round of trade talks. But the tensions between developed and developing countries, along with the lack of a coordinated strategy on the part of the US and the EU, slowed progress. Amid chaos outside and discord inside the meeting rooms, the meeting broke up without agreement on a new round. The new multilateral trade system was in danger of proving itself dysfunctional, perhaps through over-reaching its base of political support, after only six years of operation. But eventually, after a period of 'confidence building' all members agreed at the Doha Ministerial, in November 2001, to launch a new round of talks. To emphasize that the developing countries could expect their issues to remain on the front-burner, the round was labeled the Doha Development Agenda

(DDA). After a disappointing 'mid-term' review of progress in Cancún in September 2003, the DDA was back on track, if a little behind schedule, by the summer of 2004. But three of the Singapore issues had been dropped, leaving only trade facilitation on the negotiating table. Environmental issues were confined to discussion in a Trade and Environment Committee and not central to the negotiations.[18] Labor issues were excluded altogether, besides an exhortation to the WTO secretariat to liaise with the International Labour Office.[19] The expansion of the scope of the WTO appeared, at least for the moment, to be halted.

The structure of the multilateral trade system
What are the main characteristics of the institution that creates and guards the multilateral trade system? The WTO is structured as an intergovernmental organization with a small secretariat. It remains self-consciously 'member-driven' and controlled through the trade officials of member states, though in practice national parliamentarians and lobbyists frequently interact with WTO officials and non-governmental organizations are increasingly included at least at the discussion stage of trade issues. The governing body is the General Council, comprising representatives from all members. It can meet at the official or the ministerial (political) level, and is responsible for taking all major decisions. Many members have permanent representation in Geneva, but some smaller countries choose to send trade officials from capitals for important meetings. The General Council also meets as the Dispute Settlement Board, and so presides over both the legal and legislative functions of the WTO. In addition, as the Trade Negotiating Committee, the Council also initiates and closes trade rounds and meets periodically to review their progress.

Reporting to the General Council are Councils for the various component agreements: the Goods Council (GATT), the GATS Council, the TRIPS Council and the TRIMS Council. In turn, Standing Committees as created by the various agreements report to these bodies, including an Agriculture Committee, an SPS Committee, a TBT Committee, and so on. Though there is provision for voting on the Council, in practice decisions are taken by consensus (defined as none present objecting).

The Secretariat, located in Geneva, functions primarily as an organizer of meetings, an institutional memory, and a provider of information to the countries. The Secretariat does play a role as facilitator in negotiations and disputes, and the Director General has traditionally developed a close relationship with the Geneva ambassadors that allows for some informal consultation and information exchange. Unlike the staff of the World Bank or the International Monetary Fund, the WTO secretariat does not engage in extensive research or country advisory work.[20]

Through the expanded mandate given the GATT/WTO system in the Uruguay Round, a number of other trade-related bodies have been brought in to the orbit of the WTO. Among these are three that deal with various aspects of health and safety regulations in the area of food and agricultural products, the Codex Alimentarius Commission (CODEX), the International Plant Protection Convention (IPPC), and the International Office of Epizootics (OIE). Improved relations with the 'other' Geneva based trade organization, the United Nations Commission on Trade and Development (UNCTAD) has greatly helped to avoid the tensions between North and South that characterized the 1970s. The one institution that suffered by the introduction of the WTO was the World Intellectual Property Organization, WIPO, which was the guardian of the various conventions on copyrights and patents. Without the power of sanctions, WIPO had proved ineffective in obliging countries to adopt these intellectual property protections.[21]

The current state of the multilateral trade system

So what is the state of the multilateral trade system at this time? On the positive side, the legal and institutional structure is firmly in place, based on the Marrakesh Treaty that established the WTO. The underlying rules are embodied in the GATT and the GATS, along with the TRIPS. No major country has called for any significant changes in these basic rules. The increased interest of developing countries in the operation of the system, though no doubt motivated in part by the increased obligations that they have incurred, is surely a positive sign for any institution that purports to be global. The fact that those countries that are not yet members are apparently willing to join, even if to do so means making significant modifications to their domestic institutions, suggests that membership of the WTO is still regarded as a necessary if not sufficient condition for attracting foreign investment.

But the institution is nevertheless under significant stress. A major challenge to the basic logic of the system comes from the progressive weakening of the MFN principle. This shows up in two different ways: the increasing attraction of preferential trade agreements (PTAs), and the tendency towards more pervasive 'special and differential treatment' for groups of countries. Free trade agreements among WTO members have proliferated even as the multilateral system has developed. Though the economic impact of these PTAs varies, they all divert attention and diplomatic resources from the multilateral system. So long as they remain useful to governments, the WTO as an institution cannot adopt an agenda to curb such agreements. But it could embrace them and exploit the synergies while avoiding as much as possible the conflicts. This may be one important item for the agenda after the current DDA.

Special and Differential Treatment for developing countries has a long history in the GATT and an accepted place in current trade relations. But two concerns keep arising. First, the category of 'developing country' is nowhere defined in the WTO. That designation is self-declared by countries, leading to a natural reluctance to 'graduate' to developed country status. The need to face this issue has been emphasized by the increasing success in trade of countries such as India, China and Brazil, for whom developed countries are less than eager to give non-reciprocal benefits in trade talks. Indeed, those countries that do need extra time, or special consideration, may be disadvantaged by the spreading of such treatment to all developing countries. It may be time to limit the scope of such SDT elements, particularly non-reciprocity in trade talks. Reciprocity is becoming more firmly established in regional trade agreements, as the developing countries offer to developed country trade partners the benefits of full reciprocity in exchange for greater assurance of access to markets. The same deal seems possible at the multilateral level.

But quite apart from the difficulty of defining a developing country a second concern is what concessions should one give to those countries that do not merely delay their full integration in the trade system and make them less attractive for investment? Certain structural problems exist in developing countries that make them particularly vulnerable to rapid liberalization, and it has long been recognized that not all countries have the capacity to take advantage of export possibilities. But if open economies grow faster, an underlying premise of the trade system, then encouraging countries to delay opening may be perpetuating asymmetries rather than reducing them. Permissive SDT needs to be matched with positive policies to encourage participation of developing countries, including developing supply capacity and transferring technology. In addition, regulatory systems differ among countries, and the capacity to implement agreed regulatory frameworks can be lacking in developing countries. But again the approach to this problem could combine some relief from obligations with assistance to develop the necessary regulatory capacity.

The decision-making procedures of the WTO are also being called into question by many members, as well as by NGOs concerned about access.[22] Calls for democratic processes in intergovernmental organizations are somewhat misleading, as the legitimacy of the decisions derives from that of the member governments. But ownership of the system by all the members is desirable, and that requires each country to feel that it has an opportunity to be heard. Many developing countries have objected, in particular, to the so-called 'green room' meetings held at crucial times during a negotiation that involve only a few countries. It is difficult to see how crucial compromises can be worked out in plenary sessions. The trade-off between efficiency and inclusiveness is inevitable, but the progress of the WTO requires that all members feel informed and consulted. The old notion of GATT as a traders club for the industrial countries has given way to another model, but the details have yet to be agreed.[23]

The dispute settlement process is also under some scrutiny, though radical changes seem unlikely in the near future.[24] Three different criticisms have been leveled against the DSU. The first is that the procedure is biased against small countries, who can less easily afford the legal costs and, if they win, cannot easily impose the trade sanctions that would be necessary to persuade the larger countries to adjust their policies. The second issue is the possibility of a clash between the legal and the political aspects of the WTO. Some have noticed the emergence of a legal culture in the WTO that encourages litigation rather than negotiation.[25] It is not difficult to foresee reduced political support for the institution if this were to be taken too far. A third question is whether trade sanctions are intended as a penalty for transgression, designed to enforce a judgment of the membership, or a compensation for non-compliance, that can be chosen as an alternative to the change in policy that would be required. Clearly, the way in which countries approach this question will indicate the extent to which the 'flexibility' of the GATT remains in the more legally complete WTO.

Perhaps most fundamentally, the nature of the organization is also under some question. The WTO currently is a 'system guardian' responsible for the set of rules that govern world trade. The premise on which it was set up is that trade is beneficial if governments restrict their actions to a limited set of policies designed to minimize the imposition of costs on others. But this may not benefit all countries equally, and may not redress inequalities or promote sustainable development. Many would argue that the body should be following a 'results-oriented' strategy, by judging rules by their contribution to development rather than their neutrality and liberality. But this would clearly change the support for the trade system in developed countries, where selling the trade rules as good for developing countries is unlikely to generate support. Neither is it obvious that the Secretariat can reshape itself as a development agency. It has no mandate for work with individual countries, other than assistance with understanding obligations. But there certainly could be a place for more consistency between advice given by aid and development agencies and the obligations under the WTO.

The current state of the WTO serves to illustrate the strengths and weaknesses of the multilateral system as it has developed in the post-war period. It requires the active support of major economic powers and yet has to be run in a way that does not alienate middle-sized countries and impose impossible burdens on smaller members. The GATT was successful largely because it allowed the hegemons room to balance domestic political interests with the conduct of global strategies. Moreover, there was a broad coincidence of interests between the US and the EU that carried the GATT through crises. The WTO could be equally successful if its tighter rules, that impinge on domestic interests, were seen to be reasonable price to pay for a more structured and inclusive trade system. But this requires a broader consensus both within major countries and across the membership, and this consensus is proving difficult to obtain. Leadership is shifting from the US and the EU to a group of countries with a major stake in the stability of the system. But it is not clear whether this change in power structure will be easy for former trade powers to accept, and the domestic political support to be maintained.

Much may rest on the successful outcome of the Doha Round currently underway. But starting a round is easier than bringing it to a conclusion. Starting a round of trade negotiations requires a degree of ambiguity to maintain a consensus. But finishing a round needs precision and firm commitments, typically involving intensive negotiations among the leading countries. So the issue of leadership and political commitment becomes crucial to the success of the Doha Round, and by extension to the future of the multilateral trading system.

Acknowledgments

The author would like to acknowledge his debt to John Barton, Judith Goldstein and Richard Steinberg, co-authors of a book on the Multilateral Trade System (Barton *et al*, 2005). They should not be held accountable, however, for ideas expressed in this current chapter.

Notes

1. The links between domestic politics and trade rules are explored in Goldstein (1998), and Goldstein and Martin (2000).
2. Other chapters in this book deal with the rational for trade agreements and the relationship between size and enthusiasm for such agreements.
3. The economic arguments are covered in detail in Hoekman and Kostecki (2001).
4. Arguments for coordination of legal structures are found in Trebilcock and Howse (1995) and in Barton, *et al*. (2005).
5. See Bidwell and Diebold (1949) for a contemporary analysis of the emergence of the post-war trade system.
6. For a fuller discussion of the issue of flexibility in the GATT see Barton *et al*. (2005).
7. Agriculture was an exception to this harmony, along with steel and later civil aircraft. Trade disputes continue in these areas.
8. The legal structure introduced in the Uruguay Round is discussed in full in Jackson (1998), and the impacts of this transformation are reviewed in Victor and Weiner (2002).
9. The basic structure of the GATT, as well as its early development, are discussed in Dam (1970).
10. See the discussion of discrimination in Hudec and Southwick (1999) and the economic critique of regional discrimination in Srinivasan (1998).
11. Of course, the instrument used at the border has significant implications for the type and generosity of domestic economic assistance programs, so a tariffs-only regime is not without its domestic impacts.
12. For a critique of how the anti-dumping agreement has performed and what might be needed to improve it, see Lindsey and Ikenson (2002). Sykes (2003a and 2003b) deals with the issues of subsidies, countervailing duties and safeguards.

13. This reciprocity in negotiations has an important domestic function as well. It engages the export sectors in trade talks in a way that counters the pressure of import competing sectors for continued protection.
14. The nature and implications of this expansion are discussed fully in Barton *et al.* (2005).
15. For a detailed discussion of how agriculture had been treated in the GATT, see Josling *et al.* (1996). The story of the Uruguay Round negotiations is told in Croome (1995). For more information on the TRIPS Agreement on intellectual property protection, see Gervais (1998). Barton (2001) discusses the rationale for including intellectual protection rules in trade agreements. Maskus (2000) gives a comprehensive account of this issue.
16. Graham and Richardson (1997) give an extended discussion of the merits of including competition policy in trade rules.
17. Many developing countries were actively involved in constructing regional trade systems at this time, and deepening the multilateral system was not so high a priority.
18. For detailed discussion of the trade and environment debates see Esty (1994) and Steinberg (2002).
19. The trade and labor issues are discussed in Elliot (2000) and Cleveland (2003).
20. Coordination with UNCTAD is facilitated by the joint responsibility for the International Trade Center (ITC).
21. A discussion of the relationship between the WIPO and the WTO is to be found in Beier and Schricker (1989).
22. See Blackhurst (2001) and Blackhurst *et al.* (1999) for detailed discussions about changing the decision process.
23. Compare Curzon and Curzon (1973) with Kerr (2002).
24. See Davey (2001) for a commentary on the expanded scope of the dispute settlement system. Lawrence (2004) discusses many of the shortcomings of the current system.
25. See Barfield (2001) for a critique of the sovereignty issues stemming from the legal culture, and Weiler (2000) for the tension between diplomats and lawyers.

References

Baldwin, Richard (1996), 'A Domino Theory of Regionalism,' in Richard Baldwin, Pentti Haaparanta and Jaakko Kiander (eds), *Expanding Membership of the European Union*, Cambridge, UK: Cambridge University Press, pp. 25–48.

Barfield, Claude (2001), *Free Trade, Sovereignty, Democracy: The Future of the World Trade Organization*, Washington, DC: The AEI Press.

Barton, John H. (2001), 'The Economics of TRIPS: International Trade in Information-Intensive Products,' *The George Washington International Law Review*, 33(3), 473–501.

Barton, John, Judith Goldstein, Tim Josling and Richard Steinberg (2005), *The Evolution of the Trade Regime: Politics, Law and Economics of the GATT and WTO*, Princeton NJ: Princeton University Press.

Beier, Friedrick-Karl and Gerhard Schricker (1989), 'GATT or WIPO? New Ways in the International Protection of Intellectual Property.' *IIC Studies*, **11**, New York: VCH Publishers.

Bello, Judith Hippler (1996), 'The WTO Dispute Settlement Understanding: Less is More,' *American Journal of International Law*, **90**, 416.

Bidwell, P. W and W. Diebold Jr. (1949), 'The United States and the International Trade Organization,' *International Conciliation*, **49**, 187–239.

Blackhurst, Richard (2001), 'Reforming WTO Decision-Making: Lessons from Singapore and Seattle,' in Klaus Gunter Deutsch and Bernhard Speyer (eds), *Freer Trade in the Next Decade: Issues in the Millenium Round in the World Trade Organization*, London: Routledge.

Blackhurst, Richard, Bill Lyakurwa and Ademola Oyejide (1999), 'Improving African Participation in the WTO,' prepared for WTO/World Bank Conference, available at www1.worldbank.org/wbiep/trade/WTO_2000.html.

Cleveland, Sarah H. (2003), 'Why International Labor Standards?' in Robert J. Flanagan and William J. Gould IV (eds), *International Labor Standards: Globalization, Trade and Public Policy*, Stanford, CA: Stanford University Press.

Croome, John (1995), *Reshaping the World Trading System: A History of the Uruguay Round*, Geneva: World Trade Organization.

Curzon, Gerard and Victoria Curzon (1973), 'GATT: Traders' Club,' in *The Anatomy of Influence*, Robert W. Cox and Harold K. Jacobson (eds), New Haven, CT: Yale University Press, pp. 298–333.

Dam, Kenneth W. (1970), *The GATT: Law and International Economic Organization*, Chicago, IL: Chicago University Press.

Davey, William J. (2001), 'Has the WTO Dispute Settlement System Exceeded Its Authority?' *Journal of International Economic Law*, **4**, 79.

Elliott, Kimberly A. (2000), 'Getting Beyond No . . .! Promoting Worker Rights and Trade,' in Jeffrey J. Schott (ed.), *The WTO After Seattle*, Washington, DC: Institute for International Economics, pp. 187–204.

Esty, Dan (1994), *Greening the GATT*, Washington, DC: Institute for International Economics.

Gervais, Daniel J. (1998), *The TRIPS Agreement; Drafting History and Analysis*, London: Sweet & Maxwell.

Goldstein, Judith (1998), 'International Institutions and Domestic Politics: GATT, WTO and the Liberalization of International Trade,' in Anne O. Krueger (ed.), *The WTO as an International Organization*, Chicago, IL: University of Chicago Press, pp. 133–52.

Goldstein, Judith and Lisa Martin (2000), 'Legalization, Trade Liberalization, and Domestic Politics: A Cautionary Note,' *International Organization*, **54**(3), 603–32.

Graham, Edward M. and J. David Richardson (1997), *Global Competition Policy*, Washington, DC: Institute for International Economics.

Hoekman, Bernard M. and Michel M. Kostecki (2001), *The Political Economy of the World Trading System: The WTO and Beyond*, Oxford: Oxford University Press.

Hudec, Robert E. and James D. Southwick (1999), 'Regionalism and the WTO Rules: Problems in the Fine Art of Discriminating Fairly,' in Miguel R. Mendoza, Patrick Low and Barbara Kotschwar (eds), *Trade Rules in the Making: Challenges in Regional and Multilateral Negotiations*, Washington, DC: Brookings/OAS.

Jackson, John H. (1998), *The World Trade Organization: Constitution and Jurisprudence*, London: Royal Institute of International Affairs.

Josling, Tim, Stefan Tangermann and T. K. Warley (1996), *Agriculture in the GATT*, London: Macmillan.

Kerr, William (2002), 'A Club No More – The WTO after Doha,' *The Estey Centre Journal of International Law and Trade Policy*, **3**(1), 1–9

Lawrence, Robert Z. (2004). *Crimes and Punishments? An Analysis of Retaliation Under the WTO*, Washington, DC: Institute of International Economics.

Lindsey, Brink and Dan Ikenson (2002), 'Reforming the Antidumping Agreement; A Road Map for WTO Negotiations,' CATO Institute Trade Policy Analysis 21, Washington, DC: CATO Institute Center for Trade Policy Analysis.

Maskus, Keith (2000), *Intellectual Property Rights in the Global Economy*, Washington, DC: Institute for International Economics.

Srinivasan, T. N. (1998), 'Regionalism and the WTO: Is non-Discrimination Passé?' in Anne O. Krueger (ed.), *The WTO as an International Organization*, Chicago Press, pp. 329–49.

Steinberg, Richard H. (2002), 'Understanding Trade and the Environment: Conceptual Frameworks,' in Richard H. Steinberg (ed.), *The Greening of Trade Law: International Trade Organizations and Environmental Issues*, Boulder, CO: Rowman and Littlefield.

Sykes, Alan O. (2003a), 'The Economics of WTO Rules on Subsidies and Countervailing Measures,' The Law School, University of Chicago, John M. Olin Law and Economics Working Paper No. 186 (2nd series).

Sykes, Alan O. (2003b), 'The Safeguards Mess: A Critique of WTO Jurisprudence,' The Law School, University of Chicago, John M. Olin Law and Economics Working Paper No. 187 (2nd series).

Trebilcock, Michael J. and Robert Howse (1995), *The Regulation of International Trade*, London: Routledge, pp. 1–24.

Victor, David G. and Rebecca U. Weiner (2002), 'A Great Transformation in World Trade Law: Can the WTO Stay Afloat,' in Barry Krissoff, Mary Bohman and Julie A. Caswell (eds), *Global Food Trade and Consumer Demand for Quality*, New York: Kluwer Academic/Plenum Publishers, pp. 33–41.

Weiler, J. H. H. (2000), 'The Rule of Lawyers and the Ethos of Diplomats: Reflections on the Internal and External Legitimacy of WTO Dispute Settlement,' Harvard Jean Monnet Working Paper 9/00, Cambridge, MA: Harvard Law School.

8 Overview of trade agreements: regional trade agreements
Nicholas Perdikis

Introduction

The majority of WTO members are also participants in at least one regional trade agreement (RTA). The popularity of RTAs among trading nations is not in doubt. Since the early 1980s there has been a surge in their number. The WTO claims that 250 RTAs were notified to it by the end of 2002. Of these 130 were ratified after 1995 with an additional 70 in operation but not yet ratified. The WTO estimates that by the end of 2005 if the RTAs that are planned or under negotiation come on stream the total number in existence could be in the region of 300 (WTO 2004 a,b,c,d).

This chapter will examine the reasons behind this growth, their relationship to and the potential effect on the multilateral trading system, and the way GATT/WTO rules have dealt with them.

The scope of Regional Trade Agreements (RTAs)

The Dictionary of Trade Policy Terms describes Regionalism or the process by which RTAs come about as 'actions of governments to liberalise or facilitate trade on a regional basis, sometimes through free trade areas or customs unions'. The WTO definition is, however, both more specific and more general. It is more specific because its provisions relate to the conditions of preferential trade liberalization. The meaning is more general because RTAs may be concluded between countries that are not geographically proximate (WTO, 2004e). RTAs can vary in both their coverage and in the depth of preferential treatment they accord their members. The movement in modern RTAs is not just towards the removal or reduction of tariffs and quantitative restrictions but for deeper forms of integration. These are increasingly covering the regulations governing intra bloc trade. This may include the harmonization and adoption of common health and safety standards, safeguard provision, common customs rules and administration. They may also extend to competition, industrial policy and environmental policy as well as rules regarding government procurement. A widening array of services trade is often included in these preferential agreements. The adoption of a common currency or the fixing of exchange rates between national currencies may also be a feature. The European Union (EU) certainly displays the characteristics of an advanced and sophisticated RTA in that the provisions of its treaties deal with all the issues just mentioned.

Several forms of RTA exist. Economists generally identify four standard types. The simplest is the Free Trade Area (FTA). In this the participants agree to eliminate the barriers to trade between one another on either one or several product categories such as manufactures. While barriers are eliminated between participants each member pursues its own independent trade policy with non-members. This can lead to potential problems. Non-member exporters can direct their products to their target market via a member country that has low trade barriers for onward distribution to one that has high trade barriers. To prevent this, members of free trade areas set up elaborate and complicated rules to prevent their trade policies being undermined, these are the so called rules of origin. FTAs are, therefore, not without their bureaucratic costs.

The next form of RTA is the customers' union. Essentially this is an FTA but one that operates an agreed common trade policy against non-members. This often takes the form of a common external tariff (CET). A customs union is a deeper form of integration than the FTA. In forming a customs union countries give up an element of their economic and political sovereignty. In so doing while individual sovereignty is reduced collective sovereignty is gained. The customs union thereby increases its economic and political power *vis à vis* other trade partners or neutralizes that of other RTAs. The acquisition of power and the thwarting of that of others has often been an important reason for the formation of RTAs. The North American Free Trade Area (NAFTA) was to some extent a reaction against the economic deepening of the EU via its single market programme. In Asia, the Association of South East Asian Nations (ASEAN) in its economic form was developed as a reaction to the growing power of the EU and integration in North America. Similar reasoning underlies the development of Asia-Pacific Economic Co-operation (APEC).

A further and deeper form of RTA is the common market. This institution is essentially a customs union but one that allows the free movement of capital and labour as well as goods and services. This form of integration allows these factors of production to migrate and seek their highest return in the RTA. By allocating resources more efficiently factor productivities are raised and the growth rate increased. Internal tensions can arise from the distributional issues that result and often collective regional policies are introduced to deal with these. The EU's regional development fund is an example of this. An individual country's sovereignty is reduced further by this form of RTA as a further element of domestic policy, the control of capital and labour flows, is lost to a central authority. The expectation is that the consequent loss of individual sovereignty is outweighed by the economic and political power gain by increasing collective sovereignty.

An economic union is the ultimate form of an RTA. It requires that countries harmonize their fiscal and monetary policies as well as their broader economic and social legislation. The idea here is that companies and workers engaged in economic activities throughout the union face the same economic conditions. All artificial barriers are thereby removed. While an economic union does not require a single currency for its operation, merely the fixing of exchange rate parities will suffice, it is often easier and less costly to adopt one. The EU's euro is a current example of this. In this type of RTA the loss of individual economic and political sovereignty is considerable. Again the benefit is the enhanced economic and political power of the group. The EU is an example of such an RTA although it could be argued that because it lacks the harmonization of tax rates and some member states are not members of the euro it cannot be considered an economic union.

What has been outlined above are a set of ideal models. In the world economy, as we have indicated, there are variants to these ideals. One assumption made is that the RTA that is formed is amongst equals or the members are treated as equals in decision making. This may not always be the case and RTAs can develop in a different way. The 'hub and spoke' idea fits this well. In this form of integration an economy may develop a set of separate economic agreements with a host of other economies. The larger or more powerful economy represents the hub of a wheel while the spokes represent the separate agreements that run out from the hub to the other countries. These arrangements can be supplemented by agreements between the countries that make up the spokes. They may, in addition, differ substantially one with another thus a whole web of overlapping agreements can result. Examples of this form is the set of agreements that the EU has developed with its former colonies; the so-called African, Caribbean and Pacific countries or ACP and the countries of North Africa and the Middle East. These are known as the Euro-Med Agreements.

Regional trade agreements: some history

RTAs are not a new or post-Second World War phenomenon as is sometimes thought. RTAs first began to appear in the nineteenth century with the Anglo-French commercial treaty of 1860 (Irwin 1992). The preferential trading arrangements that these countries granted one another were quickly sought by other countries. The British granted these on a Most Favoured Nation (MFN) basis. The French in contrast were keen to develop bilateral trade agreements with its trading partners. These eventually led to a plethora of bilateral measures which in turn developed into an open multilateral system. This system came to an end on the outbreak of the First World War.

The open multilateral system was not restored after the end of the war. To the contrary and with the onset of the depression of the 1930s a more closed system established itself. To some extent countries tried to maintain some of the benefits of openness by trading with neighbours through the formation of RTAs. This was particularly so in Europe.

After the Second World War while the principal thrust of international economic policy was to establish an open multilateral economic order, the pursuit of RTAs was seen as a complementary activity. This movement was particularly strong in Europe with the formation of the European Economic Community (EEC), the forerunner of the EU in 1956 and the European Free Trade Area (EFTA) in 1957. The perceived success of the EEC in raising the growth rate of its members encouraged the setting up of similar bodies in other areas and continents. In Latin America, the Latin American Free Trade Area (LAFTA) was brought into being while Africa spawned the Economic Community of West African States (ECOWAS) and the East African Community (EAC) to name but two. The Middle East saw the formation of the Arable Common Market (ACM) and in the Pacific the Australia–New Zealand Free Trade Area (ANZFTA). The success of these RTAs could not always be assumed. LAFTA, ECOWAS and the EAC did not bring the rewards expected. This was largely the result of the adoption of inappropriate policies that failed to liberalize trade between them and a lack of co-ordination.

A second wave of RTA formation can be detected from the late 1980s onwards. This came about for several reasons. The first was the dissatisfaction felt by some countries, in particular the United States, with the progress of multilateral trade negotiations. The second is the fear that the multilateral trading system could be dictated to by a powerful inward looking EU. This certainly motivated wider economic integration in North America and influenced policy makers in Asia. A third factor was the idea of linking slowly growing economies to those with higher growth rates in order to improve their development.

Regional trade agreements and the multilateral trading system

RTAs are by their nature discriminatory. By conceding preferences to their members they discriminate against non-members. This cuts across the basis of the multilateral trading system which is summed up by the Most Favoured Nation (MFN) clause of the WTO/GATT system. This clause requires all signatories of the GATT to extend any concessions or preferences granted to one signatory to all signatories. Recognizing the political and economic realities of the international trading system both the GATT and later the General Agreement on Services (GATS) allowed exemptions to the MFN clause (WTO 2004e).

The GATT and RTAs

In terms of the GATT, RTAs are allowed under Article XXIV. The conditions under which they are allowed are as follows. First, when RTAs are established on average trade barriers are not higher than before the formation (Article XXIV:5). This condition attempts to ensure that the restrictions placed on imports from non-member states do not reduce the volume of imports significantly. In other words that trade diversion is minimized. The extent to which this is achieved is dependent on the height of the original restrictions and the concessions granted to fellow members of the RTA. The higher the external barriers and the greater the concessions the greater the trade diversionary effects.

Sub-paragraphs namely Article XXIV:5 and XXIV:5b dealt with the different effects on non-member states brought about by the formation of customs unions on the one hand and free trade areas on another. The formation of a customs union requires member states to harmonize their individual tariff rates against non members when they adopt a CET. Article XXIV:5a requires that trade barriers must not be 'on the whole' any higher or more restrictive than prior to the RTAs formation. The words 'on the whole' have led to numerous interpretations and disputes between the signatories of the GATT.

The situation for an FTA is more straightforward. In an FTA each member retains its own tariff structure against non-member states. This may lead to disputes and disagreements between the members which can only be solved by adopting complex rules of origin. The retention, however, by each member of its own foreign economic policy towards non-members makes the GATT rule easy to operate in practice. Article XXIV:5b decrees that barriers applied by each participant must not be raised in relation to non-member states when the FTA is formed.

The second condition allowing RTAs requires that when they are formed tariffs and non-tariff barriers are removed on substantially all intra-regional trade in goods within a reasonable length of time. This is required in order to maximize the trade creation effects and to prevent countries establishing RTAs and thwarting the MFN principle in their trade with their partners (Finger 1993). This sub-paragraph though does not attempt to ameliorate the impact on non-member states which could well be adverse.

The third condition requires that all RTAs are notified to the WTO Council. This is to ensure that the RTAs meet the GATT criteria outlined above. The scrutiny of RTA has now been devolved to the Committee of Regional Trade Agreements (CRTA). Whether this approach will prove fruitful is open to question given past experience. Up to the period of the late 1980s only four working parties set up by the council for trade in goods to examine the compatibility of RTAs with GATT rules could agree that they had been satisfied. The remainder, looking at over 50 RTAs, could neither agree nor disagree as to whether they satisfied GATT rules (Hoekman and Kostecki 2001). While allowing non-member states of RTAs and other interested parties to make their views known, the effect of the examination of RTAs can be said to have been limited.

The reason for this can be explained by the political and economic power of the proposed RTAs. In the case of the EEC the GATT decided not to examine its formation. Several reasons account for this. Had the GATT concluded that its formation was contrary to its rules the member states could well have withdrawn from GATT (Snape 1993). This would have seriously weakened its operation and put in jeopardy the multilateral trading system. Another reason was the approval of the EEC's formation by the United States for wider political and economic reasons. It was willing therefore to see this exception to the multilateral trading system created. The result, however, was that a precedent was established which weakened the GATT's control over the formation and policing of RTAs.

As mentioned above, Article XXIV:5a is open to various interpretations. The words 'substantially all trade' lack quantification while the way that trade policy and its effect is evaluated is unclear. Further what time period can be placed on a 'reasonable length of time' is also indeterminate and open to discussion (Hoekman and Kostecki 2001).

We can see, therefore, that for economic, political and interpretative reasons the GATT has not been able to control or monitor the establishment of RTA as institutions. It can, however, through its Trade Policy Review comment on their trade policies.

By the early 1990s it was recognized that there were problems with the GATT's processes in evaluating RTAs. In 1994, the GATT established the Understanding on the Interpretation of Article XXIV. This reaffirmed the view that RTAs should enhance trade between the members of the group while not raising barriers to non-member states. This was emphasized further with regard to the expansion of an existing RTA (GATT 1994).

The Understanding also clarified the criteria and procedures used to assess and evaluate new or expanding RTAs and improved the transparency of all RTAs notified to the GATT under Article XXIV.

The method of assessing the impact of RTA formation was also made more explicit. The WTO was put in charge of collecting the statistical material necessary for an evaluation to be made. This was to be carried out by assessing the effect of the change in the weighted average of tariff rates and customs duties on a line by line, country by country, basis.

In cases where a potential new member of a customs union is required to raise bound tariffs Article XXIV:6 requires that it enter negotiations and offer compensatory adjustments to the affected parties. In its negotiations it can offer any reductions that might arise if other potential members have to reduce their tariffs. Where such compensation is deemed insufficient, then the Understanding requires that the customs union reduced tariffs on other lines or offer direct compensation. The Understanding also makes provisions if the parties cannot agree on compensation. If there is no agreement within a reasonable period from the commencement of the negotiations then the customs union can amend or remove the concessions on offer. The affected parties can also react by imposing penalties or withdrawing concessions of an equivalent value from the customs unions participants. By legitimizing retaliation countries are under pressure to come to an agreement.

A ten year maximum was also set by the 1994 Understanding for the implementation of an RTA. Longer transition periods were allowed but these were considered exceptional. The working parties were also given authority to examine and pronounce on interim agreements regarding the time period within which the RTA was to be completed and the measures required for its completion. Where interim agreements did not include a plan and schedule the working party had the power to recommend one. Unless the negotiating parties to an RTA meet the recommendations of the working party then they are not allowed to implement it. The implementation of its recommendations is also subject to review.

The GATT Understanding tightened up considerably the rules surrounding RTAs. The authority for examining the compatibility of RTAs with the rules of the GATT passed to the newly founded Regional Trade Agreements Committee in 1995. Although all RTAs falling under the ambit of Article XXIV are still notified to the Council for Trade in Goods once it has adopted the terms of reference the agreement is passed on to the CRTA for examination. This examination has two functions. The first is to ensure transparency so that agreements are not made in or kept secret. The second is to see if agreements are consistent with the WTO's rules. The examination is carried out using information provided by the members of the RTA either in written or oral form. Once the facts have been established the secretariat draws up an examination report. Under the rules of the CRTA the examination report is sent out for consultation after which, if agreed, it is passed up to the WTO for adoption. A lack of consensus has, though, prevented any examination report from being adopted since 1995.

There are several reasons as to why this state of affairs exists. First, the wording and rules of the WTO with regard to RTAs is still imprecise and open to interpretation. Second, WTO rules are absent with regard to areas of importance to RTAs. For example, there is a lack of rules on the operation of preferential rules of origin. Third, there are discrepancies between the rules of the WTO and those of many RTAs.

This state of affairs vexed the members at the WTO ministerial meeting at Doha. It was felt that given the extent to which members were party to RTAs and given their potential role for economic development, the issues needed resolving. The Doha declaration set a deadline for the RTAC's deliberations.

RTAs and development – the Enabling Clause
The potential of RTAs in promoting economic development was recognized by the international community and was formalized in 1979. In that year, the so called Enabling Clause was adopted which allowed developing countries to establish agreements that did not meet the conditions enshrined in Article XXIV. Essentially, developing countries were allowed to enter into agreements that while opening up trade did not require them to liberalize 'substantially' all trade. It further allowed them to offer preferences to other developing countries (Hoekman and Kostecki 2001).

The General Agreement on Trade in Services and RTAs
While the GATT Article XXIV deals with the effect of RTA formation on the trade in goods, Article V of the General Agreement on Trade in Services (GATS) as its name implies covers services. Like the GATT the GATS allows countries to discriminate in their trade in services. As in the GATT, this is conditional and subject to surveillance.

The three conditions laid out in Article V are first, that there must be substantial coverage of the sectors involved. Substantial here means in terms of numbers of sectors, the trade volumes affected and supply modes involved. Second, that the participants 'provide for the absence or elimination of substantially all discrimination . . . between or among the parties, in the sectors covered' (GATS, Article Vb). It requires, in other words, the elimination of existing or new discriminatory measures. Third, the formation of an RTA must not lead to higher trade barriers against non-member states.

The GATS approach is in several respects weaker than that of the GATT. First, the GATS refers to sectoral coverage whereas the GATT requires liberalization in 'substantially all trade'. Second, the GATS does not relate trade in services to free trade. It deals principally with the specific commitments made by prospective members of an RTA under the GATS. Third, there are several loopholes that allow prospective members to deviate from multilateralism. One example of this is Article V:2 which allows agreements over the trade in services to be influenced by 'the wider process of economic integration amongst member states' (Hoekman and Kosteki 2001). Article V:3 also allows developing countries to discriminate against non-member states' companies even if they are operating within the RTA. These weaknesses in the GATS allow national governments to pander to, and not stand up against, domestic vested interests. They also allow them to discriminate further against non-members than under the GATT.

Challenging the operation of RTAs
Despite the difficulties encountered in verifying the compliance of RTAs with WTO rules, countries have been very reluctant to challenge their operation or use the WTO dispute settlement procedures. The India–Turkey textile and clothing case is an exception. When Turkey joined the EU's customs union it adopted its quantitative restrictions against India for these products. The WTO disputes panel set up to adjudicate found that Turkey's actions were incompatible with its obligations under GATT Articles XI and XIII. Turkey defended its actions on the basis of GATT Article XXIV and appealed against the ruling. The Appellate Body upheld the panel's views and also found that Turkey's actions were incompatible with Article 2.4 of the Agreement on Textiles and Clothing. The panel's interpretation of GATT Article XXIV was, however, questioned by the Appellate Body. Its view was that panels should first consider whether an RTA complies with Article XXIV before other GATT provisions are considered.

Why countries are so reluctant to challenge RTAs trade regimes under the GATT rules is an intriguing question. It could be due to several factors. First, as so many countries belong to RTAs themselves the trade diversion effects might be small compared with the trade creation effects of their own RTA. Given that challenging another RTA's policies is not costless in terms of the time and resources required, the benefits to be derived from pressing a claim may not be worth the costs involved. Second, again given that most countries belong to an RTA, challenging the rules may bring about retaliations. Again, the perceived losses may not be worth the presumed benefits.

The welfare effects of RTAs
The popularity of RTAs raises questions about their impact not only on non-member states but also on the development of the multilateral trading systems. This second question asks essentially whether the world economy will develop via RTAs into a free trade multilateral system quicker than it would via multilateral WTO negotiations.

State impact questions: The effect on non-member states and the world economy
To understand the effect of the formation of an RTA on non-members and the world economy we have to make use of the concepts of trade creation and trade diversion. These concepts were developed by Viner (1950) and they form the basis of any analysis of the effect of RTA formation.

Assume that two countries decide to form an RTA. Initially tariffs are applied in a non-discriminatory fashion. This is no longer the case once they form an RTA. If they reduce tariffs on one another's goods to zero even if they keep the old tariff levels against their other trading partners then they are discriminating in favour of one another's products and against those of their trading partners. Assume further that production takes place under constant costs. If one of the RTA partners now imports goods from the other instead of producing them at home, or reduces its own production as a result of price competition, then trade is created between the two. If one of the RTA partners replaces its imports from the non-RTA partner with those from a higher cost RTA partner then trade is diverted. While trade creation increases welfare, trade division reduces it.

From the point of view of world welfare a trade creating RTA increases world welfare but a trade diverting RTA reduces it. A trade creating RTA is, therefore, a positive move towards an open multilateral trading systems while a trade diverting RTA is the opposite.

The relative size of trade creation and trade diversion is dependent on several factors. The first factor is the initial size of the protective tariff and the size of its reduction. High initial tariffs suggest that the domestic market is supplied mainly if not exclusively by domestic suppliers. As tariffs on RTA partners' products are cut, prices fall and its firms capture a larger share of the market. Consumers gain while domestic firms exit the market. Concentration on specialization takes place as the lower cost producers replace those with higher costs.

The second factor is the similarity in demand patterns between the countries that make up an RTA. The greater the similarity between markets, the larger the potential gains from trade creation through specialization. High income countries benefits will accrue mainly through intra-industry trade specialization as their demand is stronger for differentiated goods. Poor countries benefit more the more dissimilar they are, since they engage in inter-industry trade to a greater extent and RTAs allow them to specialize on the production and export of goods in which they have a comparative advantage.

The final factor that determines the overall gains from RTA formation is the height of the external tariffs after it is established. The lower the tariffs on non-member imports the smaller the losses from trade division. These benefits can also be acquired if the low cost producing nation is a member of the RTA.

It has been suggested that RTAs are more unlikely than not to be trade creating rather than trade diverting. It is also suggested that even trade diversion need not be welfare reducing (Summers 1999). The reasons for holding these views are fourfold. First, empirical evidence suggests that the bulk of existing and proposed RTAs are amongst countries that trade most with one another. As a result, they are trade creating. Second, trade diversion can only be negative if trade is diverted to a higher cost supplier. If trade is diverted to a country whose industries have a similar cost structure then there is no negative welfare effect. Third, trade creation effects will be enhanced in the longer term through dynamic economies of scale effects and competition. These are more likely to be greater than, and unlikely to be damaged by, trade diversion effects. Fourth, the greater and more longer term gain are more likely to appear via the adoption and harmonization of economic policies and legislation that has an economic impact. Some non-trade diversionary effects are more than likely to be outweighed by these longer term advantages.

Do RTAs lead to multilateral free trade?: dynamic issues
Economists tend to agree that a multilateral free trade system is the most welfare enhancing of all possible systems. When discussing RTAs, the question that arises is do they lead to multilateral free trade? This is what is often called a dynamic time path question (DeMelo and Panagariya 1992). For international policy makers it means that RTA formation should be allowed to continue until they finally coalesce into one bloc thereby bringing about universal free trade. For international policy makers this is a crucial question. Will RTAs eventually coalesce into one world RTA in which case free trade will be brought about or will it remain fragmented leaving the world short of achieving its welfare potential (Bagwell and Staiger 1998)?

Analysis of these issues has required the development of theoretical models (Bhagwati 1993; Summers 1999). One model, developed by Krugman (1993), begins with the premise that the world is divided into a large number of identical countries trading one differentiated product with many different varieties. Each country produces one variant and imports the rest. The world then divides itself into several identical RTAs. Each RTA then imposes an optional tariff structure of the others. World welfare is then maximized if there is just one bloc because there is free trade, or when there are very many blocs. This case comes about because the more blocs there are the more the optimal tariff will approach zero. Krugman's analysis implies that as the number of blocs rises beyond one world welfare falls and continues to do so until it reaches a minimum until after which it begins to rise. Krugman, via simulations, suggests that world welfare is minimized when the number of RTAs is three.

Krugman's result suggests that RTA formation would lead the world to a high level of welfare and it would remain at that high level. Krugman's model is highly theoretical and as Srinivasan (1993) shows allowing for different sized RTAs and how and when they are formed can lead to different results.

Bhagwati (1993) suggests that to examine the dynamic question properly requires an examination of the attitudes facing the various interest groups or stakeholders in the RTA. In particular, how they perceive the gains or losses they will acquire through its expansion. Bhagwati's (1993) view is that large blocs will be resistant to further enlargement. This would be due to several reasons. The first is that governments will perceive the costs of enlargement to outweigh the benefits. The market is large enough for domestic companies to achieve economies of scale so why bother. Second, domestic companies will support this view as they are reluctant to accept further competition by the inclusion of companies that are more efficient. The potential losers will lobby against expansion (Winters 1999).

Protagonists for the formation of RTAs would counter these arguments with one of their own. They would claim that RTAs would lead to free trade quicker than the multilateral process. A few large blocs would be able to negotiate with one another far more easily than the large numbers involved in multilateral negotiations. They would internalize national interest issues and overcome the free rider problems associated with multilateral negotiations. As a result, a free trade outcome would come faster and more certainly.

Counter arguments abound but come back to Bhagwati's thesis that the larger the bloc the greater the economic power and the more tempting it is to adopt restrictions against non-member states.

The potential size and composition of an RTA has been examined by applying the theory of clues to this question (Buchanan 1965; Olson 1965; Padoan, 2001). The theory suggests that formation and size are dependent on the marginal costs and benefits facing the potential and existing members of an RTA. These may be made up of both internal and external economic and political factors.

Empirical evidence on this important question is mixed. The European Union (EU) and its forerunners the European Community (EC) and the European Economic Community (EEC) have consistently brought down trade barriers between the member states. The most recent attempts at this, the 1992 single market programme and the adoption of a single currency amongst the inner core of members as well as the Madrid Treaty are witness to this. In contrast stand the blocs formed in Latin America, Africa and the Middle East which, until recently, became negative forces for liberalization. One can also point to the EU's Common Agricultural Policy (CAP) as an example of a barrier to multilateral liberalization and a restraint on agricultural trade (Dr Melo and Panagariya, 1992).

Dealing with RTAs – maximizing the gains minimizing the losses

Whatever economists say about RTAs they seem to be here to stay and have become popular once again as vehicles for both promoting economic growth and development as well as cementing political change and stability. These features can be found in the recent moves to RTA formation. In particular one can see these arguments deployed in the discussion over the enlargement of the EU to embrace the former communist, centrally planned economies of Central and Eastern Europe. They were also prevalent in the development of RTAs in Latin America and Africa.

If there are both gains and losses involved in RTA formation, the economic question is how can the gains be maximized and losses minimized. To achieve this within the existing multilateral framework would require the reform of GATT Article XXIV and the GATS.

One step that could be taken is that the GATT only allows customs unions by banning other forms of RTAs. This would ensure that countries wishing to form an RTA would have to adopt the trade restrictions of the partner with the lowest trade barriers. The requirement that in a customs union all countries impose a common external tariff (CET) would ensure trade liberalization. This positive move occurred when the EC expanded to include Greece, Portugal and Spain. It has happened again with the recent inclusion of the Central and Eastern European countries.

Another benefit of a customs union over a free trade area is that it does not require rules of origin and bodies to enforce and adjudicate on them. Also, interest groups become fragmented as they have to lobby for customs union policies rather than having to focus on those of a specific country.

Articles dealing with contingent protection, anti-dumping and export restraints could be enhanced further in order to reduce the power of RTAs in formulating and imposing these barriers.

A further possibility, albeit a very radical one, is that RTA approval should be based on them being unable to exclude any country from membership that wishes to join. This would ensure that low cost producers could not be kept out of a proposed RTA. In this way, the trade diversionary effects of RTA formation would be eliminated. This is a very radical suggestion because RTA would not be able to exclude potential members on political or cultural grounds. The EU is facing a dilemma along these lines regarding the accession of Turkey, a country that has a poor record on human rights and democracy.

These suggested proposals also disguise the difficulties involved in enforcing international agreements. Governments constantly contravene WTO rules. With so many members of the WTO belonging to RTAs, one has to ask the question whether there is a willingness to enforce let alone propose changes to the existing GATT rules.

Summary and conclusions
The establishment of RTAs has long been a controversial fact of international economic life. RTAs can take many forms, each of which has different economic and political implications for the involved member states. There are also implications for non-members in that the formation of an RTA inevitably means discrimination against them. RTA formation, therefore, cuts across the principles of both the GATT and GATS which have non-discrimination and MFN at their core. This has been accommodated formally by allowing RTAs under Article XXIV of the GATT and Article 5 of the GATS. These exceptions are in recognition of the political realities of the international trading system.

Whether RTAs are good or bad for their participants, the non-members and for the wider multilateral trading system has long been debated by economists. Measuring trade creation against trade diversion has been one way of calculating their effect on members and non-members alike. The effect on the multilateral system as to whether RTAs eventually lead to a free trade system or not has only recently been examined formally. The theoretical models developed and deployed to answer this question are still in their infancy. Their conclusions are also not very robust and remain open to debate.

Policy makers, while recognizing that there may be benefits to both the participants and non-members as well as the multilateral trading system, find it difficult to formulate policies that substantiate trade creation and eliminate trade diversion and maintain the momentum towards achieving free trade. Acceptance of such policies requires the acceptance of international rules by which nation states have to abide. The current acceptance of the situation where existing WTO rules are open to interpretation suggests that its member states are not willing to go down this path. The way the RTAC recommendations are viewed and accepted by the WTO membership will reveal the way RTAs are likely to behave in the future. One thing is certain and that is the RTAs have, do and will form an important part of the international economic landscape.

References
Bagwell, K. and R. W. Staiger (1998), 'Will Preferential Agreements Undermine the Multilateral Trading System?' *Economic Journal*, **108** (449), 1162–82.
Bhagwati, J. (1993), 'Regionalism and Multilateralism: An Overview', in J. De Melo, A. Panagariya and D. Rodrick (eds), *New Dimensions in Regional Integration*, Cambridge: Cambridge University Press.
Buchanan, J. (1965), 'The Economic Theory of Clubs', *Economica*, **33**, 1–14.
De Melo, J. and A. Panagariya (1992), *The New Regionalism in Trade Policy*, London: World Bank and Centre for Economic Policy Research.
Finger, J. M. (1993), 'GATT's Influence on Regional Agreements', in J. De Melo, A. Panagariya and D. Rodrick (eds), *New Dimensions in Regional Integration*, Cambridge: Cambridge University Press.
GATT (1994), *The Results of the Uruguay Round of Multilateral Trade Negotiations: The Legal Texts*, Geneva: GATT.
Hoekeman, B. M. and H. M. Kostecki (2001), *The Political Economy of the World Trading System*, Oxford: Oxford University Press.

Irwin, D. A. (1992), 'Multilateral and Bilateral Trade Policies in the World Trading System: An Historical Perspective', paper delivered to the World Bank and CEPR Conference 'New Dimensions in Regional Integration', 2–3April, Washington, DC.

Krugman, P. (1993), 'Regionalism: Some Analytical Notes', in J. De Melo, A. Panagariya and D. Rodrick (eds), *New Dimensions in Regional Integration*, Cambridge: Cambridge University Press.

Olson, M. (1965), *The Logic of Collective Action*, New Haven, CT: Yale University Press.

Padoan, P. C. (2001), 'Political Economy of New Regionalism and World Governance', in M. Telo (ed.), *European Union and New Regionalism*, Aldershot: Ashgate.

Snape, R. (1993), 'History and Economics of GATT's Article XXIV', in K. Anderson and R. Blackhurst (eds), *Regional Integration and the Global Trading System*, London: Harvester-Wheatsheaf.

Srinivasan, T. N. (1993), 'Comment on Krugman', in J. De Melo, A. Panagariya and D. Rodrick (eds), *New Dimensions in Regional Integration*, Cambridge: Cambridge University Press.

Summers, L. H. (1999), 'Regionalism and the World Trading System', in *Policy Implications of Trade and Currency Zones*, Kansas: Federal Reserve Bank.

Viner, J. (1950), *Customs Union Theory*, New York: Carnegie Endowment for International Peace.

Winters, L. A. (1999), 'Regionalism vs Multilateralism', in R. Baldwin, D. Cohen, A. Sapir and A. Venables (eds), *Marketing Integration, Regionalism and the Global Economy*, Cambridge: CEPR, Cambridge University Press.

WTO (2004a), *Regional Trade Agreements*, http://www.wto.org/english/traptop_e/region_e/region_e.htm.

WTO (2004b), *Regional Trade Agreements: Scope of RTAs*, http://www.wto.org/english/traptop_e/region_e/scope_rta_e.htm.

WTO (2004c), *Regional Trade Agreements: Facts and Figures*, http://www.wto.org/english/traptop_e/region_e/region_e/regfac_e.htm.

WTO (2004d), *Understanding the WTO: Cross-cutting and New Issues. Regionalism: Friends or Rivals?*, http://www.wto.org/english/the to_e/whatis_e/tif_e/bey1_e.htm.

WTO (2004e), *Regional Trade Agreements: Rules. The WTO's Rules*, http://www.wto.org/english/traptop_e/region_e/regral_e.htm.

9 The breadth of integration arising from trade agreements

Peter W. B. Phillips

Introduction

International trade has been and likely always will be a critical factor in the economic, social and political development of nation states. Ultimately, trade agreements and regimes integrate markets – from the earliest times to the present day, national governments and imperial powers have sought to use trade rules to bind others to their power system in order to enhance their development. The process of negotiating and enforcing international agreements has changed twice in the last century. In the early 1900s, the role of the imperial powers diminished, and individual trading countries and specific commodity groups took the initiative to define the trade system to support their national or industrial interests (Phillips 2001). This accelerated after the Second World War, with the proliferation of commodity agreements, international technical agencies and national, regional and multilateral trade agreements. While these agreements accelerated integration in selected areas, the rate and range of integration varied widely, with some sectors highly integrated (for example manufactured goods) and others largely not (for example agriculture). The signing of the World Trade Organization (WTO) Agreement in 1995 reasserted a strong integrationist focus in trade matters, as members of the new organization henceforward were compelled to accept all of the wide-ranging international arrangements. Countries could no longer cherry-pick to comply with those arrangements that suited their own interests, while ignoring those that were less beneficial. Now, virtually all aspects of trade (and by extension, many areas that traditionally were viewed as domestic concerns) are increasingly integrated in a common set of rules and markets.

In that context, many have expressed concerns that the economic, social and political agendas of the large countries – often equated with the US, European Union, and at times the OECD – will compel smaller, less powerful countries to integrate into the global system. This chapter examines a number of specific concerns. First, some worry that many countries have little or no effective choice in how fast to liberalize and integrate into the global trade system. In the past, countries could choose which international agreements to join and when to join them. Many smaller and less developed countries would join the General Agreement on Tariffs and Trade (GATT) but not some of the technical agencies and agreements – such as the World Intellectual Property Conventions and the FAO/Codex food safety agencies. This would enable them to pick only those elements that had the greatest potential benefit for the country. It is becoming increasingly difficult for countries wanting to trade to remain outside the aegis of the WTO. A couple of options – entering into regional trade arrangement with partners that may yield higher benefits and accessing the general system of preferences available to lesser developed countries – offer some flexibility for smaller and poorer countries. This chapter will examine the practical matter of accession and membership in an effort to identify what degrees of freedom remain for smaller

94

countries. Meanwhile, some have argued that once inside, many of the smaller and less developed countries have little or no opportunity to influence the general direction of the international trade regime because the negotiating process effectively shuts them out. This chapter will examine the challenges facing many smaller countries as they attempt to put their position forward. Finally, there is a common belief that the WTO dispute settlement system is a blunt instrument that can compel smaller, weaker countries to conform to the interests of the international system or the largest traders. This chapter will review the operation of the dispute settlement mechanism (DSM) to identify the real risks of this.

International integration

International integration is a dynamic process whereby the economic and social, political, cultural and normative dimensions of a nation converge with those dimensions of other nations. It occurs either implicitly through cultural convergence (for example multinational corporations, immigration, the global entertainment industry, the internet, international sports or tourism) or explicitly through governments entering into treaties, international institutions, global standards and trade agreements.

International integration elicits strong emotional responses from many. At the extremes, some view international integration as the 'natural' extension of 'progressive' practices from the developed world to lesser developed regions (for example Romer 1990) while others see it as an insidious undermining of national sovereignty and cultural integrity (for example Council of Canadians, nd). Supporters of international integration believe that collective action among independent nation-states can lead to greater overall gains or avoid overall losses that often arise when nations act alone, guided only by their own self-interest. Critics simply see integration as a corrosive force that erodes national or domestic economic and social distinctiveness and autonomy.

States can choose a variety of strategies to accelerate or control the rate of integration. Most nations have attempted to find a balance in the level of integration they pursue, reserving some matters as merely domestic concerns (for example culture), engaging in bilateral or regional agreements on other matters (for example environment or some sectoral trade arrangements) and opening more generally through multilateral processes (for example the WTO). Similarly, countries have some control over the depth of integration into the international system, choosing either to limit integration to issues that extend from their borders outward (for example tariffs and import quotas) or to engage in arrangements that explicitly restrict certain domestic practices (for example subsidies) or require change in domestic policies and industries (for example government procurement). In that context, there is a spectrum of possible integrative options, ranging from shallow, regional arrangements (for example the NAFTA) to global, deep arrangements, such as the Cartegna Protocol on Biosafety (see Table 9.1)

Table 9.1   Illustrative examples of the range of international integration

Level of integration	Depth of integration	
	Shallow	Deep
Regional	NAFTA	EU
Global	WTO	CPB

States use various strategies to influence the gains or losses of international integration. Few countries are consistently pro or anti integration. Prospective winners from integration often pursue global trade systems to solidify their positions (for example the so called *Pax Romanica, Britannica* and *Americana* cited by Gilpin 2001), encouraging liberalized flows of goods and factors of production. These countries have tended to choose shallow integrative options (such as the NAFTA and WTO), allowing them to leave their domestic policies unchanged, but often forcing others to revise their systems to conform to the norms embedded in the international system. Ostry (1997) offers a perfect example of this from the Uruguay Round, noting that the US negotiating team effectively wrote the Trade Related Intellectual Property Agreement (TRIPS) to mirror the US system of IP, requiring no changes by the US but major reforms by many other countries. Other countries may choose deep integration for tactical reasons. European nations, for instance, have made impressive strides in creating a continental union of 25 member states that provides a variety of mechanisms that further common economic, social, cultural and political goals. Globally, there have been a variety of efforts (for example the Cartegna Protocol) to develop common rules that protect social and cultural goals from being disciplined by international economic institutions and regimes.

History of integration through international trade
International trade has been for a long time one way to extend a country's influence on competitors and partners. Going back into the earliest recorded history one can identify the important role of trade, and by extension, the significant efforts by governments and others to benefit from defining the rules of trade.

There is ample evidence of the important role trade played in the evolution and enrichment of the pre-classical, classical and modern empires. The millennia of empires can be categorized as a period when 'might was right' with the imperial power (large or small) establishing the rules and structures for trade, almost always in order to control the economy and society and to enrich the social elites and rulers of the empires. There was clear and direct integration through trade – the goal was not to spread the wealth but to enrich the core (the rulers and elites) at the expense of the periphery. The Egyptian empire spanned the Nile and spread into the Mediterranean, establishing a common rule of law, common weights and measures and a set of practices for the efficient trade in many common products. As early as 3200 BC there is evidence of Egyptians importing cedars from Phoenician traders. With the decline of the Egyptian empires, the Phoenician empire emerged in about 1100 BC as the dominant 'merchant mariners' in the region, trading a variety of commodities and products around the Mediterranean, aided and assisted by the establishment of maritime cities in what is now the Middle East, along the north coast of Africa, in Sicily and in Spain. First the Greek empire under Alexander the Great and then the Roman empire replaced the trading rules of the earlier systems, culminating in a pan-European system of governance and trade that realized unprecedented wealth and power. While there was a hiatus in imperial structures during the feudal age, empires again emerged on the global stage in the 1400s, as the major European powers refocused their competitive efforts on carving up the rest of the world as empires and colonies. Trade within the individual imperial preferential systems – British, Spanish, Portuguese, Dutch, German and Italian – was often relatively free, but trade between the systems was relatively less attractive and frequently discouraged or even impeded. Each imperial system imposed a currency system, most had their own unique sets of weights and measures, all had their own transportation infrastructure and, through their laws, each provided means of adjudicating disputes. While trade integrated regions within the empires, competition between empires escalated. Irwin (1996) notes that the philosophers and economists throughout history have supported and rationalized the dominant power systems, justifying the structure and nature of the trade relationships – be they state led, free market or mercantilist.

The waning of imperial power in the later part of the nineteenth century opened the way for a significant change in trade rules. Beginning after 1850 and accelerating into the early 1900s individual trading countries (for example the US) and specific commodity groups (for example the dairy industry) took the initiative to redefine the trade system to support their national or industrial interests. A wide range of purpose built – what we would now call *sui generis* – rule systems were developed to enable greater trade under more predictable and competitive terms. International treaties were negotiated and signed to protect and enable trade in intellectual property rules, beginning as far back as 1885. Countries such as the US negotiated bilateral trade arrangements with other countries, such as Canada, which previously had conformed almost exclusively to the Imperial Preferences of the British Empire. Some of these arrangements simply dealt with border measures, but many imposed higher integration, with agreements specifying production and processing methods and allowable measures to manage domestic markets (for example various treaties between the US, Canada and the UK to manage fish stocks in the Atlantic and Pacific). Groups of commodity producers, in the first instance represented by their national governments but increasingly represented by leading companies, meanwhile sought to define the terms of engagement in international trade for their specific goods by specifying appropriate standards for product attributes, public health and safety and, at times, terms of trade and domestic production targets to manage periodic gluts and shortages (for example the International Office of Epizootics [OIE] to deal with animal health in 1924). This trend to purpose built systems accelerated after the Second World War, with the proliferation of commodity agreements (for example the International Wheat Agreement in 1949) and a wide range of international agencies such as the Food and International Plant Protection Convention (1952), the Food and Agriculture Organization (1945), the World Health Organization (1948) and the *Codex Alimentarius* Commission (1963). In some ways, the GATT in 1948 was simply another purpose built organization, in its case with a mandate to liberalize trade for manufactured goods; most of the other products, all services and trade in all factors of production (labor, capital and intellectual property) were exempt from the agreement. Even though successive rounds of negotiation in the following 40 years attempted to address many of the exemptions to the GATT, any resulting arrangements were usually formalized outside the aegis of the GATT and, consequently, allowed piecemeal development and implementation of standard trade rules across all markets and regions.

The Uruguay Round (1986–1994) fundamentally changed the direction and scope of international trade. The WTO Agreement essentially rolled up most of the purpose built systems from the preceding 100 years, adding a few new subjects (such as trade in services and government procurement), and made them all subject to the four pillars of the GATT treaty – the most-favored-nation principle; national treatment; transparency; and dispute settlement. Taking as the base the General Agreement on Tariffs and Trade (GATT), which largely focused on manufactured goods, the new Organization added an ambitious agreement on agriculture (which converted quotas to tariffs and then bound and targeted to reduce overall tariff levels, domestic trade distorting subsidies and export subsidies), incorporated and expanded a number of the Understandings from the Tokyo Round (that is those relating to sanitary and phytosanitary measures (SPS) and technical barriers to trade (TBTs), the multifiber agreement on textiles and clothing and trade-related investment measures (TRIMS)), incorporated the provisions of the World Intellectual Property Office and its related treaties through the agreement on trade-related aspects of intellectual property rights (TRIPS), offered new rules of origin, introduced a new agreement on trade in services (GATS) and implemented a series of procedural measures related to making trade less uncertain (for example agreements related to Art. VI, Anti-dumping, Art. VII, customs valuation, preshipment inspection, import licensing procedures, subsidies and countervailing and safeguards). The WTO Agreement also implemented for the first time a binding dispute settlement system, where expert panel decisions would be implemented unless the General Assembly in plenary session unanimously rejected the decision (under the GATT, if any single member state, including one of the disputing parties, challenged a decision, it would be suspended, which meant few decisions were ever adopted). One final provision was a decision of the negotiators to formalize collaboration between the WTO and its sister Bretton Woods institutions, the International Monetary Fund and the World Bank. Increasingly the pressure was on countries to be a member in all three institutions, rather than simply those that offered the greatest benefit to the country.

This larger package of obligations had three immediate effects. First, many countries that were members of only some of the purpose-built systems were now obligated to conform universally to the entire package. Countries could no longer pick and choose which trade arrangements to join and enforce. Second, there was less incentive to stay out of the GATT/WTO world. Increasingly, there was less strategic value in partial trade relationships. Both the costs of non-conformity and the benefits of membership rose. Third, many of the new trade rules went beyond prescribing border measures and imposed either constraints or obligations on member states to adjust their domestic policies to conform. Essentially, countries that previously diverged from the norm were being required to integrate or lose.

Does membership in the WTO force integration?
While the history paints a convincing picture of trade being a highly integrative policy, the actual influence of various trade measures on individual countries to conform and integrate with the global system is not discernible without further review. Four specific issues warrant investigation: the rights and obligations of membership; the special provisions for Least Developed Countries (LDCs); regional trade arrangements; and dispute settlement practices and outcomes.

The rights and obligations of membership
Membership involves both rights and obligations arising from accession and from the opportunity to help to direct and craft the future of the agreement. There is a reasonable argument to be made that LDCs and some of the lower and middle income countries may be forced to integrate into a system that is not unambiguously in their own best interest.

As noted previously, since implementation of the WTO, membership is now an all or nothing choice. Countries, once they pass any transition periods and evolve from being a lesser developed country, are no longer allowed to select which parts of the system to accept. Now they must adopt the entire package. Many have argued that while this makes great sense for developed nations and perhaps even for the largest developing nations, many smaller and less developed countries could be disadvantaged by the all-or-nothing process. Lanjouw (2002), for example, has noted that OECD countries adopted strong patent rights for pharmaceutical drugs at a much higher level of development than many LDCs. He notes that in the 1976–1992 period, 11 OECD member states adopted stronger patent protection, with prevailing per capita GDPs of $10900 to $40000. In contrast, he identified nine major developing countries that are being asked to adopt higher protection much earlier in their development. China, for example, extended rights in 1992/3, with a per capita GDP of only $424. India, Pakistan and Egypt have per capita GDPs of less than $1200, and were required to implement by 31 July 2006 the provisions in the TRIPs agreement, which included extension of patents to inventions from other countries. Other areas of the WTO Agreement and its sub-agreements could similarly be argued to be less advantageous to LDCs than developed nations. If the GATT model of purpose built rules prevailed, these countries could accede only to those provisions that fit with their stage of development and trade prospects.

Meanwhile, there is some doubt about whether the negotiating process is appropriate to deal with LDC concerns and interests. Quite clearly in the early rounds of GATT negotiations the process was predominantly one of reciprocal negotiating between the key exporters and importers related to key issues and key markets. A country made bids and offers with key traders to liberalize specific areas; once bilateral agreements were set, they were multilateralized through the most-favored-nation principle. In this way the negotiations focused on those trade issues that had the greatest commercial importance. The strong reciprocity of interests in continued international trade in those products among those countries improved the likelihood of success. Disproportionately this process paired the United States with other OECD countries in the key negotiations, effectively disenfranchising LDCs and low- and middle-income countries. Beginning in the Kennedy Round and continuing through the Tokyo, Uruguay and Doha Rounds, there has been a shift in the negotiating process. In the first instance, there has been a move away from bid and offer negotiating toward a formula-based system of identifying overall goals and objectives, against which countries then bind specific trade measures. These formulas offer fewer opportunities for discrete issues to be addressed, and instead increase the pressure for overall liberalization and integration of markets. By the same token, the introduction of a wide range of new negotiating issues that have significant domestic implications – for example SPS, TBT and TRIPs – has created a conundrum for many LDCs and developing countries. These areas, which mostly involve developing standards of performance and market access, do not fit with the formula model of negotiation but rather require an ability to bring forward a functioning system to compare and contrast with others, in the pursuit of a common base. Phillips and Khachatourians (2001), citing FAO (1998) data, have noted that many non-OECD countries – including LDCs, various low- and middle-income countries and most transition economies – lack operating, transparent and accountable administrative systems for managing intellectual property, sanitary and phytosanitary issues and technical barriers to trade. For example, in 1998, only 25 percent of states had national legislation for plant breeders' rights, about one-third of African and Asian nations did not have any quarantine rules for seeds or animals, a minority of countries outside the OECD had seed certification or seed quality legislation and fewer than one in eight had national crop research programs that could assess and analyze any attendant risks in new agricultural varieties. In the absence of effective domestic capacity, these countries are completely removed from any negotiations to develop product or performance standards that will underpin trade in these products.

Special provisions for LDCs
The purpose built GATT system that evolved between 1948 and 1994 was dominated by developed country issues and concerns. Between 1948 and 1961, OECD countries dominated the GATT in both absolute numbers and in relative terms. Between 1962 and 1994, the number of developing and lesser developed countries rose sharply, as decolonization created more independent states in Africa, the Middle East and Latin America. While issues of concern to developing nations were aired in the negotiations over that period, the agreement remained dominated by the issues of OECD member states. With the implementation of the WTO Agreement beginning in 1995, there has been a push to complete the membership of the organization, mostly by bringing into the fold key Asian markets (for example China) and the transition economies from the former Comecon Pact. As of 24 October 2004, 147 states had negotiated membership in the organization and another 28 nations had observer status, which implies they are likely to seek accession within five years (see Table 9.2).

The total membership of the WTO is now clearly dominated in number terms by countries with development concerns and the organization has worked to accommodate their most pressing concerns. While there are no WTO definitions of 'developed' or 'developing' countries, the WTO allows countries to self-select themselves as needing assistance (generally the country granting any preference decides whether to accept or reject a country as developing). In 2004, 32 member states of the WTO were listed as LDCs: Angola, Bangladesh, Benin, Burkina Faso, Burundi, Cambodia, Central African Republic, Chad, Democratic Republic of the Congo, Djibouti, Gambia, Guinea, Guinea Bissau, Haiti, Lesotho, Madagascar, Malawi, Maldives, Mali, Mauritania, Mozambique, Myanmar, Nepal, Niger, Rwanda, Senegal, Sierra Leone, Solomon Islands, Tanzania, Togo, Uganda and Zambia (eight additional LDCs were in the process of accession to the agreement, including Bhutan, Cape Verde, Ethiopia, Laos, Samoa, Sudan, Vanuatu and Yemen while

Table 9.2   *Date of admission of 147 member states as of 24 October 2004, by status of nation state*

	OECD	Africa/ Middle East	Asia	Latin America	Transition Economies	Other
1948–1961	19	5	5	8	0	0
1962–1994	10	38	7	22	2	2
1995–2004	1	4	7	4	11	3
Total	30	47	19	34	13	5
Pending in 2004	0	12	5	2	9	0

Source: WTO (2004b)

Equatorial Guinea and São Tomé and Principe were WTO Observers). In aggregate, the WTO estimates that those LDCs that are members accounted for only $34 billion of trade in 2000, equal to about 0.55 percent of total world trade that year.

Developing country status in the WTO brings certain rights. In the first instance, most developing countries can avail themselves of the Generalized System of Preferences (GSP), which provides for greater market access than afforded to larger and wealthier states (UNCTAD 2004). Some WTO Agreements also provide LDCs with longer transition periods before they are required to fully implement the provisions (for example TRIPs provided LDCs with ten years to implement the provisions, rather than the one year schedule for developed countries), LDCs are eligible to receive technical assistance to comply with the WTO and some agreements provide commitments or measures to increase trading opportunities for developing countries (for example the MultiFibre Agreement members committed to consider favorable quota treatment for small suppliers and least-developed countries).

The WTO negotiating process has also attempted to provide for differential benefits for LDCs. At the Fourth Ministerial Conference in Doha, Qatar, in November 2001, WTO member governments agreed to launch a new 'development' round of negotiations. Since then, much of the negotiating effort has focused on addressing LDC concerns, such as a balance-of-payments exception (clarifying less stringent conditions in GATT for developing countries if they restrict imports in order to protect their balance-of-payments), market-access commitments (clarifying LDC eligibility to negotiate or be consulted on quota allocation) and an array of derogations that will either allow LDCs to deal more proactively with domestic and rural development or to engage in and help to define the new technical rules of trade (for example in the SPS standards and measures).

Regional Trade Agreements
One derogation from the WTO MFN principle available to all countries is the right to enter into a regional trade agreement (RTA), where preferences within the agreement are not automatically multilateralized to all WTO members. While there are popular reports of thousands of RTAs, as of May 2004, only about 250 RTAs have been notified to the GATT/WTO. Over 170 duly notified and authorized RTAs are currently in force and an additional 70 are estimated to be operational although not yet notified. The WTO Secretariat estimates that by the end of 2005 the total number of RTAs could approach 300 if all the RTAs reportedly planned or already under negotiation are concluded.

RTAs generally involve either a free trade area, a customs union or, increasingly, a services agreement. A free-trade area (under GATT Art. XXIV) provides for RTA members to lower or eliminate trade barriers among themselves while maintaining their own, individual WTO-bound commitments against non-RTA partners (for example the NAFTA). A customs union (under GATT Art. XXIV) usually involves eliminating all trade measures between RTA members but erecting a common set of tariffs and quotas (which would then be bound under the WTO) against non-RTA members (for example the EU). A services agreement (under GATS Art. V) would reduce barriers for trade in selected services among RTA members, without offering those benefits to others (for example the CARICOM agreement). Of the 208 RTAs notified as of May 2004, 141 involve FTAs, 14 involve CUs and 34 involve services.

The WTO reports that the coverage and depth of preferential treatment varies. More recent RTAs tend to go far beyond tariff-cutting exercises – they provide for increasingly complex regulations governing trade in goods (for example with respect to standards, safeguard provisions and customs administration) or provide preferential regulatory frameworks for trade in services. The most sophisticated RTAs are major integrative instruments, providing regional rules on investment, competition, environment and labor.

An examination of the 208 notifications as of May 2004 shows that about 70 percent of the RTAs involve one or more OECD countries. Most OECD arrangements involve EU, North America, Australia or Japan and provide for preferential arrangements among themselves or with other selected strategic partners (for example Israel, selected South American nations and key trading partners in their region, such as New Zealand with Singapore). The second largest group of notified RTAs involves the transition economies in Eastern Europe and the former Soviets. The Comecon trade bloc had a wide range of preferential regional trade arrangements that remain valuable to some former members. As these countries join the WTO, they are required to notify any preferential deals. As of May 2004, 36 preferential arrangements have been approved. The remaining 25 RTAs that have been notified represent an effort by pairs or groups of countries within Africa, the Middle East, Asia and Latin America to create closer regional integration, even if at the expense of trade with larger and more developed countries.

Overall, the provisions that allow RTAs cannot be said to forestall or limit integration, but rather to redirect the direction and scope of integration toward various strategic options (regional or sector) and away from global integration. Hence, they offer one avenue for smaller and less-developed countries to control their level, depth and rate of integration into the global economy.

Dispute settlement procedures and outcomes
As noted, the processes for handling trade disputes have been strengthened in the WTO, making it far more likely that countries that do not comply with the terms of the agreement will be prosecuted and either directed to conform or to be subject to sanctions and retaliation. This 'big stick' has the potential to accelerate the integration implied by the WTO as countries are expected to be more likely to comply with the real threat of costs of non-compliance.

While the theory would suggest that smaller countries would be most at risk, the evidence does not show that. Between 1 January 1995 and 12 October 2004 member states launched 317 disputes in the WTO. The vast majority of the cases involved developed, OECD member states challenging other OECD member state's policies. An analysis of the cases shows that 72 percent of the cases were brought against the US, EU or other OECD countries. No cases during the period were brought against any of the 32 LDCs. Of the 90 cases brought against low and middle income countries, 60 were brought by OECD members while 30 were brought by other low and middle income countries (see Table 9.3). Looking just at the 21 US cases launched against lower and middle income countries during this period, the strategy becomes clearer. The US launched cases against Brazil (4), Argentina (4), Philippines (3), India (3) and one each with Chile, China, Egypt, Indonesia, Pakistan, Romania and Venezuela, each which is either middle income country or a low income country with a large population and hence proportionately large market. The US has never launched a case at a market smaller than US$100 billion.

Table 9.3   Distribution of 317 dispute settlement cases launched between 1 January 1995 and 12 October 2004

		Case brought by				
		US	EU	Other OECD	Other	Multiple
Case brought against	US	–	26	33	22	3
	EU	28	–	13	22	3
	Other OECD	27	16	16	17	1
	Other	21	23	16	30	0
	Total	76	65	78	91	7
Pending		0	12	5	2	9

Source: WTO (2004b)

Table 9.4   WTO DSM cases, 1 January 1995 to 12 October 2004

	Brought by				Brought against			
	US	EU	Other OECD	Other	US	EU	Other OECD	Other
1995	5	2	3	9	3	7	10	2
1996	15	7	11	9	9	6	15	13
1997	17	15	8	5	9	10	11	16
1998	9	16	11	7	7	15	12	10
1999	9	7	12	3	11	4	5	11
2000	8	7	4	11	9	2	3	16
2001	1	1	4	19	8	4	7	8
2002	4	3	11	16	18	6	6	4
2003	2	4	12	10	7	8	6	7
2004[a]	5	2	3	2	3	4	3	3
Total	75	64	79	91	84	66	78	90
Total (%)	24	20	25	29	26	21	25	28

Note: [a] Cases filed as of 12 October 2004.

Source: WTO (2004b)

Perhaps what is most revealing is that the use of the DSM has begun to change in recent years. In the first six years of the operation of the agreement, the US and EU dominated as the major initiator of trade disputes. Low and middle income countries used the DSM less frequently. Beginning in 2000, the non-OECD members began to aggressively use the DSM. Looking at the targets of cases, it is interesting to note that lower and middle income countries were a major target through 2001, but since then the focus has shifted to opening the US. Rather than becoming a big stick in the hands of the large and wealthy, the DSM would appear to be becoming a leveling device, enabling smaller economies to push back on the integrationist agenda of larger, wealthy countries (see Table 9.4).

Conclusions

Two points are worth noting when considering whether the international trade system embodied in the WTO is a major integrative force in the global economy.

First, one must keep in mind that trade policy is only one of the many factors that can contribute to integration. It is hard to determine how much integration we would have had in the absence of the liberal trade regime embodied in the WTO. Remember that integration is being furthered by a wide range of formal and informal arrangements. The combination of multinational corporations, the global entertainment and media world, the internet, international tourism and immigration, among other factors, have combined to create a cohort of 'global citizens' who work, live and play in a multinational world. This world is underpinned by our international governmental and non-governmental organizations, the increasing global academy, global sports, global cultural and media stars and multinational executives. While still small, this group of globalists is a major force for integration. Few if any of these integrative forces can be attributed to the liberal trade regime. Thus, liberal trade rules may be less of a cause and more of a result of the evolution of the global society. More work will be needed to determine the causal relationship between liberal trade and global economic integration.

Second, the evidence noted above would suggest that there are a range of pressures resulting from the WTO Agreement in 1995 that are simultaneously increasing the pressure for integration and affording new options for managing and controlling integration. The WTO would appear to have furthered integration by its comprehensive structure, the new cooperation between the WTO and other Bretton Woods Systems and the fact that many of the 29 specific sub-agreements go beyond addressing border measures and actually prescribe domestic policy. But it is important to keep a few points in mind. First, these institutions actually provide a more enabling environment than prevailed under the old imperial systems. Second, relatively small and underdeveloped countries are almost immune from the more integrative aspects of the agreement, partly due to their formal derogations (for example GSP, transition periods, RTAs) and partly due to the simple fact that their markets are simply too small to justify a trade action against them.

References

Council of Canadians (nd), www.canadians.org.
FAO (1998), 'State of the World's Plant Genetic Resources for Food and Agriculture', Appendix 1, Rome: FAO.
Gilpin, R. (2001), *Global Political Economy: Understanding the International Economic Order*, Princeton, NJ: Princeton University Press.
Irwin, D. (1996), *Against the Tide: An Intellectual History of Free Trade*, Princeton, NJ: Princeton University Press.
Lanjouw, J. (2002), 'Intellectual Property and the Availability of Pharmaceuticals in Poor Countries', CGD Working Paper No. 5. Washington: Centre for Global Development.
Ostry, S. (1997), *The Post-Cold War Trading System: Who's on First?* Chicago: A Twentieth Century Fund Book, The University of Chicago Press.
Phillips, P. (2001), 'Food safety, trade policy and international institutions', in P. Phillips and R. Wolfe, *Governing Food: Science, Safety and Trade*, Montreal: McGill University Press/Queens School of Policy Studies, pp. 27–48.
Phillips, P. and G. G. Khachatourians (2001), *The Biotechnology Revolution in Global Agriculture: Invention, Innovation and Investment in the Canola Sector*, Wallingford and Cambridge, MA: CABI, p. 360.
Romer, P. (1990), 'Endogenous technological change', *Journal of Political Economy*, **98**:5(2), S71–S102.
UNCTAD (2004), 'About GSP', at http://www.unctad.org/Templates/Page.asp?intItemID=2309&lang=1.
WTO (2004a), 'Regional Trade Agreements', at http://www.wto.org/english/tratop_e/region_e/region_e.htm.
WTO (2004b), 'Understanding the WTO', at http://www.wto.org/english/thewto_e/whatis_e/tif_e/tif_e.htm.

Recommended reading

Winham, G. (1986), *International Trade and the Tokyo Round Negotiations*, Princeton, NJ: Princeton University Press.

WTO (1995), 'The Final Act', at http://www.wto.org/english/docs_e/legal_e/legal_e.htm.

WTO (2002), TN/RL/W/8/Rev.1 1 August 2002 (02-4246) 'Negotiating Group on Rules Original: English compendium of issues related to regional trade agreements Background Note by the Secretariat', Revision.

10 Trade agreements: depth of integration
Nicholas Perdikis

Introduction
This chapter describes the principal forms of Regional Trade Agreements (RTAs) and compares and contrasts their particular features. To illustrate these issues existing and past RTAs will be referred to and used as examples. While the main focus of this chapter will be the economic characteristics of RTAs, political causes and effects will also be touched upon. This is inevitable as the formation of even the simplest form of RTA requires the agreement of sovereign entities – countries – and has consequences for different sections of society or interest groups within those countries.

A simple taxonomy of Regional Trade Agreements
Economists identify four basic forms of RTA (World Bank, 2000). These range from the most simple – the free trade area (FTA), to the customs union (CU), the common market (CM) and on to the final and deepest form, the economic union. This last form is often referred to as economic and political union signifying not only the economic aspects of the relationship but also the depth of political integration that is required from member states to make it operational.

The Free Trade Area
The simplest form of economic integration is FTA. The FTA is the most popular form of economic integration amongst countries forming Regional Trade Agreements, accounting for approximately 90 per cent of them. In this form the member states agree to remove all barriers to trade in either goods or services, or both, between them. In its present theoretical form, artificial impediments to trade are not allowed to interfere with the free flow of goods and services between the participants. In practical terms no tariffs, quotas, subsidies or administrative restrictions are allowed to distort the trade between the members. Each participating country is allowed to pursue its own trade or foreign economic policy against non-members of the FTA. In this way the restrictions placed on the products of non-members may vary between the members.

The ability to follow its own foreign economic policy does or can give rise to problems. Non-member countries' exporters may be able to overcome discrimination against their products by exporting via the member or members with the lowest levels of protection. In this way, they can still penetrate the more highly protected markets. To preclude non-member countries' exporters from adopting these transhipment strategies, the members of an FTA usually agree a set of rules to deal with this possible occurrence. These rules are often very complex. Often they have to take into account products that arrive from non-member states having undergone some form of processing or finishing in a member state. Under these circumstances, the value added has to be calculated and an appropriate allowance made before the tariff rate is applied. These so called *rules of origin* usually result in a lower tariff being placed on products that are subject to some processing or finishing in member states than those that are applied on exports coming from non-member states via a member with lower restrictions. To administer their rules of origin, FTAs have to set up costly bureaucratic structures. The most enduring and at one time the most prominent FTA, the European Free Trade Area (EFTA), had a very elaborate system of rules of origin. These were enshrined in its Stockholm convention. The North American Free Trade Area (NAFTA) has similar rules.

As the members of an FTA have their own sets of domestic regulations with regard to health, safety, production and so on, conflicts can arise between them. They usually adopt dispute settlement rules to deal with these potential issues. In NAFTA disputes can be dealt with via their own agreed procedures or those of the WTO (Kerr 2005).

The Customs Union

The bureaucratic costs of administering complex rules of origin have led policy makers to suggest the adoption and application of a common trade policy against non-member states. This can be summed up as a common external tariff (CET). If adopted this would turn a FTA into a Customs Union (CU). The CET is, however, shorthand for common external trade policy as a CU has to deal not just with tariffs but quotas, anti dumping legislation, variable levies, voluntary export restraints (VERs) as well as domestic policies that impinge on trade relations with non-member states. Essentially, a CU is an FTA but one that has a common external trade policy. As we have seen above, FTAs have to adopt rules of origin to deal with imports from non-member states. This raises some interesting questions as to whether rules of origin and a CET are equivalent and have the same welfare effects on the economies involved. It has been shown that this is not the case.

The formation of a CU and its adoption of a common external trade policy administered by a central body does lead to an erosion of the participating states' economic and political sovereignty. This is inevitable as the member states have to compromise to work out and adopt a common position and then accept the outcome of any trade agreements reached on its behalf by a central body. Countries are willing to accept this reduction in individual sovereignty in order to increase collective power or sovereignty. Countries, by sinking their differences and adopting common positions, may be able to achieve more than negotiating individually with trade partners. This was one of the reasons behind the establishment of the EEC in 1956 and its subsequent evolution into the European Union (EU) as well as the widening of its CET to cover the majority of trade issues. The EU is not the only customs union. The current Andean pact made up of Bolivia, Colombia, Ecuador and Peru in South America is also a customs union and imposes a CET of between 5 and 20 per cent on imports arising from non-member states (*The Economist* 1991a).

The Common Market (CM)

This form of integration is deeper than the CU because it incorporates the free movement of capital and labour as well as goods and services into its structure. It is a deeper form of integration because it requires a greater degree of harmonization of domestic policies between the member states. For the movement of capital not to be influenced artificially by different taxes and incentives between the members of the CM requires commonality of treatment. Similarly, to facilitate the free movement of labour requires recognition of qualifications and the harmonization of employment policy.

From its inception the EEC considered itself as a CM since it allowed for the free movement of capital and labour. The reality of the situation, however, was different. The Cecchini Report on the barriers to completing the single market certainly highlighted the lack of policy harmonization and set 1992 as the date for achieving the goal (*The Economist* 1991b).

Economic union

This is the deepest form of economic integration short of countries merging with one another to form a single state. As its name implies large areas of economic and, therefore, political action are merged and dealt with by a central authority. This form of integration leads to an even greater loss of individual economic and political sovereignty. This is particularly so where the member states adopt a common currency.

An economic union is in many respects an amalgam of the other forms of economic integration outlined above. It is a free trade area in that goods are allowed to flow freely between member states. It is also a customs union because it adopts a common external tariff if not a common foreign economic policy. It is also a common market since the factors of production, essentially capital and labour, are also allowed to migrate freely in order to obtain their highest returns. An economic union is all those things plus the complete fixing of exchange rates between member states or the adoption of a common currency. Adopting a common currency turns an economic union into a monetary union as well.

Adopting a single currency is often seen as a way of eliminating the transactions costs that companies and individuals incur when converting one currency into another. Where trade with partners is highly integrated and constitutes a high proportion of overall trade adopting a single currency makes economic sense. A common currency will also make prices transparent to consumers and producers across the union. Highlighting price differences in this way increases competition amongst producers. It also increases competition between countries as potential locations for foot loose foreign direct investment.

An economic union also requires countries to coordinate and harmonize their fiscal policies. The need to operationalize these requirements leads to authority being vested in supranational bodies where decisions are made either on the basis of consensus or majority voting. Devolving power to supranational bodies and adopting their decisions is what reduces a member state's individual sovereignty. The purpose of accepting this reduction is the gain in collective sovereignty or economic and political power. The increased leverage that results can lead to greater gains for individual states than if they try to achieve their goals independently.

The European Union is considered to be an economic union albeit an imperfect one. Not all its member states have adopted its single currency, the euro. A notable absentee from the Euro zone is the UK. The harmonization of fiscal policy and government expenditure it is also not complete.

The high degree of coordination required and the intervention of supranational bodies in domestic policies can lead to tensions between the member states. Again, this is seen very clearly in the European Union. Government subsidies to state owned industries, in particular airlines but also transportation equipment, has led to conflicts between the member states and the European Commission – one of the EU's supranational institutions. The threat of and actual imposition of fines has not stopped this behaviour. Optouts and rebates have also been given to member states in order for them to square the realities of domestic politics and membership of the European Union. Here again, the

UK is an example. It has been given a rebate on its contribution to the European Union budget. More recently France, Germany and Italy have run budget deficits in excess of the 3 per cent demanded by the operational rules of the European Monetary System.

The economic and political case for and against Regional Trade Agreements
There are both economic and political reasons why countries seek to form or join RTAs. We will now discuss the economic arguments and then move on to the political reasons for forming RTAs.

The economic case for RTAs
The basis of the economic case lies in standard normative trade theory which suggests that free trade leads to an improvement in economic welfare. Economic integration implies the opening up of trade with one set of trading partners while continuing or increasing discrimination against others. In this way it is an economic state lying between total free trade on the one hand and total discrimination on the other. Since it is short of total free trade a policy pursuing economic integration through the formation of an RTA implies a second best policy (Lipsey 1957). A first best policy would be one adopting free trade with all trading partners.

Pragmatically, it also has to be recognized that a world of free trade is unlikely. The opening up of world trade is dependent on multilateral discussions held under the auspices of the WTO. The speed with which the trade in goods and services can be opened up depends on the willingness of the participants to enter into discussions. National and sectoral interests may well act as a powerful brake on these negotiations. An organization like the WTO with such a large national membership may find it difficult to proceed quickly in promoting, negotiating and implementing the outcome of trade rounds. Both the Uruguay and Doha Rounds are examples of this. To achieve some of the benefits of free trade, countries may find it useful to form RTAs with trade partners (Ethier 1998). Two sets of benefits can be said to arise. These are static and dynamic.

The static benefits arise from what is called trade creation (Viner 1950). These appear from the replacement of high cost domestic supplies in an economy by low cost suppliers from within the RTA. They can also occur when high cost foreign suppliers are replaced by lower cost suppliers from within the RTA. The benefits to the members of the RTA arise from the increase in domestic consumer surplus as a result of lower domestic prices.

These trading creating effects have to be offset against the trade diversionary effects that result from RTA formation. If lower cost foreign suppliers are replaced by higher cost RTA suppliers then the costs can outweigh the benefits. The extent to which trade creation outweighs trade diversion depends on the similarity or overlap between the economies forming the RTA and whether low cost producers are part of it. The greater the degree of overlap the more opportunity there is for reallocating resources efficiently between the members along the lines of comparative advantage.

In addition to these static allocative reasons, dynamic factors also play their part in conferring benefits to RTA members. The reduction of trade barriers gives rise to increased competition and, therefore, weakens and threatens existing monopoly positions. Increased competition not only reduces prices to consumers but spurs companies to reduce their costs and use inputs more efficiently. That, in turn, increases competition (Krugman, 1991a, 1991b; Frankel, 1997).

The larger market also has a dynamic impact. Domestic companies will now find it easier to export their goods to other member markets. In time, companies begin to regard the whole RTA economy as their domestic market. Producing for this larger market may allow companies to acquire economies of scale of a static and dynamic nature. These may be both internal and external to the companies involved (Corden 1972).

A larger market and the potential of scale economies may also allow firms to specialize in producing goods for market segments that were not considered viable prior to integration. Trade between the members of an RTA can then become more of the intra-industry type. Specialization as a result of increased trade will be on varieties or types of a particular product rather than on different products. This type of trade specialization has been observed by a number of researchers (Balassa 1965; Verdoorn, 1960).

The positive impact that improved resource allocation and economies of scale will have on economic growth and, hence, the growth of the domestic markets will make the RTA attractive to foreign direct investment (Rivera-Batiz and Romer 1991; Grossman and Helpmann 1991).

Foreign investment may also increase as companies fear being left out if the RTA should turn protectionist in the future (Whalley 1998). This can also act as a stimulant for seeking membership of existing RTAs or forming rival groups. The formation of NAFTA can be seen in that light as can the establishment of MERCOSUR. Mexico had little to gain from establishing a free trade area with the US and Canada as trade barriers were low. The risk that remaining outside of such a group and losing its existing position to future potential members acted as a catalyst in its application (Ethier 1998).

RTAs, by enlarging the size of the domestic market, reduce both risk and uncertainty and hence increase domestic investment in general. Further benefits also arise from the capital and labour mobility associated with common markets. Capital and labour moving from areas of surplus, and therefore earning low returns, to areas where there are shortages, will raise returns accordingly.

A further economic reason for the formation of an RTA is the benefit that participants may obtain by exploiting collectively their economic power as monopolists or monopsonists via improvements in the terms of trade.

Larger size also confers greater bargaining power on RTA members *vis-à-vis* non-member states. In this way RTAs act as devices for coordinating economic policies but in particular trade policies towards non-members.

Enhancing and furthering economic reforms can also act as a factor contributing towards RTA membership and formation. By committing to an agreed set of arrangements a government can enhance its credibility as a reformer (Maggi and Rodriguez-Clare 1998). This may also provide it with ammunition to fight and ward off domestic sectional interests. Arguments of this nature certainly lay behind the entry of Greece, Spain and Portugal to the EU and more recently the accession of the Central and Eastern European Economies. These outcomes provide wider economic benefits than those traditionally associated with RTA formation (Fernandez and Portes 1998; Tornell and Esquirel 1997)

The political case for RTAs
The political dimension in the formation of RTAs should never be overlooked. By linking their economies together so that they become more interdependent, countries reduce the likelihood of conflict between them. By developing a common economic purpose and

acting in concert to promote and protect it a group of nations can enhance their international bargaining power and hence sovereignty. Political power will follow and enhance economic power (Schiff and Winters 1998).

The formation of RTAs can also be viewed as the outcome of interest groups seeking to improve their position *vis-à-vis* rivals both in their own domestic economies and within other potential members (Grossman and Helpman 1995). It is also suggested that the long term viability of an RTA is dependent upon the extent to which interest groups in favour of it contribute positively towards its continuation.

The current EU owes much of its origins to Western Europe's desire to establish a system that locked the economies of France and Germany together so that they were never likely to go to war against one another again.

The EU also owes its development to the desire of Western European leaders to develop an economy that would rival that of the US. The aim here was to enhance the potential of European companies so that they could meet the challenges of US industries and reduce Europe's dependence on them.

The founders of the EU also believed that developing a successful and growing Western European economy would help to prevent it from drifting towards communism and ultimately falling under Russian control. Events in Central and Eastern European countries that had been liberated by the Russians worried the leaders in Western Europe.

The Europeans also believed that developing an economic entity that could rival the power of the US and Russia would ensure its political independence. While sympathetic towards the US in terms of economics and politics, they did not wish to be dominated by it.

The political aspect of integration in Western Europe was further enhanced by the EU's insistence that member states had to be and remain democracies in order to be member states. This requirement has been an important feature of its programme of expansion. States seeking accession see this as a guarantee of their democratic system and a defence against potential dictators. It has loomed large in the desire for membership in Greece, Spain and Portugal in the 1980s and more recently in the accession of the Central and Eastern European states.

Similar political arguments have featured in the formation of RTAs in Africa, Latin America, the Middle East and Asia to a greater or lesser degree. In the Middle East the Gulf Cooperation Council (GCC) began its life more as a political entity to cope with Britain's withdrawal from the Persian Gulf. It then developed an economic dimension embracing a free trade area and possibly a common currency in the future. ASEAN also came into existence primarily as a political military alliance (Yeung *et al.* 1999). The withdrawal of Britain from its presence east of Suez and the defeat of the US in Vietnam persuaded the pro-market nations in South East Asia to come together in a defensive alliance. An economic dimension was added later to promote the commercial cooperation amongst the member states.

The economic and political case against RTAs

The economic arguments   Here the economic arguments are mainly based on the trade diversion effects of RTA formation (Viner 1950). Trade division can exert a negative influence if high cost goods from RTA members replace those from lower cost foreign suppliers. In this way the welfare benefits of RTAs are reversed and the members are made worse off rather than better.

RTA may also reduce economic welfare by setting in train a set of retaliatory policies by non-member states. These may lead to the elimination of the terms of trade effect and the overall reduction in both bloc and world welfare. An extensive literature exists that can show this in theoretical terms (Krugman 1991b; Richardson 1994; Panagariya and Findlay 1996; Mayer 1981).

Whether RTA formation is a way to promote trade and overcome the delays in multi-lateral trade negotiations can also be questioned. Multilateral negotiations may take longer because they involve more countries but their potential gains are greater. It is also a fact that RTA formation can also be delayed because of disagreements amongst potential members.

If RTA formation allows governments to resist sectional interests, enhance domestic economic reform and establish its credibility then the same can be said of entering into multilateral agreements.

From the above, we can see that the economic arguments for RTA formation are not clear cut or unequivocal. It may be the case that rather than overcoming sectional interests they may establish themselves at the bloc level. Furthermore, the security arguments for RTAs also apply to multilateral liberalization.

The political arguments　If the political will is not present to lead to trade liberalization, then the benefits of trade liberalization will not appear from RTA formation. Evidence of this phenomenon can be seen in the failure of the Arab Common Market and also in the MERCOSUR free trade area.

Why should the political will to liberalize trade not exist or weaken when an agreement has been reached? There are several reasons. The first is ideology. If belief in liberalization and the benefits of the market system are not strongly held then political vacillation can result.

Second, those who are likely to lose out from RTA formation may acquire political power and prevent the process of integration. Liberalization results in both winners and losers. In Ricardian analysis, for liberalization to be successful the winners must compensate the losers and still feel better off. In practical terms this would require a third party, namely the government, to step in and transfer some of the gains via taxation. The reality may, however, be different. The winners may not be easy to identify and tax. Even if they can be identified, the government may be reluctant to tax the winners if they are also its principal supporters. In this political atmosphere if the losers can gain the support of the government then the process can be stopped if not halted and reversed.

Who would be the winners and who would be the losers? The winners would be, in the first instance, the consumers who gained from lower prices and an increase in consumer surplus. It would also be those producers and their workers whose exports increased as a result of trade liberalization within the RTA. The losers would be those domestic companies that lost out to foreign competition and lower prices; those who experienced a loss of producer surplus. As the gains of RTA formation and liberalization are often slow to appear but the losses are concentrated by industry and region the latter are more obvious and specific. If the losers can concentrate their efforts politically, they may be able to form a coalition of interested parties to fight the proposals successfully.

A case against RTAs can also be built on theoretical grounds. Essentially, this view suggests that in the initial stages of RTA formation the more obvious and, hence, trade creating RTAs are formed. In latter stages, the less obvious and, hence, principally trade diverting appear which leads to a decline in world welfare. This is then in contrast to the belief that RTAs are a positive, albeit second best, welfare enhancing form of trade liberalization (Bhagwati 1993). While WTO rules can limit the trade diversionary effects of RTA formation, their existence is still a possibility.

Who should join RTAs?

Having outlined the economic characteristics of RTAs and the arguments for and against their formation, can we deduce anything specific about who should join one, their size, depth, width and the external policy to be adopted? The World Bank in a policy report on trade blocs tried to come up with some answers to these questions (World Bank 2000).

It attempted to answer the 'who should join a RTA' question using four hypothetical scenarios. The first deals with a middle income developed or transitional economy contemplating joining a high income bloc or country. It is assumed that the bloc accounts for a high percentage of the middle income country's exports. In this case, the political reasons for joining would be high and would ensure the 'locking in' of the country's political system with that of the bloc. If it tried to renege on its agreement, the consequences for the middle income country in terms of economic outcomes could be severe. On the economic front the benefits to the middle income country could be substantial. These would arise from both the static and dynamic reallocation of resources as well as inflows of direct investment from the larger partner, especially if it is a low cost location for a wide range of economic activities. There is one caveat, however; companies from the middle income country may relocate to the richer partner if it has better access to technology, R&D and those activities that benefit from agglomeration. Trade diversion may also be an issue although an unlikely one given the size of the bloc. Another possibility may be the loss of tariff revenues.

For the high income country or bloc the advantages of joining with a middle income country may not be as great but they could be positive in both the economic and political sphere. Improved resource allocation via competition could be beneficial as could finding lower cost locations for domestic industries. Political benefits might also flow in the sense of securing borders and cementing friendly economic and political systems. Examples of this type of integration include the recent accession of the former communist countries of Central and Eastern Europe into the EU.

The second scenario deals with the formation of an RTA between large middle income countries. On the economic front there could be substantial benefits from integration. These could arise from enhanced resource allocation, economies of scale, terms of trade effects and improved attractiveness to footloose foreign direct investment (FDI) and technology transfer. Relocation of industries is also a possibility but would depend on the difference in both comparative and competitive advantage between the member states. Benefits could also arise on the political front. There would be gains to countries from the growth in political power, cooperation, security, as well as locking in policies and dealing with domestic vested interests.

As well as the benefits, there may be costs from integration that would need to be weighed up. These would involve trade diversion and loss of government resources from reduced tariffs. MERCOSUR may be an example of an RTA between middle income countries resulting in net costs rather than benefits accruing to its members (Yeats 1996).

The third scenario put forward by the World Bank team is the formation of an RTA between low income countries. In this scenario, the real economic benefits could be large especially if size allows scale economies to be secured. Positive benefits from enhanced competition and nationalization can also arise. FDI inflows and technology transfer could also result if market size has been an inhibiting factor. Political benefits could appear, in particular, with regard to enhancing the external power and perception of the bloc.

Costs, however, could also feature from the integration of low income economies. Development could become uneven amongst the members in particular if one has an initial advantage over the others. This could also lead to a loss for some members as development is diverted to the more successful country. To ensure cohesion in such RTAs mechanisms are needed to compensate losers. Politically, the gains may not be as great as first perceived. Weak economic benefits may lead members of the RTA to seek more beneficial ties.

An RTA which was not a success, although it has recently been revived, was the East African Community (EAC). It was established in 1967 by Kenya, Tanzania and Uganda. The EAC was essentially a common market with free trade, a common external tariff, harmonized monetary and fiscal policies and fixed exchange rates. It also had a role in the coordination of development planning between the member states. Tensions quickly grew between them, however, as disparities in growth rates developed and investment funds were skewed towards Kenya. These were financed by tariff revenues and, as a consequence, Tanzania and Uganda were potential losers of development funds. Whether the EAC was doomed to failure is a moot point (Eken 1979). For an RTA to be a success in trade creating terms, the potential has to exist. It is unlikely that trade between the members was being inhibited by trade restrictions.

The last scenario contemplated is that of a low income country joining a high income country or bloc. In this scenario the low income country can gain politically and economically. Political benefits would be associated from security, wider cooperation and the 'locking in' of reforms. The last of these could be very important in holding back domestic interest groups opposed to reform. The sanctions a powerful partner could impose could well force an opposing group to think twice before carrying out any action. Economic benefits for the low income country would arise from its access to a high income market and offering itself as a low cost base for footloose producers.

The costs need also to be considered. On the political front, the fear may be that the richer partner is not that interested in the domestic politics of the low income partner. As a result, the threat that the high income country or bloc would intervene to sustain reforms may not be credible. In the economic sphere, the required reduction in tariffs could lead to a reduction in government revenues. The benefits from improved access to the richer markets may not arise if transport costs are high and if the appropriate infrastructure is not available to promote exports. The extent to which these costs can be minimized depends to some extent on the depth of integration between the two parties. If the high income country or bloc can compensate the low income partners, to help with transport and infrastructure, then positive gains can be achieved. This would, however, depend on its political willingness to involve itself. If the rich bloc has some 'moral' obligation through previous involvement or perceives some strategic interest, this may come about and the benefits may be maximized.

Single or multiple membership?

Allied to the previous issue is the question how many RTAs should a country join? There are numerous instances of countries belonging to more than one bloc or blocs being affiliated to other blocs. A prime example of this is the EU whose members states are collectively members of the European Economic Area (EEA) along with EFTA and other countries. They are also participants in the EU's Euro-Med agreements with North African and Middle Eastern Countries.

The EU is not the only example. In Central and Latin America many of the countries are also involved in overlapping agreements. For example, some of MERCOSUR's members are also full participants in APEC and the Latin American Integration Association. Similarly, in Africa there are many such overlapping organizations. The same is true of East Asia where again the ASEAN group is also part of APEC.

There may be benefits, but also several costs, associated with being a member of multiple RTAs. For example, being at the centre of a 'hub and spoke' agreement would be attractive as a location for companies who wished access to several markets otherwise denied them. This could be a major benefit to a country in enabling it to enhance its comparative and competitive advantage.

The costs could be felt by both private business and the government. Being part of several RTAs with different rules of origin and so on could lead to confusion and uncertainty amongst the business community, both domestic and foreign. This would hinder both trade – exports and imports – as well as investment, again domestic and foreign. The resource requirements on governments attempting to coordinate and deal with a multiplicity of rules and regulations can also be considerable. This may be particularly so in poorer countries. Governments may also find their focus on policy issues defined when having to deal with several RTAs, thus preventing them from dealing with deep seated economic problems.

Recent RTA formation in Africa also offers a warning over their potential lack of success. Since trade between African countries is small, the main benefits are supposed to arise from their dynamic impact. It has been suggested that these may not arise because of the difficulties in administering these RTAs (Shaver 1999). Further, they have not only overlapping memberships but also different objectives and strategies, conflicting rules and regulations as well as other inconsistencies. As a result, trade and foreign direct investment is impeded as are the longer term dynamic outcomes.

The issues discussed above can influence an existing RTA considering expansion or widening to accommodate new entrants. Improving the level of integration or depth amongst existing members may have to be traded off against expansion and accepting new members. One way of limiting the costs to existing members is to require new entrants to accept the existing rules. The EU applies this procedure with new members having to implement its entire package of policies. This is the so-called 'acquis communitaire'. While this may be an attractive way to proceed for existing members, it may make accession less desirable from the point of view of new entrants (Gaisford *et al.* 2003).

RTAs and external trade policy

Countries forming or wishing to join a RTA have to consider their external trade policy towards non-member states and how it should be implemented. For instance should they have independent external trade policies or should they adopt a common approach? In other words should they pursue an FTA approach or consider forming a CM? Also of crucial importance will be the height of the barriers adopted against non-member states. High external tariffs will increase the possibility of trade diversion, lower potential consumer benefits, reduce competition, distort the efficient allocation of resources and lead to agglomeration diseconomies (Ades and Glaeser 1985; Krugman and Hanson 1993; World Bank 2000). In contrast, liberalization can bring with it adjustment costs which may be substantial. These may be considered unacceptable to policymakers. However, not accepting the adjustment costs may continue or enhance an inefficient economic structure such as may be the case in MERCOSUR (Yeats, 1996).

Choosing between forming or joining a CU or FTA is bound up with countries' attitudes towards sovereignty. As noted above, CUs avoid the establishment of costly rules of origin and bureaucracies to administer them. It has been estimated that administering the rules of origin that applied to EEC–EFTA trade cost between 3 and 5 per cent of free on board prices (Herin 1986). As long as the members of a CU can agree on the external tariff rate to be applied and how the revenues are distributed, this is a better form of RTA.

Since the bulk of RTAs are FTA and not CUs, it must mean that there are also costs that apply to this form. These costs, as implied, deal with sovereignty and the difficulty of reaching consensus amongst the members. Applying a CET requires agreement regarding its height and the distribution of the proceeds. To administer these will require the setting up of supranational institutions and the ceding of national sovereignty to them. The whole procedure may be difficult and politically unacceptable to the individual members. It is evident that this has been, and still is, the case even in established CUs (World Bank 2002). In the EU budgetary contributions are contentious. In the GCC consensus over the common external tariff has been difficult to achieve while in CARICOM there were considerable delays in its implementation. Difficulties of a similar nature have arisen in the Central American Common Market (CACM). For the first 30 years of its life, the EU allowed its individual members to administer their own non-tariff barriers such as quotas in order to ameliorate adjustment costs and placate vested interests (Winters 1992, 1993).

Choosing between an FTA and a CU
Linked to the previous issue is another regarding the form an RTA should take and the relationship that should be pursued. We touched on this issue earlier when outlining a taxonomy for RTAs. There we suggested that CUs have lower costs in administering trade policy. Here we will examine the effect these institutions have in setting the height of external tariffs.

FTAs may create a downward pressure on tariffs for three reasons. The first suggests that one way to limit or eliminate trade diversion is to reduce tariffs on non-member states. The second deals with the differential in tariff rates between members and what this implies for government revenues. If goods can enter via partners with lower tariffs then it makes sense for a country to lower its tariffs to recapture the revenues it is losing through trade deflection. Third, maintaining high tariffs against imports that are used in the production of exports makes them uncompetitive. As a result tariff reductions are a sensible policy option.

CUs, however, may encourage an upward movement in tariffs. This can be for several reasons. The first is that by coming together the members of a CU increase their collective economic power. They are, therefore, able to exploit this by increasing their trade restrictions on non-members and shift the terms of trade in their favour. Second, if members are willing to acquiesce in protecting the interests of particular individual members then trade restrictions can be enhanced. This can also arise if in the decision making process members can veto proposals that are perceived to be counter to their national interests. Third, sectoral interests may be enhanced rather than diminished as a result of CU formation. Concerted pressure from these groups may be difficult to withstand. This may be particularly so if the group seeking protection is relatively homogeneous such as agricultural producers.

The depth and width of bloc formation

Another issue that is pertinent in bloc formation is the choice of depth and width of coverage of the arrangements.

The long term gains from membership in a bloc arise essentially from the removal of barriers that segment markets. The removal of trade barriers alone may not be enough to open up markets and enhance competition amongst firms across borders. To achieve these gains may require a deeper form of integration than just forming an FTA. This may not be a simple choice as deepening has its costs. Issues that need resolving cover topics such as the members' maintenance of contingent protection, border controls, national regulations and public procurement. In general, these have the effect of protecting the domestic market from foreign competition, albeit from partners in a trade bloc. The extent to which these are removed or harmonized shows the commitment a bloc has towards gaining the dynamic benefits and its willingness to give up individual sovereignty to achieve them.

The choice of the width of coverage of the agreements also has costs and benefits associated with it. FTAs usually restrict their coverage to manufactures although some cover agriculture. In other words, they cover trade in goods. Other areas such as the liberalization of investment flows (capital movements), services and the harmonization of fiscal and monetary policies also need consideration. Allowing liberalization in the area of services can bring many benefits to the bloc through an improved allocation of resources as well as better returns to owners. It also signals a more positive policy stance which may encourage greater cross-border investment. The opening up of trade in services, while adversely affecting domestic suppliers, may be beneficial to local producers that use these services intensively. Harmonizing fiscal and monetary policies may establish a so called 'level playing field' between producers and enhance real competition. In this way 'false' comparative advantages that have arisen from differences in tax regimes can be stopped.

Summary and conclusion

This chapter has outlined the main forms of RTAs ranging from the simplest, the FTA, through to the Economic and Political Union, the deepest form, and their specific features. Both economic and political reasons deployed for and against their formation have also been examined. Issues regarding a bloc's membership, external trade policy, choice of structure and depth and width of integration have also been discussed. Throughout this chapter the theoretical work has been illustrated by referring to existing RTAs. Empirical evidence has been used to underscore the points made. It is clear from the topics covered that the RTAs of whatever depth cannot be said to be good or bad unequivocally for individual members. A great deal depends on the circumstances. What is clear, however, is that belonging to many overlapping RTAs may not be beneficial to individual countries. Multiple memberships may lead to a muddying of the waters rather than clarification.

References

Ades, A. E. and E. L. Glaeser (1985), 'Trade and Circuses: Explaining Urban Giants', *Quarterly Journal of Economics*, **110**, 198–259.

Balassa, B. (1965), *Economic Developments and Integration*, México: D. F. Centre de Estudios Monetarios Latinoamericanicos.

Bhagwati, J. (1993), 'Regionalism and Multilateralism: An Overview', in J. De Melo, A. Panagariya and D. Roderick (eds), *New Dimensions in Regional Integration*, Cambridge: Cambridge University Press.

Corden, W. M. (1972), 'Economies of Scale and Customs Union Theory', *Journal of Political Economy*, **80** (3), 465–75.

Eken, S. (1979), 'Break Up of the East African Community', *Finance and Development*, **16** (4), 36–40.

Ethier, W. (1998), 'Regionalism in a Multilateral World', *Journal of Political Economy*, **106** (6), 1214–45.

Fernandez, R. and J. Portes (1998), 'Returns to Regionalism: An Analysis of Non-traditional Gains from Regional Trade Agreements', *World Bank Economic Review*, **12** (2), 197–220.

Frankel, J. A. (1997), *Regional Trade Blocs in the World Economic System*, Washington, DC: Institute for International Economics.

Gaisford, J. D., W. A. Kerr and N. Perdikis (2003), *Economic Analysis for EU Accession Negotiations – Agri-food Issues in the EU's Eastward Expansion*, Cheltenham, UK and Northampton, MA, USA: Edward Elgar.

Grossman, G. M. and E. Helpman (1991), *Innovation and Growth in the Global Economy*, Cambridge, MA: MIT Press.

Grossman, G. M. and E. Helpman (1995), 'The Politics of Free Trade Agreements', *American Economic Review*, **85** (4), 667–90.

Herin, J (1986), 'Rules of Origin and Differences between Tariff Levels in EFTA and the EC', Occasional Paper No. 13, European Free Trade Association, Secretariat, Geneva.

Kerr, W. A. (2005), 'Trade Dispute Mechanisms: the NAFTA and the WTO', in N. Perdikis and R. Read, *The WTO and the Regulation of International Trade: Recent Trade Disputes between the European Union and the United States*, Cheltenham, UK and Northampton, MA, USA: Edward Elgar.

Krugman, P. R. (1991a), 'The Move Towards Free trade Zones', *Economic Review*, 76, Federal Reserve Bank of Kansas, Kansas City, pp. 5–25.

Krugman, P. A. (1991b), 'Is Bilateralism Bad', in E. Helpman and A. Ragin (eds), *International Trade and Trade Policy*, Cambridge, MA: MIT Press.

Krugman, P. and G. Hanson (1993), 'Mexico–US Free Trade and the Location of Production', in P. Garber (ed.), *The Mexico-US Free Trade Agreement*, Cambridge: Cambridge University Press.

Lipsey, R. G. (1957), 'The Theory of Customs Unions: Trade Diversion and Welfare', *Economica*, **24** (93), 40–46.

Maggi, G. and A. Rodrigues-Clare (1998), 'The Value of Trade Agreements in the Presence of Political Pressure', *Journal of Political Economy*, **106** (3), 574–601.

Mayer, W. (1981), 'Theoretical Considerations on Negotiating Tariff Adjustments', *Oxford Economic Papers*, **33** (1), 135–53.

Panagariya, A. and R. Findlay (1996), 'A Political Economy Analysis of Free Trade Areas and Customs Unions', in R. Feenstra, D. Irwin and E. Grossman (eds), *The Political Economy of Trade Reform: Essays in Honour of Jagdish Bhagwati*, Cambridge, MA: MIT Press.

Richardson, M. (1994), 'Why a Free Trade Area? The Tariff also Rises', *Economics and Politics*, **6** (1), 79–96.

Rivera-Batiz, L. A. and P. M. Romer (1991), 'Economic Integration and Endogenous Growth', *Quarterly Journal of Economics*, **106** (2), 531–56.

Schiff, M. and L. A. Winters (1998), 'Regional Integration as Diplomacy', *World Bank Economic Review*, **12** (2), 271–95.

Shaver, R. (1999), 'Trade: An Engine of Growth for Africa', *Finance and Development*, **36** (4), 26–29.

The Economist (1991a), 'The Business of the American Hemisphere', 24 August.

The Economist (1991b), 'One Europe, One Economy', 30 November.

Tornell, A. and G. Esquirel (1997), 'Political Economy of Mexico's entry into NAFTA', in T. Ito and A.O.Krueger (eds), *Regionalism versus Multilateral Trade Arrangements*, Chicago, IL: Chicago University Press.

Verdoorn, A. J. (1960), 'The Intra-bloc Trade of Benelux', in E. A. G. Robinson (ed.), *Economic Consequences of the size of Nations*, London: Macmillan.

Viner, J. (1950), *Customers Union Theory*, New York: Carnegie Endowment for International Peace.

Whalley, J. (1998), 'Why do Countries Seek Regional Trade Agreements?', in J. Frenkel (ed.), *The Regionalisation of the World Economy*, Chicago, IL: Chicago University Press.

Winters, L. A. (1992), 'The Welfare and Policy Implications of the International Trade Consequences of 1992', *American Economic Review*, **38** (2), 104–8.

Winters, L. A. (1993), 'The European Community: A Case of Successful Integration', Discussion Paper No. 775, Centre for Economic Policy Research, London.

World Bank (2000), *Trade Blocs*, World Bank Policy Research Report, Oxford: Oxford University Press.

Yeats, A. J. (1996), *Does MERCOSUR's Trade Performance Justify Concerns about the Global Welfare – Reducing Effects of Free Trade Arrangements? Yes!*, Washington, DC: World Bank.

Yeung, M. T., N. Perdikis and W. A. Kerr (1999), *Regional Trading Blocs in the Global Economy: The EU and ASEAN*, Cheltenham, UK and Northampton, MA, USA: Edward Elgar.

11 Trade creation and trade diversion: analyzing the impact of regional trade agreements
Lindsay Kendall and James Gaisford

Introduction

There has been a proliferation of regional trade agreements (RTAs) in recent years. As of the end of November 2005, the World Trade Organization (WTO) was notified of 186 regional trade agreements (RTA) and it was estimated that by the end of 2006 almost 300 RTAs may be notified (WTO 2006). An RTA is a group of two or more countries or other territories that reduce or eliminate trade barriers for each other but leave higher barriers in place for outsiders. In the case of a free trade area, each member country removes trade barriers on internal trade, but maintains its own external trade barriers. Common external trade barriers are added with customs unions and other arrangements involving closer regional economic integration such as common markets and economic unions.[1] Since each participant grants other member countries preferential access to its own markets, any RTA inherently discriminates against outside countries.

Non-discrimination, however, has been a central tenet of the multilateral trading system since the inception of General Agreement on Tariffs and Trade (GATT) in 1947. With respect to tariffs, for example, each member of the GATT is usually required to grant 'most-favoured nation' (MFN) status to each other GATT member, such that the lowest tariff rate available to any country is extended to all. While clearly in violation of the MFN principle, RTAs have always been explicitly permitted by the GATT subject to certain conditions. External barriers are not permitted to rise and internal trade barriers must be eliminated on substantially all trade within a reasonable time frame, which in most circumstances has come to mean 10 years (WTO 1999). RTAs are also allowed by the newer General Agreement on Trade in Services (GATS), which along with the GATT, is now housed under the umbrella of the WTO.

While the discriminatory feature of RTAs raises concerns for outside countries, there are also important issues for member countries inside an RTA. Even if a country is ultra small so that free trade is its optimum policy, the theory of the second best implies that if tariffs are to be left in place for some outside countries, it is generally not best to reduce tariffs to zero for the other inside countries (Lipsey, 1960). Viner (1950) analyzes the conflicting forces affecting economic welfare that arise from the formation of an RTA under the headings of 'trade creation' and 'trade diversion'. Trade creation occurs when new trade arises between member countries because of the reduction in internal trade barriers. Trade diversion exists when imports from a low-cost outside country are replaced by imports from a higher-cost partner country because the partner has preferential access to the market and does not have to pay tariffs. At unchanged world prices, trade creation is beneficial for the member countries, considered jointly, but trade diversion is harmful. Since any particular RTA will have a combination of both trade creation and trade diversion effects, Viner (1950) concludes that it is not possible to draw unambiguous conclusions concerning how RTAs affect economic welfare.

Not surprisingly, there has been considerable debate over whether the forces of trade creation or trade diversion are likely to dominate. On the one hand, opponents of trade blocs, such as Bhagwati and Panagariya (1999), take a 'stumbling blocs' view that trade diversion is a serious concern. Opponents also worry that overlapping RTAs appear to be increasing the complexity and reducing the transparency of the world trading system. In addition, it is also claimed that the formation of RTAs has made progress toward multilateral trade liberalization more difficult for political as well as economic reasons. On the other hand, proponents of trade blocs, such as Krugman (1991), take the 'building blocs' view of trade blocs. In this view, trade creation usually dominates trade diversion because RTAs frequently build on natural trading relationships where transport and transaction costs are low. Further, the enlarged markets resulting from RTAs provide small countries a vital opportunity to exploit economies of scale.

In this chapter we consider trade creation and trade diversion in detail. We begin in the simplest possible context with a thorough theoretical analysis of RTAs in a static competitive world economy. Subsequently, we move beyond the static competitive model and finally we briefly consider empirical evidence on trade creation and trade diversion.

Trade creation and trade diversion in a static competitive world

We analyze a simple static world economy that consists of three countries: A and B, which enter into an RTA, and W, which comprises the rest of the world. There are many markets, all of which are competitive. On some, both A and B export and, on others, they both import, but on the markets of greatest current interest, one country imports and the other exports.[2] For simplicity, we focus on sample markets where it happens that country A imports and country B exports, but we emphasize that there are likely to be other similar configured markets where the trade pattern is reversed.[3]

We assume that import tariffs are the only trade policy instruments that are in use and, thus, imports are directly subject to distortion whereas exports are not. For this reason our principal focus is on whether imports rather than exports are created or diverted by the formation of the RTA. As we examine various market situations for evidence of import creation and/or import diversion, we proceed in two steps. First we systematically examine the impact of the formation of RTAs conditional on constant world prices. If both country A and B were (ultra) small relative to the rest of the world, then this first step alone would suffice. In general, however, world prices will change. Second, for each market we consider the likely impact on world prices and the subsequent impact on economic welfare in each of the member countries and in the rest of the world.[4] To keep our analysis as simple as possible we assume that the RTA that is formed by A and B is a free trade area where each partner maintains its original tariff structure.

In the diagrammatic analysis in Figure 11.1 and subsequent figures, P is the price axis and TV is the trade volume or quantity traded axis. In drawing the import demand curve of country A, DM_A, negatively sloped, and the export supply curve of country B, SX_B, positively sloped, we are taking a general case where neither country is (ultra) small relative to the other. Further, the underlying supply curves in each country have non-infinite elasticities reflecting rising marginal costs in production. While it has become traditional to pursue a diagrammatic analysis of trade creation and trade diversion where

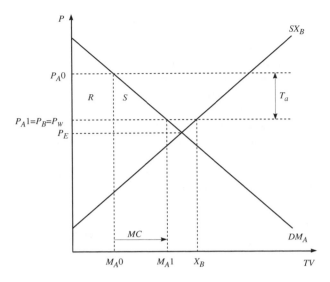

Figure 11.1   Pure trade creation

the exporting partner has a horizontal or perfectly elastic export supply curve, we believe that dispensing with this restriction leads to stronger insights. In Figure 11.1, P_W is the world price that is assumed to prevail prior to the formation of the RTA between A and B, and P_E is an exclusive-trading price that would arise if A and B traded only with one another on this market, holding prices on other markets constant.

Pure import creation
We begin our market analysis by considering Figure 11.1, which is a market where country B is a low-cost supplier for A. By this, we formally mean P_E is less than P_W or that the price at which B would sell to A in an exclusive trading arrangement is lower than the world price. While the world price is P_W, the initial tariff-ridden price in country A is P_A0 given that A's tariff is T_A per unit imported. Of course, Country B receives the world price for its exports such that P_B is equal to P_W. Country A's initial imports are M_A0, and Country B's initial exports are X_B. The difference, $X_B - M_A0$, reflects the imports demanded by the rest of the world at the initial world price.

When countries A and B form an RTA, A removes its tariff on goods from B and the domestic price in A falls until it is equal to the world price. Conditional on the world price remaining constant at P_W, the domestic price in Country A falls to P_A1 and its imports rise to M_A1. This increase in imports associated with the removal of the tariff-distortion on imports can be called import creation or, more simply, trade creation. In Figure 11.1, the arrow labeled MC shows the extent of this import creation for country A. The exports of country B remain unchanged at X_B. Given the constant world price, the reduction in A's domestic price is associated with a gain in net consumer surplus or importer surplus for the private sector equal to $R+S$ dollars, but the removal of the tariff causes a reduction in government revenue equal to R dollars. Thus country A experiences an overall gain in economic welfare or total surplus equal to S dollars, which is unambiguously positive.

Since the price and total surplus remain unchanged in the exporting country *B*, the gain of *S* dollars by *A* also represents the level of joint gains for *A* and *B* from the formation of the RTA conditional on a constant world price. Here, *S* represents an efficiency gain from pure import creation.

The world price, however, is not likely to remain constant. While the overall exports of *B* remain unchanged at the initial world price, the creation of new imports shown by the arrow, *MC*, implies that net exports available to the rest of the world, *W*, from *A* and *B* have been reduced. Since this net-export restriction represents a reduction in the net supply from *A* and *B* to *W*, there is excess demand on the world market. The world price, thus, is likely to rise on this market. Such an increase in the world price will reduce economic welfare in the rest of the world. As an importing country, *A* also loses from an increase in the world price, but *B* gains. Moreover, there are unambiguous joint gains for *A* and *B* from an increase in the world price because *B* exports more than *A* imports making the gains of the former larger than the losses of the latter.

On a market where the exporting partner is a low-cost producer and, thus, there is pure trade creation, countries *A* and *B* typically experience a joint overall gain because they gain jointly both from the formation of the RTA at a constant world price and from an increase in the world price. The overall effect on the importing partner is ambiguous since it gains from RTA formation but loses from an increase in the world price. The overall impact on exporting partner *B* is typically positive because an increase in the world price is beneficial while the formation of the RTA is neutral. Conversely, the overall effect on the rest of the world is typically negative because, while the formation of the RTA is neutral, a world price increase is harmful.

Pure import diversion

In Figure 11.2, we turn to a market situation where country *B* can be considered to be a high-cost supplier for *A* because the exclusive trading price at which country *B* could supply *A*, P_E, is greater than country *A*'s initial tariff-ridden domestic price, P_A. Country *B* initially receives the world price for its exports such that P_B0 is equal to P_W. Country *A*'s initial imports are M_A, and Country *B*'s initial exports are X_B0. The difference, $M_A0 - X_B$, reflects the exports supplied by the rest of the world at the initial world price.

When the RTA is formed and *A* removes its tariff on goods from *B*, *A*'s domestic price remains unchanged at P_A conditional on the world price remaining constant at P_W. This is because country *A* will continue to import some product from the rest of the world at the tariff-ridden price P_A rather than face the higher price P_E, which would arise if it chose to import exclusively from *B*. Since *A*'s domestic price remains constant, its imports will remain constant at M_A as well. Country *B*, however, now has preferential access to *A*'s market and, thus, the new price that *B* prevails for its exports and for its own domestic market, P_B1, is equal to P_A. Consequently, *B*'s exports rise to X_B1. For *A*, this represents import diversion. Some low-cost tariff-paying imports from *W* are replaced by high-cost tariff-free imports from *B*. The arrow labeled *MD* in Figure 11.2 shows the extent of import diversion or trade diversion.

Since the domestic price remains unchanged in *A*, there is no change in the importer surplus or net consumer surplus obtained by the private sector. Tariff revenue, which was initially equal to $V + Y + Z$ dollars, falls to *Z* dollars. Consequently, there is a decline in both government revenue and total surplus equal to $V + Y$ dollars in country *A*. The price

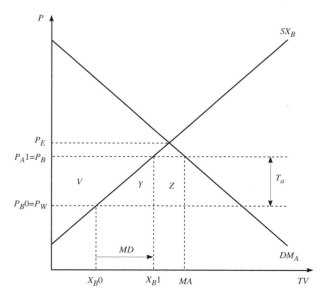

Figure 11.2   Pure trade diversion

increase experienced by exporting country B, however, generates an increase in both private-sector exporter surplus (that is, net producer surplus) and total surplus equal to V dollars. Conditional on the constant world price, therefore, there is an overall loss of joint total surplus for A and B equal to Y dollars on this market, where B is a high-cost exporter and there is pure trade diversion. Here, Y represents an efficiency loss due to pure import diversion.

It should be observed, once again, that the world price is not likely to remain constant. Since A has diverted its imports toward B and away from W as shown by the MD arrow in Figure 11.2, the rest of the world is faced with an exactly corresponding net import restriction from A and B. The reduction in net demand by A and B implies that there is excess supply on the world market at the initial world price making a decline in the world price likely. Such a decline in the world price, considered on its own, will hurt both B and W because they are exporters, but it will be beneficial to A because it is an importer.

Considering the overall impact of the formation of the RTA and the likely price reduction in a market where the exporting partner is a high cost supplier, the rest of the world loses, but joint impact on the partners is ambiguous. The joint impact of RTA formation is negative, but a world price reduction has a positive joint impact. The overall impact on the importing partner is ambiguous by analogous reasoning. Meanwhile, the exporting partner stands to gain overall provided that the final price in the importing partner remains above the initial world price.

Contemporaneous trade creation and diversion
In the final market situation to be considered, which is shown in Figure 11.3, B is a mid-cost supplier for A in the sense that the exclusive-trading price for the two countries, P_E, lies below the tariff-ridden price in A, P_A0, but above the world price, P_W. Given that the

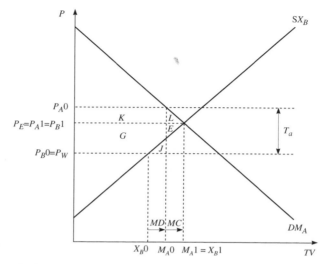

Figure 11.3   Trade diversion with trade creation

initial domestic price in Country A is P_A0, its initial imports are M_A0. Country B's initial price, P_B0, is equal to the world price and thus its initial exports are X_B0. Since X_B0 is less than M_A0, the difference reflects imports supplied by the rest of the world, W, at the initial world price.

As a result of the formation of an RTA, the participating countries always have the same domestic prices for products that they trade such that P_A1 is equal to P_B1. Further, when A and B form an RTA on the market shown in Figure 11.3, they will trade exclusively with one another assuming that the world price remains constant, such that A's imports, M_A1, are equal to B's exports, X_B1. This is because it is in A's interest to buy only from B at a price of P_E rather than continuing to purchase some product from W at the higher tariff-ridden price, P_A0. Overall, existing imports are diverted as shown by the arrow, MD, but new imports are also created as shown by the arrow, MC.

At an unchanged world price, the private sector in importing-country A gains importer surplus equal to $K+L$ dollars due to the decline in the domestic price and the government loses $G+K+J$ dollars due to the disappearance of tariff revenue. The change in total surplus for country A, therefore, is $L-[G+J]$ dollars, which in principle is ambiguous but happens to be negative in Figure 11.3. Exporting-country B experiences an unambiguous gain in both exporter and total surplus equal to $E+G$ dollars. The change in joint total surplus attributable to the formation of the RTA is $[L+E]-[J]$ dollars, which is ambiguous in principal and happens to be positive in Figure 11.3.[5] Here, $L+E$ represents an efficiency gain due to import creation and J is an efficiency loss due to import diversion.

Of course, as Countries A and B withdraw their net imports from the world market at the initial world price of P_W, a state of excess supply will prevail making a decline in the world price likely. This will clearly be harmful to the rest of the world. A small decline in the equilibrium world price would be associated with a state of autarky or no imports for W, but a sufficiently large decrease in the equilibrium world price decline would be associated with the re-opening of net exports by A and B.

It is certainly possible to construct mid-cost situations where M_A0 is less than X_B0 and the difference reflects exports supplied to the rest of the world at the initial world price. In this case, there is only import creation and no import diversion as a result of the formation of the RTA. Countries A and B will continue to cut off their net imports harming W. While the impact on B continues to be positive and the impact on A continues to be ambiguous, it is straightforward to show that there are unambiguous joint gains for A and B together because area J disappears from the analysis.

Overarching considerations
Given that there are many goods, each partner is likely to be subject to trade creation and trade diversion both on markets where it is an importer and on markets where it is an exporter. Even in the context of a simple static analysis where markets are competitive, theory does not predict unambiguous joint gains for countries that enter into RTAs of the types which are typically seen and described in Chapter 8. Because of trade diversion, joint losses cannot be ruled out. Additional problems with a mal-distribution of gains or losses across countries may also arise. The prognosis is generally worse for excluded or outsider countries, because external trade tends to be restricted as the insiders trade more with one another, whether due to trade diversion or trade restriction.[6] This does not imply, however, that internal trade diversion and/or external trade restriction are inevitable.

In theory, RTAs could be constructed so as to avoid any welfare losses. Consider the formation of a customs union where external trade barriers are harmonized. Kemp and Wan (1976) show that, if the common external tariff is set appropriately, the member countries can obtain unambiguous gains without hurting the rest of the world. In particular, suppose that external tariffs are configured to keep the aggregate external trade volumes between insiders and outsiders at their initial levels. This immediately assures that world prices will be constant and outside countries remain equally well off. Kemp and Wan show that for the member countries there exists a feasible set of transfers across individuals and countries that allow all individuals to afford their original consumption bundles. Since prices inside the customs union will have changed, individuals will be able to substitute to superior consumption bundles, which implies that there are unambiguous gains. Krishna and Panigariya (2002) show that the analysis can be generalized to the case of a free trade area. In this case, each member country re-sets its own tariff structure to maintain constant trade volumes with outside countries as a group. Once again, world prices and levels of economic welfare in outside countries remain constant. An additional advantage of the more general Krishna and Panagariya analysis is that it does not rely on transfers across countries. While the GATT/WTO rules for the formation of RTAs require that external barriers do not increase on average, the analysis in Kemp and Wan (1976) and Krishna and Panigariya (2002) suggest that a requirement to preserve external trade volumes would be superior on economic grounds.[7]

Even when an RTA is not designed to eliminate trade diversion, the forces of trade creation are more likely to dominate the forces of trade diversion under some circumstances than others. To begin with, trade barriers matter, whether they are policy-made or natural. Where initial tariffs are high, trade creation is likely to be dominant (Laird 1999). For example, if the initial tariff is prohibitive, there is only trade creation. On the one hand, if final tariffs are lowered either due to the formation of a customs union (De Melo *et al.* 1993) or as an endogenous policy response (see Richardson 1993), then trade diversion will be reduced. On the other hand, if the RTA flexes its muscles and attempts to exercise its increased market power with respect to world prices by raising final tariffs, then trade diversion will become more pronounced (see Krugman 1991). Trade creation will also tend to dominate when transport and transaction costs are low with insiders and high with outsiders. In the limit if such costs are prohibitive with outsiders, there can only be trade creation (Laird, 1999). Krugman (1991) points out that countries in close geographic proximity have relatively low transport costs and thus tend to make 'natural' RTAs.

The larger is a country's RTA-partner, the more likely that trade creation will be dominant. A large partner is more likely to be a low-cost producer, which is able to export additional products to the rest of the world after satisfying a country's import demands at the world price. The less similar is a partner country or the more complementary its patterns of comparative advantage, the more likely it is to be a low-cost exporter leading to greater trade creation. For this reason, RTAs between developing and developed countries may tend to be beneficial (De Melo *et al.* 1993).[8] When examining products that are imperfect substitutes, Head and Ries (2004) reason that the more substitutable are domestic goods with those offered by RTA-partner countries, the greater the trade creation. Contrariwise the less substitutable are domestic goods with those offered by outside countries, the smaller the trade diversion.

The analysis of trade creation and trade diversion in a static competitive world economy also masks some vital features. In a dynamic model, the formation of an RTA may both create new investment and divert investment from an outsider into the RTA. On the one hand, to the extent that the RTA members experience more rapid growth there will be dynamic trade creation gains as trade grows both between insiders and with outsiders. Further, there may be endogenous gains from learning and improved technical integration from deeper integration among member countries (Laird 1999). On the other hand, outside countries could experience dynamic losses if they grow more slowly due to the diversion of investment.

When markets are imperfectly competitive, the gains from greater market integration through the formation of RTAs appear to be extremely important, especially to small and medium-sized economies. As discussed further in Chapter 13, market integration increases the range of imported plus domestic varieties available to consumers. Meanwhile, rationalization typically occurs in each individual country. The output of surviving varieties tends to increase, driving down average costs and realizing economies of scale. Moreover, there are typically pro-competitive gains. More intense competitive pressure in an integrated market within an RTA tends to generate efficiencies by driving prices closer to marginal costs.

The empirics of trade creation and trade diversion

There is a growing body of empirical literature that examines trade creation versus diversion. There are three empirical methodologies that are frequently used. The first methodology relies on an examination of trade shares before and after an RTA comes into effect. As Clausing (2001) points out, a major flaw with such studies is that they implicitly assume that the trade pattern between the partners would not have changed in the absence of the formation of the RTA signed.

A second more useful methodology for investigating the formation of RTAs involves *ex post* econometric analysis with so-called 'gravity' models. While gravity models do incorporate many explanatory variables into the explanation of bilateral trade flows, they must be used with care. For example, the dummy variables that are intended to pick up trade creation and/or trade diversion may inadvertently pick up other commonalities between country pairs. The third important methodology for studying the formation of RTAs involves *ex ante* analysis using computable general equilibrium (CGE) models. While the results from CGE models are sensitive to the assumptions that they incorporate and the data they employ, such models are useful in distinguishing between trade creation and trade diversion effects. Gravity models and CGE models are discussed in detail in Chapter 5. We proceed by briefly considering a selection of empirical studies from around the world.

Clausing (2001) and Romalis (2005) have examined the trade creating and trade diverting effects of the Canada–US Free Trade Agreement, which has been subsumed into the North American Free Trade Agreement. Clausing (2001) used disaggregated trade data because the large variations in initial tariffs across commodities for both countries could lead to misleading results if tariffs were aggregated across commodity groups. The model reveals evidence of substantive trade creation, but there is no statistically significant evidence of trade diversion. By contrast, Romalis (2005) does find evidence of trade diversion when employing a more sophisticated empirical approach to deal with rapidly growing trade with emerging markets such as China. Nevertheless, trade creation continues to outweigh trade diversion.

Bayoumi and Eichengreen (1995) used a gravity model to assess trade creation and trade diversion arising from economic integration in Europe. While the European Free Trade Association (EFTA) was found to be mainly trade creating, the expansions of the European Union (EU), with the exception of the additions of Spain and Portugal, were found to cause significant trade diversion. Grinols (1984) also finds that the United Kingdom experienced significant trade diversion when it entered the EU.

Bohara *et al.* (2004) focus on the MERCOSUR agreement between Argentina, Brazil, Paraguay and Uruguay. While they find evidence of significant trade diversion, their endogenous tariff approach, which follows Richardson's (1993), suggests that there may be secondary trade creation as external tariffs are reduced. This appears consistent with observed unilateral reductions by Argentina and the agenda for common external tariffs for MEROSUR as a whole. Carrère (2004) uses a gravity model to examine the impact of African trade agreements in a framework that incorporates the Economic and Monetary Union of West Africa and the Economic and Monetary Community of Central Africa. Regional trade agreements in Africa, which appear to be predominantly trade diverting, in fact may be mainly trade creating when monetary features are considered. Roberts (2004) uses a gravity model to examine the trade creating and trade diverting potential of a proposed RTA between China and the Association of Southeast Asian Nations, ASEAN. The analysis suggests that trade costs between the potential members are more significant than geographical distance in determining bilateral trade flows, suggesting that there may be considerable room for trade creation if an RTA is formed.

Robinson and Thierfelder (2002) examine the results from several studies using CGE models. Despite the differences in assumptions across studies, they conclude that RTAs typically have larger trade creating effects than trade diverting effects for member countries. This, perhaps, is not surprising since CGE models generally go beyond the realm of static competitive theory. CGE models sometimes incorporate dynamic elements and they generally move the empirical analysis into the realm of imperfect competition allowing for gains associated with greater market integration.

Conclusion

It is tempting to interpret the rapid spread of RTAs as evidence that: (a) in reality, trade creation trumps trade diversion, and (b) therefore, RTAs are a boon to the international commercial system. Even if the first part of this conjecture is true and it is individually rational for countries to enter into RTAs, the second part does not automatically follow from the first. In the extreme, a prisoners' dilemma is possible where the cumulative impact of all RTAs is mutually harmful for all countries (Krugman 1991). More reasonably, the gains that some countries obtain from any RTAs in which they are included might not compensate for the harm that they experience as a result of those from which they are excluded.

Consequently, the analysis of trade creation and trade diversion in this chapter suggests a cautious assessment of regional trade agreements. On the one hand, a cynical view of RTAs appears to be unwarranted, especially when one considers the likely additional benefits of market integration when markets are imperfectly competitive. Moreover, there may be substance to Krugman's (1991) view that RTAs such as NAFTA and the EU constitute natural trading blocs that are predominantly trade creating. On the other hand, it appears unwise to be sanguine about the formation of RTAs. The proliferation of RTAs has seemingly complicated the international trading system and reduced transparency for businesses. Any net benefits from the reduction in trade barriers within each RTA may be have been largely nulified by increases in transaction costs that occur when business are confronted with an overlapping muddle of RTAs. Further, for any countries such as Japan that might remain on the sidelines without partners, the brave new world of RTAs may be particularly harsh.

Notes

1. Chapter 8 considers different types of RTAs in more detail.
2. In principle, the formation of an RTA could lead a country to switch between importer and exporter status, but we ignore this complication. Markets where both partners import are also of considerable interest. At constant world prices, the joint welfare of the partners will frequently rise. Consider a free trade area and suppose that *A* has a higher tariff than *B*. If *W* can circumvent *A*'s tariff by shipping through *B* or displace *B*'s domestic production into *A*'s market, there will be a joint efficiency gain for *A* and *B*. (Free trade areas frequently adopt rules of origin to prevent tariff circumvention as discussed in Chapter 12.) A similar joint efficiency gain occurs in the case of a customs union that adopts the lower tariff in *B*. In all these cases, subsequent increases world prices are likely because *A* demands more at the lower price. Such a price increase will be beneficial to *W*, but harmful to *A* and *B*. Consequently, the overall impact will be positive for *W*, but ambiguous for *A* and *B* when considered individually or jointly. Further details are provided in Chapter 12.
3. To implement the analysis when there are in principle many goods, we assume that changes in income only affect the consumption of a numeraire good that is exported by both countries. This allows the use of a simple (net) consumer and producer surplus approach to policy assessment where it is to be understood that we would move sequentially through the markets in the economy changing one price at each step.
4. We caution that in a multi-market context, excess world demand (supply) on some particular market at the original world prices does not automatically imply that the price will rise (fall) on that market to reach the new world equilibrium.
5. Notice, in Figure 11.3, it happens to be the case that there are joint gains for *A* and *B* even though *A* loses.
6. It is worth noting that the rest of the world may experience favourable changes in world prices on markets where both *A* and *B* import as detailed in an earlier footnote.
7. Feenstra (2004, ch. 6) provides a useful restatement of the Kemp and Wan (1976) and Krishna and Panigariya (2002) analysis of unambiguously beneficial RTAs.

8.   However, the more dissimilar are the countries, the greater the likely adjustment costs and effect on income distribution.

References

Bayoumi, T. and B. Eichengreen (1995), 'Is Regionalism Simply a Diversion? Evidence from the Evolution of the EC and EFTA,' NBER Working Paper 5283.

Bhagwati, J. and A. Panagariya (1999), 'Preferential Trading Areas and Multilateralism – Strangers, Friends, or Foes?,' in *Trading Blocs: Alternative Approaches to Analyzing Preferential Trade Agreements*, J. Bhagwati, P. Krishna and A. Panagariya (eds), Cambridge, MA: MIT Press.

Bohara, A. K., K. Gawande and P. Sanguinetti (2004), 'Trade Diversion and Declining Tariffs: evidence from Mercosur,' *Journal of International Economics*, **64**, 65–88.

Carrère, C. (2004), 'African Regional Agreements: Impact on Trade with or without Currency Unions,' *Journal of African Economies*, **13**(2), 199–239.

Clausing, K. A. (2001), 'Trade Creation and Trade Diversion in the Canada–United States Free Trade Agreement,' *Canadian Journal of Economics*, **34**(3), 677–94.

De Melo, J., A. Panagariya and D. Rodrik (1993) 'The New Regionalism: A Country Perspective,' in *New Dimensions in Regional Integration*, J. De Melo and A. Panagariya (eds), Cambridge: Cambridge University Press.

Feenstra, R. C. (2004) *Advanced International Trade: Theory and Evidence*, Princeton, NJ: Princeton University Press.

Grinols, E. L. (1984), 'The Thorn in the Lion's Paw: Has Britain Paid Too Much for Membership in the Common Market,' *Journal of International Economics*, **16**, 271–93.

Head, K. and J. Ries (2004), 'Regionalism within Multilateralism: The WTO Trade Policy Review of Canada,' *The World Economy*, **27**(9), 1377–99.

Kemp, M. C. and H. Wan Jr. (1976), 'An Elementary Proposition Concerning the Formation of Customs Unions,' in *Three Topics in the Theory of International Trade: Distribution, Welfare and Uncertainty*, M.C. Kemp (ed.), Amsterdam: North Holland.

Krishna, P. and Panagariya, A. (2002) 'On Necessarily Welfare-Enhancing Free Trade Areas,' *Journal of International Economics*, **57**, 353–67.

Krugman, P. (1991), 'The Move to Free Trade Zones,' in *International Economics and International Economic Policy: A Reader*, 2nd edition in P. King (ed.), New York: McGraw Hill.

Laird, S. (1999), 'Regional Trade Agreements: Dangerous Liaisons?' *The World Economy*, **22** (9) 1179–200.

Lipsey, R. G. (1960), 'The Theory of Customs Unions: a General Survey,' *Economic Journal*, **70** (279), 496–513.

Richardson, M. (1993), 'Endogenous Protection and Trade Diversion,' *Journal of International Economics*, **34**, 309–24.

Roberts, B. A. (2004), 'A Gravity Study of the Proposed China–ASEAN Free Trade Area,' *The International Trade Journal*, **18** (4) 335–53.

Robinson, S. and K. Thierfelder (2002), 'Trade Liberalisation and Regional Integration: The Search for Large Numbers,' *The Australian Journal of Agricultural and Resource Economics*, **46** (4), 1377–99.

Romalis, J. (2005), 'NAFTA's and CUSFTA's Impact on International Trade,' NBER Working Paper 11059.

Viner, J. (1950), *The Customs Union Issue*, New York: Carnegie Endowment for International Peace.

WTO (1999), *World Trade Organization: the Legal Texts*, Cambridge, UK: Cambridge University Press.

WTO (2006), Web document, World Trade Organization, Regional Trade Agreements. Available at: http://www.wto.org/english/tratop_e/region_e/region_e.htm.

12 Rules of origin and tariff circumvention
Sarah Lang and James Gaisford

Introduction

Tariff circumvention occurs when an outside country attempts to ship goods to a country inside a free trade area via a second member country, which has a lower tariff, so as to avoid a higher tariff at the final destination. Consider an example loosely based in history where Poland had a high tariff on tomato paste and the Czech Republic had a lower tariff. The two countries participated in a free trade area – the Central European Free Trade Agreement (CEFTA) – where goods could be shipped tariff-free between the countries, but each country maintained its own external trade barriers. Outside countries such as China, then, would appear to have had an incentive to ship through the Czech Republic when they exported tomato paste to Poland provided that the tomato paste qualified for tariff-free access from the Czech Republic to Poland and the additional transport and transaction costs were negligible. Such shipments through the Czech Republic would circumvent the higher Polish Tariff.

One of the primary roles of 'Rules of Origin', which identify the country where a good is deemed to have originated, is to prevent such tariff circumvention. When appropriate rules of origin were incorporated into CEFTA to identify the tomato paste as a good from China rather than the Czech republic, then the tomato paste was no longer exempt from the Polish tariff. Consequently, the incentives for shipment through the Czech Republic disappeared.

This chapter explores the use of rules of origin in the context of regional trade agreements (RTAs). In addition to providing a mechanism to forestall tariff circumvention, however, rules of origin have the potential to act as a new form of protectionism in two related ways. First, stricter rules of origin typically reduce the extent of new trade creation in final goods between member countries within a free trade area. Second, stricter rules of origin also lead to greater trade diversion with respect to trade with outside countries in intermediate goods because there are significantly increased incentives to produce intermediate goods within an RTA so that final goods will not be subject to tariffs.

We begin by considering when and why tariff circumvention is likely to be a problem. We then consider the roles of rules of origin and the criteria that are applied in determining the country in which a good originates. Prior to concluding, we examine a simple tariff circumvention case that involved the shipment of Brazilian citrus products to the US through Caribbean Basin countries and a more complex case that involved a rules-of-origin dispute between Canada and the US over Honda automobiles.

When is tariff circumvention a 'problem'?

Situations of tariff circumvention and related situations such as (import) quota circumvention cannot occur when an RTA adopts common external barriers. Consequently, customs unions, common markets and economic unions, such as the EU (European Union) do not have to worry about tariff circumvention. Further, the 'single market' of the EU eliminates virtually all customs-related procedures from internal borders. Tariff circumvention, therefore, is only a problem in free-trade areas and other similar preferential trading situations such as the US Caribbean Basin Initiative where the participating countries maintain their own different tariffs and non-tariff barriers.[1]

Within free trade areas, tariff circumvention is regarded as a problem for two reasons. First, and most obviously, the government of the high-tariff country loses tariff revenue. Second, tariff circumvention provides unintended trade liberalization for outsider countries without any reciprocal concessions. These two considerations have an interesting implication in the likely event that trade policy is politically motivated. Suppose that when governments set tariffs, they focus predominantly on producer interests and their own revenue, while largely ignoring consumers. If there were no mechanism in place to prevent tariff circumvention, it would always be individually rational for higher-tariff countries in an RTA to lower their tariff and slightly undercut the lowest-tariff member country. Taken to its extreme, this would lead to a free-trade Nash equilibrium where all external as well as internal tariffs were completely removed.[2] Such an extreme non-cooperative outcome is unlikely in reality since the countries are already assumed to be cooperating in a free trade area. Nevertheless, the analysis does suggest that there will be strong incentives to expand coordination to prevent tariff circumvention either indirectly, by harmonizing external trade barriers, or directly.

The above analysis may also appear to suggest that, when tariff circumvention occurs, the combined government revenue of the two countries will fall. This, however, is not necessarily true. Imports may rise sufficiently to counteract the lower tariff rate and give rise to an increase in combined government revenue of the member countries. Further, not only is national welfare likely to rise in the low-tariff country, which obtains extra revenue when tariff circumvention occurs, but national welfare could also rise in the high-tariff country. For example, suppose that the tariff rate is equal to zero in the low-tariff country and the high-tariff country is an ultra-small country with no power whatsoever over the world price. From the perspective of the high-tariff country, tariff circumvention has the same effect as a unilateral move to free trade. For a small country, moving from a positive tariff regime to free trade always increases national welfare. In general, such a welfare gain for the high tariff country is more likely the lower is the tariff rate applied by the low-tariff country and the smaller its own influence over the world price.

Figure 12.1 helps to clarify the analysis of tariff circumvention. Countries A and B, which might represent Poland and the Czech Republic from the initial tomato paste example, both import from the rest of the world. The import demand curves of A and B are DM_A and DM_B respectively, and the world price is P_W, which for the moment is assumed to be constant. Country A's tariff, T_A, is larger than B's tariff, T_B, and therefore, A's initial domestic price prior to the formation of the free trade area, P_A0, is greater than B's initial domestic price, P_B0. The initial imports of Country A are M_A0, while those of Country B are M_B0. Consequently, the initial tariff revenue of A is $F+J$ dollars and that of B is H dollars. If A and B form a free trade area, then in country B, the domestic price remains at P_B0 and the net level of net imports remains at M_B0. If there are no provisions to prevent tariff circumvention, all imports to A will be shipped through B. This causes a decline in the domestic price in A to P_A1, which is equal to P_B0. The influx of additional imports arising due to tariff circumvention, which are shown by the arrow labeled C/D in Figure 12.1, increase the level of imports to M_A1.

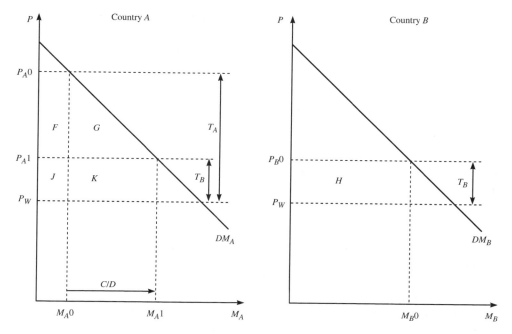

Figure 12.1   Tariff circumvention and import displacement

The only change from the formation of the free trade area for country B is that it collects tariff revenue on the imports of M_A1 destined for A as well as its own net imports of M_B0. Consequently, government revenue and overall welfare, or total surplus, increases by $J+K$ dollars for Country B. Since government revenue declines in A by $F+J$ dollars, the change in revenue for the two countries jointly is $K-F$, which happens to be positive in Figure 12.1 but could be negative in other situations. In Country A, the private sector experiences an unambiguous gain in net consumer surplus or importer surplus equal to $F+G$ dollars due to the lower domestic price. Aggregating the changes in importer surplus and government revenue gives a change in total surplus of $G-J$ dollars in Country A, which could, in principle, be positive or negative. Figure 12.1 has been constructed to show a special case where area G exceeds area J so that here is a gain in A's overall welfare from tariff circumvention. Considered together, the two countries experience an unambiguous economic efficiency gain of $G+J$ dollars conditional on a constant world price. Since country A now demands more, however, the world price will tend to rise. Since this hurts countries A and B individually and jointly, the overall changes in welfare, which arise from tariff circumvention and the induced change in the world price, are ambiguous for country B and for the countries considered jointly as well as for A.

While tariff circumvention does not automatically run counter to a country's national interest, it is incongruous with the typical political reality where the vested interests of producers are a key driver of trade policy. Member countries in a free trade area, thus, are very unlikely to allow tariff circumvention to persist. Before proceeding, however, it is crucial to note that simply eliminating tariff circumvention often will not forestall the arbitrage process shown in Figure 12.1. If the domestic production in B is greater than or equal to M_A1, then products legitimately originating in B will fully displace imports from the rest of the world in A's market, while imports from the rest of the world will compensate for the displacement of B's domestic production in its own market. After this import displacement the net imports of B are still M_B0 and the imports of A are still M_A1! While the political appearances may have changed, eliminating tariff circumvention may have no economic effects whatsoever and, at best, is likely to have only limited effects.[3]

Roles for rules of origin
Rules of origin (ROOs) are central to controlling tariff circumvention. It is important to distinguish between preferential and non-preferential ROOs. National governments implement non-preferential ROOs unilaterally whereas preferential ROOs are typically a feature that is included in RTAs between countries. Non-preferential ROOs are clearly necessary for keeping trade statistics and for country of origin labeling, but they are also important for identifying products with countries for government procurement purposes, antidumping and countervailing duty cases, administering import quotas and tariff-rate quotas, and so on. Preferential ROOs define the products eligible for tariff free access between member countries in an RTA or similar preferential trading arrangement. As such, it is preferential ROOs that are the primary focus of this chapter.

Since ROOs have gradually evolved with the global trading system, they went unmonitored by the GATT for many years. During this unregulated period, governments began to use ROOs for protectionist purposes with increasing frequency (LaNasa III 1995). Stringent preferential ROOs, for example, tend to divert intermediate as well as final good production inside RTAs so that the final goods will qualify for tariff-free movement within the RTA. In 1987 the US International Trade Commission (ITC) advanced suggestions to place disciplines on the use of ROOs (Morici 1992: 2), and eventually, the Uruguay Round negotiations led to an Agreement on Rules of Origin under the World Trade Organization (WTO) umbrella. The agreement deals substantively with non-preferential ROOs, but it also includes an annex on preferential ROOs. Both types of ROOs are supposed to be transparent, impartially applied, non-trade distorting and defined using a positive standard stating what does 'confer origin' (WTO 1999).

How rules of origin work
A central tenet of both preferential and non-preferential ROOs is that the country that is designated as the origin for a good should be the one 'where the last substantial transformation has been carried out' (WTO 1999: 214). The two primary criteria used to determine where the 'last substantial transformation' occurred are: (a) the change of tariff classification test and (b) the ad valorem or percentage test. The specified operations test is a third method that is sometimes used, often in conjunction with one or both of the other procedures. Within a single RTA, such as the North American Free Trade Agreement (NAFTA), each criterion is often used in different sectors.[4]

The ad valorem *criterion*
The *ad valorem* or percentage test calculates the percentage of the product's cost that is designated as originating in a particular country – say a preferred partner country within

an RTA. Basically by adding up the value of country-specific inputs and comparing this with the total cost of production, the *ad valorem* test establishes the percentage of the product's costs attributable to the partner. If this percentage meets the requirement, then the product is considered to originate in the partner and, therefore, will receive duty-free status. For example, for passenger automobiles NAFTA uses an *ad valorem* test that requires 62.5 percent of the net cost to come from a NAFTA country.

While the *ad valorem* test has empirical benefits, it's not problem-free. First, the definition of the *ad valorem* test requires setting up standard calculations that estimate the user cost of capital or contribution of capital to total cost. Differences in calculation procedures can cause differences and disagreements in measurements. Furthermore, different industries may be deemed to warrant different *ad valorem* cutoffs because of diversity in manufacturing processes. These different percentage requirements allow for industry lobbyists to argue for changes in the percentage tests to protect their interests as we discuss further below.

The *ad valorem* criterion is frequently accompanied by a *de minimus* or general tolerance rule and it sometimes include roll-up or roll-down provisions in assessing the origins of intermediate inputs used in the production of a final good. A general tolerance rule simply allows an imported input to be ignored if it constitutes a sufficiently low percentage of the cost of a product. Roll-up and roll-down systems are somewhat more complex. Of course, if one country used an input from a second country to produce an intermediate good, the intermediate good would be designated as a product of the first country provided that it satisfied the *ad valorem* criterion. If the intermediate good were then used in manufacturing a final product, a role-up rule would allow the intermediate good to be counted as having 100 percent content from the first country (Ghoneim 2003: 607). Consider an example from DeHousse *et al.* (2002) relating to the Egyptian–European Partnership Agreement, in which textiles and apparel from Egypt receive preferential access to the EU. Suppose that fibers from an outside country such as China are spun into yarn in Egypt and that the spinning process accounts for 60 percent of the cost of the yarn, which exceeds EU's *ad valorem* threshold for the yarn to be considered Egyptian. If the yarn were shipped to Italy to be used as an input to embroider shirts, the yarn would be treated as 100 percent Egyptian using the roll-up rule. On the other hand, using a roll-down provision, the yarn would be treated as 0 percent Egyptian if it failed to meet the EU's *ad valorem* threshold. Since Egypt is a preferred country, the role-up rule would then allow a greater proportion of other inputs to originate outside the EU in this particular example. Roll-up and roll-down provisions also ease the computational problems in implementing *ad valorem* tests since only the preceding step of production is considered.

The change of tariff classification criterion

The change of tariff classification test is the second important methodology employed in ROOs. This is the default test in NAFTA, which applies except where *ad valorem* and/or other methodologies are specified for products such as automobiles and auto parts, and textiles and apparel. The change in tariff classification test generally uses the Harmonized (Tariff) System, which separates products into major categories called chapters and then further separates them into subcategories called classifications and then further subcategories called headings and subheadings. In order for a product to be considered to originate in a given country, say a preferred country in a free trade area, it must go through a change in category due to a production process in the preferred country. Depending on the product, the extent of the required change will differ. Where some products only require a change in their subheading, others will require a classification change in order to be labeled as a preferred-country product (Morici 1992: 8–9). Nevertheless, the benefit of the change of tariff classification is that all countries using the Harmonized System will have uniform and transparent product tests. Like the *ad valorem* test, however, the change of tariff classification test leaves opportunities for governments to administer these tests in a protectionist way.

The specified operations criterion
A third methodology that is used in rules of origin is the specified operations test where a product is deemed to originate in a country if it has undergone specific steps in manufacturing or processing. For instance, as part of its non-preferential ROOs for textiles, the US permitted a 'four operations rule' in determining the country of origin. The four operations rule stated that a textile was considered to originate in a country if '[d]yeing of fabric and printing, [was] accompanied by two or more of the following operations: bleaching, shrinking, fulling, napping, decating, permanent stiffening, weighting, permanent embossing or moireing' (Dehousse *et al.* 2002: 71). Continuing with an example from Dehousse *et al.* (2002), a scarf made from Chinese silk that was cut and woven in China, could then be exported to Italy where the scarf was dyed, printed, shrunk, and permanently embroidered (embossed). Under the four operations rule, such a scarf would be labeled as originating in Italy. The protectionist potential of seemingly innocuous changes in ROOs is illustrated by the US decision to terminate the four operations rule in 1996. Overnight the identical scarf in the example would have become a Chinese product. Consequently, it would be subject to much stricter US quotas on Asian textiles and apparel and the style premium associated with Italian products would be lost (Dehousse *et al.* 2002: 75). The change in the US ROOs initiated a major trade dispute with the EU, which was eventually resolved by the partial reinstatement of the four operations rule. To protect the American cotton and wool textile industries, however, the new US ROOs excluded wool and some cotton accessories from the four operations rule (Dehousse *et al.* 2002: 80).

Preferential rules of origin in practice
The attempt to liberalize global trade by forming free trade areas and other similarly structured preferential trading arrangements has created trade problems as well as benefits for the countries involved. Two case studies – the first where the political dimension is relatively innocuous and the second where the underlying politics is more pernicious – illustrate how preferential ROOs have been used within RTAs.

World citrus markets in the 1980s
In 1983 against the backdrop of the Cold War, the US government implemented the Caribbean Basin Initiative in an attempt to improve the economies of 27 poor neighboring Caribbean countries by reducing tariffs to increase trade (Fairchild 1988: 94). Even with the reduction of tariffs on citrus products, less fertile soil conditions in the Caribbean countries meant that the US industry still had relatively low costs. Consequently, the

Caribbean Basin Initiative did not threaten much direct harm to the US citrus industry, even though there was a significant increase in citrus imports. The real danger to the US citrus industry came in the form of tariff circumvention. Brazil, a large producer of citrus and citrus products, could easily circumvent tariffs by shipping its produce through Caribbean countries (Fairchild 1988: 94). Given that the Caribbean countries are conveniently located between Brazil and the US, Brazilian citrus exports would undergo a minimal addition in transportation costs if they were shipped via a Caribbean country. In this situation, the Brazilian citrus products could circumvent the US tariff.

Not surprisingly, the US citrus industry complained, and in the late 1980s preferential ROOs were introduced into the Caribbean Basin Initiative to prevent tariff circumvention. Since minimal processing was involved in the Brazilian citrus case, the solution to simple tariff circumvention was relatively straightforward. In other more complicated manufacturing cases, the issues become considerably more complex and depend crucially on whether intermediate inputs from outside countries have undergone 'substantial transformation' in member countries.

Honda automobiles case in the 1990s

In 1989, partially to take advantage of the new Canada–US Free Trade Agreement (FTA), the Honda Motor Company became the first major Japanese auto manufacturer to set up assembly plants in North America. Sales of the Honda Civic surged so that it quickly became the top seller in its class in North America causing serious concern to the 'Big-Three' American automakers, General Motors, Ford and Chrysler (Cantin and Lowenfeld 1993: 379).

Under the Canada–US FTA, auto products had to meet a 50 percent North American content requirement to obtain duty-free status (External Affairs Canada 1987). Civic engines were manufactured in the US using imported Japanese parts and US aluminum and iron. The engines were then shipped to Canada where they were assembled into the final Honda Civic product. A large proportion of the Civic cars were then exported back to the US. Honda claimed both the engines and the cars met the *ad valorem* content requirement for duty-free cross-border movement. Government decisions on these claims were finally announced in 1992. Whereas Canada accepted that the engines were a US product, the US did not accept that the cars were Canadian. As a result, Honda was charged over $17 million in back payment for tariffs on the Civics imported to the US from Canada (Cantin and Lowenfeld 1993: 380).

The dispute over Hondas hinged on the use of roll-up and roll-down systems (Inama 2004). Honda insisted that under the change in tariff classification and *ad valorem* criteria, the US-manufactured engines met the 50 percent threshold to move tariff-free to Canada and, using the roll-up rule, the engines could be considered 100 percent North American in the calculation of the North American content of the cars. Ironically, US Customs maintained that the engines did not meet the 50 percent requirement and, thus, were subject to a roll-down to 0 percent in the calculation of the North American content of the cars. By applying the roll-down system, US Customs calculated that the Civics had only 45.87 percent North American content (Cantin and Lowenfeld 1993: 381).[5]

While there appear to have been questionable calculations both by Honda and the US government, political considerations are central to this dispute over ROOs (Cantin and Lowenfeld 1993: 380). Honda, a Japanese multinational corporation, contended that capricious policy by the US was increasing their costs. The Canadian government was worried that, simply to avoid US tariffs, Japanese automakers would favor US locations for future assembly plants at the expense of Canada and Canadian jobs. In addition to generating government revenue and potentially furthering future job-creation in the US, the strict US government stance on ROOs placated the politically-important Big-Three American auto producers, which gained a competitive boost from the increased trade costs of their Japanese rival.

This dispute was resolved indirectly through the NAFTA negotiations, which concluded in 1994. The required North American content ROO for the auto industry was progressively bumped up to 62.5 percent. NAFTA also dissolved some rules that allowed for political manipulation, such as roll-up and roll-down systems (see, Morici 1992, and Johnson n.d).[6]

Conclusion

While governments frequently extol the virtues of Regional Trade Agreements, preferential rules of origin may often dilute the potential benefits. In order to prevent tariff circumvention of the type that arose in the Brazilian citrus case, it is understandable that preferential rules of origin become a foundational element of free trade areas and other preferential trading arrangements where the participating countries maintain their own tariffs and non-tariff barriers. Nevertheless, similar or even identical economic effects may arise from import displacement even if tariff circumvention is eliminated by rules of origin. Further, compliance with preferential rules of origin entails significant transaction costs for businesses, which reduce both trade volumes and gains from trade. As the Honda case clearly demonstrates, rules of origin also create the potential for an entirely new class of trade disputes.

Moreover, political pressure often results in stringent rules of origin that have two types of protectionist effects. First and most obviously, the extent of internal trade creation between participating countries in downstream goods is limited. Some exporters or potential exporters are disqualified from tariff-free cross-border access because the proportion of intermediate imports from outside countries that they use is deemed to be too high. In the Honda case, for example, impediments to trade in cars arose because of questions with respect to the origin of their engines. This diminution of trade creation occurs even in cases where the pattern of tariff rates on intermediate goods is either neutral or biased against the would-be exporting member (that is, the member wishing to export the final good has a tariff on the intermediate input that is greater than or equal to that in the member that would receive the final good).

The second type of protection that arises from preferential rules of origin is that there is trade diversion away from outside countries for upstream or intermediate goods. In order to be able to move downstream goods on a tariff free-basis between members, there is a greater incentive to produce upstream inputs within the RTA.[7] Indeed, even in an RTA with common external trade barriers, preferential rules of origin can be put in place with the protectionist effect, if not the intent, of limiting internal trade creation and accentuating external trade diversion.

The analysis in the chapter points to a variety of significant problems with preferential rules of origin. While the WTO Agreement on Rules of Origin provides some disciplines to non-preferential rules of origin, the extent of direct coverage for preferential rules of origin is limited to an Annex. Current moves to clarify the multilateral disciplines for rules of origin are certainly useful, and future moves to tighten them would be constructive as well. In the meantime, however, there is an obvious alternative to excessive reliance on preferential rules of origin for countries that are serious about regional trade liberalization. When RTAs are formed, the role of preferential rules of origin can be minimized if the member countries choose to adopt common external trade barriers and, thus, integrate beyond the level of a free trade area to at least the level of a customs union. Countries should definitely consider this customs-union alternative.

Notes

1. Different types of RTAs are discussed in depth in Chapter 8.
2. This is reminiscent of a standard Bertrand price-setting oligopoly with homogeneous goods.
3. We have seen that eliminating tariff circumvention has no economic effect if B's domestic production is greater than or equal to $M_A 1$. By extension, eliminating tariff circumvention will be fully effective in preserving the initial domestic price in country A only if B's domestic production would be less than or equal to $M_A 0$ at a price of $P_A 0$, and it will preserve all of A's initial tariff revenue only if B's domestic production would be equal to zero at a price of $P_A 0$.
4. Other methodologies dealing more directly with the tariff circumvention problem are possible. From its inception the GATT has specified a net tariff approach where the only the difference in tariff payments must be paid when a product originating from an outside country is shipped directly from a low-tariff country to a high-tariff country within a free trade area without transformation. Such a procedure could be extended to cases where goods are produced in member countries using raw materials or components from outside countries. A major flaw in this system, and with ROOs in general, is the significant transaction costs required for compliance.
5. In a further twist, the US was simultaneously battling France over the North American content of the Honda Accord engine. The Accord engines were manufactured at a separate US plant from the Civic engines. France contended that the Accord engines, which were manufactured in a separate plant from the Civic engines, did not meet the necessary content requirements to be considered a US product. The US, however, claimed that these engines did meet the American-content requirements, and consequently, that the engines should not be subject to Japanese quota restrictions on exports to the EU (see Inama 2004: 19).
6. It has been suggested that tight rules of origin coupled with regional value content requirements seriously eroded Mexico's net benefits from NAFTA (Morici 1992: 16–17). For example, Mexico's potential advantage in labour-intensive assembly and manufacturing plants was weakened by because of strict limits on the use of non-North American parts and components.
7. Calculations provided by Cadot *et al.* (2002) appear to suggest that the preferential ROOs within NAFTA do exert considerable protectionist drag on the potential gains from trade liberalization.

References

Cadot, O., J. deMelo, A. Estevadeordal, A. Suwa-Eisermann and B. Tumurchudur (2002), 'Assessing the Effect of NAFTA's Rules of Origin,' Web document, Laboratoire d'Economie Appliquee, June. Available at: http://www.inra.fr/Internet/Departements/ESR/UR/lea/document.htm.

Cantin, F. P. and A. F. Lowenfeld (1993), 'Rules of Origin, The Canada–U.S. FTA, and the Honda Case,' *The American Journal of International Law*, **87**(3), 375–90.

Dehousse, F., K. Ghemar and P. Vincent (2002), 'The EU–US Dispute concerning the New American Rules of Origin for Textile Products,' *Journal of World Trade,* **36**(1), 67–84.

External Affairs Canada (1987), *The Canada-US Free Trade Agreement*, Ottawa, Ontario, Canada: The International Trade Communications Group.

Fairchild, G. (1988), 'The Impact of US Government Policies on the Import, Export and Distribution of Citrus,' *Journal of Food Distribution Research*, February, 91–8.

Ghoneim, A. F. (2003), 'Rules of Origin and Trade Diversion: The Case of the Egyptian–European Partnership Agreement,' *Journal of World Trade*, **37**(3), 597–692.

Inama, S. (2004), 'Rules of Origin in International Trade,' Paper presented at 'Intensive Course on Rules of Origin,' Asian Development Bank, Bangkok, 6–9 September, available at: http://www.adb.org/Documents/Events/2004/Intensive-Rules-Origin/program.asp.

Johnson, J. R. (n.d), 'NAFTA and the Trade in Automotive Goods,' Web Document, Goodman & Goodman and the Fraser Institute. Available at: http://oldfraser.lexi.net/publications/books/assess_nafta/auto_goods.html.

LaNasa III, J. A. (1995), 'An Evaluation of the Uses and Importance of Rules of Origin, and the Effectiveness of the Uruguay Round's Agreement on Rules of Origin in Harmonizing and Regulating Them,' Web Document New York University School of Law, Jean Monnet Center. Available at: http://www.jeanmonnetprogram.org/papers/96/9601ind.html.

Morici, P. (1992), 'NAFTA Rules of Origin and Automotive Content Requirements,' Web Document, University of Maine and Fraser Institute, Nov. 18. Available at: http://oldfraser.lexi.net/publications/books/assess_nafta/origin.html.

WTO (1999), *World Trade Organization: the Legal Texts*, Cambridge, UK: Cambridge University Press.

13 Economies of scale, imperfect competition and market size

Michael Benarroch

Explaining the causes and consequences of international trade has been a central focus of both the theoretical and empirical literature dealing with international trade. Prior to the 1980s, trade theorists generally employed two international trade models, the Heckscher–Ohlin–Samuelson Model (HOS) and the Ricardian Model, to help understand the world of international economics. Both of these models use a market structure characterized by perfect competition and constant returns to scale (CRS) in production. These models predict that trade will occur across countries with either factor endowment or technological differences, and across countries that export 'different goods', inter-industry trade. By 1980 however, there was a growing body of empirical evidence that pointed to the fact that not all trade followed this pattern (Grubel and Lloyd 1975).

While trade models based on perfect competition shaped trade policy prior to 1980, models with imperfect competition, 'New Trade Theory', have gained prominence since that time. These new theories have spawned a generation of trade models based on imperfect competition in product markets, increasing returns to scale (IRS) in production and intra-industry trade (IIT), trade across similar goods. This innovation in trade theory has led to an analysis of international trade and policy with market structures such as oligopolies, monopolies, and monopolistic competition (MC). A central feature of this literature is that trade can occur across either similar countries, countries with the same technologies and factor endowments, or across 'similar goods', intra-industry trade.

With this in mind, the purpose of this chapter is to consider the causes and consequences of IIT rather than inter-industry trade. While there are many models of imperfect competition that can generate IIT, this chapter will only consider the impact of monopolistic competition on the international trade literature. The main focus of the chapter will be to explain how IIT and monopolistic competition can alter the basic predictions of trade theory with respect to the effects of trade liberalization on the pattern of trade and gains from trade.

The chapter proceeds as follows. The next section provides a brief overview of the measures used to compute the value of intra-industry trade. The third section presents an overview of the model of monopolistic competition and its predictions for the pattern of trade and gains from trade. In the fourth section new directions for research are discussed. In particular, the model is used to show how trade liberalization with IIT and MC can be used to explain the rising wage gap between skilled and unskilled labour and the impact of trade liberalization on the environment.

Measuring intra-industry trade

Intra-industry trade refers to two way trade between countries but across the same or similar products. This type of trade can occur across horizontally differentiated products, goods that are slightly differentiated but have similar prices, such as toothpaste, laundry detergent or candy bars, or it can occur across products that have different characteristics and prices, vertically differentiated IIT, for example, automobiles.[1]

An empirical measure of IIT trade first appeared in Balassa (1966) but it was Grubel and Lloyd (1975) who developed a simple Index (*I*) that has become the standard measure of the extent IIT in the literature. According to Grubel and Lloyd the IIT index for any given industry, *i*, is given by:

$$I_i = 1 - \frac{|X_i - M_i|}{X_i + M_i} \tag{13.1}$$

where X_i is the value of exports and M_i is the value of imports in any industry *i*. To ensure that the value of the index is always between zero and one, $0 \geq I \geq 1$ the numerator is given by the absolute value of exports minus imports. A value of $I_i = 1$ suggests that all trade in the industry is IIT. That is, the value of exports in the sector is equal to the value of imports. Alternatively, a value of zero implies that there is no IIT in the sector.

One of the advantages of this index is that it can be used to measure intra-industry trade at any level of aggregation. The IIT Index can be aggregated, or summed, across a particular industry or country, in which case one would take a weighted average of trade across all sectors.[2] At the two-digit level of aggregation, *i* represents entire industries such as food and live animals, manufactured goods, machinery and transport equipment and so on. At lower levels of aggregation, *i* consists of a more refined definition of an industry such as meat and meat preparations, dairy products and birds' eggs, rubber manufactures, metalworking machinery, and so on.

Equation 13.1 can be used to calculate values for IIT across countries. Table 13.1 reports the aggregate value of *I* for eight different countries and three time periods employing two-digit World Bank SIC data. The data clearly show that IIT is both highly prevalent across countries and increasing in importance. In all the countries, the index shows that the degree of IIT has risen over time. Moreover, for six of the eight countries the index of IIT exceeds 0.7 indicating that over 70 per cent of trade at the two digit industry level is intra-industry trade.

Though the Grubel and Lloyd Index has become the standard measure of IIT within the international trade literature, it is not without its shortcomings. First and foremost,

Table 13.1   Grubel–Lloyd intra-industry trade index

Country	1980	1990	1999
Argentina	0.33	0.36	0.41
Canada	0.65	0.71	0.74
France	0.86	0.87	0.87
Germany	0.68	0.77	0.80
Great Britain	0.80	0.87	0.87
Japan	0.33	0.41	0.51
South Korea	0.60	0.60	0.72
United States	0.75	0.78	0.78

Source: Trade data is from the *World Bank Trade and Production Database 1976–1999*

the index is very sensitive to the level of aggregation. The greater the level of industry aggregation employed the higher is the value for *I*. Conversely, the degree of IIT declines or completely disappears at greater levels of industry aggregation. This occurs because a large degree of two-way trade occurs at lower levels of aggregation, for example across the category of food and live animals, but as the definition of the industry becomes more refined, for example articles of natural cork which exists at the four digit level of aggregation, there is less IIT. A second problem with the Grubel–Lloyd measure is that without overall trade balance the value of exports cannot be equal to the value of imports so that the aggregate IIT Index can never equal one. In this case, the measure is biased downwards. Grubel and Lloyd (1975) suggest adjusting the index value upwards as the trade imbalance increases to overcome this problem. There is however, little consensus in the literature as to how to correct for the problem of trade imbalance.[3]

Monopolistic competition and intra-industry trade

In this section, and the remainder of the chapter, a simple model of monopolistic competition and IIT is developed and employed to explain the role of IIT and highlight the differences between the standard trade model with inter-industry trade and the model with IIT. The model is based primarily on Krugman (1979, 1980) and Helpman and Krugman (1985).

There are a number of defining features of the monopolistically competitive trade model that differ from those found in the standard trade models. To begin, consider the production side of the model. It is assumed that that there exists only one good in the world, a differentiated good produced with monopolistic competition.[4] There are many varieties, *n*, of this differentiated product and it is produced in at least two countries. This differentiated good is produced within one sector, or industry, but each variety of the good has slightly different characteristics. Under the assumption that consumers desire to consume many different varieties of the good, the possibility of trade across varieties, intra-industry trade, arises. In the standard HOS trade model conversely, all goods are assumed to be homogeneous so that a country trades one type of good for another, inter-industry trade.

Second, it is assumed that all firms regardless of location employ the same technology to produce all varieties. This technology exhibits increasing returns to scale at the firm level. As firm level output expands, average costs decline. Given that the market is characterized by monopolistic competition, there is free entry into the market. If firms are earning positive economic profits new firms enter the market. This implies that in equilibrium, economic profits equal zero. Moreover, because there are increasing returns to scale at the firm level, each variety of the differentiated good is produced by only one firm. Under these assumptions, average costs are a positive function of three factors, the number of firms in the industry, unit costs and fixed costs. Average costs, on the other hand, are inversely related to market size.[5]

On the demand side, it is assumed that consumers have a love of variety.[6] This implies that consumers desire to consume some of each variety of the differentiated good. Consumers thus purchase some of every variety. To simplify matters further, assume that each consumer spends a constant fraction of their income on each variety so that demand for each variety of the differentiated good is the same. In equilibrium, where supply is equal to demand, each variety is then produced in equal amounts at the same average cost and price. Under this scenario, increased competition will cause prices to decline. As the number of firms, or varieties, expands price must decline in order to clear the market. Further, price is directly related to unit or marginal costs.[7]

The model thus treats each differentiated good symmetrically on both the demand and supply side so that price is the same across all firms. Setting average costs equal to price yields the equilibrium number of varieties for a given market size and unit cost. Under this framework, the number of firms falls as unit costs rise and increases as market size expands.

In this highly symmetric world where all firms employ the same technology and face the same demand conditions, trade is not driven by comparative advantage, since prices are the same for all varieties. Nevertheless, there still exist potential gains from international trade. In particular, if one assumes that there are two countries each producing a set of differentiated products, international trade serves two important functions: (a) it expands the size of the market by allowing producers in each country to gain access to foreign markets; and (b) it increases the number of varieties available to consumers. Both of these results serve to put downward pressure on the price level for each variety.

In the trading equilibrium, as in the closed economy, each variety is produced by only one firm. Each country thus completely specializes over a particular set of varieties. In opening to trade, some firms in each country, however, shut down (for example across goods that are common to both countries). If one assumes that both countries are initially the same size, that is they each produce n number of varieties in autarky, the total number of firms in the world in the trading equilibrium will be less than the number in autarky, $n^T < 2n$.[8] With the market doubling in size, each firm's output expands so that both average costs and the price level decline. Consumers are made better-off because they gain access to a greater variety of goods at lower prices.

It is important to note that in this simple model, all trade is IIT. Each country completely specializes in a range of varieties of the differentiated good, and then exports these varieties to the foreign country in return for foreign varieties. Which goods are produced in each country, however, cannot be determined without introducing additional restrictions into the model.

This simple framework can easily be expanded to include a second homogeneous good produced with constant returns to scale. In a world with two goods in which both the homogeneous and the differentiated good are produced with two factors of production, skilled and unskilled labour for example, it can be shown that each country will produce a set of differentiated goods and the homogeneous good.[9] If the homogeneous good is intensive in unskilled labour and the countries have different relative endowments of skilled and unskilled labour, the country that is relatively well endowed in unskilled labour will export both the homogeneous product and a set of varieties of the differentiated product. It would, however, be a net importer of the differentiated good, that is it imports more varieties of the good than it exports. The country well endowed in skilled labour would export only varieties of the differentiated good though it would produce both goods. Within this framework, there is both intra-industry and inter-industry trade. The IIT is motivated by economies of scale and love of variety, whereas the inter-industry trade occurs due to differences in endowments and comparative advantage. This model thus, contains features of the standard HOS approach and the IIT trade framework.

The inability of the IIT monopolistic competition model to determine a pattern of comparative advantage was in part the focus of Krugman (1980). In this paper, Krugman extends the monopolistic competition model to include transport costs. He finds that in a world with increasing returns and transportation costs, there is an incentive to locate production closest to the market where demand is largest.[10] This holds regardless of whether the good is a traded or nontraded. This incentive arises because producers desire to avoid transport costs and try to maximize the available firm level economies of scale. Countries consequently tend to export those goods, or varieties of goods, for which they have the largest domestic demand and, consequently, the lowest production costs. The pattern of trade, and comparative advantage, is driven by domestic tastes or what Krugman called the 'Home Market Effect'.

As in the previous model, market size once again matters. Smaller countries will tend to have lower wages to compensate for both their smaller market size and absence of economies of scale. Further, under this framework countries can be incompletely specialized in a particular variety. The higher are the transport costs relative to the size of the firm level economies of scale the less likely that a country will be completely specialized in a variety.[11]

Applications of the intra-industry trade model

The basic model of IIT and monopolistic competition outlined above is now commonly employed in the international trade literature. In addition to its theoretical applications, numerous authors have empirically tested the results and assumptions of the model. In this section it is not my intent to review either the theoretical or empirical literature on IIT and monopolistic competition, rather I will discuss two recent theoretical papers that link changes in trade policy to both the growing wage gap between skilled and unskilled labour and to the environment.

The first of these extensions deals with the growing wage gap between skilled and unskilled labour. There is now ample evidence that the wage gap between skilled and unskilled labour is expanding across a wide range of both developed and less developed countries (*Economist* 1996, 1999; Wood 1994; Das 2002; Zhu and Trefler 2001). Much of the literature on the wage gap has concentrated on identifying factors that have caused this widening gap. One of these explanations contends that for the United States, the growing gap has been driven by trade liberalization across skill-intensive goods (Leamer 1996). While this type of argument may be true for a particular country like the United States, it cannot explain the simultaneous expansion in the wage gap across many countries. Under the HOS framework, and as predicted by the Stolper–Samuelson Theorem, trade liberalization across goods using skilled labour abundantly would lead to a rising relative wages for skilled labour in skilled-labour abundant countries but the opposite in skill scarce countries. The empirical evidence however, points to a widening gap across many, though not all, skill scarce and abundant countries. The question then arises as to how trade economists can reconcile this dilemma?

In two recent papers, Beaulieu *et al.* (2004a,b) adopt the model of monopolistic competition and IIT to reconcile this dilemma. To explain the growing wage gap between skilled and unskilled labour they consider a model with two factors of production, skilled and unskilled labour. There are two goods, a homogeneous good produced with constant returns to scale and using unskilled labour intensively, and a differentiated good produced with monopolistic competition and employing skilled labour intensively. Tastes and technology are identical across countries and symmetric across varieties of the differentiated good and demand is uniform for each variety. As a result, a common output of each variety of the differentiated good is demanded and supplied by every country so that the domestic price of each variety is the same across all countries.

What differentiates the model in this section from that outlined previously is that there are now trade barriers on both goods in each country. Introducing trade barriers raises the possibility that prices may not be equal across goods, varieties, or countries. The trade barriers are represented by $\tau_{jc} \geq 1$ where j represents either the homogeneous good, y, or a variety of the differentiated good, n, and $c = h, f$ for the home or foreign country. For any imported product, a value of $\tau_{jc} \geq 1$ implies that there is an *ad valorem* import tariff on the variety or good. If one considers varieties of the differentiated product, the tariff then raises the price of an imported product at home, $p_{nh} = \tau_{nh} p_{nf}$.

Adjusting for relative differences in protectionism afforded to the homogeneous good, and assuming that the traditional good is the numeraire, the relative price of an imported differentiated good to the numeraire at home is raised when the home country applies a tariff on the product or when the foreign country protects its traditional good. In the case of the latter, protectionism for the homogeneous good in the foreign country raises supply of the homogeneous good in the foreign country so that the relative prices of the differentiated varieties rise. Likewise, protectionism for the traditional good at home lowers the relative price of the imported good at home.[12] The relationship between price and the extent of protectionsism also implies that if countries apply different tariffs rates domestic prices need not be equal across varieties.

As in Krugman (1995), the model developed above allows for both IIT across the varieties of the differentiated good as well as inter-industry trade between the differentiated and homogeneous good. Beaulieu *et al.* (2004a, b) find that multilateral trade liberalization across all countries engaged in IIT can, however, have very different results compared to the predictions of the HOS model. In particular, they find that this type of trade liberalization has the same effect on the wage gap across all countries engaged in IIT. In essence, since all countries export the differentiated good, multilateral trade liberalization causes the relative demand for the differentiated good to rise in every country, not just one country as in the HOS model. As a result, the relative prices of the differentiated varieties rise across all countries. Since the differentiated good is intensive in skilled labour, standard Stolper-Samuelson results suggest that the relative wage for skilled labour rises and the wage gap expands in all countries engaged in IIT. Unlike the HOS model where countries trade different products and experience the opposite effects on wages from trade liberalization, a model with IIT in which all countries export similar products, suggests that the wage gap can increase simultaneously across many countries with trade liberalization. The main requirements for this to occur are that countries be diversified (produce both types of goods), engage in IIT and liberalize trade across the differentiated product.

A second similar application of the model can be used to examine the effects of IIT trade on the environment. The use of the IIT model in this respect is motivated by two recent empirical findings. First, Antweiler *et al.* (2002) find empirical evidence showing that trade can be beneficial to the global environment in the sense that it leads to lower pollution. They explain this empirical result with a theoretical model that shows that higher pollution taxes resulting from increases in income from trade, lead to lower pollution. Second, Frankel and Rose (2004) find that there is no empirical evidence to support the creation of pollution havens resulting from trade liberalization. Pollution havens arise under the HOS model because trade liberalization leads to higher production of pollution intensive goods in countries with lax environmental policies and lower production of pollution intensive goods in countries with stricter environmental policies. Pollution intensive industries consequently, tend to agglomerate in countries with lower environmental standards.

An IIT model similar to the one developed to explain the growing wage gap between skilled and unskilled labour can also be applied to the case of the environment.[13] Several modifications to the model must however, be made to adapt the model. Specifically, one must assume that the two goods are distinguished in terms of their pollution intensity, that is, the degree to which they generate pollution as a by product of production. In particular, assume that the homogeneous good is more pollution intensive so that it generates more pollution per unit of production than the differentiated product.

As in the wage gap model, multilateral trade liberalization across all varieties of the differentiated good and all countries is found to have similar effects across countries. A lower tariff raises the relative demand of the differentiated product thereby increasing its relative price. This leads to not only a global expansion in output of the differentiated good but an increase in output for each country. Since the differentiated good is less pollution intensive than the homogeneous good, higher output of the differentiated good causes pollution levels to fall in every country. Multilateral trade liberalization thus causes production and the generation of pollution to move in the same direction in all countries. The model consequently, provides an alternative explanation to that found in Antweiler, Copeland and Taylor (2002) as to why trade liberalization can lead to lower pollution. In particular, the model shows that even without pollution taxes rising with trade, trade liberalization can lead to lower global pollution. Moreover, since multilateral trade liberalization causes changes in pollution to move in the same direction across all countries, this model of IIT provides a theoretical explanation for the empirical results found in Frankel and Rose (2005). IIT trade liberalization leads to a cleaner environment without the creation of 'Pollution Havens'. With all countries experiencing the same relative price changes, there is no incentive for 'dirty industries' to agglomerate in one country.

Summary and conclusion

The incorporation of imperfect competition and economies of scale into the international trade literature spawned both new directions for research and new insights into the causes and consequences of international trade. Rather than trade being limited to occurring between dissimilar countries producing distinctly different goods, international trade theorists were able to explain the growing volume of trade that was occurring both across similar countries and products. The chapter showed how a market structure characterized by monopolistic competition can give rise to intra-industry trade. The benefits of IIT were found to be dependent on market size and the available economies of scale. Expanding international trade provides producers with the ability to gain access to a larger market and thus increase production thereby taking advantage of the economies of scale to lower costs. Consumers are found to also benefit from trade liberalization because a greater variety of goods are made available at a lower cost.

While the monopolistic competition models used in the literature, and examined in this chapter, tend to be highly stylized, they still provide students of international trade with important insights. Arguments in favour of freer trade now centre on domestic producers gaining access to greater world markets to expand output and lower costs. This argument rests crucially on the availability of economies of scale in production. Likewise, it is often argued that consumers benefit from freer trade because liberalization will allow them have greater choice in consumption. Once again this prediction finds its roots in trade models with imperfect competition and IIT.

Notes

1. See Krugman (1980) for a model of IIT with horizontally differentiated products and Lancaster (1980) for a model of IIT with vertically differentiated products.
2. See Chapters 5 and 6 in Greenaway and Milner (1986) for a review of aggregation issues.
3. Further, suggestions for adjusting the index are reviewed in Greenaway and Milner (1986).
4. At the end of this section and in the next section of the chapter this assumption will be relaxed to allow for two goods.
5. See Krugman and Obstfield (2004) Chapter 6 for an explicit version of the model.
6. The love of variety utility curve first appeared in Dixit and Stiglitz (1977).
7. With monopolistic competition firms set prices above marginal costs.
8. The assumption of identical countries is not necessary and is assumed in this case only to simplify the analysis.
9. One could also, assume that the goods are produced with labour and capital, see Krugman (1995).
10. Note that a similar result can be derived if one assumes that countries impose tariffs or other trade restrictions rather than transport costs.
11. For empirical evidence on the home market effect see Head and Reis (2002), Davis and Weinstein (1999) and Weder (1995).
12. The exact relationship between price and the relative tariff rates is

$$p_{nh} = \frac{\tau_{yf}}{\tau_{yh}}\tau_{nh}p_{nf}$$

13. See Benarroch and Gaisford (2004) for complete details of such a model.

References

Antweiler, Werner, Brian R. Copeland and M. Scott Taylor (2001), 'Is Free Trade Good for the Environment,' *American Economic Review*, **91**(4), 877–908.

Balassa, Bella (1966), 'Tariff Reductions and Trade in Manufactures Among the Industrial Countries,' *American Economic Review*, **56**, 466–73.

Beaulieu, Eugene, Michael Benarroch and James Gaisford (2004a), 'Trade Barriers and Wage Inequality in a North–South Model with Technology Driven Intra-Industry Trade,' *Journal of Development Economics*, **75**, 113–36.

Beaulieu, Eugene, Michael Benarroch and James Gaisford (2004b), 'Intra-Industry Trade Liberalization and Trade Policy Preferences,' University of Calgary Department of Economics Working Paper, 2004–06.

Benarroch, Michael and James Gaisford (2004), 'Intra-Industry Trade Liberalization and the Environment,' University of Calgary Department of Economics Working Paper, 2004.

Das, S. P. (2002), 'Foreign Direct Investment and the Relative Wage in a Developing Country,' *Journal of Development Economics*, **67**, 55–77.

Davis, Donald R. and David E. Weinstein (1999), 'Economic Geography and Regional Production Structure: An Empirical Investigation,' *European Economic Review*, **43**(2), 379–407.

Dixit, Avinish and Joseph Stiglitz (1977), 'Monopolistic Competition and Optimum Product Variety,' *American Economic Review*, **67**(3), 297–308.

Economist (1996), 'Trade and Wages', 7 December, page 74.

Economist (1999), 'Global Pay', 8 May, Survey following page 56.

Frankel, Jeffrey A. and Andrew K. Rose (2005), 'Is Trade Good or Bad for the Environment? Sorting Out the Causality,' *Review of Economics and Statistics*, **87**(1), 85–91.

Greenaway, David and Chris Milner (1986), *The Economics of Intra-Industry Trade*, New York: Basil Blackwell.

Grubel, Herbert G. and Peter J. Lloyd (1975), *Intra-Industry Trade: Theory and Measurement of International Trade in Differentiated Products*, London: Macmillan Press Ltd.

Head, Keith and John Reies (2002), 'Increasing Returns Versus National Product Differentiation as an Explanation for the Pattern of US–Canada Trade,' *American Economic Review*, **91**(4), 859–76.

Helpman, Elhanan and Paul Krugman (1985), *Market Structure and Foreign Trade: Increasing Returns, Imperfect Competition and the International Economy*, Cambridge, MA: MIT Press.

Krugman, Paul (1979), 'Increasing Returns, Monopolistic Competition, and International Trade,' *Journal of International Economics*, **9**, 469–80.

Krugman, Paul (1980), 'Scale Economies, Product Differentiation, and the Pattern of Trade', *American Economic Review*, **70**(5), 950–59.

Krugman, Paul R. (1995), 'Increasing Returns, Imperfect Competition and the Positive Theory of International Trade,' in G. M. Grossman and K. Rogoff (eds), *Handbook of International Economics*, Vol. **3**, Amsterdam: Elsevier; 1243–80.

Krugman, Paul and Maurice Obstfeld (2003), *International Economics: Theory and Policy Sixth Edition*, Boston, MA: Addison Wesley.

Lancaster, Kelvin (1980), 'Intra-Industry Trade under Perfect Monopolistic Competition,' *Journal of International Economics*, **10**(1), 151–75.

Leamer, Edward E. (1996) 'Effort, Wages and the International Division of Labor,' NBER Working Paper W5803, Cambridge, MA: National Bureau of Economic Research.

Weder, Rolf (1995), 'Linking Absolute and Comparative Advantage to Intra-Industry Trade Theory,' *Review of International Economics*, **3**(3), 342–54.

Wood, Adrian (1994), *North–South Trade, Employment, and Inequality: Changing Fortunes in a Skill-Driven World*, Oxford: Clarendon Press.

Zhu, S. C. and D. Trefler (2001), 'Ginis in General Equilibrium: Trade, Technology and Southern Inequality,' National Bureau of Economic Research Working Paper No. 8446.

14 Trade in services
Eugene Beaulieu

Introduction

International trade in services has become a major policy issue in both developed and developing countries. The international (or offshore) outsourcing of some service activities has attracted considerable media attention in the developed world as white-collar workers in the service sector face increased international competition from outsourcing.[1] A recent article in the *Wall Street Journal* (2003) reported that white collar workers in the service sector have become a force in the anti-free trade lobby. Another article in the *Wall Street Journal* (2004) points out that it is very difficult to measure the number of jobs that are being lost to outsourcing but this number appears to be growing. The rapid spread of service trade caught many off guard. As Thomas Friedman (2005) metaphorically states in his book on globalization, he woke up one day and found that the world is flat. Friedman spends time discussing services that used to be strictly considered non-traded in nature, but are now traded internationally. He is not talking about haircuts. Rather he provides examples of software development, call centers and accounting work.

All of this attention to international trade in services may seem peculiar as, until recently, services have been treated in economic analysis as the proverbial non-tradable. Compared to goods, services are non-tradable in the sense that many services are non-storable and therefore must be produced where they are consumed. The classic example of such a non-traded service good is a haircut.

Much of the recent attention afforded trade in services is linked to the rapid growth of this previously non-traded activity. Although trade in services and foreign investment in service sectors have been growing rapidly, they started from small bases. Services remain the most closed sector of the world economy by conventional measures of openness. This is partially due to the aforementioned non-tradable nature of services, but in addition, service trade continues to be a highly protected sector of the economy in most countries. Services were excluded from the multilateral negotiations until the Uruguay Round of the General Agreement on Tariffs and Trade (GATT) and the reduction of trade barriers in the service sector faces many hurdles in the current Doha Round of negotiations. Service trade will continue to be adversely affected if the Doha Round fails to make substantive progress.[2]

Although the rapid growth in service trade has drawn the attention of both the popular media and academic literature, trade in services deserves close attention for three additional reasons. First, although services are still not as widely traded as agricultural and manufactured goods, the service sector is the largest sector in most developed and many developing countries. Second, services are even more important than their relative size implies because services are inputs into most other business activity. Third, there are some important differences between services and goods that have conceptual implications relevant for policy makers.

This chapter provides an overview of the salient aspects of trade in services and discusses what makes services trade distinct from goods trade. The chapter then provides an overview of recent trends and developments in service trade including attempts to liberalize this trade.

Overview of trade in services

What are services?

There are important conceptual and practical differences between goods and services. Nicolaides (1989) defines a service as a transaction involving an agreement to perform certain tasks. As the ubiquitous haircut example illustrates, services tend to have an intangible quality and often (though not always) require the physical presence of both client and service provider. Based on this definition, the nature of services is such that a number of issues arise in thinking about international trade in services. Services tend to be non-tradable because they are non-storable. However, the service sector encompasses much more than haircuts and similar activities. Service activities once considered non-tradable, such as accounting, have become more widely traded internationally. Copeland (2002) provides an excellent overview of the conceptual issues related to services, and more specifically international trade in services.

There are two important differences between services and goods that are not always considered, especially when one refers to haircuts as an example of services. First, services are often used as an input into the production process. Think of telephone services or accounting. In fact, so-called 'commercial services' are the largest group of industries in the service sector in most countries. Commercial services are primarily intermediate inputs. Since services are a key input into the production process, policies that affect services may have profound effects on productivity. Countries with inefficient service provision, thus, tend to have lower productivity in the manufacturing, agriculture and government sectors.

A second important difference between goods and services that is often overlooked is that services tend to be differentiated products, whereas some goods are homogeneous in nature and other goods are differentiated. Rauch (1999) classifies goods according to whether they are differentiated or homogeneous. Homogeneous goods are traded on exchanges where price differences directly reflect relative scarcity. On the other hand, differentiated goods are not traded on exchanges and price differences reflect differences in characteristics and quality that may obscure price signals. A typical differentiated good is difficult to trade internationally because of the informational difficulties. For example, according to Rauch (1999: 9) shoes are a typical differentiated product and as such

> do not have reference prices. Any observed price at another location must be adjusted for multidimensional differences in characteristics, and the adjustment depends on the varieties of shoes available at that location and the distribution of consumer preferences over varieties at that location. I claim that these informational demands are too great to permit international commodity arbitrage.

Rauch (1999) uses a gravity model to present empirical evidence that proximity and commonalities such as language and cultural background are more important for international trade in differentiated products than for trade in homogeneous goods. He finds that in 1990 approximately 65 percent of goods trade was in differentiated products. By the same criteria used by Rauch, 100 percent of service trade is in differentiated products. It is not only the non-storability aspect of services that make it difficult to trade services internationally but also that services are differentiated goods.

An important insight of the work by Rauch (1999) is that networks and search (with respect to matching between customers and differentiated goods providers) are important aspects of trade in differentiated goods and hence for trade in services. In this context there is a role for 'social capital' in the international trade of services and for personal contacts and relationship building in determining the geographic distribution of economic activity. Moreover, if there are unintended spillovers of information in networking and search then there may be a rationale for export-promotion policies.

Not only are services in principal differentiated products, but it is important to distinguish between different types, or modes, of service transactions. Unlike trade in goods, not all trade in services is based on moving the product from an exporter in one country to an importer in another country. This is only one type of service transaction. The General Agreement on Trade in Services (GATS) identifies four modes of service trade: (a) the standard cross-border trade familiar to trade in goods where physical interaction of the buyer and seller is not required; (b) consumption abroad where a client travels to the service provider (that is tourism); (c) commercial presence where the service provider sets up a facility in the client's home country; and (d) the temporary movement of natural persons where the service provider goes to the client. Signatories to the GATS are permitted to limit liberalization commitments to one or more of the four modes of service supply.

Although the different modalities give countries some flexibility when negotiating liberalization in services trade, they also complicate the negotiations. Since many types of service trade cannot be embodied in a good that is traded across borders, issues of trade policy in services often relate to international migration or investment. Only the first modality involves delivery of the service across international borders, which is typical of international trade similar to trade in goods. The other three modalities require the international movement of persons and/or international investment.

In addition to the hindrance that the different modalities place on liberalizing trade in services there are two other aspects of services that make negotiating liberalization in services difficult: some services are public goods and many service sectors face domestic regulation. For example, traditional service sectors like finance, electricity, water and telecommunications are regulated industries in almost all countries and several of these services are frequently publicly provided. Moreover, services often involve domestic regulatory issues and government policies that occur inside borders. Most goods trade avoids this issue and the policy impediments to trade in goods are 'border' policies. On the other hand, trade policy issues concerning services are commonly referred to as issues of market access. The most significant commercial policy affecting international transactions in services are domestic regulations rather than border measures. Countries tend to restrict market access for service providers through discriminatory treatment contained in laws and domestic regulations rather than through border tariffs or taxes. Therefore, liberalizing trade in services will affect domestic laws and regulations. This makes services negotiations difficult and sensitive for governments, and makes arriving at international agreements a long and complex process.

Measuring trade in services

Services have become the largest and most important sector in most economies in the world. It is estimated that the services sector now represents 60 percent of GDP on average in the Americas. For example, according to Copeland (2002), 73 percent of Canadian employment is in services, while only 14 percent of Canada's international trade is in services. This pattern is not just true of developed countries. While services have become an important part of the domestic economy in both developing and developed countries alike, services continue to represent a relatively small share of exports and imports. According to a recent report by UNCTAD (2003, p. 97), services represent 72 percent of GDP in developed countries and 52 percent in developing countries. McGuire (2002: 2) reports that the service sector typically encompasses between 40 and 60 percent of GDP and employment in developing economies and between 60 and 80 percent in developed countries.

The services sector is extremely heterogeneous including a large number of activities ranging from architecture and telecommunications to air and even space transportation.[3] Services are generally divided into 11 different industries: Business Services; Communication Services; Construction and Related Engineering Services; Distribution Services; Educational Services; Environmental Services; Financial Services; Health-Related and Social Services; Tourism and Travel-Related Services; Recreational, Cultural and Sporting Services; Transport Services; and Other Services Not Included Elsewhere. It is difficult to measure trade in services, but some data are available. According to recent statistics from the WTO (2004a) 'other commercial services' – primarily made up of business and financial services – are the largest and fastest-growing category of trade in services. These commercial services made up almost 40 percent of trade in services in 1990 and constituted over 45 percent of total trade in services by 2002. In 1990, transportation made up just less than 30 percent of services trade, while travel services were just over 30 percent. Transportation and travel services declined in relative importance between 1990 and 2002. In 2002 the three main types of trade in services were transportation services (22 percent), travel services (31 percent) and other commercial services (47 percent).

Table 14.1 Share of goods and commercial services in the total trade of selected regions and economies, 2002

	Exports			Imports		
	Value Total $ billion	Share Goods (%)	Commercial services (%)	Value Total $ billion	Share Goods (%)	Commercial services (%)
World	7900	80.1	19.9	7810	80.2	19.8
North America	1258	75.5	24.5	1640	84.9	15.1
Latin America	414	86.4	13.6	408	84.1	15.9
Western Europe	3336	77.1	22.9	3147	77.3	22.7
C./E. Europe/ Baltic States/CIS	379	84.2	15.8	358	81.8	18.2
Africa	173	82.1	17.9	165	75.6	24.4
Asia	2097	84.7	15.3	1913	80.8	19.2

Notes: Billion dollars and percentage, based on balance of payments data. Trade in goods includes significant re-exports or imports for re-exports. It is likely that measures of trade in commercial services is understated.

Source: World Trade Organization: 'International Trade Statistics 2003'

As Table 14.1 indicates, by 2002 total world trade in goods and services reached US$7900 billion and service trade was approximately 20 percent of world exports and imports. Notice that in Table 14.1 that trade in services is at least 13 percent of trade on average across all regions in the world. Services trade represents a larger share of export trade in North America (24.5 percent) than anywhere else. The services share of trade is 22.9 percent in Europe and 13.6 percent in Latin America. Almost 18 percent of African trade is in services. Services make up a larger share of total African imports (24.4 percent) than anywhere else. Service imports into North America represent 15.1 percent of North American imports. Both developing and developed countries are significantly engaged in services export and import trade. According to the WTO, services make up over 30 percent of trade in some Latin American and Asian countries.[4]

Although trade in services is growing rapidly, the sector remains relatively closed by the conventional metric of trade relative to output. According to the World Trade Organization (2004b), only one-tenth of service output enters world trade whereas trade in goods is over 50 percent of goods production. International trade in services has become a larger share of total world international trade but international trade in services is still only a small share of the world production of services. This sets services apart from agriculture and manufacturing.

In 2000 the value of cross-border trade in services amounted to US$1435 billion, or about 20 percent of total cross-border trade.[5] This measure of trade in services under-estimates the true size of international trade in services because a large proportion of service trade takes place through foreign establishments located in the export market. This mode of international trade in services, however, is not recorded in balance-of-payments statistics. The telecommunications industry provides a good example. Until recently the telecom industry in most countries was closed to foreign competition and in many countries the telecoms were state-run. Many countries have now liberalized their telecom industries and have opened the industry to foreign investment. According to UNCTAD (2003, p. 117) the communications, transport and storage industry had the fastest growing foreign direct investment (FDI) of all service industries across all countries. Thus, this service sector grew significantly due to changes in government policy, but the transactions are not recorded in trade statistics.

As discussed above, the nature of services implies that there is a non-traded element in services. Some services, such as haircuts, require proximity to clients. Since services are differentiated goods, proximity, language and networks are important factors in determining the extent of the service market for firms. International trade in such services is also likely to be under-reported because it falls under GATS Mode 4 involving the temporary movement of persons. This type of service conducted across countries does not pass through customs houses at international borders and therefore some service trade is not included in the international trade data.

Barriers to services trade
However, the non-traded nature of some services and the under-reporting of trade in services does not tell the entire story of why services are such a closed sector. The service sector faces high levels of protection at the border and often faces domestic regulations that impede market access. The non-traded nature of many service products means that until recently, services were not on the table in multilateral negotiations of tariff

reductions. These factors combine to make services one of the most protected sectors in the world economy. Hufbauer and Warren (1999) computed tariff equivalent estimates for industrial, agriculture and service sectors in several countries. They found that some service sectors like transportation and storage had 'tariff equivalents' of over 100 percent in countries such as the United States and Canada and the estimates were even higher for Brazil (143 percent) and Mexico (182 percent). Service sectors are typically afforded much higher levels of protection than are found in industrial and agricultural sectors. Only sugar has a level of protection as high as protection in the transport and storage sector.

It is important to realize that tariff estimates on broad sectors are a very superficial way of examining the impact of protection afforded the service industry. Chen and Schembri (2002) point out that measuring trade restrictions in services is a very complicated affair. They provide an overview of measuring barriers to trade in services and provide several measures of barriers and conclude that barriers in services are very high.

Liberalizing trade in services

Until recently services have not been included in negotiated agreements to reduce protection. They were not included in bilateral and regional agreements until the Canada–US Free Trade Agreement (CUSTA) in 1989 and the North American Free Trade Agreement (NAFTA) in 1994. Services were included in the Uruguay Round of the General Agreement on Tariffs and Trade (the GATT) negotiations that produced the General Agreement on Trade in Services (GATS).

There has been and continues to be a great deal of interest among a large cross-section of countries in liberalizing services trade. Interest in services trade liberalization has been strong since services became an important part of the NAFTA and this interest expanded throughout the 1990s. A large number of countries have completed some form of trade liberalization in services through bilateral (or sub-regional) arrangements. Many countries are part of the so-called 'progressive liberalization' of services trade at the multilateral level through the GATS. However, liberalization of service trade is illusive because many service sectors face domestic regulations that hamper liberalization and make negotiations difficult.

The liberalization of trade in services continues to be negotiated under the GATS as the economic importance of services continues to increase within and between countries. In Doha in 2001, WTO members agreed that countries would submit initial requests for market access commitments in services. Negotiations continue today but are characterized by a North–South divide where developing countries are limiting areas of discussion under market access.

Not only is the inclusion of services a recent phenomenon but a number of service sectors have been excluded both from regional and bilateral agreements as well as the GATS. For example these agreements exclude government services when they are provided on a non-commercial basis and are not open to competition between one or more service suppliers. Therefore, excluded services include services such as education and health care that are frequently provided almost exclusively by the government on a not-for-profit basis.[6] Other industries such as telecommunications have typically been either run or regulated by governments and until recently have been excluded from international liberalization.

Given the importance of trade in services to both developed and developing countries and the high levels of protection in service sectors it is not surprising that the need for multilateral liberalization is widely accepted. Stephenson (2001) argues that recent consensus on the need for the liberalization of trade in services is also partly explained by the expanded information and capacity for negotiating and understanding the implications of liberalized trade in this sector that has resulted from the GATS negotiations.

This general consensus that 'something oughtta be done' to reduce impediments to trade in services has been translated into a great deal of activity in this area. However, liberalizing trade in services is a complicated issue and is not simply a matter of reducing the tariff as was the case for most merchandise trade.

Potential gains
As discussed in detail above there are two important trends in the services sector that are having profound implications for international trade. First, services have become more tradable. The type of non-traded services, such as haircuts, is a declining share of the total services sector. Second, the service sector in most countries is becoming an increasingly important input into manufacturing, agriculture and services.

The structure of the economy in most industrialized countries has changed in the recent decades. Using very broad measures, the Canadian economy, for example, has moved from an economy dominated by resources and manufacturing to one where services play a major role. The share of services in Canada's GDP increased from 44.5 percent in 1951 to 65 percent in 1997, while the corresponding share for agriculture and resources has declined from 18.8 percent to 6.9 percent over the same period. At the same time, there was an important shift from intermediate inputs being comprised of 'goods' to intermediate inputs being comprised of 'services'. Beaulieu and Chen (2005) show that the share of goods as intermediate inputs decreased from 57 percent of total intermediate inputs in 1980 to 48.5 percent in 1997. Consequently, the share of services in intermediate inputs increased from 42 percent to 51 percent of total intermediate inputs over the same period.

Liberalization in services trade has important implications for less developed countries. First, imported services might complement rather than substitute for domestic services. Second, they economize on scarce domestic skilled labor that is then freed for other uses. Third, imported services may allow countries to obtain what is not otherwise available and would take considerable time and/or resources to develop. Fourth, imported services may provide crucial missing inputs that allow a country to produce and export goods in which the country has a natural comparative advantage except for the missing input.[7]

Efficiency in the export of goods of all kinds depends critically upon the quality and cost of available services. Exporters of agricultural and other basic commodities are adversely affected by inefficient or expensive banking, insurance, telecoms and transport services. Removing barriers to trade in services will likely lower prices, improve quality, and increase the variety of service products available. McGuire (2002) provides a very good survey of the literature measuring the gains from liberalizing services. First he points out that it is very difficult to measure and model the effects of liberalization in services because the models have to incorporate the various modes of trade in services. Furthermore, there is not very good information on transactions in some modes of service trade and data on restrictions in services trade is difficult to obtain and interpret. Nevertheless, McGuire (2002) surveys the studies that have been completed and a common result in these studies is that there are substantial global real income gains from liberalization in services and the gains are typically larger that those derived from liberalizing trade in agriculture and manufacturing combined.[8]

Developing countries stand to gain substantially from liberalizing their trade in services, mainly due to the productivity improvement resulting from increased imports of high-quality, differentiated, intermediate services inputs. Dee and Hanslow (2000) employ a dynamic CGE model to examine the impact of liberalizing services, agriculture and manufacturing and find that the world as a whole will be better off by about US$260 billion annually from eliminating all post-Uruguay Round trade restrictions. More than half of this, US$133 billion, would come from liberalizing services trade. Only 20 percent of the total (US$51 billion) will come from liberalizing agricultural, and 32 percent (US$83 billion) from liberalizing manufacturing. Developing economies will stand to gain US$130 billion annually from this policy change.

Konan and Maskus (2004) examine how service liberalization differs from goods liberalization in a developing economy. Their work focuses on Tunisia where, despite recent trade liberalization, service sectors remain largely closed to foreign participation and are provided at high cost relative to many other developing nations. The authors use a computable general equilibrium (CGE) model to examine the impact of liberalizing services trade with respect to restrictions on cross-border supply (mode 1 in the GATS) and on foreign ownership through foreign direct investment (mode 3 in the GATS). They find that a reduction of services barriers in a way that permits greater competition through foreign direct investment generates larger welfare gains than goods trade liberalization. Service liberalization also entails lower adjustment costs than goods-trade liberalization. Moreover, services trade liberalization stimulates economic activity in all sectors. Most of the liberalization gains come from opening markets for finance, business services, and telecommunications because these are key inputs into all sectors of the economy.

According to the World Trade Report of the WTO (2004b), there may be significant benefits from liberalizing international trade in services through the facilitation of the temporary movement of persons across national borders (Mode 4 of the GATS). According to the report, temporary labour movement can bring significant gains to national economies in three ways: (a) by stimulating other kinds of trade; (b) by supporting technology transfer and human capital development; and (c) by smoothing out cyclical variations in the demand for labor. An important aspect of temporary movement versus permanent migration is that temporary presence avoids the deeper economic and social problems associated with migration.

The issue of sovereignty and domestic policies/regulations
Article VI of GATS provides a basic framework for minimizing the distortions of trade created by domestic regulation. Under the provisions of Article VI new regulations that affect services bound by national commitments are to be 'administered in a reasonable, objective and impartial manner' (GATS Article VI, para. 1). To paraphrase Article VI member countries must provide procedures for the review of the regulation at the request of service suppliers (GATS Article VI, para. 2a); and must be 'based on objective and transparent criteria' (GATS Article VI, para. 4a); must not be 'more burdensome than necessary to ensure the quality of the services' (GATS Article VI, para. 4b); and in the case of licensing procedures must not in themselves restrict the supply of the service (GATS Article VI, para. 4c).

Structural change and globalization have created a need for regulatory reform in services under the WTO. Technological advances have led to an explosion of new goods and services. Many of these goods and services have difficulty entering markets where regulations mandate the use of goods and services based on current technologies, in order to satisfy various environmental, health, or safety concerns. Such regulations may distort trade and competition by preventing enterprises or consumers from accomplishing desired social goals by more efficient means.

New insights into the economics of regulation may make it possible to design more economically efficient regulations. Much has been learned about the incentive structures created by various techniques of regulation and their relative effectiveness in achieving desired social objectives. Too often regulatory systems seek to achieve social objectives by controlling entry into the industry by new suppliers and producers, while attention really needs to be on the behavior of suppliers with respect to particular regulatory objectives.

The globalization of production and markets has increased the cost of maintaining large national differences in regulatory standards and created pressures for harmonizing standards. Such globalization makes economic sense only where national regulations allow the adoption of the technologies, information systems, and standards across national frontiers. Large differences in national regulations that have a direct bearing on the operation of globally integrated networks or production systems add to the cost of doing business internationally. Thus domestic regulatory issues resonate strongly in the international trade of services.

Recent developments

There has recently been a great deal of activity in services negotiations. Services were included under WTO in 1995 as well as NAFTA. Like the Agreement on Agriculture, the GATS includes a so-called 'built-in agenda' whereby members are required to enter successive rounds of negotiations aimed at progressive liberalization. At Doha in November 2001, WTO members agreed to adopt the 'Negotiating Guidelines and Procedures' which stipulate that countries submit initial requests for market access commitments. Countries agreed to adopt a request-and-offer approach as the main mechanism to negotiate specific commitments on market access, national treatment and additional commitments. The submission of members' initial requests in June 2002 was the beginning of the market access phase of negotiations. Participants have been exchanging bilateral initial requests since then.

The approach to liberalization in services in the GATS is known as a 'positive list', or 'bottom-up', approach. In this approach countries schedule voluntary commitments that they can re-negotiate. According to Stephenson (2002: 3) this has led to 'a situation of very unequal obligations and undertakings in the services area'. A major shortcoming of this approach is the lack of transparency. It is impossible to get information about a sector or service in a country if that sector or service is not included on the list.

An alternative approach is the 'negative list', or 'top-down', approach. Under the 'negative list' approach in which all services and service sectors are included and considered free of trade restrictions unless they are placed on a list of exclusions or reservations. According to Stephenson (2002), most regional agreements in the Americas have adopted the 'negative list approach'. Stephenson (2002) shows that only the 1997 ASEAN agreement and the MERCOSUR adopted the positive-list approach while all the others, including NAFTA, adopted the negative-list approach. However, even MERCOSUR has moved away from the positive-list approach to adopt a hybrid 'list-or-lose' approach. According to Stephenson and Prieto (2001) the MERCOSUR adopted a variation of the positive list approach whereby annual rounds of negotiations based on the scheduling of increasing numbers of commitments in all sectors (with no exclusions) are to result in the elimination of all restrictions to services trade among the members of the group within ten years.

Another important difference between the approaches to services liberalization found in the GATS and among regional agreements is in the treatment of services and investment. In the GATS, investment is treated as one of the service modes described above. That is, investment in services entails a commercial presence (the third mode). The MERCOSUR also follows this approach. In contrast, many agreements treat investment rules in a separate chapter from disciplines on goods and services. This is the approach taken by NAFTA and the subsequent NAFTA-type agreements.

Lack of progress in the GATS

One major problem with the GATS – and perhaps with the positive-list approach – is the lack of progress. There are only a very limited number of sectors included on the national schedules (the positive-lists). According to a recent report by the International Centre for Trade and Sustainable Development (ICTSD) and the International Institute for Sustainable Development (IISD) (2005) almost all WTO members have received initial requests from 90 different countries. Negotiations have moved into the 'revised offer' stage. However, there is dissatisfaction among member countries because the quality of the offers is unsatisfactory in many cases. Therefore, most members feel that insufficient progress has been made.

As with trade in goods, the lack of progress at the multilateral level has led to the simultaneous occurrence of a large number of bilateral, sub-regional and regional negotiations. This large number of negotiations is challenging and complex for the countries involved. However, capacity to produce success in this context does not appear to be the biggest hurdle at this point. The failure in Cancun and lack of progress since then suggests that the biggest hurdle for reducing trade impediments in services is the linking of all negotiations to agriculture. Some developing countries have directly linked the level of ambition in services to the level of ambition attained in other areas of negotiations like agriculture.

On the other hand, developing countries want movement on Mode 4 to be de-linked from movement on Mode 3. That is, many developing countries are pushing for progress on the 'movement of natural persons' (Mode 4) because this is considered a modality that offers considerable benefits to these countries. However, most of the Mode 4 offers are linked to commercial presence (Mode 3). India, China and Brazil have led a group of 18 developing countries striving to move forward on Mode 4 by de-linking the two modes and removing a number of restrictions on the movement of persons.

Although there is consensus in principle on liberalizing service trade, there still appears to be some disagreement on the approach to be taken. Many developing countries prefer the 'positive-list' approach while the developed countries prefer the 'negative-list' approach. Moreover, there is a further divide between developed and developing countries: developing countries do not want market access matters to include negotiations on issues such as safeguards, domestic regulations, subsidies and government procurement.

The most controversial issue in the Doha Round negotiations on services has been a strong push by developed countries including Australia, the US and the EU to adopt a mandatory minimum market access commitment in services. This is known as a benchmarking approach. Benchmarking is an attempt to increase the level of commitment by setting numerical targets for services that members must commit to liberalize. The benchmarks include different targets for developed and developing countries. Most developing countries disagree with this approach arguing that mandatory market access commitments are contrary to the very nature of the GATS which explicitly allows countries to liberalize services according to their individual situations and national policy objectives.

However, there are still some reasons for optimism. The liberalization of trade in services is not as controversial as trade in agriculture. There is some common ground (and support) among North and South countries for GATS. The Chair of GATS is attempting to reconcile differences between countries. The November 2005 draft ministerial text draws up the post-Hong Kong program to conclude any outstanding initial offers as soon as possible and conclude negotiations by the end of 2006. In addition there has been significant progress at regional and sub-regional level. From 1994, when NAFTA was signed, to 1999, 14 sub-regional arrangements were concluded in the Americas that included disciplines on trade in services.

Conclusion

There are four important features of the service sector that have been highlighted in this chapter. First, services have become the largest productive sector in most economies and a large share of service output is used as inputs into the production of all goods and services in the economy. Second, services are a growing part of world trade and investment, but the service sector remains the most closed sector of the economy. While services remain relatively closed in part due to the non-tradable nature of services, there is more to the story. Third, there has been considerable interest and effort by most countries in the liberalization of trade and investment in services. However, the fourth feature of the service sector is that it remains highly protected due to explicit protectionist measures and due to the fact that many services are the subject of domestic regulations.

Although international trade in services is growing rapidly, services are by far the most 'closed' sector in the world economy as measured by the ratio of imports and exports to output. While the economics literature is not yet too far out of line treating services as the quintessential 'non-tradable', it is important to recognize that service trade has come to comprise a substantial share of international trade and production for both developed and developing countries. Nevertheless, the level of protection afforded trade in services remains very high compared to other sectors. The need in principle for multilateral reductions in such barriers is not controversial for many WTO member countries, but due to the nature of trade in services, liberalization is a complicated and drawn out process where progress has been slow. Trade and investment liberalization in services has been difficult to implement.

Notes

1. In this chapter I follow the economics literature and use 'outsourcing' to refer to 'offshore outsourcing'. Technically 'outsourcing' can more broadly refer to any activity that is contracted out to another firm – and 'offshore' refers to contracting to a firm operating in a different country. Feenstra (2004: 100) points out that splitting apart the production process across several countries is also referred to as 'production sharing', 'fragmentation', 'vertical specialization' and 'slicing the production chain'.

2. Progress in the Doha Round of WTO negotiations remains difficult in spite of the fact that the Hong Kong Ministerial in 2005 was moderately successful at least in relation to the failure in Cancun in 2003.
3. Note that this is a different notion of services heterogeneity than discussed above in the context of Rauch's (1999) analysis of differentiated products. The current point is that there are different types of services, or in other words, different industries within the service sector. In the differentiated products context, there is product differentiation within these different service industries.
4. This is not reported in Table 14.1. See WTO (2004a) 'International Trade Statistics 2003'.
5. See the WTO (2006) document 'GATS – Fact and Fiction'.
6. See Stephenson and Prieto (2001).
7. See Markusen, Rutherford and Tarr (2001).
8. McGuire cites results from the following studies: Benjamin and Diao (1998, 2000); Brown *et al.* (1996); Chadha (2001); Chadha *et al.* (2000); Dee and Hanslow (2000); DFAT (1999); Hertel *et al.* (1999); and Robinson *et al.* (1999)

References

Beaulieu, Eugene and Shenjie Chen (2005), 'Trade in Services,' in William A. Kerr and James D. Gaisford (eds), *Trade Negotiations in Agriculture: A Future Common Agenda for Brazil and Canada?* Part of 'Turning Points: Occasional Papers in Latin American Studies Series,' pp. 177–99. Calgary: University of Calgary Press.

Benjamin, N. and X. Diao (1998), 'Liberalizing Services Trade in APEC: A General Equilibrium Analysis with Imperfect Competition,' *The Economic Implications of Liberalising APEC Tariff and Non-Tariff Barriers to Trade*, Washington, DC: US International Trade Commission.

Benjamin, N. and X. Diao (2000), 'Liberalizing Services Trade in APEC: A General Equilibrium Analysis with Imperfect Competition,' *Pacific Economic Review*, 5(1), 49–75.

Brown, D., A. Deardorff and R. Stern (1996), 'Modelling Multilateral Liberalization in Services,' *Asia-Pacific Economic Review*, 2, 21–34.

Chadha, R. (2001), 'GATS and the Developing Countries: A Case Study of India,' in Robert M. Stern (ed.), *Services in the International Economy: Measurement and Modelling, Sectoral and Country Studies, and Issues in the WTO Services Negotiations*, Michigan, MI: University of Michigan Press.

Chadha, R., D. Brown, A. Deardorff and A. Stern (2000), 'Computational Analysis of the Impact on India of the Uruguay Round and the Forthcoming WTO Trade Negotiations,' Discussion Paper No. 459, School of Public Policy, University of Michigan.

Chen, Zhiqi and Lawrence Schembri (2002), 'Measuring the Barriers to Trade in Services: Literature and Methodologies,' Trade Policy Research 2002, http://www.dfait-maeci.gc.ca/eet/research/TPR_2002-en.asp.

Copeland, Brian R. (2002), 'Benefits and Costs of Trade and Investment Liberalization in Services: Implications from trade theory,' Trade Policy Research 2002, http://www.dfait-maeci.gc.ca/eet/research/TPR_2002-en.asp.

Dee, P. and K. Hanslow (2000), 'Multilateral Liberalisation of Services Trade,' Productivity Commission Staff Research Paper, Ausinfo, Canberra, http://www.pc.gov.au/research/staffres/multilatlib/index.html (accessed 15 October 2001).

Department of Foreign Affairs and Trade (DFAT) (1999), *Global Trade Reform: Maintaining Momentum*, Canberra: DFAT.

Feenstra, Robert C. (2004), *Advanced International Trade: Theory and Evidence*, Princeton, NJ and Oxford: Princeton University Press.

Friedman, Thomas L. (2005), *The World is Flat: A Brief History of the Twentieth Century*, New York: Farra, Straus and Giroux.

Hertel, T., J. Francois and W. Martin (1999), 'Agriculture and Non-agricultural Liberalisation in the Millennium Round,' Paper presented at the Global Conference on Agriculture and the New Trade Agenda from a Development Perspective: Interests and Options in the WTO 2000 Negotiations, sponsored by the World Bank and WTO, Geneva, 1–2 October.

Hufbaur, Gary and Tony Warren (1999), 'The Globalization of Services: What has Happened? What are the Implications?' in Gerhard Fels (ed.), *The Service Economy: An Engine for Growth and Employment*, Dresden: Institut der Deutschen Wirtschaft Koln.

International Centre for Trade and Sustainable Development (ICTSD) and the International Institute for Sustainable Development (IISD) (2005), 'Doha Round Briefing Series: Hong Kong Update,' Vol. 4, November.

Konan, Denise Eby and Keith E. Maskus (2004), 'Quantifying the Impact of Services Liberalization in a Developing Country,' World Bank Policy Research Paper no. 3193.

Markusen, J., T. F. Rutherford and D. Tarr (2001), 'Foreign Direct Investment in Services and the Domestic Market for Expertise,' NBER Working Paper No. 7700, Cambridge, MA.

McGuire, Greg (2002), 'Trade in Services – Market Access Opportunities and the Benefits of Liberalization for Developing Economies,' United Nations Conference on Trade and Development (UNCTAD) Policy Issues in International Trade and Commodities Study Series No. 19.

Nicolaides, P. (1989), *Trade in Services*, London: Royal Institute of International Affairs.

Rauch, James E. (1999), 'Networks versus Markets in International Trade,' *Journal of International Economics*, **48**, 7–35.

Robinson, S., Z. Wang and W. Martin (1999), 'Capturing the Implications of Services Trade Liberalisation,' Invited Paper at the Second Annual Conference on Global Economic Analysis, Ebberuk, Denmark, 20–22 June.

Stephenson, Sherry M. (2001), 'Non-Tariff Barriers and the Telecommunications Sector,' OAS Trade Unit Studies Working Paper. http://www.oas.org/.

Stephenson, Sherry M. (2002), 'Can Regional Liberalization of Services go Further than Multilateral Liberalization under the GATS?' OAS Trade Unit Studies Working Paper. http://www.oas.org/.

Stephenson, Sherry M. and Francisco Javier Prieto (2001), 'Evaluating Approaches to the Liberalization of Trade in Services: Insights from Regional Experience in the Americas,' OAS Trade Unit Studies Working Paper, http://www.oas.org/.

UNCTAD (2003), *Back to Basics – Market Access Issues in the Doha Agenda*, Geneva: United Nations publication, Sales No. E.03.II.D.4.

Wall Street Journal (2003), 'Skilled Workers Sway Politicians with Fervor Against Free Trade', Michael Schroeder and Timothy Aeppel, 10 October, p. A1.

Wall Street Journal (2004), 'Data Gap – Behind Outsourcing Debate: Surprisingly Few Hard Numbers; Counting Jobs Moving Abroad Is a Complicated Task; Benefits Are Less Tangible; One Report: "A Little Wobbly",' Jon E. Hilsenrath, New York, NY: 12 April, p. A.1.

World Trade Organization (WTO) (2004a), 'International Trade Statistics 2003' http://www.wto.org/.

World Trade Organization (WTO) (2004b), *World Trade Report, 2004*, Geneva.

World Trade Organization (WTO) (2006), 'GATS – Fact and Fiction,' http://www.wto.org/english/tratop_e/serv_e/gats_factfiction_e.htm.

15 Trade-related intellectual property rights, trade flows and national welfare
Olena Ivus

Introduction

The protection of intellectual property rights (IPRs) is one of the most controversial issues in today's global economy. There is a vigorous ongoing debate about the strength of national systems of patent and copyright protection that is of considerable importance. Proponents of more stringent protection argue that differences in IPRs protection constitute a form of non-tariff barriers to trade in products containing a patentable innovation and that lax patent systems of many developing countries represents blatant free-riding, which distorts natural trading patterns and reduces the ability of firms to transfer technology abroad. Proponents of less stringent protection argue that strengthening global IPRs will bestow market power on inventing firms, thus enhancing the profits of the monopolistic foreign firms at the expense of domestic welfare and would constitute a barrier to legitimate trade in imitative products (Taylor 1993; Gaisford and Richardson 2000).

The continuing debate over the role of IPRs in trade, growth and development has resulted in numerous initiatives through international organizations to harmonize, strengthen and broaden the level of protection for IPRs all over the world. One outcome of multilateral negotiations was an agreement on Trade-Related Aspects of Intellectual Property Rights (TRIPS) of 1994, which was approved as a part of the Uruguay Round that established the WTO. The TRIPS provides minimum standards on IPRs for all WTO members.

The growing importance of the issue of IPRs has resulted in a proliferation of empirical and theoretical research analyzing the effect of protecting IPRs on national welfare, technological transfers, trade volumes and economic growth. This chapter explains key features of the protection of IPRs in the global economy. It begins by presenting the rationale for intellectual property protection in a closed economy. Attention then shifts to the impact of IPRs on national welfare in a world economy that is becoming increasingly global rather that isolated. The impact of more stringent intellectual property laws and enforcement on international trade volumes is subsequently discussed. Finally, a selection of empirical studies pertaining to intellectual property protection and trade flows is examined to determine if the theoretical conclusions are supported by the empirical evidence.

Protecting intellectual property rights in a closed economy

To demonstrate arguments for and against granting patent protection in a closed economy, consider Figure 15.1, where the domestic market for a patentable product is illustrated. In the absence of patent protection for this product, the competitive price would be P_C^* and, given the demand for the product is represented by the curve D, equilibrium output Q_C^* will result. Welfare maximization in a single market would require that

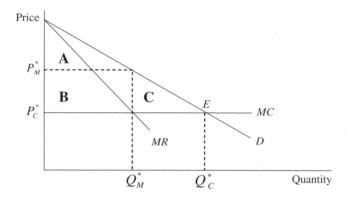

Figure 15.1   Welfare effects of monopoly price discrimination

the market price for a product is equal to the marginal cost (MC) of production. The diagram shows a simple case where the marginal cost is constant and, thus, is equal to the average cost of production. Since price is then equal to average cost, this implies zero economic profits at the production stage. The sunk cost of expenditures on research and development, however, are not covered. Consequently, there is no pecuniary incentive to engage in innovation and the product would not be developed by competitive industry in the absence of policy action. Clearly, this competitive outcome is not efficient. In this system, market price fails to provide the proper signals to economic agents because it does not take account of the costs of inventing. This, in turn, implies that the market would underinvest in new ideas and information, as research and development involves additional costs and results in negative profits for innovators.

Hence, the most compelling argument usually presented in favor of intellectual property protection, say through patents, is that it provides an incentive to undertake research and development activities and fosters the dynamic benefits associated with the production of knowledge. Providing patent protection enables an innovator to exercise temporary monopoly power over the market for the patentable product and to earn a return on the invention. In this scenario, monopolistic price P_M^* will be established on the market and a patent-holder will garner the profit on production represented by the area **B**. The monopoly profits will provide some return on the cost of invention. Thus, it seems that the outcome of this standard monopoly pricing model may justify the arguments in favor of strong patent protection.

However, there is a negative side of this story. In contrast to the efficient solution described above, in the monopolistic framework consumers and society as a whole are clearly worse off. The consumer benefits decrease from area **A + B + C** to **A** in Figure 15.1. In other words, with monopolistic power in the market, consumers enjoy less output at a higher price. IPRs protection endows a patent-holder with a monopoly on the use of patented products which, in turn, leads to monopoly distortions of consumer choice. In addition, it may be argued that patents are an imperfect method of fostering invention (Deardorff 1992). An optimal patent system fails to promote all worthwhile inventions,[1] since the creation of only those innovations for which expected net gains in monopoly profit exceed the research and development costs will be initiated. Furthermore, the welfare of a country depends on the average level of product improvement. While strong patent rights increase this average level of product improvement by stimulating innovation, they may also inhibit innovation by preventing a wider dispersion of new technology. In this case, the outcome is the following: fewer publicly available technologies, lower levels of technological spillovers, and, consequently, possibly higher per unit research costs for all firms. In this sense, incomplete patent protection may be optimal. With less restrictive patents, more technologies would remain in the public domain, which, in turn, would allow for more widespread availability and application of innovation (Diwan and Rodrik 1991; Falvey *et al.* 2002). Further, in practice, patent laws help to protect the innovators from imitation by increasing the price of infringing goods, but they fail to grant the perfect protection theorists often assume. For example product 'masquing' technologies are common in practice (Taylor 1993).

In summary, in choosing its IPRs policy a country that acts in isolation will look for the optimal balance between the benefits from enhancing the incentive to innovate, on one hand, and costs of monopoly distortions and lower diffusion of new technology and innovation, on the other. The final policy choice will be some intermediate level of patent strength.

IPRs and national welfare in a global context

With national economies becoming increasingly affected by the forces of globalization and the resulting increase in the cross-border trade, investment and the transfer of information, there is a growing recognition of the importance of technology and knowledge spillovers for economic growth. As a result, IPRs have become an issue of international concern.

As we concluded in the previous section, if each country acts in isolation when establishing its system IPRs, they will search for the optimal level protection that suits their own circumstances. However, in contrast to the case of a closed economy, where the country's patent strength affects only domestic economic agents, in a global market, patent protection in one country affects welfare in other countries. Thus, a country's choice of its level for IPR protection is now dependent on the choices of other countries and its choice affects other national markets.

Falvey *et al.* (2002) note that the way patents are applied tends to push countries to choose extreme patent strengths. Even for two identical countries,[2] it is not individually rational to choose patent systems of identical strength. In order to provide an insight for this statement, consider a world of two identical countries A and B. If the countries had identical patent systems, firms from A would have half the sales in country B and *vice versa* assuming no transportation and transaction costs associated with the international transfer of goods. If country A has a lax patent system, however, it may make eminently good sense for the country B to choose tighter patent procedures. By doing so, B will completely control the sales in its domestic market plus half of the sales in A. In addition, by choosing stronger patent protection, country A provides global incentives for innovation that would not otherwise exist. Alternatively, if country A has a stringent patent system, it is rational for the country B to choose weaker patent protection. In this case, B will not bear the costs of the monopoly distortions, will reap the benefits of free riding and enjoy the higher level of average product improvement due to greater tolerance of imitation. Hence, in a Nash equilibrium, where each country adopts an individually rational strategy and does not want to deviate from this, one country will have a strong patent system and the other one will have weaker patent protection.

From a global perspective, the resultant Nash equilibrium is sub-optimal, because intellectual property protection is under-provided. The reason for this is that each country ignores the benefits that its tighter protection generates for the other countries. As neither side takes into account these positive spillovers, less than the efficient incentives for innovative activity are provided on a worldwide basis. This result can be contrasted with the outcome which arises in the presence of an institutional framework that has the objective of achieving international cooperation (Gaisford and Richardson 2000).

Whenever the two countries are not symmetric with respect to their characteristics, there are further reasons why it is optimal for them to choose patent systems of different strength. That is why it comes as no surprise to observe that the strength of IPRs protection varied across the globe prior to the TRIPS which standardized patent length internationally. These differences, being more acute between developed and developing countries, resulted in a dispute about the increase in IPRs protection during negotiations to establish common worldwide standards. The basic economic issue that underlies the conflict between the North (that is the developed countries) and the South (the developing countries) is not difficult to understand.

The developed countries argued for the stricter enforcement of IPRs on the grounds that lax patent protection in developing countries allowed for a greater possibility of free riding on the part of local firms, which competed with innovating firms from developed countries. Clearly, tighter protection of IPRs laws and their enforcement in the South would be profitable for the North. It would reduce the ability of domestic firms in the South to imitate technologies embodied in foreign products and, consequently, would result in increased costs associated with infringement. In this way, innovators in the North would be more protected from imitators in their export markets, encouraging additional production and exports of patentable products. The resulting higher monopolistic profits would expand the set worthwhile research and development activities leading to innovations that otherwise would not have taken place as soon. In contrast, the strong imitative abilities and weak patent rights in the South do not allow the innovator to discriminate internationally and reap additional profits. In addition, the differences in the protection of IPRs across the countries constitute a form of non-tariff barrier to trade. For example, for the producer to sell its patentable product internationally, it is necessary to obtain an array of independent national patents, which entails considerable expenses.

For the developing countries there exists a strong free-riding motive because the vast majority of innovative activities take place in the North and the South is mainly a consumer of invented products. The more lax is the protection of IPRs, the less developing countries have to pay for the innovated products. If innovative ideas diffuse freely and the capacity for imitation is high, a close substitute will be produced in the South. Not only are such products likely to be sold domestically at a price lower than would be charged by the foreign monopoly, but they may also be exported to other countries with weak IPRs.[3] In such a situation, it is independently rational for a developing country to provide little protection or no protection whatsoever since the new products can be obtained at competitive prices in any case. Of course, this argument considers only the short run because it does not recognize the disincentive effect on innovation in the North and, hence, that there will be less innovations available to pirate in the future.

The issue of IPRs became controversial in the mid-1980s as the proportion of the value of goods constituted by intellectual property began to rise. For those interested in strong international protection for intellectual property, the existing international conventions pertaining to intellectual property were found wanting. In 1883, the Paris Convention for the Protection of Industrial Property was founded to coordinate patents and in 1886 the Berne Convention for the Protection of Literary and Artistic Works was formed to coordinate copyrights. In order to administer both the Paris and Berne conventions, the World Intellectual Property Organization (WIPO) was established in 1967. In the 1980s developed countries' frequent frustration with the voluntary nature of the WIPO led to the inclusion of trade-related IPRs on the negotiating agenda for the Uruguay Round of GATT talks. In 1994, the TRIPS agreement was concluded, imposing additional requirements on all WTO members (Gaisford and Richardson, 2000). A major facet of the TRIPS is cross-agreement retaliation through the WTO whereby retaliatory trade measures on goods can be imposed on countries that fail to protect the intellectual property of foreign firms (Boyd *et al.* 2003; Kerr 2003). As countries wishing to be part of the WTO cannot opt out of the TRIPS, an enforcement mechanism has been added to the multilateral system for the protection of intellectual property.[4]

The TRIPS agreement was vigorously supported by most developed countries but was extremely controversial for many developing countries. Gaisford and Richardson (2000) argue that the provisions of the TRIPS agreement constitute 'a fundamental and ill-advised departure from the traditions built up through many rounds of GATT negotiations' (p. 138). Successive GATT agreements have required symmetric reductions in tariff protection across the countries allowing for the rates of final tariff protection to be asymmetric in according to a country's development status. Hence, some forms of discrimination in favor of developing countries were provided. On the contrary, the TRIPS agreement required asymmetric increases in the durations of intellectual property protection to establish common world standards for patents and copyrights. The only significant concession in favor of the developing countries was longer periods of grace for implementation.

The acrimonious debates over the TRIPS agreement resulted in a considerable research effort to find an answer to the question of how more stringent patent protection will affect the distribution of welfare, trade flows, technology transfer and growth across countries. One prominent study, Deardorff (1992) showed that the extension of patent protection from the North, where innovation takes place, to the South, which only consumes innovative products, unambiguously increases the welfare of the inventing countries but may decrease the welfare of the developing countries. Moreover, the decline in the South's welfare may far exceed the increase in the North's welfare. In this case, there will be adverse effects for the world as a whole arising from stronger patent protection. With time, as the coverage of patent protection is extended to more and more countries in the world, there will be a definite loss in the world welfare. This is due to the fact that the number of additional innovations that can be stimulated by extending patent protection diminishes with an increase in the number of markets covered. Thus, after a certain threshold, the costs of extending patent protection will outweigh the benefits. As a result, it may be optimal to limit patent protection geographically.

Further, Deardorff (1992) demonstrated that even if the world's efficiency does initially improve from extending more stringent patent systems, it is because of the North's relatively high gains at the expense of the rest of the world. However, for the developing countries, the benefits from increased economic activity are not strong enough to outweigh the losses from monopoly power and lower dispersion of new technology. This argument provides a formal rationale for the opposition of developing countries to the proposals for more stringent patent protection.

Another pioneering theoretical study by Chin and Grossman (1990) found that more stringent intellectual property protection may or may not enhance global welfare. They demonstrated that there is a conflict of interest between developed and developing countries such that it may be in the South's interest to evade rather than enforce the protection of IPRs.

The arguments above strongly rely on the assumption of identical demands for invented goods in both countries. However, in reality the developed and developing countries have different technological needs or tastes and, therefore, the inventions demanded by different countries can be different. Diwan and Rodrik (1991) assume that North and South have differences in distributions of preferences over the range of potential innovated products. This, in turn, implies a greater incentive for the South to protect IPRs, because tighter patent protection in the South now implies a larger proportion of scarce research and development resources will be allocated to the invention of goods that are of particular importance to its consumers. To put it differently, more stringent property protection in the South leads to a tighter fit between innovated technologies and the preferences of its population. This additional incentive can at least partially offset the strong free-riding motive the South would have in case of identical technological needs and tastes.

The model by Diwan and Rodrik (1991) suggests that the restrictiveness of the prevailing patent laws in the South has important implications for the welfare of both regions. More stringent patent protection in the South affects the welfare of the North and the South in two directions: (a) through the magnitude of profit transfers from the South to the North; and (b) through the change in the range of innovated technologies. The second impact is of particular interest as it suggests that the stringency of intellectual property protection affects not only the quantity of the products innovated, but also their quality. In other words, the South's more stringent patent rights will facilitate the invention of technologies more appropriate to their own preferences and may skew the range of innovations away from Northern preferences. In this vein, Gaisford *et al.* (2001) examine the impact of IPRs in agricultural biotechnology on the trade patterns. The authors note that there exists substantial potential for the innovations that are more appropriate to the local needs of developing countries that are left unexplored. One reason for this is the low levels of income and resulting low demand in developing countries. Therefore, the degree to which the extension of patent protection in the South will alter the range of products innovated remains problematic. Merely suggesting that the South could reap greater benefits by protecting intellectual property more vigorously, because it will stimulate the invention of more 'local' technologies, leaves the vital question of affordability unanswered. Are the developing countries able to pay monopolistic prices for more 'appropriate' innovated products, such as drugs to combat tropical diseases, and to reap the benefits of extended protection? If the answer to this question is doubtful, as the HIV/AIDS crisis in Africa seems to suggest, then the debate regarding extending patent protection in poor developing regions may be a moot point.

The theoretical results of the welfare analysis by Diwan and Rodrik (1991) imply that a benevolent global planner would assign identical rates of patent protection to the North and South only if their welfare levels are weighted equally, that is when the global welfare function is strictly utilitarian. In addition, the results of their numerical simulations suggest that when the poor South's welfare is given priority, as in the case of an egalitarian global welfare function, the North should be required to provide a higher level of patent protection.

The findings of the previous models critically depend on the assumption of how the information about the innovated product is transmitted. If one assumes that information is costlessly spread from the North to the South and the South's level of imitation is high, then the same product may be produced in the South with no patent protection whatsoever. However, in reality, innovative ideas do not diffuse without cost. Consequently, extending patent protection may be beneficial for the developing countries to the extent that it stimulates the transfer of technology (Deardorff 1992).

To investigate how the stringency of the South's patent protection affects the level of unintentional technology transfer, a North–South model is developed by Taylor (1993). He adopts a leader–follower (Stackelberg) framework where the North is the first to move and to set its output and 'market-made' barriers to imitation, such as physical masking techniques in order to deter local imitators. It is assumed that both institutional and market-made barriers to imitation affect Southern costs of production. In this respect, southern production costs are increasing in the strength of the South's patent protection and in the level of the North's efforts at masking product technology. The results of the model indicate that vigilant intellectual property protection by the South reduces the need of firms in the North to invest in masking their product's characteristics and, consequently, leads to higher flow of unintended technology transfers. This increase in the transfer of technology to the South would enhance the productivity of resources employed in the South and, hence, raise output in the South. Conversely, laxly enforced intellectual property laws in the South would call forth defensive reactions from the side of innovative firms, which can limit technology transfer to the South. This represents a Pareto-inferior position for the world economy. The North is diverting resources into strategies to reduce imitation and the South, in its turn, is employing resources to uncover the 'embodied technology'. The analysis suggests moving away from this situation through the use of a mechanism to protect IPRs more vigorously will be beneficial for both the developed and the developing countries. The world welfare is maximized at some intermediate level of patent strength.

Taylor (1994) employs a two-country endogenous-growth model to investigate the effect of intellectual property protection on world trade, technology transfer and growth. His analysis leads to the conclusion that laxly enforced patent laws in developing countries: (a) reduce the incentive for inventors to implement best practice research techniques; (b) decrease the willingness of innovators to transfer technology abroad; (c) reduce global research and development activities; and (d) slows global economic growth. The stark move from a symmetric protection regime to an asymmetric one brings a loss in export opportunities for the developed countries, where innovating firms are concentrated, and distorts the patterns of trade in both goods and research and development. In addition, a move to asymmetric protection eliminates technology transfer between the countries and, consequently, slows down the rate of technological progress in all industries in the developing countries. The welfare of both regions may fall in the move to an asymmetric

IPRs regime. On the contrary, if the levels of intellectual property protection are equalized across countries, innovative firms will have an incentive to transfer technologies abroad, the allocation of the world technical resources will improve and, in many cases, world economic growth will rise. Thus, the paper by Taylor (1994) argues that there is substance to the claims of the developed countries.

In contrast to Taylor (1994), Grossman and Lai (2002) examine an optimal government policy for intellectual property protection in the framework of a simple model of endogenous innovation. They found that the harmonization of patent systems is neither necessary nor sufficient for the efficiency of the global patent regime. This result is consistent with a study by Gaisford and Richardson (2000), which addresses problems caused by the establishment of a harmonized world level of intellectual property protection under the TRIPS agreement. These authors argue that, given the existing asymmetry in innovative capacity across countries in the world, the common international standards for IPRs protection established by the TRIPS are not likely to be mutually beneficial. The move to the uniform worldwide standards worsens the positions of the developing countries both absolutely and relative to the developed countries. The developing countries potentially suffer significant losses in their national welfare and would comply with TRIPS requirements only under the threat of WTO trade sanctions. Alternatively, a mutually beneficial efficient solution can be achieved with asymmetric intellectual property protection where lower levels are allowed for developing countries and higher are required for developed countries. To support this statement, the authors develop a partial-equilibrium, game-theoretic model, which focuses on patent lengths. The results of the model simulations imply that a move to symmetric levels of patent protection will lead to a 40–47 percent decline in the net welfare benefits from innovation in the developing countries. At the same time this change is unambiguously welfare enhancing for the North.

IPRs and trade volumes

The issue of the trade-related IPRs has gained more importance as the share of high technology products in total world trade has increases from 12 percent in 1980 to 24 percent in 1994 (see Braga and Fink 1999). The main findings of the theoretical studies establish that IPRs are related to international trade flows. The theoretical literature alone cannot provide clear prediction on the direction of the impact of greater intellectual property protection on international trade flows.

To analyze the influence of the level of IPRs protection on international trade flows, Maskus and Penubarti (1995) developed a model in which a dominant exporting firm competes with a fringe industry in a particular market. The fringe industry is capable of imitating the dominant firm's production process and produce competing goods. The paper shows that the optimal response of an exporting firm to a marginal strengthening of intellectual property laws by an importing country could be to either increase or decrease its exports. This is because there is a tradeoff between enhanced market power and greater market size. In other words, the results of the model indicate that no unambiguous theoretical prediction can be made about the effects of strengthening IPRs protection on international trade flows because there are two opposing effects. On one hand, a stronger level of IPRs protection decreases the level of imitative activity in the importing country. This increases the demand faced by the exporting firm, encouraging it to export more to the local markets. This is known as the market expansion effect. On the other hand, stronger protection of IPRs grants monopoly power to the exporting firm by assuring exclusive rights for its products and technologies. This allows the firm to behave more monopolistically and export less. The latter effect is known as the market power effect. Thus, the impact of the imposition of stronger IPRs protection depends on the relative importance of the two countervailing effects.

The market expansion effect lies at the heart of the numerous initiatives from the side of international organizations to harmonize and strengthen the level of IPRs around the world. The developed countries contend that differences in intellectual property protection constitute a form of non-tariff barriers to trade, which distorts natural trading patterns. Thus, the asymmetries in national standards of IPRs protection are thought to negatively affect trade between countries. However, the market power effect provides support for the developing countries' counter argument. From their point of view, a more stringent IPRs system would provide monopoly power to the foreign firms and decrease foreign exports to their domestic markets. In addition, such requirements would constitute a barrier to legitimate trade in imitative products and substantially restrict the exports of developing countries in 'IPR sensitive' industries.

According to Smith (1999), the relative strength of the market-power and market-expansion effects depends on how exporters respond to the threat of imitation (or its absence) in the importing country. Table 15.1 describes the relationship between threat of imitation and market power and expansion effects. The table entries describe the threat of imitation as an interaction between imitative abilities and level of IPRs protection in the country. As is summarized by Shevtsova (2004), the numbers in the cells rank the threat of imitation from weakest (1) to strongest (4). A stricter patent system is expected to primarily generate an increase in market power in importing countries with a weak threat of imitation (Group 1) because few substitutes are available. For these markets, enhanced patent protection increases the monopoly power of innovative firms by ensuring exclusive rights to their technologies. Higher prices then follow from a restriction in the supply of exported goods. By contrast, in importing countries where there is a significant threat of imitation (Group 4), the market-expansion effects are expected to be dominant if the patent system becomes stricter because imitation is made more difficult. Reductions in masking costs incurred by innovative firms then lead to greater exports. In situations with a moderate threat of imitation (Groups 2 and 3), it is not possible to make an unambiguous prediction concerning the impact of more stringent intellectual property protection on trade flows.

Table 15.1   *Relationship between threat of imitation and market power and expansion effects*

	Weak IPR protection		Strong IPR protection	
Weak imitative abilities	2.	Moderate threat of imitation; ambiguous effect (+/−)	1.	Weak threat of imitation; market power effect (−)
Strong imitative abilities	4.	Strong threat of imitation; market expansion effect (+)	3.	Moderate threat of imitation; ambiguous effect (+/−)

Source: Smith (1999)

In general, theoretical analysis provides few definitive priors on how stronger intellectual property protection will affect international trade flows. Further, there are important additional complications. First, an innovative firm's response to an increase in intellectual property protection will depend on the structure and strength of the trade policy regime in the importing country. Second, a firm's decisions about the volume of exports to a particular market are interdependent with its decisions to service the market through licensing or foreign direct investment (see Horstmann and Markusen 1987). All this implies an imperative for empirical analysis to ascertain how enhanced intellectual property protection by an importing country will affect trade volumes.

Maskus and Penubarti (1995) examined the influence of differences in national patent laws on international trade. A positive relationship was found between manufacturing exports of OECD countries and the level of IPR protection in importing countries. This relationship was found to be stronger in developing countries with significant abilities to imitate and weaker in small developing countries with low incomes. From these results the authors conclude that for bigger developing countries with stronger imitative abilities the market expansion effect dominates, causing the exporting country to export more due to the expansion of market size. Conversely in small, low-income developing countries, the enforcement of the level of IPRs protection enhances the market power effect, which in turn causes the exporter to exercise more market power. Consequently, its export volumes increase by a smaller proportion than in the first case. A study by Ferrantino (1993) using US data also provides empirical evidence in support of a positive relationship between trade volumes and the level of intellectual property protection in importing countries as proxied by the duration of patent rights.

Smith (1999) showed that, while US exports are sensitive to intellectual property protection in importing countries, the relationship is more complex. There is a positive relationship for importing countries with strong infringement abilities due to the domination of the market expansion effect and negative in the case of importing countries with a low threat of imitation because stronger intellectual property protection enhances the market power effect, stimulating US exporters to reduce their exports to those markets. In addition, Smith's results indicate that IPRs have a market expanding effect on US exports to countries in the lower-middle income per capita group, which is consistent with the findings by Maskus and Penubarti (1997). These patterns prevail in the majority of manufacturing industries and in the aggregate for patent-sensitive industries. Smith (2002) also obtained similar results in an additional study focusing on the effects patent rights have on US exports in three drug industries: biological products, medicinals and botanicals and pharmaceuticals.

Rafiquzzaman (2002) studied the impact of national differences in the level of protection of patent rights on international trade flows using Canadian manufacturing export data. He found that stronger IPRs protection induces Canadian firms to export relatively more to high-income countries than to low-income countries. In addition, Canadian exports are biased against those importers that pose a weak imitative threat due to the market-power effect and biased toward those importers that pose a strong imitative threat due to the market-expansion effect. Wisniewski (2003) contributed new empirical evidence on the sensitivity of US exports of biotechnology related agricultural inputs to national differences in IPRs protection. This study provided some support for the market-expansion hypothesis for field crop seeds and significant support for the market-power hypothesis for both field crop seeds and agricultural chemicals. Wisniewski also found that the relationship between the strength of IPRs and trade was not sensitive to a country's ability to imitate. It is worth noting that Wisniewski's findings for the biotechnology related agricultural industry are different from the results for manufacturing industry described above. This suggests that findings for manufacturing products may not be applicable to the agri-food sector.

Conclusion

Despite the fact that a great deal of effort has already been expended in the attempt to shed light on the debates over IPRs, there are still some aspects that require a more detailed theoretical and empirical investigation. It is apparent that existing empirical studies focus on industries at fairly high levels of aggregation. Thus, more empirical work is needed at the level of disaggregated industries or even the firm level. For example, trade in agricultural products warrants further attention. Knowledge of the performance of firms and industries in this field is becoming increasingly important to policy makers as the amount of intellectual property embodied in agricultural products increases due to the potential for widespread application of agricultural biotechnology. As the existing theoretical and empirical studies do not provide unambiguous predictions related to more stringent IPRs protection, reliable normative policy recommendations remain elusive.

Acknowledgments

This chapter is partially based on 'Intellectual Property Rights and Agricultural Trade Volumes' by Olena Ivus, Laura Loppacher and Yevgeniya Shevtsova, presented at the Canadian Agriculture Innovation Research Network Conference at the University of Calgary, March 2005.

Notes

1. An invention is considered to be worthwhile as long as the consumer benefits exceed the costs of research and development.
2. The countries are identical in terms of number of firms and market size.
3. Traded good are subject to the patent strength of both the importing and exporting countries and must satisfy the stronger of two systems. Exporting the imitated product to a country with stronger patent rights would infringe the patent in the destination country (Falvey *et al.* 2002).
4. The efficacy of this enforcement mechanism has been questioned by Yampoin and Kerr (1998).

References

Boyd, S. L., W. A. Kerr and N. Perdikis (2003), 'Agricultural Biotechnology Innovations versus Intellectual Property Rights – Are Developing Countries at the Mercy of Multinationals?' *The Journal of World Intellectual Property*, **6**(2), 211–32.
Braga, C. P. A. and C. Fink (1999), 'How Stronger Protection of Intellectual Property Rights Affects International Trade Flows', World Bank Policy Research Working Paper No. 2051 (February), http://ssrn.com/ abstract=569254.
Chin, J. C. and G. M. Grossman (1990), 'Intellectual Property Rights in North–South Trade', in: R. W. Jones and A. O. Krueger (eds), *The Political Economy of International Trade: Essays in Honor of Robert E. Baldwin*, Cambridge, MA: Basil Blackwell.
Deardorff, A. V. (1992), 'Welfare Effects of Global Patent Protection', *Economica*, **59**, 35–51.
Diwan, I. and D. Rodik (1991),'Patents, Appropriate Technology and North–South Trade', *Journal of International Economics*, **30**, 27–47.
Falvey, R., F. Martinez and G. Reed (2002), 'Trade and the Globalization of Patent Rights', GEP Research Paper No. 02/21 (September) http://ssrn.com/abstract=413263.
Ferrantino, M. J. (1993), 'The Effects of International Property Rights on International Trade and Investment,' *Weltwirtschaftliches Archiv*, **129**(2).

Gaisford, J. D. and R. S. Richardson (2000), 'The TRIPS Disagreement: Should GATT Traditions Have Been Abandoned?' *Estey Centre Journal of International Law and Trade Policy*, **1**(2), 137–69.

Gaisford, J. D., R.Tarvydas, J. E. Hobbs and W. A. Kerr (2001), 'Biotechnology Piracy: Rethinking the International Protection of Intellectual Property', University of Calgary, Department of Economics Discussion Paper Series No. 2001–06 (October).

Grossman, G. M. and E. L.-C. Lai (2002), 'International Protection of Intellectual Property', NBER Working paper 8704.

Horstmann, I. and J. Markusen (1987), 'Licensing versus Direct Investment: A Model of Internalization by the Multinational Enterprise,' *Canadian Journal of Economics*, **20**(3), 464–81.

Kerr, W. A. (2003), 'The Efficacy of the TRIPS: Incentives, Capacity and Threats', *The Estey Centre Journal of International Law and Trade Policy*, **4**(1), 1–14.

Maskus, K. E. and M. Penubarti (1995), 'How Trade Related are Intellectual Property Rights?' *Journal of International Economics*, **39**, 227–48.

Maskus, K. E. and M. Penubarti (1997), 'Patents and International Trade: An Empirical Study,' in K. E. Maskus, P. M. Hooper, E. E. Learner and D. Richardson (eds), *Quiet Pioneering: Robert M. Stern and His International Economic Legacy*, Ann Arbor MI: University of Michigan Press.

Rafiquzzaman, M. (2002), 'Impact of Patent Rights on International Trade: Evidence from Canada', *Canadian Journal of Economics*, **35**, 307–30.

Shevtsova, Y. (2004), *The Impact of Intellectual Property Rights Protection on International Trade: The Case of Transition Economies*, Kiev: Economics Education and Research Consortium.

Smith, P. J. (1999), 'Are Weak Patent Rights a Barrier to US Exports?' *Journal of International Economics*, **48**,151–77.

Smith, P. J. (2002), 'Patent Rights and Trade: Analysis of Biological Products, Medicinals and Botanicals, and Pharmaceuticals', *American Journal of Agricultural Economics*, **84**(2), 495–512.

Taylor, S. M. (1993), 'TRIPs, Trade and Technology Transfer', *Canadian Journal of Economics*, **26**, 625–37.

Taylor, S. M. (1994), 'TRIPs, Trade and Growth', *International Economic Review*, **35**, 361–81.

Wisniewski, S. L. W. (2003), 'Effects of Foreign Intellectual Property Rights on US Bilateral Exports of Biotechnology Related Agricultural Inputs', Prepared for presentation at AAEA Annual Meeting, July.

Yampoin, R. and W. A. Kerr (1998), 'Can Trade Measures Induce Compliance With TRIPs?' *Journal of the Asia Pacific Economy*, **3**(2), 165–82.

PART III

TRADE POLICY
INSTRUMENTS

16 Trade distortion: border measures versus domestic support

James Gaisford

Introduction

Governments intervene in markets in wide-ranging ways and most of these interventions, either by design or accident, affect international trade. This chapter provides an overview and primer on how two broad types of policy intervention affect national and international markets. First, we analyze border or international trade measures such as import tariffs and export subsidies, which directly alter or distort international trade flows. Second, we investigate domestic support measures such as production subsidies, which directly affect firms on the supply side of the market and indirectly affect trade flows. Subsequent chapters provide a detailed treatment of many types of border measures and domestic support measures. For simplicity, we focus on competitive markets although most of the key insights that are developed carry over to more complex situations with imperfect competition. For ease of exposition, we adopt a single market or partial equilibrium approach where the international market that we examine is assumed to have a negligible impact on the rest of the world economy.[1]

Policy interventions in markets tend to have pervasive effects on the consumption and production decisions of households and firms. Trade flows, whether imports or exports, subsequently will be affected. Rational consumers will choose the quantities they consume such that the additional or marginal benefit is equal to the price. Consequently, a policy-induced increase in the price facing consumers will necessarily reduce the quantities that consumers demand, and ultimately, either reduce imports or increase exports as the case may be. Meanwhile, profit-maximizing competitive firms will choose to produce where the price is equal to marginal cost or cost of the last unit produced. Whenever a policy measure either raises the price received by producers or lowers their marginal cost, therefore, firms will choose to increase the quantities that they supply. Consequently, exports will rise or imports will decline. Since firms can enter or exit an industry in the long run, the price facing producers must be equal to the average cost in a long-run equilibrium so that firms break even. Whenever a policy measure either raises the price or reduces the long-run average costs, there will be additional entry, and thus additional long-run output from the industry.[2] Once again, exports will rise or imports will fall. The numerous channels through which market interventions affect trade suggest that it may be difficult to find de-coupled subsidies, which have no trade impact at all.

Politics, of course, is frequently at the heart of government interventions in markets. Governments frequently trade off special interest groups against one another and the national interest as part of the political processes involving elections, lobbying, and so on. The intent is often to support industry or occupational groupings, which are strongly associated with particular sectors of the economy. Most often the support or protection offered by governments is 'reactive' in the sense that lobbying is more likely to be successful when the sector is in distress, whether due to international competitive pressures, labor-saving technological change or declining demand. Disadvantaged groups, such as farmers or textile workers, and well-organized groups, such as unions, frequently also tend to be more effective in lobbying governments for support. Sometimes the impact of policy measures on trade flows is deliberate, but this is certainly not always the case. While it is understandable, and often equitable, that sensitive special interests receive support, the trade impact of support policy on international trade flows frequently harms corresponding interests in foreign countries.

There are two other secondary objectives that may underlie some of the market interventions that we will investigate. First, governments could conceivably intervene in world markets purely in pursuit of their own national interest. In this case, governments would deliberately manipulate trade flows to generate terms of trade improvements that serve their national interest, albeit at the expense of the rest of the world. Second, governments may also intervene in markets in an attempt to correct market failures and restore efficiency. In this case, the effects on production consumption and trade are generally well intended and, arguably, reasonable.

With the political-economy motive and/or the national-interest motive for policy it may be broadly individually rational for each country to intervene in markets but the international trade repercussions are such that it may be mutually beneficial for countries to agree to international trade disciplines or rules that constrain these interventions. While these prisoners' dilemma features of the conduct of trade policy were discussed in Chapter 6, the purpose at hand is to investigate how sample border and domestic support measures work.

Border measures

We use a competitive market framework to explore border measures that protect the domestic industry in Figure 16.1. In both panels, D and S represent demand and supply curves of the 'Home Country', and Pw is the world price. We use a two-step analysis: first, we assess the impact of policy conditional on the world price remaining constant, and second, we consider how the resultant trade distortions will affect world prices. The left-hand panel of Figure 16.1 shows a case where Home is an importer and the right-hand panel shows an alternative case where Home is an exporter. In both the import and export cases, Home supplies quantity $Qs0$ and demands quantity $Qd0$ in an initial free-trade situation. In the import case, the quantity demanded exceeds the quantity supplied leading to imports of $Qm0$ under free trade, while in the export case, the quantity supplied exceeds the quantity demanded resulting in exports of $Qx0$.

We can now proceed to consider the implementation of border measures by the Home country. In the import case, a tariff or import tax of Tm dollars per unit will raise the domestic price, Ph, above the world price, Pw, such that the domestic price is equal to the world price plus the tariff. In the export case, an export subsidy of Sx dollars per unit will have the same effect.[3] Here it is clear that an export subsidy will lead to a higher price for suppliers, but a moment's reflection indicates that consumers will also have to pay this higher price because they are not subsidized. In fact, the export subsidy is even more closely related to the tariff than it might at first appear. A tariff, or some similar measure, must accompany the export subsidy to prevent Home consumers from purchasing from foreign sources, or even re-importing domestic output, at the world price, Pw, which is

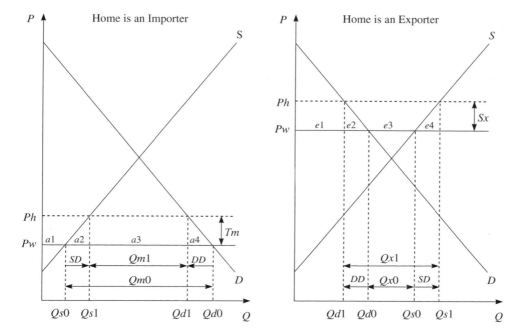

Figure 16.1   Border measures

lower than the domestic price, *Ph*. In both the import and export cases, the border measure raises quantity supplied by the domestic industry to *Qs*1 and decreases the quantity demanded to *Qd*1. While consumers are hurt by these border measures, the support provided by the higher domestic price is beneficial to producers. Either the tariff or the export subsidy effectively insulates suppliers from the world price and, thus, protects their interests.[4]

The increase in the quantity supplied will become larger over time because, in the long run, new firms can enter the industry and existing firms can adjust the use of capital and other inputs, which may be fixed in the short run (see Gaisford and Kerr 2001, ch. 2). In terms of Figure 16.1, the long run supply curve is flatter making supply more responsive to price or more elastic in the long run. This implies that the long run decline in imports or increase in exports will be larger in magnitude.

The arrows labeled *SD*1 and *DD*1 in Figure 16.1 reflect the supply and demand distortions introduced by the border measures. As a result of the supply and demand distortions, imports fall to *Qm*1 in the left panel and exports rise to *Qx*1 in the right panel. Consequently, the border measures have a definite impact on trade at the initial world prices. Unless the home country is the proverbial small country with no influence over the world price, this is not the end of the story. Either less import demand or more export supply will put downward pressure on the world price. Although consumers in the rest of the world will gain from the lower world price, foreign producers will be adversely affected, causing likely political fallout. Border measures that protect domestic producers thus tend to have a 'beggar-thy-neighbour' impact on foreign producers, which frequently leads to trade conflict.[5]

Other border measures can be analyzed in a manner similar to tariffs and export subsidies. There are many types of non-tariff barriers (NTBs) that affect imports in a qualitatively similar manner to tariffs. These include: (a) variable levies, which are variable tariffs that absorb variations in the world price so as to maintain a constant domestic price; (b) quantitative barriers, such as domestic import quotas and foreign voluntary export restraints (VERs); (c) tariff-rate quotas (TRQs) or tariff quotas, which are a hybrid of tariffs and quotas involving a low within-quota tariff and a high over-quota tariff. Import subsidies and export taxes, by contrast with tariffs and export subsidies, reduce the domestic price below the world price and harm the interests of domestic producers. Politics being what it is, export taxes and especially import subsidies are more rarely utilized.[6]

The multilateral trading rules of the General Agreement on Tariffs and Trade (GATT), which is now under the broader umbrella of the World Trade Organization (WTO), seek to place disciplines on the use of border measures because of their often unintended trade-distorting impact. Efforts have been made to convert non-tariff barriers to importation into tariffs because tariffs are more transparent for businesses, they are easily configured to be non-discriminatory and they tend to be less distortionary when markets are not competitive. As well as this so-called tariffication process, the successive rounds of GATT negotiations have also aimed at reducing tariffs. Export subsidies are prohibited by GATT rules in all areas except agriculture. The Uruguay Round negotiations, which were concluded in the mid-1990s, led to the first limits on the use of export subsidies in agriculture, and further action in this regard is a key goal of the current Doha Round (WTO 1999).

Understandably, the disciplines placed on border measures by the GATT and WTO have not lessened lobbying by producer interests when sectors have come under pressure from international competition, declining demand and/or labor-saving technological change. One consequence has been increased emphasis on domestic support measures in many sectors such as agriculture.

Domestic support

Figure 16.2 assists in the analysis domestic support measures. Once again, the left panel shows a case where Home imports and the right panel shows a case where it exports. We begin the analysis with a domestic price equal to *Ph*. If border measures are not in place the domestic price will be equal to the world price. We leave open the possibility, however, that border measures, such as those analyzed above, are already in place and that, as a consequence, *Ph* exceeds the world price. Prior to the implementation of any production measure, the quantity supplied by the domestic industry in Home is $Qs1$ and the quantity demanded is $Qd1$ in both panels of the figure. Consequently, imports are $Qm1$ in the left panel and exports are $Qx1$ in the right panel.

Now consider the impact of the implementation of a production subsidy. For the moment, we hold the underlying world price, and thus the domestic price, constant. From the preceding analysis, recall that domestic price depends only on the world price and any border measures that may already be present. If border measures are present, they too remain constant in our analysis of the implementation of a production subsidy. Given that the government provides *Ss* dollars per unit of output, domestic producers are willing to accept a lower domestic price as indicated by the subsidy-adjusted supply curve S'. Consequently, the subsidy causes an increase in output to $Qs2$ in both panels. Further, the

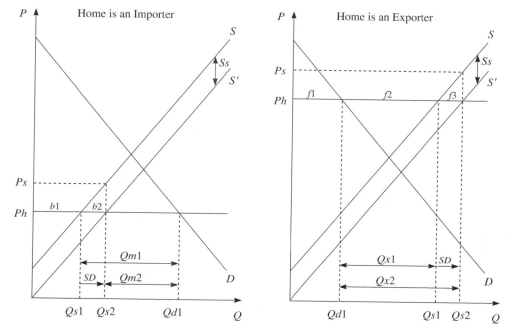

Figure 16.2   Domestic support

subsidy-inclusive supply price obtained by domestic suppliers, *Ps*, is equal to the domestic price plus the production subsidy.[7] Since the supply price rises, producers are better off because of the subsidy.[8]

Instead of the production subsidy, where the supply price would vary over time with any movements in the world price, the government could fix *Ps* as an intervention price, and then offer deficiency payments to cover the difference between the domestic price and the intervention price. Another mode of domestic support is to subsidize the use of inputs. In such a case, the subsidy-adjusted supply curve *S'* reflects the lower marginal cost of production with subsidized inputs rather than a subsidy of *Ss* paid on output. Domestic output still rises to *Qs2*, but the supply price remains equal to the domestic price, *Ph*, in this case.

It should be observed that the production subsidy or domestic support measure does not affect consumption provided that the world price remains constant. With the domestic price constant at *Ph*, the quantity demanded by domestic residents remains at *Qd1* in both panels of Figure 16.2. Although domestic support measures of the type being analyzed here have a smaller impact on trade than a comparable border measure because there are only supply distortions and no demand distortions, trade effects remain. In both panels of Figure 16.2, the arrows labeled *SD* indicate supply distortions arising from the domestic support policy. As a result of the supply distortion, imports fall to *Qm2* in the left panel and exports rise to *Qx2* in the right panel. In turn, there will be downward pressure on the world price as a result of either a decline in Home's imports or an increase in its exports. Consequently, domestic support, like border measures, tends to have a beggar-thy-neighbor impact on foreign producers.[9]

Exceptions to this rule can, however, be found. Consider, for example a land 'set aside' in agricultural production where producers are subsidized to reduce the use of an input, namely land. In this case, though producers are supported, their marginal costs rise and the subsidy-adjusted supply curve shifts up rather than down in Figure 16.2. This leads to lower output, greater imports or reduced exports and, thus, upward pressure on world price. While a trade distortion remains, world prices tend to rise, generating benefits to producers in 'neighboring' countries.

Since domestic support measures typically have a trade distorting impact, they too are subject to disciplines in the GATT and other related WTO supervised agreements. While domestic subsidies that are deemed to cause minimal trade distortion are permissible, those that cause more significant trade distortions such as production subsidies are actionable as unfair trade practices. For example, an exporting country that uses production subsidies can be subjected to countervailing duties applied by importing countries. Until the Uruguay Round, there were no disciplines on domestic support in agriculture. While the resulting Agreement on Agriculture has limited the use of countervailing duties on actionable subsidies during an adjustment period, it has also required that each country reduce its aggregate measure of support (WTO 1999).[10] Once again, multilateral agreement on trade disciplines for domestic support measures does not remove domestic political pressures to provide support when producer groups are struggling against hard times. This leads to the question of whether it is possible to design de-coupled domestic support measures that do not distort trade.

De-coupled domestic support?

Proponents of de-coupled support contend that subsidies based on past actions, such as historic production in an earlier reference period, involve little if any trade distortion. Subsidies based on past production have been used in agriculture in the US and other countries (Kerr 1988; Gaisford *et al.* 2003). Provided that such a subsidy is not anticipated, it tends to have a minimal impact on the behavior of firms in the short run. The producer price remains equal to the domestic price, *Ph*, in Figure 16.2. Further, the marginal costs of each firm, which govern their supply behavior, do not change so that the industry supply curve *S* is not affected. Consequently, domestic output remains unchanged at *Qs*1 in spite of the presence of the support policy. Further, provided that historic production is highly correlated with current production potential, the support will generally reach its target.

It is difficult, however, to maintain de-coupled support on an ongoing basis. Since the most likely objective is to support current producers, the base period for determining subsidies may be revised from time to time and businesses may be required to have an ongoing minimum presence in the industry to maintain their eligibility for subsidies. Either of these features creates problems. Clearly, there may be an added incentive to produce at present if this year's output may eventually be rolled into a new base-period output for determining future subsidies. In effect, the expected future benefit from an extra unit of output today lowers the effective current marginal cost leading each firm to produce more. In Figure 16.2, the industry supply curve shifts down to *S'* with trade-distorting consequences.

If a firm is required to have an ongoing presence in the industry, there are also problems. In Figure 16.3, we assume that there are quality differences across firms in some firm-specific input such as management capability or land. As the industry expands, less efficient firms with higher marginal and average costs enter. This leads to the upward sloping long-run supply industry supply curve S in the left panel and creates differential rents for the superior firms that enter first. Suppose that, in the past, the world price was Pw and the domestic industry was in a long-run equilibrium producing an output of Qs. At that time, the marginal firm – the last and weakest firm to have entered the industry – had long-run average and marginal costs shown by AC and MC respectively in the right panel of Figure 16.3. Consequently, the marginal firm produced output qs, where the price, Pw, was equal to the minimum long-run average cost, $minAC$. Notice that the marginal firm was maximizing its profit since price was equal to marginal cost and it was just content to be in the industry because price was equal to average cost.

Suppose that the present world price has since fallen to Pw' and consider the long-run equilibrium that would eventually arise in the absence of policy intervention. The previous marginal firm, and all others with minimum long-run average costs in excess of Pw', would exit the industry. Further, the remaining firms with minimum long-run average costs less than or equal to Pw' would reduce their outputs, moving down and to the left along their long-run marginal cost curves. Consequently, in the absence of support policy, the industry output in the new long-run equilibrium would be Qs'.

Now suppose that the government offers a lump sum payment based on past production that reduces the marginal firm's long-run average costs to AC''. The payment happens to be just sufficient to allow the past marginal firm to survive at the lower world price, but in the new long run equilibrium that eventually arises its output is reduced to qs''. No firms exit the industry, though they – like the marginal firm – all reduce their outputs as they

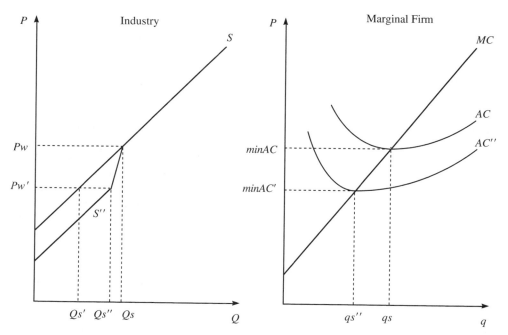

Figure 16.3   Allegedly de-coupled support in the long run

move down and to the left along their marginal cost curves. In Figure 16.1, the long-run equilibrium output for the industry is now Qs'', which exceeds the output of Qs', which would prevail in the absence of payment based on historic output. Consequently, trade is distorted in the long run. It should be observed, however, that a subsidy on current production would have shifted the marginal as well as the average cost curve downward, leaving the long-run outputs of the marginal firm and the industry unchanged from the past at qs and Qs respectively. Thus, the subsidy based on historic production remains less trade distorting than a comparable subsidy based on current production, but it is no longer 'de-coupled'. Subsidies paid for research and development and other non-production activities, which have a negligible trade distorting effect in the short run, also have a significant impact entry or exit decisions. In the long run, therefore, few if any domestic support measures are fully de-coupled from output and trade.[11]

Warranted domestic subsidies?
Before concluding, it is important to consider whether policy measures that affect domestic production or consumption, and thus international trade, are ever economically justifiable.[12] Indeed, in cases of market failure, such policy measures can be warranted on economic efficiency grounds. For example, in the debates over so-called multifunctionality and non-trade concerns in the WTO Doha Round trade negotiations on agriculture, the EU and countries such as Japan and Norway have argued that support policy is warranted because so-called externalities have led to divergences between the private and social costs of production (Gaisford *et al.* 2003: 87). More specifically, it is claimed that there may be external benefits from agricultural activity related to flood control, the amenity value of rural countryside, etc. In Figure 16.2, suppose that the S curve reflects private costs while the S' curve reflects social costs. In this case, the production subsidy of Ss dollars per unit, which leads to an output of $Qs2$, would be warranted on economic efficiency grounds because it equates the price with the marginal social cost of agricultural output.

There have been two important criticisms of such externalities arguments. First, the externalities may be negligible in magnitude and the argument may be primarily a protectionist subterfuge. Second, even if the externalities are substantial, it is better to subsidize or tax as close to the source as possible. Subsidies, if they are warranted, should be paid for flood-control or amenity-enhancing activities rather than for agricultural production *per se*. While both criticisms have potential merit and should be taken seriously (Gaisford *et al.* 2003: 87), it remains true that some subsidies are warranted on economic efficiency grounds. Unfortunately, there is not always a close correspondence between the domestic subsidies that are permissible under the rules of the multilateral trade system and those that are warranted on economic efficiency grounds (Gaisford and McLachlan 1999).

Conclusion
Border measures and domestic support measures usually have an affect on international trade flows. Very often, but not always, policies put in place to support industry-related interests in one country, have a beggar-thy-neighbor, impact on producers in the same sector in the rest of the world. Subsidies paid for land set asides and environmental improvements, however, have the opposite effect provided that they reduce domestic

output. There have been attempts to de-couple support policy from current production decisions by basing payments on non-production activities, such as research and development, or past actions, such as historic production levels. On the one hand, if such support policies are intended only for a short duration during a temporary crisis or to facilitate orderly downsizing of a domestic industry, the prognosis for minimal trade-distortion is favorable. On the other hand, if the policies are to be ongoing, the goal of de-coupled support appears almost certain to be illusory. Further, even if de-coupling were possible, it would not be a panacea. Subsidies that affect production or consumption, and thus trade, may be warranted in cases of market failure.

Notes

1. The analysis is readily reinterpreted in the two-good general-equilibrium context, where explicit equilibrium in one market implies equilibrium in the other market due to a convenient property known as Walras' law. For a thorough introduction to the partial equilibrium approach to international trade analysis, see Chapter 2 of Gaisford and Kerr (2001).
2. Here the so-called user cost of capital, which enters into the average cost, includes the costs associated with risk and forgone interest. Thus, a reasonable return on capital is included.
3. The analysis of *ad valorem* or percentage tariffs and export subsidies is equivalent. In this case the domestic price is equal to world price multiplied one plus the tariff or export subsidy rate.
4. Assuming a constant world price, the quantitative gains and losses resulting from a tariff or export subsidy can be examined using Figure 16.1. Using the left panel to consider the tariff, the increase in the domestic price from Pw to Ph causes a gain in producer surplus of $a1$ dollars, an increase in government revenue of $a3$ dollars, a decline in consumer surplus of $a1+a2+a3+a4$ dollars and an overall loss in total surplus equal to $a2+a4$ dollars. Thus, there is a supply-side distortionary loss of $a2$ dollars and a demand-side distortionary loss of $a4$ dollars. Using the right panel to examine the export subsidy, the increase in the domestic price from Pw to Ph causes a gain in producer surplus of $e1+e2+e3$ dollars, a decrease in government revenue of $e2+e3+e4$ dollars, a decline in consumer surplus of $e1+e2$ dollars and an overall loss in total surplus equal to $e2+e4$ dollars. Thus there is a supply-side distortionary loss of $e4$ dollars and a demand side distortionary loss of $e3$ dollars. See Chapter 2 of Gaisford and Kerr (2001).
5. When home is an importing country, the decrease in the world price represents a terms-of-trade gain. If the tariff is sufficiently small, the terms-of-trade gain will outweigh the distortionary losses and the country will gain. Excessive tariffs, however, will reduce national welfare in Home. Since the rest of the world is exporting, the decline in the world price represents a terms-of-trade loss, which reduces overall welfare. When Home is an exporting country, the decrease in the world price represents a terms-of-trade loss for the country, which is additional to the distortionary losses. Consequently, an export subsidy always reduces Home's national welfare. Meanwhile, the rest of the world experiences a terms-of-trade gain and, thus, is always better off overall (see Gaisford *et al.* 2003: 54–61).
6. There is extensive further discussion on border measures in this volume: aspects of tariffs are discussed further in Chapters 17, 19 and 20; export subsidies and related matters are discussed in Chapters 26, 28 and 30; issues linked to import quotas, VERs, and TRQs are discussed in Chapters 22–25, and export taxes are discussed in Chapter 21.
7. The analysis of a percentage or *ad valorem* subsidy is qualitatively equivalent. In this case the producer price is equal to domestic price multiplied one plus the production subsidy rate.
8. Assuming constant world and domestic prices, the quantitative gains and losses resulting from a production subsidy can be examined using Figure 16.2 (see also Gaisford *et al.* 2003: 78–84). In the left panel where Home is an importer, the increase in the supply price from Ph to Ps causes a gain in producer surplus of $b1$ dollars, a loss in government revenue of $b1+b2$ dollars, and a decline in total surplus equal to $b2$ dollars, which reflects a supply-side distortionary loss. In the right panel where Home is an exporter, there is a gain in producer surplus of $f1+f2$ dollars, a decrease in government revenue of $f1+f2+f3$ dollars and an overall supply-side distortionary loss of $f3$ dollars. If the production subsidy is superimposed on a tariff or export subsidy, the earlier analysis in Figure 16.1 changes slightly because the final quantity supplied will be at $Qs2$, which is greater than $Qs1$. In the case of an import tariff in the left panel of Figure 16.1, the tariff revenue will fall as area $a3$ shrinks and the supply-side distortionary loss will increase as area $a2$ expands. In the case of an export subsidy in the right panel of Figure 16.1, the supply-side distortionary loss increases as area $e4$ expands. This also increases the government outlay on export subsidies.
9. When Home is an importer, the decline in the world price represents a terms-of-trade gain for it but a terms-of-trade loss for the rest of the world. If the production subsidy is sufficiently small, Home's terms

of trade gain will outweigh its distortionary loss, and it will experience an overall welfare gain. If the subsidy is excessively large, however, Home will lose overall. When Home is an exporter, the decline in the world price will represent a terms-of-trade loss for it and a gain for the rest of the world. Consequently Home will lose on an overall basis from the production subsidy, but the rest of the world will gain. (For further details, see Gaisford *et al.* 2003: 78–84.)

10. Issues related to production subsidies are examined in detail in Chapter 27 and countervailing duties are explored in Chapter 33.
11. Even in the short run, there is a snag if there is an ongoing presence required in the industry. If the world and domestic prices are sufficiently low that some firms would have temporarily shut down by electing not to produce at all, they may remain open simply to collect subsidies. As a result, even short-run industry output will not be decoupled.
12. Consumption measures, such as consumption taxes and subsidies, can be analyzed in a manner analogous to the production measures. A consumption tax, for example, raises the demand price above the domestic price. This reduces in the quantity demanded leading to greater exports or reduced imports, and downward pressure on the world price.

References

Gaisford, J. D. and W. A. Kerr (2001), *Economic Analysis for International Trade Negotiations: The WTO and Agricultural Trade*, Cheltenham, UK, and Northampton, MA, USA: Edward Elgar.
Gaisford, J. D., W. A. Kerr and N. Perdikis (2003), *Economic Analysis for EU Accession Negotiations: Agri-Food Issues in the EU's Eastward Expansion*, Cheltenham, UK, and Northampton, MA, USA: Edward Elgar.
Gaisford, J. D. and D. L. McLachlan (1990), 'Domestic Subsidies and Countervail: the Treacherous Ground of the Level Playing Field', *Journal of World Trade*, **24**(4), 55–78.
Kerr, W. A. (1988), 'The Canada–United States Free Trade Agreement and the Livestock Sector: The Second Stage Negotiations', *Canadian Journal of Agricultural Economics*, **36**(4), 895–903.
WTO (1999), *World Trade Organization: the Legal Texts*, Cambridge, UK: Cambridge University Press.

17 Tariffs: national welfare and distributional issues
Jean-Philippe Gervais and Bruno Larue

Introduction

Broad globalization forces are pressuring governments throughout the world to eliminate trade barriers and lower tariffs. In essence, the work started after World War II to lower tariffs on manufactured products is nearly complete; but agri-food trade liberalization only started in the mid-1990s. As a result, many countries still use tariffs to protect their borders from foreign competition. As such, tariffs are not obsolete trade instruments. Many reasons can be called upon to explain the persistence of tariffs in agri-food markets and in some other sectors. One strand of the literature appeals to political-economy considerations to rationalize the choice of trade instrument and the level of protection.[1]

Another factor that can explain border protection is the so-called terms of trade[2] argument. This argument dates back to the nineteenth century and is almost as old as Ricardo's principle of comparative advantage (Kemp 1966). It is based on the notion that a country that has a large enough trade volume to influence prices at which it trades can increase its level of welfare relative to the free trade benchmark by restricting trade below the free-trade level. The rationale for government intervention is a terms of trade externality because individual agents cannot by themselves exploit their joint market power. Hence, the government must step in to harness the country's market power through a tax on trade. In the case of a large policy-active importing country, the optimal import tariff in *ad valorem* terms is equal to the inverse of the foreign export supply elasticity.[3] The fact the optimal import tariff can unequivocally be welfare-enhancing for a large policy-active importing country hinges upon the assumption that there is no retaliation by foreign trade partners, that there is perfect competition in the economy and that policy commitment is credible in any dynamic setting. In reality, markets are not always competitive and foreign trading partners are seldom passive.

The current chapter is structured as follows. The next section formally defines the optimal tariff argument in its simplest form; that is when there is perfect competition, no retaliation from foreign trade partners, no uncertainty and trade policy commitment is credible. The following section relaxes the previous assumptions in our welfare analysis of tariffs. The third section addresses changes in the market structure assumption. In particular, the possibility of foreign retaliation is analyzed as well as the possibility that other policy-active importing countries simultaneously use tariffs. The role of domestic and foreign market structures are also studied in greater details. Going back to the initial setting of a single policy-active importer, the fourth section focuses on dynamic considerations by assuming that policy makers and firms do not face the same sequence of decisions and that tariff commitment is not feasible. The results from this section demonstrate the importance of trade institutions.

The fifth section discusses the impacts of uncertainty on optimal tariffs. A short discussion about the (non)equivalence of tariffs and quotas is presented. Distributional issues related to tariffs are discussed in the sixth section. The seventh section reviews empirical studies pertaining to the optimal tariff, and as such it sheds some light on the practical relevance of the optimal tariff argument. Plainly put, is it just a theoretical curiosity or does it matter to policy makers? It is argued that the answer is more complicated than a simple yes or no. While it may be difficult to increase welfare through an optimal tariff if one considers the many factors that must be accounted for before setting the tariff level, it is crucial for policy makers to recognize the incentives created by the terms of trade argument in order to understand the trade policy negotiation forum. The final section provides concluding remarks.

Defining the optimal tariff

It is now well recognized in the economics literature that a country can raise its welfare compared to free trade by restricting trade flows. Kemp (1966) credits economists such as Torrens, Mill and Sidgwick for developing the concept of the optimal tariff. Professor Bickerdike (1906) first proposed that the terms of trade advantage of the policy-active country be related to elasticity parameters. Graaf (1949) and Johnson (1951–1952) later formalized the optimal tariff argument. As mentioned in the introduction, under the assumptions of no domestic distortions and of perfect competition on domestic markets, a policy-active country can increase welfare by taxing trade. In the case of importables, the optimal tariff argument entails setting an *ad valorem* tax equal to the inverse of the foreign export supply elasticity. For a so-called small country, the exogeneity of its terms of trade implies that it is confronted with an infinitely elastic foreign export supply and that its optimal tariff is zero. In essence, any reduction in a small country's volume of imports is too small to trigger a reduction in the world price. It is not so for a so-called large country because changes in its trade volumes are sufficiently important to directly impact on world prices. For this reason, a large importing country must act to re-establish the equality between the marginal cost of its imports and the domestic marginal benefit accruing from its importing activities.

The optimal tariff argument can be illustrated using either partial equilibrium or general equilibrium frameworks. Explaining the optimal tariff argument in a standard two-good–two-countries general equilibrium framework requires the use of trade indifference curves and offer curves.[4] Trade indifference curves are community indifference curves defined in terms of excess demand and excess supply. The first welfare theorem of economics states that if there are no distortions in the domestic market, a competitive general equilibrium is Pareto optimal. In the context of a trade equilibrium, the marginal rate of substitution between two commodities should equal the domestic marginal rate of transformation for welfare to be maximized. The curve U^{ft} in Figure 17.1 illustrates the combination of imports of good F and exports of good M for which these conditions hold (Wong 1997). Indifference curves which are higher and to the left correspond to higher levels of welfare for the economy.[5] The ratio of world prices is represented by the slope of the segment tangent to the indifference curve. For a small country, this ratio is constant; and free trade is optimal because the foreign rate of transformation (the terms of trade) equals the marginal rate of substitution (and the marginal rate of transformation in the absence of domestic distortions).

Figure 17.1 also illustrates both countries' offer curves; that is the general equilibrium export supply functions. The difference between a partial equilibrium excess supply function and an export supply function in a general equilibrium setting is that the former shows how

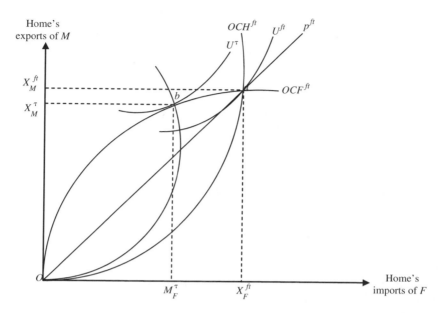

Figure 17.1

supply changes when only the output price changes while all other prices remain constant. Conversely, the general equilibrium export supply function shows how exports change following a change in relative commodity prices. As such, an offer curve represents the combinations of exports and imports that a country will choose at different relative prices. The curves OCH^{ft} and OCF^{ft} respectively represent the offer curves of the Home and Foreign countries under a *laissez-faire* scenario. The free trade equilibrium is represented by point *a*.

The optimal tariff entails a shift in the Home country's offer curve. For a given world price, a tariff reduces both exports and imports; and will also change the equilibrium terms of trade. In Figure 17.1, the shift in the Home country's offer curve will yield a new equilibrium point (b) if the Foreign country adopts a *laissez faire* policy (that is, no retaliation). This new trade equilibrium yields a higher welfare for the Home country (that is, $U^{\tau} > U^{ft}$). It is worth noting that this optimal tariff equilibrium can be supported with a number of different instruments. The point is that a policy-active country, wishing to make the foreign country undertake a particular level of trade, can achieve this with a tariff or an import quota or identical consumption tax and production subsidy.

Two caveats must be discussed at this stage. First, income distribution issues have been purposely ignored in the previous general equilibrium framework by appealing to the second welfare theorem and the assumption of zero administrative costs to redistribute income through lump sum transfers.[6] The relationship between tariffs and income distribution will be discussed later. Moreover, the optimal tariff increases welfare in the policy-active country at the expense of the rest of the world which sees its terms of trade worsens. The next section will look at retaliation from foreign trading partners.

Graaff (1949) first noted that the optimal tariff argument can entail negative trade taxes (that is, import or export subsidies). Horwell and Pearce (1970) provide an example in which substitution effects in supply and demand in the context of $N (> 1)$ goods entail at least one optimal tariff to be negative. The problem in a multi-commodity setting is that the optimal tariff structure is not unique. Bond (1990) analyzes more formally how the standard optimal tariff result can be extended to the general N good-case. He showed that, under fairly loose conditions, all goods cannot be subsidized in the optimal tariff structure. If all goods are gross substitutes, the most protected good must be an import good and the least protected commodity must be an export good. Moreover, certain conditions also ensure that all importables are more protected than export goods. Young (1991) shows that if certain regularity conditions on the foreign offer curve hold, the optimal tariff will be positive on average.

The role of domestic and world market structures
The remainder of the chapter relaxes the basic assumptions made in the previous section. Consider now the possibility of retaliation by the Foreign country. Figure 17.2 analyzes the retaliation equilibrium as explained by Johnson (1953–1954). The simultaneous use by the Foreign country of an export tariff and by the Home country of an import tariff induces both offer curves to shift inward. The 'tariff-war' equilibrium is at point b and welfare for the Home country is lower than in the no-retaliation scenario (that is, $U^R < U^\tau$). Note that the example in Figure 17.2 also implies that welfare under retaliation is lower than the free-trade scenario. The example also suggests that free trade is not optimal from the Foreign country's perspective given that its trading partner is using a tariff. It is however possible to construct an equilibrium in which the optimal tariff under retaliation will increase welfare of one of the two countries (but not both) with respect to the free trade situation. Syropoulos (2002) spelled out the sufficient conditions for a country to prefer a non-cooperative tariff equilibrium under retaliation over free trade.

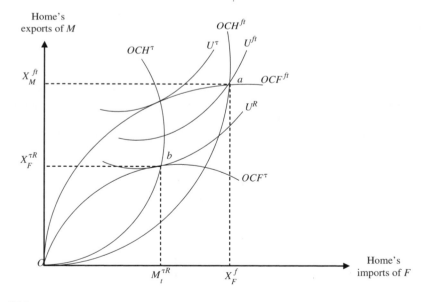

Figure 17.2

Raimondos-Moller and Woodward (2000) also showed that when a small country trades with a single foreign partner that is large (in the trade sense), the former can gain by committing to a non-zero tariff in order to force the large policy-active country to adopt a lower trade tax. This strategy is appealing for the small country because it forces the large country to be less aggressive in its attempt to improve its terms of trade. This mitigating strategy is better welfare-wise than a *laissez-faire* policy.

Consider next the case in which $N > 1$ importing countries have purchasing power on the world market and face passive exporting countries. We can assume that the rest of the world's excess supply consists of many small exporting nations that cannot influence their terms of trade. This strategic game between policy-active importers was first introduced by Bergstrom (1982) and later analyzed by Karp and Newbery (1991, 1992)[7] and Gervais and Lapan (2001). Bergstrom (1982) analyzed a situation in which policy-active importing countries set their trade instrument given their belief about the type of instrument the other importers will use. When the strategy space is restricted to the use of a tariff, the non-cooperative equilibrium entails lower tariffs for each country than in the situation when they collude and act as a single monopoly importer. Each country would be better off if it implemented the collusion strategy which calls for smaller levels of imports.

Dynamics can also be included in the bilateral monopoly setting. Syropoulos (1994) endogenized trade policies in a two-good, two-country world by building a two-stage game. In the first stage, both countries declare simultaneously whether they wish to move early or late. A declaration of the type [*Early(E),E*] or [*Late(L),L*] implies that both players set their trade instrument simultaneously at the first or second stage. A declaration [*E,L*] or [*L,E*] implies that one country becomes the leader while the other is the follower. The non-cooperative equilibrium of this dynamic sequence still entails positive trade flows, even when export quotas are used.

The standard rule for the optimal tariff can be substantially altered if the domestic market is imperfectly competitive. Collie (1991), Lahiri and Ono (1999) and Larue and Gervais (2002) have relaxed the assumption of perfect competition in the domestic market. Larue and Gervais (2002) derive welfare-maximizing and revenue-maximizing taxes for several domestic market configurations. In all of their settings, foreign firms are price-takers whether they sell directly to domestic consumers or to domestic importing firms. In one particular setting, they assume imperfect competition among domestic firms and importing firms. Barriers to entry in importing activities can be maintained through discretionary import license allocation mechanisms or other institutional/market features. This is not uncommon for example in agri-food markets that are protected by Tariff-Rate Quotas (TRQs).[8] If domestic firms behave *à la* Cournot and exert leadership *vis-à-vis* foreign firms, the optimal import tariff is generally higher than the standard optimal tariff (defined as the reciprocal of the foreign export supply elasticity).[9] The argument is relatively easy to understand if one realizes that a tariff can always be decomposed into a production subsidy and a consumption tax on the importable good. There are two market failures; the terms of trade externality and imperfect competition on the domestic market. The former encourages the taxing of consumption and the subsidizing of production at the same rate while the latter exert pressure to subsidize production because not enough output is produced domestically.

If domestic firms are involved in production and trade, the welfare-maximizing tariff can be negative, provided that the number of firms is small. The government's problem is one of product sourcing. It wishes to encourage domestic sales by subsidizing imports, thus lowering the domestic firms' marginal cost to generate more competitive pricing decisions. This incentive to subsidize imports must be weighted against the incentive to tax imports. Of course, because there are two market failures, the first-best solution would also entail using both a domestic policy to curb market power (such as a price ceiling) and a tariff.

The zero tariff/free trade policy prescription for a small country is not robust to changes in market structure assumption. For example, Katrak (1977) assumed that a single foreign firm was supplying a small open economy. The importing country can increase its welfare by taxing imports if certain demand conditions are met, thus shifting rent from the foreign firm. The import tariff raises the cost structure of the foreign monopolist. Starting from a free trade situation a small import tariff will increase the domestic price, but will lower the foreign monopolist's supply price. The importing country's improved terms of trade allows for the tariff revenue to more than compensate for the loss in consumer surplus. Kolev and Prusa (1999) extended the previous setting by assuming that the importing country has incomplete information about the foreign monopolist's cost structure. They found that the policy prescription of Katrak is not robust to various information settings. Jones and Takemori (1989) extend the possibilities for a small country to use an import tariff by considering various forms of imperfect competition in foreign countries. With imperfectly competitive suppliers, a small country might be able to improve its terms of trade if its market is segmented from that in supplying countries.

The case of a small economy extracting rents from a foreign monopolist paved the way to the profit-shifting argument pioneered by Brander and Spencer (1985). It is well known in the literature that if a firm from country A and a firm from country B have identical unit costs, Cournot conjectures, and compete in a third market, the optimal policy for governments A and B is to subsidize exports even though it runs counter to the standard argument that export subsidies depress world prices.[10] However, Eaton and Grossman (1986) demonstrated that if the few domestic and foreign firms engage in Bertrand price competition, the policy-active government can raise welfare by taxing exports. This sensitivity of the results to a change in conjectures has long been considered a devastating blow to the relevance of strategic trade policies. However, Maggi (1996) developed a general framework in which firms invest in their capacity of production in a first stage before competing in prices in a second stage. If it is costly (cheap) to adjust capacity once the initial investment has been made, then the game between the firms resembles a one-shot Cournot (Bertrand) game. Maggi showed that in this setting, a capacity subsidy is always optimal regardless of the 'apparent' conduct mode.

Time consistent tariffs and welfare
As pointed out by Staiger (1995), an optimal trade policy is bound to lack credibility if there is a sufficient degree of discretion in policy setting. Lapan (1988) pointed out that the standard optimal tariff is not time consistent when production decisions are made before consumption and trade decisions and a government can readjust its tariff between production and marketing decisions. This setting is particularly relevant in agricultural markets, but the same issue would arise if there was a lag between capital/investment decisions and labor decisions. From an *ex-post* perspective, that is once production decisions are made, the foreign export supply elasticity is lower than the *ex-ante* elasticity. Therefore, policy makers have an incentive to set *ex-post* tariffs at

a higher level than they would if they could precommit to the *ex-ante* tariff. Foreign and domestic producers deduce that the *ex-ante* tariff is not time consistent and adjust their production accordingly. As a result, foreign production ends up being lower than if the large country could have committed to the *ex-ante* optimal tariff and both countries end up worse off. The importance of the timing assumption is immediate once it is recalled that a tariff can always be decomposed into a production subsidy and a consumption tax on the importable good. The pre-commitment solution is welfare superior to the no-commitment solution.

Figure 17.3 illustrates the implications of the time consistent tariff when a policy-active importer cannot credibly commit to its trade policy in a partial equilibrium framework.[11] The segment *ED* is the excess demand of the domestic country and *ES^{ea}* is the standard excess supply function. The height of *ED* is the maximum willingness to pay for one more unit of imports while the height of the excess supply function represents the marginal cost of exports for foreign suppliers. Because the Home country is large enough, it faces an upward supply function and thus the *ex-ante* marginal cost of imports from an *ex-ante* perspective (that is, before production and consumption decisions are made) is represented by *MC^{ea}*. Free trade equilibrium is represented by point *a*. It is assumed that the Foreign country adopts a policy of *laissez-faire*.

The optimal tariff implies an equilibrium in which marginal benefits equal marginal costs (point *b*). The optimal tariff if the policy-active importer can commit to its policy is τ^{ea}. Consider the case in which the policy-active government can revise its tariff once production decisions are made. The foreign export supply elasticity is *ES^{ep}*; and it is less elastic than *ES^{ea}* due to the fact that production can no longer be adjusted. Time consistency of the policy requires that foreign firms correctly anticipate that the policy-active government

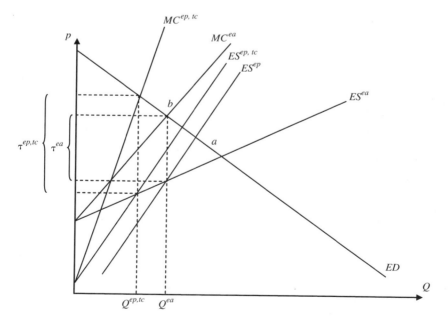

Figure 17.3

will revise its policy once production decisions are made. With perfect foresight, foreign producers fully anticipate the time consistent tariff and decrease their production accordingly which results in the shifting of the *ex-post* excess supply function to $ES^{ep,tc}$. The optimal *ex-post* tariff is $\tau^{ep,tc}$. It is easy to verify that the policy-active government loses from the inability to precommit.[12]

Gervais and Lapan (2002) examined the robustness of the previous conclusions when there are $N\ (>1)$ policy-active importing countries in the word market as in Bergstrom (1982). In their setting, *ex-post* tariffs are still higher than *ex-ante* tariffs because the residual export supply curve elasticity faced by each country is lower *ex-post*. However, the no-commitment situation may be welfare increasing for policy-active importers compared to the *ex-ante* equilibrium because the inability to commit offsets the negative welfare effect due to the non-cooperative behavior of policy-active importing nations.

Tariffs and uncertainty

There is a vast literature on the setting and welfare implications of tariffs under uncertainty. Many studies are centered on tariffs-quota welfare comparisons (see Fishelson and Flatters 1975; Dasgupta and Stiglitz 1977; Pelcovits 1976; Young 1980; Young and Anderson 1982, among others). It should not be inferred from such comparisons that restricting trade is always better than free trade under uncertainty. As mentioned above, tariffs and quotas are equivalent under perfect competition and perfect information in the sense that the import vector generated by the tariff vector, if realized through a set of quotas, will generate an implicit tariff vector identical to the tariff policy. Under uncertainty, tariffs are generally considered welfare superior to quotas because tariffs lead to arbitrage of imports across states of the world. The ranking can be reversed for example if real income fluctuations are greater under the tariff. If individuals are risk averse, the fluctuations in income reduce the attractiveness of the tariff compared to the quota. The common weakness in all of these studies is that it is never explained why there is protection in the first place. The usual practice is to compare tariffs and quotas under an expected imports constraint or some other non-economic objective. The results are usually sensitive to the variable anchoring the comparisons and the source of the uncertainty. Lapan and Choi (1988) provide a ranking of tariffs and quotas under an import-induced externality (for example, pollution) for a small country facing foreign price uncertainty and domestic production disturbances. When the external damage function is linear in imports and the indirect utility function is linear in income, their model reduces to the standard expected welfare criteria. In the more general case, quotas are more likely to dominate tariffs when the price elasticity of demand for imports or the elasticity of the marginal external damage function is large.

Similar to the uncertainty case, there exists a sizeable literature that studies the non-equivalence of trade policies under various non-economic objectives. Bhagwati's (1965) standard result on the non-equivalence of tariffs and quotas when the domestic production is controlled by a monopolist is a classic example. For a quota and a tariff yielding the same volume of imports, the quota triggers a higher price and lower consumption of the good than the tariff. However, for a quota and a tariff yielding the same domestic price, output under a tariff is higher than under a quota which may be an advantage or a disadvantage for the tariff relative to the quota depending on the positioning the marginal cost of production relative to the marginal cost of imports.

If we go back to the topic of national welfare, a number of interesting results can be established. Syropoulos (1994) showed that, in a bilateral world market with retaliation, import quotas do not replicate the tariff equilibrium and thus that these two policies are never equivalent if both countries restrict trade. Unlike what had been argued by Rodriguez (1974), quotas do not asymptotically eliminate trade in a trade war. The extreme result derived by Rodriguez had been an important reason to favour tariffs in the selection of an instrument of protection. The point made by Syropoulos (1994) is that sequential equilibria Pareto dominate Rodriguez's equilibrium. Once the timing of policy announcements is endogenized, it is easy to show that the Rodriguez equilibrium is not subgame perfect. Grant and Quiggin (1997) have endogenized the type of tariff used by a large country in a bilateral framework. They assume that each country has an export supply function subject to a random shock. In equilibrium, the optimal tariff rule is given by the common inverse elasticity rule. However, given the structure of export supply functions, the optimal tariff policy in equilibrium varies from a specific tariff (semi-log linear schedules), to an *ad valorem* tariff (constant elasticity schedules) or to a quadratic tariff (linear export schedules). Their model can explain the ubiquity of *ad valorem* trade taxes in the real world. They argue the popularity of *ad valorem* tariffs is evidence that policy makers believe that export supply functions are characterized by constant price elasticities. Since all countries observe their own shock but not the other countries' shock, the equilibrium of the game is one in beliefs. It may not be the case that the export supply schedules literally exhibit constant price elasticity. It may just be that the perception of policy makers is shaped by numerous econometric or computable general equilibrium studies which have used a log-linear specification to estimate export supply schedules.

Tariff and income distribution
Distribution issues related to the optimal tariff have been assumed away to this point using a representative consumer model and the assumption that the tariff revenue is distributed in a lump-sum manner. In 1949, Metzler (1994) pointed out that changes in a country's terms of trade are closely related to the distribution of national income. Bhagwati and Johnson (1961) were perhaps the first to explicitly analyze the case in which consumers are not homogeneous, thus allowing for changes in domestic prices through terms of trade variations to redistribute real income between consumers. Chang and Michael (1988) relax the assumption that consumers are identical by assuming that consumers have different endowments and preferences. Under these assumptions, the optimal tariff calls for the marginal utilities of income among all consumers to be equal. If the tariff revenue can be distributed in this optimal way, the optimal tariff in the many consumers case is identical to the formula of the optimal tariff under the representative agent assumption. If the optimal income redistribution scheme cannot be implemented, a second-best situation arises and the optimal tariff will generally not be equal to the orthodox optimal tariff. Even though the second-best tariff formula can be reconciled in some instances with the standard formula, the tariffs will not be equal because the equilibrium terms of trade will be different and thus the elasticity of the foreign export supply function will also be different.

In the Chang–Michael framework, tariffs emerge as second-best instruments because redistribution is a not a choice variable and the manner with which the tariff revenue is distributed to consumers is exogenous. The role of tariffs as second-best instruments is certainly not unique. For example, Eaton and Grossman (1986) analyze tariffs as a partial substitute for insurance markets. In a world where there are asymmetries in tastes or endowments or when agents must commit to certain activities before uncertainty is resolved, insurance markets have an important role in re-establishing the case for free trade for a small country facing uncertain terms of trade. If risk sharing agreements between private agents are difficult to implement, perhaps because of moral hazard, tariffs may be used as instruments to redistribute income and bring about an improvement over *laissez-faire*. The first best policy would entail redistributing income without affecting producers' or consumers' prices. Another second-best example involving tariffs is found in Choi and Lapan (1991). They analyze the optimality of tariffs in the provision of a public good that enters the utility function of consumers when a small economy is facing random terms of trade and domestic taxes are not feasible. In this instance, the optimal tariff for a small country is not zero.

Melvin (1987) considers the regional implications of tariffs in a Heckscher–Ohlin model when two regions within a country have different factor endowments ratios and are separated by great distances, like Eastern and Western Canada. Cross-hauling takes place at the country level and changes in the country's terms of trade benefit one region and hurt the other. Tariffs can be used to redistribute income directly from one region to another through the distribution of the tariff revenue, but they have other distribution-like effects through their impact on factor prices. Furthermore, the effects of a tariff cannot be duplicated by consumption and production taxes/subsidies.

It would be odd to say nothing about the effects of tariffs as a redistributive policy without saying a few words about the farm sector. After all, it may be difficult to reconcile the high level of protection in agri-food markets with welfare-maximizing arguments. Moschini and Sckokai (1994) argue that free trade is always welfare-superior to some tariff protection for a small country which redistributes income to farmers using de-coupled payments financed with a distortionnary taxation system. This highlights the fact that tariffs are not second-best instruments but third-best policies to redistribute income (Dixit and Norman 1980).

Finally, time consistency issues arising from using tariffs as a redistributive tool should also be acknowledged. Staiger and Tabellinni (1987, 1989) consider the credibility issue arising from the use of tariffs as a redistributive tool. In their setting, the government wishes to redistribute income between two sectors using an import tariff. Their results are similar to Lapan's (1988) conclusions that the time consistent trade policy involves more protection.[13]

Computing the optimal tariff structure

Given the various policy prescriptions implied by the terms of trade argument, it is only fair to ask if the whole optimal tariff argument has any practical policy value. Krugman and Obstfeld (2003: 224) wrote: 'The terms of trade argument against free trade, then, is intellectually impeccable but of doubtful usefulness. In practice, it is emphasized more by economists as a theoretical proposition than it is used by governments as a justification for trade policy.' Yet, Bagwell and Staiger (2002: 11) 'give primary emphasis' to the terms of trade approach in their most influential book on the economics of the world trading system. In spite of the orthogonal views on the merit of the terms of trade motivation to trade policy, it is nevertheless important to briefly summarize the literature on applied studies. The empirical studies can be divided according to two broad methodologies.

First, a few authors used econometric modelling to estimate the optimal tariff structure for policy-active countries. For example, Yousef (2000) estimates what might have been the optimal export tariff on Egyptian cotton exports in the early twentieth century. All econometric specifications used in the paper demonstrate that the optimal export tax was positive and that Egypt could have collected significant revenues had it not implemented a free trade policy. Other researchers have used Computable General Equilibrium (CGE) models to estimate the optimal tariff structure of small and large economies. With respect to the former, Abrego (2003) showed that the optimal tariff structure of the Costa Rican economy entails a combination of small tariffs that can be either positive or negative. Conversely, the Antebellum period[14] in the United States often serves as an example of the potential terms of trade gain for a large country exercising its dominant position on world markets. James (1981) argues that the optimal tariffs generated by a CGE model were superior to the actual average tariffs from 1821 to 1860 and that this difference did in fact widen up over that period. Conversely, Harley (1992) argues that the tariffs had no important terms-of-trade effects. Tariff protection had a significant effect in American industrialization because of the protection granted to American manufacturing firms.

Lee and Roland-Holst (1999) contend that bargaining strengths of Japan and the United States are asymmetrical and that the US would benefit from a tariff war in which both countries would use their optimal tariffs. This example serves to illustrate how asymmetry in trade negotiations setting can help understand cooperative outcome. Japan benefits more from US unilateral tariff liberalization than bilateral liberalization. Thus, it has an incentive to maintain its trade barriers. The potential threat of retaliation by the United States in that case can lead to the implementation of a cooperative agreement between the two countries. Other CGE estimates can be found in Hamilton and Whalley (1983).

Concluding remarks

This chapter has reviewed the optimal tariff argument under different assumptions related to world, domestic and foreign market structures, information settings, dynamics and redistributive objectives. It also provided a brief review of some applied studies that computed the optimal tariff structure for some economies. The initial optimal tariff argument referred to the possibility for a large country to improve its terms of trade by restricting trade below the free trade level. Obviously, this argument can be challenged on many fronts. Perhaps, the most important critique of the concept relates to its applicability in the real world. While it is fair to say that the information requirement to implement an optimal tariff structure may be excessive, the literature still offers deep insights on the various forces involved under trade liberalization talks. On this matter, a promising avenue of research has recently emerged (see for example Bagwell and Staiger 1999, 2001) in which terms of trade incentives are balanced against political-economy motives for protection to analyze trade policy decisions of policy-active countries.

Notes

1. For readers interested in this topic, Rodrik (1995) provides an excellent survey of political-economy models applied to trade policy.
2. Terms of trade are defined as the ratio of a country's export prices to its import prices. It is generally well understood that an increase in a country's terms of trade increases trade benefits for that country.

3. The Lerner (1936) symmetry theorem states that, in a general equilibrium framework, this equilibrium can be supported through the use of an export tariff.
4. Another way, attributed to G. Harberler, makes use of the production possibility frontier, the foreign country's offer curve and standard indifference curves. The disadvantage of this approach is that it is not nearly as convenient as the approach with offer curves and trade indifference curves to analyze scenarios involving retaliation.
5. By definition, the level of social welfare is constant along a trade indifference curve. The positive slope and convexity of a trade indifference curve indicate that increases in exports must be compensated by increasingly large volumes of imports. This outcome results from the fact that goods exported are foregone for domestic consumption and that welfare is conditioned only by domestic consumption.
6. In the current context, a lump-sum payment is a complete payment consisting of a single sum of money that does not distort agents' behavior.
7. These papers analyze the strategic behavior between importers of a depletable resource. There is a significant difference between the optimal tariff for an ordinary good compared to an exhaustible resource such as oil. Oil is available in a fixed amount and, if costless to extract, its supply will be inelastic. However, in a trade context, exports are not inelastic, that is there is a role for demand.
8. TRQs are multiple tier tariffs in which different tariffs are applied depending on the aggregate volume of imports. The TRQs defined in the Uruguay Round Agreement on Agriculture are two-tier tariffs.
9. We purposely leave aside the potential comparisons of *ad valorem* and specific tariffs throughout. In the standard optimal tariff case, a specific tariff is equivalent to an *ad valorem* tariff in that it yields the same welfare. There are however a number of situations in which the two instruments will not be equivalent.
10. If countries A and B have respectively n^a and n^b firms, then it would be optimal for country A to subsidize exports as long $n^a < n^b + 1$. Furthermore, the size of the equilibrium subsidy is positively conditioned by the cost advantage of country A's firms versus firms based in country B.
11. The partial equilibrium setting can be reconciled with the general equilibrium framework assuming that consumers' preferences in the home country are quasi-linear. The usefulness of the partial equilibrium analysis is that we can show directly the implications of the fixity of production (once production decisions are made) on the *ex-post* foreign supply curve.
12. Other time consistency problems were studied by Maskin and Newbery (1990) who modeled the behavior of a large importer of oil unable to commit to future tariffs in a two-period model. Karp and Newbery (1991, 1992) also analyze time consistent tariffs through infinite planning horizon models with various competition modes between domestic and foreign firms.
13. Other papers have showed how future tariff removal is usually time inconsistent if protection was either granted to provide incentives to firms to reduce their costs or to a declining industry (Tornell 1991; Brainard 1994; and Wright 1995). Karp and Paul (1998) analyzed the impact of tariff commitment on the ability to affect the reallocation of labor in a declining industry.
14. The Antebellum period in the United States refers to the decades just prior to the American Civil War.

References

Abrego, L. (2003), 'Trade Liberalization in the Presence of Foreign Direct Investment and Tax Credits: Estimates for Costa Rica', *Review of Development Economics*, **7**, 192–203.

Bagwell, K. and R. W. Staiger (1999), 'An Economic Theory of GATT', *American Economic Review*, **89**, 215–48.

Bagwell, K. and R. W. Staiger (2001), 'Domestic Policies, National Sovereignty, and International Economic Institutions', *Quarterly Journal of Economics*, **116**, 519–62.

Bagwell, K. and R. W. Staiger (2002), *The Economics of the World Trading System*, Cambridge, MA: MIT Press.

Bergstrom, T. C. (1982), 'On Capturing Oil Rents with National Excise Tax', *American Economic Review*, **71**, 194–201.

Bhagwati, J. N. (1965), 'On the Equivalence of Tariffs and Quotas', in R. E. Baldwin, J. Bhagwati, R. E. Caves and H. G. Johnson (eds), *Trade, Growth, and the Balance of Payments: Essays in Honor of Gottfried Haberler*, Chicago, IL: Rand-McNally and Amsterdam: North Holland, 53–67.

Bhagwati, J. and H. G. Johnson (1961), 'A General Theory on the Effects of Tariffs on the Terms of Trade', *Oxford Economic Papers*, **13**, 225–53.

Bickerdike, C. F. (1990), 'The Theory of Incipient Taxes', *Economic Journal*, **16**, 529–35.

Bond, E. W. (1990), 'The Optimal Tariff Structure in Higher Dimensions', *International Economic Review*, **31**, 103–16.

Brainard, S. L. (1994), 'Last One Out Wins: Trade Policy in an International Exit Game', *International Economic Review*, **35**, 151–72.

Brander, J. A. and B. E. Spencer (1985), 'Export Subsidies and International Market Share Rivalry', *Journal of International Economics*, **18**, 83–100.

Chang, W. W. and M. S. Michael (1988), 'Optimum Tariff and Its Optimum Revenue Distribution', *Economics Letters*, **28**, 69–74.

Choi, E. K. and H. E. Lapan (1991), 'Optimal Trade Policies for a Developing Country under Uncertainty', *Journal of Development Economics*, **35**, 243–60.

Collie, D. (1991), 'Optimum Welfare and Maximum Revenue Tariffs under Oligopoly', *Scottish Journal of Political Economy*, **38**, 398–401.

Dasgupta, P. and J. E. Stiglitz (1977), 'Tariffs vs. Quotas as Revenue Raising Devices Under Uncertainty', *American Economic Review*, **67**(5), 975–81.

Dixit, A. K. and V. Norman (1980), *Theory of International Trade*, Cambridge: Cambridge University Press.

Eaton, J. and G. M. Grossman (1986), 'Optimal Trade and Industrial Policy under Oligopoly', *Quarterly Journal of Economics*, **101**, 383–406.

Fishelson, G. and F. Flatters (1975), 'The (Non)Equivalence of Optimal Tariffs and Quotas under Uncertainty', *Journal of International Economics*, **5**, 385–93.

Gervais, J-P. and H. E. Lapan (2001), 'Optimal Production Tax and Quota under Time Consistent Trade Policies', *American Journal of Agricultural Economics*, **83**, 921–33.

Gervais, J-P. and H. E. Lapan (2002), 'Time Consistent Export Quotas in an Oligopolistic World Market', *Journal of International Economics*, **56**, 445–63.

Graff, J. de V. (1949), 'On Optimum Tariff Structures', *Review of Economic Studies*, **17**, 47–59.

Grant, S. and J. C. Quiggin (1997), 'Strategic Trade Policy under Uncertainty: Sufficient Conditions for the Optimality of Ad Valorem, Specific and Quadratic Trade Taxes', *International Economic Review*, **38**(1), 187–203.

Hamilton, B. and J. Whalley (1983), 'Optimal Tariff Calculations in Alternative Trade Models and Some Possible Implications for Current World Trading Arrangements', *Journal of International Economics*, **15**, 323–48.

Harley, C. K. (1992), 'The Antebellum American Tariff: Food Exports and Manufacturing', *Explorations in Economic History*, **29**, 375–400.

Horwell, D. J. and I. F. Pearce (1970), 'A Look at the Structure of Optimal Tariff Rates', *International Economic Review*, **11**, 147–61.

James, J. A. (1981) 'The Optimal Tariff in the Antebellum United States', *American Economic Review*, **71**, 726–34.

Johnson, H. G. (1951–1952), 'Optimum Welfare and Maximum Revenue Tariffs', *Review of Economic Studies*, **19**, 28–35.

Johnson, H. G. (1953–1954), 'Optimum Tariffs and Retaliation', *Review of Economic Studies*, **21**, 142–53.

Jones, R. W. and S. Takemori (1989), 'Foreign Monopoly and Optimal Tariffs for the Small Open Economy', *European Economic Review*, **33**, 1691–707.

Karp, L. and D. M. Newbery (1991), 'Optimal Tariffs on Exhaustible Resources', *Journal of International Economics*, **30**, 285–99.

Karp, L. and D. M. Newbery (1992), 'Dynamically Consistent Oil Import Tariffs', *Canadian Journal of Economics*, **25**, 1–21.

Karp, L. and T. Paul (1998), 'Labor Adjustment and Gradual Reform: When is Commitment Important', *Journal of International Economics*, **46**, 333–62.

Katrak, H. (1977), 'Multinational Monopolies and Commercial Policy', *Oxford Economic Papers*, **29**, 283–91.

Kemp, M. C. (1966), 'The Gain from International Trade and Investment: A Neo-Heckscher–Ohlin Approach', *American Economic Review*, **61**, 788–809.

Kolev, D. R. and T. J. Prusa (1999), 'Tariff Policy for a Monopolist in a Signalling Game', *Journal of International Economics*, **49**, 51–76.

Krugman, P. R. and M. Obstfeld (2003), *International Economics: Theory and Policy*, 6th Edition, Boston, MA: Addison Wesley.

Lahiri, S. and Y. Ono (1999), 'Optimal Tariffs in the Presence of Middlemen', *Canadian Journal of Economics*, **32**, 55–70.

Lapan, H. E. (1988), 'The Optimal Tariff, Production Lags, and Time Consistency', *American Economic Review*, **78**, 395–401.

Lapan, H. E. and E. K. Choi (1988), 'Tariffs versus Quotas under Uncertainty: Restricting Imports and the Role of Preference', *International Economic Journal*, **2**, 35–55.

Larue, B. and J-P. Gervais (2002), 'The Welfare-Maximizing and Revenue-Maximizing Tariffs with a Few Domestic Firms', *Canadian Journal of Economics*, **35**, 786–804.

Lee, H. and D. Roland-Holst (1999), 'Cooperation or Confrontation in US–Japan Trade? Some General Equilibrium Estimates', *Journal of the Japanese and International Economies*, **13**, 119–39.

Lerner, A. P. (1936), 'The Symmetry between Import and Export Taxes', *Economica*, **3**, 306–13.

Maggi, G. (1996), 'Strategic Trade Policies with Endogenous Mode of Competition', *American Economic Review*, **86**, 237–58

Maskin, E. S. and D. M. Newbery (1990), 'Disadvantageous Oil Tariffs and Dynamic Consistency', *American Economic Review*, **80**, 143–56.
Melvin, J. R. (1987), *The Interregional Effects of Canadian Tariffs and Transportation Policy*, Toronto: University of Toronto Press
Metzler, L. A. (1994), 'Tariffs, the Terms of Trade, and the Distribution of National Income', published in A. V. Deardorff and R. M. Stern (eds), *The Stolper–Samuelson Theorem: A Golden Jubilee*, Studies in International Trade Policy, Ann Arbor, MI: University of Michigan Press, pp. 65–93.
Moschini, G. and P. Sckokai (1994), 'Efficiency of Decoupled Farm Programs under Distortionary Taxation', *American Journal of Agricultural Economics*, **76**, 362–70.
Pelcovits, M. (1976), 'Quotas versus Tariffs', *Journal of International Economics*, **6**, 363–70.
Raimondos-Moller, P. and A. D. Woodland (2000), 'Tariff Strategies and Small Open Economies', *Canadian Journal of Economics*, **33**, 25–40.
Rodriguez, C. A. (1974), 'The Non-Equivalence of Tariffs and Quotas under Retaliation', *Journal of International Economics*, **4**, 295–8.
Rodrik, D. (1995), 'Political Economy of Trade Policy', in G. Grossman and K. Rogoff (eds), *Handbook of International Economics*, Vol. 3, Amsterdam: Elsevier North Holland.
Staiger, R. W. (1995), 'International Rules and Institutions for Trade Policy', in G. M. Grossman and K. Rogoff (eds), *Handbook of International Economics*, Vol. 3, New York: North Holland.
Staiger, R. W. and G. Tabellini (1987), 'Discretionary Trade Policy and Excessive Protection', *American Economic Review*, **77**, 823–37.
Staiger, R. W. and G. Tabellini (1989), 'Rules and Discretion in Trade Policy', *European Economic Review*, **33**, 1265–77.
Syropoulos, C. (1994), 'Endogenous Timing in Games of Commercial Policy', *Canadian Journal of Economics*, **27**, 847–64.
Syropoulos, C. (2002), 'Optimum Tariffs and Retaliation Revisited: How Country Size Matters', *Review of Economic Studies*, **69**, 707–27.
Tornell, A. (1991), 'Time Consistency of Protectionist Programs', *Quarterly Journal of Economics*, **106**(3), 963–74.
Wright, D. J. (1995), 'Incentives, Protection and Time Consistency', *Canadian Journal of Economics*, **28**, 929–38.
Wong, K-Y. (1997), *International Trade in Goods and Factor Mobility*, Cambridge, MA: MIT Press.
Young, L. (1991), 'Optimal Tariffs: A Generalization', *International Economic Review*, **32**, 341–70.
Young, L. (1980), 'Tariffs vs. Quotas under Uncertainty: An Extension', *American Economic Review*, **70**, 522–7.
Young, L. and J. E. Anderson (1982), 'Risk Aversion and Optimal Trade Restrictions', *Review of Economic Studies*, **48**, 291–305.
Yousef, T. M. (2000), 'The Political Economy of Interwar Egyptian Cotton Policy', *Explorations in Economic History*, **37**, 301–25.

Recommended reading

Grossman, G. M. (1985), 'The Optimal Tariff for a Small Country under International Uncertainty: A Comment', *Oxford Economic Papers*, **37**, 154–8.
Itagaki, T. (1985), 'Optimal Tariffs for a Large and a Small Country under Uncertain Terms of Trade', *Oxford Economic Papers*, **37**, 292–7.
McCulloch, R. (1973), 'When are a Tariff and Quota Equivalent?', *Canadian Journal of Economics*, **6**, 503–11.

18 Trade and domestic policy: conduct and modeling
John Whalley

Introduction
It is widely acknowledged that the complexity of domestic policy interventions, which influence trade flows and are now the subject of substantial international negotiation, are different in their effects from those of tariffs that are widely analyzed by trade theorists. This is especially the case in such areas as services, competition policy, environmental regulation, product standards, professional accreditation, movement of persons and transportation regulation. It also applies to those areas of agricultural policy where the trade impacts are often significant, despite the commitments in the Uruguay Round to tariffy all border measures relating to agricultural trade.

Despite such acknowledgments, however, it remains commonplace in numerical simulation exercises to analyze the impacts of potential changes in these policies using *ad valorem* equivalent tariff treatment even though estimated impacts using explicit policy representation and *ad valorem* equivalent treatments will differ. The difficulty for modelers is that the detail and subtlety embodied in this wide array of policy interventions means that some simplification is appealing. In addition, no meaningful general propositions exist in the theoretical literature as to the sign or size of the differences in predicted effects. All that can seemingly be done is to investigate the differences case by case, but even here the findings are sensitive both to the particular form of model used as well as the model parameterization employed. As a result, there is relatively little in the literature that provides guidance as to the seriousness of the pitfalls and the degree to which *ad valorem* tariff equivalent treatment is misleading.

This chapter overviews three examples of numerical simulation exercises where explicit representations of policy interventions are compared to *ad valorem* equivalent modeling and draws on these examples to frame a broader discussion. The picture that emerges is that there are large quantitative and even qualitative differences in predicted impacts. In the absence of other firm guidance, these examples suggest that where interventions differ from tariff rates, *ad valorem* representation can be undertaken in numerical trade modeling only with substantial caveats. Policy differences do in fact matter, and consequently, modeling differences are warranted.

Geographical extension of free trade zones as a form of trade liberalization
The first example of comparison of explicit model representation and *ad valorem* equivalent modeling draws on a recent paper by Ng and Whalley (2004), which analyzes the geographical extension of pre-existing free trade zones as a form of trade liberalization. The authors assess how this form of trade liberalization compares to more conventional trade liberalization involving the lowering of national tariffs covering the whole economy in which zones are absent. They also draw comparisons with earlier literature on free trade zones such as Hamada (1974), Rodriguez (1976) and Young (1992).

A key assumption in the Ng and Whalley analysis is that in some countries, such as China, it is administratively feasible to operate movable internal trade barriers, and that some mechanism exists for the progressive enlargement of free trade zones within these countries. This can be through the sequential addition of cities or portions of an economy to a pre-existing free-trade or export-processing zone. The form that progressive liberalization will take during the implementation period for China's WTO accession commitments in key service areas such as banking, insurance and telecoms (see Whalley 2003) provides the motivation for the systematic comparisons undertaken by Ng and Whalley (2004). For these service items, protection through a tariff is not feasible as there is no customs clearance for international trade in the relevant service. Prior to WTO accession, China's domestic markets in these areas were protected by regulatory arrangements, which relied on licenses and limits on the extent of foreign participation, especially in the degree of ownership in joint ventures. Since licenses are inherently discrete instruments of protection, they have been converted into continuous instruments of progressive liberalization in these service areas by allowing for an expansion in their geographical coverage over the five-year implementation period (that is, by expanding over time the number of cities where foreign presence is allowed). Limits on allowable foreign participation (and ownership) are also to be progressively raised over time.

Ng and Whalley assume that such schemes are possible to implement even though in reality they may be hard to administer. China, Vietnam and other countries with strong administrative control mechanisms and embedded provincial structures seem to fit this characterization. The authors do not explicitly consider inter-temporal intermediation services in their model due to the added complexity this implies, but instead limit the analysis to trade in goods. They do emphasize, however, that the themes of their analysis of trade in goods almost certainly apply to trade in services as well.

Ng and Whalley consider cases where the size (and hence the border) of the free trade zone can be varied inside an economy and numerically evaluate the welfare implications of increasing the size of free trade zones and compare this to conventional forms of trade liberalization such as a reduction in a national tariff. They analyze the welfare effects of the two types of trade policy changes (that is, *ad valorem* national tariff reduction versus expansion of the geographical size of a trade zone) where there are observationally equivalent impacts of the two policies in the sense that the changes in trade volumes are identical.

To do this, Ng and Whalley calibrate a numerical general equilibrium trade model of a small open economy to a base case free trade equilibrium data set. They then introduce both a free trade zone and a tariff and compare the outcome of an expansion in the size of the zone to that generated by an observationally equivalent reduction in a national tariff in a model without trade zones. Figure 18.1 presents a flow chart from Ng and Whalley (2004) setting out their procedures for comparing the expansion of a free trade zone with the reduction of an *ad valorem* tariff.

In the first experiment, the tariff applies to international trade for only a portion of the economy and also applies to trade internally between the free trade and protected zones. Trade policy changes involve variations in the size of the free trade zone while the tariff rate in the tariff zone remains unchanged. The second part of the analysis uses a conventional nationally based tariff with no free trade zone in which the tariff applies only at the national border and the rate is varied on all country trade.

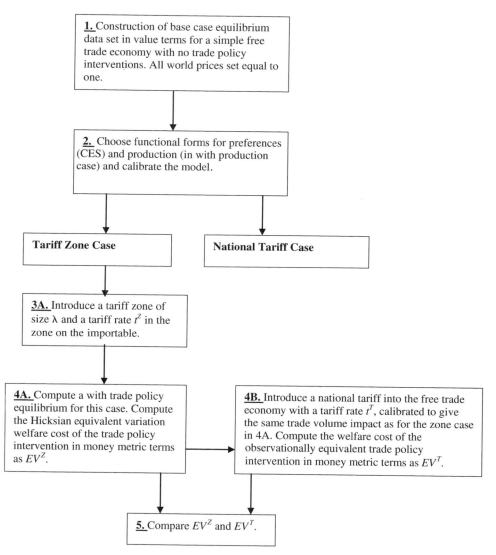

Figure 18.1   Flow chart outlining the procedures used by Ng and by Whalley (2004) in constructing observationally equivalent numerical experiments comparing national and zone based trade policy changes

The numerical simulations show that the welfare changes of observationally equivalent trade policy changes differ significantly across the two cases. There is a larger gain from the first type of liberalization pertaining to expansion of the free trade zone, reflecting both the use of a higher tariff rate on a smaller portion of trade, and the reduction in distortions across the divide between the free trade zone and the rest of the economy. Ng and Whalley explore the size of these differences both for pure exchange economies where there is no production and for models with production. Larger differences occur in the case where production is allowed due to added distortions having to do with the location of mobile factors across the two zones.

To illustrate the approach, consider a pure exchange model with fixed endowments of traded goods and focus on a small country, which cannot influence world prices. Assume a zone within the economy can be defined in which international trade can occur, while trade between the zone and the rest of the economy involves the same tariff as applies to international trade. No tariffs apply in the free trade zone, while in the tariff zone there are *ad valorem* tariffs both on international trade and trade between the zones. For simplicity non-traded goods are excluded from the analysis. (Additional mathematical details of the pure exchange model are provided in the Appendix.)

To simplify matters, the relative sizes of the two zones are represented by the relative endowments of goods in each zone (expressed in proportional terms). Suppose that the economy wide endowment is ten units of good one and 20 units of good two, and consumers in the free trade zone have six units of good one and 12 units of good two, while those in the tariff zone have four and eight units. Thus, the tariff zone covers 40 percent of the whole country. A simple treatment is to normalize the size of the whole economy to one and let λ denote the fraction of the economy in the tariff zone. In the example above, the sizes of the free trade and tariff zones are $1-\lambda = 0.60$ and $\lambda = 0.40$ respectively. Because the relative sizes of the two zones are allowed to vary, it further simplifies things to assume that all consumers in both zones have identical homothetic preferences where relative demands do not depend on income. Trade liberalization in this economy can involve the geographical expansion of the free trade zone, a change in the tariff rate, or some combination of these. If we increase the size of the free trade zone with a given tariff from $1-\lambda$ to $1-\lambda'$ rate where $\lambda > \lambda'$, the size of the free trade zone increases while the tariff zone shrinks.

The impact on consumer welfare in each area of the economy is evaluated in two steps. First, general equilibria are calculated for before and after a trade policy change, such as the change from λ to λ'. Since endowments are evenly distributed within each zone and the relative sizes of zones reflect relative population sizes, it is easy to compute the consumption of each good before and after liberalization. Second, the welfare changes for consumers located in each area are computed using rigorous Hicksian money-metric welfare measures known as equivalent variations (EVs). The welfare change for the whole economy is then computed by summing these money metric measurements, which are expressed as a percentage of the economy-wide pre-change income.

Ng and Whalley (2004) calibrate the conventional small-country trade model without trade policy interventions to a free trade base case data set. In the case of a pure exchange economy, the model is as described above, with the size of the tariff zone set equal to zero (that is $\lambda=0$). They then evaluate the welfare impacts of two types of trade policy change. In the first case (the tariff zone case), they introduce a tariff zone of size λ equal to 0.55 and a tariff rate t^Z of 0.6 in the zone for the importable. They next compute an equilibrium for this case, and compare it to the original free trade equilibrium to generate a money metric measure of the welfare impact of the trade policy change. An observationally equivalent national tariff (t^T) is then introduced into the free trade calibrated model giving the same impact on trade volumes as in the tariff-zone case. This trade-impact equivalent national tariff rate is calculated to be about 0.30 for both the pure exchange and production cases. They then compute a money metric measure of the welfare impact for this intervention.

Ng and Whalley's results show that the welfare costs of imposing a geographically restrictive tariff scheme (the tariff zone case) are almost two times larger than those from a conventional national tariff with observationally equivalent trade effects (the national tariff case). This reflects both the use of a higher tariff rate on a smaller portion of trade, and the introduction of distortions across the divide between the free trade zone and the tariff zone when modeling the tariff zone case. On the other hand, there is a relatively lower national tariff applying at the national border and there are no internal distortions within the country. Thus, the welfare impacts of observationally equivalent trade policy changes differ across the two cases.

Ng and Whalley conclude that if trade liberalization is achieved through geographical expansion of free trade zones, policy analyses that study such liberalization in national tariff-equivalent terms can be highly misleading. Although more complex inter-temporal and spatial models are needed to study the liberalization of trade in services in sectors such as banking, telecom and transportation, which are associated with Chinese WTO accession, the work of Ng and Whalley suggests that analyzing liberalization of this form in tariff-equivalent terms, as is typically done in the modeling literature, is not a satisfactory way to proceed.

Border delays and trade liberalization

The second case study of explicit trade barrier representation and *ad valorem* equivalent modeling draws on work dealing with border delays by Cudmore and Whalley (2005). The motivation for this study is that in a number of lower income and transition economies significant delays at the border when achieving customs clearance are commonly observed (for example, Hare 2001; Wolf and Gurgen 2000). This can be due to complex customs formalities, which sometimes are continually changing, capacity constraints to process imports given limited facilities, and/or corruption at the border. In some African economies, there are reported delays of three to six months to achieve customs clearance, although this is perhaps extreme.

The thrust of the argument in Cudmore and Whalley is that if such delays are significant and the length of the delay is endogenously determined, then trade liberalization through tariff reductions that increase the length of the queue can be welfare worsening. Tariff reductions, as have occurred in recent years in the Commonwealth of Independent States (CIS) of the former Soviet Union, may thus be bad policy if customs clearance issues are not first addressed. Cudmore and Whalley show this for a small country case in a simple general equilibrium model where there is a physical constraint on the volume of imports, which can be admitted. They then analyze extensions where corruption occurs, and finally where some imports are perishable. Cudmore and Whalley apply their analysis to data on Russian trade for the late 1990s. The results emphasize that not only is it best to deal with border and administrative delays first, before engaging in trade liberalization, but also the quantitative orders of magnitudes for the costs involved can be large.

Cudmore and Whalley begin by formalizing the interactions between border delays and trade liberalization in a simple pure exchange economy, which is a price taker on world markets. Mathematical details of this simple model are provided in the Appendix. Cudmore and Whalley also extend the model to capture additional mechanisms through which border delays and trade liberalization can interact. One such mechanism is the presence of corruption. Another elaboration is differential impact of queuing on different commodities when perishable commodities are more adversely affected by queuing than non-perishable commodities. The differential border delays that arise across commodities lead to added distortionary costs.

Using this simple framework, Cudmore and Whalley make some calculations using Russian data to explore the possible quantitative orders of magnitude involved with analysis of trade liberalization that incorporates border delays. The delays reported in the Russian case appear to be lengthy and a major restraint on trade. Cudmore and Whalley's calculations serve to underline the point that if tariff reforms occur with no attention being paid to administrative considerations and border delays, liberalization can be welfare worsening, rather than welfare improving as in conventional models. Importantly, this suggests that there are costs rather than benefits from trade liberalization in such cases and that these costs can be substantial. Here again, analyzing trade liberalization using conventional tariff based models can also be misleading, and in this specific case the sign might even be wrong.

US wheat programs and program participation

A final case study that compares *ad valorem* treatment versus explicit trade barrier representation is drawn from Whalley and Wigle (1990). They show that modeling agricultural programs involves surprising complexities, and that overly simple *ad valorem* modeling can again be misleading. They illustrated this by discussing the modeling of price supports paid to US wheat farmers in the late 1980s. At this time price support for produers of wheat, as well as corn, grain, sorghum, oats, barley and rye, in the United States were mainly provided through commodity loans and deficiency payments (USDA 1987). These programs jointly had the effect of raising prices received by farmers.

Under the Commodity Loan program, the Commodity Credit Corporation (CCC) made non-recourse loans to farmers using commodities (for example, wheat) as security, stored either on the farm or in commercial warehouses. These loans matured on demand, but on or before the loan's maturity date farmers had the option of regaining possession of their crop by paying off the loan plus any accrued interest, or forfeiting the stored commodities to the CCC as full payment of the loan. This component of price supports effectively operated through the setting of the loan rate.

Deficiency payments were based on the difference between the target price and the higher of the national average market price and the loan rate. This difference was multiplied by the established yield of each farmer's land to determine the total deficiency payment. Prior to 1985, established yields were frequently recalculated using a five-year moving average of the preceding years' yields on a farm-by-farm basis. Under this system, subject to a lag, higher yields implied higher deficiency payments. In effect, marginal output received the support (target) price. One of the major changes in the 1985 Farm Bill was an attempt to 'decouple' deficiency payments from output by fixing established yields.

However, acreage set asides coexisted with these two methods of price support as a condition for receiving support. To receive deficiency payments on their harvested acreage, or to gain access to non-recourse loans, farmers were required to reduce their planted acreage by a specific percentage of their base acreage. The aim of these set-aside requirements was to reduce surplus production that was thought to arise from the price supports. However, the joint effect of deficiency payments, loans, and set-asides on output and prices, and hence on market prices, was uncertain. Producers participating in the program

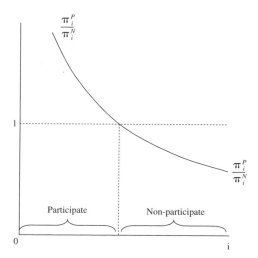

Figure 18.2   Distribution of farms between participants and non-participants in United States voluntary crop programs (Whalley and Wigle, 1990)

planted a reduced acreage but faced a higher price, giving ambiguous effects on production. Increasing the target price would increase yields of program participants, but could also increase participation, reducing planted acreage.

To assess the net effect, it was necessary to analyze farm participation decisions. In deciding whether or not to participate in support programs, individual farms compared their profits from participating in both the price support and set-aside programs with their profits if they did not participate. This is illustrated in Figure 18.2 from Whalley and Wigle (1990) where π_i^P and π_i^N represent the profits of farm i under participation (P) and non-participation (N) and, thus, π_i^P/π_i^N represents relative profits. The prices of non-land inputs affect both participation and non-participation profits, but the world market price of wheat influences only non-participation profits while the target price of wheat designated under price supports and the set-aside rate influence only participation profits. If farm i's non-participation profits exceed its participation profits such that $\pi_i^N > \pi_i^P$ or $\pi_i^P/\pi_i^N < 1$, then it will choose not to participate in the set-aside program as shown in Figure 18.2. It will, of course, participate in the reverse case where non-participation profits are lower than participation profits

In general, farms differ in a range of characteristics, including the crop in which farms had a comparative advantage, land quality, and the ease with which land and other inputs could be substituted. Typically, for any given level of target and market prices and set-aside rates, it would pay some farms to participate and others not.

If farms are ranked by their relative profits from participating and non-participating and are indexed by the subscript i, the distribution of participant and non-participant farms is described by the relative profit functions. Changes in program parameters, such as the target price of wheat and the set-aside rate, will shift these relative profit functions changing the number of participant farms. This emphasizes the importance of capturing endogeneity of program participation in any modeling of the impacts of agricultural supports.

Whalley and Wigle analyzed the effects of price supports and set-asides for wheat in the United States on both output and the terms of trade. Taking the numerical general equilibrium model of global trade in wheat reported in Trela *et al.* (1987), they embedded a richer treatment of both farm behavior and program supports in the United States. In Whalley and Wigle, the US wheat sector was comprised of a continuous distribution of farm types, leading to variations across farms in both average yields and participation decisions.

Whether farms choose to participate in any configuration of program supports and set-asides depends on the level of program support, the way marginal cost functions change as land is idled to comply with set asides, and the lump sum costs which set-aside requirements cause. For simplicity, Whalley and Wigle assumed that farms differed only in the ease of substitution between inputs measured by the elasticity of substitution, which was uniformly distributed over a pre-specified interval. Farms with higher elasticities and greater ease of substitution had higher average yields, and, given that land was a fixed factor for each farm, these farms had flatter or more shallowly sloped marginal cost functions. The parameter values they used in the model along with the data to which the model was calibrated, implied that high elasticity, high yield, farms participated in program support, while high elasticity, low yield, farms did not.

Whalley and Wigle calibrated the model to a 1981 micro-consistent equilibrium data set, and then computed counterfactual equilibria for a variety of policy changes. In particular, they compared results under two different model treatments. In the first, all policies in all countries were treated in *ad valorem* form as percentage price wedges, while in the second US Commodity programs were fully modeled as described above with endogenous voluntary participation. Under explicit program modeling, output rose when programs were abolished because the increase in production from the extra acreage planted more than offset the fall in production due to the decrease in prices received by producers originally in the program. In the *ad valorem* subsidy case, the output of the US wheat sector fell when the subsidy was eliminated so long as the world price did not rise by more than the subsidy.

The theme again is that there is a significant difference between *ad valorem* equivalent modeling and explicit policy representation, which in this situation may lead to a difference in the direction that output changes.

Conclusion

While all economic analysis inevitably involves a simplification from a more complex reality, representing trade and other policy interventions in *ad valorem* equivalent form is clearly incorrect when judged by an absolute standard. Unfortunately, we usually do not even know how misleading this treatment might be when we employ it, as we widely do in policy analysis. This chapter presents three case studies where the numerical results allow a comparison between explicit policy representation and *ad valorem* equivalent representation in observationally equivalent models. Significant differences in size of effect, and in some cases in sign, appear in the results. These results indicate the need for caution when using an *ad valorem* equivalent treatment both in analyzing trade liberalization. Since the details matter in the conduct of policy, they also matter in modeling.

References

Abrego, L., R. Riezman, J. Whalley (2001), 'How Reasonable are the Assumptions Used in Theoretical Models?: Computational Evidence of the Likelihood of Trade Pattern Changes', NBER working paper No. W8169. March.

Cudmore, E. and J. Whalley (2005), 'Border Delays and Trade Liberalization,' in. T. Ito and A. Rose (eds), *East Asian Seminar in International Trade, No. 12*, University of Chicago Press for NBER.

Hamada, K. (1974), 'An Economic Analysis of the Duty-Free Zone,' *Journal of International Economics*, **4**(3), 225–41.

Hare, P. G. (2001), 'Trade Policy During the Transition: Lessons from the 1990s,' *The World Economy*, **24**(4), 483–512.

Ng, E. and J. Whalley (2004), 'Geographical Extension of Trade Zones as Trade Liberalization: A Numerical Simulation Approach,' CESifo Working Paper.

Rodriguez, C.A. (1976), 'A Note on the Economics of the Duty-Free Zone,' *Journal of International Economics*, **6**(4), 385–88.

Trela, I., J. Whalley and R. Wigle (1987), 'International Trade in Grain: Domestic Policies and Trade Conflicts,' *Scandinavian Journal of Economics*, **89**(3), 271–83.

USDA (United States Department of Agriculture) (1987), *Government Intervention in Agriculture: Measurement, Evaluation, and Implications for Trade Negotiations*, Washington, DC: Economic Research Service.

Whalley, J. (2003), 'Liberalization in China's Key Service Sectors Following WTO Accession: Some Scenarios, and Issues of Measurement,' NBER working paper No. W10143.

Whalley, J. and R. Wigle (1990), 'Terms of Trade Effects, Agricultural Trade Liberalization and Developing Countries,' in I. Goldin and O. Knudsen (eds), *Agricultural Trade Liberalization; Implications for Developing Countries*, Paris: OECD.

Wolf, T. and E. Gurgen (2000), 'Improving Governance and Fighting Corruption in the Baltic and CIS Countries: The Role of the IMF,' *Economic Issues*, **26**, Washington, DC: International Monetary Fund.

Young, L. (1992), 'Unemployment and the Optimal Export-processing Zone,' *Journal of Development Economics*, **37**(1–2), 369–85.

Appendix

The Ng and Whalley (2004) Model

If Y_i defines the aggregate endowment of good i for the whole economy, and λ is the size of the tariff zone leaving $(1-\lambda)$ as the size of the free trade zone, then the aggregate endowments of goods in each zone are given by:

$$Y_i^T = \lambda Y_i \quad \text{and} \quad Y_i^F = (1-\lambda) Y_i \qquad i=1,\ldots,N \qquad 0 \le \lambda \le 1 \qquad (18.\text{A}1)$$

where superscript T stands for the tariff zone and F for the free trade zone.

To facilitate welfare analysis of alternative trade policies, the relative sizes of the free trade and tariff zones are assumed to also reflect the relative sizes of the population in the zones. There are therefore λ and $1-\lambda$ consumers in the tariff and free trade zones respectively. A further simplifying assumption is that the aggregate endowments of each good in each zone are evenly distributed.

All consumers are assumed to have identical CES preferences:

$$U = \left[\sum_i (\alpha_i)^{\frac{1}{\sigma}} (X_i)^{\frac{\sigma-1}{\sigma}} \right]^{\frac{\sigma}{\sigma-1}} \qquad i=1,\ldots,N \qquad (18.\text{A}2)$$

where α_i is the consumption share of good i; X_i is the quantity of good i; and σ is the elasticity of substitution in this economy. Utility-maximizing demands for goods depend upon the amount of income spent in each zone. Since consumer prices differ across the zones, the aggregate demands in each zone are:

$$X_i^j = \frac{\alpha_i I^j}{(P_i^j)^\sigma \sum_i \alpha_i (P_i^j)^{1-\sigma}} \qquad i=1,\ldots,N \qquad j=F,T \qquad (18.\text{A}3)$$

where X_i^j is the aggregate demand for good i in zone j, I^j is the income spent in zone j, and P_i^j is the price of good i in zone j.

The income in each zone I^j is given by:

$$I^F = \sum_{i=1}^{N} P_i^j y_i^F + \gamma^F R \quad \text{and} \quad I^T = \sum_{i=1}^{N} P_i^j y_i^T + \gamma^T R \qquad (18.\text{A}4)$$

where γ^j denotes the share of national tariff revenue R collected in the tariff zone accruing to zone j; $\sum_{j=F,T} \gamma^j = 1$, $\gamma^j \ge 0$. In the numerical experiments it is assumed that the tariff revenue collected in the tariff zone is only distributed to that zone. In this case, $\gamma^F = 0$ and $\gamma^T = 1$. The aggregate demand of good i for the whole economy is the sum of the aggregate demands in each zone:

$$X_i = X_i^F + X_i^T \qquad i=1,\ldots,N \qquad (18.\text{A}5)$$

Defining the net imports of each good in the tariff zone as $M_i^T = X_i^T - Y_i^T$ for $i = 1, \ldots, N$; P_i^W as the world price of good i; and t_i as the tariff on good i; the national tariff revenue, R, is given by:

$$R = \sum_i t_i P_i^W \max(M_i^T, 0) \qquad (18.A6)$$

The aggregate net import of each good for the whole country, M_i, is given by the sum of net imports for each good entering each zone:

$$M_i = \sum_j M_i^j \qquad i = 1, \ldots, N \qquad j = F, T \qquad (18.A7)$$

Since the country is modeled as a small open price-taking economy with no non-traded goods, it is simple to characterize an equilibrium. Given world prices of goods, any excess demands for goods are absorbed by imports from (or exports to) the world market. Trade balance is implied by Walras' Law, which automatically follows from utility maximizing behaviour subject to budget constraints. Given λ, an equilibrium for this economy can also be computed easily. Alternatively, given a target tariff revenue R^* and a tariff rate t in the tariff zone, λ can be endogenously determined as the relative size of the two zones needed to meet the revenue requirement and the tariff rate.

The Cudmore and Whalley (2005) Model
For expositional simplicity, all goods are assumed to be traded; the world prices for the N goods are given by $\bar{\pi}_i^w$; tariff rates on imports are denoted by t_i (but for exports, $t_i = 0$); and the direction of trade is assumed to be predetermined. The latter is a standard assumption in most theoretical trade models, although numerically the direction of trade can change when trade policies change. See Abrego *et al.* (2001) for a recent discussion of the likelihood of this assumption being false in comparisons between free trade, customs unions, and Nash equilibria.

In this economy, domestic prices depart from world prices on the import side both due to tariffs and per unit queuing costs at the border $T^q(\pi)$. For simplicity, it is assumed that these costs are the same for all goods, and that units for goods are denominated in comparable physical terms (for example tonnes). Thus, if M goods are imported and $N - M$ exported with the direction of trade remaining unchanged:

$$\pi_i^d = \bar{\pi}_i^w(1 + t_i) + T^q(\pi) \qquad i = 1, \ldots, M \qquad (18.A8)$$

Here T^q is assumed to be indexed and so is homogeneous of degree one in π and is endogenously determined.

The economy has market demand functions, $\xi_i(\pi^d, R, Q)$, and non-negative endowments, w_i, for each of the N goods, where π^d denotes the N dimensional vector of domestic commodity prices. R defines tariff revenues, and Q represents the aggregate endogenously determined queuing costs (denominated in units of the good being imported). These demand functions are non-negative, continuous, homogeneous of degree zero in π^d, and satisfy Walras' Law for all price vectors π^d:

$$\sum_{i=1}^{N} \pi_i^d[\xi_i(\pi^d, R, Q) - w_i] = 0 \tag{18.A9}$$

Assuming there is a single representative consumer in this economy, its budget constraint is given by

$$\sum_{i=1}^{N} \pi_i^d\xi_i(\pi^d, R, Q) = \sum_{i=1}^{N} \pi_i^d w_i + R - \sum_{i=1}^{M} T^q(\pi)(\xi_i - w_i) \tag{18.A10}$$

For simplicity, border delays are assumed to reflect a constraint on the volume of imports that can be processed over the period of time covered by the model (for example, one year). Thus, for now, consider this to be a physical constraint rather than one reflecting corruption or other considerations. If $\bar{C}$ represents the administratively determined physical capacity constraint on imports, then

$$\sum_{i=1}^{M} [\xi_i(\pi^d, R, Q) - w_i] \leq \bar{C} \tag{18.A11}$$

where R denotes tariff revenue, $\sum_{i=1}^{M} \bar{\pi}_i^w t(\xi_i - w_i)_i$, and $Q = \sum_{i=1}^{M} T^q(\pi)(\xi_i - w_i)$ denotes the total queuing costs.

In this model, if the capacity constraint on imports is binding then per unit queuing costs $T^q(\pi^w)$ are determined in equilibrium along with domestic prices π^d, tariff revenues, and domestic demands ξ_i. The effect of tariff liberalization will be to lower tariff revenues and increased queuing costs. In the case where tariff rates are uniform across commodities, tariff reductions simply generate a corresponding increase in queuing costs. Since the latter use real resources, tariff reducing trade liberalization will typically be welfare worsening.

The Whalley and Wigle (1990) Model

If P^W represents the target price of wheat designated under price supports, P^Z the price of non-land inputs used by all farms and λ the set aside rate; then the participation decision for farm i involved the comparison of the profit functions π_i^N, π_i^P for farm i under non-participation (N) and participation (P). For farm i, if:

$$\pi_i^N(P^W, P^Z) > \pi_i^P(P_T^W, P^Z, \lambda) \tag{18.A12}$$

then farm i would choose not to participate in the set-aside program, and it would only participate if the inequality is reversed.

For analytical convenience, it is assumed that farms differ only in the elasticity of substitution between land and non-land inputs in production. In doing so, the model abstracts from differences in land quality across farms, location (and thus transportation costs in shipping crops), and differences in comparative advantage across crop types between farms. The production technology for each farm type, i, was assumed to be constant returns, and to take the constant elasticity of substitution (CES) form:

$$g_i = B[\delta \bar{L}_i^{-\rho_i} + (1 - \delta)Z_i^{-\rho_i}]^{-\frac{1}{\rho_i}} \tag{18.A13}$$

where g_i is the output of farm type i, $\bar{L}_i$ and Z_i are land and non-land inputs, δ is a share parameter, B a units term taken to be identical across all farms, and:

$$\sigma_i = \frac{1}{1 - \rho_i} \tag{18.A14}$$

is the elasticity of substitution between inputs. Wheat-producing land (L) and other inputs (Z) were assumed to be the sole inputs in the production of wheat by any farm.

Since acreage available to each farm, $\bar{L}_i$, is fixed, producers face a two-level optimization problem. They must first choose whether or not to participate in the commodity program including any set-aside provisions. Given their participation decision, they then optimize on non-land inputs and outputs.

The profit functions from participation and non-participation are:

$$\pi_i^P = P_T^W \bar{y}_i (1 - \lambda) \bar{L}_i - P^Z \bar{Z}_i + T_i \tag{18.A15}$$

$$\pi_i^N = P^W \hat{y}_i \bar{L}_i - P^Z \hat{Z}_i \tag{18.A16}$$

where: P^W is the world market price for wheat; P_T^W is the US target price for wheat; $\bar{y}_i$ and $\hat{y}_i$ are the optimal yields under participation and non-participation respectively; $\bar{L}_i$ is the total acreage available for farm i; P^Z is the price of other inputs; $\bar{Z}_i$ and $\hat{Z}_i$ are the total amounts of other inputs used under non-participation and participation; λ is the proportional set-aside requirement; and T_i is the lump sum 'paid diversion' received by farm i, which is equal to the rental value of a pre-specified proportion of land set aside when complying with set-aside requirements. In this formulation, farm profits equal the returns to land net of input costs. Participating farms were assumed to receive the target price for incremental output, although in some model experiments the degree to which deficiency payments were coupled to current yields was varied.

Using equation 18.A13, a non-participating farm's non-land input demand is given by:

$$\hat{Z}_i = \left\{ \frac{1}{\delta} \left[B(1 - \delta) \frac{P^W}{P^Z} \right]^{\left[\frac{\rho_i}{\rho_i - 1} \right]} + \frac{(\delta - 1)}{\delta} \right\}^{\frac{-1}{\rho}} \bar{L}_i \tag{18.A17}$$

and its optimal yield is:

$$\hat{y}_i = \delta[(1 - \delta)B]^{\frac{-1}{1 - \rho_i}} \left[\frac{P^W}{P^Z} \right]^{\frac{\rho_i}{1 - \rho_i}} \bar{L}_i \tag{18.A18}$$

For a participant, the input demand is given by:

$$\bar{Z}_i = \left\{ \frac{1}{\delta} \left[B(1 - \delta) \frac{P_T^W}{P^Z} \right]^{\left[\frac{\rho_i}{\rho_i - 1} \right]} + \frac{(\delta - 1)}{\delta} \right\}^{\frac{-1}{\rho_i}} (1 - \lambda) \bar{L}_i \tag{18.A19}$$

and its optimal yield is:

$$\bar{y}_i = \delta[(1-\delta)B]^{\frac{-1}{1-\rho_i}}\left[\frac{P^W}{P^Z}\right]^{\frac{\rho_i}{1-\rho_i}}(1-\lambda)\bar{L}_i \qquad (18.A20)$$

Given the program parameters P_T, and knowing the world market price of wheat P^W, and the input price P^Z, it is possible to solve for the optimal yields and input demands under participation and non-participation. This allows for a comparison of the two profit functions equations (18.A8), (18.A15) and (18.A16), and a determination of the participation decision. This, in turn, allows input demand and outputs to be calculated.

19 Tariffication: theoretical justification and problems of implementation
Laura J. Loppacher and William A. Kerr

Introduction

Tariffication is the process whereby non-tariff barriers to trade imposed by countries are converted to tariffs which, at least in theory, provide an equivalent degree of protection to the non-tariff barrier that they replace. The principle of tariffication was enshrined in the 1947 General Agreement on Tariffs and Trade (GATT 1947) and remains a central premise of the World Trade Organization (WTO). Tariffs are pre-announced border taxes that remain in place until the country imposing them announces that they are to be altered. Their pre-announced nature provides a degree of predictability for exporters as they are able to discern if exports can be made profitably after paying the tariff. Tariffs are, hence, a subset of border taxes – other forms could be levied on a one time basis when shipments arrive at the importer's customs warehouse (greatly increasing the risk for exporters) or could be adjusted to reflect changes in international market prices. These latter are known as variable import levies which can be increased as international prices fall and decreased as international prices rise. The effect is to provide a degree of domestic price stability. Other non-tariff barriers such as import quotas, import licenses, minimum import prices, non-tariff measures maintained by state trading enterprises and administrative impediments can all provide even less transparency for exporters than tariffs. Beyond the advantage of transparency, however, there are sound theoretical reasons why tariffs are the preferred mechanism for restricting trade that has been agreed by the Member States of the WTO.

Why Tariffs?

Tariffs have long been recognized as likely to be the least trade distorting trade restrictions over time. This is because they allow for automatic adjustments in sources of imports that reflect changes in international competitiveness over the time that tariffs remain fixed. If tariffs are applied in a non-discriminatory manner (that is they are collected on the same basis regardless of the firm or country of origin) then imports will always be sourced from the least cost supplier. This is because the most competitive foreign supplier in the importer's market will be the one that has the lowest price after paying the tariff. As all firms pay the same tariff, this will be the firm that has the lowest cost – that is, is the most resource efficient.

If another supplier can lower its supply cost below that of an existing exporter, then it will become the low cost source of imports and importers will switch. This change takes place as a result of market forces and is automatic in the sense that there is no government involvement in the decision to select the most resource efficient supplier. Alternative methods of restricting imports such as import quotas require some form of government intervention to re-apportion quotas among suppliers as the competitiveness of foreign suppliers changes.[1] Bureaucrats may not be able to correctly identify the least cost supplier and the re-apportioning process may be open to rent seeking and corruption.

If the competitiveness of foreign sources of supply is increasing relative to domestic producers in the importing country, then imports will increase to reflect this change. Thus, while the distortion introduced into the market by the tariff remains, the distortion does not grow over time. In a similar fashion, if the competitiveness of domestic producers in the importing country improves over time relative to that of foreign competitors, imports automatically decline. Hence, global welfare, taking into account the distortion arising from the imposition of the tariff, is automatically maximized over the time the tariff remains in place.

The Members States of GATT 1947 and subsequently the WTO have attempted to institutionalize the use of tariffs to strengthen their role in international commercial policy. Tariffication is a well accepted principle and was more fully extended to cover most agriculture products in the Uruguay Round (1986–1994) of negotiations.[2] The WTO also requires countries to 'bind' their tariff levels once their tariff schedules are agreed. Having one's tariffs 'bound' means that the country has agreed not to raise tariffs above the agreed level in the future. This leads to greater transparency for firms engaged in international commercial activities. It also serves the goal of trade liberalization by putting an upper limit to future protection. Also enshrined in the WTO is the principle of non-discrimination whereby a country extends the same tariff rate to the imports from all other Member States thus ensuring that the low cost supplier will be the most competitive – that rate is the 'most favoured nation rate' (MFN). There has been some erosion of the dominance of the MFN rate in recent years as better than MFN rates are extended to developing countries under the General System of Preferences and tariffs are removed among members of regional trade associations (Yeung *et al.* 1999). In these cases, the development and trade liberalization benefits of allowing discriminatory tariffs are seen to outweigh the benefits of being able to access the lowest cost supplier on a consistent basis.

Tariffication is seen as having a secondary benefit in multilateral negotiations. When barriers to market access take a variety of forms, comparisons of the degree of protection are very difficult – an apples and oranges problem. This complicates negotiations to liberalize trade. As trade negotiations rely on reciprocity in offers to reduce trade barriers among trading partners, reaching agreement on what is being offered, and hence what would be the appropriate reciprocation, is difficult. If all trade barriers are converted to tariffs, then they have numeric values that can be compared. This ease of comparison would not be available from other forms of trade barriers, for example import quotas, and, hence, tariffication leads to the preferred trade restricting mechanism for negotiating convenience.

Tariffication does not, however, remove all comparison problems. This is because tariffs themselves do not necessarily have the same form. Tariffs can be collected on a per unit basis (for example $5000 per car regardless of the value of the car), an *ad valorem* basis (for example as a percentage of the unit value of the import) or may be complex (that is some combination of the two). For ease of comparison in international negotiations, *ad valorem* tariffs are preferred, when economic analysis of, for example, multilateral trade liberalization is conducted per unit and complex tariffs are often converted to their approximate *ad valorem* equivalents. These conversions are fraught with difficulties as they will vary depending on market conditions (for example if the per unit tariff on cars is $5000 and car prices are depressed, $50 000 per car, then the *ad valorem* equivalent is 10 percent; if at some other time the car market is buoyant and the price of the same car is $80 000 then the *ad valorem* equivalent is 6.25 percent).

Problems with tariffication

While tariffs are, in theory, the preferred means of protection and enshrined in multilateral agreements, arriving at appropriate conversions of non-tariff barriers through tariffication has proved a contentious international issue. This is because there is no agreed standardized method for determining the 'equivalent degree of protection'. As with other areas of trade law where ambiguity leads to Member Countries being able to avoid their commitments to liberalize, the process of tariffication has allowed countries to maintain barriers or even increase barriers to market access.

Tariffication is supposed to result in a tariff that provides an equivalent degree of protection as what was provided by the combination of all of the non-tariff barriers (NTBs) in place for a particular commodity. The problems that arose from the implementation of the Uruguay Round where it was agreed that tariffication of most agricultural products would take place will serve as an appropriate example. Modalities were established during the negotiations to guide countries in how to calculate the appropriate tariff. Stripped of all the details, the appropriate tariff to put in place would be the amount by which the domestic price was above the world price during the base period. Members chose 1986–1988 to serve as the base period. Importantly, these years were a period of depressed prices for many agricultural commodities on the world market, so the implied protection from programs like price supports was significantly higher than if prices had been closer to normal. These lower prices resulted in higher tariff bindings (Swinbank 2004).

After the completion of the Uruguay Round Agreement on Agriculture (URAA) and the establishment of new tariff schedules, a number of authors began to suggest that countries had engaged in what they called 'dirty tariffication'.[3] Dirty tariffication is when the tariff established is greater than the wedge between domestic and world prices during the base period. Ingco (1995) argues that dirty tariffication was most prevalent in sensitive sectors such as sugar, dairy and grains. Some of her findings indicate that the European Union's (EU) rice tariff was excessive by 207 percent, that the US raised base protection in sugar by 66 percent and that Canada raised tariffs relative to base period protections by 100 percent in dairy products and more than 200 percent in poultry. The benefit of this extra protection arises as a result of other Uruguay Round commitments whereby Member States agreed to tariff cuts after tariffication – 36 percent for developed countries and 24 percent for developing countries. By converting NTBs to higher 'dirty' tariffs, it meant that the commitments to tariff reduction would not lead to increased market access.[4]

Water in the tariff

The excess between the existing tariff level and the level below which market access could be expected to increase is known as the 'water in the tariff'. If negotiated reductions in tariffs are less than the water in the tariffs then no increase in market access will take place. In essence, this means that no liberalization in this commodity will take place as a result of an agreement to liberalize. The question of excess tariffs is further complicated by countries having different 'bound' and 'applied' tariff rates.

During the URAA, the negotiations centered on the maximum level a tariff could be; the 'bound' tariffs. Members have the right to choose to put in place any tariff level below the bound rate; these are known as applied tariffs.[5] Bound and applied tariffs may bear little relationship to one another except that the applied tariff must always be less than or equal to the bound tariff. In many importing countries for a range of agricultural products, applied tariffs are well below the bound level. The amount of discrepancy varies significantly between countries and commodities. If current and future negotiations at the WTO are going to result in increased market access, the reductions in bound tariffs must bring them down to below applied tariffs. If the applied tariff is not prohibitive (that is some imports are occurring at that level of tariff), the gap between bound and applied tariffs will be equal to the water in the tariff (Podbury and Roberts 2003). If the applied tariff is also a prohibitive tariff then the water in the tariff will be larger than the difference between the bound tariff and the applied tariff.[6] Figure 19.1 illustrates the two sources of water in the tariff.

In the figure, the very least bound tariffs would have to decrease for there to be a possibility of increased market access would be 15 percentage points (this would correspond to a 20 percent reduction of the tariff). This is the amount required to decrease the bound tariff to the applied level. In this circumstance, however, no trade occurs at a tariff of 60 percent. Trade would not occur until the tariff was less than or equal to the difference between domestic and world prices – 30 percent in this example. Thus, tariffs would have to decrease by 30 percentage points from the applied tariff and 45 percentage points from the bound tariff if additional market access is to be achieved. This 45 percent is the water in the tariff. Note that to reduce an initial tariff of 75 percent to 30 percent, a 60 percent cut in the tariff is required.

Water in the tariff can come from a few different sources. The first situation to consider is when applied tariffs are below the bound tariffs and trade is occurring. In this circumstance, it was likely a voluntary decision of a government to apply a lower tariff than what

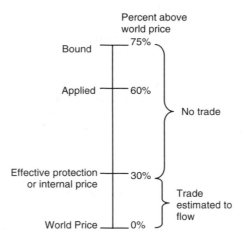

Source: Adapted from Podbury and Roberts (2003)

Figure 19.1 Illustration of Effective Protection

they had agreed upon internationally. There may be many causes of water in the tariff between the currently applied tariff and the tariff that would begin inducing trade. One possible cause of is dirty tariffication. If countries actively worked to create a higher tariff during the process of tariffication than the price wedge during the base period, this could result in a prohibitive tariff. Another possible cause is the base period that was used for determining the tariff to apply. As suggested above, it is generally acknowledged that 1986–1988 was a period of lower than average commodity prices. As such, in 1995 when all NTBs were converted to tariffs, protection increased in many cases, some to the point of causing water in the tariff (Swinbank 2004). Further, as international markets for many agricultural products exhibit considerable volatility, given that there is no standardized way to determine the price in the agreed base period, it is possible for countries to strategically choose the observations to use when calculating the base price.

The amount of water in the tariff must be acknowledged if true gains are to be achieved in market access liberalizations in agriculture. For example, although developed countries agreed to reduce their tariffs by 36 percent over six years in the URAA, if there was 40 percent water in the tariffs, there would have been no actual increase in market access. It is important to note that the amount of water in the tariff for a particular commodity being imported into a particular country will vary from year to year depending on domestic and world demand and supply conditions. In a study released in 2003, Podbury and Roberts estimate the amount of water in the tariff for a variety of agricultural products. They found there was a substantial amount of water in the tariffs in major importing countries across all ranges of present bound tariff levels. For example, for bound tariffs in the 0–15 percent range, the average water in the tariff was 37 percent and for bound tariffs in the 150–300 percent range, average water in the tariff was 75 percent. The authors conclude that if the Doha Round of negotiations results in cuts in the bound rate by similar magnitudes as those negotiated in the Uruguay Round, there would only be a minimal impact on market access. For example, in order to induce imports, a 50 percent cut in the bound tariff is needed for butter in Switzerland (Podbury and Roberts 2003), a 38 percent cut is needed for sugar in the US and 68 percent for sugar in Japan (Koester and Brummer 2003). While there has been some discussion of using applied tariffs as the starting point for tariff reduction negotiations, this idea was rejected and 'bound' tariff levels are the point of departure for tariff reduction negotiations in the Doha Round.

Podbury and Roberts (2003) find the water in the tariff varies substantially for a variety of commodities. The authors found for coarse grains, soybeans, soya oil, milk powders and to a lesser extent wheat and palm oil that the amount of water in the tariff is considerable and would require very large reductions in bound rates to increase actual market access. In addition, the effective protection provided to these products currently is quite low so even if these large cuts are made, gains available are smaller. Sugar and rice both have a large amount of water in the tariffs and would require large cuts in the bound rate if additional trade is to be induced. However, in this circumstance, both commodities are granted a high level of effective protection so if the appropriate cuts were made, significant improvements could be achieved. Cheese and beef were found to have both moderate levels of water in the tariff and tariff protection. As such, tariff cuts that actually induce additional trade are more likely in these products as the size of cut required is smaller. Finally, butter was found to have very low levels of water in the tariff for most countries, combined with high tariff levels. As such, small cuts could eliminate the water in the tariff and induce significant market access (Podbury and Roberts 2003).

Tariffication and future negotiations at the WTO

One of the primary long term objectives of undertaking tariffication was to facilitate future market access negotiations. There are many possible reduction methods to utilize in negotiations. The simplest outcome is when all tariffs are cut to a single rate. This is most common in free trade agreements where the final tariff is either very low or zero. Another simple method to use is to apply a uniform percentage reduction to all tariff lines. During the Uruguay Round, countries chose a methodology that required countries to cut tariffs by an average of 36 percent with a minimum cut on each individual tariff of 15 percent. This is now known as the Uruguay Round approach. Many countries have tariff 'spikes' in which a small number of tariff lines have very high duties. There have been approaches developed to make steeper cuts on higher tariffs and thus reduce the variance in the duties. One approach is to use a tiered method. Tariffs are put into groups according to their size and different groups are subjected to different reduction commitments with the largest tariffs being subject to the largest cuts. Countries can also utilize a mathematical formula that is designed to make steeper cuts on higher tariffs. One of the most common examples is the Swiss Formula (WTO 2005).

Conclusion

Tariffication is a central theme of the WTO and a very important component of the URAA which put trade in agricultural products on a path to conformity with general WTO disciplines. One of the primary benefits of tariffication in agriculture was greater transparency and predictability when compared to the non-tariff barriers that were used prior to the completion of the Uruguay Round. The process of tariffication, however, was far from perfect. Due to low commodity prices during the base period for determining the appropriate tariff, in some cases, protection actually increased after countries switched in 1995 from NTBs to tariffs. There have also been accusations that countries engaged in dirty tariffication to increase the tariff applied. In addition, tariff commitments only apply to bound tariffs and not applied tariffs, often meaning substantial water in the tariff that must be eliminated before any real gains in market access can occur. Negotiations in the Doha Round and beyond will centre on the reduction method that should be utilized and the magnitude of cuts made. These cuts, however, will have little market access implications if they are insufficient to eliminate the water in the tariffs.

Notes

1.   While it is possible to approximate automatic adjustments through, for example, auctioning quotas, there may still be delays between auctions.
2.   Of course, not all trade barriers are amenable to tariffication. Sanitary and phyto-sanitary that are put in place reduce the risks associated with human animal and plant diseases are one obvious example.
3.   See for example Ingco (1995)
4.   While Ingco's (1995) work has been widely cited, it has also come into question. For example, in regards to EC sugar imports, Ingco (1995) found the EC applied a rate 63 percent higher than what it should have been based on 1986–1988 world and domestic prices. Utilizing the methodology the EC notified to the other Members of the GATT, Swinbank (2004) calculated the implied tariff during 1986–1986 to be 514 ecu/tonne – 10 ecu/tonne less than the figure calculated by the EU. This difference is quite insignificant and the author suggests it is more likely from an arithmetic error than from a deliberate attempt to engage in dirty tariffication. Swinbank does acknowledge that the methodology applied resulted in an upward bias

in the level of protection but points out that the EU had notified other members of its intent to use this methodology well in advance and had carried out what it said it would do (2004).

5.   In effect, countries may increase their applied tariffs to any level up to the bound level if the competitiveness of foreign suppliers increases. Thus, it allows countries to use tariffs in a similar fashion to variable import levies. As variable import levies are now effectively banned in the WTO, this use of applied tariffs allows importing countries to circumvent another WTO commitment.

6.   There may be other strategic reasons for having applied tariff levels less than bound levels. For example, when a country enters into a regional trade association, if it is required to raise its tariff level to conform to that of the customs union it is joining, it must negotiate compensation for trading partners that would be adversely affected by the tariff increase. If bound levels are kept high, if tariffs must be raised above the applied level upon accession to the regional trade association, then compensation can be reduced or eliminated. See Gaisford *et al.* (2003) for a discussion of this strategy.

References

Gaisford, J. D., W. A. Kerr and N. Perdikis (2003), *Economic Analysis for EU Accession Negotiations – Agri-food Issues in the EU's Eastward Expansion*, Cheltenham, UK and Northampton, MA, USA: Edward Elgar.

Ingco, M. D. (1995), 'Agricultural trade liberalization in the Uruguay Round: One step forward, one step back?' Supplementary paper for the World Bank Conference on the Uruguay Round and the Developing Countries, January 1995. Washington DC: World Bank.

Koester, U. and B. Brummer (2003), 'How relevant is the failure of Cancun for world agriculture?' *Intereconomics*, **38**(5): 245–49.

Podbury, T. and I. Roberts (2003), 'Opening Agricultural Markets Through Tariff Cuts in the WTO', ABARE report for the Rural Industries Research and Development Corporation. February. available online at http://abareonlineshop.com/PdfFiles/PC12456.pdf.

Swinbank, A. (2004), 'Dirty Tariffication Revisited: The EU and Sugar', *The Estey Centre Journal of International Law and Trade Policy*, **5**(1): 56–69, available online at www.esteyjournal.com.

World Trade Organization (WTO) (2005), *Tariff Negotiations in Agriculture: Reduction Methods*, Background fact sheet, available online at http://www.wto.org/english/tratop_e/agric_e/agnegs_swissformula_e.htm.

Yeung, M. T., N. Perdikis and W. A. Kerr (1999), *Regional Trading Blocs in the Global Economy: The EU and ASEAN*, Cheltenham, UK and Northampton, MA, USA: Edward Elgar.

20 Tariff spikes and tariff escalation

André M. Nassar, Zuleika Arashiro and Marcos S. Jank

Introduction

In this chapter we discuss the concepts of tariff spikes and tariff escalation and suggest methodologies for calculation and measurement. Tariff spikes are usually imposed on products that a country considers sensitive, due to its low competitiveness in that specific sector. Despite the fact that it covers only a small portion of the total tariff lines, they can function as an effective mechanism to limit international trade. For foreign suppliers, tariff spikes affect trade by pressing prices down and restricting market access.

Although tariff spikes are broadly recognized as an obstacle to agricultural trade, they had never been fully addressed at the WTO. With the Doha Round negotiations, however, their importance has become evident.

Tariff escalation occurs when countries impose tariffs on processed products that are higher than tariffs on raw materials incorporated as inputs. By acquiring raw materials at international prices and protecting domestic processing industries, countries foster domestic industrialization while they limit trade on processed goods.

This chapter is organized in four sections, including this introduction and the final remarks. The next section addresses tariff spikes while the third section deals with tariff escalation. Both follow the same structure: conceptualization, methodology and numerical applications. A brief set of concluding comments ends the chapter.

Tariff spikes

A tariff spike – or tariff peak – can be defined as a tariff that is considerably above a pre-defined tariff cut level. Tariff peaks appear to be particularly important in the following sectors: (a) agricultural and agroindustrial products; (b) textiles and clothing; (c) footwear, leather and travel goods; and (d) the automotive sector and a few other transport and high-technology goods, such as consumer electronics and watches (UNCTAD 2000). Restrictions in these sectors have a negative effect, particularly on developing countries, as their competitiveness commonly rest in agricultural and labor-intensive exports.

There is still no consensus on the criteria to define the threshold above which a tariff peak would be characterized. Based on the related literature, we refer to two criteria for identification of tariff peaks that are also found in the WTO's *World Trade Report 2004*. The first is a general-based criterion, also called 'international peak' by the WTO (2004), valid for all countries regardless of particular characteristics of their respective tariff structures. This is the case of the definition of a tariff peak as any tariff higher than 15 percent (at the six-digit level of the Harmonized System), which is broadly utilized in international studies.[1] The other methodology is less discretionary and it is based on specific characteristics of individual tariff structures. Under such a country-specific criterion – referred to as a 'national peak' (WTO 2004) – a tariff peak can be defined as a tariff three times higher than the average tariff of a country.

Based on studies we develop on agricultural tariffs, we suggest an additional possibility to define peaks, which takes into consideration the variability within individual tariff structures. It consists of considering as peaks, tariffs higher than the sum of the average and one standard deviation.

As we will see, each methodology brings about considerably different outcomes. Despite being extensively utilized in international studies (Hoekman *et al.* 2001), the standard international cut-off level presented in the first methodology has as its main limitation the fact that it does not provide an accurate identification of protected products, within individual contexts.

In fact, a significant portion of developing and least developed countries tariffs are above 15 percent. Based on the first methodology, we may end up considering as tariff peaks a large group of tariffs that are actually close to a country average tariff and are not exceptional in its tariff structure. On the other hand, for developed countries, it may happen that some products that could be identified as sensitive through a country-specific measurement would not be captured under the general-based parameter. This helps understand why in international trade negotiations the standard cut level tends to be criticized as biased against developing countries.

Methodology

Tariff profiles vary greatly among countries. The cross-country comparison of tariff profiles is usually conducted through the utilization of standard statistical indicators such as maximum and minimum tariffs, mean, median; dispersion (standard deviation and coefficient of variation) and Gini Index. Graphic resources are also helpful tools. The most frequently used graphs are: histogram, which shows the distribution of frequencies; column and line charts with *ad valorem* tariffs on the horizontal axis; and box plot chart if the purpose of the analysis is to observe the dispersion within the tariff structure.

Regardless of the concept of tariff peak adopted or indicators used, the main challenge for cross-country comparisons lies on data gathering and the methodology of analysis. It is difficult to find complete tariff data that can be easily accessed by the public. In some cases, tariffs must be collected individually, an unviable task when we consider the need to gather information on around ten thousand tariff lines.

The next stage involves data analysis. The main methodological challenge is to deal with the complexity of tariff structures, as they are usually composed of *ad valorem* tariffs, specific tariffs, combined tariffs and tariff rates quotas (TRQs).

Until the early 1990s, countries used to apply quantitative restrictions to imports. During the Uruguay Round negotiations, they were required to transform such non-tariff barriers into tariffs through the process of tariffication. This conversion led to the emergence of a group of extremely high tariffs, corresponding mainly to products previously protected by import quantity restrictions.

Tariffication was expected to increase transparency of tariff structures and to provide a basis for negotiation of tariff reductions (UNCTAD 2000). However, various mechanisms guaranteed the maintenance of a certain level of protection to the most sensitive products. Through specific tariffs, a fixed value is charged per unit of import, instead of a percentage over the import value (*ad valorem* tariff). In the case of agricultural products, bound non-*ad valorem* tariffs (specific, combined and compound tariffs) account for 75 percent of the total of tariffs in Norway, 49.6 percent in the United States, 40.8 percent in the EU, 26 percent in Canada and 22.7 percent in Japan (WTO 2004). The introduction of TRQs was designed to provide a minimum access for products formerly subject to quantitative restrictions and products for which access was denied.[2] Nevertheless, lack of transparency in the administration of the quotas system became a major challenge. Currently, almost the totality of over-quota tariffs consists of tariff peaks.

The conversion of non-*ad valorem* tariffs into *ad valorem* tariffs is essential so that we can better depict the actual level of protection of a tariff structure. But while there is a broad recognition of the importance of the so called '*ad valorem* equivalent (AVE),' there is no consensus on how to calculate it. See Box 20.1 for an example of the complexity of determining an *ad valorem* equivalent.

A final clarification refers to the distinction between the concepts of tariff peaks and prohibitive tariffs. Following Markusen *et al.* (1995: 245), a prohibitive tariff can be described as 'the most extreme form of protective tariff,' which when applied, can effectively eliminate imports. It is usually the case that an extremely high tariff creates such a rigid barrier that effectively protects the domestic market against imports, functioning simultaneously as a tariff peak and a prohibitive tariff. However, for some products and under certain market structures, a tariff that does not correspond to a tariff peak can be characterized as a prohibitive tariff if it is sufficient to cut off imports, even if it cannot be characterized as a tariff peak.

BOX 20.1   *AD VALOREM* EQUIVALENTS (AVE) AND COMBINED TARIFFS

The Canadian tariff profile for the poultry sector is based on a mixture of combined tariffs and a tariff rate quota system. Canada imposes an in-quota tariff for chicken cuts (boneless) of 5.4 percent. The amount resulting from such tariff must be higher than Can$ 4.74 cents/kg and lower than Can$ 9.48 cents/kg. The over-quota tariff for the same product rises to 249 percent, combined to a minimum amount of Can$ 6.74/kg. What is the *ad valorem* equivalent of such specific tariffs?

In order to calculate the AVE, we use the following formula:

$$AVE = \frac{t_i}{p_w}$$

where
AVE: *Ad valorem* equivalent
t_i: nominal tariff rate on the imported good
p_w: world price for the imported good. In the absence of world price, the unit import value can be used.

We see that the AVE depends on the price and exchange rate. Suppose Canada imports chicken cuts at an average price of USD 1.8/kg, under an exchange rate of Can$ 1.2 per USD 1.0. The AVE that will be charged for in-quota imports corresponds to 4.4 percent, at the upper limit (0.0948/2.16 = 4.4 percent). Prices being the same, the AVE for the over-quota tariff will be 312 percent (6.74/2.16 = 312 percent), which is higher than the nominal rate of 249 percent.

Let us now imagine a highly competitive supplier who is able to export at a price of USD 1.4/kg. The AVE for in-quota imports will then be 5.6 percent for the upper limit, but due to the nominal tariff limitation, the imposed tariff will be 5.4 percent. The new AVE for over-quota tariff rises to 401.2 percent.

In the case of a less competitive supplier, selling at a price of USD 2.4/tonne, the AVE for the in-quota tariff will be 3.3 percent. The calculated over-quota tariff corresponds to 234 percent, but as the nominal tariff is 249 percent, this is the duty that will prevail.

Notes:

1. Nominal tariffs are identified at a minimum of eight digits of the Harmonized System. Import unit values can also be collected at eight digits. However, for world prices, there is correspondence among countries only at the six-digit level.
2. For some agricultural commodities, world prices can be collected on international trade boards – for example the Chicago Board of Trade (cereals and oilseeds), New York Board of Trade (raw sugar, coffee, cocoa, concentrated orange juice, cotton) and London International Financial Futures and Options Exchange (coffee, cocoa, wheat and white sugar) – and the UN database (COMTRADE).

Identifying and measuring tariff peaks

In theoretical terms, two typical profiles of tariff structures can be identified (Figure 20.1). The non-symmetrical profile, commonly observed in tariff structures of developed countries, is characterized by a small number of very high tariffs and a high concentration of tariffs at zero or low levels. The dispersion tends to be very high, with the coefficient of variation higher than 1 and the median tariff usually smaller than the mean tariff. The symmetrical form, most commonly found in developing countries, reflects a lower degree of dispersion. The coefficient of variation tends to be lower than 1 and the mean and median tariffs do not show significant differences. There is a clear concentration of tariffs at medium ranges, with a smaller number of tariffs at high or low ranges.

The histograms for tariff structures of the United States, EU, Brazil and India help to visualize these situations. The Y axis of the histogram shows the frequency – how often each level of tariff is counted – while the X axis indicates the level of tariff aggregated in small ranges.

In order to identify a tariff peak, the first step is to choose a cut level above which a peak is characterized. The WTO calculates the number of tariff peaks, using both the international and national criteria. Table 20.1, containing data provided at the WTO *World Trade Report 2004*, shows how each methodology – national or international peaks – brings about different results, particularly to developing and least developing countries:

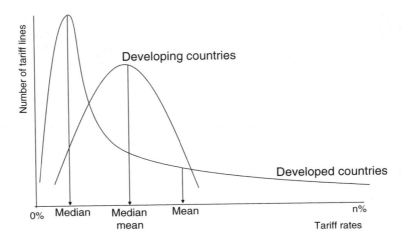

Source: Institute for International Trade Negotiations (ICONE).

Figure 20.1   Curves for hypothetical tariff profiles

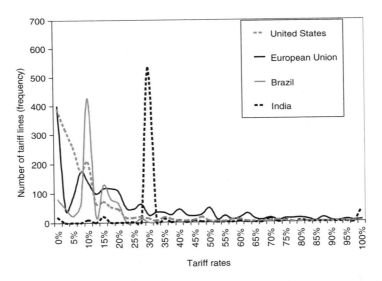

Notes: (a) applied tariffs; (b) specific tariffs were converted into *ad valorem* equivalents and calculated according to COMTRADE/UN export unit values; (c) Brazilian exceptions to MERCOSUR's external common tariff were taken into account; (d) US, EU, and India have a few tariffs above 100 per cent.

Sources: ICONE, from data provided by the US International Trade Commission; European Commission; Brazilian Ministry of Industry, Development and Foreign Trade, and Government of India.

Figure 20.2   Agricultural tariff structures: frequency of tariff rates

Table 20.1   Mean tariff and share of tariff peaks for selected WTO members

	Simple average			Share of national peak duties			Share of international peak duties		
	All	Ag	Non-ag	All	Ag	Non-ag	All	Ag	Non-ag
Developed countries									
Australia	4.1	1.1	4.6	10.1	21.1	11.4	4.2	0.0	4.8
Canada	4.1	3.0	4.3	9.8	7.8	10.6	8.2	1.2	9.3
European Union (EU)	4.4	5.9	4.2	2.5	4.1	1.5	1.9	8.2	0.9
Japan	3.3	7.1	2.7	8.8	8.6	9.9	2.7	16.1	0.7
New Zealand	3.3	1.7	3.5	6.2	15.5	6.9	4.7	0.0	5.4
United States	3.9	4.7	3.8	7.9	8.1	7.9	4.5	7.2	4.1
Developing countries									
Brazil	14.6	12.5	14.9	0.0	0.1	0.0	47.1	27.5	50.0
China	12.4	19.2	11.3	1.6	2.6	1.0	30.3	55.7	26.4
India	31.4	37.0	30.5	0.7	1.3	0.3	86.9	87.0	86.9
Mexico	17.9	23.4	17.1	0.7	4.1	0.0	54.2	47.9	55.1
South Africa	5.8	8.7	5.3	11.5	5.8	10.2	11.7	21.1	10.3
Least developed countries									
Guinea Bissau	12.0	14.2	11.6	0.0	0.0	0.0	40.9	57.0	38.1
Malawi	13.4	14.8	13.2	0.0	0.0	0.0	37.4	43.1	36.5
Mauritius	19.0	19.7	18.9	16.2	12.1	16.9	30.7	35.2	30.0

Note: Based on applied tariffs.

Source: WTO.

1. Simple tariff averages in agriculture and non-agricultural sectors are higher in developing and least developed countries than in developed countries.
2. The share of national and international tariff peaks tend to be similar in developed countries than in developing and least developed countries.
3. Tariff peaks occur more often in agriculture than in non-agricultural sectors.
4. Under the national peak criterion, tariff peaks appear as a significant problem in developed countries but less meaningful for developing and least developed countries.
5. If the international criterion is adopted, the opposite occurs. A large share of developing and least developed countries is represented by tariff peaks, while for developed countries the issue appears to be of little relevance.

Figure 20.2 presents a comparison of the agricultural tariffs for the US, EU, Brazil and India. The Y axis corresponds to tariff levels, in a descending scale, while tariff lines are represented in the X axis. All tariffs were converted into *ad valorem* equivalents, using COMTRADE/UN export unit values. Table 20.2 provides statistical indicators to the tariff profiles analyzed, including shares of tariff peaks calculated according to the different criteria presented above.

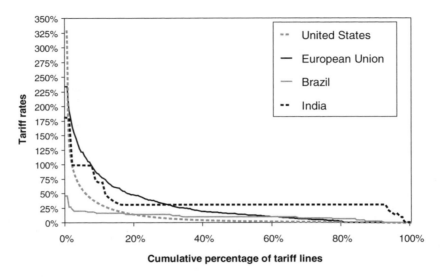

Notes: (a) applied tariffs; (b) specific tariffs were converted into *ad valorem* equivalents and calculated according to COMTRADE/UN export unit values; (c) Brazilian exceptions to MERCOSUR's external common tariff were taken into account.

Sources: ICONE, from data provided by the US International Trade Commission; European Commission; Brazilian Ministry of Industry, Development and Foreign Trade, and Government of India.

Figure 20.3   Agricultural tariff structures for selected WTO Member

Table 20.2   Statistical indicators for agricultural tariff profiles

	Brazil	USA	EC-15	India
Statistical indicators				
Mean	10.2%	12.4%	29.3%	36.9%
Median	10.0%	4.4%	14.4%	30.0%
Standard deviation	6.0%	29.8%	40.2%	25.8%
Coefficient of variation	0.6	2.4	1.4	0.7
Gini Index	0.3	0.7	0.6	0.2
Maximum tariff	55.0%	350.0%	277.2%	182.0%
Minimum tariff	0.0%	0.0%	0.0%	0.0%
Share of tariff peaks				
Three times the mean	0.3%	7.4%	8.6%	1.3%
Mean plus Std. deviation	5.6%	6.9%	12.1%	10.9%
Tariffs above 15%	16.7%	18.9%	49.6%	95.9%

Sources: ICONE elaborated with data from US International Trade Commission, European Commission, Brazilian Ministry of Industry, Development and Foreign Trade, and Government of India.

Tariff Escalation

Production processes often require the incorporation of various inputs that are produced both domestically and internationally. Changes in the import duties applied to intermediate inputs usually affect the costs of the final good and have to be taken into account in the assessment of the actual level of protection incorporated in a tariff structure.

Tariff escalation occurs when tariffs rise as we move up to higher stages of processing. In simple terms, it means that the more we increase the value-added of a good, the higher the import duty will be. As a form of protectionism, tariff escalation distorts the optimum allocation of resources. Higher import duties on processed goods artificially increase the value-added price for similar goods produced domestically, stimulating processing activities in the protected market and raising the demand for primary goods. For foreign producers, the incentives to export processed goods decrease, while the higher demand for primary inputs may stimulate their exports of commodities.

In theory, tariff escalation may reinforce specialization of developing countries in the export of commodities – with lower value added when compared to processed goods – while developed countries continue to retain larger shares of the most dynamic markets of processed goods.

The measurement of tariff escalation for specific processing chains can be performed through the calculation of the effective rate of protection (ERP). Nominal tariff rates are calculated over the value of the final product and they allow consumers to realize the price rise in the final good deriving from protection. However, nominal rates do not reflect the actual level of protection incorporated in each stage of processing. From the producers' viewpoint, the way tariffs are administered for different stages of processing or value addition provides differentiated incentives to local production of processed goods.

The vast literature that deals with the issue is unanimous in recognizing the methodological challenges related to ERP calculation (Tangermann 1989; OECD 1997; Chevassus-Lozza and Gallezot 2003). It is assumed, for instance, that productive processes are similar and that a perfect exchangeability among domestic-produced and imported inputs exists. Despite that, the ERP continues to be a reference to measure escalation (Markusen *et al.* 1995; Bureau, 2004).

Methodology

Aggregated measures reveal that countries – both developed and developing – tend to apply lower tariffs for raw materials than for semi-industrialized and industrialized goods. Table 20.3 offers a comparison of simple average tariffs for groups of products according to processing stages. For all countries examined, tariffs for raw materials are the smallest while tariffs for industrialized goods are the highest. For the United States, EU and Japan, the average tariff for industrialized goods is lower than for semi-processed goods, but the difference between them is small.

A limitation of the data presented in Table 20.3 is that it does not distinguish among various production chains. The concept of tariff escalation, however, has to be oriented towards productions chains instead of aggregated groups of products. This happens because in order to properly evaluate tariff escalation, we first need to choose a production chain and define its boundaries. Only after this procedure one can select the tariffs lines that will be analyzed.

Table 20.3   *Mean tariff for industrial products according to processing stages*

	Raw material (%)	Semi-processes (%)	Industrialized (%)
Developed countries			
Australia	0.59	4.19	5.48
Canada	0.66	3.49	4.18
European Union (EU)	0.54	4.48	3.90
Japan	0.56	4.31	3.35
New Zealand	0.33	2.10	5.38
United States	1.27	5.00	4.32
Developing countries			
Brazil	7.44	11.34	15.14
China	8.54	11.67	16.91
India	20.19	32.11	29.41
Mexico	11.10	12.87	17.36
South Africa	1.69	4.39	7.33
Least developed countries			
Malawi	9.16	10.12	15.49
Mauritius	1.56	5.14	29.91

Source: WTO.

One example is the textile production chain. We can assure that cotton is the primary product of the chain and we know that yarn, woven fabric, finished fabric, clothing and apparel are made from cotton. Nevertheless, the tariff structure of any country has at least three tariff positions for cotton, 42 for cotton yarn, 77 for woven fabrics and an even higher number for clothing and apparel. If the target is to calculate the tariff escalation in the textile sector, it is necessary first to define the extension of the production chain in order to select the tariff positions that will be compared. That involves pre-definitions such as whether clothing and apparel should be considered a part of the production chain.

As an empirical rule, we recommend that the definition of the extension of the chain be based on the content of the primary product in the final product. The analysis of tariff escalation is meaningless if the primary product is an irrelevant input in the production of the final good. In that case, even if tariffs on the final good are higher than those imposed on primary goods, it is not possible to relate the low protection over the primary good to a strategy to confer more competitiveness to the final good. Following this criteria, clothing and apparel should be excluded from the production chain, as cotton is only a secondary input on such products. On the other hand, cotton yarn and woven fabrics should be added because both are essentially made (have a high content) of cotton.

A second rule that can be followed in order to simplify the process of calculating escalation is to choose only tradable goods. When the input or the final product is a non-tradable good, trade will not occur even with a zero tariff. Calculation is still possible, but the results have no practical significance.

A third rule is to ensure that the input and the final product belong to the same production chain. Fresh fruits are inputs for juice production while table fruits are products for final consumption. As a consequence, tariffs for table fruits cannot be compared to tariffs on fruit juices in order to calculate escalations.

The dairy sector is a good case study of the complexity involved in tariff escalation. Tariffs for cheeses are usually higher than those imposed on powder milk and fluid milk. Powder milk is a tradable good but as it is rarely used as a main input for cheese production, its inclusion in the estimation of tariff escalation in the dairy sector leads to results with little practical significance. On the other hand, fluid milk is the most important raw material in the production of cheese, but as it is a non-tradable good,[3] it is inadequate to include it for the purpose of analyzing tariff escalation in the dairy sector.

The calculation of tariff escalation, therefore, is a task that requires a minimum knowledge about the production process. This is even more relevant when the effective rate of protection (ERP) is adopted to measure the magnitude of the escalation. In addition, the knowledge of the production process is fundamental because, besides tariffs, productive factors and prices for all selected products are required for the analysis.

Finally, the importance of carefully selecting tariff positions must be emphasized. For agricultural products, for instance, the incidence of quotas is quite high. When the raw material is subject to a tariff rate quota, the in-quota tariff must be selected and compared to the tariff on the intermediary and processed goods. If all the concerned goods are subject to quotas, the comparison must be based on the same type of tariff – either in-quota or over-quota. Box 20.2 provides an example of the complexity associated with calculating tariff escalation.

BOX 20.2   EFFECTIVE RATE OF PROTECTION: HOW TO CALCULATE IT?

Consider that the production of 1 tonne of instant coffee (final commodity) requires the utilization of 2.2 tonnes of coffee beans (input). International prices are US$ 6.0 for 1 instant coffee tonne, and US$ 1.6 for 1 tonne of coffee beans.

The value added – given by the difference between the price of the final commodity and the cost of input – is US$ 2.5 (US$ 6.0 − US$ 3.5 = US$ 2.5). In our example, a_i would therefore be equal to 58 percent (US$ 3.5 / US$ 6.0 = 0.58).

Let us now add tariffs to the input and the final commodity. EU imposes a 0 percent tariff on coffee and 9 percent tariff on instant coffee. European consumers would then pay US$ 6.54 for one tonne of imported instant coffee. From this total, US$ 3.5 corresponds to imported coffee beans, while US$ 2.5 is the value added and US$ 0.54/tonne results from the tariff imposed. The US$ 0.54/tonne collected tariff on imported instant coffee represents the 9 percent nominal tariff, but it corresponds to a 21.6 percent effective rate of protection because the effective tariff is calculated on the value added domestically to the instant coffee (US$ 0.54 / US$ 2.5 = 21.6 per cent).

Conceptually the ERP is given by $(V' - V)/V$, where V' is the domestic value added with a tariff on imports and V is the domestic value added under free trade. In the example, $(3.04 - 2.5)/2.5 = 21.6$ percent

Algebraically, the ERP can be calculated by applying the formula (Salvatore, 2001):

$$g = \frac{t - a_i t_i}{1 - a_i}$$

where
g: the effective rate of protection to producers of the final commodity
t: the nominal tariff rate of the final commodity
a_i: the ratio of the cost of the input to the price of the final product in absence of tariffs.
t_i: the nominal tariff rate on the imported input.

Evaluating tariff escalation

Table 20.4 presents our ERP calculations for selected agricultural chains. Escalation is characterized when the nominal tariff for the raw material is smaller than the tariffs on the processed goods. The magnitude of the escalation is measured by the ERP.

The US imposes zero tariff on soybeans, a 2.6 percent *ad valorem* equivalent tariff for oilcake and 19.1 percent for crude soybean oil. However, for each processed product examined, the ERP is higher than the nominal tariff. The ERP confirms that when relative prices between the input and the processed product are taken into account, the magnitude of the escalation is higher than the simple comparison of nominal tariffs. In other words, the ERP shows that protection for domestic producers is higher than the duty expressed on nominal tariffs.

Though nominal tariffs allow us to identify escalation, the ERP is a more appropriate measure to evaluate the magnitude of the escalation. A Chinese producer of soybean is protected by a 3 percent tariff, but the crusher enjoys an even larger protection, with tariffs of 5 percent and 9 percent for oilcake and oil respectively. For Chinese crushers, the 5 percent and 9 percent tariffs actually mean 17.3 percent and 25.2 percent of the value of domestic processing. Such effective tariffs represent a much greater level of protection than the simple comparison of nominal rates would indicate.

Table 20.4 includes examples of seven chains for eight markets. We identified a total of 42 cases of escalation, seven cases of de-escalation, and seven of homogeneous tariffs (primary and processed products with the same nominal tariff). In some cases, domestic producers actually face a negative protection, as the effective tariff for the processed product is negative.

Soybean, corn (maize) and tobacco are the sectors with a greater number of escalations (seven for the eight markets). On cocoa, six cases of escalation were identified, and for coffee, palm and wheat, escalation appears in five cases.

Coffee and cocoa are interesting examples to show how pervasive tariff escalation is. Both correspond to products that can be produced only in tropical countries. Nevertheless, non-tropical regions such as the European Union, Canada, Japan and China impose a higher protection on roasted and instant coffee, and on cocoa paste, powder and butter. The mechanism of escalation is thus used as part of a strategy to stimulate the processing of coffee and cocoa domestically.

Table 20.4 Nominal tariffs and effective rate of protection for selected agricultural chains

Sector		USA (%) NPR	USA (%) ERP	EU (%) NPR	EU (%) ERP	Canada (%) NPR	Canada (%) ERP	Japan (%) NPR	Japan (%) ERP	China (%) NPR	China (%) ERP	Mexico (%) NPR	Mexico (%) ERP	Indonesia (%) NPR	Indonesia (%) ERP	India(%) NPR	India(%) ERP
Coffee	Coffee, not roasted	0.0	n.a.	0.0	n.a.	0.0	n.a.	0.0	n.a.	8.0	n.a.	23.0	n.a.	5.0	n.a.	100.0	n.a.
	Coffee, roasted	0.0	0.0	7.5	13.6	0.5	0.9	12.0	21.7	15.0	20.7	72.0	111.8	5.0	5.0	100.0	100.0
	Coffee, extracts and essences	0.0	0.0	9.0	22.4	1.1	2.7	8.8	21.9	17.0	30.4	141.0	316.4	5.0	5.0	30.0	−74.1
Soybeans	Soybeans	0.0	n.a.	0.0	n.a.	0.0	n.a.	0.0	n.a.	3.0	n.a.	0.0	n.a.	0.0	n.a.	30.0	n.a.
	Oilcake	2.6	18.8	0.0	0.0	0.0	0.0	0.0	0.0	5.0	17.3	18.0	128.4	0.0	0.0	30.0	30.0
	Oil, crude	19.1	70.7	3.2	11.8	4.5	16.7	32.0	118.5	9.0	25.2	10.0	37.0	0.0	0.0	45.0	85.5
	Oil, refined	19.1	53.0	5.1	14.1	9.5	26.3	27.5	76.2	9.0	19.6	20.0	55.5	0.0	0.0	45.0	71.6
Palm	Palm nut	0.0	n.a.	0.0	n.a.	0.0	n.a.	0.0	n.a.	10.0	n.a.	0.0	n.a.	5.0	n.a.	30.0	n.a.
	Palm oil, crude	0.0	0.0	3.8	12.7	6.4	21.5	3.5	11.7	9.0	6.6	10.0	33.5	0.0	−11.8	100.0	264.7
	Palm kernel oil, crude	0.0	0.0	6.4	55.1	6.4	55.1	4.0	34.5	9.0	1.4	10.0	86.2	0.0	−38.1	100.0	633.2
Wheat	Wheat (exc. Durum wheat)	2.9	n.a.	0.0	n.a.	1.0	n.a.	20.0	n.a.	1.0	n.a.	67.0	n.a.	5.0	n.a.	100.0	n.a.
	Wheat flour	3.4	4.5	80.2	237.1	0.8	0.3	25.0	34.8	6.0	15.8	15.0	−86.7	0.0	−9.8	30.0	−107.0
	Pasta	6.4	7.0	25.8	31.1	4.3	5.0	23.8	23.6	15.0	16.8	10.0	9.0	5.0	6.0	35.0	36.0
	Wheat gluten	6.8	8.5	79.8	119.9	14.9	22.0	21.3	19.4	18.0	24.0	15.0	15.0	5.0	7.5	30.0	30.0
	Bran	0.0	0.0	106.3	106.3	2.2	2.2	0.0	0.0	3.0	3.0	13.0	13.0	0.0	0.0	35.0	35.0
Cocoa	Cocoa	0.0	n.a.	0.0	n.a.	0.0	n.a.	0.0	n.a.	8.0	n.a.	0.0	n.a.	5.0	n.a.	30.0	n.a.
	Cocoa paste (without defatting)	0.0	0.0	10.0	32.0	0.0	0.0	5.0	16.0	10.0	14.4	18.0	18.0	5.0	5.0	30.0	30.0
	Cocoa powder	0.5	0.5	8.0	8.0	6.0	6.0	12.9	12.9	15.0	15.0	23.0	23.0	5.0	5.0	30.0	30.0
	Cocoa butter	0.0	0.0	7.7	15.9	0.0	0.0	0.0	0.0	22.0	36.9	18.0	18.0	5.0	5.0	30.0	30.0
	Cocoa paste (defatted)	0.3	0.3	9.6	9.6	0.0	0.0	10.0	10.0	10.0	10.0	18.0	18.0	5.0	5.0	30.0	30.0
Maize	Maize (grain)	2.3	n.a.	44.9	n.a.	0.0	n.a.	0.0	n.a.	1.0	n.a.	198.0	n.a.	0.0	n.a.	60.0	n.a.
	Starch	1.9	1.4	55.8	68.0	0.0	0.0	25.0	52.7	20.0	41.1	15.0	−188.0	5.0	10.5	30.0	−3.3
	Bran	0.0	0.0	121.5	121.5	0.0	0.0	0.0	0.0	5.0	5.0	13.0	13.0	5.0	5.0	35.0	35.0
	Oil, crude	3.4	3.4	6.4	6.4	4.5	4.5	17.0	17.0	10.0	10.0	10.0	10.0	0.0	0.0	100.0	100.0

Table 20.4 (continued)

Sector		USA (%)		EU (%)		Canada (%)		Japan (%)		China (%)		Mexico (%)		Indonesia (%)		India(%)	
		NPR	ERP	NPR	ERP	NPR	ERP	NPR	ERP	NPR	ERP	NPR	ERP	NPR	ERP	NPR	ERP
Tobacco	Tobacco, stemmed/ striped	11.6	n.a.	18.4	n.a.	8.0	n.a.	0.0	n.a.	10.0	n.a.	45.0	n.a.	5.0	n.a.	30.0	n.a.
	Cigarettes	12.1	12.3	26.0	27.9	12.8	13.6	26.7	33.4	25.0	28.8	67.0	72.6	15.0	17.5	30.0	30.0

Notes: (a) nominal rate tariff (NRP) was collected from the WTO; (b) the effective rate of protection (ERP) was calculated for individual processed products, based on information provided by the private sector; (c) n.a: not applicable.

Sources: ICONE.

Another distortion caused by escalation is that it helps non-competitive raw material producers to become competitive on processed products. Their broad access to internationally priced raw materials, combined with the possibility to explore the domestic market without facing competition from foreign producers, gives producers in the protected market extra incentives to make and even export processed products. The European Union, for example, is a huge importer of soybean and soy cake, but at the same time it is an exporter of soya oil. The EU imports soybean under a zero tariff, crushes the oilseed to obtain enough oilcake for feed and exports the by-product, that is, soya oil. If escalation did not exist, part of the European crushing activities would be economically unviable.

The exercise developed here shows that there is no single rule for tariff escalation, in what concerns sectors or countries. Despite the fact that escalation was detected in the majority of the sectors examined, it has to be noted that each country develops its own strategy, according to the sectors it intends to protect.

Final Remarks

In the WTO negotiations initiated in 2001, the treatment granted to tariff peaks and tariff escalation differs depending on whether the products belong to the agricultural sector or are classified as non-agricultural goods. The Doha mandate for negotiations clearly called for the reduction or elimination of tariff peaks and tariff escalation for non-agricultural goods. However, no explicit provisions were made to address such issues in agricultural negotiations.

As a consequence, the framework for establishing the modalities in non-agricultural goods market access (NAMA) establishes that the formula for tariff reduction must incorporate mechanisms to address tariff peaks and escalation.

On the other hand, in agricultural negotiations, the treatment proposed is less ambitious. According to the framework for modalities in agriculture, the formula shall obey the rule of progressivity, based on which higher tariffs must face deeper reductions. There is, however, some flexibility for countries to select sensitive products. Particularly for tariff peaks, a tariff cap is suggested, but such limitation could exclude sensitive products.

In the case of tariff escalation, countries recognize it as trade distorting, however, the idea behind the framework is that its use should be minimized, but not necessarily eliminated.

The Doha Round brought tariff peaks and escalation to the forefront of the negotiations. This has shown the importance of methodologies that allow countries to identify, with greater accuracy, tariff peaks and to measure the magnitude of tariff escalation for a variety of sectors.

Notes

1. In a joint study, UNCTAD and WTO (UNCTAD, 2000) adopted 12 percent as the cut level. Gibson *et al.* (2001) suggest the limit of 100 percent for agricultural products, while other authors adopt 30 percent and 50 percent as the limit. This clearly shows how open to discression the definition of an internationally valid criterion can be.
2. The minimum access corresponds to the commitment undertaken at the end of the Uruguay Round, according to which future members of the WTO agreed to guarantee a minimum level of access to their markets for imported goods that corresponds to 3 percent of domestic consumption (calculated for the 1986–1988 period). Moreover, it was agreed that the access level for imported goods would be increased to 5 percent of domestic consumption by 2000 for developed countries, and by 2004 for developing countries.
3. Fluid milk is a tradable good only if commercialized as a UHT product (ultra high temperature). However, UHT milk is packed in 1 liter bottles and commercialized for domestic consumption only.

References

Bureau, J. C. (2004), 'Incidence and Impact of Tariff Peaks and Escalation of Selected Agricultural Products in Specific Markets', Technical Paper No. 33, Amsterdam, The Netherlands: Common Fund for Commodities.

Chevassus-Lozza, E. and J. Gallezot (2003), 'Preferential Agreements – Tariff Escalation: What are the consequences of the multilateral negotiations for the access of developing countries to the European market?', paper presented at the International Conference 'Agricultural policy reform and the WTO: where are we heading?', 23–26 June, Capri, Italy.

Gibson, P., J. Wainio, D. Whitley and M. Bohman (2001), 'Profiles of Tariffs in Global Agricultural Markets', *Agricultural Economic Report* No. 796. Washington, DC: US Department of Agriculture.

Hoekman, B., F. Ng and M. Olarreaga (2001), 'Tariff Peaks in the Quad and Least Developed Exports', Discussion Paper No. 2747, London: Centre for Economic Policy Research.

Markusen, J., J. Melvin, W. Kaempfer and K. Maskus (1995), *International Trade: Theory and. Evidence*, New York: McGraw-Hill.

OECD (1997), *The Uruguay Round Agreement on Agriculture and Processed Agricultural Products*, Paris: OECD.

Salvatore, Dominick (2001), *International Economics*, 7th edition, New York: John Wiley & Sons.

Tangermann, S. (1989), *Tariff Escalation in Agricultural Trade*, Forum 19,Wissenchaft Verlag Vauk, Kiel.

UNCTAD (2000), 'The Post-Uruguay Round Tariff Environment for Developing Country Exports: Tariff Peaks and Tariff Escalation', UNCTAD/WTO Joint Study, TD/B/COM.1/14/Rev.1, 28 January, Geneva.

WTO (2004), *World Trade Report 2004*, Geneva: WTO.

Recommended readings

Balassa, B. (1968), 'The Structure of Protection in Industrial Countries and its Effects on the Exports of Processed Goods from Developing Countries'. In UNCTAD, *The Kennedy Round: Estimated Effects on Tariff Barriers*, TD/6/Rev. 1. New York: United Nations.

Corden, W. (1971), *The Theory of Protection*. Oxford: Clarendon Press.

Tariff databases

Inter-American Development Bank (DataIntal)
http://www.iadb.org/intal/ingles/bdi/i-dataintalweb.htm.

FTAA Hemispheric Trade and Tariff Database
http://www.ftaa-alca.org/.

United States International Trade Commission (USITC). Tariff and Trade Dataweb
http://dataweb.usitc.gov/.

APEC Tariff Database
http://www.apectariff.org/.

21 Export taxes: how they work and why they are used

Ryan Scholefield and James Gaisford

Introduction

Governments use a variety of trade policy instruments to affect cross-border trade flows. This chapter examines export taxes. An export tax is a tax or tariff that a domestic country imposes upon its own products before they are shipped abroad. In addition to enabling a domestic government to collect revenue on exports, an export tax drives the domestic price below the world price. There are numerous political motivations for imposing export taxes, which tie in with the reduction in the domestic price change, and a potential national welfare rationale for export taxes, which is associated with a possible increase in the world price.

We begin with a general theoretical overview of how an export tax works. As in the case of import tariffs, which were discussed in several preceding chapters, the impact of an export tax on national welfare depends on whether a country is large enough to have some influence upon the world price or whether it is sufficiently small that its effect is negligible. Consequently, for countries that are able to affect the world price, there is an optimum export tax, which is analogous to the optimum import tariff. Regardless of whether an export tax affects the world price, the decline in the domestic price creates winners and losers in the domestic economy. We provide a simple example of such winners and losers using a standard two-factor, two-good (Heckscher-Ohlin) framework where the Stolper-Samuelson Theorem implies that an export tax favours the factor used intensively in the import competing sector at the expense of the factor used intensively in the export sector.

This chapter also examines practical experience with export taxes. For largely political reasons, which we will explore, export taxes are used far less frequently than tariff and non-tariff barriers to imports. Voluntary Export Restraints (VERs), which are quantity restrictions on exports, were also comparatively common until they were prohibited as a result of the Uruguay Round of the General Agreement on Tariffs and Trade (GATT). The examination of VERs in the next chapter reveals a trade impact that is very similar to an export tax, at least if markets are competitive. Even export subsidies remain more common than export taxes, despite the fact that export subsidies have been largely relegated to the agricultural sector by international trade rules since the inception of the GATT after the Second World War. As a result of the current Doha Round of World Trade Organization (WTO) negotiations, however, export subsidies may eventually be phased out completely in agriculture as well. Export subsidies are discussed in Chapter 26. While export taxes are observed less frequently in practice than many other trade measures, they *are* observed. In this chapter, we explore four case studies: Thailand's rice, Ukrainian sunflower seeds, Canadian softwood lumber, and Canadian oil under its National Energy Program.

How export taxes work

We consider a simple two-country world and we focus on a market where Home exports to the rest of the world. We can use a simple demand and supply analysis of the domestic market and, ultimately, the world market, to assess the effects of an export tax imposed by Home. On the one hand, our analysis can be interpreted in a so-called partial equilibrium context where the single market in question does not significantly affect incomes or prices in the rest of the economy. On the other hand, it is possible to interpret the analysis in a two-good *general* equilibrium context where the economy as a whole is in balance. The two-good general equilibrium interpretation is possible because a useful property known as Walras' Law implies that if the first market – shown in our diagrams – is in equilibrium, so too is the second market. To simplify the general equilibrium interpretation, it is useful to assume that demand is independent of income for the good that is shown explicitly and that prices are measured relative to the other good. In both the partial and general equilibrium approaches, we assume that markets are competitive. Since both interpretations are theoretically consistent, there is a useful dual-purpose element in the analysis that follows.

Export taxes in the archetypal small-country case

We use Figure 21.1 to assist in the analysis of an export tax in the special, but simple, case where Home is a very 'small country'.[1] In fact, Home is assumed to be so small relative to the rest of the world that it cannot influence the world price, P^*, at all. The demand and supply curves of Home are represented by D and S. Free trade prevails in the initial equilibrium before Home implements its export tax. Since the initial domestic price in Home, Pi, is equal to the world price, P^*, the initial quantities supplied and demanded are QSi, and QDi respectively. The initial quantity exported, therefore, is QXi, the amount by which the quantity supplied exceeds the quantity demanded.

Now suppose that Home introduces a final export tax equal to Tf dollars per unit. An equivalent analysis would follow with an *ad valorem* or percentage export tax rather than

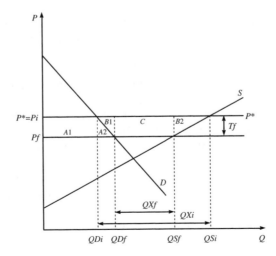

Figure 21.1   An export tax in the small-country case

a (dollar) per-unit tax. The introduction of the export tax reduces the final domestic price in Home to *Pf* and results in a situation where the domestic price plus the export tax is equal to the world price. This implies that producers in Home receive the domestic price whether they sell to Home consumers at *Pf* or sell to the rest of the world at *P**, but pay the government *Tf*. The lower domestic price, *Pf*, results in: a decrease in the quantity supplied to *QSf*, an increase in the quantity consumed to *QDf*, and a decline in exports to *QXf*. Since exports are being taxed, this reduction is to be expected.

While the export tax is clearly harmful to producers, it is beneficial to the government, which collects additional tax revenue, as well as to consumers. These losses and gains are readily quantifiable. In Figure 21.1, there is a loss in net benefits to suppliers or producer surplus, equal to *A*1 + *A*2 + *B*1 + *B*2 + *C* dollars that occurs because of the reduction in the domestic price from *Pi* to *Pf*.[2] Meanwhile, the price reduction implies a gain in net benefits to demanders, or consumer surplus, equal to *A*1 + *A*2 dollars.[3] The government collects *C* dollars since the newly created tax revenue is equal to the export tax, *Tf*, multiplied by the quantity exported, *QXf*. Aggregating across producers, consumers and the government, Home experiences a loss in total surplus equal to *B*1 + *B*2 dollars. Consequently, we can conclude that if Home is a small country, it will suffer an efficiency loss from imposing a distortionary tax wedge on the market.

Export taxes in the general case

While the analysis in Figure 21.1 applies strictly to a very small country that has no influence over the world price over any quantities that it could feasibly export, the analysis may provide a reasonable approximation for other less extreme situations where countries do not have much market power. Nevertheless, in general, countries may have a perceptible influence on the world of the exported good. This general situation is somewhat more complex. In Figure 21.2, there are separate panels showing demand and supply in the Home market on the left, demand and supply in the rest of the world on the right and international trade in the centre. In the trade panel, the export supply curve for Home is *SX* and the demand for imports curve of the rest of the world is *DM**.[4] The fact that the import demand curve of the rest of the world is negatively sloped rather than horizontal or perfectly elastic is the novel feature of this analysis. As the rest of the world imports more from Home, the world price it is willing to pay now falls; it no longer remains unchanged.

The initial free-trade equilibrium that exists prior to the implementation of Home's export tax is at the intersection of the export supply curve of Home and the import demand curve of the rest of the world. As we will see, world markets are in balance at this point. In the initial free-trade equilibrium, the domestic price in Home, *Pi*, is equal to the world price, *Pi**. The initial quantities supplied and demanded in Home are *QSi* and *QDi*, while the corresponding quantities in the rest of the world are *QSi** and *QDi**. The difference between output and consumption in Home, *QXi*, is exported, while the difference between consumption and output in the rest of the world, *QMi**, is imported. This situation is an equilibrium precisely because Home's exports are equal to the rest of the world's imports.

When Home imposes an export tax of *Tf* dollars on each unit that it exports, a wedge is created between the world price, represented by the height of the import demand curve of the rest of the world, and Home's domestic price, represented by the height of its export

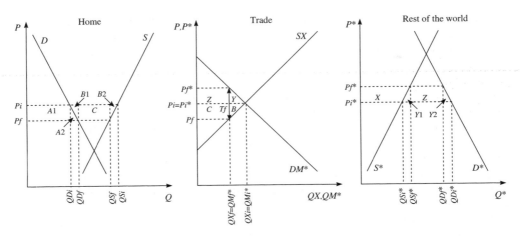

Figure 21.2   An export tax in the general case

supply curve. The two-way arrow in the centre panel of Figure 21.2 shows this export-tax wedge. As in the small-country case, the final domestic price in Home, *Pf*, is lower than the initial domestic price, but now the world price has risen to *Pf** as a result of Home restricting its exports.[5] At the lower price, Home reduces its quantity supplied to *QSf*, increases its quantity demanded to *QDf* and, thereby, restricts its exports to *QXf*. These quantity changes, of course, are qualitatively equivalent to those obtained in the small-country case. At the higher world price, however, the rest of the world reduces its quantity demanded to *QDf**, increases it quantity supplied to *QSf** and, thereby, rations the quantity of imports it demands to *QMf**, which is exactly equal to the quantity of exports supplied by Home.

In the Home market panel of Figure 21.2, we observe that suppliers suffer a decline in producer surplus equal to *A1 + A2 + B1 + B2 + C* dollars due to the reduction in the domestic price, while consumers gain *A1 + A2* dollars in increased consumer surplus. There is, thus, an unambiguous loss in exporter surplus, or net benefits to the private sector, equal to *B1 + B2 + C* dollars. The private sector experiences an unambiguous loss from the decline in the domestic price because producer interests dominate when a country is exporting; simply put, there is more production than consumption. The construction of the export supply curve implies that area *B* in the trade panel of Figure 21.2 is equal to the sum of areas *B1 + B2* in the Home market panel and that area *C* is the same in both panels. Therefore, the loss of *B + C* dollars in the trade panel also represents the private sector's change in exporter surplus. The increase in government revenue is equal to the export tax, *Tf*, multiplied by the quantity exported, *QXf*, which amounts to *Z + C* dollars in the trade panel. Aggregating across the private sector and the government, Home experiences a change in total surplus equal to *Z − B* dollars. The change in Home's total surplus is also equal to *(Z + Y) − (B + Y)* dollars, where *Z + Y* represents a terms-of-trade gain from the increase in the world price of Home's export and *B + Y* represents an efficiency loss form the introduction of the tax distortion into what would otherwise be an efficient world market. Since area *Z* happens to be larger than *B* in Figure 21.2, the export tax of *Tf* generates an overall gain for the Home country. In more intuitive terms,

Home gains from this particular export tax because the terms-of-trade gain more than offsets the efficiency loss.

While the terms-of-trade gain will outweigh the efficiency loss for a range of small export taxes as suggested by Figure 21.2, we hasten to observe that there are other situations where Home will lose because the export tax becomes excessively large. For example consider a prohibitively large export tax, which is sufficient to cut off trade entirely. In this case, the efficiency loss overwhelms the terms-of-trade gain generating an overall loss.[6] Since Home gains relative to free trade from sufficiently small export taxes but loses from sufficiently large export taxes, there is an optimum export tax somewhere in between where home exercises its monopoly selling power on world markets to its best advantage. The optimum export tax is discussed further in the Appendix.

While Home may experience overall gains or losses from the export tax, the rest of the world always loses on an overall basis. In other words, export tax, like an import tariff, is always a beggar-thy-neighbour policy. From the right-hand panel of Figure 21.2, we see that the higher world price generates a decline in consumer surplus equal to $X + Y1 + Y2 + Z$ dollars, but the gain in producer surplus is only X dollars. Consequently there is an unambiguous loss of importer surplus and total surplus equal to $Y1 + Y2 + Z$ dollars in the right-hand panel or, equivalently, to $Y + Z$ dollars in the centre panel. The overall loss experienced by the rest of the world arises because of the increase in the price of its imported good, which is a terms-of-trade deterioration from its perspective. Not surprisingly, the rest of the world experiences a terms-of-trade loss that is exactly equal in magnitude to the terms-of-trade gain in Home. Of course, this still leaves the world as a whole facing an efficiency loss of $B + Y$ dollars because the export tax distorts the world market.[7]

Winners and losers from export taxes
While governments might ideally seek to impose trade policy measures such as export taxes so as to maximize national welfare, in reality politics is rarely – perhaps never – so straightforward. In response to electoral pressures, lobbying, and so on, governments frequently play off one special or vested interest against another and against the national interest. Consequently, political-economy considerations are such that to understand trade policy in general, much more attention should be placed on the examination of winners and losers as opposed to overall national welfare. For this reason, we now focus more sharply on the likely winners and losers from export taxes.

The preceding analysis suggests that consumers tend to gain and producers tend to lose from an export tax. Applying our two-good general equilibrium interpretation with care, we can extend this to a simple economy-wide conclusion. Producers in the export sector will tend to lose relative to those in the import competing sector, while consumers that consume disproportionately more of the export good tend to gain relative to those who consume disproportionately more of the imported good. As we will see below, 'consumer interests' frequently play a significant role in the political economy of export taxes. Nevertheless, supply-side interests usually tend to dominate in the formulation of trade policy in general and should not be neglected here.

As the above analysis suggests, in the short run the interests of firms in the import competing sector and the factors they employ would be well served by an export tax, while the interests of those in the export sector would be harmed. In the long run, however, entry or exit eliminates abnormal profits or losses for firms in competitive industries.

Consequently, it is the underlying factor groups, rather than firms, that will be the winners and losers in the long run. Further, such factors may be mobile between sectors at least to some degree. In a two-good general equilibrium setting, factors used specifically or intensively in the export sector will tend to lose from an export tax, while those used intensively in the import-competing sector will tend to gain. For clarity, suppose that there are two factors, skilled labour and unskilled labour, as well as two goods. Further, let us assume that unskilled labour is always used intensively relative to skilled labour in the production of Home's export good compared with its import-competing good. The Stolper–Samuelson theorem (Stolper and Samuelson 1941) implies that the decrease in the domestic price of Home's export will unambiguously increase the real wages of skilled labour and reduce the real wages of unskilled labour. This result arises because the contracting export sector releases a relatively high proportion of unskilled labour relative to the needs of the expanding import-competing sector generating excess supply of unskilled labour and excess demand for skilled labour. Meanwhile, the increase in the world price will reduce the real wages of unskilled labour and increase the real wages of skilled labour in the rest of the world.[8]

The fact that in both the short run and the long run the supply-side interests that are associated with the export sector lose from the export tax helps explain why export taxes are rather uncommon. Although the interests of supply-side groups that are associated with the import-competing sector are advanced by an export tax, it appears more natural and certainly more transparent for such groups to lobby for a tariff applied directly to imported goods.[9] Consequently, supply-side clientele for export taxes will often be absent.

Why export taxes are imposed
While our analysis suggests that lobbying for export taxes will be observed less frequently than for tariffs, this does not imply that export taxes are never used. We now examine export taxes in practice by considering four case studies that apply to a variety of sectors and countries.

Thailand's export tax on rice
Thailand imposed an export tax on rice following the Second World War but the 'rice premium' was gradually reduced during the 1970s and 1980s and eventually it was eliminated in 1986.[10] It appears that the motivation for the tax was primarily fiscal exigencies. Historically, the export tax was an important source of government revenue and foreign exchange. Further, much of the burden fell on foreigners. Indeed, in 1960 rice premiums accounted for 12 per cent of government revenue, while income tax revenue accounted for only 9.4 per cent. Only in 1966 did income tax revenue overtake the rice premium as a share of government revenue (Wong 1978). With the currency crisis of 1997, which caused a large depreciation of the Thai baht, there were calls for the renewal of an export tax to provide much-needed foreign exchange and as a way to prevent consumer price increases. With the recovery of the baht and the Thai economy growing once again, pressure to reinstate the export tax subsided.

The overall implications of the export tax for Thailand's national welfare are interesting. The international market for rice has the unusual property that only about 5 per cent of world production is actually traded. Thailand contributed approximately 26 per cent of world rice exports from 1975 to 1998 suggesting that it my have had a significant market impact (Warr 2001). Because of differentiated consumer preferences over different varieties of rice, there is additional reason to believe that Thailand could exercise a degree of market power through an export tax. Any national welfare gains from the export tax, however, must be weighed together with the redistributive consequences. Since the rural poor are net producers of rice, the reduced domestic price associated with the export tax was undoubtedly harmful and acted as a disincentive to increase and improve rice production. Given that rice production uses unskilled labour intensively, it is possible that the urban poor may also have been adversely affected in the long term. The Stolper–Samuelson theorem suggests the possibility that the additional influx of migrants to Bangkok and other cities caused by the export tax could have reduced unskilled wages by a greater proportion than the decline in rice prices. Unskilled labour in the cities as well as the countryside, therefore, may have experienced lower real wages.

Ukraine's export tax on sunflower seeds

In 1999 Ukraine imposed a 23 per cent export tax on sunflower seeds, but the rate has since been scaled back to 17 per cent (Shulha 2003) and may be further reduced as an eventual consequence of Ukraine's negotiations to enter the WTO. The central motivation behind the export tax has been to support downstream vegetable oil producers, who are the immediate 'consumers' of sunflower seeds. As the theoretical model predicts, the domestic price of sunflower seeds fell due to the export tax, making the processors more competitive. Not only did the government receive revenue from exports, but also the oil processing plants began to operate at 60–70 per cent of capacity, which was up from 30–35 per cent before the export tax (Shulha 2003).

No doubt, greater value added in the processing versus the farm sector contributed to the government's decision process. Nevertheless, there have clearly been adverse distributional consequences for seed producers, and as in the case of Thai rice, these could eventually lead to negative effects for unskilled labour more generally. Ukraine is a significant oil seed producer and, in good growing years, it has been the second largest producer of sunflower seeds in the world, accounting for about 12 per cent of world production and 20 per cent of world exports (Shulha 2003). In spite of this evidence of probable market power, Shulha (2003) has calculated that export tax rates have been excessively high; the optimum export tax appears to be in the order of 10–15 per cent with the higher rate applying only in the harvest season.

Canada's export tax on softwood lumber under the memorandum of agreement

In 1986, the US Department of Commerce threatened to rule that a 15 per cent duty should be applied to softwood imports from Canada because of alleged unfair subsidies.[11] Rather than face such a US import tariff, Canada negotiated a Memorandum of Understanding (MOU) with the US, where Canadian authorities agreed to collect a 15 per cent export tax on softwood lumber. In terms of private-sector impact in both countries, the 15 per cent import tariff and the 15 per cent export tax would be similar. Canadian prices would fall and US prices would rise leading to gains for Canadian consumers and US producers at the expense of Canadian producers and American consumers. The export tax, however, allowed Canada to keep the tax revenue. Since an export tax depresses domestic prices and decreases producer surplus relative to free trade, Canadian producers pressured their government leading Canada to unilaterally terminate the MOU in 1991. In response the Department of Commerce imposed a 6.5 per cent countervailing duty, which was eventually overturned leading to a refund of the duties. Nevertheless, in 1996 the two nations concluded a new deal called the Softwood Lumber Agreement (SLA), which included a mixture of export quotas and taxes. This allowed for a set amount of Canadian lumber to enter the US market tax free, and any amounts above the set amount would be subject to gradually increasing export taxes (Zhang 2005; Kinuncan and Zhang 2003). This agreement expired in 2001, and in the absence of a new negotiations, the US Department of Commerce eventually imposed a 27.22 per cent antidumping and countervailing duty on Canadian softwood lumber (DFAIT Canada 2002). Canada has challenged this through the North American Free Trade Agreement (NAFTA) and the WTO.

Canada undoubtedly has market power in the North American softwood lumber market since Canadian lumber exports to the United States amount to approximately 60 per cent of US domestic production (DFAIT Canada 2002). In spite of strong evidence that Canada experienced overall gains relative to free trade under both the MOU and the SLA (see Begley *et al.* 1998; Zhang 2005; Kinuncan and Zhang 2003), Canada has long favoured a free-trade policy in softwood because of the benefits to Canadian producers.[12] The US, on the other hand, seems set on protecting its producers whether through its own tariffs under the auspices of antidumping and countervailing duties, or through Canada agreeing to export taxes or similar policies.

Canada's export tax on oil under the National Energy Program
Another example of Canadian export taxation occurred under the National Energy Program (NEP). In addition to an export tax on oil (Gainer 1976), this programme also included: a Petroleum and Gas Revenue Tax of 8 per cent on net operating revenues; a Natural Gas and Gas Liquids Tax which was created to tax all natural gas sales, including those to export markets; and a price ceiling for oil at the wellhead (Jenkins 1986). The NEP had predictable effects. During the volatile oil market that existed in the late 1970s and early 1980s, the NEP did succeed in keeping oil prices in Canada below the world level and it also redistributed government revenue from the provincial government in oil-rich Alberta to the federal government. While the lower domestic price for consumers was intended, the NEP also had the standard effect of increasing consumption, decreasing production and reducing net-exports. The decrease in domestic production activity, however, was an undesired side effect of the policy, which led to a variety of efforts to mitigate the reduced incentives for production and exploration (Jenkins 1986). Declining world oil prices, rising industry pressure and increasing federal-provincial tension eventually led to the termination of the NEP in the mid-1980s.

Conclusion
Export taxes create government revenue, while depressing domestic prices, reducing output and increasing consumption. In addition, if a country is large enough to have some market power, the world price will typically rise and foreigners will bear some of the burden of the tax. This opens the door to an increase in national welfare provided that the tax is kept sufficiently small. Since export taxes reduce access to world markets by restricting exports, they run counter to the vested interests of producer groups associated with the export sector. Such sectoral producer interests would, consequently, favour

export subsidies rather than taxes. As a result, export taxes are much less frequently observed than import tariffs even though both policies restrict trade. Nevertheless, it is not difficult to find examples of export taxes. As the case studies show, export taxes have been applied to a wide variety of goods by countries at all levels of development for diverse but predominantly political reasons.

Notes

1. A similar diagrammatic analysis can be found in Shulha (2003).
2. The producer surplus associated with a particular quantity supplied is equal to the difference between producers' revenue and their opportunity cost. The opportunity cost, in turn, is measured by the cumulative area under the supply curve up to the quantity in question. This implies that the change in producer surplus resulting from a change in price is typically equal to the area inside the supply curve between the two prices. Of course, a price decrease implies a loss in producer surplus and *vice versa*.
3. The consumer surplus associated with a particular quantity demanded is the difference between consumers' total willingness to pay, measured by the area under the demand curve up to the quantity in question, and their actual expenditures. This implies that the change in consumer surplus resulting from a change in price is typically equal to the area inside the demand curve between the two prices. By contrast with producer surplus, consumer surplus rises if the price declines.
4. At any domestic price, the supply of exports for Home reflects the difference between the total quantity supplied by domestic producers and the quantity demanded by domestic consumers. Consequently, Home's export supply curve reflects the excess supply or horizontal gap between Home's supply and demand curves at each price. By analogous reasoning, the import demand curve of the rest of the world reflects the excess demand or horizontal gap between its demand and supply curves at each price.
5. In the two-good general equilibrium case where income changes do not affect the demand for Home's exported good in either country, the world price must rise. This will typically, but not always, be the case in more general situations where income does affect demand. In general, the export supply curve could become backward bending and it will shift as a result of changes in income from trade taxes.
6. Note that in this case the efficiency loss is equal to the entire area inside the export supply and import demand curves in the trade panel of Figure 21.2, while the terms-of-trade gain is equal to the smaller area above the initial price line and inside the import demand curve.
7. It is interesting to observe that, when income effects on demand are absent for the market in question, an import tariff by the rest of the world equal to Tf would lead to exactly the same price and quantity changes and exactly the same changes in private sector welfare as the Home's export tax. While the efficiency loss to the world economy would also be the same for both policies, the impact on government revenue and overall national welfare does depend on which country applies the tax. When there are income effects on demand, however, this equivalence between Home's export tax and the rest of the world's tariff breaks down because the market impact does depend on where the tax revenue accrues.
8. For a modern treatment of the Stolper–Samuelson theorem, see Feenstra (2004, ch. 2).
9. In a competitive two-good general equilibrium setting, any trade restriction that can be accomplished by restricting imports through a tariff could also be accomplished with an equal percentage export tax. In principle, then, an omniscient rational interest group should be indifferent to which sector receives a trade tax. In more complex economies, however, seeking equivalent protection by applying tax instruments to a range of other sectors, rather than a group's own sector, becomes politically more problematic. Consequently, when lobbying for protection it appears to be a much safer and more obvious strategy for an interest group to focus on policies that are applied to its own sector.
10. The export premium was administered as a fee paid for obtaining an export license. Commercial exporters then had to buy rice at prices 15 per cent to 20 per cent higher than the domestic price and they were subject to punitive official exchange rates (Wong 1978).
11. There has been a lengthy series of Canada US softwood lumber disputes. Institutional differences between Canada and the United States forestry regulation have been at the heart of these disputes. For example, in Canada the provincial governments own about 94 per cent of timberlands and charge a stumpage fee for lumber companies to harvest wood. By contrast, in the United States, rights to harvest lumber from public or private lands are generally sold through a competitive bidding process. The government administered stumpage fees in Canada are often significantly lower than the prices for cutting rights auctioned in the US, but Canada has more abundant forest resources. Other features such as the British Columbia provincial government's export ban on logs have added to the controversy. The US has generally contended that Canada engages in unfair trade practices by dumping and providing unfair subsidies, while Canada has repeatedly argued that its exports are based on comparative advantage and that it has been the victim of unfair harassment by the US (see DFAIT Canada 2002, and Zhang 2005).

12. Kinuncan and Zhang (2003) show that, in theory, it is possible that Canadian producers could have gained relative to free trade under the SLA due to the export quota rents that accrue when Canadian firms with export licences sell at the high US price. Zhang (2005) shows that the empirical evidence strongly suggests that Canadian producers actually lost relative to free trade under the SLA, though less than under the MOU or US tariff regimes.

References

Begley, J., J. Hughes, J. Rayburn and D. Runkle (1998), 'Assessing the Impact of Export Taxes on Canadian Softwood Lumber,' *Canadian Journal of Economics*, **31**(1), 207–19.

DFAIT (Department of Foreign Affairs and International Trade) Canada (2002), 'Canada–US Softwood Lumber Trade Relations,' Web Document: http://www.dfait-maeci.gc.ca/trade/eicb/softwood/menu-en.asp.

Feenstra, Robert (2004), *Advanced International Trade: Theory and Evidence*, Princeton, NJ: Princeton University Press.

Gainer, Walter D. (1976), 'Western Disenchantment and the Canadian Federation,' *Proceedings of the Academy of Political Science, Canada-United States Relations*, **32**(2), 40–52.

Jenkins, B. (1986), 'Reexamining the "Obsolescing Bargain": A Study of Canada's National Energy Program,' *International Organization*, **40**(1), 139–65.

Kinnucan, H. W. and D. Zhang (2004), 'Incidence of the 1996 Canada–US Softwood Lumber Agreement and the Optimal Export Tax,' *Canadian Journal of Agricultural Economics*, **52**, 73–88.

Shulha, T. (2003), 'Measuring the Cost of Protection in Ukrainian Sunflower Seed Industry,' MA Thesis, National University 'Kyiv-Mohyla Academy', Economics Education and Research Consortium.

Stolper, W. F. and P. A. Samuelson (1941), 'Protection and Real Wages,' *Review of Economic Studies*, **9**, 58–73.

Warr, P. G. (2001), 'Welfare Effects of an Export Tax: Thailand's Rice Premium,' *American Journal of Agricultural Economics*, **83**(4), 903–20.

Wong, C. M. (1978), 'A Model for Evaluating the Effects of Thai Government Taxation of Rice Exports on Trade and Welfare,' *American Journal of Agricultural Economics*, **60**(1), 65–73.

Zhang, L. (2005), 'The Canada–US Softwood Lumber Dispute,' MA Thesis, University of Calgary, Department of Economics.

Appendix: The optimum export tax

The optimum export tax requires the marginal cost of exports, which is given by the height of the export supply curve, to be equal to the marginal benefit or marginal revenue from exports. The marginal revenue is less than the world price given by the height of the import demand curve. While the world price is received when an additional unit of exports is sold, the world price is bid down for all preceding units and revenue is lost on these intra-marginal units. Consequently the marginal revenue from exports curve must lie below the import demand curve. In Figure 21.2, if the marginal revenue curve, which is not drawn to avoid clutter, happened to intersect the export supply curve where exports are equal to QXf, then Tf would be the optimum export tax.

A somewhat tedious but straightforward mathematical argument can be used to establish that the optimum *ad valorem* export tax is inversely related to the responsiveness or elasticity of the rest of the world's import demand with respect to the world price. The marginal cost of exports can be written as $MCX = P = P^*/(1 + t)$, since the world price is equal to the domestic price marked up by the export tax such that $P^* = (1 + t)P$. Given that the total revenue from exports is $TRX \equiv P^* \times QX = P^* \times QM^*$, small changes in total revenue must be in conformity with $dTRX = P^* \times dQM^* + QM^* \times dP^*$. Given that equilibrium changes in imports and exports are equal, such that $dQX = dQM^*$, the marginal revenue from exports is given by $MRX \equiv dTRX/dQX = P^* \times [1 - (1/\varepsilon^*)]$, which is less than the world price. Here, $\varepsilon^* \equiv (P^* \times dQM^*)/(QM^* \times dP^*)$ measures the elasticity of the rest of the world's import demand with respect to the world price. Equating the marginal cost of exports and the marginal revenue from exports yields $t = 1/(\varepsilon^* - 1)$ after simplification. Using the two good interpretation of our analysis, it happens that $t = 1/(\varepsilon^* - 1)$ is the expression for Home's optimum import tariff as well as its optimum export tax. That is to say, Home's optimum export tax is equal to its optimum tariff; either – but not both – can be used to achieve optimum trade restriction.

22 Import quotas and voluntary export restraints
Stefan Lutz

Introduction

Import quotas[1] are limitations on the quantity of a particular good that can be imported into the country within a specified time.[2] Import quotas are administered by a domestic government agency.[3] Quotas may be absolute quotas in the sense defined above or they may be tariff-rate quotas. In the latter case, the quota amount can be imported at a reduced tariff rate. Both types of quotas can be set globally or against specific countries. A total import prohibition effectively amounts to a quota of size zero.

If the quota is implemented by the government of an exporting country, then it is called a Voluntary Export Restraint (VER). Typically, VERs are requested from a specific exporting country because the importing country's industry seeks protection. Therefore, VERs are often negotiated bilaterally. The degree of 'voluntariness', hence, depends on the relative bargaining power (economically and otherwise) of the countries involved. As long as neither quotas nor VERs are sold, the economic effects of quotas and VERs are largely the same. Therefore, VERs will only be discussed explicitly in this chapter where significant differences arise.[4]

The remainder of this chapter is organized as follows. The next section gives an overview of theoretical research on quota effects. The third section analyzes quotas under perfect competition. Quotas on import competition in the presence of domestic market power are presented in the fourth section. This is followed by an extensive treatment of quotas in markets with quality-differentiated oligopolies in the fifth section. Empirical evidence is discussed in the sixth section. The last section provides a conclusion.

Some theoretical results concerning quotas

According to recent theoretical studies, quotas on foreign competition will increase qualities, prices and profits of both domestic and foreign firms under fairly general assumptions.[5] These results obtain, since a quota imposes on firms a degree of collusion that they could not obtain otherwise. In doing that, it raises the marginal profitability of quality for both firms at the former free-trade qualities; and it does so even if the quota is not binding. Therefore, the quota also changes the nature of oligopolistic competition. This is the oligopolistic analogue to the case of a domestic monopoly (Bhagwati 1965). However, theoretical research by Krishna (1987), Das and Donnenfeld (1989), and Herguera *et al.* (2000), suggests that a quota could also lead to quality downgrading for either domestic or foreign quality. Krishna analyzes a monopoly, while both the latter approaches assume a duopoly with Cournot competition, that is firms choose quantities strategically,[6] in the last stage of the industry-game. The duopoly studies differ in the exact timing of the games analyzed.

Krishna (1989) emphasizes the importance of the form of last stage game for the resulting payoff functions of the firms. Important attributes are the chosen strategic variables (prices, quantities), the form of the restrictions or policy variables (quotas, tariffs), the sequencing of the game (simultaneous, Leader–Follower, quality first or quality jointly with price, and so on). She shows that a quota will still lead to increased prices and profits for both firms for the case of differentiated substitute products and simultaneous price competition. But the price equilibrium will now involve mixed-strategies on the part of the domestic firm. However, she does not analyze the previous stage of quality choice, treating quality in effect as unchanged. Given the general thrust of current research results, however, effects on quality are of particular interest. Vertical quality differentiation ('high' versus 'low' product quality) between substitutable products is, of course, an important dimension in international trade, since trade in differentiated but substitutable products (intra-industry trade) has grown most in recent decades.

Choosing product quality in a first investment stage followed by direct market competition has been applied in studies by Herguera *et al.* (2000) as well as by Lutz (2005); the former study incorporates Cournot competition whereas the latter analyzes the Bertrand case. Regardless of the form of market competition in the last stage – price or quantity choice – a quota close to the free-trade import quantity will lead to quality downgrading by the high-quality firm and reduction of domestic consumer surplus irrespective of whether the importer produces the higher quality. When the foreign firm is the low-quality producer, the profit and domestic welfare results for the Cournot and Bertrand cases are also consistent. Similarly for both model variants, a tightening of the quota leads to declining import quality and profits while domestic quality and profits will rise.

Quotas under perfect competition

This section deals with the imposition of a quota in a single competitive market. The resulting price and quantity changes and their effects on profits and consumer surplus are described.[7] One major aspect of the effect of the imposition of a quota is that they are exactly equivalent to those of a tariff – reducing trade to the quota level.

In Figure 22.1, let D denote aggregate domestic import demand, S^* denote aggregate foreign export supply, M denote import quantities, and P denote prices. Under free trade, the import volume would be M_f sold at price P_f. A quota of M_q will reduce foreign export supply to M_q and the effective supply price to P_t^* while domestic import demand will only equal M_q at a domestic price P_t. Define now $P_t^* = P_t - t$, then t is the effective quota rent, or cost of imposing the quota.

Note that we could get the same market result by imposing a (specific) import tariff equal to t. In the case of a tariff, of course, the government would earn tariff revenues of $(t * M_q)$ paid for in part by domestic consumers $((P_t - P_f) * M_q)$ and in part by foreign producers $((P_f - P_t + t) * M_q)$. In the case of a quota, the distribution of burdens will be identical to that of a tariff, but the distribution of revenues – the quota rents – depends on the quota allocation system used by the government. If the government sells the quota at price t per unit to the foreign firms, net benefits and burdens will be identical to the tariff case, since foreign firms can then sell at price P_t in the domestic market, but have to pay t per unit sold for the privilege.

In the case of a Voluntary Export Restraint, that is a quota effectively administered by the foreign government, the quota rents accrue to the foreign government if it sells the export rights or to the foreign firm if they get assigned export rights without payments. Note however, that the area between domestic demand and foreign supply not covered by

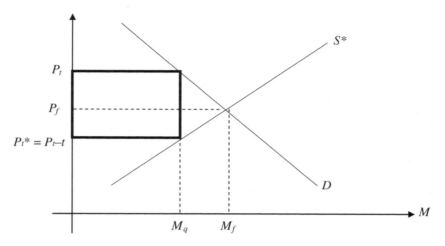

Figure 22.1   A quota under perfect competition

the quota rent ($t^* M_q$), namely the triangle [$t^* (M_f - M_q)$]/2, represents the net welfare loss of the quota operation. It is mainly caused by the reduction in trade resulting from the imposition of the quota.

Quotas on foreign import competition in the presence of domestic market power
Domestic market power is generally threatened by international trade. A domestic monopoly would have to supply under perfect competition conditions if the international market for its good was perfectly competitive and no trade restrictions applied. However, a quota on that foreign competition can restore the domestic supplier's monopoly power. This is the case covered in this section.[8]

In Figure 22.2, let P and Q denote price and quantity of the good in question. Total demand is given by D and the domestic monopolist's marginal cost curve is given by MC. Without a quota, residual demand faced by the domestic producer is any amount at world price P_w, that is residual demand is horizontal. Imposition of a quota changes the domestic producer's residual demand into D', which reverts to total demand D for any price below the world price. Hence, with the quota, the domestic supplier's marginal revenue is now MR'. Maximizing (residual) monopoly profits then leads to the choice of production quantity Q_q at price P_q. Under free trade, the domestic firm would have offered instead the larger amount Q_w at a lower price P_w.

While the quota always gives the domestic producer the possibility to gain additional monopoly profits, it does not necessarily lead to a reduction in production and sales. The quantity effect depends on the relation between the world price and unit cost c_q at the profit-maximizing choice. If the world price ends up being lower than this cost after imposition of the quota, then domestic production quantity will be increased rather than reduced. This can be the case for quotas whose impact on the quantity imported is large since they would tend to give the domestic firm relatively more market power.

Here, because of the domestic firm's potential monopoly status, the equivalence between tariffs and quotas no longer holds. When we compare the effects of a tariff and a quota that would lead to the same level of imports, then the quota leads to a lower

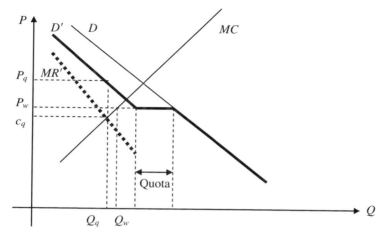

Figure 22.2   An import-competing monopolist

quantity supplied by the domestic supplier and a higher price being charged. The basic reasoning here is that a quota reduces the total domestic demand for the good, but the domestic supplier is now (again) a monopolist on this residual demand and chooses the monopoly solution by setting residual marginal revenue equal to marginal cost. On the other hand, in the case of a tariff low enough to (potentially) allow imports, i.e. the supply price plus tariff would still have to be below the potential domestic monopoly price, the domestic supplier cannot charge a higher price due to the threat of imports. This threat is effectively taken away by the quota.

In the case of a potential domestic oligopoly instead of a monopoly, the qualitative results of the monopoly case still apply, but to a lesser extent. A quota would restore the oligopolistic power of the domestic firms who would compete strategically with each other on the resulting residual demand curve.

Oligopolies, product quality and quotas

Product quality is a strategic variable for the firm that can be influenced by trade policy[9] and especially by quotas or VERs. The conceptual economic framework that explicitly includes these vertical quality aspects in the analysis is provided by models of vertical product differentiation.

In an early study, Falvey (1979) showed that a quantitative restriction on trade would lead to quality upgrading on the part of a multi-product monopolist. The quota places a shadow price on any unit of the high or the low quality goods. Any increase in the quality of any of the goods reduces the shadow price of the restriction. Hence, raising quality as a response to the quantitative restriction is profitable for the monopolist assuming that the marginal consumer values quality increments less than the average consumer.

For the case of a monopolist serving a destination market, the effects of quotas on the endogenous product choice of a monopolist have been examined.[10] In this case, quality is a factor that raises the willingness to pay for any given output. Depending on the rationing rule implied by the quota the marginal consumers left out after the quota may be the high valuation or the low valuation consumers. If only the low valuation marginal consumer is excluded from the market after the quantitative restriction then the monopolist raises the average quality of the products as a response.

In the presence of oligopolies, the theoretical results are more complex than in the monopoly case. Three major cases with respect to competitive conduct by firms can be distinguished.

First, when firms simultaneously choose the quality and the quantity of their products in an international oligopoly market, the quotas may lead to quality upgrading depending on the initial location of the firms in the quality ladder. If the foreign (quota-restricted) firm is the high-quality producer after the quota is imposed, it will increase the quality attached to its good since total sales in the market decrease and marginal revenue is increasing in the quality. Consumers are willing to pay a higher price if the quality offered is higher. However, the foreign firm would reduce its quality as a response to a quota if it already was the low-quality producer. The domestic firm responds to a quota by increasing its quality if it produces the low quality initially or by downgrading if it produces the high quality initially.[11] The driving force behind these results lies in the competition-reducing effect of the quota. However, firms' responses to a quota are not insensitive to variations in the timing of market interaction.

Second, quality determination can take place in an earlier stage as a long-run choice, while the quantity (or price) competition takes place in the short run.[12] This implies that the quality choice is treated as a sunk investment in the short run when quantities are chosen. Assuming short-run quantity competition (Cournot competition), a quota may lead to quality downgrading by both firms as presented in Herguera *et al.* (2000). While the domestic firm may choose not to compete aggressively in the quality stage since it knows the foreign firm is restricted, the foreign firm simply lacks the sales to finance a higher quality level.[13]

Using a similar approach, but assuming that firms choose price strategically when offering their products in the market (Bertrand competition),[14] Lutz (2005) showed that a quota on foreign competition set at a quantity close to the free-trade level will generally lead to quality-upgrading of the low-quality firm and quality-downgrading of the high-quality firm. Furthermore, the quota will cause an increase in average product quality, a reduction of quality differentiation, and a reduction of domestic consumer surplus, irrespective of whether the foreign firm produces the higher or lower quality.[15]

The effects of a quota on industry profits and domestic welfare, however, depend crucially on the direction of international vertical quality differentiation. If the foreign firm produces low quality, both firms' prices and profits will rise but domestic welfare will fall. The fall in domestic welfare is due to three effects: high quality decreases, prices rise, total quantity bought (of both goods) falls. The last effect reduces market participation (share of consumers buying either good) to such an extent, that this negative effect overcompensates for an increase in average quality. The increase in average quality is the result of the reduced market share of the low-quality product.

If the foreign firm produces high quality, foreign profits will fall. The foreign firm is bound by the quota, but it cannot profitably increase its already high and costly quality. Since its quantity must be reduced, it actually needs to decrease its quality. However, the domestic low-quality firm increases quality substantially. This leads to a decrease in quality-adjusted price of the low-quality good while the high quality good becomes relatively more expensive. For the consumers as a whole, these two effects almost cancel out.

Therefore, domestic consumer surplus declines only to a small degree, and domestic profit gains will lead to an overall increase of domestic welfare.

Regardless of the form of market competition in the last stage – price or quantity choice – a quota at the free-trade import quantity will lead to quality-downgrading by the high-quality firm and reduction of domestic consumer surplus irrespective of whether the importer produces the higher quality. When the foreign firm is the low-quality producer, the profit and domestic welfare results for the Cournot and Bertrand cases are also consistent. Similarly for both model variants, a tightening of the quota leads to declining import quality and profits while domestic quality and profits will rise.

Further, for both forms of market competition, a quota may also lead to leapfrogging, that is a reversal of the order of product qualities in the market.[16] A quota set close to the free trade level of exchange will not induce any leapfrogging, although it leads to small changes in the quality choices. There are, however, positive quota levels such that the initially high-quality foreign producer finds it no longer profitable to maintain its previous level of quality since the market share it will enjoy in the products market is expected to be too small. It may therefore decide to downgrade the quality of its products even below the quality offered by the domestic rival. In this case, the domestic government may achieve a Pareto improvement by inducing leapfrogging if the resulting profits shifted to the domestic firm outweigh possible consumer losses due to reduced sales. In consequence, trade policy can cause a discontinuous change in the behavior of the firms in the quality as well as in the quantity (or price) dimension.

Empirical evidence

As mentioned at the beginning of the chapter, quotas on foreign competition may increase qualities, prices and profits of both domestic and foreign firms under fairly general assumptions. This view has also found widespread empirical support, for example, for the automobile industry (Feenstra 1984, 1985, 1988, 1993; Goldberg 1992, 1994). Similar findings have been forwarded by Boorstein and Feenstra (1991) for the steel industry, by Aw and Roberts (1986, 1988) for the footwear industry, and by Anderson (1985, 1991) for the cheese industry. Mintz (1973) found that US quotas on meat, dairy products, textiles and sugar led to increased import qualities. Markusen *et al.* (1995) summarize some evidence about the cost of protection.[17] They state that existing numerical estimates of the welfare cost of non-tariff barriers (such as quotas or VERs) typically find the welfare losses to be quite moderate as a percentage of national income. However, these estimates tend to understate losses since they ignore dynamic (long-run) effects of the trade barriers. In what follows, the cases of the US car market and the international Multi-fibre Agreement are discussed as important examples.

The US car market and Japanese imports

In the early 1980s, US customers demand for cars shifted from domestic cars to more fuel-efficient Japanese cars. This was in part a response to rising fuel prices due to the second OPEC oil price shock. Since this demand shift lead to more imports while reducing US auto-makers' sales, the US auto-industry lobbied for protection. This resulted in the United States Trade Representative negotiating with Japan what eventually became a series of regularly renewed VER agreements that lasted until the early 1990s. In addition, Japanese car imports were also subjected to tariffs. In response, Japanese car makers upgraded the quality of imported vehicles.[18] Additional means of circumventing the quota restriction were also employed. Japanese car producers sold unassembled cars to Korean and Taiwanese manufacturers, who in turn exported the assembled (mostly 'Japanese') cars into the US market. Furthermore, in time, Honda, Mazda, Mitsubishi, Nissan and Toyota all established assembly plants to the US. Arguably, the US automobile industry might still be affected by the consequences of 'asking for' and obtaining protection in the form of quantitative restrictions.[19]

Textiles and the Multi-fibre Agreement
The Multi-fibre Agreement (MFA) was created in the early 1970s as the result of a series of multilateral negotiations between importers and exporters of textile products. It was renewed periodically until its phasing out was agreed on during the GATT Uruguay Round.[20]

The MFA specified quotas from all major textile exporters to all major textile importers. In specifying these quotas, the MFA limited international competition for import-competing textile producers in the European Union and in the US. These European and US producers had come under increasing pressures from Asian imports since the 1960s and had therefore lobbied successfully for protection. As a result, consumer choice in the importing countries was restricted while economic growth in the mostly less developed exporting countries was hindered.[21]

Summary and conclusions
As a rule, quotas and VERs harm consumers by restricting market supply while raising prices. At the same time, they generally tend to raise prices and profits of both the domestic firms and the foreign, quota-constrained firms. This is the case, since the quota acts as a facilitating device for collusion between the domestic and foreign supplier. For the same reason, no profit shifting from the foreign to the domestic firms takes place and the burden of the quota is borne by domestic consumers.

The gain to foreign producers could, in principle, be appropriated by the domestic government if it decided to sell the quota rights instead of offering them for free on a first-come-first-served basis. Still the total net welfare effect for all affected countries would be negative.

These results generally hold when product characteristics and quality are fixed. In the long run, when adjustments of product qualities as a response to quotas or VERs take place, cases can arise where some profit shifting would take place and foreign firms could actually be harmed by a quota or VER. While a country applying a quota may gain more, its trading partner loses more and again the net welfare effect would be negative.

Given these observations, it is probably to be welcomed that the use of quantitative restrictions has been progressively restricted by multilateral agreement at the GATT and subsequently the World Trade Organization.

Notes
1. For an introduction and definitions, see also Suranovic (1999), Chapter 10 and Markusen *et al.* (1995), Chapter 16.
2. The author gratefully acknowledges the continued support of the Center for European Integration Studies (ZEI), Bonn.

3. In the USA, for example, most quotas are administered by the US Customs Service and many apply to agricultural products.
4. Important past examples of VERs are those established for Japanese cars in the US automobile market and those negotiated in the framework of the Multifibre Agreement. Both cases will be discussed in more detail later in this chapter.
5. Rodriguez (1979), Falvey (1979), Das and Donnenfeld (1987) and Krishna (1987) deal with cases of perfect competition or monopoly. Other studies take oligopolistic competition into account while assuming exogenously fixed product qualities (Leland 1979, Shapiro 1983) or homogeneous goods (Deneckere *et al*. 2000). Harris (1985) and Krishna (1989) model, in effect, horizontal product differentiation without analyzing effects on quality.
6. For an introduction to strategically oriented trade policy, see Brander (1995).
7. See also Helpman and Krugman (1989), Chapter 2 and Markusen *et al*. (1995), Chapter 16.
8. See also Helpman and Krugman (1989), Chapter 3 and Markusen *et al*. (1995), Chapter 16.
9. See for example, Levinsohn (1988), Feenstra (1993) and Menzler-Hokkanen (1994).
10. See Krishna (1987) and Spence (1975).
11. See Das and Donnenfeld (1987) and Ries (1993).
12. As in Herguera *et al*. (2000).
13. Corresponding tariff effects are analyzed in Herguera *et al*. (2002).
14. The basic model used here is already well-known; see Shaked and Sutton (1982), Ronnen (1991), Choi and Shin (1992), Motta (1993), Lutz (1996) and Boccard and Wauthy (1998).
15. Note that Herguera *et al*. (2000) report that a quota at the free-trade level will lead to quality decreases of both firms, regardless of which firm produces higher quality, here such a quota leads to quality upgrades by the low-quality producer.
16. See Herguera and Lutz (1998).
17. A general summary on evidence about the effects of trade policy can also be found in Leamer and Levinsohn (1995) while main international rules and institutions for trade policy are presented in Staiger (1995).
18. See for example Feenstra (1993) and Goldberg (1992, 1994).
19. For informal, but more comprehensive stock-taking of the US car industry's historical performance, see for example Ingrassia and White (1995) or Maynard (2003).
20. The General Agreement on Tariffs and Trade (GATT) evolved in successive negotiation rounds often named after the places where they were initiated. The Uruguay Round ended in 1994.
21. See for example Keesing and Wolf (1980) and Morkre (1984).

References

Anderson, J. E. (1985), 'The Relative Inefficiency of Quotas: The Cheese Case,' *American Economic Review*, **75**(1), 178–90.

Anderson, J. E. (1991), 'The Coefficient of Trade Utilization: The Cheese Case,' in: R. E. Baldwin (ed.), *Empirical Studies of Commercial Policy*, Chicago: University of Chicago Press.

Aw, B. Y. and M. J. Roberts (1986), 'Measuring Quality in Quota-Constrained Import Markets: The Case of US Footwear,' *Journal of International Economics*, **21**(1/2), 45–60.

Aw, B. Y. and M. J. Roberts (1988), 'Price and Quality Level Comparisons for US Footwear Imports: An Application of Multilateral Index Numbers,' in R. C. Feenstra (ed.), *Empirical Methods for International Trade*, Cambridge, MA: MIT Press.

Bhagwati, J. (1965), 'On the Equivalence of Tariffs and Quotas,' in R. E. Baldwin, J. Bhagwati, R. E. Caves and H. G. Johnson (eds), *Trade, Growth and the Balance of Payments: Essays in Honor of Gottfried Haberler*, Chicago, IL: Rand McNally.

Brander, J. A. (1995), 'Strategic Trade Policy,' in G. M. Grossman and K. Rogoff (eds), *Handbook of International Economics, Volume 3*, Amsterdam: Elsevier.

Boccard, N. and X. Wauthy (1998), 'Import Restraints and Quality Choice under Vertical Differentiation,' CORE Discussion Paper 9819.

Boorstein, R. and R. C. Feenstra (1991), 'Quality Upgrading and its Welfare Cost in US Steel Imports,' in E. Helpman and A. Razin (eds), *International Trade and Trade Policy*, Cambridge, MA: MIT Press.

Choi, C. J. and H. S. Shin (1992), 'A Comment on a Model of Vertical Product Differentiation,' *Journal of Industrial Economics*, **40**(2), 229–31.

Das, S. P. and S. Donnenfeld (1987), 'Trade Policy and its Impact on Quality of Imports: A Welfare Analysis,' *Journal of International Economics*, **23**, 77–95.

Das, S. P. and S. Donnenfeld (1989), 'Oligopolistic Competition and International Trade: Quantity and Quality Restrictions,' *Journal of International Economics*, **27**(3–4), 299–318.

Deneckere, R., D. Kovenock and Y. Y. Sohn (2000), 'Quotas and Tariffs with Endogenous Conduct,' *Industrial Organization*, **9**, 37–68.

Falvey, R. E. (1979), 'The Composition of Trade Within Import-Restricted Categories,' *Journal of Political Economy*, **87**, 1105–14.

Feenstra, R. C. (1984), 'Voluntary Export Restraint in US Autos, 1980–81: Quality, Employment and Welfare Effects,' in R. E. Baldwin and A. Krueger (eds), *The Structure and Evolution of Recent US Trade Policy*, Chicago, IL: Chicago University Press.

Feenstra, R. C. (1985), 'Automobile Prices and Protection: The US–Japan Trade Restraint,' *Journal of Policy Modelling*, **7**, 49–68.

Feenstra, R. C. (1988), 'Quality Change under Trade Restraints in Japanese Autos,' *Quarterly Journal of Economics*, **103**(1), 131–46.

Feenstra, R. C. (1993), 'Measuring the Welfare Effect of Quality Change: Theory and Application to Japanese Autos,' NBER Discussion Paper No. 4401.

Goldberg, P. K. (1992), 'Product Differentiation and Oligopoly in International Markets: The Case of the U.S. Automobile Industry,' mimeo, Princeton University.

Goldberg, P. K. (1994), 'Trade Policies in the US Automobile Industry,' *Japan and the World Economy*, **6**(2), 175–208.

Harris, R. (1985), 'Why Voluntary Export Restraints are "Voluntary",' *Canadian Journal of Economics*, **18**(4), 799–809.

Helpman, E. and P. R. Krugman (1989), *Trade Policy and Market Structure*, Cambridge, MA: MIT Press.

Herguera, I. and S. Lutz (1998), 'Oligopoly and Quality Leapfrogging,' *The World Economy*, **21**(1), 75–94.

Herguera, I., P. Kujal and E. Petrakis (2000), 'Quantity Restrictions and Endogenous Quality Choice,' *International Journal of Industrial Organization*, **18**(8), 1259–77.

Herguera, I., P. Kujal and E. Petrakis (2002), 'Tariffs, Quality Reversals and Exit in Vertically Differentiated Industries,' *Journal of International Economics*, **58**, 467–92.

Ingrassia, P. and J. B. White (1995), *Comeback: The Fall & Rise of the American Automobile Industry*, New York: Simon & Schuster.

Keesing, D. B. and M. Wolf (1980), *Textile Quotas against Developing Countries*, London: Trade Policy Research Centre.

Krishna, K. (1987), 'Tariffs vs. Quotas with Endogenous Quality,' *Journal of International Economics*, **23**, 97–122.

Krishna, K. (1989), 'Trade Restrictions as Facilitating Practices,' *Journal of International Economics*, **26**, 251–70.

Leland, H. E. (1979), 'Quacks, Lemons, and Licensing: A Theory of Minimum Quality Standards,' *Journal of Political Economy*, **87**, 1328–46.

Levinsohn, J. (1988), 'Empirics of Taxes on Differentiated Products: The Case of Tariffs in the US Automobile Industry,' in R. Baldwin (ed.), *Trade Policy Issues and Empirical Analysis*, Chicago, IL: NBER.

Leamer, E. E. and J. Levinsohn (1995), 'International Trade Theory: The Evidence,' in G. M. Grossman and K. Rogoff, *Handbook of International Economics, Volume 3*, Amsterdam: Elsevier.

Lutz, S. (1996), 'Vertical Product Differentiation, Quality Standards, and International Trade Policy,' CEPR Discussion Paper No. 1443.

Lutz, S. (2005), 'The Effect of Quotas on Domestic Product Price and Quality,' *International Advances in Economic Research*, **11**(2), 163–73.

Markusen, J., J. Melvin, W. Kaempfer and K. Maskus (1995), *International Trade: Theory and Evidence*, New York: McGraw-Hill.

Maynard, M. (2003), *The End of Detroit: How the Big Three Lost Their Grip on the American Car Market*, New York: Random House.

Menzler-Hokkanen, I. (1994), 'Empirical Comparisons of Quality Measures in International Trade,' in I. Menzler Hokkanen (ed.), *Quality Change and Competitiveness in International Trade*, Helsinki: Helsinki School of Business Administration.

Mintz, I. (1973), 'US Import Quotas: Cost and Consequences,' American Enterprise Institute for Public Policy Research.

Morkre, M. E. (1984), 'Import Quotas on Textiles: The Welfare Effects of United States Restrictions on Hong Kong,' Bureau of Economics Staff Report to the Federal Trade Commission.

Motta, M. (1993), 'Endogenous Quality Choice: Price vs. Quantity Competition,' *Journal of Industrial Economics*, **41**, 113–32.

Ries, J. C. (1993), 'Voluntary Export Restraints, Profits, and Quality Adjustment,' *Canadian Journal of Economics*, **26**(3), 688–706.

Rodriguez, C. A. (1979), 'The Quality of Imports and the Differential Welfare Effects of Tariffs, Quotas and Quality Controls as Protective Devices,' *Canadian Journal of Economics*, **12**, 439–49.

Ronnen, U. (1991), 'Minimum Quality Standards, Fixed Costs, and Competition,' *Rand Journal of Economics*, **22**(4), 490–504.

Shaked, A. and J. Sutton (1982), 'Relaxing Price Competition Through Product Differentiation,' *Review of Economic Studies*, **49**, 3–13.

Shapiro, C. (1983), 'Premiums for High Quality Products as Returns to Reputations,' *Quarterly Journal of Economics*, **98**, 659–79.

Spence, M. (1975), 'Monopoly, Quality and Regulation,' *Bell Journal of Economics*, **6**, 417–29.

Staiger, R. W. (1995), 'International Rules and Institutions for Trade Policy,' in G. M. Grossman and K. Rogoff (eds), *Handbook of International Economics, Volume 3*, Amsterdam: Elsevier.

Suranovic, S. (1999), 'International Trade Theory and Policy Lecture Notes,' Washington, DC: George Washington University.

23 Tariff rate quotas
David Skully

Definition

A tariff-rate quota (TRQ) is a two-level tariff. During a specified period, it allows a specified volume of imports at the lower tariff and charges additional imports the higher tariff. In many languages TRQs are called 'contingent tariffs' which emphasizes that the tariff applied is contingent on the cumulative volume of trade.[1]

A TRQ has four components: (a) an in-quota tariff (also called a low-tier tariff); (b) an over-quota tariff (also called a high-tier tariff); (c) a quota that specifies the volume of imports charged the in-quota tariff; and (d) a method of administration.

For example, a TRQ could allow one million tonnes of salt to be imported at a one-cent-per-kilo tariff and charge a one-dollar-per-kilo tariff on any additional salt imports. Since a dollar-per-kilo tariff on salt would likely prevent imports beyond one million tonnes, this TRQ appears to be no different from a regular or absolute quota of a million tonnes. The distinction is that under an absolute quota it would be legally impossible for imports to exceed the million-tonne quota, whereas a TRQ allows imports to exceed the one-million-tonne quota. It might be economically irrational to import at the higher tariff, but it is legally possible.

Mechanics

Figures 23.1, 23.2 and 23.3 illustrate how a TRQ imposes disincentives on trade. The two-level tariff results in a stepped import supply function. Imports within the quota are charged the lower tariff (t), and over-quota imports are charged the higher tariff (T). This results in a vertical step when the quota volume (Q) is filled.

The level of domestic demand for imports and the world price jointly determine which of the TRQ elements constrains imports. Figure 23.1 plots three import demand curves. If there is no demand for imports at the world price, none of the TRQ elements constrains imports: there would be no imports even with free trade – D1. Similarly, if there is no import demand at the in-quota tariff rate $(1 + t)$, domestic demand remains the binding constraint – D2. A small reduction in the in-quota tariff will not increase imports, but a large reduction could make the in-quota tariff binding. When import demand intersects the in-quota tariff – illustrated by D3 – a volume of $M(t)$ is imported and the domestic market price equilibrates at $1 + t$. In-quota tariff revenue equals t times the volume of imports, represented by the shaded rectangle.

Figure 23.2 illustrates import demand constrained by the quota: the import volume is Q and the domestic price is $1 + t + r$, where r represents the per unit quota rent. The per unit quota rent is the difference between the domestic price (the price an importer can sell the product in the domestic market) and the world price inclusive of the in-quota tariff (what it costs an importer to purchase the product on the world market and pay the tariff).

Figure 23.3 illustrates over-quota imports. The over-quota tariff determines the volume of imports at $M(T)$ and the domestic price equals $1 + T$. When there are over-quota

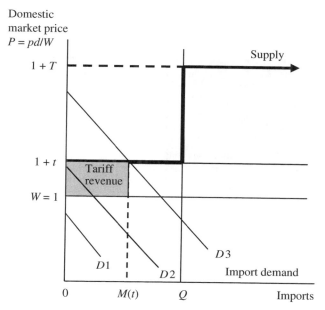

Figure 23.1   In quota tariff binding

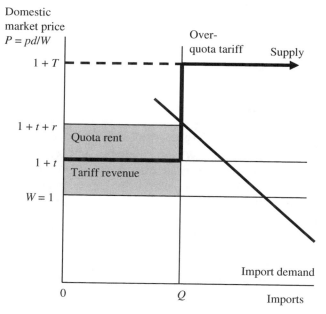

Figure 23.2   Quota binding

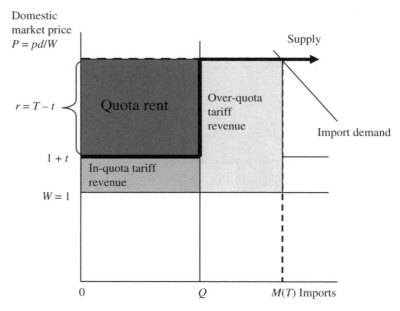

Figure 23.3   Over-quota tariff binding

imports, imports within the quota are charged the in-quota tariff and imports beyond the quota are charged the over-quota tariff. Thus there are two shaded rectangles of tariff revenue in Figure 23.3.

In-quota imports can be imported for $(1 + t)$ and sold on the domestic market for $(1 + T)$ so the per unit quota rent, r, equals $(T - t)$. The shaded rectangle labeled 'quota rent' represents the total value of quota rents.

Why tariff quotas?

The primary instruments of trade policy examined in economics texts are tariffs and quotas; there is little or no mention of tariff-rate quotas. This general neglect was justified because, until the establishment of the WTO in 1994, tariff-rate quotas were infrequently employed; quotas were far more commonly used. What happened in 1994 is addressed below. The fact remains that governments did impose tariff quotas prior to 1994 and this leads to the question: why would a government choose to use a TRQ rather than a tariff or a quota?

Anderson and Young (1982) answer this question by assuming that a TRQ is a solution; they work backwards to identify the problem or problems that a TRQ solves. They find that a TRQ can maximize domestic welfare if there is sufficient uncertainty about fluctuations in import market conditions. The intuition is that there is a critical volume of imports beyond which imports become 'too much'. Imposing an absolute quota is one solution to this problem but a TRQ can often do better. Unlike an absolute quota, a TRQ allows over-quota imports and can generate tariff revenue. This revenue can balance (at the national level) the social disutility or domestic displacement over-quota imports may cause. So, a TRQ, under certain circumstances, can provide a better outcome than either a quota or a tariff alone.[2]

The historical record on TRQ uses points to a different, although related motivation. Anderson and Young examine a TRQ applied to imports from all sources. In practice, however, TRQs tended to be allocated to specific countries or even particular firms. They were typically used to govern specific bilateral trade flows. TRQs are often imposed to preserve or protect pre-existing commercial relationships from other changes in trade policy such as the initiation of a free trade agreement or changes in the membership of a customs union.

For example, the first TRQ on record is a Belgian tariff quota on the import of cast iron from Luxembourg.[3] It was established in 1839 when the territory of Luxembourg, formerly under Dutch rule, was divided along linguistic lines: part was transferred to Belgium and the remainder became the Grand Duchy of Luxembourg. The geographic division of Luxembourg threatened to sever longstanding commercial relationships in the iron and steel industry. The TRQ for cast iron allowed these pre-existing commercial relationships to continue at traditional volumes. Belgium applied its standard (higher) tariff to trade beyond the tariff quota volume. Providing *limited* preferential market access to a specific trading partner or partners is the reason many TRQs exist.

The Uruguay Round, 'tariffication' and TRQs

In 1994, the Uruguay Round of trade negotiations concluded with the establishment of the World Trade Organization (WTO) and several WTO/GATT-related agreements. The Agreement on Agriculture, in particular, forbade the use of quantitative trade restrictions (that is, bans and absolute quotas) and required existing quantitative restrictions on agricultural products to be converted into tariffs, a process known as 'tariffication'. Because the WTO considers tariff quotas to be tariffs and not quantitative restrictions, many WTO signatories chose to 'tariffy' or transform their quantitative restrictions with TRQs. Indeed, for agricultural products alone, the Uruguay Round resulted in over 1400 new TRQs.[4]

The WTO/GATT does not consider TRQs to be quantitative restrictions because they do not limit import quantities absolutely. One may always import by paying the over-quota tariff. This opportunity is not possible with a regular quota. If an over-quota tariff makes imports prohibitively expensive, it yields the same import volume as a traditional quota. But if the difference between domestic and international prices exceeds the over-quota tariff, the over-quota tariff is not prohibitive, and the tariff quota results in a different volume of trade than does a standard quota. Were a standard quota in place, expanding the volume of imports over the restricted quantity would be impossible. Because of this (frequently slight) difference, a tariff quota is in theory less restrictive than an absolute quota.

Because they combine tariff and quota elements and are technically considered a form of tariff, Uruguay Round negotiators presented TRQs as an optional intermediate step in the transformation of quantitative restrictions and other non-tariff barriers into pure tariffs. This facilitated negotiations: it gave exporters greater (although limited) market access and it allowed importers to postpone substantive liberalization until later negotiations.

WTO tariffication led to two kinds of TRQs – minimum access and current access. Minimum access TRQs provide a minimum volume of market access – in general, 5 percent of average domestic consumption in the three-year base period, 1986–1988. For example, if base consumption were 100 000 tonnes of butter, then 5-percent minimum access is 5000 tonnes. Current access TRQs ensure that tariffication did not diminish the volume of market access allowed prior to the Uruguay Round: they preserve pre-existing preferences.

Bilateral trade agreements and TRQs
Besides the WTO the expanding number of bilateral, regional and other Free Trade Agreements is another source of new TRQs. The North American Free Trade Agreement (NAFTA), and the Euro-Mediterranean Association Agreements (EMAAs) both include numerous bilateral and multilateral TRQs.[5] The US–Chile free trade agreements includes TRQs for beef, various dairy products, tobacco, tires, cotton, copper, hotel and restaurant chinaware. Most of these 'sensitive product' TRQs also have safeguards and surge protections. These are additional tariffs – beyond the over-quota tariff – that can be imposed if import prices fall below specified levels or if import volumes exceed specified volumes.

Many TRQs are phased in gradually. For example, the US–Chile FTA, effective January 2004, allowed Chile to export 300 tonnes of butter to the United States duty-free; additional exports face an over-quota tariff of $1.541/kg. Each year the in-quota volume increases by 3 percent (compounded): in 2014 the quota reaches 590 tonnes and in 2015 unlimited imports are allowed. The over-quota tariff on butter is also liberalized but on a different schedule: it remains fixed at $1.541/kg for seven years. Starting in 2011 the over-quota tariff rate is reduced by 20 percent each year (not compounded), becoming zero in 2015. Such provisions allow negotiators to state that the agreement fully liberalizes trade, although full liberalization is deferred 12 years.

The US–Australia FTA, effective January 2005, allows Australia butter duty-free access to the US market within a tariff quota. Unlike Chile the over-quota tariff is not liberalized: it is fixed at $1.541/kg. Nor is the TRQ ever fully liberalized: the in-quota volume begins at 1500 MT in 2005 and increases at a 3 percent annual compound rate, indefinitely. In 25 years (2029) the in-quota volume doubles to 3046 MT. The agreement allows either party to initiate negotiations for 'modifying market access commitments' for dairy TRQs in 2024.

Liberalizing TRQs
If a TRQ is an initial transitional step between a quota and a tariff (or full liberalization), then what is the next intermediate step? Is there a best way to liberalize an existing TRQ? If one defines 'best' to mean increasing market access then the answer is simple. Determine which of the three elements (t, T, Q) constrains imports; relax the binding constraint to increase market access. There are other criteria to consider beyond market access, however. If one is concerned about improving the efficient allocation of resources globally, then one must examine whether TRQ liberalization increases quota rents and how rents are distributed – this is the task of TRQ administration.

TRQ administration involves distributing the rights to import at the in-quota tariff. Whoever obtains such rights can make a risk-free profit equal to the domestic price less the world price inclusive of the in-quota tariff. Rents indicate that the demand to import within the quota is greater than the supply of quota: thus the necessity to ration or administer the TRQ.

That rents can bias trade and cause an inefficient allocation of resources can be illustrated by a simple rationing example. Suppose two types of firms can supply a market:

low-cost and high-cost. Low-cost firms have a cost of production less than or equal to PL. High-cost firms have a cost of production of $PH > PL$. If demand is not rationed the market price is PL and only low-cost firms supply the market. When a binding quota is imposed the market price increases to PH. At PH high-cost firms will enter the market. The quota rent of $PH - PL$ per unit is sufficient to cover their higher cost of production. When high-cost firms displace low-cost firms we observe an inefficient use of resources. Global welfare would be improved if high-cost firms could be excluded from the market. If quota rents could be neutralized or taxed away, then high-cost firms would have no incentive to enter the market.

Any TRQ liberalization that increases quota rents can also increase the risk that high-cost suppliers will displace low-cost suppliers. We can examine how the impact of liberalizing t, T, and Q depends on market conditions.

t: Reducing the in-quota tariff t expands market access when the in-quota tariff is binding (Figure 23.1). But when Q or T is binding, reducing t only increases rent, it provides no additional market access (Figures 23.2 and 23.3).

Q: Increasing the quota Q increases the probability that the in-quota tariff will be the binding constraint (Figure 23.1). But when Q is binding, increasing the in-quota volume usually increases rents – unless demand is inelastic – or unless it causes t to become the binding constraint (Figure 23.2). Similarly, when T is binding, quota expansion increases rents (Figure 23.3).

T: Reducing the over-quota tariff T is always a positive action. It cannot increase rent; if the quota fills or over-fills reducing T reduces rents. If T is the binding constraint, it increases market access (Figure 23.3).

For most TRQs the relationship between import demand and in-quota volume is relatively stable. When t is the binding constraint on imports in one year, it tends to remain the binding constraint in subsequent years. Similarly, if the in-quota volume binds – if Q or T bind and generate rents – in one year, it tends to bind in the next year. Skully (2001) found that, for agricultural TRQs notified to the WTO, over 80 percent of low-fill TRQs remain low-fill the next year; and over 80 percent of filled quotas also fill the following year. These findings suggest that one could make the form of TRQ liberalization contingent on the typical fill level of a TRQ.

Fill rates
The fill rate of a quota or TRQ is the ratio of actual in-quota imports to the potential in-quota volume, in a given period. For example, if a TRQ allows 1000 tonnes and in-quota imports are 473 tonnes then the fill rate is 47.3 percent. Fill rates are simple to calculate en masse. One creates a database with in-quota imports in one column and in-quota volumes in another; division yields fill rates. These data can usually be downloaded from various official trade organizations – national ministries, UNCTAD, WTO.

Fill rates are the most common indicator constructed for TRQs; unfortunately, it is not clear what a fill rate indicates. A low fill rate (also called 'underfill') can indicate that there is not sufficient demand for imports to fill the quota – the situation illustrated in Figure 23.1 – this is a neutral or even positive interpretation. However, low fill rates are sometimes interpreted negatively: that the quota is not filled is viewed as an indication that market access is being somehow inhibited. The implicit, but false, assumption is that a TRQ should fill. TRQs are supposed to permit market access – the opportunity to import within quota – they do not obligate the importing country to import at least the TRQ volume. Quota rights can be allocated in a way that prevents the quota from filling although there is sufficient import demand. For example, suppose quota rights were given to the national salt monopoly and the salt monopoly decides not to import competing salt. Or, an importing country could impose fees and bureaucratic impediments to getting in-quota import licenses. Both examples result in low fill rates (or underfill) not related to market demand.

Fill rates alone do not tell us much. If we can find data to calculate the difference between domestic prices and world prices, we can make some plausible inferences. If the domestic price is less than the world price plus the in-quota tariff, then there is no rational reason for there to be imports. Analogously, if the domestic price is, say, 30 percent greater than the world price plus the in-quota tariff and we observe a low fill rate, then it is reasonable to conclude that something besides the in-quota tariff is limiting import demand. The next step is to examine how the quota is administered and how licenses or foreign exchange are issued: there are many reasons why a quota can underfill unrelated to the TRQ itself.

The World Trade Organization publishes occasional studies of TRQ fill rates and TRQ administration: some patterns of quota fill emerge (WTO 2001, 2002). For example quota rights that are assigned to state trading enterprises (STEs) tend to have relatively high fill rates. This seems counterintuitive: one would expect STEs to minimize import competition, like the salt monopoly mentioned earlier. However, causality runs in two directions: the method of administration can influence the fill rate and the expected fill rate can determine the method of TRQ administration an importing government selects. Many STEs exist solely to administer the import of an important and sensitive commodity – if imports were not important a specialized agency would not have been created – such commodities are inherently likely to fill the quota.

Unenforced TRQs
Often TRQs are enforced as applied tariffs. This means that the importing government chooses not to impose the over-quota tariff: all imports are charged the in-quota tariff. Almost half of 1400 agricultural TRQs notified to the WTO are administered as applied tariffs. Why would a country choose to do this? There are two related answers. First, with tariff schedules many countries maintain 'bound tariffs' – these are the maximum rates that they have agreed to charge to their trading partners – and 'applied tariffs' – the rates actually charged. Governments are free to reduce tariffs unilaterally or choose not to apply them; cutting tariffs does not justify retaliation by their trading partners nor can claims for compensation be credibly made. But if governments raise tariffs above their bound (negotiated) levels, they are liable to retaliation and demands for compensation. This incentive asymmetry makes negotiating high levels of protection an attractive strategy; it provides the government with greater trade policy discretion.

The countries that most commonly administer TRQs as applied tariffs are countries that, when they negotiated the TRQs, knew that there was a reasonable probability that they would join a customs union or undergo some similar change in trade regime. For example, Norway, Iceland, Poland and Hungary account for a large share of agricultural

TRQs, and almost of these TRQs are administered as applied tariffs. All four countries were likely to joint the European Union: Poland and Hungary did join, Norway and Iceland have occasional referenda on whether to join. The TRQs allowed Poland and Hungary to maintain relatively high levels of bound protection while operating a relatively liberal applied tariff regime. When they harmonized their tariff regimes with that of the European Union they did not have to increase their bound rates. In this way they avoided having to negotiate concession with other, non-EU trading partners.

The second, related reason for not imposing the over-quota tariff is to maximize discretion over trade policy. When the government finds imports to be desirable it does not impose the over-quota tariff; this allows a large volume of imports. In years when imports are not desirable, the over-quota tariff is imposed; this can limit imports to the in-quota volume, if the over-quota tariff is prohibitive or provide addition tariff revenue if it is not. This situation is similar to that posited by Anderson and Young (1982); the difference is that they assume the over-quota tariff is always applied.

Choosing to import over-quota

One final TRQ quirk is the phenomenon of importers choosing to import at the over-quota rate rather than the in-quota rate. This is not common, but it does happen; here is why.

Often to import at the in-quota rate one must incur formal and informal transactions costs – applications, delays, uncertainty, other paper work, fees paid to private brokers or even bribes. If these (unit) costs exceed the difference between the over-quota tariff and the in-quota tariff, then the rational choice is to pay the higher tariff and be done with it. Evidence of this requires examining imports at the eight-digit or ten-digit tariff code level. Tariff quotas are typically listed in tariff schedules as two distinct tariff lines. For example, in the US tariff schedule, the tariff code (line) for in-quota butter is 0405.10.10 and that for over-quota butter is 0405.10.20. The former requires in-quota rights (however allocated); the latter does not, one can import over-quota whether or not the in-quota tariff has filled. So, for these reasons, it is possible to observe a low (in-quota) fill rate and imports – the sum of in-quota and over-quota imports – in excess of the quota.

Notes

1. For example: French-*contingent tarifaire*; German-*Zollkontingente*; Polish-*kontyngenty taryfowe*; and Spanish-*contingente arancelario*. The terms 'tariff quota' and 'tariff-rate quota' are employed interchangeably in the literature and in this chapter. Technically, tariff quota is a more accurate description as it allows for specific tariffs; while tariff-rate quota could be narrowly interpreted to include only *ad valorem* tariffs.
2. They also find that TRQs can solve foreign exchange allocation problems. Anderson (1988) reprints Anderson and Young (1982) among other relevant articles.
3. Heuser (1939) and Rom (1979) provide extensive detail on the actual administration of protection and preference.
4. The GATT-1947 forbids quantitative restrictions, however, GATT signatories had long resisted applying this discipline to agricultural trade.
5. There is a growing literature examining the European Union's import regime for fruits and vegetables. See Cioffi and dell'Aquila (2002) and Garcia-Alvarez-Coque (2002).

References

Anderson, J. A. (1988), *The Relative Inefficiency of Quotas*, Cambridge, MA: MIT Press.
Anderson, J. A. and L. Young (1982), The Optimality of Tariff Quotas under Uncertainty, *Journal of International Economics*, **13**(3/4), 337–51.
Cioffi, A. and C. dell'Aquila (2004), The Effects of Trade Policies for Fresh Fruit and Vegetables of the European Union, *Food Policy*, **29**(2), 169–85.

Garcia-Alvarez-Coque, J. M. (2002), Agricultural Trade and the Barcelona Process: Is Full Liberalisation Possible? *European Review of Agricultural Economics*, **29**(3), 399–422.

Heuser, H. (1939), *Control of International Trade*, Philadelphia: Blakiston's Son & Co., Inc.

Rom, M. (1979), *The Role of Tariff Quotas in Commercial Policy*, London: Macmillan.

Skully, D. (2001), Liberalizing Tariff-rate Quotas, *Background for Agricultural Policy Reform in the WTO: The Road Ahead*, USDA, Economic Research Service, ERS-E01-001 [www.ers.usda.gov].

World Trade Organization (2001), *Tariff Quota Administration Methods and Tariff Quota Fill*, Geneva: G/AG/NG/S/8/Rev.1, 18 May 2001 [www.wto.org].

World Trade Organization (2002), *Tariff and Other Quotas*, Geneva: TN/AG/S/5, 21 March 2002 [www.wto.org].

24 Quota administration
David Skully

Introduction

Quota administration concerns how the rights to import within a quota are distributed. Quota administration is fundamentally a rationing problem. There are many ways to ration, some are more efficient than others. There are three general types of quota administration: market-based or auction allocation, rule-based allocation, and discretionary allocation.

This chapter first considers the superior efficiency of market-based allocation; that is, rationing a fixed supply among competing demands by market-determined prices, either auction bids or market-clearing prices. Market allocation provides the benchmark against which to evaluate other allocation methods.

Rule-based methods can be reduced to algorithms. The most common rule-based systems are license on demand and first-come-first-served. Historical allocation, in which quota rights are allocated based on some characteristic in an 'historical' base period, for example, a country's average market share in a given three-year period, is a rule-based system; but it has a discretionary element because one must choose among characteristics, base periods, and averaging methods.

Discretionary methods cannot be reduced to rules or algorithms. In such a system the quota administrator is not constrained to follow an explicit (or, at any rate publicly available) rule. The allocation can be arbitrary. Often discretionary allocation involves the government of the importing country granting quota administration powers to some private or non-governmental organization.

Finally, it should be noted that quotas are sometimes not enforced. The standard treatment of a quota is a trade restriction imposed unilaterally by the government of the importing country that prevents imports from exceeding a specific quantity. Unilateral imposition has become a relatively rare occurrence: most existing quotas (or TRQs) result from a multilateral or bilateral negotiation process. They are particularly common in free-trade agreements. Quotas (or TRQs) are often framed in 'minimum access' terms: they specify that the importing country must allow its trading partner(s) the opportunity to sell at least the minimum volume specified. The government of the importing country is free to allow imports to exceed the minimum-access volume. Many quotas (or TRQs) exist to provide the potential for a government to protect a domestic industry without having to worry about retaliation. Such quotas provide latent protection: they are not enforced unless there is a surge of imports or some other change in market or political conditions that causes the government to invoke its latent protective power.

Rationing and efficiency

The welfare analysis of quota administration is illustrated in Figure 24.1. We assume that the importing country is a 'small country': its imports are not sufficiently great to influence the world price. The relevant portion of the international supply curve is a horizontal segment at the world price (W). At the quota volume Q the supply curve turns vertical.

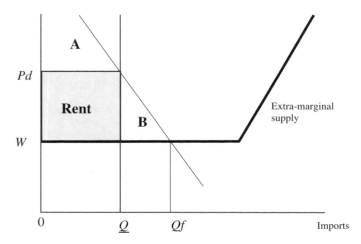

Figure 24.1   Quota administration

Suppose import demand is sufficient for the quota to bind and consider the differences between a quota and free trade. With free trade, an unlimited quantity may be imported at the world price. The domestic market clears with imports of QF; the domestic price equals the world price, $P = W$; and all demand inframarginal to W is satisfied. The large triangle below the demand curve and above the world price is the economic surplus gained from importing QF, that is, the sum of areas labeled: $A + \text{Rent} + B$.

The quota limits imports to $\underline{Q}$ and the domestic market price increases to Pd. This reduces domestic welfare. Domestic consumers' surplus is reduced to the triangle labeled A. The area 'Rent' represents the arbitrage profits from the opportunity to import $\underline{Q}$ units at the world price, while the domestic market value is Pd.

Quota rents are neither good nor bad, they simply exist as the result of rationing the opportunity to bridge the gap between domestic and world prices. However, unless the government of the quota-imposing country provides some means for allocating the right to import within the quota, there will be no clear title to these rents. The rent will be a common property resource, and, as such, its existence stimulates wasteful rent-seeking behavior. The purpose of quota administration is to order an otherwise potentially chaotic rent-seeking situation.

Textbook treatment of quotas assumes, often implicitly, that quota rights or import licenses are efficiently distributed. This assumption results in a figure similar to 24.1 where quota rents are a rectangle with a base equal to the quota volume, $\underline{Q}$, and a height equal to Pd – Corden (1971: 201) notes that the simple treatment 'assumes that import licenses are transferable between firms and there is a market in licenses.' Other necessary assumptions include lack of monopoly ownership of import licenses.[1] These are strong assumptions. If they do not hold, then outcome can be far inferior to the efficient allocation of Figure 24.1.

A market is efficient if all buyers and sellers to the left of the intersection of the supply and demand curves can find each other and exchange. These traders are inframarginal to the market price. In Figure 24.1 when there is no quota and $Pd = W$, inframarginal buyers are those to the left of Qf: they have a willingness to pay that exceeds the market-clearing price, W. Buyers outside the margin or *extramarginal* buyers, represented on

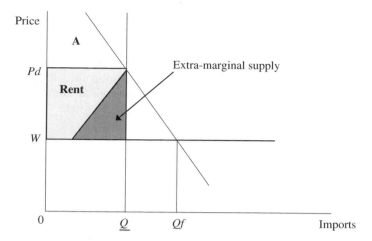

Figure 24.2   Quota administration

the demand curve right of equilibrium, have a willingness to pay less than the market-clearing price. Similarly, inframarginal suppliers have a willingness to accept less than the market-clearing price; extramarginal suppliers, represented on the supply curve where it rises above W, right of equilibrium, have a willingness to accept greater than the market-clearing price. The displacement of inframarginal traders by extramarginal traders is the primary source of inefficiency in quota administration. The availability of quota rents provides an incentive for extramarginal traders to enter the market. Market-based administrative methods, auctions for example, remove the incentive posed by quota rents and thus remove the risk of displacement. The more quota administration deviates from market-based administrative methods, the greater the risk of displacement and the lower the allocative efficiency.

Figure 24.2 provides an example of quota allocation with displacement. It starts from the same free trade situation shown in Figure 24.1 but assumes that the quota is open to whomever ships before the quota is filled. This is a first-come, first-served allocation system. Anyone who has lined up to buy popular concert or game tickets has participated (as a buyer) in a first-come, first-served allocation system. Because the quota results in a domestic price of $Pd > W$, suppliers inframarginal to Pd but extramarginal to W have an incentive to enter this quota-rationed market. The shaded triangle in Figure 24.2 shows that part of what we would normally assume to be rent is not rent but rather the production costs of firms extramarginal to Pd (the area under the supply curve but above W). This shaded triangle represents an inefficient allocation of resources due to the displacement of efficient firms by less efficient – higher-cost, extramarginal – firms.

In summary, if a quota is binding and imports are limited to $\underline{Q}$, the greatest domestic surplus possible is $A +$ Rent. The next section shows that auctioning quota rights can approximate the efficient allocation.

Market-based allocation methods

Suppose quota rights are limited to importers: we are rationing demand. To maximize domestic surplus, given a quota constraint on imports, extramarginal buyers must be excluded. This is the beneficial, discriminatory role that prices play in markets. The quota rent and the incentive it transmits induces inefficiencies. In Figure 24.1 demand inframarginal to Pd but extramarginal to W will find it attractive to import. If there were no quota rents, only buyers inframarginal to W would enter the market and welfare would be maximized. An auction neutralizes quota rents. The opportunity to buy something for W and sell it for Pd is worth $R = Pd - W$. Buyers inframarginal to Pd will bid at least R for the opportunity; buyers extramarginal to Pd will bid less than R; and the required (beneficial) discrimination is realized.

In a quota auction, consumers would bid, at the margin, $R = Pd - W$, the difference between the domestic price Pd (given imports of Q) and the world price. If all winning bids are charged the marginal winning bid (uniform price auction) then auction revenue equals the area of the shaded rectangle labeled 'rent'. The consumers who obtain the quota rights are those with a willingness to pay of at least Pd. These consumers realize a consumer surplus equal to the area A. The domestic economy realizes gains from trade equal to the auction revenue plus A. This allocation is identical to the allocation that would result from the tariff-equivalent of a quota (given market conditions).

The tariff equivalent is simple to calculate if one knows both W and Pd: the specific tariff $= Pd - W$; and the *ad valorem* tariff $= (Pd - W) / W$. This equivalence between tariff and quota, however, only holds if the quota is allocated efficiently. Either tariff calculated above can reproduce the quota allocation shown in Figure 24.1; but no single tariff can reproduce the allocation shown in Figure 24.2.

Tradable quotas
It is critical to distinguish between the distribution of trade and the distribution of rents. When importing is the only way to gain quota rents, the distribution of rents determines the distribution of trade. But rents can be decoupled from the act of importing if quota rights (import licenses) can be resold or traded once they have been initially distributed. Tradable quotas remove, or at least greatly reduce, the potential displacement-caused inefficiency generated by rent-seeking actions. When resale is allowed, the final distribution of rent will differ from auction allocation only in that the quota rent (quota sales revenue) is captured by private agents rather than by the government. Suppliers inframarginal to W who receive quota rights keep them; suppliers extramarginal to W who gain quota rights in the primary allocation (tend to) sell them. Essentially the auction revenue (rent) is redistributed from the government or auction authority to private agents.

It is the distribution of rents that motivates the politics of quota administration. Quota administration is fundamentally a political decision; many competing interests claim entitlement to quota rents. Tradable quotas are a means of distributing rents to selected groups while, at the same time, allowing market forces to match inframarginal traders with quota rights. Tradable quotas have become an increasingly common instrument in fisheries management and, with the Kyoto Protocol to the UN Framework Convention on Climate Change, an emerging means of pollution management and control.

The interesting analytical work on tradable quotas is not found in the international economics literature; rather, because of products and activities involved, it is found in journals like: *Marine Policy*, the *Journal of Environmental Economics and Management*, *Energy Policy* and *Energy Economics*. The goal of rationing in a fisheries context is to limit the 'catch' to a sustainable amount. Fishing boats (or firms) are allocated shares of the total quota, usually based on their historical share of the catch or share of harvest capacity. Recipients can use (fish) their quota, they can purchase more quota from other recipients, or they can sell some or all of their allotment. High-cost operators typically choose to sell to lower-cost operations; the high-cost operators cease to operate, but they get to keep the receipts (rents) from selling their quota allocation. Such payments to less efficient operators facilitate industry-wide coordination efforts: it allows equity considerations to be addressed while allowing for efficient resource allocation. Tradable quotas in pollution control operate in a similar manner. First, greenhouse-gas emissions permits are allocated among polluting operations based on some historical measure; once initially allocated, permit trading commences; permits migrate from less-efficient to more efficient operations.

If auctions are such a wonderful way to allocate quotas, then why are import quotas so seldom auctioned? There are several possible and related reasons. First, auctions outperform other rationing methods only if the market is sufficiently liquid – if the market has a large volume of trade and several competing traders. As a market becomes less liquid, its capacity to function as a price-discovery mechanism deteriorates. Those commodities for which active futures or cash markets exist are excellent candidates for quota auctions. If illiquidity diminishes the relative efficiency of an auction, then other methods, license on demand, for example, might be more efficient, and thus preferable. This is a Coasian argument: sometimes markets are a more costly means of exchange than non-market mechanisms.

Second, there is a political explanation. Auctions are markets and they are hard to control. If the government administering the quota has strong preferences about which countries or firms receive quota rights and rents, then it will probably not choose to auction quota. Similarly, if a government prefers to transfer quota rents to a certain group rather than collecting the rents as auction revenue, it will not auction. As shown below, discretionary allocation provides the importing government or industry the greatest control over the distribution of rent and of trade.

A third argument is that auctions are recognized as the ideal quota administration mechanism but have yet to be widely adopted because of concern about retaliation and WTO consistency. The concern is as follows: auctioning quota generates auction revenue; auction revenue might be considered tariff revenue; if it is considered tariff revenue, then a quota auction could violate the auctioning country's tariff commitments. It is very unlikely that a WTO panel would censure auctions. An auction, unlike a tax, is quid pro quo. The winning bidder gains ownership of something of equal or greater value than the amount paid – the quota rent rebates the auction bid. Thus it is not tax on imports nor is it a tariff.

The fourth argument concerns notions of fairness. Kahneman *et al.* (1986) examined the perceived fairness of auctions as allocation mechanisms. They posed the following hypothetical to a random sample: Suppose you are at a toy store the week before Christmas and the manager announces that one item of that season's in-demand gift has been discovered in the storeroom. The store auctions the toy to the highest bidder. Suppose the $20 toy goes for $200. They then ask (under two conditions): do you feel that this is fair? When the toy store keeps the $180 as rent respondents answer 3 to 1 that the auction is not fair. When told that the toy store will donate the $180 rent to UNICEF, however, the response changes: 3.5 to 1 say it is fair. So, the legitimacy of using an auction as a rationing device may depend on how the auction revenue is used. If it is put in general revenue (like tariff revenue) it might be perceived as illegitimate. But if it is used for some worthy cause (or simply destroyed) then it is likely to be viewed as legitimate.

Rule-based administration
Rule-based quota administration can be represented by set of rules or an algorithm. This section examines three commonly-used rule-base allocation systems: license on demand, first-come-first-served (FCFS) and historical allocation.

License on demand
License-on-demand allocation generally operates in the following manner. Before the quota period begins, potential importers are invited to apply for import licenses. Applicants specify the quantity of imports they desire to import. After the application deadline passes the quota administrator calculates the total volume of (valid) import requests. Call the sum of all import application requests Q^*. If $Q^* \leq Q$ then the quota is not binding and all valid applicants receive a license to import the amount requested. If $Q^* > Q$ then the quota is binding. To ration license supply among license demand, application quantities are reduced proportionally by the factor $k < 1$. If one applies for q^* units and the quota is binding, then a license is granted for kq^* units of imports.

Many countries also specify a minimum license amount, so that the allocation rule reads: kq^* units but no less than 'm' units. This minimum quantity rule can prevent the distribution of licenses that are too small to be commercially useful. For example, a license to import 1 kg of gold or 1 kg of truffles might be of commercial use; but a license to import just 1 kg of cement is commercially useless. The value of 'm' depends on the transport economics of the particular commodity.

The proportional reduction of license requests complicates importing. First, if a trading firm accurately states its desired import volume and the quota is binding, it receives less quota than desired. So, there is an incentive to overstate license requests. A recent example of strategic overstating of license requests involves the European Central Bank. Each week the ECB sells short-term notes to provide liquidity for the Euro-based banking system. The ECB began, in January 1999, by announcing a fixed interest rate for that week's notes and the amount of notes it wished to sell (at a fixed price), and requested interested buyers to submit applications stating the amount of notes they wished to purchase. Because the ECB notes were in considerable demand applications greatly exceeded supply. By mid-1999, the applications were about 20 times the amount offered; thus k was about 5 percent. Over-bidding prompted more over-bidding and, by May 2000, k had fallen below 1 percent. The system had become unmanageable: On 8 June 2000 the ECB (2000) announced that it would switch to an auction-based system. The interest rate is now determined by competitive bidding and the over-bidding problem ceased.

From the perspective of allocative efficiency, license on demand fails to prevent the displacement of inframarginal traders by extramarginal traders when the quota is binding. Allowing resale of licenses reduces the risk of displacement.

First-come-first-served
The standard first-come-first-served (FCFS) allocation allows imports until the quota fills. This is a familiar rationing mechanism: many retailers advertise low prices 'while supplies last' or for the 'first X shoppers'. Such offers are designed to create queues. Such

queues have a positive externality for retailers – it amplifies advertising. For import quotas, FCFC-induced queues can make administration difficult and contentious. Some quotas fill in a matter of minutes or hours; since most countries have more than one port of entry this poses an information management problem. On the supplier side, potential exporters may avoid shipping if they believe that the quota is close to being filled and they perceive a high risk of being stuck with freight at the border. This rational risk-aversion can inhibit in-quota imports.

Finally, FCFS allocation can induce import surges and disrupt markets. These can cause: (a) an unnecessary dip in domestic prices; (b) unnecessary domestic storage costs; and (c) other costs induced by queuing. FCFS, because it ties rents to the act of exporting early, makes resale or tradability impractical; an alternative would be issue tradable permits on a FCFS basis. Permits would be resold to low-cost suppliers who could use market signals to determine when during the period of permit validity to export.

Historical allocation
Historical allocation is most commonly applied when a quota-imposing country chooses to assign quota to specific suppliers – countries or sometimes specific firms. The convention is to grant quota to suppliers in proportion to their average share of the import market during a period prior to the imposition of the quota. Article XIII of the GATT, 'Non-Discriminatory Administration of Quantitative Restrictions', governs the administration of quotas and tariff quotas: this article remains in force under the WTO. Article XIII: 2(d) says that when a country chooses to assign quota to specific suppliers (called a supplier quota) it should endeavor to do so in a way the meets the approval of all interested parties. If that proves impractical, then it should allocate quota rights in proportion to supplier market shares in some prior representative period. Article XIII was written in 1947 and it reflects the accumulated wisdom of generations of negotiators. It recognizes that there is an infinite number of ways to divide a pie and that it is very hard to gain unanimous consent on one particular division. The prior-market-share rule, although imperfect, has been deemed practical and legitimate.

An obvious problem with the prior-market-share rule is that things change: suppliers can gain or lose comparative advantage. Ideally, one would reallocate quota shares to reflect such changes. But this proves difficult to negotiate; suppliers who face an erosion of their quota shares tend to be adamantly opposed to any change. As a result, historical allocation is infrequently revised.

For example, quota shares for US sugar imports were first allocated in 1934 based on average trade shares in 1931–1933. Save for wartime controls, these supplier shares persisted until 1948 when minor adjustments were made to the shares of the two major suppliers, Cuba and the Philippines. The 1961 trade embargo imposed on Cuba forced a reallocation of the large Cuban share. It was reallocated in 1965 to countries (other than the Philippines) based on trade shares in 1963 and 1964. This allocation remained until 1974 when the quota system was terminated. A brief quota-free interlude ended when a quota was re-imposed in 1982 on the basis of trade shares during 1975–1981. These quota shares were tariffied unaltered into a TRQ in 1995 that remains in effect. Each major reallocation was prompted by an economic or political shock that, in each case, altered the structure of the sugar market. Despite this, the allocation of shares was based on the pattern of trade prevailing before the change.

The country allocation of the US sugar TRQ provides a clear example of the displacement of efficient sugar producers by inefficient sugar producers. The 1975–1981 base period witness unusually high sugar prices; and many countries high-cost producers were able to export sugar to the United States. These high-cost suppliers are inframarginal to Pd – the US domestic price (about 45 cents/kg) – but extramarginal to W – the world price (between 10 and 25 cents/kg). The US sugar TRQ requires that in-quota exports be the domestic production of the exporting country. This prohibits the resale or transfer of quota between countries and ensures that the displacement of efficient exporters persists.

Discretionary allocation
Discretionary allocation methods are those that do not follow an explicit or transparent rule or algorithm. This class is defined by negation and thus resists generalization. But some generalization is possible. Governments sometimes grant discretion over quota administration to quasi-governmental or non-governmental organizations. For example, the national paperclip council or the national cabbage-producers board is granted the power to allocate the (quota) rights to import competing products. But even in extreme cases, such as granting quota administration power to the Prime Minister's sister-in-law, the deputized quota administrator must choose some means of allocation. There is not that many practical and politically-viable ways to allocate: very often market-based (exchanging for cash or political favors) or rule-based allocations are adopted. Two examples follow.

First, when Japan, at the insistence of the United States, imposed a Voluntary Export Restraint (VER) on its automobile exports to the United States in 1981, the task of allocating this export quota fell to MITI – the Japanese Ministry of International Trade and Industry. MITI has never explained how it made its allocation; however, the firm-specific shares of automobile exports to the United States after the VER closely (but not perfectly) match the shares observed in 1979, prior to the VER. It appears that MITI invoked the historical market-share allocation rule.

Second, the United States government has granted discretion over which US firms gain the right to export milled and brown rice within the US share of the European Union's rice TRQ to the Association for the Administration of Rice Quotas, Inc. (AARQ). The AARQ was organized specifically to allocate rice quota. It is a registered Export Trading Company; this allows it to coordinate the export activities of competing US firms without violating US Antitrust laws – it is an authorized export cartel. The AARQ auctions the quota (TRQ Certificates); the following is from the rice quota tender closing 1 December 2004:

> TRQ Certificates will be awarded to the highest bidder(s). Any person or entity incorporated or domiciled in the United States is eligible to bid. The minimum bid quantity is 18 metric tons. Performance security (the lesser of $50 000 or the total value of the bid) must be submitted with each bid.

This auction rations the quota rights to inframarginal firms; it also maximizes AARQ revenue. The AARQ distributes the auction revenue to US rice exporting firms in proportion to their current market shares of US rice exports.

These two examples do not prove that all discretionary methods devolve into market-based or rule-based allocations. They do indicate that the transformation is likely and that, when attempting to understand an apparently opaque allocation system, it is probably worth investigating the hypothesis that the allocation is rule or market based.

Note

1. Corden (1971) is an exception in the literature: a considerable portion of two chapters on quotas are devoted to the problems of import licensing, pp. 199–238. Vousden (1990), in contrast, devotes a full chapter to quotas without ever considering how quota rights are allocated, pp. 60–83.

References

Corden, W. M. (1971), *The Theory of Protection*, Oxford: Oxford University Press.

European Central Bank (2000), 'The Switch to Variable Rate Tenders in the Main Refinancing Operations', *Monthly Bulletin*, July, 37–42.

Kahneman, D., J. L. Knetsch and R. Thaler (1986), 'Fairness as a Constraint on Profit Seeking: Entitlements in the Market', *American Economic Review*, **76**(4), 728–41.

Vousden, N. (1990), *The Economics of Trade Protection*, New York: Cambridge University Press.

Recommended reading

Bergsten, C. F., K. A. Elliot, J. J. Schott and W. Takacs (1987), *Auction Quotas and United States Trade Policy*, Washington, DC: Institute for International Economics.

Skully, D. W. (2001), *Economics of Tariff-Rate Quota Administration*, Economic Research Service, US Department of Agriculture. Technical Bulletin No. 1893.

Trela, I. and J. Whalley (1995), 'Internal Quota Allocation Schemes and the Costs of the MFA', *Review of International Economics*, **3**(3), 284–306.

25 Capitalization of trade policy benefits
William A. Kerr

Introduction

When the partial equilibrium approach is used to evaluate trade policy measures, the analysis is often undertaken from a short-run perspective. For many of the questions for which answers are sought, the short-run perspective is sufficient. In other cases, however, if longer-run adjustments are not taken into account, important implications and complications are ignored. These long-run adjustments often lead to misestimates of the distortions arising from the imposition of trade barriers (Gaisford *et al.* 2003) and complicate negotiations to reduce or eliminate trade barriers that were imposed in the past and have remained in place over long periods (Gaisford and Kerr 2001). One of the most important of the latter long-run effects arising from the imposition of trade-distorting measures is the capitalization of trade policy benefits.

What is capitalization?

A vital insight that arises from approaching the examination of changes in a trade policy regime from a long-run perspective is that the benefits of policies will be capitalized into the value of relatively fixed assets. While it is often convenient to approach the analysis of trade policy from the starting position of competitive static long-run equilibrium, where all firms in the industry have the same cost structure, in fact industries are seldom at or near equilibrium due to differences in the abilities or predilections of firms to acquire or utilize new technologies (Grilliches 1957; Quan and Kerr 1983), lags in the exit process of firms and because industries are not competitive allowing for the ongoing existence of firms with different costs. Hence, in a situation of competitive disequilibrium or with some non-competitive industrial structures, firms' costs structures can vary considerably. When protection from foreign competition is requested and granted, it is often only a subset of inefficient firms that require protection. For example, in agriculture it is well known that trade (and other) policy benefits go to many firms that do not need assistance (Tweeten 1970; Tweeten 1994). As trade policies tend to raise prices received by firms in the protected industry, trade policy can lead to super-normal (or economic) profits for some firms. This can be illustrated in Figure 25.1, which depicts an efficient firm in a competitive industry[1] that will benefit from a policy change. Assume that a change in a trade policy regime leads to an increase in the price received for the firm's output of P_w to P_d. For the moment assume that this is an industry where a production quota is required before output can be produced (such as dairy farming in the European Union or Canada (Kerr, 1987–1988)).[2] Further, assume that the original farmer received the quota at no cost when the milk quota regime was initiated. It will be shown that this lack of an initial purchase price does not imply that the production quota has no value.

Suppose that the farm's long-run average cost curve was lac^0 prior to the change in the trade policy regime and the implementation of production quotas. This cost curve continues to represent production costs (and any other non-quota costs). The farm's

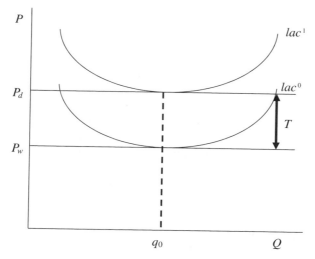

Figure 25.1   Rents produced by trade policy

production quota of q_0 entitles it to revenue that exceeds production costs by the area given by $(P_d - P_w) \times q_0$ in Figure 25.1. This difference between revenue and production cost is properly viewed as rent attributable to the production quota itself – those without production quotas cannot benefit from the trade policy induced price increase. Thus, the rent generated by a unit of quota is equal to $P_d - P_w$. Adding the cost of renting units of the quota for one period to the other costs of production in the period leads to the quota-inclusive long-run average and cost curve, lac^1.

Let us examine the rents generated by production quotas from another perspective. As the quota is essential for production, it will be valuable to prospective buyers. If the total quantity of output is fixed by the government, the only way a new entrant can produce is to acquire quota from an existing farmer who has quota. Assume that the existing farmer is willing to sell and leave the industry. The question is how much will new entrants be willing to pay to acquire the quota above and beyond the purchase price of the farm? To begin with, consider how much an entrant would pay to rent the quota rights for one period. The question to ask, for example, is whether a prospective entrant would be willing to pay an amount that would increase its costs from lac^0 part of the way to lac^1 to rent the quota. At price P_d, the entrant would still earn super-normal profits and it would certainly be worthwhile to incur the additional costs of purchasing quota. Of course, another prospective buyer with the same cost efficiency would be willing to purchase the quota at a slightly higher price. As long as there are sufficient numbers of buyers competing to acquire quota, the price of quota will rise until it reflects the costs associated with lac^1. New entrants earn normal profits and so do not benefit from the programme.

This picture is too simple, however, because it shows the firm in only one production period. As the quota will be expected to generate rents in future time periods, the purchase price of the quota will represent the discounted stream of future earnings. This is why milk quotas in Canada and the EU have high purchase values (Barichello 1996). The interest cost on the money borrowed to purchase the quota or the forgone interest on funds diverted into the acquisition of the quota represents an ongoing cost for the new entrant. In the most extreme case where the quota is expected to generate these rents in perpetuity, the purchase price or present value of q_0 units of quota would be $[(P_d - P_w) \times q_0]/r$, where r is the discount or interest rate. Since the discount rate is a proper fraction, the purchase price of the milk quota is much larger than the one-period rents.[3]

Any attempt to lower the level of trade policy support – decreasing price below P_d – will lead to capital losses for new entrants who purchased quota rights, given that they have costs reflected in lac^1. Clearly, entrants who joined the industry after the trade policy was imposed will resist any attempt to reduce programme benefits as it threatens the value of their assets. Firms that received their quotas at no cost will have had an increase in their asset value and will also resist any change. Banks may have lent against the value of the asset and face the risk of default as the borrower's debt obligations exceed the value of the asset used as security. Similar capitalization will take place when, for example, firms receive allocations of import quotas from the state at no cost which allows them to import at the international price and sell in the domestic market at the higher quantity restricted domestic price. If quotas are expected to remain in place over long periods and can be traded among firms, efficient firms will have an incentive to purchase the rights to import from inefficient firms at a price equal to the capitalized value.

When quotas do not exist, the value of the trade policy that raises the domestic price from P_w to P_d will be capitalized into other fixed assets. In the case of agriculture, for example, this is usually land. The price of land is bid up as prospective entrants attempt to acquire land with which to enter into production. The inevitable bidding up of the price of fixed assets eventually chokes off the incentive to enter the industry and determines the limits of the long-run supply response.

We can now explicitly incorporate short-run and long-run supply behaviour into the analysis of trade policy. Figure 25.2 can be used to re-assess the impact of a tariff of T dollars per tonne on imports. As a result of the tariff-induced price increase there is a reduction in consumption from Q_d^0 to Q_d^1 tonnes and a loss in consumer surplus of $a + b + c + d + e + f + g$ $(a + \ldots + g)$ dollars. In the short run, output increases from Q_s^0 to Q_s^1 tonnes and imports fall from $Q_d^0 - Q_s^0$ tonnes to $Q_d^1 - Q_s^1$ tonnes. Since the short-run increase in producer surplus is a dollars and the short-run tariff revenue is $d + e + f$ dollars, there is an efficiency loss equal to $b + c + g$ dollars.

In the short run, some producers are earning super-normal profit. This acts as a signal for the entry of new low-cost producers. Over time, industry output gradually expands to the long-run level of Q_s^2 tonnes. Although consumption remains equal to Q_d^1, imports fall to $Q_d^1 - Q_s^2$. In the long run, the increase in producer surplus which accrues as rents is $a + b + d$ dollars. The tariff revenue is f dollars. The loss in consumer surplus, however, is still $a + \ldots + g$ dollars. The long-run efficiency loss from the tariff, $c + e + g$ dollars, is larger than the short-run efficiency loss. The extra producer surplus of $b + d$ dollars that arises in the long run is insufficient to compensate for the decline in government (tariff) revenue of $d + e$ dollars. Thus, the short-run efficiency loss of $b + c + g$ dollars is less than the long-run efficiency loss of $c + e + g$ dollars.[4]

In Figure 25.2, the additional rents to industry assets such as land that arise from the tariff are shown by area $a + b + d$. In the long run, when entry eliminates super-normal profits, the entire change in producer surplus is shifted upstream and accrues as higher rents paid to inputs. It is these additional rents that get capitalized into higher land values.

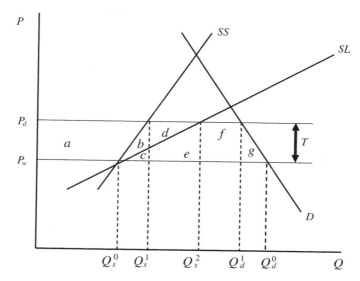

Figure 25.2   The long-run impact of a tariff

In the most extreme case where these rents are expected to continue in perpetuity, land values will increase by $[a + b + d]/r$ because of the tariff.

The lesson is that any unwarranted expansion will be difficult to reverse after the fact, due to vested interests in the inflated value of the assets. Since trade policy benefits in many countries have in reality been capitalized into asset values, there is likely to be considerable policy inertia making trade liberalization negotiations extremely difficult.

Capitalization and trade liberalization

In many countries, sectors such as agricultural have been supported by a vast assortment of trade policy and domestic support measures that distort trade. The effect of trade policy is to raise the home market price above the world price, while the effect of domestic support is to raise producer prices above the home market price and/or reduce production costs relative to the home market price. The benefits of higher prices tend to become capitalized into the value of assets that are used intensively or exclusively in the protected industry. The capitalization of the benefits of past trade policy initiatives have a profound effect on trade liberalizing negotiations.

If the protection provided by trade policy was removed as a result of trade negotiations, asset values would eventually return to their original levels. Thus, surviving firms of the efficient type and subsequent entrants who buy the now fixed asset such as land would again be viable in the long run. However, this does not lessen the short-term disruption that would face efficient producers or reduce the real resource costs that would be associated with bankruptcy. It would also be of little consolation to existing efficient firms who are likely to face financial ruin.

In the event of insolvency, firms – whether efficient or inefficient – typically face devastating capital losses as well as the loss of current income. Prior to the Uruguay Round, for example, agriculture operated under GATT waivers and countries were allowed to provide farmers with policy benefits in the form of protection from imports, export subsidies and trade-distorting domestic subsidies. The value of those benefits was capitalized into the value of farmland. The Uruguay Round Agreement on Agriculture made modest progress in limiting trade-distorting policy measures, but high levels of support remain. Gaisford and Kerr (2001) report that the total annual support provided to agriculture in the European Union in 1998 was US$129.8 billion, in the United States it was US$47.0 billion and in Japan U$49.1 billion. The annual support will typically exceed the extra policy-induced annual rents, but they are likely to be of the same order of magnitude. They make simple back-of-the-envelope estimates of capitalization by assuming that rents are 75 per cent of the policy-induced receipts of producers and discounting at the fairly high real rate of interest of 8 per cent to allow for the fact that there is a risk that the support measures will be removed, this would put policy-induced capitalization at US$1.217 trillion for the European Union, US$0.441 trillion for the United States and US$0.461 trillion for Japan.

The policy-inflated value of assets such as farmland becomes part of firms' assets, but the real question is who benefits from the support measures over the long run? The major beneficiaries are those who owned the assets at the time the policies were put in place and who subsequently sold their assets. New entrants paid for those trade policy benefits when they purchased assets such as land and do not receive ongoing benefits from the existence of the policy.

The capitalization of trade policy benefits makes it difficult to abandon support. These are real costs that must be met by those firms that purchased high-priced assets. Many will have borrowed to pay for assets such as land and the mortgage payments are an ongoing expense. Abandoning the trade policy will mean a depreciation in the value of assets and threaten the financial viability of recent entrants.

In addition, financial institutions will have lent against the value of assets such as farmland. Removal of the trade policy could lead to widespread defaults on loans and threaten financial institutions with a high proportion of, for example, agricultural loans in their portfolio. Japan is particularly sensitive to this problem given the long duration and high levels of protection provided by its agricultural policies and its recent experience with financial institutions that had lent against overvalued urban real estate. In Japan and the European Union, there has been policy-induced overinvestment in the agricultural input and processing sectors. Further, in the European Union there has been a dramatic overinvestment in storage facilities as surplus product has been purchased by intervention agencies. Any reductions in support arising from trade negotiations threaten these investments as well.

Conclusions

While capitalization is not often formally mentioned in trade negotiations, it will dramatically affect the underlying substance of the negotiations. Put simply, it is politically impossible to abandon directly affected firms and firms in linked sectors. Any concessions that are made are likely to come in the form of gradual reductions in support and/or compensation to firms for the removal of support. For example, the post-Uruguay Round movement by a number of countries with historically high levels of trade restricting and distorting policies in agriculture to direct payments to farmers that entail similar or even higher levels of budgetary expenditures can be interpreted as an attempt to defend farmers' asset base.

Notes

1. The assumption of a competitive industry does not materially alter the result.
2. The assumption of a production quota is used only to simplify the exposition of the effect on a fixed asset. This assumption is subsequently relaxed.
3. Alternatively, if an asset is expected to generate a flow of net earnings of B for T years at a discount or interest rate of r, its purchase price or net present value will be:

$$NPV = \sum_{i=1}^{T} \frac{B}{(1+r)}$$

Thus if a milk quota is expected to generate annual rents of 100 000 for five years when the interest rate is 5 per cent, the purchase price of the quota will be: $100\,000.00 + 95\,238.10 + 90\,702.95 + 86\,383.76 + 82\,270.24 = US\$454\,495.05$. If the asset is expected to generate a perpetual flow of earnings, its net present value will be: $NPV = B/r$. Thus, if a milk quota is expected to generate annual rents of US\$100 000 forever with the interest rate at 5 per cent, the purchase price of the quota will be: US\$2 000 000.
4. A similar long-run analysis for an export subsidy can be found in Gaisford and Kerr (2001).

References

Barichello, R. R. (1996), 'Capitalizing Government Program Benefits: Evidence of the Risk Associated with Holding Farm Quotas', in J. M. Antle and D. A. Sumner (eds), *The Economics of Agriculture Volume 2: Papers in Honor of D. Gale Johnson*, Chicago, IL: University of Chicago Press, 283–99.

Gaisford, J. D. and W. A. Kerr (2001), *Economic Analysis for International Trade Negotiations*, Cheltenham, UK and Northampton, MA, USA: Edward Elgar.

Gaisford, J. D., W. A. Kerr and N. Perdikis (2003), *Economic Analysis for EU Accession Negotiations – Agri-food Issues in the EU's Eastward Expansion*, Cheltenham, UK and Northampton, MA, USA: Edward Elgar.

Grilliches, Z. (1957), 'Hybrid Corn: An Exploration in the Economics of Technical Change', *Econometrica*, **25**, 501–22.

Kerr, W. A. (1987–1988), 'Quotas and Uncertainty: Canada and the UK Compared', *Farm Management*, **6**(8), 317–25.

Quan, D. C and W. A. Kerr (1983), 'Truncated Estimates for Incomplete Technological Change in the Canadian Cattle Industry', *American Journal of Agricultural Economics*, **65**(3), 581–6.

Tweeten, L. (1970), *Foundations of Farm Policy*, Lincoln, NE: University of Nebraska Press.

Tweeten, L. (1994), 'Is it Time to Phase Out Commodity Programs?' in L. Tweeten (ed.), *Countdown to 1995: Perspectives for a New Farm Bill*, Anderson Publication ESO 2122, Columbus, OH: Department of Agricultural Economics, Ohio State University.

26 Direct and indirect export subsidies
James Rude

Introduction

Members of the World Trade Organization (WTO) place a high priority on containing and eliminating the use of export subsidies. An export subsidy is conditional upon the recipient exporting the product or service that is being subsidized. The WTO takes a broad view of the definition of a subsidy as 'a financial contribution by a government or any public body within the territory of a Member that confers a benefit' (WTO 1999). Given this very broad definition an export subsidy can include direct payments, the granting of tax relief, the granting of low interest loans, disposal of government stocks at below-market prices, subsidies financed by producers or processors as a result of government actions, marketing subsidies, transportation and freight subsidies, and subsidies for commodities contingent on their incorporation in exported products (ERS 2003). Despite a WTO prohibition on subsidies that are contingent on export performance (WTO 1994a Article 3) these subsidies persist in markets for agricultural products and capital goods. Agricultural export subsidies get special attention in the WTO because there is no outright prohibition on these subsidies in this sector, and the Agreement on Agriculture puts limits on existing export subsidies and prohibits the use of new export subsidies.

Export subsidies are viewed as among the most disruptive impediments to the operation of international markets. These subsidies punish domestic consumers and taxpayers, and may have detrimental effects for competing exporters. They also distort the allocation of resources within a subsidizer's market and across international borders. Given the broad scope of potential export subsidies and the fact that not all types of potential programs have the same trade distorting effects, this chapter classifies export subsidies as either direct or indirect subsidies. Direct subsidies are considered to provide an explicit price subsidy to either the exporting or importing agent, lowering the price of the traded good. Indirect subsidies provide non-price benefits that ultimately lower the final cost to importer. This chapter will address two types of potential indirect export subsidies: government backed export credit arrangements and the possibility to use food aid to dispose of surplus production in select markets.

The second section of this chapter describes the impacts of and motivations for direct export subsidies that are targeted and non-targeted. This section also describes how these direct subsidies are disciplined in the WTO. The third section discusses indirect export subsides. The motivation for and impacts of government sponsored export credit arrangements and international food aid are presented. This section also describes how these indirect programs are disciplined in the WTO. The final section of the chapter presents concluding remarks and comments on some of the possible WTO reforms that are currently being negotiated.

Direct export subsidies

A direct export subsidy provides an explicit price discount that effectively lowers an importer's traded price for the product or service in question. These discounts not only include bonuses paid by government agencies to increase exports but also transportation, handling and inspection services that are provided on more favorable terms for exports than on goods for sale within the country (Annand *et al.* 2001). These price discounts can be further classified as non-targeted programs and programs that are targeted at individual countries.

Regardless of how the program is targeted, a direct export subsidy has the effect of raising producer and consumer prices in the domestic market of the subsidizer. This raises production and reduces consumption redirecting the good from the domestic market to the world market. The impact of increased exports on international markets depends on whether the subsiding country is a price taker (small country assumption) on international markets or if its sales affect international prices (large country assumption). If the subsidizing country is a price taker its actions will not affect international markets.

Economics of non-targeted export subsidies

The impacts of non-targeted export subsidies on prices, quantities and the welfare of individual agents are described in standard trade textbooks (Vousden 1990). Export subsidies create a net welfare loss for the exporting country because the loss of consumer welfare plus the cost to the government for the subsidy expenditure exceeds the gains to producers.[1] If the societal costs of an export subsidy exceed its benefits why would governments use these instruments?

There are a variety of justifications for direct export subsidies that range from economic to non-economic objectives. The economic rationales center on using export subsidies to offset other distortions such as competitor's export subsidies or tariffs administered by importers. In practice, arguments about offsetting distortions don't hold because of administrative costs or other unintended consequences.[2] The non-economic arguments are more mercantilist in nature, where governments attempt to expand exports, diversify markets or preserve market shares. However, export subsidies are not necessarily the most efficient method of achieving these objectives (Panagariya 2000). In agriculture export subsidies are frequently used to dispose of surplus stocks that result from other types of domestic subsidy programs.

Economics of targeted export subsidies

With a targeted export subsidy the effect of the price subsidy is specific to selected markets.[3] A targeted subsidy imposes less of a welfare cost because it is offered to only part of the market. The effectiveness of the targeting depends on whether the principles of price discrimination are followed. It is conceivable that welfare in the subsidizer's market could increase if the subsidy is targeted at the most elastic market so that small subsidies will result in relatively large increases in sales. In this case, the additional producer revenue may make up for the cost of subsidy plus the loss in consumer surplus for a net welfare gain in the exporter's market. Abbott *et al.* (1987) used a general equilibrium model to show the conditions where a targeted export subsidy can increase welfare in the subsidizer's market. Bohman *et al.* (1991) also used a general equilibrium model which recognized the theoretical possibility of a welfare enhancing targeted subsidy but they viewed the welfare gain as unlikely. In this model the welfare effects depended on the market position of a third neutral country and its market share. If the third country is an exporter, both the subsidizer and the third country suffer a welfare loss. Even if the third country is an importer, the welfare effect on the subsidizer will be negative unless the targeted importer has small market share or a higher than normal income elasticity of demand.

Targeted export subsidies, unlike general export subsidies, increase prices in more than just the subsidizing country so that prices (consumer and producer) in non-targeted markets can increase while the price in the targeted market declines. Abbott *et al.* (1987) found that both the subsidizing country and rival exporters might achieve higher domestic prices if the targeting is effective.

The evidence on the effectiveness of targeted export subsidies is at best mixed. For instance Anania *et al.* (1992) found that the targeted US Export Enhancement Program was not effective and the US exports increased minimally at a great cost to the government. No exporting country gained from the Export Enhancement Program and the intended loser, the European Union (EU), was only slightly harmed.

Trade policy discipline for export subsidies
An amendment to the General Agreement on Tariffs and Trade (GATT) in 1955 directed the contracting parties to stop granting subsidies on exports of non-primary goods.

However, for primary (agricultural) products the contracting parties were only admonished to 'seek to avoid' using export subsidies and when subsidies were used the impact on exports should be of no 'more than an equitable share of world export trade in that product' (Jackson 1997: 286). Of course 'equitable' was a subjective, ill-defined concept and export subsidies proliferated.

The prohibition on non-primary product export subsidies was not enforced until 1962 and at that time not all countries (mostly developing countries) were prepared to adopt the prohibition. The 1979 GATT Subsidies Code reiterated the prohibition and featured an annex titled 'Illustrative List of Export Subsidies' that helped to add precision to the definition of prohibited practices with a list of examples. The 1994 Uruguay Round Agreement on Subsidies and Countervailing Measures (SCM) required all WTO Members to stop using export subsidies. This requirement now included developing country Members who were given eight years to phase out their export subsidies.[4] Also included in the prohibited category are local content requirements, where subsidies are contingent upon using domestic products rather than imported goods, in a production process. Export subsidies for primary agricultural products continue to be treated differently and are disciplined through the Agreement on Agriculture. The SCM Agreement also provides for an expedited dispute settlement mechanism with respect to prohibited subsidies. The fact that complainants are not required to demonstrate injury or prejudice and are just required to establish that the subsidy belongs in the prohibited category, demonstrates the gravity with which the WTO views export subsidies (Jackson 1997: 292).

A significant achievement of the Uruguay Round Agreement on Agriculture was the introduction of discipline on agricultural export subsidies. Under the Agreement on Agriculture, the use of existing export subsidies must be reduced and no new export subsidies are allowed. As well, the Agriculture Agreement follows the SCM Agreement by providing a clearer definition of what an export subsidy is (export subsidies are defined in Article 9.1). The subsidies include direct export payments contingent on export performance; sales of governments stocks at less than acquisition prices; export payments financed through government action including payments financed by producer levies, and subsidies on goods incorporated into export products (WTO 1994b Article 9).

Article 3.3 of the Agreement on Agriculture places a limit on agricultural export subsidies measured in terms of the volume of and expenditures on subsidized exports. The key features are:

- A base period (1986–1990) was used to establish base volumes and expenditures for the 25 Members that notified the WTO of products that received export subsidies and were to be subject to the reduction commitment.
- Developed countries agreed to reduce the volume of exports subsidized by 21 percent, relative to the notified base, and to reduce the expenditure on export subsidies by 36 percent, relative to the notified base, by 2000.
- Developing countries agreed to reduce the volume of exports subsidized by 14 percent and the expenditure on export subsidies by 24 percent by 2004.

Direct export subsides have been used mainly, but not exclusively, by developed countries. Among the notified subsidizers the EU has been the most dominant user of export subsidies. The Agreement includes certain temporary exemptions for developing countries, allowing them to subsidize marketing costs and internal transport (Article 9.4).

The experience over the Uruguay Round implementation period is that the protective measures associated with export subsidies have fallen much faster than either domestic support or border measures. Since the base period, there have been major reductions in levels of export subsidies used. For instance, during the base period 55 percent of world wheat markets involved export subsides, but by 1998 this share was only 14 percent while the value of wheat export subsidies declined by 83 percent over this time period (Podbury *et al.* 2001: 33). Since 1998 there has been no significant resumption in the use of export subsidies for wheat. Export subsidies for all grains declined dramatically because the US stopped using the Export Enhancement Program and the EU dramatically reduced its use of export restitutions. The EU was able to use less export subsidies because of domestic policy reforms which reduced internal support prices for grains. For all agricultural commodities the value of export subsidies declined by 64 percent between the base period and 1998 (Podbury *et al.* 2001: 32).

Despite the reduction in the use of export subsidies, the success of the Agreement on Agriculture commitments, in terms of disciplining export subsidies, remains qualified. There are several reasons for this qualified success. First, the commitment levels are referenced to a base period that is not representative of the use of export subsidies in historic agricultural markets (Podbury *et al.* 2001: 40–47). The period 1986–1990 was a time when both the EU and US used export subsidies to reduce mounting domestic stocks of grain. Export subsidies prior to and subsequent to this period were lower. Given that the reduction commitments were determined with unrepresentative base, some Members have the potential to increase the use of notified export subsidies if they choose to.

Second, built in flexibility allows countries the liberty to redistribute subsidies to minimize liberalization. While there are expenditure and quantity limits only one of these constraints is likely to be binding, so the per unit subsidy is not rigidly bound which allows Members some flexibility in meeting their commitments. As well, some Members have provided their subsidy reduction commitments at a very aggregate level and therefore can move subsidies between individual products and still meet their commitments (de Gorter *et al.* 2003).

Third, there is also a concern that tighter controls on export subsidies than on other measures have encouraged members to shift support to other potentially distorting measures.[5]

Fourth, there is the possibility of circumventing the export subsidy commitment by using indirect export subsidies.

Indirect export subsidies
The problem with disciplining direct export subsidies is that Members can then attempt to use indirect methods to support their exports. The use of indirect export subsidies includes the use of food aid programs, actions of state trading enterprises, publicly underwritten export credits, export promotion activities, and possibly even a combination of domestic policy instruments that act like an export subsidy. All of these alternative instruments have multiple policy objectives in addition to promoting exports. These programs can have beneficial aspects, as well as trade distorting aspects, and the welfare impacts are more difficult to measure. This chapter will discuss two of these indirect measures: government supported export credit programs and food aid.

Export credit programs
An export credit arrangement occurs when a foreign buyer is allowed to defer payment on an imported good or service. Private financial institutions handle most of the financing associated with export credit arrangements. Government involvement takes the form of providing guarantees, insuring the financial transaction, directly subsidizing the interest rates, or even making credit directly available. This involvement may result in loan conditions that are better than those offered by the market thereby reducing the importer's cost of financing and possibly resulting in increased trade (Rude 2000).

Government involvement in these financing arrangements is only loosely justified. Skully (1992) suggests that the provision of government supported export credit guarantees is usually attributed to correcting market failures in the provision of insurance. The market failures are vaguely defined as arising from political risks or excess commercial risks but the absence of a market is not necessarily evidence of a market failure.[6]

If government involvement in credit financing cannot be justified from an economic perspective, do these programs involve a subsidy element? Export credit arrangements can be used to make the terms of the sale more attractive than the terms provided by a rival exporter. Interest rate subsidies and direct provision of credit at less than commercial terms have a direct subsidy element. However, most government involvement in credit arrangements involves credit guarantees or insurance. It can be argued that if the guarantee removes any risk for the lender, the borrower may freely default on the loan. So the loan guarantee transfers risk of non-repayment from the exporter to the agency providing the guarantee. When an exporter has a better credit rating than a perspective importer, the exporter may offer the importer a more favorable interest rate than is otherwise available. The guarantee will reduce the importer's risk premium and lower the cost of buying the commodity. Therefore, the credit guarantee provides an implicit interest rate subsidy (Baron 1983). In addition to the implicit interest rate subsidy, export credit agencies often do not charge the exporter the full insurance cost of guaranteeing the credit sale. So there can be an insurance premium subsidy as well.

The problem of finding the implicit subsidy value of the credit guarantee has been addressed by a number of authors (Baron 1983; Raynauld 1992; and Hyberg *et al*. 1995). All the these studies have the common element of measuring implicit interest rate subsidies as a function of the difference between the interest rate adopted by the credit agency and a reference market interest rate. The question that remains is: What is the appropriate reference interest rate? This rate should correspond to the actuarially fair rate of interest associated with expected potential default by the borrower in question. An actuarially fair rate of interest ensures that the present value of the expected sum of payments for the recipient country just equals the cash value of the commodity at the time of delivery. If there is no subsidy, then an actuarially fair interest rate would be applied (Rude 2000).

The price faced by the borrowing country on a credit sale should be higher than the price paid by a cash customer. This difference should account for the opportunity cost of funds and the risk associated with the borrower. If these costs are not accounted for, there is an export subsidy and the price discount is measured as the difference between the true unit export value and what the importer actually pays (Baron 1983). Once the interest rate subsidy can be put into terms of price subsidy the impact of the subsidy can be determined in the same manner as a direct export subsidy.

As a general rule, a credit arrangement applies to a specific country, so the effects of the implicit price subsidy should be modeled as a targeted export subsidy (Skully 1992; Vercammen 1998). As with direct targeted export subsidies, the welfare effects in the subsidizers' market depend on whether the targeting follows the principles of price discrimination. Export revenues for a third-country exporter may increase if a sufficient portion of its sales are to non-targeted markets and if prices in these markets increase more than prices in targeted markets are depressed.

Under certain other conditions, an implicit interest rate subsidy may lead to higher traded prices. If the export credit program relaxes the importer's budget constraint the program may have a demand inducing effect. To the extent that the program expands demand rather than competes for market share, traded prices will rise (Young *et al.* 2001). One of the conditions for demand to expand is the existence of a liquidity constraint such as when the importer is unable to obtain credit under any other terms. So how prevalent are liquidity constraints? The Organization for Economic Cooperation and Development (OECD 2001) reports on a survey of participants in the Export Credit Arrangement that the bulk of officially supported agricultural export credits were provided for trade between developed OECD countries where credit constraints are not perceived to be a problem.

For industrial products, the government involvement in export credit arrangements is disciplined by the SCM. The Illustrative List of Export Subsidies provides a listing of prohibited export subsidies, including 'the provision by governments . . . of export credit guarantee or insurance programmes . . . at premium rates, which are inadequate to cover the long-term operating costs and losses of the programmes' (SCM Annex I paragraph j) and subsidized interest rates (SCM Annex I paragraph k). However, an export credit practice will not be considered an export subsidy if the export credit arrangement is in compliance with the OECD's Arrangement on Guidelines for Officially Supported Export Credits (the 'Arrangement') (OECD 1998).

The 'Arrangement' places limits on the terms and conditions under which export credits can be provided. It applies to export credits with a repayment term of two or more years. The 'Arrangement': (a) lays down maximum repayment periods; (b) establishes minimum interest rates thereby limiting their use as a vehicle for subsidy; (c) restricts coverage to a maximum of 85 percent of the export contract value; and (d) establishes minimum premium benchmarks.

Since all agricultural export subsidies are exempted from the disciplines of the SCM, agricultural export credit arrangements are also not subject to these disciplines. Furthermore, agricultural export credit arrangements are also excluded from the OECD 'Arrangement'. Rather Article 10 paragraph 2, of the Agreement on Agriculture, commits WTO Members to work toward an international agreement on disciplines for export credits, export guarantees and export credit insurance programs. These negotiations have, to date, not been successful.

Food aid
The concern with food aid is the possible circumvention of the agricultural export subsidy disciplines. While export subsidies are one release valve to dispose of surplus domestic production, food aid shipments provide another avenue to vent this surplus. The objectives of most food aid programs are typically humanitarian to address shortfalls of food availability in less developed countries and to deal with the associated problems such as under-nutrition. However, history has shown that food aid shipments tend be higher when the food supply is in surplus than when markets are tight. So when can food aid shipments be used as an indirect export subsidy?

In broad terms food aid can take three forms: cash grants, in-kind shipments of food and sales of food on concessional terms. Cash donations are perfectly fungible in that the grant simply increases the recipient's budget constraint and should not distort resource allocation or disrupt the development of normal commercial distribution channels. Earmarked aid is potentially more distorting in that because of the transfer of food the recipient country may transfer resources out of agriculture to other sectors of the economy. This can harm domestic producers in the recipient country and may displace the sales of competing exporters. Concessional sales involve long-term credit on non-commercial terms and/or sales at purchase prices below market value. As with export credits these special terms involve an implicit subsidy. This subsidy may be quite large, given the length of term of a typical concessional sale. The impact of these subsidies on world markets should be relatively limited since food aid has a relatively small share of international markets (Podbury *et al.* 2001: 80). Food aid may also create additional demand for agricultural commodities, and upward pressure on prices, if the aid reaches consumers who would not have been in the market without the program.

From a trade policy perspective the concern is that food aid shipments may displace commercial shipments. Paragraph 4 of Article 10 of the Agreement on Agriculture requires that international food aid shipments not be conditional or tied directly to the recipient country buying commercial exports from the donor. However, the practice of using aid as a subsidy is more subtle. Food aid shipments tend to increase when stocks are high (see Podbury *et al.* 2001: 80 and Young *et al.* 2001: 34).

Article 10 also requires that the food aid transactions be carried out in accordance with the FAO 'Principles of Surplus Disposal and Consultative Obligations' and, where possible that food aid be provided in grant form (donations of food or cash). Finally, aid provided on concessional terms should be consistent with Article IV of the Food Aid Convention of 1986. While this article sets down details of how the transactions can be made, it does not provide a deterrent against food aid being used to displace commercial sales (Podbury *et al.*: 85–86).

Food aid is offered through both bilateral and multilateral (primarily the UN World Food Program) channels. The multilateral arrangements are not a concern with respect to surplus disposal and additional disciplines should not be necessary. However, the majority of food aid is provided through bilateral arrangements (Podbury *et al.*: 82–3). The major donors are the large industrial countries that face surplus production. As a consequence, bilateral arrangements are more supply driven than demand driven and the volume of shipments tend to vary with respect to market conditions.

Any attempts to reform the provision of food aid will have to recognize the legitimate objectives of the programs while limiting the use of the transfers for surplus disposal. Programs that target the requirements of people in need and provide direct grants rather than conditional terms should be less distorting, both for international markets and with respect to the long-term viability of domestic agriculture in the recipient country.

Concluding remarks and the way forward

Export subsidies can take many forms including direct transfers, subsidized credit arrangements, and surplus disposal through food aid. Since these instruments affect both consumer and producer decisions they tend to be more distorting than domestic programs that are aimed at a subset of agents. The extent to which these programs distort international markets depends on whether the subsidizer is a large country with respect to its ability to affect world prices. Targeted export subsidies, in theory, should be less distorting (in terms of the subsidizing country's net welfare and with respect to international markets) than general export subsidies, but in practice the impacts are probably not that different from non-targeted subsidies.

Trade policy authorities have paid more attention to direct export subsidies than indirect subsidies. These direct subsidies are prohibited for non-primary products. WTO Agricultural export subsidies disciplines are aberrant in that existing direct export subsidies are still permitted although expenditures and volumes are capped. Whether or not direct export subsidies will be prohibited in agriculture depends on the outcome of ongoing WTO negotiations. If elimination is not possible in the Doha Development Round of negotiations, other questions must addressed such the establishment of a new base for reduction commitments, the size of the reduction commitment, whether the commitments will continue to apply to both volumes and expenditures and questions about how much flexibility Members would be allowed in implementing the new commitments.

If direct export subsidies eventually are prohibited, then the concern shifts to the circumvention of the subsidy disciplines. Both government-supported export credits and food aid can be used to compete in international markets and to benefit a particular exporter at the expense of its competitors.

Currently, government-sponsored export credit programs for industrial products are disciplined in the WTO Agreement on Subsidies and Countervailing Measures with disciplines contained in an OECD export credit 'Arrangement'. There are no similar rules for agriculture. Although negotiators were directed to negotiate a similar arrangement for agricultural export credits at the OECD, at this time such an arrangement does not seem possible and the discipline will likely be written into the modalities of a reformed Agreement on Agriculture. In a new agreement export credit and insurance would likely have to be provided on 'commercial terms', with limits on the duration of credit, benchmarks for interest rates, and minimum insurance premiums. The term limits, for agricultural products, with respect to government sponsored credit arrangements should be shorter than for industrial products because food is less durable and more perishable than other goods. Other aspects of potential credit arrangement disciplines, for agriculture, should be similar to the existing OECD 'Arrangement'.

The Agreement on Agriculture's provisions on food aid should be tightened. There is a general understanding that food aid for humanitarian purposes is essential. Proposals have been put forward to limit donations to cash and that in-kind aid should be channeled through the appropriate international bodies. Whatever forms the disciplines take, negotiating them will be a delicate balancing act between humanitarian needs and a liberalized market system.

Notes

1. Note that if the exporting country has international market power in that its exports can influence traded prices, the subsidy will depress the world price and increase the size of the government expenditure beyond the size that it would be for a small price taking country.
2. Panagariya (2000) argues against responding in kind to competitor's export subsidies because adding a new distortion does not offset the existing distortion. An attempt to neutralize the distortion of a tariff in an importer's market is more theoretically plausible because Lerner's symmetry theorem (export subsidies and tariffs have opposite effects). Panagariya argues that the symmetry does not hold in practice because of the added costs of administering the subsidy, the potential for importer retaliation with a countervailing duty, and because of rent-seeking activities as agents avoid tariffs or inflate their claims for export subsidies.
3. See the technical appendix of Rude (2000) for a brief description of the economics of targeted export subsidies.
4. Members with a per capita GNP of less than $1000 are exempted from the prohibition on export subsidies.
5. Definitely the larger WTO Members, the USA and the EU, have shifted funding to domestic support measures that that are not subject to the reduction commitment (that is the so called green and blue box measures). These measures are understood to be less distorting than export subsidies.
6. Dixit (1987, 1989) finds that moral hazard and adverse selection do provide reasons for the failure of the complete development of private markets for bearing the risks of international transactions. However, neither moral hazard nor adverse selection motivates the complete absence of insurance markets.

References

Abbott, P. C., P. L. Paarlberg and J. A. Sharples (1987), 'Targeted Agricultural Export Subsidies and Social Welfare', *American Journal of Agricultural Economics*, **69**(4), 723–32.

Anania, G., M. Bohman and C. A. Carter (1992), 'United States Export Subsidies in Wheat: Strategic Trade Policy or Expensive Beggar-Thy-Neighbor Tactic?' *American Journal of Agricultural Economics*, **74**, 532–45.

Annand, M., D. F. Buckingham and W. A. Kerr (2001), *Export Subsidies and the World Trade Organization*, Saskatoon: Estey Centre Research Paper, Number 1.

Baron, D. (1983), *The Export-Import Bank: An Economic Analysis*, New York: Academic Press.

Bohman, M., C. A. Carter and J. H. Dorfman (1991), 'The Welfare Effects of Targeted Export Subsidies: A General Equilibrium Approach,' *American Journal of Agricultural Economics*, **73**, 693–702.

de Gorter, H., M. Ingco and L. Ruiz (2003), 'Export Subsidies: Agricultural Policy Reform and Developing Countries', World Bank Trade Note 8, Washington DC.

Dixit, A. (1987), 'Trade and Insurance with Moral Hazard', *Journal of International Economics*, **23**(3–4), 201–20.

Dixit, A. (1989), 'Trade and Insurance with Adverse Selection', *Review of Economics Studies*, **56**(2), 235–47.

ERS (2003), 'WTO: Glossaries', World Trade Organization Briefing Room, Economic Research Service, United States Department of Agriculture, http://www.ers.usda.gov/briefing/wto/glossaries.htm.

Hyberg, B., M. Smith, D. Skully and C. Davison (1998), 'Export Credit Guarantees: the Commodity Credit Corporation and US Agricultural Export Policy', *Food Policy*, **20**, 27–39.

Jackson J. H. (1997), *The World Trading System: Law and Policy of International Economic Relations*, Cambridge MA: MIT Press, 279–303.

OECD (1998), *Arrangement on Guidelines for Officially Supported Export Credits*, Paris: Organization for Economic Co-operation and Development.

OECD (2001), *An Analysis of Officially Supported Export Credits in Agriculture*, Paris: Organization for Economic Cooperation and Development.

Podbury, T., I. Roberts, A. Tielu and B. Buetre (2001), 'Agricultural Export Measures in WTO Negotiations', Australian Bureau of Agriculture and Resource Economics, Research Report 01.02.

Panagariya, A. (2000), 'Evaluating the Case for Export Subsidies', Policy Research Working Paper 2276, World Bank, January.

Raynauld, A. (1992), *Financing Exports to Developing Countries, Development*, Paris: Centre of Organisation for Economic Co-operation and Development.

Rude, J. (2000), 'Reform of Agricultural Export Credit Programs', *The Estey Journal of International Law and Trade Policy*, **1**, 66–82.

Skully, D. (1992), 'Price Discrimination and State Trading: The Case for US Wheat', *European Review of Agricultural Economics*, **19**, 313–29.

Vercammen, J. (1998), 'Export Credit as a Mechanism for Price Discrimination', *Canadian Journal of Economics*, **31**, 279–94.

Vousden, N. (1990), *The Economics of Trade Protection*, New York: Cambridge University Press.

WTO (1994a), *Agreement on Subsidies and Countervailing Measures*, Geneva: World Trade Organization.

WTO (1994b), *Agreement on Agriculture*, Geneva: World Trade Organization.

WTO (1999), 'Subsidies and Countervailing Measures: Overview', Geneva: World Trade Organization, http://www.wto.org/english/tratop_e/scm_e/subs_e.htm.

Young, L. M., P. C. Abbott and S. Leetma (2001), 'Export Competition: Issues and Options in the Agricultural Negotations', International Agricultural Trade Research Consortium Commissioned Paper No. 15.

27 Production subsidies
Karl D. Meilke and John Cranfield

Introduction

Production subsidies are one of the most common forms of government intervention in the economy. Most countries provide financial support and protection for a wide range of economic activities that serve to increase the output of these industries above what would be supplied at world market prices. Examples include industries as diverse as culture (symphonies, authors, artists), agriculture and aerospace. In turn, the economic instruments used to provide production incentives are as diverse as a politician's imagination. However, the primary instruments all fall into one of four categories:

- *Market price supports* that keep both producer and consumer prices above world price levels. Market price supports provide an incentive for producers to supply more and consumers to consume less than they would at world prices. These 'distortions' in production and consumption lead to a loss in economic welfare (Houck 1986; Just *et al.* 1982). Market price supports are common in the agricultural sectors of many developed countries and have traditionally played an important role in the regulated prices charged by taxis, cable TV and local phone service.
- *Deficiency payments* to producers can be used to bridge the gap between a regulated floor price and lower world market prices. Deficiency payments distort domestic production decisions but consumers are allowed to purchase the product at world prices. Deficiency payment schemes or 'stabilization policies' abound in agriculture (OECD 2003).
- *Input subsidies* are often provided to firms to allow them to lower the cost of production inputs. Perhaps the most commonly subsidized production input is credit – where firms in selected industries; firms of a certain size; or firms having a particular form of ownership structure are allowed to access capital at reduced rates. In developing countries it is not uncommon to subsidize the cost of fertilizer or other agricultural inputs.
- *Government tax policy*, through the provision of tax concessions, can also be used to subsidize the production of certain industries. This forgone tax revenue is often linked to the use of certain inputs, like high technology; provided to subsidize research and development activities; provided to stimulate the production of natural resources like oil and gas; or provided to stimulate the production of environmentally friendly products like ethanol. However, regardless of the motivation, tax incentives provide an indirect subsidy to favored industries.

While production subsidies are pervasive in modern economies it is not altogether obvious why this topic is included in a book dealing with trade policy. The answer lies in the fact that production subsides provided to meet local objectives can have external effects that harm foreign firms by lowering prices and curtailing their production. It is in the analysis of these 'external' effects where the economics of domestic and trade policies become intertwined.

This review proceeds as follows. In the next section the motivation for production subsidies are examined. The economics of the four general types of production subsides are discussed in the third section. This discussion is conducted using the standard perfectly competitive, perfect arbitrage trade model.[1] The authors have decided not to provide the three panel trade diagrams that illustrate the statements made in the text, but keen readers are invited to visualize them in their minds or to sketch them on a notepad. The conclusions from this exercise are not surprising, namely that domestic production subsides can distort trade. Consequently, in the fourth section we review the WTO rules and remedies, as they apply to production subsidies.

Why production subsidies?

There are four primary reasons for production subsidies: redistributing income; correcting for market failures; rent-seeking behavior by producers and national security concerns. If redistributing income is the primary objective of government policy then this goal is best achieved using lump-sum transfers.[2] Lump-sum transfers should be designed so potential recipients cannot modify their behavior to affect who gets the transfer, or the size of the transfer. In this way lump-sum transfers should not change the optimal allocation of resources in the economy.

Many economic policies, including production subsidies, are justified on the basis of correcting for a perceived market failure. The most common justifications involve the replacement of 'missing markets', correcting for negative externalities, augmenting the impact of positive externalities and restricting cut-throat competition.[3] Using agriculture as an example, it can be argued that investment decisions involve long lags and that a complete set of futures and risk markets do not exist to hedge the risk farmers face. Hence, there may be a role for government to provide income stabilization and crop insurance programs to replace the missing markets (Rude 2001). However, in most cases, the missing market argument does not survive close scrutiny. Farmers, in particular, have shown that they will not participate in government stabilization and crop insurance schemes unless they contain a large subsidy element (Chen and Meilke 1998). This suggests that income transfers are the primary motivation for using the program.

Another market failure argument used to justify production subsidies is that the industry receiving the subsidy provides a positive externality that is not reflected in the price it receives for its output in the market place (Paarlberg *et al*. 2002). If farms provide habitat for wild birds and animals that are valued by society and this externality is not reflected in the price of farm output, then it is argued that this market failure should be corrected by subsidizing the production of agricultural products that will also result in more habitat. The validity of this argument hinges on if the agricultural output is required to provide the habitat. If not, then the appropriate policy response is to pay farmers for providing the habitat but not to pay more than free market prices for agricultural output.

Price setting (above free market levels) and regulation are often justified as a means of eliminating 'cut-throat' competition that would drive prices and profits to unacceptably low levels. Presumably, this is the argument that is made to justify highly regulated taxi cab prices and the entry barriers that accompany them.

Rent seeking behavior can also help explain why production subsidies are provided to some industries and not to others. There is a vast literature on rent-seeking behavior but the idea is simple (Buchanan *et al.*, 1980; de Gorter *et al.* 1992; Mueller 2003; Schmitz *et al.* 2002; Tollison 1982). Industries and firms within industries compete for the import protection, production subsidies and tax breaks that governments provide. This lobbying process often involves highlighting the economic hardships that would result from a failure to provide financial support. Politicians react to the demand for subsidies by supplying protection to those industries and firms whom they feel will provide the votes needed to insure their reelection. Because the benefits of protection are concentrated either in a single industry, concentrated in a relatively small group of firms, and/or concentrated geographically, the gains from lobbying to maintain or expand protection to individual firms and their workers are large (Swinnen and de Gorter 1993). Conversely, the costs of providing protection (which might be several times larger than the gains) are usually dispersed over a large number of consumers and/or taxpayers and seldom amount to more than a few dollars, or even cents per consumer/taxpayer. Hence the rational response of the losers is to do nothing. Finally, once support has been provided to an industry it tends to get capitalized into fixed assets and this makes the removal of the support even more difficult.

A fourth justification for supporting the output of some industries relates to national security. This is most obvious in the case of support provided to industries closely related to the military, for example, aircraft, shipbuilding and aerospace. However, support for food production in many countries is also justified on the basis of national food security, for example, rice production in Japan.

Having examined the motivation for production subsidies it is time to turn attention to the effects of these policies.

The effects of output subsidies

Consider an importing country that has a market price support higher than the world price level. The economic effects of a market price support program are similar to those of a tariff in that they raise prices for domestic consumers and producers, reduce imports and cause world prices to be lower than they otherwise would be. In welfare terms, domestic consumers lose and domestic producers gain while third country producers lose and third country consumers gain. Market price supports remain an important policy instrument in some sectors, especially agriculture, but the conditions that allow them to exist are slowly being removed.

In order to operate a market price support program the importing country must have border measures that prevent the cheaper imported product from flowing into the domestic market. Traditionally, an import quota, a state trading importer or a variable levy system was used to keep out unwanted imports and to protect the higher domestic price. Import quotas were eliminated on agricultural products in the Uruguay Round and replaced by tariff rate quotas or high bound tariffs. Unfortunately, in many cases the over-quota tariffs are so high that tariff rate quotas have the same economic effects as an import quota (Boughner *et al.* 2000; de Gorter and Sheldon 2000; Moschini 1991). Still, the Uruguay Round fixed the number of tariff lines to which tariff rate quotas apply and hopefully the Doha Development Round will result in a significant lowering of over-quota tariffs and no expansion in the number of commodities covered. In countries where applied tariffs are lower than bound tariffs, an importer could vary its applied tariff in order to protect a domestic market price support program, or use a state trading importer to restrict imports in order to protect the higher domestic price.[4]

The lack of transparency and government budget expenditures makes a market price support program attractive to importers. Effectively consumers bear the cost of the program, in comparison to programs that involve a smaller trade distortion but entail highly visible government expenditures. There are two major differences between a market price support program and a tariff only regime. First, unless tariffs are high enough to completely eliminate imports, the importers' price and the quantity traded will fluctuate with world market prices under a tariff regime. This means that the domestic market shares in the price instability generated in the world market, and imports more as world prices fall and imports less as prices rise. With a market price support program domestic prices are fixed and the quantity imported adjusts as the importers supply and demand curves shift over time. In essence, the country shifts its instability in production and consumption onto the world market (Zwart and Blandford 1989; Zwart and Meilke 1979). For example, the United States maintains a market price support program for sugar that keeps its domestic price fixed and considerably higher than the world market price. Over time United States sugar imports, largely from developing countries, have fallen significantly causing world prices to be lower and more variable than they would be in the absence of the United States program.

Second, a tariff generates government revenue equal to the per unit tariff times the number of units imported. With a market price support program there is a gain (often called an import rent) equal to the value of the tariff revenue but in most cases it is not collected by the government. Generally, this gain is captured by firms in the importing country through the allocation of import rights to historical importers, or by creating a monopoly importer (Skully 1999; Meilke *et al.* 2001).[5] Occasionally, the import rent is given to firms in the exporting country which under certain conditions can make them lobby for the importer to keep its protection (Boughner *et al.* 2000).

While the economics of a market price support program operated by an importing country are similar to a tariff, what if an exporter adopts a market price support program? If an exporter wants to use a market price support program it needs an import barrier to keep out the cheap foreign product, and it needs to find a way to sell something that is expensive at home and cheap abroad. There are not a lot of options on how to do this. The most obvious way is by providing export subsides. While export subsidies are illegal in the WTO, except for agriculture, if the importer does not challenge the market price support regime the offending exporter has only to fear WTO challenges by competing exporters. Hopefully, the Doha Development Round will result in the elimination of export subsidies for agriculture and impose increased discipline on the use of export credits and guarantees. When this process is complete the use of market price supports without domestic production controls should be largely eliminated.

Since the use of a market price support program by an exporter can be expensive and invites a WTO challenge, exporters have looked for other instruments that have the effect of raising producer prices, boosting output and supporting producers' income. An obvious instrument is a deficiency payment. With a deficiency payment the government sets a minimum price producers will receive for a commodity, but consumers are allowed to continue to purchase at world market prices. If world prices are below the minimum price set by the regulators then domestic producers receive a per unit payment equal to the difference between the domestic minimum producer price (floor price) and the world price. A deficiency payment program results in a domestic supply curve that becomes vertical at any price below the floor price. This means domestic production is higher than it otherwise would be when market prices are below the floor price and as a result exports are larger. However, consumers are allowed to purchase the commodity at world market prices as prices fall. Hence, the cost of the deficiency payment program is borne by domestic taxpayers and increases as world prices fall. In general, the welfare costs of a deficiency payment program are less than for a market price support because domestic demand decisions are not distorted (Houck 1986).

Just as with market price support an importing country will gain economic welfare as a result of an exporter's deficiency payment program but the importing country's producers will not be happy. For competing exporters the drop in the world market price will cause welfare losses – especially to producers, who will mount pleas for similar levels of support, and raise justified claims that they should not have to compete against the treasuries of rich countries.

The effects of input subsidies
Output price subsidies are the most obvious way to increase the supply of a particular product but a similar effect can be accomplished using input subsidies (Gardner 1988). Input subsidies also have the advantage of being less obvious than market price support or deficiency payment schemes and hence less libel to face trade actions. Credit subsidies and other forms of input subsidies are especially important in developing countries that have less mature capital markets than developed nations. The effect of an input subsidy is to make it cheaper for a firm to produce at any given level of output. Assuming the subsidy is used by an exporter the rightward shift in the exporter's supply curve also shifts its excess supply curve to the right by an equal amount. The increased supply at every price level causes the world price to fall and the quantity traded to rise. The welfare effects for the exporter are an increase in consumer surplus and an increase in producer surplus, but these increases are not large enough to cover the cost of the input subsidy to taxpayers. The effects on importers are familiar by now, a gain to consumers, a loss to producers and a net gain to society resulting from the price decline. In fact, an input subsidy has exactly the same economic effect as a per unit output subsidy.

The above discussion becomes more complex if it is assumed that the shift of the supply curve is not caused by the direct subsidization of the cost of an input (for example, lower interest rates or lower fertilizer prices) but by publicly funded research (Norton and Davis 1981). If the shift in the supply curve is the result of improved productivity resulting from government funded or government subsidized research, it is possible for there to be net gains to society from this investment and it justifies the special treatment of this type of expenditure in the Agreement on Subsidies and Countervailing Measures (ASCM).

Production externalities provide another potential argument for the use of input or output subsidies (Peterson *et al.* 2002). For example, many consumers are concerned about animal welfare. Animal friendly production technologies are available but they entail higher per unit production costs. In this situation, the production of meat and animal welfare are jointly produced. If you want meat you only have two choices – you can use traditional technology, or more expensive animal friendly technology. If society decides that farmers must use the higher cost technology, and the border is open so meat can be imported at world market prices, then domestic producers are at a competitive disadvantage because of the high cost technology that they are forced to use. To compensate, the government could subsidize the cost of the new technology, or it could provide a deficiency payment to local farmers to restore domestic production to where it would be using the old technology.[6]

Note that the existence of an externality does not justify the use of border measures to correct for it (Paarlberg *et al.* 2002). In fact, it is difficult to concoct examples where domestic production subsidies are required to correct for the externality because the output and the positive externality are seldom jointly produced. The ASCM does make allowance for nonactionable subsidies provided to meet environmental goals but they have to satisfy strict criteria.

Production subsidies when output is limited
The above discussion makes it clear that production subsides can have adverse trade consequences. In addition, when production subsidies are provided on an unlimited quantity of output they can be very expensive. At their most perverse such subsidies can switch a country from being an importer of a product at world market prices to an exporter; at massive potential costs to domestic consumers and taxpayers. For this reason, countries have searched for ways of providing income support that minimize the trade distortions inherent in higher than free trade prices and that are fiscally prudent.

Consider a country that wants to use a market price support program to raise producer prices above world market levels and at this price the country is an exporter. If the country cannot afford to use export subsidies and/or fears a WTO challenge, it can limit domestic output to the quantity consumed domestically at the high internal price through production quotas or licenses. This is essentially the way the Canadian milk market is regulated (Meilke *et al.* 1998). In this situation, it is less clear if there is a trade distortion. Domestic consumers are consuming less than they would at world market prices, but domestic output is also limited. Discovering if a country with a market price support program, coupled with domestic supply control, is importing less or exporting more than at world market prices is a challenging empirical task. Most of the 'gains' to producers under domestic supply control come in the form of production quota rents. The original recipients of the production quota get a windfall gain, but this gain becomes a cost of production for all future producers. Again, the country must have tariffs or other border measures high enough to keep cheap foreign products from coming into the domestic market. As a result, the producers of this commodity become ardent protectionists in an effort to maintain their production quota rents. If a country wants to provide income support to producers of a product that does not have significant border protection it can still do so, in a minimally trade distorting fashion, by limiting the quantity on which payments are based.

Production subsidies and the WTO
Given that production subsidies can be trade distorting, what does the WTO have to say about them? Traditionally, the GATT/WTO has been most concerned with what happens at the border and its key principle is one of non-discrimination. Imported and domestic products should be accorded the same treatment; except the imported product may be subject to a negotiated import tariff that applies to all foreign products regardless of

source. In tackling the issue of domestic subsidies defining the word 'subsidy' has proven troublesome (Jackson 1997). Taken to its logical extreme, any government expenditure involves a subsidy. However, it seems clear that most government programs that provide services to its citizenry such as infrastructure, health care, national defense, fire and police protection are of no concern to third countries. Hence, the WTO has to delineate those domestic subsidies that have the potential to harm third countries from those that are a sovereign country's right.

The beginning point of the discussion is GATT'47 where the original Contracting Parties stepped very gingerly into the minefield of domestic subsidies as codified in Article XVI. Article XVI (Subsidies) says that a country that grants or maintains a subsidy that increases its exports or decreases its imports should notify the Contracting Parties about the effects of the subsidy and the reasons for the subsidy. If any Contracting Party felt it had suffered serious prejudice as a result of another country's domestic subsidy it should consult with the country granting the subsidy to discuss the 'possibility of limiting the subsidization'. So while GATT'47 acknowledged that domestic subsidies might harm other countries, the disciplines on them were extremely weak. Jackson traces the evolution of GATT laws applying to domestic production subsidies since 1947, so for this review it is sufficient to jump ahead to GATT'94 and the Agreement on Subsidies and Countervailing Measures (ASCM). Through this Agreement, domestic subsidies were brought under significantly tighter disciplines.

The ASCM begins by defining a subsidy.[7] The ASCM says that a subsidy shall be deemed to exist if there is a contribution by a government or public body. This may entail: (a) direct or indirect transfer of funds; (b) forgone government revenue; (c) provision or purchase of goods or services, other than general infrastructure; or (d) income or price support. However, the ASCM limits the government programs that are actionable by saying the programs must confer a benefit to a specific firm or industry.

In determining if a subsidy is actionable, the ASCM is organized along a traffic light system (Hufbauer and Erb 1984; Jackson 1997). Red light (prohibited) subsidies include export subsidies and subsidies contingent on the use of domestic rather than imported products. These types of subsidies are beyond the scope of this chapter.

Green light subsidies (non-actionable) include all subsidies that are not specific. Such subsidies include those for research that cover only a specified portion of the costs, assistance to disadvantaged regions that are part of a regional development plan, and certain forms of assistance to adopt to new environmental requirements. The 'specificity' test is designed to remove from potential WTO challenge those general tax measures and programs that apply uniformly to all firms in the economy or at least to all firms in a sector of the economy. In economic terms, the programs may not involve lump-sum transfers but because they are generally available they are deemed to have only a minimal effect on resource allocation and production decisions. In addition, there are a large number of specific subsidies that are not going to be challenged because their trade effects are minimal. Subsidies provided to starving poets are unlikely to be challenged because it would be difficult to prove injury. High prices for taxi cabs in Las Vegas are not going to be challenged because, if anything, they will result in people gambling in the Bahamas instead of Las Vegas. In addition, as shown above, importing nations generally benefit from the specific subsidies provided to producers in exporting nations, and are often happy to accept their 'cheap' output. However, especially in developed countries, industries harmed by third country production subsidies are quick to yell 'foul' and their political representatives are quick to listen. As a result, government subsidies targeted to specific industries that are engaged in trade, risk being subjected to countervailing duties and/or challenged at the WTO.

Yellow light (actionable) subsidies are by default anything that isn't red or green. However, for a WTO challenge of domestic subsidies to be successful the subsidies must: (a) injure the domestic industry of another Member; or (b) result in the nullification or impairment of benefits accruing to another Member; or (c) cause serious prejudice to the interests of another Member.[8] An importing country that feels it has been harmed by the subsidies of another WTO member has two potential remedies under the ASCM: (a) asking that a WTO dispute settlement panel be convened to rule on the subsidy under dispute; and/or (b) seeking a countervailing duty to 'offset' the injury its producers face as a result of the unfair trading practice.[9] The situation is different if an exporter feels it is being harmed by the production subsidies used in an importing nation, or by a competing exporter. In this case, a countervailing duty is of no use and it must take its case directly to the WTO. Countervailing duty cases (CVD) are far more numerous than WTO subsidy cases. This frequency of occurrence arises because CVDs are tried under domestic contingency protection laws and it is easier to prove injury when you are an importer.[10] Subsidy cases brought to the WTO have involved aircraft, cotton, dairy products, ships and sugar.

The ASCM also specifies the remedies that are available to combat unfair trading practices. The most popular measure, a countervailing duty, has exactly the same effect as a tariff, raising the price of the imported product in the domestic market. Because of the way subsidies are measured and duties calculated, the protection a countervailing duty gives to domestic producers is almost always higher than what is necessary to offset the 'injury' (Moschini and Meilke 1992; van Duren 1991). This is another reason why countervailing duties are so popular. In addition, once in place, countervailing duties have long lives.[11] In contrast, if a country wins a subsidy dispute at the WTO the defendant is asked to bring their policies in compliance with WTO rules. If a defendant does not comply with the WTO panel decision it can either provide compensation or risk having the Member winning the case apply countermeasures. The record of Members bringing their policies into compliance has been relatively good. Hence, a successful WTO challenge can eliminate the offending measure while a countervailing duty puts economic pressure on the exporter to remove the unfair subsidies.

Conclusions

As indicated at the beginning of this chapter, production subsides are one of the most common forms of government intervention in the economy. The rationale underlying the use of production subsidies range from redistributing income; correcting for market failures; rent seeking behavior by producers to national security concerns. Regardless of their reason for being, production subsidies will continue to influence international trade flows. Whether this affect results in trade disputes, and corresponding settlement measures, depends not only on the economic rationale underlying the production subsidy and its indirect effect on trade, but also on the political landscape of the players involved. Assuming a fair and balanced playing field is not necessarily an option, as many countries (typically developed countries) possess the political and fiscal wherewithal to influence outcomes, trade flows and world prices. Unfortunately, it is often producers in low income countries who pay the price for the policies of rich countries. These countries are also the ones least able to draw upon the trade remedies contained in the WTO rules.

Notes

1. Strategic trade policy that is focused on imperfectly competitive markets is not dealt with in this chapter.
2. Even lump-sum transfers involve the distortion caused by collecting and redistributing tax revenue (Moschini and Sckokai, 1994).
3. The economics of externalities is covered in depth in Cornes and Sandler (1996).
4. In theory state trading importers should not allow domestic prices to exceed world prices by more than their bound *ad valorem* tariff rate.
5. Skully (1999) discusses the various ways import quota rights can be allocated.
6. The compensation should not exceed the cost of using the new technology which raises difficult measurement issues.
7. There are a number of qualifications and exemptions allowed for in the ASCM that are not mentioned in this discussion. Many of these relate to developing countries and to the agricultural sector that is subject to the rules contained in the Agreement on Agriculture (AoA). However, the due restraint clause in the AoA has expired leaving this sector's policies more open to challenges than previously (Steinberg and Josling, 2003).
8. Serious prejudice involves total *ad valorem* subsidization of a product exceeding 5 percent; subsidies to cover operating losses sustained by an industry or enterprise, other than non-recurrent one-time measures; or direct forgiveness of debt.
9. A member country also has recourse to anti-dumping duties that are covered in another chapter in this Handbook as well as provisions that cover fairly traded imports (Wainio 2003).
10. Member countries' contingency protection laws should be based on those in the ASCM.
11. The ASCM introduced a sunset measure that had not existed before.

References

Boughner, D. S., H. de Gorter and I. M. Sheldon (2000), 'The Economics of Two-Tier Tariff-Rate Import Quotas in Agriculture,' *Agricultural and Resource Economics Review*, **29**(1): 58–69.
Buchanan, J. M., R. D. Tollison and G. Tullock (eds) (1980), *Toward a Theory of the Rent-Seeking Society*, College Station, TX: Texas A&M University Press.
Chen, K. and K. D. Meilke (1998), 'A Reevaluation of Canada's Safety Net Programs for Agriculture,' *Canadian Journal of Agricultural Economics*, **46**(1): 37–52.
Cornes, R. and T. Sandler (1996), *The Theory of Externalities, Public Goods and Club Goods*, Cambridge: Cambridge University Press.
de Gorter, H., J. D. Nielson and G. C. Rausser (1992), 'Productive and Predatory Public Policies: Research Expenditures and Producer Subsidies in Agriculture,' *American Journal of Agricultural Economics*, **74**(1): 27–37.
de Gorter, H. and I. M. Sheldon (2000), 'Issues in the Administration of Tariff-Rate Import Quotas in the Agreement on Agriculture in the WTO: An Introduction,' *Agricultural and Resource Economics Review*, **29**(1): 54–7.
Gardner, B. L. (1988), *The Economics of Agricultural Policies*, New York: Macmillian Publishing Co.
Houck, J. P. (1986), *Elements of Agricultural Trade Policies*, New York: Macmillan Publishing Co.
Hufbauer, G. C. and J. S. Erb (1984), *Subsidies in International Trade*, Cambridge, MA: The MIT Press.
Jackson, J. H. (1997), *The World Trading System* (2nd edn), Cambridge, MA: The MIT Press.
Just, R. E., D. L. Hueth and A. Schmitz (1982), *Applied Welfare Economics and Public Policy*, Englewood Cliffs, NJ: Prentice-Hall.
Meilke, K. D., R. Sarker and D. Le Roy (1998), 'The Potential for Increased Trade in Milk and Dairy Products between Canada and the United States Under Trade Liberalization,' *Canadian Journal of Economics*, **46**(2): 149–71.
Meilke, K. D., J. Rude, M. Burfisher and M. Bredahl (2001), 'Market Access: Issues and Options in the Agricultural Negotiations,' Commissioned Paper 14. International Agricultural Trade Research Consortium, St Paul, MN.
Moschini, G. (1991), 'Economic Issues in Tariffication: An Overview,' *Journal of Agricultural Economics*, **5**(1): 101–20.
Moschini, G. and K. D. Meilke (1992), 'Production Subsidy and Countervailing Duties in Vertically Related Markets: The Hog-Pork Case Between Canada and the United States,' *American Journal of Agricultural Economics*, **74**(4): 951–61.

Moschini, G. and P. Sckokai (1994), 'Efficiency of Decoupled Farm Programs under Distortionary Taxation,' *American Journal of Agricultural Economics*, **76**(3): 362–70.

Mueller, Dennis C. (2003), *Public Choice III*, Cambridge: Cambridge University Press.

Norton, G. W. and J. S. Davis (1981), 'Evaluating Returns to Agricultural Research: A Review,' *American Journal of Agricultural Economics*, **63**(4): 685–99.

OECD (2003), *Agricultural Policies in OECD Countries: Monitoring and Evaluation*, Paris.

Paarlberg, P. L., M. E. Bredahl and J. G. Lee (2002), 'Multifunctionality and Agricultural Trade Negotiations,' *Review of Agricultural Economics*, **24**(2): 322–35.

Peterson, J. M., R. N. Boisvert and H. de Gorter (2002), 'Environmental Policies for a Multifunctional Agricultural Sector in Open Economies,' *European Review of Agricultural Economics*, **29**(4): 423–43.

Rude, J. (2001), 'Under the Green Box: The WTO and Farm Subsidies,' *Journal of World Trade*, **35**(5): 1015–33.

Schmitz, A., H. Furtan and K. Baylis (2002), *Agricultural Policy, Agribusiness and Rent Seeking Behaviour*, Toronto: University of Toronto Press.

Skully, D. (1999), *The Economics of Tariff-Rate Quota Administration*, Economic Research Service, US Department of Agriculture, Washington, DC, September.

Steinberg, R. H. and T. E. Josling (2003), 'When the Peace Ends: The Vulnerability of EC and US Agricultural Subsidies to WTO Legal Challenge,' *Journal of International Economic Law*, **6**(2): 369–417.

Swinnen, J. F. M. and H. de Gorter (1993), 'Why Small Groups and Low Income Sectors Obtain Subsidies: The "Altruistic" Side of a "Self-Interested" Government,' *Economics and Politics*, **5**(3): 285–93.

Tollison, R. D. (1982), 'Rent Seeking: A Survey,' *Kyklos*, **35**(4): 575–602.

Van Duren. E. (1991), 'An Economics Analysis of Alternative Countervailing Duties,' *Journal of World Trade*, **25**(1): 91–105.

Wainio, J., L. M. Young and K. D. Meilke (2003), 'Trade Remedy Actions in NAFTA: Agriculture and Agri-Food Industries,' *World Economy*, **26**(7): 1041–65.

Zwart, A. C. and D. Blandford (1989), 'Market Intervention and International Price Stability,' *American Journal of Agricultural Economics*, **71**(2): 379–88.

Zwart, A. C. and K. D. Meilke (1979), 'The Influence of Domestic Agricultural Policies on International Price Stability in the World Wheat Economy,' *American Journal of Agricultural Economics*, **61**(4): 434–47.

28 Strategic export subsidies
Stefan Lutz

Introduction

Export subsidies are payments by the government to support the export of a specified product. They typically take the form of a fixed payment per unit exported (a specific subsidy) or of a payment as a percentage of export value (an *ad-valorem* subsidy).[1]

Most countries provide subsidies to agricultural products as a support for domestic farmers.[2] However, as a result of the Uruguay Round, participating countries have agreed to set quantity ceilings by commodity and budgetary limits to possible export subsidies.[3]

Under perfect competition, an export subsidy normally decreases the price of the exported good abroad, but raises the price of the exportable at home. The situation described here is for a 'large' country, that is a country which does affect its terms of trade – the ratio of price of exportables to price of importables – by its own supplies and demands in the world markets. Here, exporters and foreign consumers gain while domestic consumers and foreign competing producers lose. Since the subsidy is costly, government will have 'negative revenues'. Note in particular that in the case of a subsidy the terms-of-trade effect will go 'in the wrong direction' since the subsidy and its supply effect will tend to decrease the world price of the exportable, adding another element to the domestic welfare loss. As a consequence, summing up all the welfare effects for the country applying the subsidy reveals that national welfare falls. Since the subsidy introduces a price distortion leading to misallocation of resources, the gross welfare effect is negative, even if the gain of foreign consumers (and the loss of foreign producers, of course) is taken into account. In the case of a 'small' country – one where world prices of its exportables and importables are unaffected by the policy – there will be no welfare losses due to world price changes, but the negative result of a net welfare loss still remains. In this case, domestic consumers are not harmed, but profit gains by domestic producers are less than the total cost of the subsidy and the loss to consumers.

According to Brander (1995), 'strategic trade policy [is] trade policy that conditions or alters a strategic relationship between firms'. This relationship refers to the situation when firms 'have a mutually recognized strategic interdependence', as is normally the case in an oligopolistic market. In an oligopolistic market, the number of supplying firms is so small that everyone recognizes and reacts on a change of strategy – such as a price change or a change in quantities offered.

In particular, if a domestic industry competes with foreign producers in a third export market, unilateral export subsidies by the domestic government can serve to shift market share and profits from the foreign competitors to the domestic industry. The net welfare effect for the subsidizing country may be positive even if the resulting terms-of-trade effect is negative.[4] This can be the case in oligopolistic markets where domestic firms and foreign firms compete for their respective exports in a third market by choosing quantities to be exported.

However, this result is far from stable. If firms compete by setting prices rather than quantities, export subsidies will always lead to domestic losses. Domestic welfare will also decrease if the subsidy is set too high, if the number of domestic firms gets rather larger, or if the foreign government retaliates with a similar subsidy of its own. Generally, these results carry over to the case of reciprocal markets, where foreigners sell their products in the home market while domestic firms export into their competitors' markets. While GATT rules prohibit export subsidies by developed countries on industrial products, it may be very difficult in practice to identify all such subsidization. As a consequence, subsidies for industrial products remained a practice even among developed countries. In addition, over time, direct export subsidies were replaced by domestic policy measures achieving similar effects. A major instrument of this kind is the subsidization of research and development.[5]

The remainder of this chapter is organized as follows. The next section discusses perfect competition, while the third section introduces the oligopolistic case with exports into a third market. In the fourth section, the case of reciprocal exports into each other's markets is presented. Empirical applications of export subsidies are briefly reviewed in the fifth section. Alternative instruments, such as research and development subsidies are covered in the sixth section. The last section concludes.

Export subsidies under perfect competition[6]

Under perfect competition, an export subsidy will always help the domestic industry, but will never benefit a country on the whole. The main reason is that subsidy outlays by the government will always be greater than profit gains by the subsidized industry. When the country is 'small', that is when it cannot affect world prices of its exportables and importables by its own export supply and import demand, domestic welfare is not directly affected by world price changes. The effects on exporters and on government outlays are illustrated in Figure 28.1.

Let S be domestic export supply and D^* world net demand at fixed world price P_w. Let the domestic market price be $P_s = P_w + s$, where s is the per-unit subsidy, so that the home industry receives a per-unit revenue equal to the world price plus the subsidy rate. The quantities exported under free trade and under the subsidy regime, respectively, are given

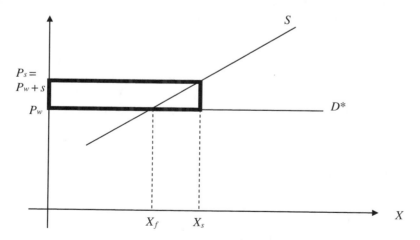

Figure 28.1   Export subsidy under perfect competition: small country

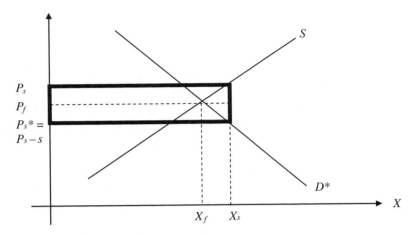

Figure 28.2   Export subsidy under perfect competition: large country

by X_f and by X_s. Hence the cost of the subsidy is given by the area of the rectangle (s * X_s). However, the increase in domestic industry profits is given by that subsidy amount minus the excess cost beyond world price of the additional exports, that is minus the triangle lying under the supply curve between X_f and X_s. Hence total welfare loss is equal to $[(X_s - X_f) * s/2]$.

The situation described above is for a 'small' country, that is a country which does not affect its terms of trade – the ratio of price of exportables to price of importables – by its own supplies and demands in the world markets. In contrast, a 'large' country will affect its terms of trade by its own export supply – here specifically the world price of its exportable will decrease, that is the terms-of-trade effect will go 'in the wrong direction' and therefore will add another element to the domestic welfare loss.

In Figure 28.2, again let S be domestic export supply and D^* world import demand. World demand is now downward sloping so that the free-trade world price P_f is now determined by the intersection between demand and supply. Let the domestic market price be P_s again, but now the price paid by foreigners will be $P^*_s = P_s - s$, where s is the per-unit subsidy. The reduction in price from P_f to P^*_s is the (negative) terms-of-trade effect. Note also, that at home, the price of the exportable rises to P_s;[7] domestic consumers would consequently be hurt in the process. The total welfare loss increases compared to the 'small'-country case. In both cases, there is a deadweight loss of $[(X_s - X_f) * s/2]$, corresponding here to the triangle between X_f, X_s, P_s, and P_f. In addition, there will be another loss term caused by the terms-of-trade effect and corresponding to the area $(P_f - P_s) * X_f$ plus $(P_f - P_s) * (X_s - X_f) \sim /2$.

In summary, under perfect competition, an export subsidy per se cannot be used to raise the net welfare of a particular country, however it may still increase profits and international market shares of the subsidized industries.[8]

Profit shifting when competing in exports to a third market[9]

Under imperfect competition the foreign industry as well as the domestic industry may make positive economic profits from the outset.[10] These profits are the outcome of

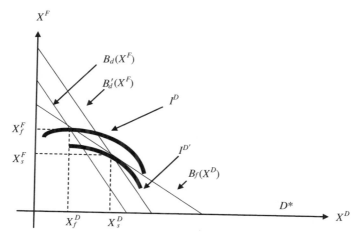

Figure 28.3   Export subsidy in a Cournot Duopoly

strategic interaction between all competing firms and, therefore, introduce the incentive for strategic trade policy by governments. Governments' policy interaction here is called 'strategic trade policy' since it alters the strategic relationship between domestic and foreign firms to give the former a competitive advantage. A major goal of these policies is to enable the domestic industry to increase its profits (and market share, and so on) to the detriment of the foreign industry's profits (and market share, and so on); if successful, this is called 'profit-shifting'. Profit shifting may be a possible outcome of trade policy even if the resulting terms-of-trade effect is negative, that is if the policy leads to a reduction of the domestic industry's export prices.

The mechanics of profit-shifting are easily illustrated using simple duopoly market where a domestic firm and a foreign firm compete for their respective exports in a third market. Firms' products are assumed to be identical so that they are perfect substitutes for each other as far as consumers in the export market are concerned. Firms compete by choosing their quantities shipped to the market and sell both at the same resulting equilibrium price. The strategic interaction between firms arising from such a situation is illustrated in Figure 28.3, where X^D denotes domestic exports and X^F denotes foreign exports, $B_d(X^F)$ and $B_f(X^D)$ denote the so-called Cournot reaction functions of the firms, and I^D is one of the domestic firms' iso-profit curves.[11] The Cournot reaction functions give firms' profit-maximizing quantity choice given the competitors' quantity chosen; so $B_d(X^F)$ shows the profit-maximizing quantities chosen by the domestic firm at any level of foreign quantity X^F. A market equilibrium is reached, where the two reaction functions intersect (at X^F_f, X^D_f), since either firm maximizes profits given the other firm's choice.[12]

At the equilibrium without subsidies X^F_f, X^D_f, the slope of the domestic iso-profit curve I^D at the equilibrium is horizontal. Since domestic profits unambiguously increase as the foreign firm's quantity offered falls, moving below a given iso-profit curve increases profits. As a consequence, this equilibrium is not the outcome with maximal profits along the foreign firm's best response. This maximum would be at X^F_s, X^D_s, where the domestic iso-profit $I^{D'}$ is just tangent to the foreign firm's best response.

In theory, the domestic government could now choose a specific export subsidy such that the domestic firm's new reaction function goes straight through X^F_s, X^D_s, thereby increasing and in effect maximizing attainable domestic profits net of the subsidy. Domestic welfare would be unambiguously increased by this measure while the foreign industry would lose profits. Coincidentally, consumers in the third market gain by both a reduced price and an increase in total quantities sold.[13]

However, this result is far from stable. If the subsidy is set too high, it will shift $B'_d(X^F)$ further and to the right of the intersection of the initial domestic iso-profit curve with the foreign best response, leading to a decrease in domestic profits net of subsidies. Furthermore, with domestic and foreign oligopolies, the outcome depends on the relative size of the domestic *vis-à-vis* the foreign industry. As the number of domestic firms N gets large relative to the number of foreign firms, N^*, a domestic subsidy increases the output of all domestic rivals thus depressing possible domestic profit increases. In the limit, as N gets very large, none of the domestic firms makes any profits and there is only a negative terms-of-trade effect.[14]

If firms compete by setting prices rather than quantities, that is they compete in a Bertrand market, export subsidies will always lead to domestic losses.[15]

Lastly, if the foreign government retaliates with subsidies of its own, both industries' profits net of subsidies will fall. Hence both countries involved in that kind of trade war will suffer welfare losses, whereas consumers in the third market gain due to increases in quantities and falling prices.[16] This situation constitutes a typical 'prisoner's dilemma' for the governments involved since either government has an incentive to set a positive subsidy but in the resulting outcome both countries will end up with welfare losses as a result.[17]

Strategic exports subsidies and retaliation in reciprocal markets[18]

If exporters compete in reciprocal markets, that is the domestic industry exports into the foreign industry's home market and *vice versa*, the results discussed for a third-market situation still hold under fairly general assumptions.[19] The case of tariffs has been analyzed explicitly for a Cournot oligopoly in Brander and Spencer (1984). Export subsidies in reciprocal markets are analyzed in Dixit (1984, 1988).

In the case of reciprocal markets, the damaging results of conflicting trade policies are somewhat alleviated by their positive effects on consumers. For a symmetric case, where home and foreign markets as well as home and foreign industries are of the same size, half of consumer benefits resulting from identical export subsidies set by both countries would accrue to domestic consumers. The remaining question, of course, is whether these consumer benefits could make an international subsidy war beneficial for the home country.

Brander and Krugman (1983) show that international oligopolistic markets may exhibit market outcomes with cross-hauling of identical products out of and into the foreign market, even in the presence of trade costs.[20] This has been labeled 'reciprocal dumping', since the domestic industry's price charged abroad will be typically less than its domestic price plus the transport cost. Since trade here leads to a beneficial increase in competition in each market while incurring additional trade costs, the net effect is ambiguous. This effect is normally negative at very high trade costs and positive at very low trade costs. In particular, if trade costs are just prohibitive so that no trade occurs, then a marginal decrease of these costs introducing trade would lead to welfare losses. What follows directly from this analysis is that with very high trade costs, any export subsidies set at identical levels by both governments would be welfare reducing since their effect would be equal to that of the trade cost reduction analyzed here minus the additional outlays for the export subsidies.

Using a similar argument, it can be shown that if trade costs are close to zero, a small export subsidy, again set identically by both governments, could improve welfare for each country. However, strategic interaction between governments would again lead to a 'prisoner's dilemma' result where both governments set high subsidies and all countries lose due to excessive 'reciprocal dumping'.

Some empirical evidence

Since 1956, GATT rules prohibit export subsidies by developed countries on industrial products. Primary products, such as agricultural products are exempt from this prohibition. Furthermore, developing countries may also subsidize industrial products to temporarily support the viability of an otherwise nonviable, emerging industry.[21]

Since it is extraordinarily difficult in many cases to actually identify if export subsidization is taking place, subsidies for industrial products remained a practice even among developed countries. Brander (1995) suggests cases of interventionist policies applied by countries such as Japan, Korea and France. In the United States, these policies included three major elements. Research and development in the university research sector has been subsidized publicly. Second, defense and space programs are publicly funded. Third, the Export–Import Bank of the US has provided export subsidies to high-tech industries, including the aircraft industry.[22]

GATT/WTO takes account of this reality by allowing defensive or retaliatory mechanisms in cases where illicit subsidies are identified. Central to these measures are countervailing duties, which may be applied by a country on illegally subsidized imports. Consequently, subsidies and countervailing duties are covered under the same international legal agreements.[23]

Trade in agricultural products is still subject to substantial export subsidies. This is especially the case in the European Union. In Europe, export subsidies are an integral part of the Common Agricultural Policy (CAP) designed to support local farmers. The CAP absorbs over 40 percent of the EU's budget and contains export subsidies of several billion euros annually. The United States has also provided agricultural export subsidies in the order of magnitude of one billion dollars yearly. In the 1980s, the prevailing agricultural trade war between the US and the EU significantly depressed the world price of many agricultural goods. Since the GATT Uruguay Round concluded with only an interim agreement on reducing agricultural subsidies, new rounds of agricultural negotiations began in the year 2000. As Gaisford and Kerr (2003) report, initial positions by the major agricultural trading nations were very diverse and there still seemed to be little chance to come to an agreement. While some reduction of outlays on the support of agricultural goods was agreed upon, a major part of the concerned trade in agricultural goods is still open to negotiation.

Domestic industrial policy as alternatives to export subsidies[24]

Since direct subsidies on exports of industrial products are prohibited under general GATT rules, countries might have an incentive to use domestic policies to achieve similar results. Under general conditions, the results of a particular export subsidy of, say, an amount of s

per unit of exports, can be replicated by a combination of a production subsidy of s per unit and a domestic consumption tax of the same per-unit amount. However, subsidizing production directly also entails a direct subsidy to that part of production that is subsequently exported.

In contrast, if government support takes one of the forms discussed in the previous section – for example providing public-sector research, offering government contracts, or subsidizing firms' own investments in research and development, the case of an illicit export subsidy is much harder to verify.

The case for research and development subsidies instead of export subsidies was first considered by Spencer and Brander (1983). In cases where unilateral export subsidies are optimal for a country, research and development subsidies are only second-best. But in contrast to export subsidies, unilateral research and development subsidies are welfare-improving for the applying country irrespective of the nature of the product-market competition. This welfare-increasing effect is remarkably robust, as has been noted by Leahy and Neary (2001).[25] But when reciprocal markets are considered, again there is not yet convincing evidence that all countries involved can win from a research and development subsidy race.[26]

Summary and conclusions

Export subsidies per se may benefit a particular industry or economic sector, but they often do not improve the overall welfare of the country applying them. Nevertheless, benefits to specific sectors of an economy, such as agriculture in the EU, continue to provide powerful motives for continued application of these policies. Due to current international trade agreements, export subsidies prevail only in agriculture and in infant-industry protection by developing countries. Among developed countries, subsidies benefiting industrial products are more likely to take the form of investment or research and development subsidies. Subsidies on investments or research and development are, at least as a unilateral measure, much more robust in providing a welfare benefit to the country applying them. These benefits are probably much less sure when other countries are sufficiently powerful to consider retaliation.

Acknowledgements

The author gratefully acknowledges the continued support of the Center for European Integration Studies (ZEI), Bonn.

Notes

1. For a general introduction, see, for example, Suranovic (1999), Ch. 10, Helpman and Krugman (1989), Ch. 2, Markusen *et al.* (1995), Ch. 15.3.
2. For example in the United States the former Export Enhancement Program (EEP) and in the European Union the Common Agricultural Policy (CAP). The European Union spends by far the most on these kinds of subsidies with in excess of USD 4 billion per year.
3. Export subsidies on industrial products have been prohibited for most products under General Agreement on Tariffs and Trade (GATT) rules since 1956 but permitted for primary products such as agricultural products. On export subsidies for agricultural products, see Gaisford and Kerr (2003). World Trade Organization (WTO) and GATT trade agreement documentation is available under www.wto.org. US trade policy information is available under www.usitc.gov and under www.ita.doc.gov.
4. See Brander and Spencer (1985), who cover the case of firms competing by setting quantities (Cournot).
5. See Spencer and Brander (1985), Neary and Leahy (2000), Leahy and Neary (2001).
6. See Markusen *et al.* (1995), Ch. 15.3, Helpman and Krugman (1989), Ch. 2.3.

7. Because the opportunity cost of selling the exportable at home is the export revenue forgone, that is foreign price plus the subsidy.
8. Note that if the country question can affect its terms of trade, the optimal unilateral policy here would even be a (small) export tax, where tax revenue paid by foreigners due to the change in export price outweighs domestic welfare losses.
9. See Brander (1995), Section 3, Helpman and Krugman (1989), Ch. 5.
10. While under perfect competition, all firms make 'zero profits' which means that they just earn enough to afford their owners the average market return on capital invested.
11. The iso-profit curve gives the locus of combinations of domestic and foreign quantities where domestic profits stay constant at some fixed level.
12. This is called a Nash-equilibrium in quantities or Cournot–Nash equilibrium.
13. Total quantity increases given a move along the foreign firm's reaction function, since a given quantity increase by the competitor will be countered by an underproportionate decrease in own quantity accompanied by falling prices.
14. See Brander (1995), Section 3.2.3. Note also that this result is reversed if N stays small but N^* gets very large.
15. See Helpman and Krugman (1989), Ch. 5.3.
16. See Helpman and Krugman (1989), Ch. 5.6.
17. See Brander (1995), Section 3.2.1., Brander and Spencer (1985).
18. See Brander (1995), Section 4, Helpman and Krugman (1989), Ch. 5.6), Brander and Spencer (1984).
19. See Brander (1995), Section 4.4.
20. In the current context, trade costs are transport costs and all other additional expenses arising from exporting a particular good.
21. See www.wto.org. Countries that are specifically allowed to use industrial export subsidies include Bolivia, Cameroon, Congo, Côte d'Ivoire, Dominican Republic, Egypt, Ghana, Guatemala, Guyana, India, Indonesia, Kenya, Morocco, Nicaragua, Nigeria, Pakistan, Philippines, Senegal, Sri Lanka and Zimbabwe.
22. For a detailed discussion of further cases, see Cohen and Zysman (1987) and Tyson (1992). In the US, the International Trade Commission presents information on countervailing duty investigations under www.usitc.gov. Information on countervailing duty decisions is also available under www.ita.doc.gov.
23. See Staiger (1995), Section 7.1 and the 'Agreement on Subsidies and Countervailing Measures' at www.wto.org.
24. See Eaton and Grossman (1986).
25. For more evidence on this, see also Bagwell and Staiger (1994), Maggi (1996), Neary and Leahy (2000), Jinji (2003) and Herguera and Lutz (1998, 2003).
26. However, Jinji (2003) presents a reciprocal market case with differentiated products and two governments simultaneously improving welfare due to subsidizing.

References

Bagwell, K. and R. W. Staiger (1994), 'The Sensitivity of Strategic and Corrective R&D Policy in Oligopolistic Industries,' *Journal of International Economics*, **36**, 133–50.

Brander, J. A. (1995), 'Strategic Trade Policy,' in G. M.Grossman, and K. Rogoff, *Handbook of International Economics, Volume 3*, Amsterdam: Elsevier.

Brander, J. A. and P. R. Krugman (1983), 'A "Reciprocal Dumping" Model of International Trade,' *Journal of International Economics*, **15**, 313–23.

Brander, J. A. and B. J. Spencer (1984), 'Tariff Protection and Imperfect Competition,' in H. Kierzkowski (ed.), *Monopolistic Competition and International Trade*, Oxford: Clarendon Press.

Brander, J. A. and B. J. Spencer (1985), 'Export Subsidies and Market Share Rivalry,' *Journal of International Economics*, **18**, 83–100.

Cohen, S. S. and J. Zysman (1987), *Manufacturing Matters: The Myth of the Post-industrial Economy*, New York: Basic Books.

Dixit, A. K. (1984), 'International Trade Policy for Oligopolistic Industries,' *Economic Journal*, **94** supplement, 1–16.

Dixit, A. K. (1988), 'Anti-dumping and Countervailing Duties under Oligopoly,' *European Economic Review*, **32**, 55–86.

Eaton, J. and G. M. Grossman (1986), 'Optimal Trade and Industrial Policy under Oligopoly,' *Quarterly Journal of Economics*, **101**, 383–406.

Gaisford, J. D. and W. A. Kerr (2003), 'Deadlock in Geneva: The Battle Over Export Subsidies in Agriculture,' *International Economic Journal*, **17**(2), 1–17.

Helpman, E. and P. R. Krugman (1989), *Trade Policy and Market Structure*, Cambridge, MA: MIT Press.

Herguera, I. and S. Lutz (1998), 'Oligopoly and Quality Leapfrogging,' *The World Economy*, **21**(1), 75–94.

Herguera, I. and S. Lutz (2003), 'The Effect of Subsidies to Product Innovation on International Competition,' *Economics of Innovation and New Technology*, **12**(5), 465–80.

Jinji, N. (2003), 'Strategic Policy for Product R&D with Symmetric Costs,' *Canadian Journal of Economics*, **36**(4), 993–1006.

Leahy, D. and J. P. Neary (2001), 'Robust Rules for Industrial Policy in Open Economies,' *Journal of International Trade and Economic Development*, **10**(4), 393–409.

Maggi, G. (1996), 'Strategic Trade Policies with Endogenous Mode of Competition,' *American Economic Review*, **86**, 237–58.

Markusen, J., J. Melvin, W. Kaempfer and K. Maskus (1995), *International Trade: Theory and Evidence*, New York: McGraw-Hill.

Neary, J. P. and D. Leahy (2000), 'Strategic Trade and Industrial Policy Towards Dynamic Oligopolies,' *Economic Journal*, **110**, 484–508.

Spencer, B. J. and J. A. Brander (1983), 'International R&D rivalry and industrial strategy,' *Review of Economic Studies*, **50**, 707–22.

Staiger, R. W. (1995), 'International Rules and Institutions for Trade Policy,' in G. M. Grossman and K. Rogoff, *Handbook of International Economics, Volume 3*, Amsterdam: Elsevier.

Suranovic, S. (1999), 'International Trade Theory and Policy Lecture Notes,' Washington, DC: George Washington University.

Tyson, L. (1992), *Who's Bashing Whom: Trade Conflict in High-technology Industries*, Washington, DC: Institute for International Economics.

29 Government procurement
Linda M. Young

Introduction
The sheer size of government procurement elevates interest in the economic efficiency and the domestic and international welfare consequences of how governments purchase goods and services. Government procurement accounts for nearly 20 percent of GDP in some countries, and all levels of government, including national, subnational and municipal governments are large purchasers of goods, services and construction services. Scrutiny over government procurement used to be exercised largely on the domestic level, with concern about policies favoring domestic suppliers over foreign ones, and the effectiveness government procurement to achieve social goals. Finally, there is perpetual concern over the possibility of corruption influencing the award of government contracts.

Domestic governments continue to reform and improve their government procurement systems to reduce costs and raise standards of efficiency, transparency and competition. Attention devoted to government procurement has heightened on the international level. Multilateral institutions, such as the World Bank, have increased efforts to assist developing countries to improve their government procurement systems as part of a larger endeavor to improve governance. Some transition economies are challenged to meet standards for their government procurement systems in order to join the European Union (EU). The World Trade Organization (WTO) is working on an agreement to create standards for transparency in government procurement, an initial stage to move toward a comprehensive multilateral agreement to open government procurement to international trade from the current limited, plurilateral agreement.

This chapter will discuss efforts to improve government procurement systems on both the domestic and the international level, as the two are deeply connected.

How significant is government procurement?
The OECD (2002) has undertaken a comprehensive study on the size of government procurement. Their objective is to provide information and analysis to support the WTO negotiations on government procurement by estimating the amount of government procurement that can be traded. National accounts data, available for a wide range of countries, are used to estimate the value of goods and services purchased by the government. The OECD estimates that for all levels of government, total expenditures are 19.96 percent of GDP for OECD countries, valued at US$4733 billion US dollars (Table 29.1). For non-OECD countries, total government procurement accounts for 14.48 percent of GDP, valued at US$816 billion. The authors note that this is equivalent to around 82 percent of 1989 world merchandise and service exports. Subtraction of expenditures on defense and employee compensation produces estimates of the potentially tradable market for government procurement of 7.57 percent of GDP for OECD countries and 5 percent for non-OECD countries, valued at US$1795 and US$287 billion respectively.

Table 29.1   Government procurement ratios in OECD and non-OECD countries

General government	Percent of GDP (weighted average)		Value (US$ billions)	
	OECD	non-OECD	OECD	non-OECD
Consumption expenditure	17.09	14.12	4053.1	4849.0
Less compensation	6.31	4.82		
Less defense	14.17	9.54		
Less compensation and defense	4.73	2.09		
Total expenditure	19.96	14.48	4733.8	816.9
Less compensation	9.17	6.89		
Less compensation and defense	7.57	5.10	1795.3	287.7

Source: OECD (2002)

If non-core defense items were opened up for foreign competition, then the size of the market would significantly expand.

Other methods have been used to estimate the size of government expenditures, but these methods are hampered by inconsistent data making it difficult to produce cross country comparisons or aggregates (Audet 2002).

Rules for government procurement
Rules for government procurement are enacted by domestic governments and a great deal of variation has existed between countries. The United Nations Commission on International Trade Law (UNCITRAL 2004) developed model law for government procurement of goods, construction services and services. This work, begun in 1989, culminated in the adoption by the UN General Assembly of the UNCITRAL Model Law on Procurement of Goods, Construction and Services (Hunja 1998; Beviglia-Zampetti 1997). This model law provides a set of 'best practices' for countries seeking to update or reform their government procurement practices. In particular, transition economies and developing countries have adopted variants of the model law for their government procurement systems. Beviglia-Zampetti (1997) concludes that the model law balances the need to accommodate social objectives with mechanisms to create competition and trade.

Many authors discuss the procedures required to create a competitive and transparent system of government procurement (Arrowsmith 2003; Evenett 2002; Arrowsmith and Davies 1998). Central to government procurement policies are rules governing the process of tendering for contracts, evaluating bids, making awards, and notifying unsuccessful applicants. Another key ingredient of best practices is provision for redress by suppliers who submitted a bid but were not awarded a contract (Hunja 1998).

The type of tendering used is a key factor determining the level of transparency and competition in the award of government contracts to businesses (Mattoo 1997). There are three types of tendering producing different levels of competition and transparency. In open tendering all interested suppliers are invited to submit bids. Selective tendering is when the government has screened suppliers to ensure they meet criteria and the bid is open only to screened applicants. Finally, limited tendering is when the contracting agency elicits a bid from specific suppliers and there is no open competition.

How domestic bias is introduced

Most governments hold conflicting objectives for government procurement policy. As pressure on government spending has increased, many governments have placed a premium on achieving value for money. In most conditions, this goal is best achieved through transparent and open access to government contracts resulting in competitive outcomes and low prices. At the same time, realization of a fully competitive system is frequently comprised by the government's desire to achieve social goals, such as assisting disadvantaged groups within their society.

Governments also frequently adopt policies that favor domestic suppliers as a whole *vis-à-vis* foreign suppliers, with a desire to give domestic industries assistance and to keep government funds in the domestic economy. Many policies have been used to accomplish these ends including price preferences, whole or partial import bans, or additional requirements on foreign suppliers, such as requiring technology transfer, local content or investment. More covert forms of discrimination against foreign suppliers include selective tendering to unofficially exclude foreign suppliers, and publishing tenders or writing technical specifications in a manner to make it difficult for foreign suppliers to compete (Trebilcock and Howse 1995).

The most extreme form of preference for domestic firms is a ban on foreign suppliers. Baldwin and Richardson evaluate import bans in a frequently referenced 1972 work. Their insight is that if the amount demanded by the government is less than domestic supply, then the ban will not distort the economy. In this case, based on a perfectly competitive market with constant returns to scale, government demand is satisfied by domestic suppliers, and excess private demand is satisfied by imports. In essence, a shift in government demand to domestic suppliers is offset with an equal shift in domestic demand for imports, leaving both production and consumption unchanged.

Baldwin and Richardson's early work provides a springboard for further analysis of the impact of government procurement policies. Trionfetti (2000) argues that developing countries are less likely to produce the services and manufactured goods demanded by the government. If local supply is small relative to demand, then it is more likely that policies creating a domestic bias will distort markets. In the developed country context, Arrowsmith (2003) notes that Baldwin's insight has limited applicability to the actual markets in which government procurement occurs. She notes that a large portion of government purchasing occurs in sectors characterized by increasing returns to scale and monopolistic competition.

A policy frequently used by governments to create domestic bias is a price preference. In this case foreign bids are accepted only if the lowest bid is a specified percentage lower than the most competitive domestic bid. Deltas and Evenett (1997) find that price preference policies generate only modest welfare gains at best, but as firms profits increase, there are important distributional impacts. They argue that the rents obtained by domestic firms create a constituency against trade agreements that would eliminate domestic bias.

McAfee and McMillan (1989) assess the role played by imperfect information so that bidders have better information about their own costs than those of their competitors, and use a scenario in which foreign firms have lower costs than domestic firms. In the absence of discrimination, foreign firms will bid just below what they believe domestic firms will bid, even though their costs are lower. The optimal strategy by the government is to favor domestic firms with a price differential so that foreign firms must lower their bids. Both Mattoo (1997) and Arrowsmith (2003) note that this literature is similar to strategic trade policy in that government intervention may be optimal under very specific conditions. The authors note that the same cautions applied to strategic trade policy apply here, as difficulties in identifying optimal intervention, and in avoiding capture by rent-seeking special interest groups, leads to the rule-of-thumb of no intervention.

The 'Buy American Act' provides an example of a US policy that incorporates both an import ban and a price differential. The Act, implemented in 1933, bans the government from procuring goods from foreign suppliers, unless the domestic price exceeds the import price by a specified margin (WTO 1996). The price margin used varies by agency, with many civilian agencies using 12 percent and the Department of Defense using 50 percent.

The complexity and diversity of policies affecting government procurement have made it difficult for economists to estimate their impact. Instead, several studies have estimated the degree of domestic preference by comparing import penetration in the private sector with import penetration in government procurement. Baldwin (1970), Francois *et al.* (1997) and Trionfetti (2000) all take this approach under the assumption that the government will import the same percentage of consumption that the private sector does. All studies find substantial domestic preference margins in government purchasing.

Social policy
Social policy may include discrimination in favor of regions or disadvantaged groups or actions to promote human rights on a domestic or international level (McCrudden 1998). A variety of mechanisms exist to achieve these goals. A quota may be determined for suppliers meeting particular qualifications. An obligation not to discriminate on the basis of gender may simply be included in a contract with a supplier, or the supplier may need to provide statistics on the workforce gender composition, or be required to hire an equal opportunity officer, or to use preferential hiring practices. Interpretation of the compatibility of state social policy with the non-discrimination mandate in some regional trade agreements, such as EU procurement policy, is unclear and is being developed through court cases (McCrudden 1998). The effectiveness of these types of polices has not been broadly studied despite their prevalence.

Corruption
As discussed above, open and transparent government procurement systems offer benefits from competition between suppliers. Another goal of many government procurement systems is to eliminate corruption and cronyism. Government corruption can be viewed in economic terms as a problem of agency, as the government procurer is an agent for the public, but can lack adequate incentives to work on behalf of the public (Mattoo 1997). Moral hazard results in collusion between the agent and suppliers. Taxpayers, as a diffuse group, have insufficient incentive to monitor agency behavior closely enough to minimize the possibility of corruption (Laffont and Tirole 1993).

Corruption can occur through bribes paid to government officials, for example, in return for preferential treatment in inclusion of a list of qualified bidders, or writing a bid to favor a particular contractor, or for award of the bid itself. The economic impact of the bribe depends on both its size and other distortions introduced into the economy (Rose-Ackerman 1996). Rose-Ackerman argues that distortions from bribery extend beyond allocation of a contract to a party who is not the most appropriate supplier, as the need to pay bribes may pose a significant barrier to entry for some firms. Furthermore, success in bribery is likely to encourage firms to attempt to secure other benefits from the state in the same manner, and provides bureaucrats with the incentive to implement further controls.

Efforts to reduce corruption in government procurement generally include an increased level of monitoring and accountability in the award and supervision of government contracts. Work by Ades and Di Tella (1997) investigates the role of lax monitoring and lack of competition on the level of corruption. They find empirical support for a positive relationship between those variables and the level of corruption.

The World Bank has undertaken a significant initiative to assist developing countries in improvement of their government procurement systems. Hoekman (1998) estimates that on average, 18 percent of low-income developing country non-defense government procurement is funded by multilateral bank loans. These agencies have rules for government procurement to protect their loans from misuse. Tucker (1998) evaluates the procurement practices of the World Bank which offers its procurement practices as a model for developing countries and other multilateral banks. In addition, the World Bank is providing technical assistance to promoting best practices in government procurement as an essential component of good governance.

Adoption of model laws on government procurement by a government with weak or corrupt administration may be viewed with suspicion. And, as Tucker (1998: 143) notes 'A perfectly transparent paper trail can conceal corruption, suppress awkward evidence and even protect the guilty'. However, efforts to increase adherence to strict procedures and to increase transparency, as promoted by the World Bank and other entities, may increase the accountability of an administration.

Bilateral and plurilateral trade agreements on government procurement

While multilateral disciplines on government procurement have been discussed in the context of the GATT/WTO since 1947, a lack of willingness to open government procurement to trade resulted in a limited agreement signed by relatively few members. The GATT 1947 explicitly excluded government procurement from the obligation of national treatment. After the Tokyo Round, in 1981, 26 members implemented the first GATT agreement on government procurement. It applied only to trade in goods (not works or services), for contracts valued over Special Drawing Rights (SDR) 130 000, for central government entities, with an exemption granted for defense procurement. As the agreement applies only to suppliers from other signatories, it was necessary to accompany the agreement with rules of origin. This agreement did not ban 'offsets', requirements for the foreign firms to meet conditions on local content, technology licensing and investment requirements.

A new Government Procurement Agreement (GPA) was negotiated as part of the Uruguay Round Agreement (URA) and went into force in 1996. This plurilateral agreement is signed by the European Commission (with 25 member countries) and 12 other countries. Non-discrimination is the keystone of the agreement, as signatories must give foreign suppliers of products and services treatment that is 'no less favorable' than that given to their own suppliers of goods and services. Also, it must not treat a local supplier less favorably due to a foreign affiliation and ownership (WTO 2004).

As transparency is seen as the key to achieving equal treatment, the agreement specifies procedures for tendering and the award of contracts to ensure that foreign suppliers can compete on an equal basis with domestic ones. Each country signing the agreement specifies on positive lists the levels of government, the goods, services and construction services, and the contract value minimums included in the agreement. The inclusion of sub-national levels of government, and works and services in addition to supplies, has expanded coverage significantly. The value of trade under the URA GPA is estimated to increase ten-fold from the prior agreement (WTO 2004). The most significant procedural change in the new GPA is that signatories must establish timely and impartial procedures for foreign suppliers to challenge contract awards. In addition, offsets are explicitly banned.

As the agreement does not operate on the basis of the most favored nation principle, its coverage is not uniform or predictable. For example, the United States kept its program favoring small businesses as an exception to its commitments in the WTO agreement. Canada, in retaliation for US insistence on this exception, limited its commitments to the federal level, excluding procurement by provincial and municipal governments. In turn, Canada's exclusion of sub-national levels of government from the GPA means that it is denied access to the sub-national levels of government procurement in other signatories (International Trade Canada 1999).

Hoekman and Mavroidis (1997) investigate reasons why relatively few developing countries have joined the GPA. They propose that as developing countries are unlikely to gain much access to OCED country markets for government procurement, they lack motivation to join. They advise amending the GPA so that developing countries can apply price preferences for domestic suppliers, noting that the World Bank and the UNCITRAL Model law both allow price preferences. Fenster (2003) also evaluates developing country gains from liberalization of government procurement through the WTO. In contrast, he argues that the cost of compliance with transparency regulations may outweigh gains, and concludes that most of the gains to developing countries could be achieved through unilateral reform.

The WTO has created a working group to discuss a potential agreement on transparency in government procurement. This is viewed as a first step to an eventual multilateral agreement on government procurement. Evenett and Hoekman (2002) explore the gains from increased transparency. Their analysis suggests that policies fostering domestic competition may bring larger welfare gains than those from non-discrimination. This being the case, they argue that efficient government procurement is largely affected by the degree of competition in national markets, and so by competition policy and restrictions on foreign direct investment.

Regional trade agreements

Regional trade agreements including the European Union, the North American Free Trade Agreement, the Asian Pacific Economic Cooperation and several others, have reduced restrictions to trade on government procurement to different degrees. The agreement adopted by the EU in 1971 is the oldest and most comprehensive, and subsequent changes to the original legislation have increased its scope and effectiveness. The EU agreement prohibits discrimination in public procurement from member states and applies to all government procurement. The agreement recognizes that a ban on discrimination is insufficient to overcome institutional inertia and the disadvantages posed by distance, and so detailed procedures have been implemented for all stages of contract tendering and awards for supplies, works and services (Gordon *et al.* 1998). Efforts evaluating the effectiveness of the European Code note a sharp increase the number of notices published in the official journal in compliance with transparency requirements, and conclude that new entrants competing on price have resulted in public sector cost-savings. An evaluation of both intra-EU and extra-EU import penetration found that on average, import penetration increased from 6 percent in 1987 to 10 percent in 1994 (Gordon *et al.* 1998, p. 40).

The EU Code has been important both as a prototype for the URA GPA, and also for countries from Eastern and Central Europe. These countries were required to meet EU standards on government procurement for admission to the EU. In 1990, the EU launched an initiative to assess the status of government procurement in 11 countries and to develop strategies to assist them to meet EU standards (Servenay and Williams 1995).

While the EU has embraced free trade in government procurement between members to an unprecedented degree, procurement on defense remains an exception. Previous discussion on the total size of government procurement indicates that expenditures on defense are significant, and Table 29.1 indicates that the average for OECD countries is 1.6 percent of GDP. Trybus (1998) discusses the issues involved in developing a European Defense Procurement Code. Currently, materials for either civilian or military use are subject to normal rules of civil procurement, although exceptions can be made. Hard defense procurement, for items unique to military use, remains an exception to the EU code on government procurement. Trybus argues that governments face increasing costs to simply maintain their current stock of military hardware, and that infrequent, small purchases make it impossible to realize economies of scale and learning. Trybus argues that these inefficiencies in addition to reduced government budgets makes a common set of rules for defense procurement a pressing need for the EU.

Conclusions

A number of factors have converged on governments to give impetus for the improvement of their procurement systems. In some countries rising pressure on government budgets has increased the motivation for government procurement systems to be efficient and obtain value for money. Some developing countries are mandated to ensure that funds from multilateral agencies and banks are expended in conformance with standards for government procurement. Other developing countries are involved in World Bank efforts to promote good governance, and government procurement is seen as an essential component.

Regional trade agreements are another factor changing the extent of the domestic bias of government procurement systems. The EU has by far the deepest and most comprehensive agreement on government procurement that has provided a standard for many countries that have acceded or are attempting to accede to the EU.

The fragmented and patchy WTO agreement on government procurements reflects a lack of willingness on the part of many governments to open their procurement to foreign suppliers. A continued preference toward domestic suppliers, combined with the potential cost of meeting stringent WTO requirements for notification and transparency are reasons for that reluctance.

While the literature has offered theoretical insights into government procurement policies, the complexity of the policies has stymied comprehensive econometric analysis of the gains from opening to trade. However, careful analysis has verified that government procurement is a substantial percentage of GDP, and several authors have estimated that significant margin of domestic bias exists. This evidence suggests that the welfare gains from further reform are worth pursuing.

However, the most productive route to reform is likely to depend on the status of individual countries. Some countries may be able to realize substantial benefits from increasing the level of competition in their procurement systems even without opening to trade. In other countries unilateral efforts to reduce corruption by increasing transparency and accountability may yield substantial welfare gains. While some authors point out that participation in trade agreements may assist domestic governments in meeting these goals, this argument is balanced by others who discuss the potential cost of compliance. A comprehensive and multilateral trade agreement on government procurement in the WTO appears distant at this point, for governments continue to hold contradictory goals for their procurement systems. Further analysis for individual countries on the welfare cost of procurement policies incorporating social goals and domestic bias may be useful to governments poised for change.

References

Ades, Alberto and Rafael Di Tella (1997), 'The New Economics of Corruption: A Survey and Some New Results,' *Political Studies*, Special Issue, **45**(3), 496–515.

Arrowsmith, Sue (2003), *Government Procurement in the WTO. Studies in Transnational Economic Law*, Volume 16. The Hague, London, and New York: Kluwer Law International.

Arrowsmith, Sue and Arwel Davies (1998), *Public Procurement: Global Revolution*, International Economic Development Law Series, Volume 8, London: Kluwer Law International.

Audet, Denis (2002), 'Quantifying the Size of Government Procurement,' Presentation at the *WTO Symposium on Transparency in Government Procurement*, Geneva, Switzerland, 9–10 October. Available at http://www.wto.org/english/tratop_e/gproc_e/gptran_symp_oct02_e.htm.

Baldwin, Robert E. (1970), *Nontariff Distortions of International Trade*, Washington, DC: The Brookings Institution.

Baldwin, Robert and J. David Richardson (1972), 'Government Purchasing Policies, Other NTB's, and the International Monetary Crisis,' in H. E. English and Keith A. J. Hay (eds), *Obstacles to Trade in the Pacific Area: Proceedings of the Fourth Pacific Trade and Development Conference*, Ottawa: Carleton University School of International Affairs, pp. 243–63.

Beviglia-Zampetti, Americo (1997), 'The UNCITRAL Model Law on Procurement of Goods, Construction and Services,' in Bernard M. Hoekman and Petros C. Mavroidis (eds), *Law and Policy in Public Purchasing*, Ann Arbor, MI: The University of Michigan Press, pp. 273–87.

Deltas, George and Simon Evenett (1997), 'Quantitative Estimates of the Effects of Preference Policies,' in Bernard M. Hoekman and Petros C. Mavroidis (eds), *Law and Policy in Public Purchasing*, Ann Arbor, MI: The University of Michigan Press, pp. 73–89.

Evenett, Simon J. (2002), 'Multilateral Disciplines and Government Procurement,' in Bernard Hoekman, Aaditya Mattoo and Philip English (eds), *Development, Trade, and the WTO*, Washington, DC: The World Bank, pp. 417–27.

Evenett, Simon J. and Bernard M. Hoekman (2002), 'Government Procurement: Market Access, Transparency, and Multilateral Trade Rules,' Social Science Research Network (SSRN) Electronic Library, 7 October. Available at http://papers.ssrn.com/sol3/papers.cfm?abstract_id=342380.

Francois, Joseph, Douglas Nelson and N. David Palmeter (1997), 'Public Procurement in the United States: A Post-Uruguay Round Perspective,' in Bernard M. Hoekman and Petros C. Mavroidis (eds), *Law and Policy in Public Purchasing*, Ann Arbor, MI: The University of Michigan Press, pp. 105–24.

Fenster, Giovanna (2003), 'Multilateral Talks on Transparency in Government Procurement; Concerns for Developing Countries,' *IDS Bulletin*, 1 April, **34**(2), 65–81.

Gordon, Harvey, Shane Rimmer and Sue Arrowsmith (1998), 'The Economic Impact of the European Union Regime on Public Procurement: Lessons for the WTO,' in Sue Arrowsmith and Arwel Davies (eds), *Public*

Procurement: Global Revolution, International Economic Development Law Series, Volume 8, London: Kluwer Law International, pp. 27–55.

Hoekman, Bernard (1998), 'Using International Institutions to Improve Public Procurement,' *The World Bank Research Observer*, August, **13**(2), 249–69.

Hoekman, Bernard M. and Petros C. Mavroidis (1997), 'Multilateralizing the Agreement on Government Procurement,' in Bernard M. Hoekman and Petros C. Mavroidis (eds), *Law and Policy in Public Purchasing*, Ann Arbor, MI: The University of Michigan Press, pp. 289–312.

Hunja, Robert R. (1998), 'The UNCITRAL Model Law on Procurement of Goods, Construction and Services and Its Impact on Procurement Reform,' in Sue Arrowsmith and Arwel Davies (eds), *Public Procurement: Global Revolution*, International Economic Development Law Series, Volume 8, London: Kluwer Law International, pp. 97–109.

International Trade Canada (1999), 'Government Procurement,' Consultations on FTAA and WTO Negotiations, Discussion Paper, Ottawa, Ontario, May. Available at http://www.dfait-maeci.gc.ca/tna-nac/discussion/govproc-en.asp.

Laffont, Jean-Jacques and Jean Tirole (1993), *A Theory of Incentives in Procurement and Regulation*, Cambridge, MA: MIT Press, 705 pp.

Mattoo, Aaditya (1997), 'Economic Theory and the Procurement Agreement,' in Bernard M. Hoekman and Petros C. Mavroidis (eds), *Law and Policy in Public Purchasing*, Ann Arbor, MI: The University of Michigan Press, pp. 57–72.

McAfee, R. Preston and John McMillan (1989), 'Government Procurement and International Trade,' *Journal of International Economics*, **26**, 291–308.

McCrudden, Christopher II (1998), 'Social Policy Issues in Public Procurement: A Legal Overview,' in Sue Arrowsmith and Arwel Davies (eds), *Public Procurement: Global Revolution*, International Economic Development Law Series, Volume 8, London: Kluwer Law International, pp. 219–39.

Organization for Economic Co-operation and Development (OECD) (2002), 'The Size of Government Procurement Markets,' *OECD Journal on Budgeting*, **1**(4), 66 pp. Available at http://www1.oecd.org/publications/e-book/2202011E.pdf.

Rose-Ackerman, Susan (1996), 'The Political Economy of Corruption: Causes and Consequences,' *Public Policy for the Private Sector*, 74, Washington, DC: The World Bank. Available at http://rru.worldbank.org/Documents/PublicPolicyJournal/074ackerm.pdf.

Servenay, Christian and Rhodri Williams (1995), 'Introduction of a Regulatory Framework on Public Procurement in the Central and Eastern European Countries: The First Step on a Long Road,' *Public Procurement Law Review*, **4**(6), 237–54.

Trebilcock, Michael J. and Robert Howse (1995), 'Subsidies, Countervailing Duties, and Government Procurement', in Michael J. Trebilcock and Robert Howse (eds), *The Regulation of International Trade*, London and New York: Routledge, pp. 125–61.

Trionfetti, Federico (2000), 'Discriminatory Public Procurement and International Trade,' *World Economy*, **23**(1), 57–76.

Tucker, Tim (1998), 'A Critical Analysis of the Procurement Procedures of the World Bank,' in Sue Arrowsmith and Arwel Davies (eds), *Public Procurement: Global Revolution*, International Economic Development Law Series, Volume 8, London: Kluwer Law International, pp. 139–57.

Trybus, Martin (1998), 'National Models for the Regulation of the Acquisition of Armaments: Towards a European Defence Procurement Code?' in Sue Arrowsmith and Arwel Davies (eds), *Public Procurement: Global Revolution*, International Economic Development Law Series, Volume 8, London: Kluwer Law International, pp. 71–93.

United Nations Commission on International Trade Law (UNCITRAL) (2004), 'UNCITRAL Model Law on Procurement of Goods, Construction and Services with Guide to Enactment,' Vienna, Austria. Accessed 26 October from http://www.uncitral.org/english/texts/procurem/ml-procure.htm.

World Trade Organization (1996), 'Communication from the United States: Response to the Questionnaire on Government Procurement of Services.' S/WPGR/W/11/Add.6, Geneva, Switzerland, 21 October. Available at http://docsonline.wto.org.

World Trade Organization (2004), 'Overview of the Agreement on Government Procurement,' Geneva, Switzerland. Accessed 11 June from http://www.wto.org/english/tratop_e/gproc_e/over_e.htm

30 State trading agencies
Bruno Larue and Jean-Philippe Gervais

Introduction

State trading is a very controversial subject that has produced numerous frictions between countries.[1] From the creation of GATT in 1947, state traders were ubiquitous enough to warrant a GATT Article entirely devoted to this form of government intervention. Some would say that Article XVII was necessary to 'legitimize' a valuable government policy tool while others would counter that it was imperative to 'regulate' agencies that should not exist in a first best world.[2] In this spirit, Article XVII contends that state trading enterprises (STEs henceforth) must act in accordance with the general principles of non-discrimination and that commercial considerations only are to guide their decisions on imports and exports.[3] Hence, STEs are invited to behave like private firms and they are not to be used by governments to implement country-specific trade policies. As such, STEs must comply with GATT's Most Favored Nation principle and with the other GATT articles in which state trading is mentioned. The main concern is that STEs can shirk on their obligations due to difficulties in monitoring their behavior. It is feared that import STEs could provide greater protection for domestic factors of production than what their bound tariffs allow. On the export side, the concerns are about the potential to subsidize exports beyond a WTO member's obligations.

Schmitz *et al.* (1981) estimated that 91.3 percent of all wheat imports between 1973 and 1977 were imported by STEs. Abbott and Young (1999) present evidence that the share of wheat imported by STEs in the world's total for 1996 was down to 73 percent.[4] There may not be as many STEs as there were, but some are major players as they control a substantial portion of world trade for some commodities. Furthermore, many of the most recent WTO members and observers are centrally-planned and transition economies. Their growing importance in world trade in an era of rapid globalization can only magnify suspicions about STEs.[5] Consequently, state trading issues remain most pertinent in the third millennium.

The Uruguay Round which was to impose discipline in agriculture through specific objectives pertaining to domestic support, export subsidies and market access, provided a timely opportunity to revisit long-standing state trading issues. The WTO Agreement on Agriculture emerged from slow and painful negotiations that significantly delayed the conclusion of the Uruguay Round. To avoid further postponement of the conclusion of the Round, it was decided to relegate serious discussions regarding state trading to the next Round. Nevertheless, an Understanding on the Interpretation of Article XVII was produced in the Uruguay Round to clarify what an STE is and to remedy deficient reporting requirements. Hence, many of the irritants and concerns about state trading issues in GATT remain unaddressed. State trading is not limited to agricultural products, since some are involved with resource and industrial products. However, STEs seems most prevalent in agriculture. Because of that and of the fact that agricultural-focused STEs tend to illicit more controversy, most of our attention in this chapter will be devoted to STEs exporting and/or importing agricultural products.

Because Veeman *et al.* (1999) did an exhaustive survey of the literature prior to 1998, we concentrate on the post-1998 time period. We will nevertheless revisit some of the older papers. The next section attempts to define what is meant by state trading. Definitions abound in the literature (see Veeman *et al.* 1999 for a review). Since there are dissensions over what an STE is, it is not surprising that GATT signatories/WTO members have not fully complied with their obligation to submit a notification for every single state trading agency operating within their country's borders.[6] Arguments regarding the *raison d'être* of state trading agencies are also presented as it is worthwhile to review the arguments as to why a country might elect to have STEs. The third section deals with trade liberalization issues when STEs are involved directly or indirectly with exports and/or imports. Empirical evidence is presented to give the reader some ideas about the magnitude of the economic impacts of STEs. The last section offers comments about the prospects for STEs in a post-Doha environment.

What are state trading agencies and why do they exist?

Many authors have attempted to define what an STE is. Early definitions of STEs required direct government involvement in imports and/or exports (for exmaple, van Meerhaeghe 1971). Some definitions *de facto* attributed market power to STEs (for example, Kostecki 1982; Lloyd 1982). Such a restriction would greatly reduce the pool of STEs nowadays.[7] Veeman *et al.* (1999) proposed a broader definition, but for all practical purposes, the only definition that matters is the one used by the WTO.

When visiting the WTO website, the link to state trading greets us with

> state trading enterprises are defined as governmental and non-governmental enterprises, including marketing boards, which deal with goods for export and/or import. Article XVII of the GATT 1994 is the principal provision dealing with state trading enterprises and their operations. Work on this subject in the WTO is undertaken primarily by the Working Party on State Trading Enterprises.

The first part is rather uninformative. Fortunately, it is relatively easy to find a fuller definition that adds that STEs have exclusive or special rights or privileges, including statutory or constitutional powers, in the exercise of which they influence through their purchases or sales the level or direction of imports or exports.[8] In practice, the meaning of exclusive or special rights or privileges is often construed to mean single-desk selling and/or purchasing rights, but many authors have found it useful to categorize STEs according to their powers and trade distortion potential (for example, Veeman *et al.* 1999). The argument is that STEs whose domestic market can be contested and/or ones that face stiff competition on exports markets must behave like private firms to survive. It is also worth noting that STEs include not only bodies that engage in trade, but also institutions that regulate private trade.

The definition used by the WTO has practical implications. The ambiguity regarding the definition of an STE causes problems in the application of the notification requirement. As mentioned earlier, WTO members are obligated to report their STEs. The most recent list of notifications (in the Fall of 2004) indicates that in 2000, 40 of the 124 WTO members reported at least one STE while in 2003, only 12 of the 131 members had notified the WTO. It might be tempting to infer that STEs are disappearing left and right since 2000, but that would be wrong. Reporting in a timely fashion, or at all, is a problem. As these lines are being written, Canada is not on the list of countries with notifications for the years 2000–2003 even though the Canadian Wheat Board is perhaps the most notorious STE of all. Canada's most recent notification submitted in 2002 was for the year 1998. Countries are also less than forthcoming in admitting to having an STE, as convincingly demonstrated by Rude and Annand (2002) who contend that the system of grain interventions and export refunds used by the European Union (EU) fits perfectly the WTO's definition of an STE even though a notification by the EU has yet to be submitted to the WTO.

What constitutes an STE has other implications. An obvious one has to do with accession negotiations. Martin (2001) provides an excellent discussion of Chinese reforms and of the disciplines imposed on China's STEs. Another has to do with dispute settlement. If an institution fits the definition of an STE and if its behavior is not respectful of its country's GATT obligations, then it must be possible to ask for redress. Yet, Annand (2000: 8) states that between 1949 and 1999, there has never been a case that relied on Article XVII to regulate an exporting STE and that there have only been a handful of cases involving STEs at all.

Several arguments can be invoked to motivate the creation of STEs. One of them is that STEs emerge as an endogenous response to market failures. The most common example is a pre-STE situation involving a few private traders exploiting their oligopsony power over domestic producers. The story goes that producers voice their dissatisfaction about low prices and convince the government to create an STE to remedy the problem. The objective of getting better and more stable prices has been at the foundation of all marketing boards and of many STEs. The argument holds for import and export STEs alike. Regarding export STEs, let us consider the case of a large exporting country capable of influencing its terms of trade. This country might find it more convenient to influence its terms of trade by directly controlling its volume of exports through an STE than through an 'optimal' export tax imposed on a large number of small traders.[9] In this instance, it could be envisioned that an STE controlling exports and domestic sales might be able to adjust more quickly to changes in import demand than tax-setting bureaucrats. The same can be said about the ability of import STEs to adjust quickly to changes in foreign export supply elasticities.

It must be noted that the creation of an STE can create significant domestic distortions, especially if its objective is profit maximization. If the foreign import demand elasticity is constant, Markusen (1984) showed that the optimal policy is a welfare-maximizing export tax levied on a large number of producers, even when one of the alternatives is a profit maximizing STE constrained to practice marginal cost pricing on the domestic market. Unfortunately, the first best scenario may not be feasible as the elimination of an STE need not translate into a perfectly competitive domestic sector.[10] Domestic distortions are also a concern in setting a welfare-maximizing import tariff when the domestic market is served by imperfectly competitive traders and producers. Larue and Gervais (2002) show that there could be a significant departure between the 'right' welfare-maximizing tariff and the orthodox optimal tariff formula depending on the assumed market configuration. For example, when there is a single profit-maximizing domestic firm that controls imports and production, the welfare-maximizing tariff is negative if the firm's marginal cost is upward-sloping.

Krishna and Thursby (1992) analyze the welfare implications of STEs when they compete in international markets with a few private trading firms. They allow STEs to have different motivations and find that the optimal policy is independent of the objective of the STE only when arbitrage is possible and the domestic price is regulated. Otherwise, the tax/subsidy policy is affected by the objective of the STE. The analysis in Just *et al.* (1979) is very similar in spirit to that of Krishna and Thursby in the sense that it also addresses the issue of optimal tax/subsidy but in the context of a marketing board enjoying a monopoly position. Fulton *et al.* (1999) investigate the welfare implications of having an STE that practices price-pooling instead of having a few private traders. They show that under certain conditions, having an STE is less detrimental than having a few private traders.

Some authors, like McCorriston and McLaren (2001), appeal to the concept of strategic trade policy to infer an (unfair) advantage to STEs.[11] Consider the case of exporting countries selling all of their production in a third-country market through private firms. In the first stage of the game, countries make public announcements regarding their respective policies. With this knowledge, the oligopolistic firms make their business decisions in the second stage of the game. At the risk of over-simplifying the issues, it pays for a country to practice strategic trade policy when its trading partners are not likely to retaliate and when its firms have a cost advantage over their foreign rivals. In this setting, the number of domestic and foreign firms has important policy implications. Under the assumption of symmetric Cournot-playing firms, the optimal subsidy for the home country is positive, zero or negative if the number of domestic firms, n, is less than or equal to the number of foreign firms plus one ($n^* + 1$). It could be inferred that a country with only one firm, an STE perhaps, must necessarily subsidize exports. This would be correct if its government was willing to tell the whole world about it, including the WTO, before firms make their decisions. As is well-known, a cost advantage in a game with incomplete information cannot be fully exploited by the firms enjoying the cost advantage because their rivals entertain a non-zero probability that the cost advantage is not real. Therefore, the benefits of export subsidies would be watered down if the subsidies were to be kept secret. Consequently, the strategic trade policy argument is not consistent with the alleged secretive behaviour of countries with export STEs.

Hamilton and Stiegert (2002) suggest that STEs can be used to implement a rent-shifting scheme if it has a device to commit itself to a larger volume of exports than under a no-commitment scenario. The other exporters observe the commitment and react by exporting less. The profit of the STE in the equilibrium with commitment is larger than its profit under no commitment while the converse is true for the other exporters. Thus the commitment device shifts rent from the other exporters to the STE because it gives the STE the so-called first-mover (leader) advantage. The commitment device analyzed by Hamilton and Stiegert (2002) is the initial payment used by the Canadian Wheat Board. As argued above, the commitment must be public knowledge if it is to work. The initial payment passes that test. However, there are still two problems in trying to use the initial payment as a commitment device. The first one has to do with the timing of the announcement of the initial payment. If the initial payment is announced prior to planting decisions, then it can influence production and hence exports. If it is announced after planting decisions, then it cannot influence production and hence cannot be a commitment device.[12] Schmitz and Furtan (2000: 66) indicate that the initial payment was announced prior to planting between 1971 and 1991 and has since been announced after planting. The second point has to do with what Bagwell (1995) calls the observability of the commitment. He showed that a commitment may have no value if there is even a slight noise in the observation of the leader's action. In this instance, even if there could be production and export projections made from an initial payment (announced before planting), randomness in climatic conditions is likely to make the commitment quite noisy. By allowing firms to have private information, Maggi (1999) shows that rent-shifting remains possible if the noise of the observation of the leader's action is small. Otherwise, Bagwell's reasoning applies.

Larue and Lapan (1992) posit that the price of agricultural products may reflect a country-specific reputation effect due to the importers' inability to observe with perfect accuracy the quality of the goods they purchase from abroad. The country-specific reputation effect is motivated by the fact the exporting firms in a given country are subject to the same regulations and that the quality of the goods they purchase might be influenced by regional climatic conditions. In this instance, the benefits of a good reputation are shared by all exporting firms and the incentives to improve the reputation of the country decrease with the number of exporting firms. Naturally, there is no free riding when the number of exporters is one. One way to achieve that is by creating an STE. They use data on quality complaints regarding Canadian and US wheat as empirical support for their theoretical results.

Wilson and Dahl (2004) contend that STEs can better hide their terms of trade than private traders in bidding games and as such exploit information asymmetries. They use simulations to show that STEs' informational advantage is reduced when the number of 'transparent' bidders increases. In their duopoly model with asymmetric risk and risk attitude, Larue and Yapo (2000) also show that a firm exposed to less risk or with the lowest risk aversion can achieve a higher profit than under the Cournot certainty benchmark, all other things being equal. However, it is also shown that if risk is not too high, firms not too risk averse and not too asymmetric, then the ex-post profit of both firms can be higher than their profit under certainty. It is hard to know for sure whether STEs are more or less risk averse or whether they face more or less risk than private firms even though some authors might be inclined to think that government backing makes them immune to risk. One must also consider that unlike private firms, STEs face political risks. For example, large deficits and/or the disclosure that domestic consumers faced higher prices than foreign consumers could illicit a public outcry that might jeopardize the very existence of an STE.

The feasibility of correcting a market failure through an STE is generally admitted. The fear is that the internalization of the market failure might bring about bigger problems, domestically and/or internationally. The STE might be mismanaged and/or it might purposely violate the spirit of its country's international obligations. Alternatively, the STEs could be construed as a policy tool to redistribute income or to achieve various non-economic objectives, like production/self-sufficiency targets. Governments would choose to achieve their policy goals through STEs only if it was the most efficient mean available. Otherwise, STEs would soon be regarded as government failures that would eventually be corrected or terminated. The latter has indeed happened for many STEs (see Abbott and Young, 1999; and Veeman *et al.* 1999). Alston and Gray (2000) investigate this issue by assuming that governments can choose between a price-pooling STE and export subsidies paid to private traders to provide support to wheat producers. Efficient support provision is a multi-faceted concept. It can be evaluated in terms of transfer efficiency, deadweight losses and the incidence on different domestic interest groups and on third-party traders. STEs and export subsidies are similar in many ways,[13] but they have nevertheless significant differences. Export subsidies involve taxpayer funds which may be costly to collect. This argument is also common in discussions about strategic trade policies (for example, Brander, 1995). However, when price discrimination among foreign markets is not feasible and the domestic demand is less elastic than foreign demand, the STE will tax domestic consumers more heavily compared with the export subsidy. When price discrimination among international markets is feasible, the theoretical results are more ambiguous.

Some STEs have changed to remain viable policy instruments. Carter and Wilson (1997) explore hypotheses as to why two STEs that used to be very similar, like the Canadian Wheat Board and the Australian Wheat Board, have followed different evolutionary paths. Schmitz and Furtan (2000) is also a good source for readers interested in the history of the Canadian Wheat Board. Veeman *et al.* (1999) feature cases studies about Indonesia's Badan Urusan Logistik, the New Zealand dairy board, the Japanese Food Agency, the Australian Wheat Board, the Canadian Wheat Board and the Korean State Mandated Imports.

Trade liberalization with STEs and the empirical evidence

At this point, it is convenient to separate importing STEs from exporting ones. Veeman *et al.* (1999) argue that the degree of government support provided to export STEs is relatively small and that concerns over the trade-distorting behavior of import STEs is of greater concern. One such concern with importing STEs is that they might be able to reduce market access beyond the levels consistent with their bound tariff rates. In other words, by controlling the volume of import, these STEs might be able to maintain a spread between domestic and foreign prices in excess of the specific tariff equivalent. Another concern is that STEs can discriminate across foreign sources, which goes against the Most Favored Nation principle. McCorriston and MacLaren (2001) compare the impacts of trade liberalization when there are n domestic firms and m foreign ones versus a situation in which a single firm, maximizing the sum of producer surplus and rent from imports, controls both domestic production and imports. As expected, tariff cuts do not yield as large import increases in the STE scenario as in the more competitive '$m+n$' case. This is due in part to the higher level of imports prior to the tariff cut under the more competitive market structure. As argued by Abbott and Young (1999), there are many instances for which the degree of competition after the elimination of an STE has actually decreased. They also present evidence that wheat-importing STEs are not associated with higher implicit tariffs than private traders. However, their results also suggest that STEs may be less responsive to changes in market conditions in choosing their sources of supply. On that score, Chen and Brooks (1999) found evidence of non-price discrimination in Japanese wheat imports favoring Australian and Canadian wheat at the expense of US wheat.

In Larue *et al.* (1999a,b), trade liberalization scenarios through tariff reductions and the enlargement of minimum access commitments are compared. The distinguishing aspect of these papers is that the small country assumption means that imports are purchased at the world price while exports are sold at the world price minus a marketing/transport cost. Hence, exports are not ruled out a priori even though the country would be a net importer under free trade. Different assumptions are made regarding the powers of the STE over domestic production, exports and imports. It is shown that an STE is likely to export for two reasons: (a) to price discriminate when the domestic market is shielded against foreign competition by a high tariff or a tight minimum access commitment; and (b) to maintain high prices on the domestic market in response to the presence of forced imports. Price discrimination and hence exports occur under a tariff scenario only if the firm is 'efficient enough'. This behavior is motivated by profit maximization. Still, it had to be anticipated that high tariffs could prompt an STE to export or facilitate exports by private traders even if it is not entirely motivated by the quest for profit.[14] Binding minimum access commitments generally trigger a large volume of exports and hence inefficient trade because the domestic monopolist has a strong incentive to maintain the high domestic price. Exporting allows the domestic monopolist to get rid of goods that would lower the domestic price and should be regarded as an alternative to 'sleeping' on import licenses, which might occur if the minimum access commitment did not have to be filled. This follows from Cunha and Santos (1996) who have shown that a firm enjoying a monopoly position on its domestic market has incentive to outbid import traders for import licenses, even if the intent is not to use the license to import.[15] The parallel to a monopolist acquiring a patent with the intent of not using it, but to prevent others from using it, is obvious.

A problem that has not been raised before in the context of trade liberalization when imports are controlled by an STE has to do with the potential differentiated treatments of different varieties of a given product. The STE may allow some varieties to enter the domestic market and the domestic-border price differential for these varieties may be lower or equal to the bound tariff for the product. Varieties that are not allowed to enter face an equivalent infinite tariff even if the official tariff is low. Thus, the behavior of the STE could induce the entry of domestic firms that would produce varieties that would differ from the ones actually imported and, to a lesser extent, from the ones that could have been imported. The new domestic varieties would make it difficult for the varieties that had been discriminated against to enter the domestic market even if the STE ceased its discriminatory practice.[16]

Alston and Gray (2000: 65) indicate that countries with wheat marketing boards have tended to offer lower rates of producer protection than countries using export subsidies like the United States and the European Union. As mentioned above, their theoretical analysis yielded ambiguous results regarding the merit or drawback of using export subsidies instead of a price-pooling STE to provide support to wheat producers. Their simulation results show that compared to targeted export subsidies, price discrimination and pooling is a more efficient mechanism to support Canadian wheat producers. Finally, Schmitz (2002) relies on a two-region partial equilibrium model to compute the inefficiency of an export tax, an import tariff and an STE trading cotton on the Turkish economy. He concludes that the overall inefficiency is low especially considering the amount of income redistribution actually achieved.

Conclusion
The literature on state trading has always been dogmatic and unfortunately, it will most likely remain that way. The theoretical results about the relative efficiency/inefficiency caused by STEs are very sensitive to assumptions regarding the structures of domestic and international markets with and without STEs and the powers and objective(s) of the

STEs considered. The debate over STEs is very much like the debate over regional trade agreements. In both cases, economists have to use a utopic benchmark (free trade and perfectly competitive markets) to get an easy answer or to consider second (or third) best benchmarks to come up with an answer that typically begins with 'depending on' or 'if'. Furthermore, as with the debate on regional trading arrangements, there are competent economists with entrenched views on both sides of the issue. One notable difference is that regional trading agreements have rapidly grown in numbers over the last 25 years. Individual countries must find it profitable regardless of the consequences for the rest of the world. If STEs benefit from many unfair advantages and can get away with it, why aren't there more?

It is not clear what is in store for STEs in a post-Doha world. There are calls to end privileges, like cheap deficit financing and government loan guarantees, and to make STE operations more transparent, especially their pricing schemes. Large STEs would be able to finance their deficit at very competitive interest rates and as such their ability to operate profitably would not be jeopardized. Some less developed countries (LDCs) convinced that STEs play an important development role, are already asking for an exemption to potential new restrictions. In response to more transparency, WTO members with STEs have countered that the pricing practices of large private traders are not transparent either and that STEs should not face stricter requirements than their private competitors.

Notes

1. As an example, consider that between 1990 and 2002, the United States launched ten trade challenges targeting the Canadian Wheat Board (see http://www.cwb.ca/en/topics/trade_issues/cheque_insert.jsp; 28 October 2004). This high number of challenges attests of the orthogonal positions and strong resolve on both sides of the Canada–US border.
2. This view is best depicted by the following citation taken from a speech given by Leon Brittan who was then vice-president of the European Commission: 'I think that, if we are to look at international competition rules seriously, the time is ripe to consider whether this antiquated form of monopoly trading can be phased out altogether.' The speech was entitled 'Competition policy and the trading system: towards international rules in the WTO' and it was given at the Institute for International Economics, Washington DC, 20 November 1997.
3. The premise in GATT is that trade is conducted by private firms in market-based economies. Non-discrimination applies to government policies, not to firms. GATT cannot forbid firms from attempting to price discriminate, but it allows governments to impose anti-dumping measures.
4. Simonot (1997) argues that state trading has become increasingly important over time, which contrasts with the conclusion derived by Abbott and Young (1999). Perhaps, these orthogonal interpretations of the data can be reconciled by noting that Abbott and Young (1999) did not include the European Union as a wheat importing STE. Over the period under consideration, the European Union had a market share of 27 percent. Their rationale to exclude the EU was that the EU did not admit to having a wheat importing STE.
5. The most recent WTO members, Albania (2000), Armenia (2003), Cambodia (2004), China (2001), Croatia (2000), Jordan (2000), Lithuania (2001), Nepal (2004), Oman (2000) and Chinese Taipei (2002), are not exactly examples of laissez-faire economies. Furthermore, the current list of observers is dominated by former Soviet Republics, like Azerbaijan, Belarus, Kazakhstan, Russia, Tajikistan, Ukraine and Uzbekistan.
6. See http://www.wto.org/english/thewto_e/whatis_e/eol/e/wto05/wto5_9.htm#note2; 28 October 2004.
7. Kostecki (1982) argues that the terms in import or export transactions involving STEs are dictated by governments. Lloyd (1982) defines an STE as a trading organization for which the prices and/or quantities of international transactions in commodities are determined as an instrument in the pursuit of objectives of government policies. It has since been recognized that the ability of STEs to influence their terms of trade is questionable, even for large ones like the Canadian Wheat Board. Having market power to price discriminate is an advantage and this is why STE opponents usually argue that STEs do not have market power or can't be managed smartly enough to fully use their market power.
8. See for example the documentation at: http://www.wto.org/english/tratop_e/statra_e/statrad.htm; 28 October 2004.

9. Of course, STEs are not immune to time consistency issues that can arise when large policy active exporting countries set an export tax to improve their terms of trade. The welfare implications of trade policy commitment in this context are documented in Gervais and Lapan (2002).
10. Furthermore, in cases for which a handful of multinational and state trading enterprises account for the bulk of world exports, the elimination of some STEs may actually reduce the number of players and have adverse effects on importing countries.
11. The literature on strategic trade policy is beautifully reviewed in Brander (1995).
12. Nonetheless, it could possibly be used as a signaling device to reveal information about expected levels of production and exports to other imperfectly informed trading firms in foreign countries.
13. As noted by Alston and Gray (2000: 465), both policies result in producers receiving a single price for all sales that is greater than the competitive price. Both policies result in higher prices being charged to consumers in countries where demand is relatively inelastic, typically including the domestic market. Both policies would be optimized by equating marginal revenues among the markets, but because of pooling, marginal revenue is less than marginal costs. Finally, both policies involve a burden on domestic consumers, at least when the domestic demand is relatively inelastic.
14. Canada's dairy exports in the late 1990s prompted New Zealand and the United States to complain to the WTO which ruled that the Canadian Dairy Commission facilitated a subsidization scheme that breeched Canada's obligations under the Agreement on Agriculture. Larue *et al.* (1999b: 86) argue that Canada's price pooling also lowered potential returns for dairy producers.
15. The incentive to acquire import licences and the monopolist's capacity to outbid private traders is strongest when import licenses are auctioned as a block.
16. The argument does not apply when the domestic capacity to produce competing varieties is absent. For example, the *Société des Alcools du Québec* (SAQ) is a state trader with a monopoly on wine imports for the province of Quebec. It offers a very good selection of wines compared to what is offered in private stores in US states with comparable populations. However, newspapers recently reported that SAQ had been unable to negotiate prices as low as comparable large scale buyers. The love for variety is apparently strong in the market for wine because the public did not call for the privatisation of the SAQ.

References

Abbott, P. C. and L. M. Young (1999), 'Wheat-Importing State Trading Enterprises: Impacts on the World Wheat Market,' *Canadian Journal of Agricultural Economics*, **47**(2), 119–36.
Alston, J. and R. Gray (2000), 'State Trading Versus Export Subsidies: The Case of Canadian Wheat,' *Journal of Agricultural and Resource Economics*, **25**(1), 51–67.
Annand, M. (2000), 'State Trading Enterprises: A Canadian Perspective,' *Estey Centre Journal of International Law and Trade Policy*, **2**(1), 36–50.
Bagwell, K. (1995), 'Commitment and Observability in Games,' *Games and Economic Behavior*, **8**, 271–80.
Brander, J. (1995), 'Strategic Trade Policy,' in G. Grossman and K. Rogoff (eds), *Handbook of International Economics Vol. III, International Economics*, Amsterdam: Elsevier, North Holland.
Carter, C. A. and W. Wilson (1997), 'Emerging Differences in State Grain Trading: Australia and Canada,' *Agricultural Economics*, **16**(2), 87–98.
Chen, K. and H. Brooks (1999), 'State Trading and Non-price Discriminatory Trade: The Case of Japan's Wheat Imports,' *Agribusiness*, **15**(1), 41–51.
Cunha, L. C. and V. Santos (1996), 'Sleeping Quotas, Pre-emptive Quota Bidding and Monopoly Power,' *Journal of International Economics*, **40**, 127–48.
Fulton, M., B. Larue and M. Veeman (1999), 'The Impact of Export State Trading Enterprises under Imperfect Competition,' *Canadian Journal of Agricultural Economics*, **47**(4), 363–74.
Gervais, J-P., and H. E. Lapan (2002), 'Time Consistent Export Quotas in an Oligopolistic World Market,' *Journal of International Economics*, **56**, 445–63.
Hamilton, S. F. and K. W. Stiegert (2002), 'An Empirical Test of the Rent-Shifting Hypothesis: The Case of State Trading Enterprises,' *Journal of International Economics*, **58**(1), 135–57.
Just, R. E., A. Schmitz and D. Zilberman (1979), 'Price Controls and Optimal Export Policies Under Alternative Market Structures,' *American Economic Review*, **69**(4), 706–14.
Kostecki, M. M. (1982), 'State Trading in Agricultural Products by the Advanced and Developing Countries: the Background,' in M. M. Kostecki (ed.), *State Trading in International Markets*, New York: St. Martins Press.
Krishna, K. and M. Thursby (1992), 'Optimal Policies and Marketing Board Objectives,' *Journal of Development Economics*, **38**(1), 1–15.
Larue, B. and Lapan, H. E. (1992), 'Market Structure, Quality and the World Wheat Market,' *Canadian Journal of Agricultural Economics*, **40**(2), 311–28.
Larue, B. and V. Yapo (2000), 'Asymmetries in Risk and in Risk Attitude: The Duopoly Case,' *Journal of Economics and Business*, **52**, 435–53.

Larue, B. and J-P. Gervais (2002), 'The Welfare-Maximizing and Revenue-Maximizing Tariffs with a Few Domestic Firms,' *Canadian Journal of Economics*, **35**(4), 786–804.

Larue, B., M. Fulton and M. Veeman (1999a), 'On the Exporting of Import State Traders and Other Peculiar Effects of Negotiated Minimum Access Commitments,' *Canadian Journal of Agricultural Economics*, **47**(4), 375–86.

Larue, B. M. Veeman and M. Fulton (1999b), 'Protection, Price Discrimination and Inefficient Trade: The Case for Real Tariffication,' *Canadian Journal of Agricultural Economics*, Special issue: *The national and trade dairy policies: Implications for the next WTO negotiations*, **47**(5), 77–88.

Lloyd, P. J. (1982), 'State Trading and the Theory of International Trade,' in M. M. Kostecki (ed.), *State Trading in International Markets*, New York: St. Martins Press.

Maggi, G. (1999), 'The Value of Commitment with Imperfect Observability and Private Information,' *Rand Journal of Economics*, **30**(4), 555–74.

Markusen, J. R. (1984), 'The Welfare and Allocative Effects of Export Taxes versus Marketing Boards,' *Journal of Development Economics*, **14**, 19–36.

Martin, W. (2001), 'State Trading and China's Agricultural Import Policies,' *Canadian Journal of Agricultural Economics*, **49**(4), 415–28.

McCorriston, S. and D. MacLaren (2001), 'State Trading Enterprises: Some Legal and Conceptual Issues,' *Canadian Journal of Agricultural Economics*, **49**(4), 441–58.

Rude, J. and M. Annand (2002), 'European Grain Export Practices: Do They Constitute a State Trading,' *Estey Journal of International Law and Trade Policy*, **3**(2), 176–202.

Schmitz, T. G. (2002), 'Measuring Inefficiency in the Presence of an Export Tax, an Import Tariff, and a State Trading Enterprise,' *Journal of Agricultural and Applied Economics*, **34**(1), 81–93.

Schmitz, A. and Furtan, H. (2000), *The Canadian Wheat Board, Marketing in the New Millennium*, Regina: Canadian Plains Research Center.

Schmitz, A., A. McCalla, D. Mitchell and C. A. Carter (1981), *Grain Exports Cartels*, Cambridge MA: Ballinger Press.

Simonot, D. (1997), 'The Economics of State Trading in Wheat,' M.Sc. Thesis, University of Saskatchewan, College of Agriculture.

Van Meerhaeghe, M. A. G. (1971), *International Economic Institutions*, Second edition, Dordecht: Martinus Nijhoff Publishers.

Veeman, M., M. Fulton and B. Larue (1999), *International Trade in Agricultural and Food Products: The Role of State Trading Enterprises*, Ottawa, ON: Agriculture and Agri-Food Canada, Economic and Policy Analysis Directorate, April.

Wilson, W. W. and B. L. Dahl (2004), 'Transparency and Bidding Competition in International Wheat Trade,' *Canadian Journal of Agricultural Economics*, **52**(1), 89–105.

31 Administrative measures: restraining bureaucracy from inhibiting trade

William A. Kerr

Introduction

The form of non-tariff barriers is only constrained by the ingenuity of the bureaucrats charged with putting them in place. As administrative activities of governments that require a response or change of activity by firms often act as a friction[1] on the working of markets or the internal governance activities of firms (Hobbs and Kerr 1999), motivation becomes central to the discussion of administrative measures that constrain international commercial activities. This is because almost any administrative measure can be endowed with a plausible domestic rationale and, hence, it becomes very difficult to identify measures put in place simply for purposes of restricting trade. Policy makers seldom admit that their motivation for putting measures in place is the restriction of trade and, hence, attempts to curtail the trade restricting power of administrative measures must be based on alternative criteria that are inherently less than comprehensive and imperfect substitutes. In some areas of regulation, sufficient international consensus has arisen regarding the potential for abuse of administrative measures that formal agreements have been negotiated that attempt to establish rules for the imposition of trade restricting practices. This is the case for sanitary measures that relate to tradable goods that could threaten human or animal health and phytosanitary measures that relate to transborder movements of plants and plant material that pose health or environmental risks. In these cases, the World Trade Organization's (WTO) Agreement on the Application of Sanitary and Phytosanitary Measures (SPS) applies. It attempts to restrict the use of trade inhibiting measures to those which have an objective scientific basis. In the case of technical standards applied to tradable goods, the WTO's Agreement on Technical Barriers to Trade (TBT) pertains. This chapter does not deal with SPS or TBT matters.[2] To the extent that the WTO Members have agreed that other administrative measures need to be controlled, negotiations come under the broad heading of 'trade facilitation', but as yet little progress has been achieved.

A many headed devil

As suggested above, the major difficulty with administrative measures is that they can always be given a domestic policy or administrative justification. This is not to suggest that all administrative measures have been put in place for the purpose of inhibiting trade. In the vast majority of cases, one suspects, the measure is put in place to achieve a legitimate domestic policy goal or to facilitate the administration of a domestic programme – that trade is inhibited is simply an (often unforeseen) externality. International agreements recognize that domestic policies will generate these externalities. The generally agreed rule in these cases is that given that there are likely to be a number of policy options that can be used to achieve a domestic policy goal, the option put in place should be the one that yields the least trade distortion. While this rule has been accepted, it has not proved simple to implement in practice and has not been the subject to serious challenges in disputes.

The 'least trade-distorting measure' rule has not been operationalized for a number of reasons. First, policy alternatives are seldom neutral in the other costs they impose on society and in the array of benefits they deliver. As a result, policy alternatives cannot be compared on the trade distortion criteria, *ceteris paribus*. Hence, the least trade-distorting option may impose higher domestic costs than a more trade-distorting option or deliver a less preferred array of benefits. On a more practical level, domestic policy makers seldom fully work up a range of policy alternatives,[3] rather bringing forth single options to receive the official 'go ahead' for implementation. They are simply unlikely to be willing or able to commit the resources necessary to fully investigate a range of policy options. Further, as the administration of domestic policies often resides with ministries or departments that do not deal with international trade, they are unlikely to explicitly consider the trade-distorting aspects of their policy initiatives – and may well consider attempts by trade or foreign ministries to constrain their policy development activities as unwelcome and unwarranted interference (Kerr 1997). Consistency in the application of domestic policies as well as bureaucratic preferences for 'accepted ways of doing things' may also limit willingness to consider alternative policies or administrative procedures. Further, in the absence of pre-agreed formal mechanisms for consultation with trading partners, foreign objections to policies put in place without any trade inhibiting motivation may well be considered unacceptable interference in sovereignty. Of course, when the underlying motivation for the measure was the restriction of trade, one can expect a vigorous defence of the measure, as well as its structure, as an imperative of domestic policy. Hence, the main line of international defence against the abuse of administrative measures has failed to moderate their use to any significant degree.

The economic effect of administrative measures can be roughly divided into three categories: (a) those that act in a similar way to a tariff; (b) those that act in a similar manner to an import quota; and (c) those that impose costs that impact on the activities of firms in ways similar to transaction costs.[4] While these categories of trade-inhibiting administrative measures are useful as a rough guide, the measures themselves often do not slot easily into a single category and may well have compounding effects.[5] An example of a trade inhibiting administrative measure that acts in a similar manner to a tariff is a restriction on the national origin of carriers used to transport a good or range of goods. A country might justify this practice on a domestic defence imperative of having a sizable merchant fleet to provide security of supply during wartime. Of course, this would only be necessary if domestically licensed ships were not internationally competitive because, for example, of higher safety standards or wages being established and enforced for ships carrying the country's flag. Forcing imports to be carried in ships of its flag raises the cost of transporting the listed products to the importing country and, hence, raises the costs of imports; the same result as with a tariff.[6] Once in place, those domestic producers that benefit from the protection provided by carrier of origin requirement have an incentive to ensure that the regulation is retained. Hence, carrier of origin provisions may persist long after the national defence justification has faded. As another example, border inspection fees may be lumpy leading to high importing costs for smaller lot sizes (Boyd *et al.* 2003).

An example of an administrative measure that acts in a similar fashion to an import quota would be a regulation that forces all airfreight flights through a single international airport. This may be justified by the importing country as a way to assist more efficient allocation of limited resources necessary for inspection of imports, for example, customs officers. As the total number of flights that can land during a day is limited, once the total volume of traffic reaches the daily maximum, the regulation becomes a quantitative limit on imports. Beyond this limit, no imports are possible. Import competing firms will be able to raise prices as a result of the constraint on imports. Administrative measures must be found that are similar to those used to allocate import quotas, to allocate landing rights.

Some administrative measures may have aspects of both a tariff and an import quota. Return to the carrier of origin example. If the importing country put in place regulations that required some imported products to be transported in its high cost flag carriers, this would impose a tariff-like cost on exporters. If, in addition, once the regulation was put in place the importing country refused to license sufficient ships to carry the volume of trade that would be contracted at the higher transportation cost, then an import quota-like restriction on imports would also exist.

Administrative procedures that impose costs similar to transaction costs on firms that wish to engage in international commerce may simply relate to bureaucratically established procedures that greatly increase the paperwork burden. Having to secure signatures from ten different government departments before a shipment can be released from customs warehouses can impose costs in terms of extra personnel. The completion of this type of paperwork may also entail considerable delays that raise the costs of export financing and insurance. In some cases, even determining which departments from which permission to import needs to be obtained may require considerable resources – information costs. In some cases, local agents that act as transaction cost reducing facilitators may have to be hired. This was an important role of the local *compradors* that acted as the interface between western firms that engaged in the China trade in the nineteenth and early twentieth centuries. Latterly, a major area of interest at the WTO trade facilitation negotiations has pertained to improving the transparency of import regimes, particularly those of developing countries.

Removal of import licensing requirements has also been a topic for negotiation. In addition to tariffs, countries may also require that firms wishing to import certain products obtain a licence. These licences may come at a cost, thus raising the cost of importing. Further, licences may not be freely granted meaning restricted competition that provides importers with market power that can be exploited to raise the price of imports. Countries often justify import licensing systems on the basis that the government requires information on the flow of imports of certain sensitive products or to ensure that those engaged in importing meet certain standards. In a similar fashion, governments in importing countries may require exporters to employ local agents to act as their interface with the government. For example, the local agent can ensure that paperwork is completed in a proper manner and that the government has a domestic party which can be used to resolve problems with foreign products or practices. For example, as part of its tightening of security against imports of risky products in the wake of the attacks on New York and Washington on 11 September 2001, the US Department of Homeland Security required exporters of a specified list of products to employ a US agent (Kerr 2004).

The US prevents Mexican trucks from operating in the United States outside restricted border areas. Ostensibly, this is done for vehicle safety reasons, yet no mechanism exists to evaluate the safety of Mexican registered trucks. It means that once Mexican truckers enter the United States they must drop their loads and have them picked up by US truckers who carry them to destinations within the US. While the removal of this requirement was agreed to in the NAFTA, the US has failed to implement it due to fierce resistance by US trucking interests and the Teamsters Union (Cordon and Sinha 2001).

There are often domestic regulations pertaining to labelling for purposes of consumer protection or the provision of important information. The former relate to ensuring that labels are not fraudulent while the latter represent attempts to respond to consumer interest in determining the efficacy of the products they are consuming.[7] There are no mandatory international standards for such labels, which often means that countries devise their own standards. Further, consumer protection and information must often be communicated in the local language. Obtaining officially sanctioned translations can be time consuming. Even if there is no intent to limit trade, providing staff to check translations for foreign firms is unlikely to be a high priority for the use of scarce government resources. Labelling requirements are often quite specific, pertaining to size, fonts to be used, colours, placement of labels, and so on. Information on, for example, nutrition may differ considerably from that required by the country of origin of the product. As a result, the exporter may be faced with commissioning tests of the product to obtain the required information.

Prior to exporting, labels may have to be approved by the importing government. Approvals can be subject to bureaucratic delay that can give domestic producers of similar goods a first mover advantage in establishing their presence in the market, in building reputation and in setting a standard for quality. These advantages may be costly for exporters to overcome when they eventually receive permission to move their products into the market. When information is required, the efficacy of testing firms in the exporter's country, the appropriateness of the testing facilities or the evidence submitted can all be questioned by officials in the importing country. Importing countries may specify, for example, that only certain facilities in their own country can conduct tests for exhaust emissions on imported vehicles. Limiting approved facilities may endow them with market power, raising the costs for importers.

In all of the cases presented above, the motivation may be legitimate domestic policy goals or protection from imports. Further, the link between domestic regulations and their ability to restrict trade, at first glance, may not be obvious. For example, even if restricting international airfreight to a single designated airport does not lead to a constraint on inbound flights, it may lead to congestion in freight handling facilities and bonded warehouses that drives up property prices and ground rents that indirectly raise the costs of importing. In a similar fashion, when airports are located in major cities the price of land is likely to be high, raising the cost of facilities that need to be near the airport. This was a long-standing complaint with Tokyo's Narita facilities.

It has also been a long-standing complaint of US automobile manufacturers that Japanese zoning restrictions limited their ability to set up dealership networks. This was used to explain the poor sales performance of American made automobiles in Japan – although one suspects that the refusal of US manufacturers to engineer their vehicles for right-hand drive is far more important. Food retailers in the US, however, have had similar complaints regarding Japanese zoning regulations that limit the size of supermarkets to the benefit of Japan's smaller scale and labour-intensive retail sector. Japan has always contended that zoning regulations are a strictly domestic matter.

A failure of a government to act may also be construed as a trade barrier. For example, French farmers have sometimes taken direct action against imports of British lambs, stopping and intimidating lorry drivers transporting lambs as they left French ports on the English Channel or the channel tunnel. Lorries have been turned back and have even been burned. British farm groups and the British press accuse French police of failing to strictly enforce domestic laws against this sort of violence (Gordon 1991). Similar accusations of failures to act when officials or others engage in illegal or questionable activities are common in developing countries – 'turning a blind eye' when foreigners are involved.

The regulation of transborder movements of goods has long been a favourite source of corruption income. This is for two reasons. First, border crossing points tend to be few in number and relatively easy to acquire resources for control purposes – it is the most obvious manifestation of a country exercising its sovereignty.[8] Second, as foreign firms are the source of corruption income, complaints are less likely to be heeded than if they arise from domestic sources. Beyond the obvious failure to collect tariffs in return for a bribe, there are additional opportunities to garner corruption income (Shleifer and Vishny 1993) from the regulation of transborder movements of goods. The simplest, most obvious way to do this is to create a regulation that requires a bureaucratic signature. The bureaucrat is thus interposed into the transaction and can withhold the required signature to obtain the bribe. Hence, there is a direct pecuniary incentive to invent administrative regulations pertaining to the cross-border movement of goods (Wade 1985). Of course, there may be elaborate façades put in place to justify the signature that may require exporters to incur additional costs.

Corruption tends to impose transaction-like costs on firms beyond the direct bribe cost. This is because corruption is almost always formally illegal and, hence, cannot be carried out openly (Alam 1990). Thus, there are information costs imposed on firms in terms of identifying the individuals from whom permissions must be obtained, in determining the appropriate size of the bribe, understanding the mechanism for paying the bribe, and so on; there are negotiation costs associated with having someone pay the bribe – 'cash, no paper trails please' – and monitoring costs to ensure that what the bribe paid for is actually delivered. While over time exporters can acquire experience regarding the local bribery culture, the process can be very costly for exporters attempting to enter a market or for intermittent exporters. The 'learning by doing' advantage may create a degree of market power for existing exporters that further increases the wedge between world and domestic prices. Local agents can be used to reduce some of these costs, but exporters are then faced with asymmetric information problems whereby, for example, the local agent knows the appropriate size for a bribe but the exporter does not. Many of the *compradors* of the old China trade became very wealthy exploiting their information advantage.

Reducing border corruption is difficult because it is resisted by the officials who have a direct stake in the corruption income. Recognizing this, there have been international protocols negotiated that attempt to limit the ability of foreign – usually developed country – business people from paying bribes (Pierros and Hudson 1998). One suspects that these initiatives, while they may have positive externalities in terms of the governance of developing countries, further restrict trade as either bribes are not paid, limiting market access or that exporters are forced to find even more secretive and indirect methods of enabling imports. Alternatives such as hiring official agents in exporting countries to obtain all of the clearances and undertake the paperwork prior to the products being exported so that, in effect, customs is cleared before shipment, have been resisted by the bureaucracies of developing countries that see their livelihoods threatened.

Corruption costs, both direct and indirect, drive a wedge between prices in importing countries and world prices, thus providing domestic firms with protection. These firms will also have an incentive to ensure the continuation of the existing system.

Conclusions

Administrative measures can be effective in providing protection. They are difficult to control because they can be cloaked in the guise of a domestic policy or administrative imperative. Motives for the imposition of protectionist administrative measures are unlikely to be freely admitted. Further, administrative measures cannot be eliminated because legitimate domestic imperatives often have a trade restricting effect as an externality. International constraints on the use of administrative measures then centres on the measure that can achieve domestic policy goals in the least trade-restricting manner. Importing bureaucracies have little incentive to change their policies or methods of operation. The NAFTA established mechanisms for formal consultations among the member countries regarding the harmonization of domestic regulations and consultations regarding new regulations with the potential to inhibit trade. While these bodies have had some success (Freshwater 2003), they have largely been forums to 'talk and talk' as they lack any mechanisms to force a conclusion to discussions (Kerr 2005).

One possible way forward would be to allow exporting countries to suggest alternatives that would achieve the policy goals of the importing country but are less restrictive of trade. This could be done through the offices of, for example, the WTO Secretariat. The importing country could then either implement the suggestion of the exporting country or have to formally respond as to why the suggested alternative cannot be implemented. If the exporter did not accept the reasons provided, then the issue could be taken to a dispute panel for a decision. The onus to come up with a less trade-distorting alternative is then on the party that has an incentive to develop one.

As with many trade policy issues that move beyond official border measures such as tariffs and import quotas, international agreements impinge on what have been considered domestic competencies. While governments have agreed to limits on border measures, agreeing to limit their domestic prerogatives is much more difficult politically. As a result, progress on constraining the use of administrative measures will be a long and difficult process.

Notes

1. Of course, it is possible for government activities to reduce the effects of market failure or anticompetitive practices.
2. While the SPS was negotiated and implemented after the Uruguay Round and the TBT was strengthened in it, their implementation has been fraught with controversy. See for example: Hobbs (2001); Hobbs and Kerr (2002); Isaac *et al.* (2002); Kerr (2003).
3. Although a wider range of policy options may be discussed at the early stages of policy initiation.
4. See Hobbs (1996) for an introduction to the economics of transaction costs.
5. Roberts *et al.* (1999) provide a more detailed method for classifying non-tariff barriers.
6. A requirement that exports be carried in ships that carry the flag of the exporter acts in a similar fashion to an export tax.
7. See Sawyer (2004) and Rudge (2005) for studies that examine how labeling requirements can effect international trade flows.
8. Of course, the control of smuggling is a related issue.

References

Alam, M. S. (1990), 'Some Economic Costs of Corruption in LDCs', *The Journal of Development Studies*, **27**(13), 647–56.

Boyd, S. L., J. E. Hobbs and W. A. Kerr (2003), 'The Impact of Customs Procedures on Business to Consumer E-commerce in Food Products', *Supply Chain Management*, **8**(3), 195–200.

Cordon, B. and T. Sinha (2001), 'An Analysis of an Alliance: NAFTA Trucking and the US Insurance Industry', *Estey Centre Journal of International Law and Trade Policy*, **2**(2), 235–45, www.esteyjournal.com

Freshwater, D. (2003), 'Free Trade, Pesticide Regulation and NAFTA Harmonization', *Estey Centre Journal of International Law and Trade Policy*, **4**(1), 32–57, www.esteyjournal.com

Gordon, D. V., J. E. Hobbs and W. A. Kerr (1991), 'Price Integration in the EC Lamb Market: An Application of the Holmes–Hutton Test', presented at the XXI International Conference of Agricultural Economists, Tokyo, Japan, 22–29 August.

Hobbs, J. E. (2001), 'Labeling and Consumer Issues in International Trade', in H. J. Michelmann, J. Rude, J. Stabler and G. Storey (eds), *Globalization and Agricultural Trade Policy*, Boulder, CO: Lynne Rienner Publishers, Inc., pp. 269–85.

Hobbs, J. E. (1996), 'A Transaction Cost Approach to Supply Chain Management', *Supply Chain Management: an International Journal*, **1**(2), 15–27.

Hobbs, J. E. and W. A. Kerr (1999), 'Transaction Costs', in S. Bhagwan Dahiya (ed.), *The Current State of Economic Science*, 4, Rohtak, India: Spellbound Publications PVT Ltd. pp. 2111–33.

Isaac, G. E., M. Phillipson and W. A. Kerr (2002), *International Regulation of Trade in the Products of Biotechnology*, Estey Centre Research Papers No. 2, Saskatoon: Estey Centre for Law and Economics in International Trade.

Kerr, W. A. (2003), 'Science-based Rules of Trade – A Mantra for Some, An Anathema for Others', *The Estey Centre Journal of International Law and Trade Policy*, **4**(2), 86–97, www.esteyjournal.com.

Kerr, W. A. (2004), 'Homeland Security and the Rules of International Trade', *Estey Centre Journal of International Law and Trade Policy*, **5**(1), 1–10, www.esteyjournal.com.

Kerr, W. A. (2005), 'NAFTA's Underdeveloped Institutions: Did They Contribute to the BSE Crisis?', presented at the North American Agrifood Market Integration Consortium workshop No. 2, Agrifood Regulatory and Policy Institutions Under Stress, San Antonio, May, 406.

Kerr, W. A. (1997), 'Removing Health, Sanitary and Technical Non-Tariff Barriers in NAFTA', *Journal of World Trade*, **31**(5), 57–73.

Kerr, W. A. and J. E. Hobbs (2002), 'The North American–European Union Dispute Over Beef Produced Using Growth Hormones: A Major Test for the New International Trade Regime', *The World Economy*, **25**(2), 283–96.

Pierros, P. and C. Hudson (1998), 'The Hard Graft of Tackling Corruption in International Business Transactions – Progress in International Co-operation and the OECD Convention', *Journal of World Trade*, **32**(2), 77–102.

Roberts, D., T. Josling and D. Orden (1999), *A Framework for Analyzing Technical Barriers in Agricultural Markets*, Technical Bulletin No. 1876, Washington, DC: US Department of Agriculture, Economic Research Service.

Rudge, T. J. (2005), 'Increasing Regulations for Natural Health Products: An Investigations of Trade Effects', unpublished MSc Thesis, Department of Agricultural Economics, University of Saskatchewan, Canada.

Sawyer, E. N. (2004), 'The Economic Impacts of Harmonizing Organic Standards Internationally', unpublished MSc Thesis, Department of Agricultural Economics, University of Saskatchewan, Canada.

Shleifer, A. and R. W. Vishny (1993), 'Corruption', *Quarterly Journal of Economics*, **108**(3), 599–617.

Wade, R. (1985), 'The Market for Public Office: Why the Indian State is Not Better at Development', *World Development*, **13**(4), 712–32.

PART IV

CONTINGENCY AND SAFEGUARD METHODS

32 Antidumping: theory and practice, rationales and calculation methods
Carol Chui-Ha Lau

Introduction

Dumping, defined as price discrimination or below cost sales, is a commonly adopted commercial strategy that is legal for domestic firms to apply but is punishable by international trade law when conducted by firms from other countries. Antidumping (AD) legislation allows importing countries to impose import duties on such dumped imports. AD legislation has been widely used in recent years by developed and developing countries alike, perhaps due to its legality and its ease and flexibility in adoption. This chapter provides an overview of the theory and practice of dumping and AD policies. It begins by contrasting the differences in how economists and the legislative authorities view dumping, followed by some statistics on the proliferation of AD practices worldwide. The WTO rules for AD legislation and the different methods that authorities use to calculate dumping penalties are also discussed. The chapter concludes with some suggested revisions for the current legislation.

Dumping, antidumping, and international trade laws

Economists have traditionally defined dumping as international price discrimination where prices vary across national markets (Viner 1923). Price discrimination dumping occurs when a firm exports a product at an export price lower than the price that it charges in its domestic market. For example, if a Japanese firm sells widgets for 10 yen in Japan and for the equivalent of 7 yen in Canada, the Japanese firm is dumping into the Canadian market. Economic theory shows that price discrimination is a profit-maximizing strategy when the firms are faced with different demand sensitivity, or elasticity, for their products. Specifically, firms should sell at low prices to consumers who are very sensitive to a price increase and sell at a higher price to the insensitive or inelastic consumers. In the context of trade, the Japanese firm is likely to sell in Canada at a lower price than in Japan because the firm faces competition from Canadian and other international firms. Canadian domestic firms also often engage in price discrimination by selling the same products at different prices to customers based on their age, income and the quantity of purchase.

In the 1970s, the definition of dumping was legally expanded to include the export of goods at a price that falls below the firm's production costs (Das and Mohanty 1987). Economists argue that firms often cut prices to levels below their unit costs in the short run or during a recession (Ethier 1982). Selling below cost is an economically rational loss-minimizing strategy. It is perfectly legal for domestic firms to price discriminate or sell below costs in their domestic countries. Such pricing strategies are not against any anti-trust regulations. However, export firms engaging in the same practices could be faced with penalties.

Many economists argue that the only situation in which dumping should be punished is when such activities are conducted with a predatory intent. Predation refers to the instances in which a firm dumps its products into its market at cut-throat prices with the intention of driving its competitors into bankruptcy (Telser 1966). Once its competitors exit the market, the firm could become the monopolist and reap supernormal profits. Predation is illegal under anti-trust regulations because the eventual monopolistic price would be harmful to the consumers. In reality, predation across international markets is extremely unlikely to be the incentive behind dumping. With so many potential sources of supply from around the world, the probability that a single firm can establish a monopoly price in another country is extremely low, if not zero. An empirical study by Trebilcock and Hutton (1990) also suggests that international predation is at best a rare occurrence. Of all of the EU and US cases, perhaps 3 percent of these cases may exhibit the possibility of predation on the part of the exporters (*The Economist* 1998). Given the unlikely existence of predatory dumping, most economists agree that AD duties are no different from the traditional, protectionist tariff barriers that the GATT negotiations had repeatedly struggled to cut back over the past 50 years.

A minority of economists have challenged this common criticism of AD policies. Their favorable view of AD policies stems from the strategic trade theory that was made popular in the 1970s. Using models characterized with imperfect competition and game theory, some economists have demonstrated how AD policies can be used to raise the welfare of the importing countries by capturing higher levels of economic profits through import protection.[1] Provided that such gains in profits and tax revenues outweigh the loss to consumers due to higher prices, AD protection may in fact enhance the importing countries' well-being. The main shortcoming of this view is that while these models are theoretically sound, empirical studies that can prove such claims are virtually non-existent.

More importantly, the welfare gains that these theoretical studies often refer to are based on partial equilibrium analysis. These studies examine how economic profits in the protected industries could be raised with the imposition of AD duties without accounting for the price and resources allocation distortions that such protection would create. For example, AD duties imposed on steel would raise not only consumer prices but also the input prices for the steel-using industries. The steel AD duties essentially erode the competitiveness of the auto industry, and thereby magnify welfare losses. As AD protection artificially raises economic profits and attracts more workers and capital to the steel industry, these factors of production are inadvertently being diverted from other industries. Given that inefficient industries are more likely to seek protection, AD protection tilts resources allocation towards inefficient industries. In other words, AD policies benefit the industries in which a country has comparative disadvantage, while hurting the industries in which it has comparative advantage in, namely, its export sectors. In existing studies, a common conclusion is that AD policies often lead to a deterioration in the overall welfare levels for all countries involved.[2] Hence, given the absence of predatory dumping and the presence of distortionary effects from AD duties, most economists view AD legislation as simply a means to pacify domestic lobbying pressure for import protection.

International trade legislation, however, takes a rather different view on dumping. The General Agreements on Tariffs and Trade (GATT) and the World Trade Organization (WTO) regard dumping as an 'unfair' trade practice because the import-competing industry is subject to more intense competition than in the 'normal course of trade' (GATT 1986). A 'fair' export price is defined as the price that the export firm charges in its own domestic market in 'normal' trade. Trade is 'normal' if most of the export firm's domestic sales are full cost recovering. If such sales incur a loss, the 'fair' price or normal value is often an artificially constructed full cost recovering value of the goods. GATT Article VI, also known as the Antidumping Code, and subsequently the WTO Antidumping Agreement, allows import-competing industries that suffer or are likely to suffer 'material' injury from dumped products to ask for the imposition of antidumping (AD) duties on the imports. Such duties can remain in effect for a maximum of five years. Upon the expiration date, the authorities in importing countries conduct an administrative review and decide if the duties should be rescinded or renewed. Proponents of AD policies argue that such policies are necessary because they create a 'level playing field' for domestic industries, which face unfair import competition. Specifically, they contend that the exporters may be enjoying a protected market in their own countries due to monopoly, cronyism or other forms of market distortions. Such protection allows the foreign firms to reap supernormal profits in their own markets, or sanctuary markets, and then use those profits to cross-subsidize their export sales (Lindsey and Ikenson 2003). They believe that AD laws can ensure a level playing field by offsetting such artificial advantages that the exporters enjoy.

The proliferation of antidumping complaints
In spite of the fact that economists often argue against the usage of AD policies, AD duties have become central in a new wave of protectionism, partly due to the significant decrease in conventional tariff barriers resulting from previous GATT negotiations. AD legislation essentially offers a lever to domestic governments in managing pressure from domestic lobbyists. Over the past 30 years, AD complaints have emerged as the most widespread impediment to international trade (Blonigen and Prusa 2003). The number of AD measures launched by WTO member countries every year has risen dramatically from 458 in 1990 to 903 in 1995 (Lee 1997). From July 2002 to June 2003, the number of AD complaints has reached 1323 (WTO 2004). Even traditional free trade partners, such as Canada and the US, have filed numerous AD suits against each other. The most notable amongst these cases is perhaps the dispute over US AD duties on Canadian softwood lumber exports. With quotas on agricultural products and textile and apparel products being phased out over time, AD is poised to become the most significant trade barrier remaining in the WTO member countries (Blonigen *et al.* 1999). In fact, with the WTO Agreement on Textiles and Clothing having expired on 31 December 2004, the US textiles manufacturers have indicated that they would file for protection against exports from China and India (BBC 2004). It appears that with the elimination of traditional trade barriers such as tariffs and quotas over time, AD actions have increasingly become the new weapon of choice in international trade wars.

AD policies are popular because they are easy to launch and the domestic authorities have almost a free hand in calculating and imposing the duties. Only a few large firms in the import-competing industries need to file a complaint, and different levels of AD duties could be imposed on specific products from specific firms from specific countries. The process in which the authorities calculate specific duties is secretive and highly complex, and the resulting AD duties are often hefty and long lasting. For the period between 1991 and 1995, the EU AD duties averaged 29 percent, while those imposed by the US averaged 57 percent (*The Economist* 1998). Even though the WTO specifies that AD duties should expire after five years, the authorities in the import countries can easily renew the imposition of the duties. A number of US and EU cases have remained in effect for more than 20 years (Leidy 1994).

Until recently, AD actions have been mainly practiced by developed countries, such as the US, the EU, Canada and Australia. These countries possess the legal expertise in applying the GATT AD Code in the construction and application of their own AD systems. By 1990, these countries collectively accounted for approximately 80 percent of all AD actions (Macmillan 1995). Since then, the developing countries have increasingly realized that they could also impose AD duties for their own import protection or as tit-for-tat strategies. The World Bank has since assisted countries such as Egypt and Turkey in establishing AD regimes as the quid pro quo for reductions in their tariff barriers. Argentina, Brazil, South Africa and the Asian countries are also hitting back with their own AD laws. China established its AD legislation in 1997, although it has only launched 20 cases as of February 2002 (Grace *et al.* 2003). In the year 2000, developing countries initiated approximately 50 percent of all AD investigations.

A disturbing feature of AD cases is that a majority of the complaints are targeted against input materials. For the years 1995 to June 2005, about 50 percent of all the AD cases were related to the steel and chemical industries (WTO 2005a). While AD policies could indeed offer protection to the import-competing intermediate goods industries, the higher prices of such inputs would often adversely affect the competitiveness of numerous end-user industries. For example, while the imposition of AD duties on steel imports by the US government could help secure the 226 211 steel workers' jobs, almost 13 million jobs in the steel-using industries were threatened as a result of the rise in the price of steel (CITAC 1999).

AD legislation and calculation methods

The world's first AD legislation was invented by Canada in 1904. Other countries, such New Zealand (1905), Australia (1906) and the Union of South Africa (1914) soon followed. Canada's first AD law was mainly a political product. The Liberal Party of the day in Canada, which traditionally had been a supporter of free trade, was under tremendous pressure from manufacturers when it failed to raise tariffs. Meanwhile, the export-oriented agricultural interests pressured the Liberal government for tariff reductions. To accommodate such a dilemma, the Minister of Finance introduced the AD Code (Boltuck 1988). By 1921, the US, France, Britain and most of the British Commonwealth had had AD laws in place (Finger 1993).

Internationally, the League of Nations became interested in dumping in the 1920s (Pangratis and Vermulst 1994). The GATT AD Code came into effect in 1948 as a general guideline for the formation of and amendments to AD legislation for GATT signatories. GATT member countries did not concern themselves with the use of AD laws until the late 1950s (Finger 1993). AD first became an important GATT issue in the Kennedy Round (1964–1967). The AD Code of 1967 defined dumping only as international price discrimination. The subsequent Tokyo Round (1973–1979) created the AD Code of 1979, and upon the insistence of the US, it formally expanded the definition of dumping to include sales below the costs of production. The Uruguay Round (1986–1994) provided modifications to the previous AD Codes, which eventually became the WTO AD Agreement in 1994. The WTO AD Agreement serves as a general guideline for the WTO member countries in the drafting of their own AD legislation. Different countries interpret and adopt the guidelines differently, and such differences and the lack of transparencies in the implementation of the principles have since fueled the growing controversies surrounding AD practices.

An AD complaint is typically launched by an import-competing firm, which suspects its foreign competitors have dumped import-competing products. The import-competing firm must file the complaint with its domestic authorities. For example, a US firm will be launching its complaint with the Department of Commerce, while a Canadian firm will be contacting the Canadian Border Services Agency. The WTO AD Agreement states that the AD complaint has to be sufficiently supported by most of the import-competing firms, although it is at the discretion of the individual countries as to what constitute 'sufficient support'. For example, the US is silent on the specific threshold, whereas Canada requires the complaint to be supported by Canadian firms who collectively account for at least 25 percent of Canadian production. The authorities will launch an AD investigation only if the complaint is deemed valid. A complaint is valid if the import-competing firm provides 'evidence' that the imports have been dumped, although such evidence is based on the import-competing firm's own data. Upon initiating an investigation, the authorities would contact the foreign exporters for their price and cost information. The foreign firms are typically required to respond to the requests within a short period of time, often within a month. If they refuse to cooperate, the authorities may find surrogate firms from the same or other countries that export similar products. Upon the receipt of the information, the authorities will calculate the preliminary dumping margins. Dumping margins are defined as the difference between the export price and the normal value.

The WTO AD Agreement indicates that the authorities can use the following calculation methods in finding the dumping margins: (a) the Home-country selling price method; (b) the Constructed-value method; (c) the Third-country selling price method; and (d) the Ministerial Specification method. The WTO guidelines specify substantive rules for the numerous adjustments with regard to administrative expenses and transport costs that are required to arrive at comparable prices. In general, the home-country selling price method reflects the price discrimination definition of dumping, while the constructed-value method reflects below cost sales. The authorities are required to resort to the home-country selling price method whenever possible. Note that here the 'home' market refers to the foreign exporters' own domestic market. The normal value under this method is the preponderant home price that the foreign firms charge in their own market, unless their sales are not profitable, or if the home price is substantially determined by the government. In the case of the former exception, the normal value will be determined by the constructed-value method. The normal value of the products is the exporters' average production costs plus an amount for profit, and if such information is unavailable, a full cost-recovering profitable value will be artificially constructed by the authorities. In the case of the latter exception where the home price is not determined by market forces, such as in planned economies, the normal value is the full cost recovering price of the like goods sold by a third country determined under the third-country selling price method. This method is often used on exports from countries such as China and the countries of the former Soviet Union. The ministerial specification method is used when there is insufficient information for dumping margin calculations, such as when the exporters refuse to cooperate in normal value calculations, or if the information provided is incomplete. Such a situation may arise if the exporters are reluctant to disclose confidential firm-specific information, or if the costs of supplying such information are formidable. This method sets the normal value as the export price plus an amount equal to the highest dumping margin found in the period of investigation, or a weighted average margin determined for other exporters.

The WTO AD Agreement establishes that AD duties are warranted only if the importing country can show that: (a) the imports have been dumped; and (b) there is a causal link between the dumped products and material injury to the import-competing industries. It is left to the authorities in the importing country to demonstrate the causal link between dumping and injury. For example, the US International Trade Commission establishes whether the dumped products have caused or will cause material injury to the US competitors, while the Canadian International Trade Tribunal conducts injury hearings. Dumping margin calculations and injury determinations are often conducted simultaneously, and a finding of no injury will result in an immediate termination of the investigation.

If positive dumping margins and injury are found, a provisional duty equal to the whole or part of the margins will be imposed on the goods. Perhaps in an attempt to curb frivolous AD complaints, the WTO requires that the investigation to be terminated if the margin is 2 percent or less, which is considered to be *de minimis*. Otherwise, the exporters are required to pay cash or post bonds for the duty imposed. The authorities will then proceed to conduct their final investigation. Over the course of the final investigation, the foreign firms have the opportunity to submit more detailed price and cost information and to retain legal counsel. Foreign firms that are subject to AD investigations often incur significant administrative and legal costs even if they were found to be not dumping. The average length of the investigation period of AD cases is approximately one year. Opponents of AD legislation have often argued that the costs and uncertainty brought upon by an AD complaint often act as a tax on the foreign firms regardless of the outcome of the investigation. In the event that the final investigation reaches an affirmative finding for both dumping and injury, the final AD duties will be imposed on the goods for a period of at most five years. This is often referred to as the Sunset Clause. Upon its expiration date, the AD case is typically reviewed to determine whether dumping still exists, or whether the case should be terminated. All WTO member countries are also required to report to the WTO twice a year regarding their AD investigations.

The foreign firms, of course, can disagree with the calculations of the importing country. The foreign firms have the right to appeal to the WTO through the Dispute Settlement Body (WTO 2005b). The disputes typically go through a year of consultations, panel discussions and reports. Both sides of the dispute can appeal the ruling, and the party that the WTO rules against is required to cease all of its offences. In the event that the offender refuses to comply with the WTO decision, the winner of the complaint can impose sanctions on the offending country. A widely reported AD case that has been through numerous WTO appeals is the Canada–US softwood lumber dispute. Since the Softwood Lumber Agreement expired on 31 March 2001, the US has been imposing various levels of AD duties on Canadian softwood lumber imports. Canada disagreed with the US determinations, and has since brought numerous complaints and appeals to the WTO. Unfortunately, numerous WTO rulings for Canada have not deterred the US from continuing to impose AD duties on Canadian softwood lumber. To date, any possible solutions appear problematic. Meanwhile, the softwood lumber industry in Canada continues to suffer job losses which may not be warranted, while the US consumers continue to pay higher home prices as a result of the duties.

The Doha Round and reforming the AD legislation

The Doha Round WTO Ministerial Declaration in 2001 has succeeded in putting AD legislation back on the table for further negotiations. The negotiating parties can be broadly divided into two groups, the US and a group of countries somewhat euphemistically called the 'Friends of AD' (Kerr and Loppacher 2004)[3]. The US position is to clearly defend the use of AD measures, while the Friends seek more wide-ranging revisions of the legislation. Some of the Friends' proposals include the inclusion of predation as a criteria in dumping investigations, the separation of regular business cycle fluctuations from injury determinations, the requirement that a case can be launched only if 50 percent or more of the import-competing firms support such a complaint, the inclusion of below-cost foreign market sales when calculating the normal value, the imposition of a 'lesser duty' as long as such a duty is sufficient to eliminate injury, and the termination of AD duties after a period of five years. The US takes an opposing stand on all of these issues. The only agreement that the US and 'Friends' have reached is to increase the transparency of how AD duties are being calculated.

Lindsey and Ikenson (2003) have also explored various ways in which the AD legislation could be reformed. They proposed 20 different areas in which the current WTO AD legislation could be improved upon. Examples of their proposals include: the exclusion of a profit margin in the constructed-value method; the raising of *de minimis* from 2 percent to 5 percent; and a mandatory requirement to hold public interest hearings in injury determinations.

Unfortunately, the current AD laws consist of many more than 20 flaws. Exporters should also be given sufficient time to respond to the detailed questionnaires, which are issued by AD authorities in the initiation phase of cases. Exporters often produce multiple products and sell to multiple destinations. Consequently, it is highly unlikely that exporters, especially those from developing countries, would have highly disaggregated cost and price data readily available. Public interest hearings should be mandatory, and given that intermediate products such as steel and chemicals account for a large majority of the AD complaints, it is essential for the importing country's end-users of such inputs to be heard when the authorities estimate injury. In other words, perhaps the authorities should consider not only how the dumped steel imports have harmed the import-competing steel makers, but also how such AD duties may cause injury to the steel-using industries. The criteria for injury should be broadened to consider the effects on the downstream steel users. In an effort to prevent the filing of superfluous AD complaints, perhaps the legislation can require the unsuccessful petitioners to pay damages to the affected exporters, similar to tort cases, for the legal and administrative costs that the exporters have incurred.

Conclusion

Dumping, which is an economically sound practice that is commonly practiced by foreign and domestic firms alike, is punishable by international trade laws. AD policies are not grounded on the basis of preventing predation, but rather on 'leveling the playing field' for the import-competing firms when exporters are allegedly protected in their sanctuary, home markets. Consequently, current legislation does not require any proof of predation before AD duties can be imposed. The implementation of AD policies is highly complex and subjective, and the resulting dumping margins are often incomprehensible to the common observers. Most economists regard such hefty and long-lasting AD duties as simply a new form of protectionist measure. The only difference between the traditional protectionist tariffs and AD duties is that AD duties appear to be here to stay.

Notes

1.   A sizeable amount of literature has explored the strategic game theoretical benefits of AD policies. For an overview, see Blonigen and Prusa (2003).
2.   See Brannlund and Lofgren (1995), Devault (1996), Das and Mohanty (1987) and Blonigen *et al.* (1999).
3.   The members include Brazil, Chile, Columbia, Costa Rica, Hong Kong, Israel, Japan, South Korea, Mexico, Norway, Singapore, Switzerland, Taiwan and Thailand.

References

BBC (2004), 'Trouser Traders Sense Foul Play,' 1 November.
Blonigen, B., J. Flynn and M. Gallaway (1999), 'Welfare Costs of the US Antidumping and Countervailing Duty Laws,' *Journal of International Trade*, **49**(2), 211–44.
Blonigen, B. and T. Prusa (2003), 'Antidumping,' in E. K. Choi and J. Harrigan (eds), *Handbook of International Trade*, Oxford, UK and Cambridge, MA: Blackwell Publishers.
Boltuck, R. (1988), 'An Economic Analysis of Dumping,' *Journal of World Trade Law*, **21**(5), 45–54.
Brannlund, R. and K. Lofgren (1995), 'Cyclical Dumping and Correlated Business Cycles in Imperfect Markets: Empirical Applications to the Canadian Pulp and Paper Industry,' *Applied Economics*, **27**(11), 1081–91.
CITAC (1999), 'Consuming Industries Trade Action Coalition,' http://www.citac.info/steeltaskforce/map/.
Das, P. and K. Mohanty (1987), 'Welfare of the Dumping Country: A Comprehensive Ranking of Policies,' *Journal of Quantitative Economics*, **3**(1), 13–34.
Devault, J. (1996), 'The Welfare Effects of US AD Duties,' *Open Economies Review*, 7, 19–33
Ethier, Wilfred (1982), 'Dumping,' *Journal of Political Economy*, **90**, 487–506.
Finger, J. Michael (1993), 'Antidumping is where the Action is,' in J. Michael Finger (ed.), *Antidumping: How it Works and Who gets Hurt*, Ann Arbor, MI: University of Michigan Press, pp. 3–79.
GATT (1986), *The Text of the General Agreement on Tariffs and Trade*, Sales No: GATT 1986–4. Geneva.
Grace, D., A. Herwig and Y. Feng (2003), 'China's Antidumping Regime,' *World Trade Magazine*, **16**(3), available at: http://www.worldtrademag.com/CDA/Archives/bb563ae818af7010VgnVCM100000f932a8c.
Kerr, W. and L. J. Loppacher (2004), 'Antidumping in the Doha Negotiations: Fairy Tales at the WTO,' *Journal of World Trade*, **38**(2), 211–44.
Lee, P. Y. (1997), *Canadian and International Use of Anti-dumping and Countervailing Measures (1988–1995)*, Research Branch, Canadian International Trade Tribunal, Ottawa, Canada.
Leidy, M. (1994), 'Antidumping: Solution or Problem in the 1990s?' in *International Trade Policies: The Uruguay Round and Beyond*, vol. II, Washington: IMF.
Lindsey, B. and D. Ikenson (2003), *Antidumping Exposed: The Devilish Details of Unfair Trade Law*, Washington, DC: Cato Institute.
Macmillan K. (1995), 'Antidumping: Next on the Trade Agenda,' *Canadian Business Economics*, **3**, 20–28.
Pangratis, A. and E. Vermulst (1994), 'Injury in Antidumping Proceedings: the Need to Look Beyond the Uruguay Round Results,' *Journal of World Trade*, **28**(5), 61–96.
Telser, L. (1966), 'Cutthroat Competition and the Long Purse,' *Journal of Law and Economics*, **9**, 259–77.
The Economist (1998), 'Unfair Protection', 7 November.
Trebilcock, Michael and Susan Hutton (1990), 'An Empirical Study of the Application of Canadian Antidumping Laws: A Search for Normative Rationales,' *Journal of World Trade*, 123–45.
Viner, J. (1923), *Dumping: A Problem in International Trade*, Chicago, IL: University of Chicago Press.
WTO (2004), *WTO Annual Report*, Geneva, Switzerland.
WTO (2005a), *Antidumping Measures: By Sector*, http://www.wto.org/english/tratop_e/adp_e/adp_e.htm.
WTO (2005b), *Dispute Settlement Body*, http://www.wto.org/english/tratop_e/dispu_e/dispu_e.htm.

33 Unfair subsidies and countervailing duties
Katherine Baylis

Introduction

The idea behind countervailing duties (CVDs) is inherently appealing. If a foreign competitor is being 'unfairly' subsidized, the importing country can mitigate against the effect of that subsidy by imposing a CVD. The rationale appeals to the concept of fairness, and if by being available, CVD law discourages bad (distorting) behaviour by exporters, it should improve global welfare. However, as is the case with many trade tools, there is the potential for abuse, and many argue that CVDs, like anti-dumping (AD), are often used as purely a means to insulate one's domestic producers from the competition of international trade.

How does a CVD work? If an industry (a firm, union or trade association) believes its products are competing against unfairly subsidized imports, it can file a petition for CVDs. Two key components need to be determined for CVD to be imposed: first, if there is an actionable subsidy, and second (at least for signatories of the GATT subsidies code), if the domestic industry has been injured by the subsidized imports. A preliminary determination is made both in terms of the existence of the subsidy and injury. Next, the appropriate governing body (for example, the International Trade Authority (ITA) of the Department of Commerce in the United States) makes a final determination of whether there is a subsidy. Then, the government (for example, the US International Trade Commission (ITC)) determines whether the subsidies, or, in the case of the United States, the subsidized exports, have injured the domestic injury. Lastly, duties are administered.

Not all subsidies are actionable. For a subsidy to be able to trigger a CVD under the GATT, it must confer a benefit not otherwise available from the market,[1] and it must be sufficiently targeted.[2] Each of these components has been a source of legal dispute. Most subsidies do not come in the simple form of a per-unit payment, and instead are delivered by regulation, such as low fees for the use of government-owned natural resources,[3] special rules for export products in regulated markets,[4] financing provisions,[5] or certain tax provisions for sales overseas.[6] As long as the regulation confers a benefit to the recipient, where that benefit can be defined as a decrease in average cost (not only marginal costs), it can be countervailable.[7]

The 'benefit' has to be relative to what would have existed under the market. This rule raises concerns about subsidies that are intended to address some form of market failure. Although some provision is made in the GATT for partial subsidies for one-time environmental investments, other cases have been brought against subsidies that arguably addressed labour-market failures,[8] and financial-market failures.[9]

Third, if the subsidy is not explicitly an export subsidy, it needs to be found to go to a specific industry or group of industries. A problem arises from the fact that the CVD laws provide no guidance as to what constitutes a 'group' of industries, leaving the ITA considerable flexibility in assessment of targeting. For example, agriculture has been found to be more than a group of industries, so an irrigation project that benefited all farmers was not countervailable,[10] while a benefit going to producers of highly disparate agricultural commodities (hogs, cattle, apples, onions, beans, sugar and honey) was found to be 'specific' (Sykes 1989).[11]

CVD is often perceived as a less-evil brother to AD. Many lawyers and economists have argued that CVD has merit compared with AD to counteract distorting subsidies which can cause harm to an import-competing domestic industry. Further, CVD has been touted as a way to encourage 'good behaviour' on the part of countries (Finger 1993; Brennan and Pincus 1993). A number of papers, following Brander and Spencer (1983), show that countries may have the incentive to subsidize their export industries, particularly if there is market power and large fixed costs involved, which can lead to a prisoner's dilemma where all countries subsidize and none benefit. If used well, CVD could deter such behaviour (Stigliz 1997). Other commentators counter that CVD law is geared to aiding protectionism (Schwartz 1978), and argue CVD is not intended to promote efficiency but instead to provide domestic producers with an entitlement to protection (Goetz et al. 1986; Andoh 1992).

While there has been a great deal of research on AD, there has been much less written on CVD. Theoretical models have been developed exploring firms' actions and reactions to dumping, and recently there has been a flurry of empirical studies on firm behaviour before, during and after an AD case, the types of AD cases that are brought, what determines AD findings, and unanticipated effects of AD. While there are some notable exceptions, the theory and empirics of CVD are much less well explored, and much of the work that touches on CVD has been on the use of subsidies and trade protection in general.

This chapter reviews the relevant theory regarding subsidies and countermeasures, and contrasts it with the practice. The chapter begins by asking why countries might want to subsidize their industries, and why another might want to impose CVD. In the third section, CVD case statistics are presented and compared with the theory. The chapter concludes by identifying areas for future research.

Economic theory

Since subsidizing the production of a good that primarily goes to foreign consumers almost always decreases welfare, we first have to ask: Why would a country ever do it? Second, since the importing country is receiving this subsidized good that is benefiting its consumers, why would it want to tax that benefit away?

First, consider a country that imposes a production subsidy on an export good. Using a simple two-country partial equilibrium model, one can walk through the effects on demand and supply in the exporter and importer, before and after the subsidy. In Figure 33.1, demand in the exporting country (country A) is illustrated as D and supply as S, generating an excess supply curve denoted as ES^0. Similarly, in the importing country (country B), demand is denoted as D^* and supply as S^*, yielding an excess demand curve, ED^0. The price where the excess demand and supply curves intersect gives the world price, p_w^0, and quantity traded, x^0, implying country A will produce q_s^0 and consume q_d^0, exporting the excess, x^0. Country B meanwhile will produce q_s^{*0} and consume q_d^{*0}.

Now assume country A imposes a per-unit production subsidy, s. The production subsidy drives the supply curve down to S^1, shifting the excess supply curve out to ES^1. This shift drives down world price to p_w^1, leading both countries to increase their consumption (to q_d^1 and q_d^{*1} in country A and B respectively), while country B increases its

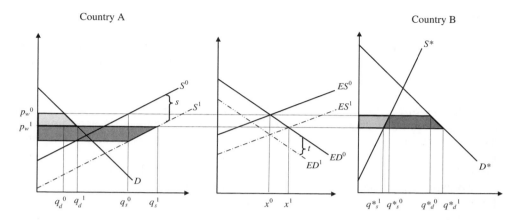

Figure 33.1   Partial equilibrium model of a production subsidy with trade

imports to x^1 and decreases its production to $q*_s^1$. The consumers in both countries receive an increase in consumer surplus, illustrated as the light-grey area in country A and the total grey area in country B. Producers in country A also gain, with an increase in producer surplus equal to the dark-grey area, while producers in country B lose by the light-grey area. Taxpayers in country A lose the per-unit subsidy times the total production, which overwhelms the gains by its producers and consumers. Meanwhile, the increase in consumer subsidy outweighs the losses by producers in country B. In short, country B is receiving a boon paid for by the treasury of country A.

Note that overall, the importer is better off because of these subsidies: it is only their producers who are suffering from this 'unfair' competition. Assume that the producers can induce the importer to impose a tariff that will counter the effect of the subsidy.[12] The tariff will shift the excess demand curve to the left (to ED^1) to return the quantity traded to x^0. The tariff, t, effectively neutralizes the trade effect of the production subsidy, and everything in country B returns to the pre-intervention situation with the exception that country A's treasury transfers income to country B in the amount of the tariff revenue. However, production and consumption in country A do not revert to the pre-subsidy situation: as the tariff drives down the price in country A by t, producers still produce more than otherwise (since their subsidy s is larger than the effect of the tariff, t) while consumers in country A reap the benefits of a further lowered price.[13]

The above model assumes that both importer and exporter are large countries and their firms do not have market power. While the latter assumption will be relaxed next, note that if the exporter is a small country, neither form of subsidy will have an effect on world price.

Strategic trade policy
Strategic trade policy describes the situation where trade policy is used to alter the strategic relationship between firms. For strategic trade policy to be possible, firms first need to have some strategic relationship, which implies they must have some market power (that is oligopoly). For a good review of the literature, see Brander (1995).

As noted above, a production subsidy will generally result in a welfare loss to the exporting country. However, if the export firm has market power, a strategic subsidy to one firm, such as an investment in research and development, can influence its competitor's actions, and therefore can result in a higher welfare. The strategic effect more than offsets the direct inefficiency of the policy; in other words, the policy decreases the inefficiency caused by the firms' actions. The intuition is that because of market power, the firm will tend to set quantity too low (to increase price), while the subsidy will induce them to produce more.

Brander and Spencer (1985) use a Cournot duopoly to illustrate a situation where two exporters are competing in a third market. The home governments of the exporting firms first choose the subsidy, and in the second period, the firms choose quantity. They start with a two good model, with labour as the only factor of production. The one good is exported and the other is a numeraire good and is produced under perfect competition. The two export firms have some fixed and marginal costs, and the domestic country, whose firm produces good x, chooses a per-unit subsidy.

If the two products are strategic substitutes, a subsidy will increase production (exports) in the domestic country and cause a reduction in the foreign country, whose firm produces good x^*. As the subsidy increases, the best-response function of the domestic firm shifts out, that is it produces more for every level of production of the foreign firm (illustrated in Figure 33.2). This results in a decrease in production by the foreign firm, with the Nash equilibrium moving from point 1 to point 2. Effectively, the domestic firm becomes a Stackelberg leader. If the two products are complements, the optimal subsidy is negative, thus the country would want to tax exports.

If the game is truly symmetric, both countries will want to impose subsidies. The structure does not change – in fact the equation for the optimal subsidy remains unchanged, the only difference being that the foreign firm's profit will also have a subsidy included in it. Thus, if the two products are strategic substitutes, both governments will subsidize production, which results in a reduction for both from the free-trade equilibrium. In short, they are in a prisoner's dilemma.[14]

In one of the other early papers on strategic trade, instead of modelling two exporting firms, Dixit (1984) considered two firms, one producing for the domestic market and the

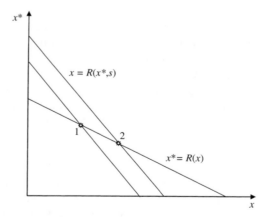

Figure 33.2   Reaction functions with Cournot conjectures before and after the export subsidy

other an importer. He showed that if a country had a cost advantage over imports, the optimal policies would be a prohibitive tariff plus a domestic subsidy. Thus, in terms of a simultaneously-chosen CVD, the tariffs do not eliminate the incentive to use strategic trade policies so the equilibrium includes both countervail and subsidy. Cheng (1988) finds this result may hold with both Bertrand and Cournot competition if goods are imperfect substitutes. When the foreign government moves first and sets an export subsidy, Collie (1991), like Dixit (1988), find that the countervailing tariff would be smaller than the subsidy, but unlike Dixit, Collie finds that the tariff is sufficient to discourage the export subsidy (Brander 1995).

One criticism of the above models has been the assumption about complete information. Real governments are unlikely to have full information, particularly about the nature of competition and firm costs. A number of papers model the choice of trade policy instruments under uncertainty about firm costs (Cooper and Reizman 1989; Qiu 1994) and the form of competition. Maggi (1996) finds that capacity subsidies can increase the home country's income regardless of whether the firms are using Bertrand or Cournot conjectures. Another criticism is that the early strategic trade models limited governments to using single-rate subsidies. A wide range of export incentives are available implying that governments can offer their exporters a menu of subsidies. Qiu (1994) finds that governments will choose a menu of policies to identify high and low cost firms. Maggi (1999) finds that with non-linear policies, the prisoner's dilemma need not hold (that is the outcome where the firms in both countries overproduce): if the outputs of the two firms are substitutes, the government can support the free-trade quantity. However this is not true with asymmetric information, which Maggi finds exacerbates the prisoner's dilemma.

Uncertainty can also affect the level of countervailing tariff. Piracha (2004), following Wright (1998), models the subsidy and countervail tariff as a two-stage game, where first the exporting government sets a subsidy (or tax) and then the importing government imposes an import tariff. He finds that in the case of complete information, the best policy is for the home government to use an export tax to decrease the magnitude of the import tariff imposed by the foreign government (and to earn tax revenue). Under incomplete information about firm costs, the firm has an incentive to reduce output from its optimal level, to signal that it is high cost, which results in the home government using a lower export tax. He argues that if the distortion is large enough (that is the low-cost firm has to reduce its production to a very large degree to mimic the low-cost producer), the country may have an incentive to subsidize exports.

Thus, strategic trade theory has provided a theoretical framework showing that under some conditions (Cournot oligopolies; producing substitutes), it may be optimal for one government to use an export subsidy and the other to use some form of countervailing tariff. This tariff may or may not be large enough to dissuade the exporting country from using the subsidy.

Political economy
A second reason for subsidies and tariffs may be political pressure. Subsidies and/or tariffs may reduce overall welfare within the country, but the government may have the incentive to adopt these policies anyway to appease certain important constituencies. Even with the most benign government objective – to maximize social welfare – decision-makers rely on interest groups for information to determine the social welfare function, implying the

country will not necessarily end up with optimal trade policy (Tharakan 1995). One problem is that although the protection afforded by trade protection is readily apparent, the welfare loss is not. The increase in price is spread among a large number of people, and the effect of trade protection on the home country's exporters is indirect and may only be felt some time later (Tharakan 1995).

Bhagwati (1971), among others, has shown that the first-best policy is one that targets the variable of interest. For example, if the government wants to increase employment in a sector, the first-best response would be to introduce a labour subsidy; the second-best would be to introduce a production subsidy, while the third-best is a tariff (Magee *et al.* 1989). Thus, a country subsidizing production may be introducing the first-best policy. However, if the country imposing the CVD is responding purely to a lobby to increase either the employment or competitive position of that industry, imposing a tariff is not the first-best policy option. If, however, the policy is intended to address the subsidized imports, it may be the efficient response.

There are a number of voting models used in political economy (for a good review of their use in trade, see Rodrik 1995). Each model results in the following conclusion: trade is not free because interest groups can influence government behaviour to transfer income to them from trade policy. However, there is a conundrum as to why there is still so much trade protection when there are more efficient ways to both get government income and more efficient ways to transfer income. Policy inertia may be one explanation. Due to the uncertainty about gains and losses, one may get votes against increased trade even though the majority would have benefited. Feenstra and Lewis (1991) propose a model where a government wants to help those industries who are hurt from a fall in world price. If the government does not know which groups lose due to the price drop, and therefore cannot use other mechanisms, such as a lump-sum transfer or a production subsidy, a tariff may be the efficient policy. Imposing a tariff will benefit those facing the price decrease yet does not have any informational requirements about individual consumption or production levels. Note these assumptions fit CVDs well since CVDs are primarily initiated due to a drop in price of imports.

Brainard and Verdier (1997) argue that if it is easier for industries to obtain protection in response to a fall in their price, it will then take longer for the industry to adjust to new technology or more competition, and it will have high long-run capacity. Thus, the specific factors of production become endogenous. This result is important to contingent protection, since it is specifically triggered by a drop in import price. Another argument is that the fact that trade may be inefficient at redistributing income and be seen as a benefit as opposed to a cost in that politicians may use fewer redistributive measures exactly because they are costly (Grossman and Helpman 1994; Staiger and Tabellini 1987).

In short, political economy explains both why a county might subsidize an industry, and why it might impose trade barriers. Firms and individuals can lobby government for favourable trade policy. Political power, size, or population mass may indicate the firms or industries that have the power to lobby for subsidies and tariffs, even if the conditions required by strategic trade theory are absent.

Liability law
Even though it is seen as the one saving grace of CVD by economists, so far we have largely ignored the fact that countervail can be used as disincentive for governments to

subsidise industries (Diamond 1989). Thus, when modelling CVD, the effect of the threat of protection on the exporter should be considered (Bhagwati and Srinivasan 1976). Firms may use contingent protection as a threat against future behaviour. For example, Tharakan (1995) found that some complainants readily admitted to having filed cases as a 'warning' to their foreign competitors. Thus, these forms of contingent protection may well be being used primarily to incite either some negotiated trade restriction or changed exporter behaviour.

CVD may be thought of as a form of litigation law – where penalties are intended to induce parties to take care in their actions and decrease the probability of injury, but the litigation mechanism is subject to abuse by those filing the claim (Baylis and Vercammen 2005). Assume for the moment that export subsidies are partially strategic and partially the result of political pressure. Further, assume that whether a domestic industry will respond with a CVD suit is stochastic. If the exporting government is overly worried about triggering a CVD, it may operate inefficiently, and not use subsidies where otherwise they would improve welfare (for example, using a subsidy to address an externality or to transfer income where a lump-sum transfer is not an option). Too little care implies the exporter is behaving too aggressively and should be held liable for damage caused in the importing country. To maximize the social welfare of both countries, the rules should encourage an appropriate amount of care and activity on the part of the exporter and an appropriate response (that is, when to file suit) by the importer.

Meanwhile, importer actions can also affect the finding of injury by engaging in aggressive price competition including lobbying for their own production subsidies.[15] Since the regulator can only view price outcomes, the more price competition on the part of the importer, the higher the probability that injury will be found. Importers and exporters may also be able to affect the probability of injury by engaging in more activity, that is increasing the quantity they export or sell domestically.

Although nominally trade rules are fault-based (that is they use a negligence rule) in that a subsidy must be shown, the rare incidence of cases failing on the initial subsidy finding would imply that the system acts more like strict liability (that is the exporter is charged the full amount of the harm, whether the exporter took care or not).[16] If actions by the importer (or importing country) can affect the degree of harm, a strict liability rule will not (necessarily) result in an optimal amount of care (Shavell 2003): although the exporter will tend to take care, the importer has no incentive to.[17]

Data: does it correspond to the theory?

It will not come as a surprise to those who study agricultural trade that the first commodity to incite the use of CVD was sugar.[18] In the nineteenth century, most European countries subsidized sugar, flour and alcohol exports, and in response, the US government imposed the first countervailing duties under the American Tariff Act (1890). The Act imposed a duty of one-tenth of one cent per lb on refined sugar that received extra subsidies over and above those received by unrefined sugar (Ehrenhaft 1958).[19] By 1894, the countervailing duty had been extended to all subsidized sugar imports and in 1897 to all subsidized merchandise imports.

Some things have not changed since the early days of CVD. The United States is still the most prodigious user of CVD (initiating 40 per cent of all cases since 1995 and with 97 duties in place at the beginning of 1995, compared with Australia with 13, Canada with seven and the EU with one). Primary and intermediate goods still make up the majority of CVD cases. From 1995 to 2003, metals made up 40 per cent of CVD cases – an unsurprising result given the dominance of steel cases, followed by agriculture with 28 per cent, then leather goods, textiles and chemicals (WTO 2005).

Marvel and Ray (1996) use the latter point to argue that strategic trade does not explain the majority of CVD cases. Primary commodities have well established industries with well-understood technology, and are unlikely to receive strategic subsidies (such as research and development), which one might find in high-tech industries.[20] Marvel and Ray also note that strategic trade theory would presumably lead to firms seeking rents when the potential rents were highest, that is when the economy was booming. However, we see petitions largely initiated at low points in the business cycle. Further, the majority of CVD cases are jointly filed with an AD case (for example, 55 per cent of all cases filed by the United States from 1980 to 2004 were filed alongside an AD case).[21] Most cases (64 per cent) were linked with other complaints on the same product that were filed against many nations simultaneously.[22] Unless all countries had some form of trade-distorting production subsidy in place at the same time, or the firm was simultaneously being subsidized and dumping, this raises concern about the use of CVD cases as a means of protecting a domestic industry that is facing increased competition, as opposed to protecting it from 'unfair' production subsidies.

If CVD cases are being used as a means of protection, perhaps the political economy model may be more appropriate. If so, one might anticipate that industries receiving CVD protection would share characteristics with firms receiving trade protection generally. There have also been a number of general empirical trade studies that have attempted to typify the industries that receive trade protection (summarized by Rodrik 1995). For example, industries receiving protection tend to be labour-intensive, low-skill, low-wage industries (Ray 1981; Marvel and Ray 1983; Anderson and Baldwin 1987; Baldwin 1989), producing consumer goods rather than intermediate goods (Baack and Ray 1983; Marvel and Ray 1983) with customers that are not highly concentrated (Pincus 1975; Trefler 1993). These industries also tend to engage in little intra-industry trade (Ray 1981; Marvel and Ray 1983).

A number of these characteristics do not generally apply to CVD cases. Many CVD cases are against intermediate goods whose consumers are highly concentrated (steel, agricultural products), and are characterized by a great deal of intra-industry trade.[23] That said, CVD cases are often in industries in decline (such as steel, agriculture), a characteristic shared by industries receiving trade protection (Marvel and Ray 1983; Mansfield and Busch 1995; Bohara and Kaempfer 1991). Does this mean that different tools for protection are applied differently across types of industries, or does that mean that as the multilateral trade agreements reduce some forms of trade protection, we see different industries receiving protection?

Above it was found that if it is easier for industries to obtain protection in response to a fall in their price, the industry will be more hesitant adopt new technology, and it will have high long-run capacity. When one compares this result against the industries that frequently appear in CVD cases, for example, steel, lumber and agriculture, one can believe that this may have in fact happened. Both lumber and steel production in North America have been accused of being overcapitalized, and have undergone significant restructuring in the past decade (lumber in Canada, which has been dealing with a CVD on its exports to its primary market, the United States, and steel production in North America, despite various forms of tariff protection).

Various other studies look at the determinants of success in CVD cases. Overall, the majority of cases were approved: 64 per cent of cases filed with the WTO since 1995 resulted in duties. Seventeen per cent were found to have no subsidy, and another 11 per cent found subsidy, but did not find injury. One question that arises is whether the determination of injury is politically motivated. In one of the few case studies of CVD, Kalt (1996) uses the Canada-US softwood lumber dispute to find that CVD findings are more influenced by politics than legal precedent. Baldwin and Steagall (1994) find that several variables that are not intuitively attached to injury also help determine the ITC outcome. For example, the higher the import penetration, and the larger the overall employment, the more likely a positive finding. Finger *et al.* (1982) and Hansen (1990) find that the ITC decisions are politically motivated, but did not explicitly test for the ITC statutory directive. On the other hand, Anderson (1993) tested four different models of ITC decision-making: two statutory and two political. The political models were found to have little predictive ability, and even when the political variables were included in the statutory models, they did not add any statistically-significant power.

A parallel question arises about the finding of subsidy. Here, the data are puzzling. One would anticipate that if a country is found to have a trade-distorting subsidy in place, other countries would launch their own cases against the subsidized exports. For example, in 1995 when Canada successfully sued against EU sugar imports, why did other sugar importers not do the same? However it is very rare to observe several countries filing CVD suits against an export from a single country. There are a few notable exceptions where several developed countries (most frequently Canada and the United States) have filed CVD cases against steel imports from developing countries.[24] Also notable is the substantial variation between countries. The United States almost always found that a subsidy was present (in slightly fewer than 90 per cent of cases) while Canada has a higher than average finding of 'no subsidy' at 31 per cent. There are very few (if any) studies looking at the determination of subsidy.

Summary

As noted in the introduction, while there has been a great deal of research, both theoretical and more recently, empirical, in AD, there has been very little work done on CVD. Perhaps it is due to the fact that with CVD, it is government behaviour not firm behaviour that is in question, or empirically, because there is a selection problem with CVD in that a subsidy needs to be found. In any case, there is a large gap in the literature that is available for researchers to address.

There is undoubtedly need for empirical work – comparing AD with CVD and comparing CVD with other forms of trade protection. Following Marvel and Ray (1996), one could look at the source of the subsidies and ask whether they are directed at lowering fixed costs or marginal costs? Marvel and Ray certainly argue that strategic trade theory only applies to a few cases, implying that there is a need for an appropriate theory to describe the others.

There is also a need to compare CVD against other forms of trade protection. There is some anecdotal evidence that the products listed in CVD cases are not typical of the products receiving other forms of trade protection. This fact raises the question as to whether CVD and other forms of trade protection are complements or substitutes. Andoh (1992) argues that one of the early rationales for CVD law in the United States was to ensure firms a constant level of protection that they had previously enjoyed with tariffs. Whether CVDs have been used as a tool for providing legally-acceptable protection as the use of other trade barriers have been constrained is an empirically-testable hypothesis.

Last, to my knowledge, very little work has been done looking at contingent protection as a form of liability law. Has it been successful in deterring 'bad' behaviour by exporters? Even if CVD is abused on occasion, and used purely as a form of trade protection, if in a sufficient number of cases it actually discourages the use of distorting subsidies, then it may be a net benefit.

Notes

1. See WTO appellate panel in *Canada-Aircraft*: Article 14, interpreting Article 1.1(b).
2. In *Carlisle Tire and Rubber Co. v. the United States*.
3. For example, the fee for cutting timber in *Canada-Lumber*.
4. For example, the creation of special export milk product classes, which allowed producers to sell both into the high-priced domestic market, and export at world prices (see *Canada-Dairy*).
5. *Canada-Aircraft, U.S.-Pasta, U.S.-Lead and Bismuth*.
6. *US-FSC (Foreign Sales Corporation)*.
7. See Goodloe (2003) on *Canada-Dairy*.
8. In *Belgium-Steel*, where there was a government subsidy for retraining workers.
9. In *Canada-Aircraft*, Brazil argued that the government loans did not charge a sufficient risk-premium.
10. See *Fresh Asparagus from Mexico*, 48 Fed. Reg. 21,618 21,621022 (1983).
11. *Live Swine from Canada*.
12. This model does not consider the use of an optimal tariff.
13. With an export subsidy, the effect of the subsidy is completely offset, and everything returns to its pre-subsidy position with the exception that the exporter transfers income in the amount of the subsidy (tariff) to the importing country. However, unlike the partial equilibrium model, consumption in the general equilibrium model actually decreases further in the exporting country. This decrease is reflecting the transfer of income from the exporter to the importer due to the combination of the export subsidy and the tariff.
14. One can expand the Brander–Spencer model to consider Bertrand conjectures, and show that an export tax is likely to be optimal when firms choose prices, as opposed to an export subsidy which is optimal when firms choose quantity (Brander 1995). Under Bertrand, the firm's reaction functions are upward-sloping – if one firm raises its price, its rival will follow suit. The taxed firm will charge higher prices for any given price charged by its rival, that is its reaction function shifts upward. This shift induces the foreign firm to also commit to a higher price, increasing welfare.

    To see why the two conjectures have two strikingly different results, consider that in the case of Bertrand competition, each firm would like to sell at a higher price, but is restricted by its belief that its rival will undercut their price and appropriate a larger share of the market. The government tax allows the domestic firm to 'credibly commit' to charging a high price, allowing the foreign firm to also raise their prices without fear that the domestic firm will aggressively compete in price. On the other hand, under Cournot competition, each firm wants to increase its quantity, but assumes its rival will follow suit, which would drive down the market price. By subsidizing exports, the government allows the domestic firm to 'credibly commit' to producing more than the pre-intervention quantity, which gives the rival the incentive to cut back on their production, to ensure price does not fall too much.
15. A problem with CVD is that it does not consider 'net' subsidies. Thus, even if an importing country has a highly-distorting production subsidy flowing to an import-competing sector, it can successfully challenge a country's exports that are subsidized to a much smaller degree. Serious prejudice is the one means by which this inequality of measures to address distorting subsidies can be addressed, however serious prejudice has been rarely used, and has even more rarely achieved successful subsidy reform (Gaisford and McLachlan 1990).
16. It is also notable that the finding of dumping/subsidy and subsequent finding of injury does not necessitate a finding of causality. Shavell (2003) finds that whether or not causality is included does not change his results on the optimality of strict liability or negligence.
17. So far I have ignored the idea of causality. Even if a country uses a strict test of negligence before allowing the case to go forward, the current rules in the United States do not test whether the action actually caused the injury, just that both action and injury occurred. Although in some instances, the additional test of causality does not change the incentives for care and activity (Shavell 2003), in other instances it may.

18. Ironically, sugar disputes between the United States and European Union continue to this day. Specifically, as of spring 2005, there are AD duties in place on EU sugar exports to the United States (USITC 2005). Antidumping and Countervailing Duty Orders in place http://www.usitc.gov/trade_remedy/731_ad_701_cvd/investigations/antidump_countervailing/index.htm.

19. What will also come as no surprise to those working in agricultural trade, at the same time the government granted its own bounty to American sugar producers.

20. It is notable that in agriculture the cases often involve processed food, not the raw product. Thus, for the agricultural cases at least, the subsidy could have come in the form of a subsidy of fixed (sunk) costs. For example, see *Delverde, SrL v. United States* 989 F. Supp. 218, 226 (Ct Int'l Trade 1997).

21. Note that cases against China, with one exception, come in the form of AD complaints. Given that the firms are often state-run, one would anticipate that they would more likely be recipients of subsidies rather than out to engage in predatory pricing. However, the United States does not apply its CVD law to non-market economies like China, as a result of the difficulty in finding (and measuring) a subsidy in a non-market economy (*Georgetown Steel Corp. v. United States*, 801 F.2d 1308 (Fed. Cir. 1986)). In *Georgetown Steel*, the Federal Circuit held as a matter of law that the CVD law could not reach subsidies granted by non-market economy governments. It was argued that these subsidies could not be countervailed because they could not be measured since there is no market benchmark and therefore prices have no real economic meaning (Magnus 2000). Instead, the United States often uses AD in cases where costs cannot be observed. Costs are constructed using data from 'similar' countries – in the case of China, wage rates from India are often used – to develop an estimate of marginal cost. Dumping is found if the price is below cost. Since the constructed costs are generally much higher than the actual costs, using this method is a surer way to obtain (higher) protection.

22. For example, New Zealand filed against canned peach exports from South Africa in 1996, and a year later, against the same product from the European Union. In 1999, the European Union filed a case against exports of synthetic polyester fibre from Indonesia, Thailand, South Korea, Taiwan and Australia.

23. Marvel and Ray (1983) note that the material injury determination for CVD only looks at import-competing firms, leaving the downstream firms and consumers out of the process. Thus, those parties who are most likely to be harmed by CVDs do not have access to the debate, which may make getting positive determinations for cases against intermediate goods relatively easy even where the duties will harm a larger portion of the domestic economy.

24. CVD cases were filed by Canada and the United States against steel exports from Brazil in 1999/00, India in 1999, 2000 and 2001, Indonesia in 1999, Thailand in 1999, and South Korea in 1998/99. The only two non-steel cases were Canada and the United States filing against Italian dried pasta imports in 1995 and the United States and European Union against dynamic random access memory semiconductors (DRAMs) from South Korea in 2002.

References

Anderson, K. and R. E. Baldwin (1987), 'The Political Market for Protection in Industrialized Countries,' in A. M. El-Agraa (ed.), *Protection, Cooperation, Integration and Development*, New York: Macmillan.

Anderson, K. B. (1993), 'Agency Discretion or Statutory Direction: Decision Making at the US International Trade Commission,' *Journal of Law and Economics*, **36**(2), 915–35.

Andoh, E. K. (1992), 'Countervailing Duties in a Not Quite Perfect World: An Economic Analysis,' *Stanford Law Review*, **44**(6), 1515–39.

Baack, B. D. and E. J. Ray (1983), 'The Political Economy of Tariff Policy: A Case Study of the United States,' *Explorations in Economic History*, **20**, 70–93.

Baldwin, R. and J. Steagall (1994), 'An Analysis of ITC Decisions in Antidumping, Countervailing Duty and Safeguard Cases,' *Weltwirtschaftliches Archiv*, **130**(2), 290–308.

Baldwin, R. E. (1989), 'The Political Economy of Free Trade,' *Journal of Political Economy*, **77**, 295–305.

Baylis, K. and J. Vercammen (2005), 'Contingent Protection as Liability Law', UBC working paper.

Bhagwati, J. (1971), 'The Generalized Theory of Distortions and Welfare,' in J. Bhagwati *et al.* (eds), *Trade, Balance of Payments and Growth: Essays in Honor of Gottfried Haberler*, Chicago, IL: Rand McNally.

Bhagwati, J. N. and T. N. Srinivasan (1976), 'Optimal Trade Policy and Compensation under Endogenous Uncertainty,' *Journal of International Economics*, **6**, 317–36.

Bohara, A. K. and W. H. Kaempfer (1991), 'A Test of Tariff Endogeneity in the United States,' *American Economic Review*, **81**, 952–60.

Brainard, S. L. and T. Verdier (1997), 'The Political Economy of Declining Industries: Senescent Industry Collapse Revisited,' *Journal of International Economics*, **42**, 221–38.

Brander, J. (1995), 'Strategic Trade Policy', in Gene M. Grossman and Kenneth Rogoff (eds), *Handbook of International Economics, Volume III*, Amsterdam: Elsevier Science: North Holland.

Brander, J. and B. Spencer (1983), 'International R & D Rivalry and Industrial Strategy,' *Review of Economic Studies*, **50**(4), 707–22.

Brander, J. and B. Spencer (1985), 'Export Subsidies and Market Share Rivalry,' *Journal of International Economics*, **18**, 83–100.

Brennan, G. and J. Pincus (1993), 'Economic Rationalist Revisited: the Case of Countervailing Duties,' Centre for International Economic Studies, Policy Discussion Paper No. 93/05, University of Adelaide, Australia.

Cheng, L. (1988), 'Assisting Domestic Industries under International Oligopoly: The Relevance of the Nature of Competition under Oligopoly,' *American Economic Review*, **78**(4), 746–58.

Collie, D. (1991), 'Export Subsidies and Countervailing Tariffs,' *Journal of International Economics*, **31**, 309–24.

Cooper R. and R. Riezman (1989), 'Uncertainty and the Choice of Trade Policy in Oligopolistic Industries,' *Review of Economic Studies*, **56**, 129–40.

Diamond, R. (1989), 'Economic Foundations of CVD Law,' *Virginia Journal of International Law*, **29**, 767–76.

Dixit, A. K. (1984), 'International Trade Policy for Oligopolistic Industries,' *Economic Journal*, **94**s. 1–16.

Dixit, A. K. (1988), 'Antidumping and Countervailing Duties under Oligopoly,' *European Economic Review*, **32**, 55–68.

Ehrenhaft, P. D. (1958), 'Protection against International Price Discrimination: United States Countervailing and Antidumping Duties,' *Columbia Law Review*, **58**(1), 44–76.

Feenstra, R. C. and T. R. Lewis (1991), 'Distributing the Gains from Trade with Incomplete Information,' *Economics and Politics*, **3**, 21–40.

Finger, J. M. (1993), 'Antidumping is Where the Action is,' in J. M. Finger (ed.), *Antidumping: How It Works and Who Gets Hurt*, Ann Arbor, MI: University of Michigan Press.

Finger, J. M., H. K. Hall and D. Nelson (1982), 'The Political Economy of Administered Protection,' *American Economic Review*, **72**, 452–66.

Gaisford, J. D. and D. L. McLachlan (1990), 'Domestic Subsidies and Countervail: The Treacherous Ground of the Level Playing Field,' *Journal of World Trade*, **24**(4), 55–77.

Goetz, C. L., L. Granet and W. F. Schwartz (1986), 'The Meaning of "Subsidy" and "Injury" in the Countervailing Duty Law,' *International Review of Law and Economics*, **6**, 17–32.

Goodloe, C. (2003), 'The WTO Case on Canadian Dairy Export Subsidies: Implications for Two-Tiered Pricing,' Presented at International Agricultural Trade Disputes: Case Studies in North America, University of Florida.

Grossman, G. M. and E. Helpman (1994), 'Protection for Sale,' *American Economic Review*, **84**, 833–50.

Hansen, W.L. (1990), 'The International Trade Commission and the Politics of Protectionism,' *American Political Science Review*, **94**, 22–46.

Kalt, J. P. (1996), 'Do Precedent and Legal Argument Matter in the Lumber CVD Cases?' *The Political Economy of Trade Protection*, National Bureau of Economic Research Project Report series, Chicago and London: University of Chicago Press, pp. 51–60.

Magee, S. P., W. A. Brock and L. Young (1989), *Black Hole Tariffs and Endogenous Policy Theory*, Cambridge and New York: Cambridge University Press.

Maggi, G. (1996), 'Strategic Trade Policies with Endogenous Mode of Competition,' *American Economic Review*, **86**, 237–58.

Maggi, G. (1999), 'Strategic Trade Policy under Incomplete Information,' *International Economic Review*, **40**(3), 571–94.

Magnus, J. (2000), 'Subsidies in the Context of China's WTO Accession,' http://www.dbtrade.com/publications/subs_china.htm.

Mansfield, E. D. and M. L. Busch (1995), 'The Political Economy of Non-tariff Barriers: a Cross-national Analysis,' *International Organization*, **49**(4), 723–49.

Marvel, H. P. and E. J. Ray (1983), 'The Kennedy Round: Evidence on the Regulation of Trade in the US,' *American Economic Review*, **73**, 190–97.

Marvel, H. P. and E. J. Ray (1996), 'Countervailing Duties,' *The Economic Journal*, **105**, 1576–93.

Pincus, J. J. (1975), 'Pressure Groups and the Pattern of Tariffs,' *Journal of Political Economy*, **83**, 757–78.

Piracha, M. (2004), 'Export Subsidies and Countervailing Duties Under Asymmetric Information,' Working Paper, University of Kent, http://ideas.repec.org/p/ukc/ukcedp/0410.html

Qiu, L. D. (1994), 'Optimal Strategic Trade Policy under Asymmetric Information,' *Journal of International Economics*, **3**, 333–54.

Ray, E. J. (1981), 'The Determinants of Tariff and Non-tariff Trade Restrictions in the United States,' *Journal of Political Economy*, **89**, 105–21.

Rodrik, D. (1995), 'Political Economy of Trade Policy', in G. Grossman and K. Rogoff (eds), *Handbook of International Economics*, Amsterdam: Elsevier Science, North Holland.

Shavell, S. (2003), 'Economic Analysis of Accident Law,' NBER Working Paper 9694, http://www.nber.org/papers/w9694.

Staiger, R. and G. Tabelleni (1987), 'Discretionary Trade Policy and Excessive Protection,' *American Economic Review*, **77**, 340–48.

Stiglitz, J. E. (1997), 'Dumping on Free Trade: the US Import Trade Laws,' *Southern Economic Journal*, **64**(2), 402–24.

Schwartz, W. F. (1978), 'Zenith Radio Corp. v. United States: Countervailing Duties and the Regulation of International Trade,' *The Supreme Court Review* (1978), 297–312.

Sykes, A. O. (1989), 'Countervailing Duty Law: An Economic Perspective,' *Columbia Law Review*, **89**(2), 199–263.

Tharakan, P. K. M. (1995), 'Political Economy and Contingent Protection,' *The Economic Journal*, **105**(433), 1550–64.

Trefler, D. (1993), 'Trade Liberalization and the Theory of Endogenous Protection,' *Journal of Political Economy*, **101**, 138–60.

Wright, D. (1998), 'Strategic Trade Policy and Signalling with Unobservable Costs,' *Review of International Economics*, **6**, 105–19.

WTO (2005), 'Countervailing Initiations by Exporter by Reporting Member', http://www.wto.org/english/tratop_e/scm_e/scm_e.htm

34 Administrative procedures, the distribution of costs and benefits, and incentives in anti-dumping cases
Richard Barichello

Introduction

Antidumping (AD) law and regulations are notoriously complex across most countries. But there are a number of characteristics of these laws and regulations relating to the process of dealing with the law that are not commonly addressed, yet still have critically important implications. They contribute to determining how the benefits and costs of AD cases are distributed among firms and countries, and give strong incentives to the various players involved to engage in certain kinds of behaviour. These responses have economic effects that likely were unintended when the laws were drafted and regulations drawn up. It is the purpose of this chapter to review a sample of such procedures, and to trace their effects. We will focus on procedures followed in the US and Canada, although many countries follow similar procedures.

This review does not cover all administrative details. We will leave aside many technical issues such as the definition of like product, the details of evidence required to show dumping and injury such as the determination of normal value and constructed cost calculations, and various practices such as zeroing and price undertakings. These are all important issues but are beyond the scope of this chapter.

The issues we examine are what might best be described as the procedures that must be followed to initiate a case, what steps are followed by government agencies, what responses are necessary by the defendant firms, who pays for these actions, how long does it take to complete a case, when do AD duties become levied, when do collected duties get refunded to firms and when do they not (including the Byrd amendment in the US), and what are the probabilities of dumping and injury being found. Then we examine the incentives these measures give to firms on both sides of a trading relationship when facing such AD procedures, including the possibility of strategic behaviour on the part of some firms.

The process of dealing with an Anti-dumping complaint [1]

To begin with, dumping is defined in the 1994 update of Article VI of the GATT as a situation 'by which products of one country are introduced into the commerce of another country (i.e., exported at a price) at less than the normal value of the products.' This kind of action 'is to be condemned if it causes or threatens material injury or materially retards the establishment of a domestic industry' (GATT 1994).

Normal value is defined as the comparable price for the same or similar product in either the home market of the exporter or in a third country, or the cost of production including an amount for profit of that product in the country of origin ('constructed cost'). When it comes to injury, the Uruguay Round Agreement added more detail to the original GATT article, giving some attention to showing clearer causation between the imports and resulting price declines that would injure domestic firms. However, in US procedures, imports only have to be one cause of injury, not even the largest causative factor in any price decline.

For anti-dumping duties to be imposed, there must be a positive determination that dumping took place and that injury occurred. The dumping duty level is set at the level of the dumping margin, the export price less normal value, divided by the export price. There is a preliminary determination for both dumping and injury, and then final determinations for the two. Dumping duties are collected from the time that positive determinations are arrived at. If a final determination reverses the finding (on either count), duties are usually to be refunded to the firms that paid them. However, the Byrd amendment in the US requires duties collected to be paid to the complainant firms. This practice has been ruled to contravene WTO rules.

Finally, there are often different government institutions involved in the two elements of an anti-dumping investigation, dumping and injury. In the US, the Department of Commerce (DOC) determines dumping and the US International Trade Commission (USITC) determines injury. In Canada, the Canada Border Services Agency (CBSA) determines dumping and the Canadian International Trade Tribunal (CITT) determines injury.

There are many related issues surrounding these points where we could elaborate further details, critical concepts, and associated procedures. In particular, an enormous amount of data often collected which taxes the investigating agencies and defendant firms. These were left out in the interest of providing a brief overview of the fundamentals. But this actual complexity is important to note because it requires experienced lawyers to put together a petition, advise on responses to data requests, and put together an adequate defence.

Time lines of an investigation

To use the antidumping law to provide relief, an industry or firm files a petition (complaint) with the DOC and the ITC (in Canada with the CBSA) to initiate an investigation. More than one producer can join the petition, and in fact producers supporting a petition must account for at least 25 per cent of domestic production, in both Canada and the US. In addition, producers expressing opposition to the petition must account for less production than that of those expressing support. This petition must offer some evidence of the dumping that is alleged to occur and the resulting injury, although these demands are not substantial.

Once an AD petition is received in the US, the ITC has 45 days to gives its preliminary decision on whether there is reason to believe that dumping is injuring or threatening to injure the domestic industry. If this determination is positive, the DOC makes its preliminary determination within 140 days, although extensions can occur. Following this preliminary decision, a final determination must be made within 75 days, with the possibility of extensions. After the final DOC determination, the ITC has 45 days further to make its final injury determination. If that is affirmative, then dumping orders are issued so that import are subject to antidumping duty deposits equal to the calculated rate of dumping. Any negative determination effectively ends the case.[2]

In other words, the time period from the initiation of the investigation to the final dumping decision is within ten months, assuming no extensions are requested. In Canada, the process is similar, and a final decision is made in 'about seven months' (CBSA 2004).

Once a preliminary decision has been made in the affirmative, which occurs in 99 per cent of cases in the US (Blonigen and Prusa 2003), dumping duties at the preliminary margin of dumping are effectively collected.

This shows the importance to petitioners of putting together a plausible case in order for their petition to land in the affirmative category rather than the alternative. Although the odds are almost certain, it is worth spending resources to better ensure an affirmative result at all stages of the investigation. This causes many petitioners to use law firms that specialize in the process. However, these costs are small compared to the costs of defending against a petition, as discussed below. And they are lower still on a per firm basis when more than one firm joins in an AD filing, because then these legal costs are split among the number of firms joining in the petition.

Probabilities of decisions in an AD case

The odds of various decisions during the AD petitioning process are important to know in order for firms to assess the (expected) value of launching an AD petition or complaint, in conjunction with a knowledge of the rules and processes being followed (as described above). One indication has just been noted, that 99 per cent of petitions receive a positive preliminary determination in the US. The situation is similar in Canada.

So what proportion of cases result in a final determination of dumping? Lindsey-Ikenson report 94 per cent. Looking at all developed country cases from 1993 to 2002 (Barichello and Malhotra 2004), 96.6 per cent of all cases initiated received a final decision of dumping. This result is almost the same if one includes all developing country data as well (96.4 per cent), although it shows some variation by industry with the steel, base metals, chemicals, and agricultural industries showing higher than average affirmative results.

In the case of injury, the results are similar, although less striking. For the US, Lindsey-Ikenson (1999–2002) report 83 per cent of final injury determinations are affirmative. For all developed countries, Barichello and Malhotra (1993–2002) report 91.7 per cent of initiated cases are judged affirmative.

Similar numbers apply to sunset reviews. For the US, 98 per cent of contested cases were determined by the DOC to have the dumping order continued, although only 72 per cent were judged affirmative in terms of injury (USITC). A similar situation prevails in Canada again. On the CBSA website it notes the length of time for which an AD duty is in effect as 'at least five years', inviting the expectation by domestic producers that sunset clauses are not very restrictive.

These data do not say that final measures (dumping duties) are levied in some 90 per cent of initiated cases. There are other circumstances that can affect the final outcome of

Table 34.1   Disposition of initiated AD cases, all industries, 1993–2002

	AD success rate	Rate of no dumping	Rate of no injury	Rate of other reasons for no final measures
Developed countries	68.3	3.4	6.5	34.6
All countries	61.9	3.6	8.3	27.7

Source: Barichello and Malhotra (2004).

an initiated case, including a price undertaking by the defendant firm (akin to a self-imposed duty by the exporter), or the case can be withdrawn for some reason. These situations are not rare; they accounted for 28 per cent of all cases for all developed countries from 1993 to 2002 (Barichello and Malhotra). The result is that final measures (duties) were applied in these data in 62 per cent of initiated cases. Using only US data, from 1980 to 1998, about 25 per cent of AD petitions were withdrawn (Blonigen and Prusa, 2003).[3]

This evidence shows quite dramatically that dumping cases are a good bet for a complainant firm seeking import protection, not only within the US but also across all developed countries. Rejections of a case in terms of a final duty determination occur less than 20 per cent of the time within the US and even less commonly across all developed countries. And temporary duties, during the period between the preliminary and final determinations, a period that usually lasts six months, if not longer, are imposed in virtually all US cases petitioned or initiated, and more than 90 per cent of the time across all developed countries. It is the case that these data differ substantially by industry sector, that some sectors have higher rates of 'success' and not surprisingly are heavier users of the AD system. A casual review of AD cases by industry shows that the steel and base metals sector, as well as chemicals, fit into this category, a finding that is well documented in the literature (Blonigen and Prusa 2003). Blonigen (2004) shows clearly that there are learning effects in using the antidumping system and that those firms that have used the system previously are more successful in using it subsequently in terms of affirmative decisions and dumping margins.

When one combines the time lines noted above with these probabilities, a clear signal is given to any firm or group of firms in an industry wishing to obtain temporary protection from imports: file an antidumping petition. This is true for at least that part of a year taken up with getting a final determination, and is likely for a five year term. The costs are relatively low in terms of the legal costs of putting together a petition or complaint. All costs of the investigation of the complaint are borne by the two (in Canada and the US) government agencies that must evaluate the petition. Yet the benefits are likely to be substantial and the risks of failing to get protection are low. Furthermore, once a firm has been through the process before, its risks of not succeeding are even lower. At this point, it appears that the AD system clearly favours petitioning firms and biases a country's trade policy towards semi-permanent ad hoc protection.

Situation facing exporting firms

The favourable treatment facing domestic firms in AD regulations can be contrasted with the situation faced by exporting firms, those alleged to be dumping. First, they must respond to the government agencies investigating the dumping petition, and this involves lengthy questionnaires, particularly from the DOC. They cover pricing on all related product lines, as well as detailed cost information on all such products, over the time period on which the investigation is based. Further, it involves not only filling out the detailed questionnaires but responding to field visits of DOC personnel to verify questionnaire data and address arguments submitted by both sides in the case. This cost is more likely to be faced by the largest firms in an industry because the DOC tends to focus on such firms in its data collection (they are termed 'mandatory respondents'). However, it is important to note that although a shared industry defence is sometimes feasible, the detailed data collection is done on an individual firm basis and the possible AD duties are set on a firm-specific basis. So unlike the situation for a petitioning domestic industry where the relatively modest legal and data collection costs are usually shared with other firms, the exporting firms, at least the larger ones, are facing large individual firm costs in addition to any shared defence costs.

The costs of not cooperating are substantial because then the DOC will use data that are alleged from the petitioner's brief or obtained by the DOC from other sources, usually adverse to the exporter's interest, with the resulting duty margin being high. So if the exporter wants to continue to export profitably to the US, it realistically has no alternative but to cooperate with and respond to the DOC's substantial requests. Not only does this take significant amounts of time for the firm's professional staff in gathering the data and working with the DOC staff but it also usually involves retaining legal, economic and accounting expertise from firms familiar with the US AD process. This usually will be very expensive. A rule of thumb that is heard on the street is that legal costs for a defending a case of normal complexity will be close to US$1 million.[4]

On top of this, the resulting decisions, based on the numbers presented above, leave small hope for exporters that the decision will be made in their favour. Almost certainly the dumping decision will be adverse to them, and they can only pin their hopes from investing seriously in the costs noted above on a slightly more probable negative injury decision, or, more likely, a lower rate of duty than was initially assessed.

The incentive these prospects give to an exporting firm are quite obvious. A Canadian greenhouse tomato firm expressed the lesson it learned from a recent AD case against it by the US as, 'We never want to go through that again'. And this came from a firm where the final decision went in its favour because there was a negative determination on the final injury decision.

Tallying up these different effects we see that almost all the benefits of this process accrue to the domestic firms that compete against imports while almost all the costs fall on the exporting firm(s). As if that were not enough, within the US there is the added issue of the Byrd amendment. This law mandates that all AD duties collected be allocated to the firms injured by the alleged dumping instead of to the US Treasury. Although this provision has been declared illegal by the WTO, it has not yet been withdrawn so is still distorting the AD process. It does so by giving an added incentive to domestic firms to make AD claims. It is in effect a bribe paid to domestic firms to encourage them to file more dumping petitions, as if the playing field was not already tilted heavily in their favour.

Implications for firm behaviour

There are two kinds of implications arising from the working of AD procedures, both analogous to what one finds in insurance markets. First, there will adverse selection in terms of which firms choose to use the AD regime. Second, firms will choose to alter their behaviour because of the existence of this kind of trade policy, a kind of moral hazard.

If a firm is weak and it wishes protection to maintain domestic competitiveness, it will be attracted to file a dumping complaint. Not only would it be attracted to the prospect of added tariff protection, but its situation as a weak firm, probably making losses, will make it more likely (than for an average firm) to achieve a positive injury determination. So the attention to injury found in existing AD rules means that weaker firms have a higher likelihood of getting AD rulings in their favour and will be more highly represented in AD cases (Prusa 2004).

Even if the firm is in only short term difficulty and knows it does not have a strong case for AD, it should go ahead and file an AD complaint because there is a high likelihood it will get a favourable (to it) preliminary ruling from which it will receive an AD duty for at least half a year, even if the final decision goes against it. This short term protection may be just what the firm needs to survive on the off-chance that this is the only protection it can obtain. Staiger and Wolak (1994) have shown that filing is a profitable strategy on the basis of preliminary relief alone; the fall in trade during just this early part of the investigation period substantially benefits the domestic industry (Blonigen and Prusa 2003).

The cost side of an AD case will also serve to select firms that use AD. Because the costs are not vastly different for large and small firms in advancing a case, yet the benefits will increase with output, there will be a bias in favour of larger firms filing AD petitions. Larger firms are also more likely to be hit by AD duties, at least in the US due to the DOC giving greater attention to collecting data from 'mandatory respondents'. Small firms are more likely to be able to 'free ride' on both sides of an AD case.

This bias is likely to carry over to differences between countries. For firms in developing countries where there are likely to be more firms without deep pockets, they would have most to fear from a costly AD case. So they would be more likely to be deterred from exporting to the US market in the first place. The cost to them of dealing with an AD case is like an entry barrier, an added fixed cost to be incurred, with the result that AD law works to reduce new entrants and hence competition in the US market.

Related to this is the possibility that there is a great deal of learning involved in responding to and initiating AD complaints. Blonigen (2004) has examined this latter hypothesis for the US and finds support for it. Firms with previous experience in filing an AD case since 1980 submit more AD filings and have more affirmative (dumping) outcomes. However, the size of AD duties is significantly smaller for more experienced firms. A probable explanation is that this indicates that in filing more cases, these firms are also filing weaker cases, for which the margins are lower. This finding is not an artefact of the larger number of steel industry cases. If you look at non-steel cases only you find the same or stronger results.

We have found no evidence of the role of experience in defending against AD complaints. This may be because there are very few experienced AD defendants; once you have had the experience of fighting an AD case as a defendant you find ways to avoid doing that again.

This raises the question of firm behaviour in responding to AD rules, or the moral hazard effect of AD rules. Again, these are likely to be different between exporters and import-competing domestic firms. For firms exporting into the US market there are clear lessons from the experience of dealing with the AD rules and investigations, whether the firm in question actually experienced this directly as a defendant or not. First, in exporting to the US, a firm would want to be careful about exporting too much, to avoid being a specific target of an investigation, and also to avoid any export surges, especially over extended periods. Second, the firm would want to hold its export prices as high as possible, and not to sell below prevailing US prices if at all possible. It turns out this is exactly what one finds in the data. Prusa (2001) has found exporters selling less to the US and selling at higher prices in those sectors where AD investigations have been made. And a variety of theoretical models also predict that the mere existence of AD laws will lead foreign firms to invest in lower capacity and therefore lower exports (and higher prices), even if there is no AD activity (Blonigen and Prusa 2003). Third, continuing the topic of pricing, there is the matter of exporting firms' response to 'administrative reviews', the practice of the DOC recalculating dumping margins periodically (as frequently as annually) by using the previous period's price and cost data. The behaviour that has been found (DeVault 1996) is that many foreign firms raise prices, thereby leading the DOC to calculate lower dumping margins in these administrative reviews with the result that lower AD duties are payable. The effect of all three of these exporter responses is to reduce imports to the market with AD duties and raise export prices in that market.

For import-competing firms in the domestic market, the lessons have been noted above. When in economic difficulty, file an AD petition. The firm will almost surely get an AD duty imposed on its competition following preliminary findings, and a high likelihood of AD duties after final determination. In fact, the weaker the firm is economically, the better its chance at proving injury.

There are other examples of strategic behaviour on the part of firms facing AD actions, aside from the more obvious direct price and export behaviour. One is to tariff-jump by way of foreign direct investment. If faced with an AD duty, invest in the US and avoid the tariff using your US plant. This has been documented empirically by Blonigen et al. (2003). Another important strategic issue is retaliation. Prusa and Skeath (2001) examine this with worldwide AD cases and find evidence of tit-for-tat behaviour. More recently, this was evident in the two tomato cases between Canada and the US during 2001–2002 where the US greenhouse growers petitioned against the Canadian greenhouse tomato exporters, followed shortly by the Canadian industry petitioning against US fresh field tomato exporters (Barichello 2004). Alternatively, forms of cooperation between importer and exporter may occur, such as an increased incentive to develop cartels between the two firms (Blonigen and Prusa 2003), and an incentive to withdraw cases due to private settlements (explaining the high level of withdrawn cases that has been observed).

Finally, there is the issue of trade, specifically import, diversion. This is not a moral hazard matter, but rather a response of other firms that could be exporting to the domestic market where AD investigations are undertaken. In those cases investigation by itself is found to reduce imports from 'named' sources, leading to increased imports from non-named or third country import sources (Blonigen and Prusa 2003; Krupp and Pollard 1996; Carter and Gunning-Trant 2004).

Conclusions

The behaviour by firms in response to antidumping regulatory processes described above has important results on the functioning of the economy in general and the trade sector in particular. The actions of petitioners in advancing more cases means more trade is subject to higher tariffs and reduced trade volumes. The responses of exporters means a smaller volume of exports to the country with AD rules and export goods entering at higher prices, both resulting in less trade and fewer gains from trade. It also means less competition in the US market, and slower exit by high cost or inefficient firms, given their comparative advantage in getting favourable AD decisions. The costs of higher tariffs may be greater with AD duties than with regular tariffs due to the greater uncertainties involved and the larger administrative costs associated with AD procedures. They may also be longer-lived due to the immunity of these tariffs from normal tariff line cuts arrived at in negotiations, and they may be more costly due to the several negative efficiency effects noted.

This impact of current AD rules and procedures on the economy, both the US and world economy, is altogether undesirable. The gains from trade arrived at over successive international trade agreements are being rolled back, increasingly, just as if there was a general increase in tariffs. What makes this trend more worrisome is that AD tariffs are increasing the dispersion of tariffs across industries, due, for example, to differences in political support and factors that relate to the antidumping regulations and how different industries can benefit from established procedures. Finally, AD laws are no guarantee that the domestic industry firms will be as well protected as hoped for by politicians and lobbyists due to trade diversion and tariff jumping.

Notes

1. A lengthy discussion of the many rules and procedures used in all phases of antidumping petitions in the US is found in Lindsey and Ikenson (2002). Some of the following discussion draws on this paper and other parts of the discussion draw on Barichello (2003).
2. Since the Uruguay Round Agreement, dumping duties are subject to a five year sunset law, whereby there is automatic termination after five years unless a sunset review is requested. A positive sunset review decision (on both dumping and injury grounds) in effect extends the duty order for five more years.
3. The observation has led to the development of theoretical models to examine the possibility of private settlements; they predict that settlements may be preferred to AD duties in a number of situations (Blonigen and Prusa 2003).
4. Another reason why legal counsel is imperative, both for defendant and petitioning firms, is that any data collected by the authorities can be accessed only by firm's legal counsel, not by the firms themselves.

References

Barichello, R. R. (2004), 'Two Cases of Tomatoes: Demonstrating the Need for Antidumping Reform,' in Andrew Schmitz, W.W. Koo and C.B. Moss (eds), *International Agricultural Trade Disputes: Case Studies in North America*, East Lansing, MI: Michigan State University Press, pp. 149–65.

Barichello, R. R. and N. Malhotra (2004), 'Antidumping, Agriculture, and the Level of Development,' December, unprocessed.

Blonigen, B. (2004), 'Working the System: Firm Learning and the AD Process,' NBER Working Paper No. 10783, September.

Blonigen, B. and T. Prusa (2003), 'Antidumping,' in E. Kwan Choi and James Harrigan (eds), *Handbook of International Trade*, Malden, MA: Blackwell Publishing.

Blonigen, B., K. Tomlin and W. W. Wilson (2003), 'Tariff-Jumping and Domestic Firms' Profits,' *Canadian Journal of Economics*, **37**, 656–77.

Carter, C. and C. Gunning-Trant (2004), 'Trade Remedy Laws and NAFTA's Chapter 12 Agricultural Trade Rulings,' in Andrew Schmitz, W. W. Koo and C. B. Moss (eds), *International Agricultural Trade Disputes: Case Studies in North America*, East Lansing, MI: Michigan State University Press, pp. 13–34.

Canadian Border Security Agency (CBSA) (2004), *What You Shoud Know About Dumping and Subidy Investigations*, Ottawa, available at: www. cbsa–asfc.gc.ca/sima/brochvre.html.

DeVault, J. M. (1996), 'US Antidumping Administrative Reviews,' *International Trade Journal*, **10**, 247–67.

GATT (1994), *Agreement on the Implementation of Article VI of Gatt*, Geneva: GATT.

Krupp, C. and P. S. Pollard (1996), 'Market Responses to Antidumping Laws: Some Evidence from the US Chemical Industry,' *Canadian Journal of Economics*, **29**, 199–227.

Lindsey, B. and D. Ikenson (2002), 'Antidumping 101: The Devilish Details of "Unfair Trade" Law,' Trade Policy Analysis Working Paper No. 20, The Cato Institute, November.

Prusa, T. (2001),'On the Spread and Impact of Antidumping,' *Canadian Journal of Economics*, **34**, 591–611.

Prusa, T. (2004), 'An Economist's Perspective on USITC Proceedings,' paper presented to 25th Annual Meeting of the International Agricultural Trade Research Consortium, St Pete Beach, FL, 5 December.

Prusa, T. and S. Skeath (2001), 'The Economic and Strategic Motives for Antidumping Filings,' NBER Working Paper 8424, August.

Staiger, R. W. and F. A. Wolak (1994), 'Measuring Industry-Specific Protection: Antidumping in the United States,' *Brookings Papers on Economic Activity: Microeconomics*, 51–118.

35 Safeguard measures and impediments to labour mobility
Lawrence Leger and James Gaisford

Introduction

The World Trade Organization (WTO) (1999: 275–82) allows countries to implement temporary safeguard measures in the form of import tariffs or quotas if they are confronted by a surge in imports that causes or threatens 'serious injury' to the domestic industry.[1] Unlike contingency measures such as antidumping duties and countervailing duties, which have been discussed in previous chapters, there is no requirement of unfair trade practices on the part of foreign firms or governments. Rather, the rationale for safeguard measures is that a country may need time, and thus temporary protection, to facilitate orderly 'structural adjustment' to a new trading reality. In the absence of unfair foreign trade practices, a country that uses safeguards must offer trade concessions of equivalent value elsewhere, or pay equivalent compensation or, by default, accept equivalent retaliation. Safeguards are normally limited to four years with any extensions requiring evidence of adjustment as well as continued evidence of serious injury. With extensions, there is an eight-year maximum duration for a single action and consecutive actions are not permitted. Developing countries receive some special treatment both if they impose safeguards and if they are subject to safeguards from other countries. The current WTO Agreement on Agriculture also includes 'special safeguard' provisions related to import levels sufficiently above the minimum access provisions negotiated in the Uruguay Round (WTO 1999: 36–8).

Depending on whether the underlying shift in comparative advantage that gives rise to an import surge is temporary or permanent, such so-called structural adjustment may entail the adoption of new technologies in the domestic industry and/or require the sector to downsize. Industrial downsizing, particularly in the case of dominant regional industries, is frequently associated with politically sensitive adjustments in labour markets. This chapter analyses various types of impediment to mobility that can lead specific labour groups to demand protection from import surges and more broadly defined trade shocks. We show that different impediments to labour mobility, which entail adjustment costs, have different social and political implications, and that while some impediments entail economic distortions, very many do not. In the case of an import surge, therefore, there is sometimes an economic efficiency argument for a temporary 'safeguard measure' to facilitate adjustment, but often there is not. While affected labour groups may lobby for trade restrictions in any case, the appropriate policy response is likely to be temporary sector- or region-specific taxes or subsidies in those cases where a safeguard measure is warranted.

In this chapter we address the impact on labour welfare of shocks to the international terms of trade, focusing on how adjustment costs might provide incentives for particular labour groups to lobby for trade protection and how policy-makers might most appropriately respond. We focus exclusively on labour welfare under the assumption that individuals can hold portfolios of capital assets, so that any sector-specific changes in returns to capital can be fully diversified.

Standard neoclassical models of international trade teach important lessons about the benefits to society of liberalized trade but they ignore significant real-world impediments to adjustment. It is assumed in such models that resources move with complete freedom in response to changes in relative prices so that a terms-of-trade shock induces an immediate full-employment adjustment. Markets for factors of production adjust to equalize the returns to any factor across all industries. For example, in a two-factor, two-good context, the Stolper–Samuelson (1941) Theorem implies that a terms-of-trade shock associated with a reduction in the relative price of the imported good will adversely affect the factor group that is used intensively in the import competing sector and favour the factor used intensively in the export sector. This leaves no relative losers or winners within either factor group. With the introduction of relocation costs, however, some sectoral labour groups may become relatively (or even absolutely) worse off after a terms-of-trade shock even if labour would experience an overall gain in the absence of such adjustment costs.

Economists have made a sufficiently strong case for the merits of trade liberalization that arguments for broad-based protectionism currently enjoy very little credibility (Perdikis and Kerr 1998). Hughes (1986) has observed that demands for protection by labour groups in fact tend to be sector specific and hardest to refuse when workers are poorly paid and their industries are regionally agglomerated and in decline. We therefore suspect that policy makers most often initiate protectionist trade measures in response to complaints arising from the adjustment costs faced by their constituents rather than for any other reason. This raises questions about the appropriate policy response when adjustment costs exist – a matter in which economic analysis has been less useful to policy makers than it might have been.

Since it is crucial to identify correctly the incentives that induce groups to demand protection (Hillman 1989), we draw on a general adjustment-costs framework developed by Leger and Gaisford (2001). We examine the circumstances in which adjustment costs may lead to an incentive for sectoral or regional labour groups to lobby for temporary or permanent protection in response to exogenous terms-of-trade shocks even when labour is mobile. We also explore the appropriate policy response to such lobbying and consider whether this could involve trade measures such as tariffs, subsidies in the form of industrial policy or more broadly-based regional intervention. We ask whether temporary anti-surge measures are indicated, and whether international trade agreements – especially the World Trade Organization (WTO) – allow appropriate safeguard measures.

We begin by outlining a standard zero-cost neoclassical model. We then consider different types of real-world adjustment cost that entail very different policy responses. This simplifies the discussion, but not reality where various frictions may occur simultaneously, possibly with different policy implications. It is for policy-makers to assess the applicability of different policies in different real-world scenarios and to select the most appropriate overall package.

The benchmark neoclassical model

The framework suggested by Leger and Gaisford (2001) extends the neoclassical model to allow for a very wide variety of adjustment costs. In the simple benchmark case it is assumed that technology is unchanging in all sectors, that the factors of production available within the economy are fixed and that distorting activities, such as collective wage-bargaining, do not occur in the labour market or elsewhere. National income is assumed to be the sum of worker incomes, which include both wages and income arising from other factors.

In the standard full-employment equilibrium, firms hire workers up to the point where individuals receive wages equal to the full value of their marginal product. The standard assumption of diminishing marginal product implies that relocation of labour between sectors causes marginal productivity to rise in the sector of origin and fall in the sector of destination. Wages therefore rise in the sector of origin as workers depart and fall in the sector of destination as workers arrive. Workers have an incentive to move between sectors as long as there is a wage differential, so that movement of labour ceases only when wages are equalized across sectors.

The only stimulus for inter-sectoral movement of labour that we consider is a shock to the terms of trade, where the relative prices of goods change in the international market. We begin by assuming that each individual's non-labour income is generated by a fully-diversified portfolio of assets. This implies that the only incentive for a worker to relocate is to earn a higher wage. In the absence of full diversification, portfolio earnings might depend on the relative prosperity of the worker's sector of employment and the mobility of sector-specific assets. For example, a worker might own land in a region in industrial decline. While the worker could relocate in pursuit of higher wages, any income from the immobile land could fall. We incorporate such complications in a later section.

A terms-of-trade shock alters the relative prices of outputs among sectors. Firms facing a rise in the price of their output receive an increase in the value of the marginal product of labour (the output produced by each additional worker is now more valuable) and are therefore both willing and able to offer higher wages to attract more workers in the pursuit of higher output. Similarly, because firms adversely affected by a terms-of-trade shock see a fall in the value of both output and the marginal product of each worker they reduce output and shed labour. An inter-sector wage differential develops, creating an incentive for workers to move. Assuming a once-and-for-all shock, a wage differential is created and labour markets begin to adjust, leading wage rates to converge. At the new equilibrium, sectors where the terms of trade have deteriorated will have shrunk while sectors with improved terms of trade will have expanded, but wages will again be equal across sectors. Whether the real wage of all workers rises or falls depends on the structure of the economy. For example, in the two-factor, two-good context, whether the wage rises or falls depends on whether or not the expanding sector uses labour intensively.

Introducing labour relocation costs

For a formal treatment of the adjustment costs described in this section the reader is referred to Leger and Gaisford (2001). If workers had identical tastes, attributes and costs-of-living, and if labour mobility were perfect, wage differentials would fully compensate for any utility change experienced by the marginal relocating worker (Rosen 1979) – for example, one could be a bricklayer in Chicago on Monday and a oceanographer in San Diego on Tuesday and experience no change in welfare. Under such circumstances, there would be no sector- or region-specific trade-policy interests; any heterogeneity in interests across the population would arise from differences in non-labour wealth. To assess the legitimacy of demands for protection from labour groups, we therefore consider differences between workers and impediments to labour mobility.

There are a number of reasons why labour may be imperfectly mobile. First, human capital may be sector-specific – bricklayers and oceanographers must be trained. Second, individuals may have different endowments of job-related natural attributes and abilities – sumo wrestlers and jockeys are not interchangeable. Third, there may be imperfections in the spatial organization of industry – fishing takes place near oceans while dry land farming takes place on the plains. This aspect of labour-market friction is often ignored in the international trade literature but its consequences can be both extremely important and subtle. For example, inter-regional relocation may entail more costly commuting patterns and changes in the provision of amenities and public goods (schools, hospital beds, utility networks and so on). The welfare of people faced with moving may also be tied to the value of immobile region/sector-specific assets such as housing (Hillman 1989). Furthermore, although housing and job-related natural abilities can both be viewed as sector-specific assets, they differ markedly in their degree of marketability. We will use the term labour market position to refer to differences in individual relocation costs arising from differences in workers' individual endowments of personal attributes or assets. Some adjustment costs can be seen as a loss in work time. For example, individuals who retrain for new jobs may have to spend time out of the labour market and the monetary cost of retraining means some wage income is channelled into educational activities that would not otherwise be undertaken. Loss of work time implies that relocation choices involve discounted streams of future benefits and costs rather than simple net wage rates. Finally, as trade unions, community leaders and the media frequently point out, industrial adjustment not only causes a loss of income for some workers but may also lead to the wholesale decline of communities and the destruction of traditional ways of life or regional heritage – externalities that are particularly difficult for politicians to deal with.

Relocation of labour evidently entails changes in both costs and benefits of employment, causing compensating wage differentials to arise at the margin in any equilibrium in which there is some inter-sector labour relocation (Tiebout 1956; Rosen 1979; Wilson 1987). When the act of changing jobs and/or relocating geographically is costly, or if workers are not identical, then the welfare effects of exogenous changes in world prices will be unequally distributed across sectors. A terms-of-trade shock may therefore make some workers worse off even when: (a) the economy as a whole gains; (b) other groups of workers gain; and (c) labour is mobile (Leger and Gaisford 2001).

These adjustment costs can be further categorized into two types. Employment costs are associated directly with a job in a new sector and are often ongoing. Many examples can be found: productivity may be reduced if an individual's innate abilities are poorly matched to a new job; commuting costs may rise if the geographical location of a new job is less convenient; the productivity of existing workers may be harmed by the mistakes of new workers and training may absorb resources. More generally, the need for training may harm productivity: in a growing industry existing workers may have to be withdrawn from production to train new arrivals; in a declining industry remaining workers may have to acquire the skills of workers who leave, and become less specialized themselves as a result. Entry/exit costs are not directly job-related but must be incurred if when employment is taken up. Often these are one-time costs associated with the move to a different geographical location. The costs of acquiring new skills – both opportunity costs and monetary tuition costs – fit into this category. Moreover, the relocation of many workers may lead to congestion in retraining facilities, pressure on local amenities and public goods in expanding regions, loss of services in declining regions, and community disruption in general.

Evidently, both employment costs and entry/exit costs have private and social cost aspects. For example, workers relocating to jobs in a new part of a city incur a private employment cost if commuting costs increase. This arises even in the absence of crowding, simply because the commuting distance is greater. However, a large regional influx of workers could cause roads to become congested, imposing an externality on all those already employed in the expanding sector in terms of longer commuting time. Similarly, entry costs arising from retraining may entail an externality if many individuals need to be retrained at any given time and, for example, they congest training facilities.

An individual's decision to relocate will be based on the private employment and entry costs they expect to face. An individual will discount the expected benefits and costs and compare their present values. If the benefits exceed the private costs, the individual will relocate. However, individuals will not consider the external costs, causing the private and social costs of adjustment to diverge when external costs are positive. The equilibrium pattern of new job uptake may therefore be inefficient and there may be a role for public policy initiatives. Of course, the social and private costs of new job uptake will diverge even when entry costs are equal to zero, if an employment costs externality exists and *vice versa*.

Finally, a worker's position in the labour market may generate employment and entry/exit costs that are either private or social. For example, individuals whose innate abilities are less suitable for employment in a given sector may have greater training needs in general. They may therefore not only face greater private costs but also create more ongoing disruption.

The adjustment-cost framework provides for many different types of entry and employment costs, which alter the rate of new job uptake relative to the zero-cost benchmark case. The multi-dimensional aspect of adjustment costs implies that it is necessary to develop policy carefully in response to given circumstances. Alternative types of relocation costs are considered in detail in the remainder of the chapter. In each case the impact of a single cost is compared with the full-employment zero-cost benchmark equilibrium.

Constant adjustment costs

The simplest case of impediments to labour mobility entails constant entry or employment costs, incurred when workers relocate between industrial sectors, where sectors may or may not be identified with regions. Adjustment costs of fixed height have been examined by Schweinberger (1979) and Fernandez and Rodrik (1991), and costs of fixed proportion have been explored by Leamer (1980), Diamond (1982) and Staiger and Tabellini (1987). Entry costs of fixed height could include one-time retraining fees or home removal costs. Similarly, employment (output) may be forgone while an individual retrains. Entry costs of fixed proportion could arise from reduced productivity during on-the-job training. These constant costs will be assumed to be independent of the individual's position in the labour market for the moment, but this assumption will be relaxed in the next section.

Assume that wages are initially equal across sectors. If a shock improves the terms of trade in sector B relative to sector A, wages will initially rise in sector B and fall in sector A, but with constant adjustment costs workers will not move unless an inter-sector wage differential emerges that is sufficient to offset the cost. This implies that relocation causes wages to converge until the differential is no larger than the relocation cost. In this case, because there are no external costs, the private and social costs of adjustment coincide and the equilibrium is efficient. For small shocks labour does not move, generating a case that is formally equivalent to either a specific-factors model (Jones 1971; Markusen *et al.* 1995: 127–41) or a fixed-factors model, depending on whether or not other factors of production are mobile. For large shocks where labour moves the model is equivalent to a Heckscher–Ohlin model (Jones 1965; Markusen *et al.* 1995: 98–126) or a specific-factors model, again depending on whether or not other factors of production are mobile.

In this case, competitive forces always generate efficient inter-sector relocation, but inequities may arise. Workers in a declining sector may become worse off, even if the shock is welfare-enhancing for the country as a whole, because the terms-of-trade gain may not offset the relative wage decline. This may lead to appeals for redress from some workers and, where industrial sectors are associated with regions, both labour leaders and local politicians may make such demands, particularly if industrial decline is due to competition from imports. However, a case for government action can only be made on grounds of equity, not on grounds of efficiency.

Optimal discretionary intervention on equity grounds entails a lump-sum subsidy to all workers initially located in the declining sector, whether they relocate or not, because a relocating worker pays the cost while a worker who does not relocate experiences a decline in wages. In practice, the government should probably rely on redistribution through progressive income taxation. The case for a protectionist policy is very weak, because a tariff or import quota would reduce overall welfare in the (small) economy by introducing distortions in both production and consumption. Further, a permanent shift in the terms of trade implies a permanent inequity, so the need for protection would be ongoing and a temporary safeguard or anti-surge measure would not be appropriate. If countries routinely implemented permanent protectionist policies in such cases, the cumulative disruptive effects on world trade could be very large. Finally, the case for industrial or regional subsidies is also weak. While they would avoid the consumption distortions arising from the use of tariffs, they would create inefficiencies in production.

Adjustment costs that depend on workers' characteristics

In this section we consider costs arising from the innate personal characteristics or aptitudes of individual workers. Individuals with different innate abilities, which are non-marketable assets, may have different natural affinities for each sector, constituting non-marketable positions in the labour force and implying imperfect mobility of labour. We focus sharply on this issue by assuming that the more an individual is suited to employment in the declining sector, *A*, the less they are suited to employment in expanding sector, *B*, and *vice versa*. Sector-specific aptitudes have been considered by: Diamond (1982), Grossman and Shapiro (1982), Mussa (1982) and Aizenman and Fenkel (1988).

Taking occupational stress as an example, we may assume that the declining industry requires independent work, creating less stress for introverts but more stress for extroverts, while the expanding sector requires teamwork, creating more stress for introverts but less stress for extroverts. As stress rises, productivity and wages fall, so that individuals with different stress levels earn different wages and effectively face different sector-specific employment costs. Of course, stress may affect utility directly through job-satisfaction but here we examine only indirect wage effects.

If we make the further simplifying assumption that all individuals can be ranked continuously with respect to introversion, then in equilibrium the most extroverted person working in the expanding sector has the highest wage (and utility) in the sector, the next most extroverted person has a slightly lower wage and so on. Similarly, in the declining sector the most introverted person has the highest wage in that sector while those with lower introversion receive lower wages. Note that at the margin of migration, where workers are indifferent to their sector of work because they receive the same total wage earnings in either sector, wages earnings are the lowest of all workers.

In this case, a positive terms-of-trade shock might again fail to offset a fall in wages in the declining sector. Workers would not relocate to the higher-wage sector if the higher wage rate failed to compensate for the reduction in their productivity in that sector – that is, they could be made even worse off by relocating. Furthermore, the welfare of some migrants may decline despite relocating – because not relocating would have been even worse. Thus, the shock may generate demands for protection or other redress, although there are again no externality effects and no efficiency grounds for intervention. More important, in this case even an equity argument for discretionary action is precarious. The simplifying assumptions made here (opposed but otherwise identical continuous distributions of innate abilities in the two sectors) may not apply in the real world, so that in general the distributions of wage earnings and utilities – equalized only at the margin of migration – may cause a terms-of-trade shock to induce an overall improvement in equity rather than a deterioration.

Adjustment costs that depend on residential location

A relocating worker may face relocation costs that arise from a change in residential location. In such a case, workers are faced with employment costs that consist of commuting and residential location costs and therefore have positions in the labour market that are defined by sector-specific marketable assets, such as housing in particular. As an example, we assume that two industries are located in different geographic areas. For simplicity, we abstract from variations in residential density, locational preferences and any other complication, to focus only on commuting distance. Since commuting absorbs real income, costs can be measured as a loss of work time that rises with distance, so workers will live as near as they can to their workplace. We assume here that the transport system is not congested, but relax this assumption later.

Suppose first that workers are renters (Leger 1993) who face different commuting costs but receive the same wage per hour worked. If there is an efficient rental market, workers will bid up the rental premium in an attempt to save commuting costs. This has two implications. First, workers at the margin of migration will pay no rental premium. Second, within a given sector, the rental payment on each residential location will be bid up until the sum of the rent plus the commuting cost is the same for each worker. Thus, all workers will receive the same wage incomes adjusted for total employment costs (that is, commuting costs plus location rents) and since there are no innate differences between workers they must have the same utility. This leads to a compensating wage differential of the type discussed by Rosen (1979) whenever commuting costs for each sector are not equal for the marginal migrant because the regions are not the same size.

Since the marginal private costs of employment are equal to the marginal social costs, workers efficiently relocate as a result of a terms-of-trade shock and the overall allocation of labour is efficient. Given also that utility is equal for all workers, neither equity across worker groups nor efficiency are justifications for government intervention in this case.

There may, however, still be people who lose after the terms-of-trade shock, because rental income in the declining sector may fall so much that it cannot be offset by the gains from trade. In this case, if landlords are not diversified, they will suffer a loss of rental income (Leger 1993) and hence a loss in the capital value of their property, as will any worker who owns their home. Property owners may therefore lobby for income compensation. Given that individuals are able to diversify their capital assets, the absence of inefficiencies means that the case for government intervention in general – and trade policy measures in particular – is weak. However, while the diversification assumption can reasonably be applied to landlords it may not be as easily applied to owner-occupiers where the value of a residence is likely to represent a very large proportion of invested income. In such a case there may be equity grounds for intervention.

Adjustment costs that depend on cumulative labour relocation

In this section, we consider employment costs that depend on cumulative relocation. Examples might include local amenities or local public goods, which are affected either positively or negatively by the quantity of employment in an area. For example, considerable regional immigration may lead to overcrowded schools and/or congested commuter routes and leisure amenities. On the other hand it may allow the creation of amenities whose per capita fixed costs were hitherto excessive. Clearly emigration will reduce congestion, but in some cases there could be negative externalities for those who continue to live in the community – for example where amenities are forced to close through lack of support. The latter is an example of a more subtle and probably more important issue, which can accompany regional or sectoral decline, namely the narrowing of friendship networks and the general loss of regional cultural heritage. Such costs have been claimed by many groups, for example in small UK mining communities after the acrimonious and socially disruptive restructuring of the coal industry in the early 1980s.

In this case, those who contemplate changing jobs do not consider the congestion costs or network effects that they impose on others, and powerful externalities are likely to exist. We elaborate by assuming two geographically separated industrial sectors where commuting within each sector is subject to congestion. Suppose that for the marginal worker in each sector there initially happens to be no difference in the private commuting costs, which are directly incurred, or external congestion costs, which are imposed on society. By construction, wages will be equal across sectors in the initial equilibrium and the resulting sectoral allocation of labour will be efficient. A shock will drive up wages in one sector and down in the other, causing the usual migration flow, but an equilibrium wage differential will remain to compensate for the emergence of higher commuting costs in the expanding region. The new equilibrium is not efficient, since relocating workers do not take account of either the congestion costs imposed on other workers in the expanding sector or the congestion relief provided for those remaining in the declining sector. In general, the private and social costs of changing jobs will diverge and competitive labour market forces will generate inefficient outcomes. In this case, the total time lost through increased congestion in the expanding sector is likely to outweigh the congestion relief in the contracting sector since more people are affected at the higher wage location. Consequently, the social cost of relocation exceeds the private cost for the marginal migrant. Thus, the equilibrium amount of labour migration is higher than the efficient level.

The general type of adjustment cost being considered here is probably among the most difficult for politicians to deal with, since there are no obvious general rules for determining a priori whether net externality effects are positive or negative in any sector or whether the net effects are opposite or similar in the various sectors. Nonetheless, divergence between social and private adjustment costs provides a rationale for government intervention on efficiency grounds. In particular, a regional/industrial system of subsidies and/or taxes could be designed to address the externalities. Depending on the context, these measures can be labelled industrial policy, regional policy or fiscal federalism. It is also important to emphasize that when costs of employment depend on sectoral employment levels, the equilibrium allocation of resources prior to a terms-of-trade shock will be inefficient in general. There is therefore a case for ongoing government intervention whether or not shocks occur. Of course, shocks would necessarily entail changes in the government's system of subsidies and taxes to maintain an efficient solution.

A valid case for safeguard or other trade-related policy measures cannot be made. Trade policy actions that attempt to address inter-regional differences in such things as congestion costs, the provision of local public goods, and so on are second-best measures leading to distortions in consumption. Further, the cumulative disruptive effects of such trade policy measures on world trade would be large because the need for such interventions would be permanent.

Adjustment costs that depend on current migration
This section draws on the analysis of Gaisford and Leger (2000) in addressing adjustment costs that depend on current migration. Sector entry costs may be affected by congestion in industry-specific skills training or elsewhere in the channels of migration. For example, there may be shortages of teachers, teacher-training places, skilled workers in the building trades, or even moving vans. Such congestion will depend on the number of workers changing jobs in any time period and will dissipate over time as migration flows gradually subside. Thus, entry costs depend on the number of workers switching jobs at any one time and affect all those who are in the process of switching.

Sector employment costs may also rise, because migration is virtually certain to disrupt both workplaces. Non-relocating workers may be forced to learn unfamiliar duties when colleagues leave a declining sector, while incumbent workers may have to help with on-the-job training in an expanding sector. In addition, untrained workers may contribute negatively to the productivity of experienced colleagues whenever there is a team element to production. Again, such disruption should dissipate over time and be correlated with current migration. Thus, sector employment costs depend on the number of workers switching jobs at any one time and affect all workers.

Since adjustment takes place over time, the benefit of changing jobs is the discounted sum of current and future inter-sector differentials in net earnings comprised of wages less employment costs. The marginal migrant is indifferent between sectors because he/she equates the one-time private entry cost with the discounted stream of benefits relative to that time period.

A terms-of-trade shock alters the stream of benefits and provides a stimulus for workers to switch to the positively-affected sector. The total benefit of relocating is greater when, (a) the initial wage differential is higher; and (b) the wage differential can be earned for longer, so we may expect migration to be greatest early on in the adjustment period. Not all potential migrants will switch jobs immediately since the entry cost rises with the current number of relocating workers (for example, a larger relocation queue intensifies congestion in the entry process). Hence relocation proceeds gradually over time, with fewer workers transferring in later periods. Future net benefits fall in any period because the current migrants further increase the downward pressure on wages in the expanding sector. Thus, both the wage differential and the cumulative number of migrants depend on the time period. As congestion and disruption gradually ease, the wage differential is gradually eliminated until there is no congestion in the entry process and no incentive to relocate. In equilibrium the sequence of migration flows will be such that migrating workers will be indifferent with respect to the time of their migration from the declining to the expanding sector.

Note that all workers initially located in the declining sector will be equally well off at the new equilibrium, whether they change jobs or not, since each migrant equates the benefit and cost of relocating. Thus, those who change jobs early pay higher entry costs but reap higher net earnings for a longer time period, while those who remain employed in the declining sector have lower net earnings but do not incur entry costs. Since congestion costs allow a temporary wage gap to develop between sectors, workers who start out in the declining sector, whether they move or not, will be worse off than workers located in the expanding sector. Workers in the declining sector may also lose in an absolute sense if the decline in their income is not offset by a positive terms-of-trade effect on the whole economy. We therefore find that there is an incentive for labour groups in declining sectors to lobby for protection against the shock.

Note also that the marginal social cost of relocation in any time period will be larger than the marginal private cost, because relocating individuals consider only their private costs – they do not consider the disruption and congestion they impose on others. Since the absolute value of the marginal social cost of migration exceeds the private cost of migration, too many workers change jobs too soon – that is, the current number of migrants always exceeds the efficient number.

Given that the inter-sector movement of workers is inefficient when current migration leads to congestion and disruption, there is finally a role for temporary safeguard or anti-surge measures in the guise of industrial or regional policy. Employment subsidies to the declining industry or region that are appropriately phased out could be used to remove the inefficiency by preventing undue disruption of the workplaces in both sectors and undue congestion of the infrastructure in the expanding region. While a system of temporary tariffs or other import restrictions could also assist in alleviating such disruption and congestion, consumption distortions would be introduced. Thus, safeguard tariffs are second-best policies even when they are appropriately phased out.

Overall policy considerations
We have argued that labour market adjustments to terms-of-trade shocks may have significant implications for labour welfare, because of impediments to labour mobility. Persistent demands for protection from labour groups may therefore be expected even

when the economy as a whole gains from a change in the terms of trade and labour is in fact mobile. In short, adjustment costs matter and should not be ignored. Indeed, policy makers are likely to be forced by their electorates into making policy responses to terms-of-trade shocks whether they wish to or not. Our intention in this chapter has been to show that the appropriate policy response to such demands for protection depends upon the nature of the adjustment cost, because some forms lead to a divergence between private and social adjustment costs while others do not. If efficiency is not affected, then no distortion is created in the economy even though there may be welfare changes that are not equitable. It has long been established (Johnson 1965) that policies aimed at correcting distortions or inequities should target their sources and that policies that introduce distortions cannot be optimal in the absence of distortions to correct. It is clear that terms-of-trade shocks may generate demands for protection on equity grounds, but policy in such cases is probably best left to the progressive income-tax system. In instances where adjustment costs create a specific distortion there can be legitimate efficiency grounds for temporary or permanent government intervention, but trade tariffs are inappropriate in any of the cases we have discussed. This is because tariffs introduce new distortions in consumption while attempting to ameliorate distortions in production.

The existing WTO rules for safeguard measures are somewhat problematic when evaluated in terms of economic efficiency. Appropriately designed subsidies that are phased out according to a pre-set timetable could restore efficiency in the face of congestion externalities arising when adjustment costs depend on the current number of individuals moving from one sector to another. Such subsidies seem less likely to be abused by government than tariffs because they are a revenue drain rather than a revenue source. Unfortunately, current international safeguard provisions permit the imposition of temporary tariffs and non-tariff trade measures, even though these are inefficient, whereas a system of temporary region- or industry-specific anti-surge subsidies, which would be optimal, may be subject to countervailing action.

The current safeguard rules, however, appear to have some teeth when it comes to avoiding unwarranted protectionism. The most elementary test concerning whether the implementation of safeguards is warranted hinges on whether there has been a terms-of-trade shock that gives rise to a sudden increase in imports or 'surge'. The US Steel safeguards imposed in June 2001 are the most notable, and perhaps notorious, safeguard case to date. These safeguards followed a long history of questionable protection afforded to the US steel industry, first mainly through Voluntary Export Restraints and later through anti-dumping actions. Throughout this history, it is hard to avoid the conclusion that the effect, if not the intent, has been to avoid labour market adjustment rather than facilitate orderly structural change. In any case, the US safeguard tariffs and tariff rate quotas, which ranged from 8 per cent to 30 per cent, were very quickly challenged by the European Union and a broad array of other countries. A WTO panel found that the US had failed to provide evidence of an import surge and that, regardless of whether existing imports were injurious or not, the criteria for safeguards had not been met. The US appealed this decision, but on almost all counts the rulings of the initial panel were upheld. Finally, two and a half years later in December 2003, the US rescinded its safeguard duties and agreed to abide by the WTO ruling. The US Steel case, thus, provides some assurance that WTO-compliant safeguards may not be open to the most flagrant forms of protectionist abuse.

Note

1. This chapter draws on the technical survey in Leger and Gaisford (2001) and takes the opportunity to update and clarify the policy analysis in Gaisford, Leger and Kerr (1999). Research assistance from Margarita Gres is gratefully acknowledged.

References

Aizenman, J. and Frenkel, J. A. (1988), 'Sectorial Wages and the Real Exchange Rate,' *Journal of International Economics*, **24**, 69–91.
Diamond, P. E. (1982), 'Protection, Trade Adjustment Assistance, and Income Distribution,' in J. N. Bhagwati (ed.) *Import Competition and Response*, Chicago, IL: University of Chicago Press.
Fernandez, R. and Rodrik, D. (1991), 'Resistance to Reform: Status Quo Bias in the Presence of Individual-Specific Uncertainty,' *American Economic Review*, **81**, 1146–55.
Gaisford, J. D, and Leger, L. A. (2000), 'Terms of Trade Shocks, Labour-Market Adjustment and Safeguard Measures,' *Review of International Economics*, **8**, 100–112.
Gaisford, J. D., Leger, L. A. and Kerr, W. A. (1999), 'Labour-Market Adjustment to Terms of Trade shocks,' in S. B. Dahiya (ed.) *The Current State of Economic Science*, Vol. 4, Rohtak, India: Spellbound Publications, pp. 2011–34.
Grossman, G. M. and Shapiro, C. (1982), 'A Theory of Factor Mobility,' *Journal of Political Economy*, **90**, 1054–69.
Hillman, A. L. (1989), *The Political Economy of Protection*, New York: Harwood Academic Publishers.
Hughes, H. (1986), 'The Political Economy of Protection in Eleven Industrial Countries,' in R. H. Snape (ed.) *Issues in World Trade Policy*, London: Macmillan Press.
Johnson, H. G. (1965), 'Optimal Trade Intervention in the Presence of Domestic Distortions,' in R. Caves, H. G. Johnson and P. B. Kenen (eds) *Trade Growth and the Balance of Payments*, Skokie, IL: Rand-McNally.
Jones, R. W. (1965), 'The Structure of Simple General Equilibrium Models,' *Journal of Political Economy*, **73**, 557–72.
Jones, R. W. (1971), 'A Three-Factor Model in Theory, Trade and History,' in J. N. Bhagwati (ed.) *Trade Balance of Payments and Growth: Essays in Honour of Charles P. Kindleberger*, Amsterdam: North-Holland.
Leamer, E. (1980), 'Welfare Computations and the Optimal Staging of Tariff Reductions in Models with Adjustment Costs,' *Journal of International Economics*, **10**, 21–36.
Leger, L. A. (1993), 'Land-Rents and the Demand for Protection,' *The International Trade Journal*, **7**, 435–62.
Leger, L. A. and Gaisford, J. D. (2001), 'Imperfect Intersectoral Labour Mobility and Welfare in International Trade,' *Journal of Economic Surveys*, **15**, 463–90.
Markusen, J. R., Melvin, J. R., Kaempfer, W. H. and Maskus, K. E. (1995), *International Trade, Theory and Evidence*, New York: McGraw-Hill.
Mussa, M. (1982), 'Imperfect Factor Mobility and the Distribution of Income,' *Journal of International Economics*, **12**, 125–41.
Perdikis, N. and Kerr, W. A. (1998), *Trade Theories and Empirical Evidence*, Manchester: Manchester University Press.
Rosen, S. (1979), 'Wage-Based Indexes of Quality of Life,' in P. Mieszkowski and M. Straszheim (eds) *Current Issues in Urban Economics*, Baltimore, MD: Johns Hopkins University Press, pp. 74–104.
Ruffin, R. and Jones, R. W. (1977), 'Protection and Real Wages: The Neoclassical Ambiguity,' *Journal of Economic Theory*, **14**, 337–48.
Schweinberger, A. G. (1979), 'The Theory of Factor-Price Equalisation, the Case of Constant Absolute Differentials,' *Journal of International Economics*, **9**, 95–115.
Staiger, R. W. and Tabellini, G. (1987), 'Discretionary Trade Policy and Excessive Protection,' *American Economic Review*, **77**, 823–37.
Stolper, W. F., and Samuelson, P. A. (1941), 'Protection and Real Wages,' *Review of Economic Studies*, **9**, 58–73.
Tiebout, C. M. (1956), 'A Pure Theory of Local Expenditures,' *Journal of Political Economy*, **64**, 416–24.
Wilson, J. D. (1987), 'Trade in a Tiebout Economy,' *American Economic Review*, **77**, 431–41.
WTO (1999), *World Trade Organization: the Legal Texts*, Cambridge: Cambridge University Press.

PART V

COORDINATING TRADE POLICY WITH DOMESTIC POLICY

36 Sanitary and phytosanitary issues
Grant E. Isaac

Introduction

As successive rounds of trade liberalization have reduced traditional market access barriers such as tariffs, quotas and other quantitative restrictions, domestic regulations – including those for food safety – have increasingly received attention as a source of trade barriers. For example, at the multilateral level concern about the potential trade distortion created by domestic food safety regulations led to the establishment of the World Trade Organization's Agreement on the Application of Sanitary and Phytosanitary Measures[1] (SPS Agreement) on 1 January 1995. Many regional trade agreements also have SPS measures built into them. The aim of such agreements is to discipline the domestic use of SPS-type food safety regulations in order to ensure that human, animal and plant safety measures are not used as disguised forms of trade protectionism. The objective in this chapter is to assess the trade rules dealing with SPS measures and to assess some of the important trade policy issues that arise.

SPS measures at the WTO

SPS measures include human, animal and plant safety and health regulations that a particular country may put into place (Isaac 2002; Marceau and Trachtman 2002). Trade tensions arise because countries differ in how they regulate resulting in SPS-related market access barriers. This potential market access barrier is explicitly recognized in the SPS Agreement which is the focus of the discussion below.

In order to understand the structure and function of the SPS Agreement, it is necessary to locate it within the broader framework for multilateral trade liberalization. The General Agreement on Tariffs and Trade (GATT 1947) was built on the principle of non-discrimination (PND), a function of the following two explicit concepts:[2]

1. the national treatment provision (Article I) which states that foreign products must be treated like domestic products;
2. the most-favoured nation provision (Article III) which states there should be no discrimination between like products originating from different countries

While not an explicit obligation, it is clear that the notion of like products is essentially a third provision in the PND (Roessler 2003; Regan 2002). The like product provision distinguishes between products and the processes and production methods (or PPM) used to create those products whereby all like products are to be treated the same regardless of the PPM used in their production. The focus on like products was to prevent the often significant differences in levels of technological development between trading partners from being used as barriers to market entry for what are essentially the same goods. Together, these three provisions mean that like products must be subject to the same regulations in a particular regulatory jurisdiction regardless of their origin or the PPM used.

While the three concepts of the PND were used in successive rounds of trade liberalization to erode traditional market access barriers to industrial products, barriers arising from domestic food safety measures were outside the scope of the GATT 1947 where signatory countries retained significant discretion to establish their own food safety and food quality regulations according to two of the GATT articles. For instance, Article XI specifically permitted regulations setting out national 'standards or regulations for the classification, grading or marketing of commodities in international trade'. Article XX(b) permitted the adoption or enforcement of measures necessary to protect human, animal or plant life or health. In an attempt to be consistent with the PND, the discretionary measures invoked under Articles XI and XX(b) were not to be applied in such a manner as to cause arbitrary or unjustifiable discrimination between countries or disguised restrictions on trade. However, this specification did not provide any discipline on the type of measure that could be implemented.

Many different interests were frustrated with the discretionary and arbitrary food safety measures applied under the GATT 1947 ranging from food exporting countries and multinational food processing and distributing companies who shared a common concern about market access barriers facing food trade to consumer organizations who wanted to ensure that as food products were increasingly traded some minimum standards of safety prevailed (Spriggs and Isaac 2001; Hooker and Caswell 1999). Therefore, the SPS Agreement employs the Risk Analysis Framework (RAF)[3] to outline permissible types of trade restricting measures that WTO Members may enact in order to protect human, animal and plant safety and health from the import of agricultural products.[4]

According to the SPS Agreement, the inalienable right of Members to protect human, animal or plant safety and health is enshrined in the Agreement:

> No member should be prevented from adopting or enforcing measures necessary to protect human, animal or plant life or health arising from:
> - the entry, establishment or spread of pests, diseases, disease-carrying organisms or disease-causing organisms;
> - additives, contaminants, toxins or disease-causing organisms in food, beverages or feedstuffs; and
> - diseases carried by animals, plants or products thereof. (SPS Agreement, Annex A)

If a legitimate justification[5] exists Members may restrict or prevent imports through the use of mandatory sanitary and phytosanitary measures. In fact, there are three important provisions of the SPS Agreement – differing from traditional trade principles – that support the unilateral establishment of SPS measures by Members.[6]

First, under the SPS Agreement, Members may discriminate against imports because of the presence of risks in the exporting country (SPS Agreement, Article 2:3). The agreement recognizes that different regions with different geographical conditions and agronomic practices face different incidences of pests and disease. As a result, it may not be possible or necessary to establish uniform SPS measures to apply to all exporters according to the PND. Instead, trade measures may need to specifically target those imports that may contaminate the domestic food supply, while other imported agricultural products may not face the same measures. Hence, Members are not required to grant either national treatment or most-favoured nation status to agricultural exporters whose products may contaminate the domestic food supply.

Second, according to the agreement, Members may also establish domestic SPS measures higher than the accepted international standard if there is legitimate justification to do so (SPS Agreement, Article 3:3). Generally, international trade agreements commit Members to adopt international standards if available; however, the SPS Agreement permits Members to establish even higher standards. That is, the SPS Agreement creates a regulatory floor but not a regulatory ceiling.

Third, under the SPS Agreement, Members may establish provisional SPS measures based on precaution, in the event that there is insufficient scientific evidence to conduct an appropriate risk assessment. The Agreement states:

> In cases where the relevant scientific evidence is insufficient, a Member may provisionally adopt sanitary or phytosanitary measures on the basis of available pertinent information, including that from sanitary or phytosanitary measures applied by other Members. In such circumstances, Members shall seek to obtain additional information necessary for a more objective assessment of risk and review the sanitary or phytosanitary measure accordingly within a reasonable amount of time. (SPS Agreement, Article 5:7)

That is, Members are permitted to establish trade barriers based on the precautionary principle. These barriers can remain in place until enough scientific evidence about the risk has been compiled.

What constitutes a legitimate justification? According to the Agreement, unilateral SPS measures must be 'based on scientific principles' and cannot be maintained 'without sufficient scientific evidence' unless it is a temporary, precautionary measure (SPS Agreement, Article 2:2). The science-based measures adopted must be proportional to the risk that is being targeted. What is important to note is that the WTO does not determine the sufficiency of scientific evidence. Instead, it defers to one of three international scientific organizations. For food safety, the relevant international institution is the Codex Alimentarius Commission (CAC), for animal safety the International Office of Epizootics (OIE) and for plant safety the International Plant Protection Convention (IPPC) (SPS Agreement, Article 5:1) (Isaac *et al.* 2001). Sufficient scientific evidence would be evidence that conforms to either the standards or the standards-setting procedures established by these organizations. The Agreement states that:

> In the assessment of risks, Members shall take into account available scientific evidence; relevant processes and production methods; relevant inspection, sampling and testing methods; prevalence of specific diseases or pests; existence of pest- or disease-free areas; relevant ecological and environmental conditions and quarantine and other treatment (SPS Agreement, Article 5:2).

Hence, the SPS Agreement requires Members to provide a legitimate justification for the adoption of measures where the justification must be congruent with a science-based approach to the assessment and management of risk in order to be trade compliant.

> When a Member has reason to believe that a specific sanitary or phytosanitary measure introduced or maintained by another Member is constraining, or has the potential to constrain, its exports and the measure is not based on the relevant international standards, guidelines or recommendations, or such standards, guidelines or recommendations do not exist, an explanation of the reasons for such sanitary or phytosanitary measure may be requested and shall be provided by the Member maintaining the measure. (SPS Agreement, Article 5:8)

In sum, a Member country with a legitimate justification for an SPS measure wields considerable international trade powers; the unilateral right under the WTO to impose trade barriers that cannot be challenged by other Members. Moreover, many regional trade agreements have adopted the multilateral SPS Agreement often with additional specifications relevant for the regional arrangement.

Trade policy issues and SPS measures
While the intended effect of the Agreement was to discipline the use of SPS measures in order to simultaneously ensure human, animal and plant safety while preventing such measures from becoming disguised trade protectionism, the actual effect has been to illustrate just how contentious is the overlap between trade liberalization rules and domestic safety and health regulations. That is, despite the fact that the SPS Agreement is written in the seemingly concise language of the Risk Analysis Framework (RAF), there are genuine differences applying the RAF in order to determine a legitimate justification (required to wield the power of the agreement).

Alternative approaches to the Risk Analysis Framework
There are two broad approaches to the RAF – the scientifically rational approach and the socially rational approach – which lead to different conceptions a legitimate justification for SPS-related market access barriers (Isaac 2002). The two approaches are illustrated in Table 36.1.

The difference between the two approaches begins with a fundamental difference in the belief about the appropriate role of science and technology in society. Scientific rationality holds that technology yields innovations and enhances efficiency; enhanced efficiency leads to economic development and growth, in turn producing higher incomes. As incomes go up, demand increases for more stringent social regulations such as for food safety and environmental protection. The result is a regulatory race to the top made possible by scientific advancements.[7] Therefore, this approach supports market access rules that are based upon scientific justifications.

Operationally, the middle column of Table 36.1 reveals that the scientifically rational approach requires a scientific justification of risk, either recognized risks (for which there are data for determining risks) or hypothetical risks (for which there are no data, but accepted analytical methods for determining risks). Substantial equivalence is used as a 'gateway' regulatory principle to determine whether or not applications using the new technologies have the same risks as applications using old technologies. If yes, then the new technology is deemed 'substantially equivalent' and regulated in the same manner as old technologies. If no, then the new technology is deemed 'novel' and regulated according to new regulations designed to identify and assess novel risks. The risks that are assessed primarily involve safety (short-term) and health (long-term) risks, rather than issues of quality or socio-economic 'risks' from the new technology. Accordingly, the regulatory burden of proof is that the technology is considered safe if – at this point – it has not been shown to be unsafe. Moreover, risk and safety are probabilistic terms; there is no such thing as either zero risk or perfectly safe under the scientific rationality trajectory. The objective of risk management is limited to the reduction and prevention of actual risks identified through scientific risk assessments, and not assuaging unsubstantiated public risk perceptions. That is, a scientific interpretation of

Table 36.1   Two approaches to the RAF

	The Risk Analysis Framework (RAF)	
	Scientific rationality	Social rationality
General regulatory issues		
Belief	Technological progress	Technological precaution
Type of risk	Recognized	Recognized
	Hypothetical	Hypothetical and Speculative
Substantial equivalence	Accepts substantial equivalence	Rejects substantial equivalence
Science or other in risk assessment	Safety	Safety
	Health	Health
		Quality
		'Other legitimate factors'
Burden of proof	Traditional: Innocent until proven guilty	Guilty until proven innocent
Risk tolerance	Minimum risk	Zero risk
Science or other in risk management	Safety or hazard-basis: Risk management is for risk reduction and prevention only.	Broader socio-economic concerns: Risk management is for social responsiveness.
Specific regulatory issues		
Precautionary principle	Scientific interpretation	Social interpretation
Participation	● Narrow, technical experts	● Wide, 'social dimensions'
	● Judicial decision-making	● Consensual decision-making
Mandatory labelling	Safety or hazard based	Consumers' right to know based

Source: Isaac (2002).

the precautionary principle is employed, whereby precaution is built into the assessments of hypothetical risks through risk-averse assumptions and likelihood functions. The scientific interpretation has a default position: if the risks are so poorly understood that an accepted risk causal–consequence mechanism cannot be built, then no hypothetical risk assessment – precautious or not – can be calculated. Hence, by default the decision would be to not go forward with the technology. Decision making is narrow in the sense that scientific experts review the risk assessment information and make the regulatory risk management decision in a judicious manner. Finally, mandatory labelling requires scientific evidence of risk or hazard to justify mandatory labels.

In contrast, the social rationality approach views science and technology not as 'drivers of economic development', but as one facet of society, where society is a normative construct composed of the preferences and concerns of all constituents. As science and technology disrupts the prevailing normative construct, this approach supports regulatory policies that ensure socially responsive technological precaution.[8] This focus on technological precaution essentially broadens the concept of legitimate justification beyond just scientific criteria.

Operationally, the social rationality approach (right-hand column in Table 36.1) permits greater scope for non-science information to be included in the determination of a legitimate justification. For example, risks are defined to include speculative risks which lack experience, data, a causal–consequence mechanism and an accepted analytical method for assessment; they are logical possibilities – irrefutable and untestable. Typically, such risks would have no standing within a science-based framework. Under the social rationality approach science only informs the decision and 'other legitimate factors' are also weighed. As a result the precautionary principle is not just a tool for scientists at the risk assessment stage, but is also a tool for the risk managers to use perhaps due to other legitimate factors. Finally, the socially rational approach supports consumers' right to know labelling measures.

Trade policy implications
With two distinct approaches to the RAF it is not hard to imagine that determining what constitutes a legitimate justification for an SPS-type market access barrier can lead to trade policy tensions. In fact, many of these SPS ambiguities are at the heart of official trade disputes. To illustrate this, consider a product approved for market access in one jurisdiction yet approval is delayed or denied in another jurisdiction.[9]

The two jurisdictions may not agree with the standards (or the standards-setting procedures) established by the international scientific organizations? This may be predicated on a view that the scientific studies were not sufficiently long-term or comprehensive enough, or that the statistical thresholds for risk were too high. Alternatively, there may be legitimate concerns about the openness of the organizations themselves (Isaac 2003b; Enders 1997). Indeed, there are many grounds on which a Member may not agree with the scientific principles underlying the SPS trade rules.

Another source of ambiguity in the SPS Agreement is associated with the 'like' products provision. It is obvious that some SPS-related risks may, in fact, be associated not with the end-use characteristics of a product but rather with the process and production methods (PPM) employed. Indeed, this is at the heart of the WTO trade disputes over both beef hormones and genetically modified crops (Isaac and Kerr 2003, 2004). In both cases the European Union has banned products from North America based on PPM technologies that Canada and the US argue have no impact on the end-use characteristics of the final product. The Agreement is relatively silent with respect to the legitimacy of PPM-based SPS market access barriers and greater clarification is required.

Differential market access rules can also result from the Agreement's Article 5(7) which permits Members to adopt temporary, precautionary bans to prevent the introduction of risks when sufficient scientific evidence is absent. The problem here does not lie with this provision; indeed, it is a necessary provision that empowers all Members to act to protect human, animal and plant safety and health in the event of a perceived crisis. The problem does lie, however, with removing the provision once it is triggered. The SPS Agreement is silent on the steps that need to be taken by a Member country that has lost international market access because trading partners have invoked this provision. For an example, consider the current case of Canada. With the discovery of a single case of BSE, Canada immediately lost access to 34 markets that – quite legitimately – established temporary, precautionary bans. Since that time, Canada believes that it has identified, isolated and eradicated the risk that any BSE-infected animals will enter the food supply. Further, animal health experts (with the OIE) have vetted the Canadian response. Yet, many important markets remain closed or are only partially open.[10] The ambiguity here arises because of an absence of a harmonized blueprint for the opening of markets after temporary, precautionary bans have been invoked. Greater clarification on how long is 'temporary' and on the quantity and type of scientific evidence that is sufficient is required in the SPS Agreement which is linked to the differences between the scientific and social rationality approaches to the RAF.

Another source of ambiguity arises from the fact that the SPS Agreement sets a regulatory floor but not a ceiling. According to the Agreement, Members are committed to both the international harmonization of SPS measures (subject to the three international scientific organizations) and to the mutual recognition of measures employed by other Members. With respect to mutual recognition, Members are committed, in principle, to granting equivalence to the SPS measures adopted by exporting countries 'if the exporting Member objectively demonstrates to the importing Member that its measures achieve the importing Member's appropriate level of sanitary or phytosanitary protection' (SPS Agreement, Article 4:1). To facilitate the process, the importing Member must be allowed to conduct a conformance assessment including inspection, testing, monitoring and evaluation of the measures in place in the exporting Member. The problem here is twofold. First, the Agreement is unclear about the timeframe that must be respected for the conformance assessment such that would-be importers are left unable to access a market because that market's officials have not yet assessed the importer's food safety system (Rege 2002; Zampetti 2000; Bhagwati and Hudec 1996). Second, the Agreement is silent on the limits that exist for countries to have their regulations substantially above other Members. Indeed, this issue is related to the discussion above, because many of the markets that continue to ban Canadian beef products – such as Japan – have domestic traceability and slaughtering regulations much more stringent that Canada's. Therefore, while there is a minimum level of sanitary and phytosanitary measures that must be met, is there a maximum defining the point where importing Member countries cannot legitimately expect potential exporting Members to achieve?

Finally, another source of ambiguity is associated with the role of socio-economic considerations in risk assessment. The SPS Agreement permits Members to establish SPS measures based on scientific risk as well as broader assessments of risk such as relevant economic factors that include:

- the potential damage in terms of loss of production or sales in the event of the entry, establishment or spread of the disease or pest;
- the costs of control or eradication in the territory of the importing Member; and
- the relative cost-effectiveness of alternative approaches to limiting risks. (SPS Agreement, Article 5:3)

Trade agreements traditionally avoid such socio-economic assessments because of the subjectivity complications that are associated with them. Indeed, it has been argued that the WTO attempts to de-politicize trade and make it a function of comparative advantage by insulating trade agreements from socio-economic assessments (World Trade Organization 1995). However, in the SPS Agreement it is recognized that imported risks to human, animal and plant safety and health are likely to have socio-economic impacts; and are perhaps quite significant. The inclusion of Article 5(3) raises significant ambiguity about how socio-economic assessments may be worked into the legitimate justifications based on sufficient scientific evidence. None of the international scientific organizations deferred to by the WTO provide much scope for socio-economic assessments, so it is unclear as to how and when they may be included in a legitimate fashion by a Member with, say, a socially rational approach to the RAF.

Looking ahead

This brief assessment of the SPS Agreement hints at two looming trade policy issues associated with the Agreement. First, given the significant power of the Agreement – it grants Members the right to take unilateral and unchallengeable trade actions against other Members if they have a legitimate justification to do so – mixed with the fact that there is significant ambiguity associated with what constitutes a legitimate justification suggests that SPS-type trade disputes will increase as Members try to mould the trade precedence to their RAF approach (Isaac 2004). Of course, trade disputes arising from sanitary and phytosanitary measures take the WTO into the unfriendly environment of having to assess the trade compliance of domestic safety and health regulations. If two Members have differential market access rules, then a WTO dispute resolution panel must essentially decide whose safety and health regulations are more appropriate from a trade point of view (Correa 2000). Given that domestic safety and health regulations are inextricably linked with domestic political economy factors, it is unlikely that an offending Member can simply change their regulations to meet the trade obligations. Therefore, a rise in SPS trade disputes presents a complex and controversial challenge for the WTO (Caldwell 1998; Nivola 1997).

Second, as SPS trade disputes polarize WTO Members a likely response will be the regionalization of SPS measures. Members with similar approaches to the RAF will find comfort in a regional arrangement that entrenches and protects their approach from the approach that comes to dominate the multilateral level (Pangariya 1999; Baldwin 1997; Sager 1997; WTO 1995). It has been argued that this regionalization has already occurred with respect to the transatlantic trade of genetically modified crops (Isaac 2003a; Isaac 2002). Dissatisfied with the multilateral market access rules for these products, the European Union and some of its Members States have put in place so-called SPS-Plus measures which incorporate many dimensions of the socially rational approach to regulating (Isaac 2002). The unfortunate effect of such a regionalization of SPS measures is that it becomes a stumbling block to multilateral trade disciplines rather and stepping stone (Isaac 2002a; Drache 1996).

Conclusion

The SPS Agreement was clearly an innovative inclusion in the WTO with its mandate to ensure the protection of human, animal and plant health while simultaneously establishing disciplines on the legitimate use of such measures. Yet, significant challenges remain in reconciling competing approaches to the Risk Analysis Framework and in removing the ambiguities associated with the operationalization of the Agreement. If these differences and ambiguities are allowed to turn from tensions to disputes, then WTO dispute settlement decisions are likely to polarize Members and promote the regionalization of the SPS measures at the expense of multilateral disciplines. If, however, proactive trade policy efforts are undertaken to deal with the tensions before they become disputes, then the SPS Agreement may just fulfil its ambitious but laudable mandate.

Notes

1. Agreement on the Application of Sanitary and Phyto-Sanitary Measures, Uruguay Round of Multilateral Trade Negotiations Legal Texts, pp. 69–84 (the 'SPS Agreement').
2. For further discussions of the Principle of Non-Discrimination and its provision see Fauchald (2003), Regan (2003), Ehring (2002), Hoekman (2002), Laird (2002), Marvoidis and Cottier (2000) and Horton (1997).
3. First presented in 1983 by the US National Academy of Sciences (1983), the RAF sought to inject science into the development of regulations for advanced technologies by decomposing regulatory development into three stages: risk assessment, risk management and risk communication. According to the RAF, the regulatory challenge is to maximize the benefits of technological progress while minimizing the risks through technological precaution.
4. Unsafe imports can jeopardize human safety and health either directly by making imported foodstuffs unsafe, or indirectly by infecting domestic food inputs including livestock and agricultural plants that are part of the domestic food chain. There is a crucial distinction to note. The SPS Agreement targets measures taken to protect the domestic food supply, not measures taken to target overall domestic biodiversity. In this sense, the SPS Agreement relates to food safety measures only, not environmental protection measures, although in practice this distinction is blurred.
5. The meaning of a legitimate justification will be discussed below.
6. The SPS Agreement is, of course, a complex agreement and the discussion in this chapter provides only a general introduction to how the agreement operates.
7. The normative and theoretical roots of scientific rationality – from a regulatory perspective – may be found in neoclassical economics. For a discussion on the role of technology in society according to neoclassical economics see Grossman and Helpman (1991). For a general discussion on the 'scientific rationality' of neoclassical economics see Blackhouse (1994).
8. The normative and theoretical roots of social rationality – again, from a regulatory perspective – may be found in *Risk Society Theories*; for a discussion see Beck (1992) and Giddens (1994).
9. Examples can include genetically modified organisms (Isaac and Kerr 2003; Isaac 2002; Perdikis *et al.* 2001; Buckingham and Phillips 2001; Zedalis 2001; Hagen and Weiner 2000; Runge and Jackson 2000; Kerr 1999) or hormone-treated beef (Kerr and Hobbs 2002; Spriggs and Isaac 2001; Sundberg and Vermulst 2001; Bureau *et al.* 1997a, 1997b).
10. In September 2003, the USDA announced the Canadian producers could export boneless meat from animals younger than 30 months to the US, however, trade in live cattle or boned meat cuts was not reinstated.

References

Baldwin, R. E. (1997), 'The Causes of Regionalism', *The World Economy*, **20**(7), 865–88.

Beck, U. (1992), *Risk Society: Towards a New Modernity*, London: Sage Press.

Bhagwati, J. N. and R. Hudec (1996), *Fair Trade and Harmonization*, Cambridge, MA: MIT Press.

Blackhouse, R. E. (1994), *Economists and the Economy: The Evolution of Economic Ideas* (2nd edn), New Brunswick, NJ: Transaction Publishers.

Buckingham, D. E. and P. W. B. Phillips (2001), 'Hot Potato, Hot Potato: Regulating Products of Biotechnology by the International Community', *Journal of World Trade*, **35**(1), 1–31.

Bureau, J. C., S. Marette and A. Schiavina (1997a), 'Trade, Labels and Consumer Information: The Case of Hormone-Treated Beef', Contributed Paper at the XXII Conference of the IAAE. IAAE, Sacramento.

Bureau, J. C., S. Marette and A. Schiavina (1997b), 'Non-Tariff Barriers and Consumers' Information: The Case of US–EC Trade Disputes on Food Products', *INRA Working Paper Series – August*, INRA, Versailles.

Caldwell, D. J. (1998), *The WTO Beef Hormone Ruling: An Analysis*, Washington, DC: Community Nutrition Institute.

Correa, C. M. (2000), 'Implementing National Public Health Policies in the Framework of the WTO Agreements', *Journal of World Trade*, **34**(5), 89–121.

Drache, D. (1996), 'Dreaming Trade or Trading Dreams: The Limits of Trade Blocs', in W. Bratton, J. McCahery, S. Picciotto and C. Scott (eds), *International Regulatory Competition and Coordination: Perspectives on Economic Regulation in Europe and the United States*, Oxford: Clarendon Press, pp. 417–43.

Ehring, L. (2002), 'De Facto Discrimination in World Trade Law National and Most-Favoured Nation Treatment or Equal Treatment?' *Journal of World Trade*, **36**(5), 921–77.

Enders, A. (1997), *Openness and the WTO*, Winnipeg: International Institute for Sustainable Development.

Fauchald, O. K. (2003), 'Flexibility and Predictability Under the World Trade Organization's Non-Discrimination Clauses', *Journal of World Trade*, **37**(3), 443–82.

Giddens, A. (1994), 'Living in a Post-Traditional Society', in U. Beck, A. Giddens and S. Lash (eds), *Reflexive Modernism*, Cambridge: Polity Press.

Grossman, G. M. and E. Helpman (1991), *Innovation and Growth in the Global Economy*, Cambridge, MA: MIT Press.

Hagen, P. and J. B. Weiner (2000),'The Cartagena Protocol on Biosafety: New Rules for International Trade in Living Modified Organisms', *Georgetown International Environmental Law Review*, **12**, 697–717.

Hoekman, B. (2002), 'The WTO: Functions and Basic Principles', in B. Hoekman, A. Mattoo and P. English (eds), *Development, Trade and the WTO: A Handbook*. Washington, DC: The World Bank, pp. 41–9.

Hooker, N. and J. Caswell (1999), 'A Framework for Evaluating Non-Tariff Barriers to Trade Related to Sanitary and Phytosanitary Regulations', *Journal of Agricultural Economics*, **50**(2), 234–46.

Horton, L. (1997), 'Internationalization of Food and Veterinary Medicine Regulation', in R. P. Brady, R. M. Cooper and R. S. Silverman (eds), *Fundamentals of Law and Regulation*, Washington, DC: FDLI, pp. 381–484.

Isaac, G. E. (2002), *Agricultural Biotechnology and Transatlantic Trade: An International Political Economy Analysis of Social Regulatory Barriers*, Cambridge, MA: CAB International Publishing Inc.

Isaac, G. E. (2003a), 'Regional Trade Agreements: Food Safety and Eco-labelling Regulations', in G. Sampson and S. B. Woolcock (eds), *Regionalism, Multilateralism, and Economic Integration: The Recent Experience*, Tokyo: United Nations University/Institute of Advanced Studies, pp. 227–52.

Isaac, G. E. (2003b), 'Increasing the Openness of Trade Policy: Challenges and Implications', *Journal of International Law and Trade Policy*, **4**(1), 58–74.

Isaac, G. E. (2004), 'The SPS Agreement and Agri-Food Trade Disputes: The Final Frontier', *Journal of International Law and Trade Policy*, **5**(1), 43–55.

Isaac, G. E. and W. A. Kerr (2003), 'Genetically Modified Organisms and Trade Rules: Identifying Important Challenges for the WTO', *The World Economy*, **26**(1), 43–59.

Isaac, G. E. and W. A. Kerr (2004), 'Bioprospecting or Biopiracy? – Intellectual Property and Traditional Knowledge in Biotechnology Innovation', *The Journal of World Intellectual Property*, **7**(1), 35–52.

Isaac, G. E., M. Phillipson and W. A. Kerr (2001), *International Regulation of Trade in Products of Biotechnology*, Research Project No. 2, Estey Centre for Law and Economics in International Trade, Saskatoon, Canada.

Kerr, W. A. (1999), 'International Trade in Transgenic Food Products: A New Focus for Agricultural Trade Disputes', *The World Economy*, **22**(2), 245–59.

Kerr, W. A. and J. E. Hobbs (2002), 'The North America–European Union Dispute Over Beef Produced Using Growth Hormones: A Major Test for the New International Trade Regime', *The World Economy*, **25**(2), 283–96.

Laird, S. (2002), 'Market Access Issues and the WTO: An Overview', in B. Hoekman, A. Mattoo and P. English (eds) *Development, Trade and the WTO: A Handbook*, Washington, DC: The World Bank, pp. 97–104.

Marceau, G. and J. P. Trachtman (2002), 'The Technical Barriers to Trade Agreement, the Sanitary and Phyto-Sanitary Measures Agreement and the General Agreement on Tariffs and Trade: A Map of the World Trade Organization Law of Domestic Regulation of Goods', *Journal of World Trade*, **36**(5), 811–81.

Marvoidis, P. and T. Cottier (2000), *Regulatory Barriers and the Principle of Non-Discrimination*, Ann Arbor, MI: University of Michigan Press.

National Academy of Sciences, Committee on the Institutional Means for Assessment of Risks to Public Health, Commission of Life Sciences (1983), *Risk Assessment in the Federal Government: Managing the Process*, Washington, DC: National Academy Press.

Nivola, P. (1997), *Social Regulations and the Global Economy*, Washington, DC: Brookings Institution Press.

Panagariya, A. (1999), 'The Regionalism Debate: An Overview', *The World Economy*, **22**(4), 455–76.

Perdikis, N., W. A. Kerr and J. E. Hobbs (2001), 'Reforming the WTO to Defuse Potential Trade Conflicts in Genetically Modified Goods', *The World Economy*, **24**(3), 379–98.

Regan, D. H. (2002), 'Regulatory Purpose and "Like Products" in Article III:4 of the GATT (With Additional Remarks on Article III:2)', *Journal of World Trade*, **36**(3), 443–78.

Regan, D. H. (2003), 'Further Thoughts on the Role of Regulatory Purpose Under Article III of the GATT', *Journal of World Trade*, **37**(4), 737–60.

Rege, V. (2002), 'Theory and Practice of Harmonization of Rules on Regional and Multilateral Bases: Its Relevance for the World Trade Organization Work on Trade Facilitation', *Journal of World Trade*, **36**(4), 699–720.

Roessler, F. (2003), 'Beyond the Ostensible: A Tribute to Professor Robert Hudec's Insights on the Determination of Likeness of Products Under the National Treatment Provisions of the General Agreement on Tariffs and Trade', *Journal of World Trade*, **37**(4), 771–81.

Runge, C. F. and L. A. Jackson (2000), 'Labeling, Trade and Genetically Modified Organisms', *Journal of World Trade*, **34**(1), 111–22.

Sager, M. A. (1997), 'Regional Trade Agreements: Their Role and the Economic Impact on Trade Flows', *The World Economy*, **20**(2), 239–52.

Spriggs, J. and G. E. Isaac (2001), *International Competitiveness and Food Safety: The Case of Beef*, Cambridge, MA: CAB International Publishing Inc.

Sundberg, D. and E. Vermulst (2001), 'The EC Trade Barriers Regulation – An Obstacle to Trade?' *Journal of World Trade*, **35**(5), 989–1013.

World Trade Organization (1995), *Regionalism and the World Trading System*, Geneva: WTO Secretariat.

Zampetti, A. B. (2000), 'Mutual Recognition in the Transatlantic Context: Some Reflections on Future Negotiations', in P. Marvoidis and T. Cottier (eds), *Regulatory Barriers and the Principle of Non-Discrimination*, Ann Arbor, MI: University of Michigan Press.

Zedalis, R. J. (2001), 'Labeling of Genetically Modified Foods: The Limits of GATT Rules', *Journal of World Trade*, **35**(2), 301–47.

37 Technical barriers to trade
Jill E. Hobbs

Introduction

Technical barriers to trade (TBT) have become an important non-tariff barrier to trade. Technical barriers to trade emerge when domestic policies imposing regulations, technical standards, testing and certification procedures, or labelling requirements impinge on the abilities of exporters to access a market. This chapter explains how technical barriers to trade arise, examining key economic issues related to why these barriers emerge, and their trade-restricting economic impacts. Institutional responses to TBT are discussed, including the role of the WTO Agreement on Technical Barriers to Trade and the role of international bodies, such as the Codex Alimentarius Commission, in building consensus on standards.

Although the terms are often used interchangeably, the WTO TBT Agreement distinguishes between a technical regulation and a standard on the basis of compliance. Regulations are mandatory requirements: imports failing to conform to a technical regulation may be prohibited from a market, whereas standards are voluntary. Imports failing to meet voluntary standards may be allowed into a market, but may garner little market share if consumers prefer products that meet local standards (WTO, 1998).

Technical regulations and standards, including labelling regulations, are an integral part of domestic policy initiatives to protect and inform consumers, employees and other firms. Technical barriers to trade can include requirements for labelling the presence of a product attribute, certification requirements, packaging requirements, technical specifications, and so on. These regulations become a barrier to trade if exporters are forced to meet different standards to access markets in different countries, and/or if they lack the technical capability to comply with a technical regulation.

The WTO deals with these barriers through its Technical Barriers to Trade (TBT) Agreement. The agreement recognizes countries' rights to adopt standards that are appropriate for domestic policy objectives that include the protection of consumer interests and the protection of the environment. Nevertheless, it attempts to prevent the use of nefarious technical barriers as a means to protect domestic industries against competition from imports. This is a difficult path to tread. Determining whether a trade-restricting measure is driven by a response to domestic protectionist interests, or for genuine consumer or environmental protection is often fraught with difficulty. Similarly, evaluating the potential economic outcomes of a new technical standard or labelling requirement in terms of social welfare impacts for consumers, domestic producers and exporters poses challenging measurement issues. To understand the trade policy implications of how technical barriers to trade emerge and how they are resolved, the underlying economic rationale for standards and technical regulations are first examined.

Asymmetric information and externalities: is there a market failure?

Labelling reduces information (search) costs for consumers. Some forms of labelling have direct consumer protection benefits, such as requirements for labelling the presence of food allergens, or health warnings on cigarettes. Other forms of labelling relate to the identification of process attributes that may be difficult for consumers to detect but are important to consumers for ethical reasons, such as the use of child labour, or harvesting techniques that threaten an endangered species.

The economic rationale behind policy-induced labelling and technical standards is to correct market failure due to information asymmetry and negative externalities. Labelling is often used to redress inequities in access to information. When information is asymmetrically distributed, markets deliver inefficient outcomes. If buyers are uncertain about the true quality of a good offered by a seller, the price they are willing to pay reflects this uncertainty. Unchecked, this quality uncertainty leads to lower average market prices, a reduced incentive for sellers of high quality goods to enter the market, and a dominance of 'lemons' on the market (Akerlof 1970).

The analysis of asymmetric information and product quality builds on the work of Nelson (1970) and Darby and Karni (1973), which distinguished between goods with search, experience and credence attributes. For search attributes, the information enabling consumers to make an informed purchase decision is plentiful. For example, the attribute can be evaluated prior to purchase by visual inspection, such as the colour of a shirt. Information asymmetry and the resulting market failure is not usually a problem for search attributes, and corrective policy actions are not usually necessary (Caswell and Mojduszka, 1996). The quality of an experience attribute can only be determined after purchase and consumption, such as the tenderness of a steak or the fuel-efficiency of a used car. Repeat purchase and reputation effects are relied upon to signal quality to consumers (see Stiglitz 1989; Klein and Leffler 1981; Shapiro 1983). Sellers are less likely to cheat if they expect to be in a repeat-purchase relationship with the buyer, or if buyers can enter the market sequentially and inform one another of product quality, for example through consumer reporting magazines and websites. Firms can signal their intention to supply high quality experience goods by investing in firm-specific sunk assets that are observable to consumers (Klein and Leffler 1981).

In the case of credence attributes, private sector reputation-based mechanisms for quality signalling are ineffective. The information asymmetry inherent in credence goods means that consumers cannot assess quality even after consumption, such as ethical attributes related to how a product was produced, for example child labour standards, animal welfare standards, the presence of absence of genetically modified organisms (GMOs) in food. Lemons-type market failures can be avoided by transforming credence attributes into search attributes through identification, certification and labelling. This can occur through private or public sector certification and labelling (Roe and Sheldon 2002). Accurate and credible labelling improves the efficiency of markets by allowing resources to be allocated to the production of goods and services according to consumer preferences.

Firms have an incentive to reveal high quality attributes through labelling but will not voluntarily disclose low quality. In fact, it is argued that firms have an incentive voluntarily to reveal all positive information relevant to consumer purchase decisions. Sceptical consumers will infer that if positive attributes are not identified in a label, they are not present, or are of low quality (see Grossman 1981). The 'unfolding theory' argues that the process of competitive disclosure results in explicit claims about all positive product attributes, enabling consumers to infer the (lower) quality of foods that do not have quality claims (Ippolito and Mathios 1990).

The private market may fail to reveal true quality through labelling (either directly or indirectly by default) if the value to consumers of the information (as reflected in their willingness-to-pay), is less than the costs to the firm of providing that information. The market may also fail to provide this information if the negative quality attribute is shared by an entire product category. Without the ability to remove the negative attribute, individual firms do not have an incentive to inform consumers of its presence (Golan and Kuchler 2000). The market can also fail to discipline firms who misrepresent their product by inaccurately labelling a credence attribute when it is difficult for consumers to verify the accuracy of the labelling. Cheating includes either mislabelling the presence of a positive attribute or failing to identify the presence of a negative attribute. In these cases, regulatory intervention to correct the market failure can include public certification, monitoring and enforcement.

While labelling can address problems of market failure stemming from asymmetric information, it is less effective as a tool to correct production externalities or achieve social objectives. The market may undervalue the externality, and there is an incentive for individual consumers to free-ride. For example, the introduction of genetically modified (GM) crops imposes externality costs on the non-GM sector. At the farm level this includes steps to reduce the risk of cross-contamination or co-mingling with GM crops. Segregation and identity preservation costs arise in the downstream supply chain in preserving the integrity of the non-GM attribute. A mandatory labelling requirement for GM foods, while perhaps addressing consumer information asymmetry, will not correct the production externalities from the introduction of GM technology (Golan and Kuchler 2002).

Regulators may also introduce labelling requirements in an effort to maximize net social benefits with respect to a specific social objective, such as child labour, animal welfare or protection of endangered species. As Golan and Kuchler (2002) point out, however, the problem is that the resulting change in consumption behaviour often under-reflects true social values. Different individuals place different values on these social objectives and a consumer can free-ride on the socially-responsible purchasing decisions of others. Instead, regulatory intervention in the form of a required standard or technical specifications can address the externality directly. For example, if the objective is to reduce vehicle-related pollution, domestic policymakers could introduce a regulation requiring all cars to have a catalytic converter, rather than relying on the identification of cars without catalytic converters as environmentally damaging and hoping that consumers take the environmental effect into consideration when making a vehicle purchase decision. Addressing the externality directly may be more effective.

In summary, standards and regulations, in particular labelling, perform a number of economic functions. They reduce search costs for consumers, facilitating the flow of market signals reflecting consumers' preferences to producers. Labels and standards also perform a consumer protection function, identifying potentially harmful ingredients or providing information that enables consumers to make healthier consumption choices (for example nutrition labelling). Labels reduce information asymmetry with respect to credence attributes, or identifying process attributes such as the labour standards used to produce a product, or the environmental, ecological or animal welfare impact of production practices. These labels enable consumers to express their ethical preferences through consumption decisions. Whether mandatory labelling of these attributes is effective in achieving social objectives with respect to labour standards, the environment, farm animal welfare, and so on is debatable. Credible labels, based on recognized standards, also facilitate market signals with respect to credence products whose quality is otherwise difficult to verify, such as organic products.

How do technical barriers inhibit trade?

Domestic regulations can become a barrier to trade in a number of ways (see Gaisford and Kerr 2001; Hobbs 2001). First, they can raise the cost of imported goods by directly increasing the cost of production for exporters. Changes in labelling or packaging requirements, or different requirements across different markets can necessitate expensive package redesign, or require separate production runs using different packaging or labelling materials for different markets, making it more difficult for exporters to achieve economies of scale. Meeting multiple standards in multiple export markets may be prohibitively costly, or it may not be technically feasible for an exporter to meet two sets of technical standards; for example, different requirements for the handling and storage of raw food products in food processing plants. If these requirements are mutually exclusive (such as requiring physically different processing/storage facilities), exporters are forced to choose between potential export markets.

Mandatory labelling requirements may also impose verification costs on exporters. Verifying label claims often entails supply chain segregation and monitoring costs in the form of identity preservation, record-keeping, auditing suppliers, and so on. In addition to verifying the presence of a positive quality attribute, verification costs can arise in proving that a product does not have to be labelled. For example, where mandatory labelling of GM content is in place, exporters of non-GM food may have to prove that their product is not derived from GM ingredients.

Labelling regulations restrict the use of specific product names. The European Union has specific regulations related to Protected Geographical Indication (PGI) and Protected Designation of Origin (PDO) products where there may be a link between the characteristics of the product and the region in which it is produced (Zago and Pick 2002). Geographical indicators are a special class of trade rules that allow countries to restrict the use of geographic nomenclatures to goods produced in that region using 'traditional' production methods. This is most commonly applied to food products, such as local breads, beers, cheeses, meats, olive oil and so on. Only products from the designated region, verified as adhering to specified production practices, are allowed to use the PGI. Countries could close their borders to an imported good that flouts a domestic PGI.

The potential conflict between genuine domestic policy goals related to informing consumers, versus the protection of domestic firms, is apparent in PGIs and PDOs. Geographical indications inform consumers about a credence characteristic and therefore provide information to assist the efficient functioning of a market for that characteristic. PGIs and PDOs can also be subverted to introduce backdoor protection to domestic firms who have an incentive to lobby for the extension of PGIs/PDOs to their class of products. Given the intellectual property component of PGIs and PDOs, these labelling restrictions are dealt with under a separate agreement on Trade Related Aspects of Intellectual Property (TRIPS), rather than under the WTO TBT agreement.

Labels can also harm imports by implying quality differences where none exist. This could be the case for mandatory country-of-origin labels if consumers perceive all imports to be inferior. Evidence from experimental markets for food products suggests that consumers sometimes view imported products as inferior (for example Hoffman 2000; Schupp and Gillespie 2001), although the reverse could also be true where a country has established a reputation for high quality, for example Italian shoes, French wines and so on. Falvey (1989) models reputation effects in an international trade context, showing that knowledge of country of origin may indeed play a valuable non-protective role in providing information to consumers. If imports truly are of a lower safety standard, however, countries could restrict these imports directly for consumer protection purposes. Relying on country of origin labels to protect consumers is only effective if consumers have accurate information, or a clear reputation signal, regarding the comparative safety/quality levels of products from different countries. Falvey (1989) shows that minimum quality standards can also be welfare-enhancing if they reduce reputation establishment costs for exporters.

Clearly, some consumers prefer to purchase domestic products for ethical reasons, such as supporting domestic industries, or if they remain uncertain about the quality of imported products. It is argued that if there is a strong consumer demand for country of origin information, there will be a market-driven incentive (price premium) for domestic firms to label their products as produced domestically (Golan *et al.* 2000). Following Grossman (1981), we can assume consumers will therefore infer that products without a voluntary origin label are imported. In the absence of cheating through mislabelling, this weakens the economic justification for mandatory country of origin labelling.

Trade barriers based on complex technical standards or labelling requirements pose particular challenges for developing countries who often lack the resources, scientific infrastructure or expertise to meet these standards. If verification, scientific testing or inspection by a government agent or independent third party is required for access to an export market, developing countries are often at a disadvantage.

The WTO TBT Agreement
Standards and labels can emerge voluntarily in the private sector as a tool of product differentiation in a competitive environment. It should also be clear, however, that market failure resulting from information asymmetry generates mandatory regulations, standards and labelling requirements as genuine domestic policy responses to market inefficiencies. Two problems arise in the international trade policy arena. First, mandatory labels and technical regulations with genuine domestic policy objectives related to consumer protection or market inefficiencies may inadvertently restrict imports. Second, regulatory intervention in the guise of consumer protection may in reality be protecting domestic industries from import competition. Distinguishing between measures with genuine consumer protection objectives from those designed to protect domestic industries poses a challenge that can lead to trade tensions.

At the close of the Uruguay Round of GATT negotiations, new trade rules governing technical barriers to trade emerged in the form of the WTO Technical Barriers to Trade (TBT) Agreement. The TBT Agreement tries to ensure that standards, regulations, testing and certification procedures do not become unnecessary barriers to international trade (WTO 1998). The agreement recognizes countries' rights to adopt standards that are appropriate to achieve domestic policy objectives related to consumer protection, environmental protection, and the protection of animal, plant or human life.

The TBT Agreement applies the core GATT non-discrimination principles of most-favoured nation status and national treatment to domestic technical regulations that affect imported goods. In other words, technical regulations cannot discriminate against imported goods in favour of 'like' domestic products, and cannot discriminate in favour of one country's exports over the exports of like products from another country. Critical to the application of these rules is the definition of a like product, which the 1994 GATT Agreement defined as a directly competitive or substitutable product. The basis for determining what constitutes like products has evolved over time through GATT/WTO case law. The general criteria, established by a 1970 GATT working party, specify that 'like' products should have similar physical characteristics, be substitutes in their end-use function, be treated as similar for the purposes of tariff classification and be used as substitutes by consumers, as determined by the magnitude of their cross-elasticity of demand (Read 2004).

The definition of like products is inherently product-based. For tangible product attributes, such as technical specifications in motor vehicles, or the thread-count in textiles, determining a like product should be fairly straightforward. This is not the case for labels or standards based on intangible process attributes related to the means by which the product was produced or procured, for example, products of agricultural biotechnology, so-called 'dolphin-safe' tuna, or goods produced using specific labour standards. While these goods could be close substitutes in a physical sense, they may not be viewed as close substitutes by discerning consumers. Consumers with strong preferences regarding agricultural biotechnology may not be willing to substitute between non-GM and GM soybean products. Consumers with strong preferences regarding the use of child labour may not be willing to substitute between textiles certified as produced without the use of child labour, and (physically) similar textiles produced in a country where the use of child labour is common.

For ethical or perceived safety reasons, there may be genuine consumer preferences for specific process attributes. However, the WTO cornerstone principle of non-discrimination implies that countries cannot apply national standards to processes used in the production of imported products (unless it violates intellectual property rights). Often referred to as Process and Production methods (PPMs), this issue is a particularly challenging area for trade policy. In developed countries, success in dealing with other trade irritants has served to focus consumer interest on PPMs. The means by which products are produced is increasingly important to consumers (Read 2004). This has led to calls to regulate PPMs through environmental and social regulations. Extending the WTO rules to cover PPMs would be controversial. Regulation related to PPMs is particularly vulnerable to potential fraud associated with documentation, monitoring and traceability. The potential for increased regulatory complexity as a source of trade disputes is also a concern (see Read 2004).

The root cause of these new trade irritants lies in a fundamental shift in the demand for protection. The simple neoclassical trade model underlying the WTO predicts that consumers benefit from trade liberalization. Most economists accept the basic premise that freer markets, with fewer trade barriers and more competition, *ceteris paribus*, should lead to lower equilibrium prices and a gain in consumer welfare. While there may be a transfer of economic surplus from domestic producers to domestic consumers and to exporters, the standard neoclassical model predicts a net gain from trade liberalization. Under these circumstances, consumers would never ask for protection from imports.

While consumers undoubtedly benefit from lower prices, the simple neoclassical model also assumes perfect information and homogeneous goods. In reality, information asymmetry exists, goods are heterogeneous and consumers are diverse in their preferences for different qualities. The straightforward prediction of an unambiguous gain in consumer surplus from trade liberalization no longer holds in the presence of information asymmetry. *Ceteris paribus* no longer reigns. The introduction of imports with an unknown quality dimension can result in a loss in consumer surplus for consumers with strong preferences if the adverse quality effect outweighs the beneficial price effect. The market for lemons problem emerges. As a result, consumers may demand protection from imports.

The WTO, and its predecessor the GATT, were predicated on the notion of domestic producers as the chief proponents of protection. The new reality is that either domestic producers or consumers could be the drivers of domestic policies to restrict imports. Disentangling genuine consumer concerns, rooted in information asymmetry with respect to credence attributes, from capricious use of regulations to restrict imports for the benefit of domestic producers is fraught with difficulty.

Recognizing the costs that different standards and regulations can impose on exporters, the TBT Agreement encourages the adoption of international standards. Examples of independent standards bodies include the ISO (the International Organization for Standardization), the International Telecommunication Union (ITU), the International Electrotechnical Commission (IEC) and the Codex Alimentarius Commission, which establishes international consensus on food standards. Codex, for example, does not have enforcement powers, instead it focuses on achieving common agreement on food standards and labelling issues. This has become particularly important as the purpose of labelling has broadened beyond simply consumer protection with a safety emphasis, to include provision of information to consumers.

Ideally, harmonization to an internationally-agreed standard reduces search costs for consumers, encourages competition without stifling innovation, and increases consumer welfare. Lack of technical compatibility generates barriers to trade. Television sets suitable for the European market are not saleable in North America due to differences in colour broadcasting formats; cars manufactured for the UK or Japanese markets need to be right-hand drive, whereas those destined for most other European markets and North America must be left-hand drive vehicles (WTO 1998). Developing international consensus on common standards through international institutions reduces barriers to trade.

While harmonization to one standard would reduce costs for exporters, the process of harmonization may not be feasible or may impose costs that are too high. Consider the implications of the UK or Japan converting to driving on the right-hand side of the road. When harmonization of technical standards is not feasible, or is not economically viable, or where consumers have strong preferences for their domestic standards precluding harmonization, granting equivalence is an alternative solution. Countries accept that technical regulations different from their own fulfil the same policy objectives, and are therefore deemed equivalent (WTO 1998). For example, two countries may have the same policy objective of protecting the environment through the reduction of vehicle emissions. However, one country chooses to achieve this objective through requiring all vehicles to be equipped with a catalytic converter. Another country achieves the same objective by requiring the use of diesel engines in motor vehicles. If the two countries agree that their technical regulations are equivalent in intent and effect, if not in implementation, then the export of cars from one country to another can occur without manufacturers in each country having to modify their vehicles to satisfy the regulatory requirement of the trading partner (WTO 1998).

Equivalency agreements reduce costs for firms. Nevertheless, an equivalency agreement notwithstanding, some consumers may still believe that domestically-produced products are superior – a perception that domestic industries are likely to encourage. This depends to some extent on the credibility of foreign certification and standards agencies. In the case of organic food standards, Lohr and Krissoff (2002) show that harmonization of accreditation standards or equivalency agreements alone are not sufficient to guarantee welfare maximization from international trade in organics. If consumers do not accept the equivalency of imported and domestically produced (organic) goods, welfare gains will be sub-optimal. Sawyer (2004) found that consumers in the US, the UK and Canada declared a strong preference for their domestic standard for organic food over the standards of the other two countries. However, despite this declared preference, in a subsequent choice experiment, most consumers were unable to identify their domestic standard and (unknowingly) exhibited a preference for the features of the organic standard from one of the other countries. The credibility of certifying agencies and standards bodies in exporting countries are important in determining the social welfare gains from equivalency agreements.

Unlike trade measures related to animal, plant and human health that are dealt with under the Agreement on Sanitary and Phyto-Sanitary (SBS) Barriers, for the TBT it is not possible to defer to a scientific justification for a technical regulation or to insist on a scientifically-based risk assessment. In the absence of harmonization to an international standard or negotiation of equivalency agreements, the TBT Agreement attempts to prevent the capricious use of technical requirements to restrict trade through 'regulatory proportionality'. The costs of complying with import requirements, such as packaging and labelling regulations, must be proportional to the purpose of the standard. Thus, the costs of complying with the regulation should not exceed the benefits that consumers derive from the additional labelling information or packaging requirements. The import requirements should be no more trade-restrictive than is necessary. In the absence of market data, measuring the potential benefit of labelling or technical requirements that are not yet (or only recently) in place requires that economists rely on other methodologies for measuring consumer willingness-to-pay, such as stated preference methodologies or experimental auctions.

Conclusions

Technical barriers to trade arise due to differences in technical standards and regulatory requirements between countries. Mandatory labelling, packaging requirements, technical specifications and certification and testing requirements are all examples of potential technical barriers to trade. Governments may introduce standards and regulatory requirements to achieve genuine domestic policy goals related to consumer protection and information provision. Labelling is often a response to asymmetric information regarding the presence, absence or quality of a credence attribute, and serves to correct a market failure. Technical regulations and standards may also be a direct policy response to an externality.

Labelling and technical regulations can increase costs for exporters and inhibit trade. While the WTO TBT Agreement recognizes the right of a member country to introduce regulations and standards that protect consumers, these measures should be non-discriminatory, transparent and adhere to the regulatory proportionality principle. A number of trade disputes over technical regulations, standards and labelling have arisen in recent years, including disputes related to labelling dolphin-safe tuna, the effect of shrimp fishing practices on endangered sea turtles, differences in gasoline emission regulations, disagreements over the definition of a sardine, and so on (see for example, Read 2004; Goldberg and Hogan 2002). All of these disputes have been resolved through recourse to the TBT Agreement.

Science and technology are continually evolving, delivering innovations with the promise of new or enhanced products, more efficient production techniques or more accurate monitoring of the environmental or human health impacts of production processes. Innovation will create ongoing regulatory questions regarding whether new technical standards or labelling policies are justified, or existing regulations are obsolete. Innovation breeds new market opportunities; it also breeds winners and losers among adopters and non-adopters of the technology, and inevitable protectionist pressure from the non-adopters. Trade policy will also need to evolve continually to address trade-distorting labelling polices, technical standards and regulatory requirements in the face of new innovations.

References

Akerlof, G. A. (1970), 'The Market for "Lemons": Qualitative Uncertainty and the Market Mechanism', *Quarterly Journal of Economics*, **84**, 488–500.

Caswell, J. and Mojduszka, E. M. (1996), 'Using Information Labeling to Influence the Market for Quality in Food Products', *American Journal of Agricultural Economics*, **78**(5), 1248–53.

Darby, M. R. and Karni, E. (1973), 'Free Competition and the Optimal Allocation of Fraud', *Journal of Law and Economics*, **16**(1), 67–88.

Falvey, R. E. (1989), 'Trade, Quality Reputations and Commercial Policy', *International Economic Review*, **30**(3), 607–22.

Gaisford, J. D. and Kerr, W. A. (2001), *Economic Analysis for International Trade Negotiations: The WTO and Agricultural Trade*, Cheltenham, UK and Northampton, MA, USA: Edward Elgar.

Golan, E. and Kuchler, F. (2002), 'Labelling Biotech Foods: Implications for Consumer Welfare and Trade', in B. Krissoff, M. Bohman and J. A. Caswell (eds), *Global Food Trade and Consumer Demand for Quality*, New York: Kluwer Academic/Plenum Publishers, pp. 197–208.

Golan, E., Kuchler, K. and Mitchell, L. (2000), *Economics of Food Labelling*, Agricultural Economic Report No. 793, Economic Research Service, US Department of Agriculture, Washington, DC, http://www.ers.usda.gov/publications/aer793/.

Goldberg, R. A. and Hogan, H. F. (2002), 'Codex Alimentarius and Food Labeling', *Harvard Business School Case*, 9-903-417, Boston, MA: Harvard Business School Publishing.

Grossman, S. J. (1981), 'The Informational Role of Warranties and Private Disclosure About Product Quality', *Journal of Law and Economics*, **24**(3), 461–83.

Hobbs, J. E. (2001), 'Labeling and Consumer Issues in International Trade', in H. J. Michelman, J. Rude, J. Stabler and G. Storey (eds) *Globalization and Agricultural Trade Policy*, Boulder, CO: Lynne Rienner Publishers Inc., pp. 269–85.

Hoffman, R. (2000), 'Country of Origin – A Consumer Perception Perspective of Fresh Meat', *British Food Journal*, **102**(3), 211–29.

Ippolito, P. M. and Mathios, A. D. (1990), 'The Regulation of Science-based Claims in Advertising', *Journal of Consumer Policy*, **13**(4), 413–45.

Klein, B. and Leffler, K. B. (1981), 'The Role of Market Forces in Assuring Contractual Performance', *Journal of Political Economy*, **89**, 615–41.

Lohr, L. and Krissoff, B. (2002), 'Consumer Effects of Harmonizing International Standards for Trade in Organic Foods', in B. Krissoff, M. Bohman and J. A. Caswell (eds), *Global Food Trade and Consumer Demand for Quality*, New York: Kluwer Academic/Plenum Publishers, pp. 209–28.

Nelson, P. (1970), 'Information and Consumer Research', *Journal of Political Economy*, **78**(2), 311–29.

Read, R. (2004), 'Like Products, Health & Environmental Exceptions: The Interpretation of PPMs in Recent WTO Trade Dispute Cases', *The Estey Centre Journal of International Law and Trade Policy*, **5**(2), 123–46, http://www.estejournal.com.

Roe, B. and Sheldon, I. (2002), 'The Impacts of Labeling on Trade in Goods That May be Vertically Differentiated According to Quality', in B. Krissoff, M. Bohman and J. A. Caswell (eds), *Global Food Trade and Consumer Demand for Quality*, New York: Kluwer Academic/Plenum Publishers, pp. 181–95.

Sawyer, E. N. (2004), 'Economic Impacts of Harmonizing Organic Standards Internationally', unpublished M.Sc. thesis, Department of Agricultural Economics, University of Saskatchewan.

Schupp, A. and Gillespie, J. (2001), 'Consumer Attitudes Towards Potential Country-of-Origin Labeling of Fresh or Frozen Beef', *Journal of Food Distribution Research*, **32**(3), 34–44.

Shapiro, C. (1983), 'Premiums for High Quality Products as Returns to Reputations', *Quarterly Journal of Economics*, **98**, 659–79.

Stiglitz, J. E. (1989), 'Imperfect Information in the Product Market', in R. Schmalensee and R. Willig (eds), *The Handbook of Industrial Organization*, Amsterdam: North Holland, pp. 769–847.

World Trade Organisation (WTO) (1998), *The World Trade Organization: A Training Package*, (Module 3, Goods: Rules on NTMs), The World Trade Organization, http://www.wto.org/english/thewto_e/ whatis_e/ eol/e/wto03/wto3.pdf (Accessed 30 November 2004).

Zago, M. and Pick, D. (2002), 'The Public Provision of Information: A Welfare Analysis of European Products with Geographical Indications and Products with Designations of Origin', in B. Krissoff, M. Bohman and J. A. Caswell (eds), *Global Food Trade and Consumer Demand for Quality*, New York: Kluwer Academic/Plenum Publishers, pp. 229–43.

38 Ethical issues in trade
Grant E. Isaac

Introduction

Consumption decisions are a function of a product's price and non-price attributes. The former refer to the product's price relative to other 'like' products as well as the price of complementary products. The latter refer to the product attributes such as the process and production methods (PPM) employed relative to competing 'like' products and complementary products. They can include both safety-related attributes[1] and non-safety-related attributes, often called technical attributes.[2]

Technical attributes broadly include various product requirements and specifications (which may include process and production methods), testing protocols, certification standards, and packaging and grading (which includes labelling issues such as country of origin, symbols, markings and terminology). It also includes conformity assessments – important for mutual recognition efforts – which are any procedures used, either directly or indirectly, to determine that relevant requirements in technical regulations (mandatory requirements) and standards (voluntary requirements) are fulfilled by foreign suppliers to the domestic market. Such requirements can include: sampling; testing and inspection; evaluation, verification and assurance; registration, accreditation and approval.

A distinct subset of technical attributes – which may called ethical attributes – focus on how products were processed or produced with respect to particular values. For instance, consumers may wish to know the environmental impact of the product across its entire life cycle to ensure congruence with an environmental ethic. Or they may wish to know if certain labour standards or, perhaps, animal welfare standards were achieved during the good's production. Or they may wish to know if particular technologies are embodied in the product such as the biotechnological techniques of genetic modification.

While ethical attributes are certainly crucial in a consumption decision, they do not enjoy an equal standing with price attributes from a trade policy point of view. Recall, the economic rationale for trade liberalization is rooted in an assumption that consumers are the ultimate and unambiguous beneficiaries of comparative advantage-based trade allowing them access to the highest quality goods produced in the most cost-efficient manner. Accordingly, it is assumed that the only consumer concern is with the end-price of a product relative to other 'like' products which are grouped according to the end-use characteristics and not according to the embodied PPM. The objective of this chapter is to assess the trade policy issues associated with technical, ethical attributes such as labour, animal welfare or environmental standards.

Ethical attributes and international trade

In order to understand how technical, ethical measures are dealt with under international trade rules it is important to understand the principle of non-discrimination (PND) (Fauchald 2003; Hart and Dymond 2003; Roesseler 2003; Isaac 2002; Regan 2002; Marvoidis and Cottier 2000; Zampetti 2000; Howse and Trebilcock 1999; Howse 1998).

Embodied in the PND are two explicit provisions – the national treatment provision and the most-favoured nation provision – and one implicit provision for 'like' products. The national treatment (NT) provision (GATT Article I) stipulates that foreign products must be subject to the same commercial market access rules as 'like' products produced in the domestic market (Roessler 2003; Isaac 2002). The most favoured nation (MFN) provision (GATT Article III) stipulates that all foreign 'like' products be granted the same market access treatment as those foreign 'like' products from the country granted market access on the most favourable terms (Fauchald 2003; Ehring 2002; Isaac 2002).[3] In both the NT and the MFN discussions is the term 'like' products. Therefore, while not an explicit obligation 'like' products have become a *de facto* third provision under the PND. According to this provision, goods are grouped with respect to their end-use and not with respect to the process and production methods (PPM) used in their manufacture (Roessler 2003; Isaac 2002; Laird 2002; Regan 2002; Marvoidis and Cottier 2000). The rationale is that as goods – and not their process and production techniques – are traded, the rules for international trade should deal only with goods leaving the decisions regarding relevant PPM to the comparative-advantage conditions prevailing within each jurisdiction. Such a focus prevents (or at least limits) protectionist trade barriers from being put in place to protect, for example, capital-intensive textile manufactures in developed countries from imports produced in developing countries based on labour-intensive technologies. Essentially, the objective of this concept is to remove the level of economic development from the market access consideration.

The PND – with its three provisions of 'like' products, NT and MFN – may be thought of as a default principle for legitimate market access rules. That is, unless otherwise exempted in a particular trade agreement all domestic policies should apply equally to all 'like' goods of domestic or foreign origin.

Applying the PND as a baseline principle for international trade policy has been challenged as new types of domestic policies such as technical, ethical measures have begun to emerge on the trade agenda in the form of non-tariff barriers (NTB) (Isaac and Kerr 2003; Regan 2003; Hufbauer *et al.* 2002; Isaac 2002; Marceau and Trachtman 2002; Wilson 2002; Phillips and Isaac 2001; Hooker and Caswell 1999; Roberts *et al.* 1999; Daly and Kuwahara 1998; Bureau *et al.* 1997a, 1997b; Mahe 1996; Majone 1990). Technical measures are intertwined with domestic concerns and as such are not as amenable to a rigid interpretation of the PND (Gamberale and Mattoo 2002). For instance, consider the separation between the end-use of a product and its PPM. Indeed, it is obvious from the discussion above that technical, ethical issues such as labour, animal welfare and environmental standards are often associated entirely with the PPM of a product. Yet, such domestic measures may favour domestic producers who have adopted the acceptable PPM while disadvantaging foreign producers who have not violated the NT provision. Similarly, such measures may favour only a few – but not all – foreign producers violating the MFN provision.

Simply imposing an orthodox view of the PND upon ethical measures is risky for the international trading system because such measures are often driven not by the traditional producer interests calling for protectionism but instead by consumer, environmental or social development organizations. Such organizations have not traditionally had a voice in the trade policy advisory system – remember consumers were perceived as unambiguous winners from trade liberalization (Isaac 2002; Perdikis *et al.* 2001). For these groups, trade liberalization rules that discipline, for example, domestic environmental protection regulations are viewed as invasive and corrosive to domestic regulatory autonomy (Isaac 2003a, 2003b; Hobbs *et al.* 2002; Jha 2002; Waincymer 2001; Correa 2000; Hagen and Weiner 2000; Phillips and Kerr 2000; World Trade Organization 1999; Caldwell 1998; Enders 1997; Ferrantino 1997; Horton 1997; Schoenbaum 1997; Cheyne 1995; Spracker and Lundsgaard 1993; Sinclair 1973). According to this perspective trade protectionism – not trade liberalization – is a valid and socially acceptable goal (Jha 2002; Howse 1998).

Therefore, in dealing with the emergence of technical, ethical measures the international trading system has faced a delicate balance between upholding its mandate of market access liberalization based on the PND on the one hand and remaining sensitive to the differences in market conditions among Member States on the other. To achieve this balance, the response has been one of accommodation; to identify legitimate violations to the PND that cannot be captured by traditional producer protectionist interests. The relevant WTO Agreement is the Agreement on Technical Barriers to Trade (TBT Agreement).[4] In the sub-sections that follow, the TBT Agreement is first assessed followed by an assessment of the manner in which PPM are dealt with under the agreement.

The TBT Agreement
As discussed previously, the Agreement on Technical Barriers to Trade (TBT Agreement) deals with technical product quality issues such as technical product requirements and specifications, testing protocols, certification standards, and packaging and grading. It also includes conformity assessments – important for mutual recognition efforts – which are any procedures used, either directly or indirectly, to determine that relevant requirements in technical regulations (mandatory requirements) and standards (voluntary requirements) are fulfilled by foreign suppliers to the domestic market. Such requirements can include: sampling; testing and inspection; evaluation, verification and assurance; registration, accreditation and approval – a broad set of issues.

Concern about the potential impact of technical measures upon international trade has been voiced at the multilateral level since the mid-1970s. The primary concern was that technical measures might be used either to restrict market access or to confer an advantage to domestic products in the domestic marketplace in a discretionary manner with no real discipline on their application.

The Tokyo Round of the GATT introduced international trade disciplines on technical measures through the Technical Barriers to Trade Code. The essence of the TBT Code was to establish international obligations on technical regulations, standards and conformance assessments for both transparency and notification based on the PND (Organization for Economic Cooperation and Development 1994). Yet, exporters had concerns with its scope. They wanted to see the TBT Code – which only applied to a limited number of developed contracting parties – strengthened and extended to cover all contracting parties. As a result, negotiations in the Uruguay Round produced the TBT Agreement.

The TBT Agreement[5] deals with both mandatory (technical requirements) and voluntary (standards) measures. Voluntary standards are subject to the *TBT Code of Good Practice for the Preparation, Adoption and Application of Standards* which urges Members to take their best endeavours to ensure that voluntary trade-restricting measures are subject to the same principles and rules as mandatory standards (TBT Agreement, Article 4 and Annex 3). The Code urges Members to use international standards as a basis for national voluntary standards and to participate fully in the preparation of international standards.

According to the TBT Agreement Members are allowed to establish trade-restricting measures in order to protect human, animal and environmental health and safety and to ensure the quality of imported products – the so-called 'legitimate objectives' – provided that the measures do not unnecessarily obstruct international trade (TBT Agreement, Article 2:2). Legitimacy is defined according to the two provisions listed below.

First, Members are required to base their national standards on international measures established by international standards-setting bodies (TBT Agreement, Article 2:4). When internationally agreed standards cannot be adopted due to geographical, climatic or technological reasons, the Member must publish the draft measures in order to allow potentially affected foreign producers an opportunity to respond to them (TBT Agreement, Article 2:9). It is anticipated that concerns of exporters will then be incorporated into any subsequent measures.

Second, the TBT Agreement requires that, where applicable, national measures should be scientifically justifiable (TBT Agreement, Article 2:2). The Agreement includes specified criteria that Members must account for in formulating technical measures in order to ensure that measures do not create unnecessary regulatory barriers to trade. Although the TBT Agreement requires that measures should be scientifically justifiable, the problems with determining appropriate scientific risk assessment procedures for non-safety issues and other legitimate objectives, such as labelling, are enormous. As a result, the scientific justification principle under the TBT Agreement is considerably weaker than under the SPS Agreement potentially permitting technical barriers. For instance, under the TBT Agreement labelling standards can prevent deceptive marketing practices that adversely impact informed consumerism, but since scientifically justifying adverse impacts on informed consumerism is difficult, such measures do not really require a science basis for justification.

Technical measures for ethical concerns including labour, animal welfare and environmental standards raise important trade issues due to their inherent focus on process and production methods (PPM). This is discussed next.

The TBT Agreement and PPM
A particularly controversial issue under the auspices of the TBT Agreement is associated with the 'like' products provision of the PND and its focus upon the end-use characteristics of products not upon the manner in which the product was processed or produced. As consumers increasingly demand to know the PPM of a product, domestic regulations have evolved to meet this demand.

The relationship between technical PPM and international trade was investigated in both the Tokyo and the Uruguay Rounds of multilateral trade negotiations. In the Tokyo Round, Contracting Parties differed as to how they thought PPM should be dealt with. On one hand, some Contracting Parties sought to have PPM included in the TBT Code to prevent circumvention of the GATT trade principles by technical regulations. The aim was not to prevent the use of PPM in product standards such as labelling requirements, but to have some discipline on their use.

Other Contracting Parties, such as developing countries, did not want to have PPM included in the Code at all so that any PPM used to ban trade would be in violation of the TBT Code. That is, they did not want any linking of trade and the technical measures because that would – in essence – link trade patterns to the level of economic development in spite of the fact that the level of economic development may be the primary source of comparative advantage for the developing country (for example, abundant and cheap labour). Many developing countries argued – with some justification – that the industrialized countries developed without technical controls such as environmental measures and labour standards yet now that they have all the benefits conferred by industrialization, especially higher incomes, they can afford to demand more income elastic protection through PPM-based trade measures. The claim is that this makes the industrialization process harder for the developing countries because such measures may favour particular PPM or technologies that are not employed and/or not available to developing country producers. Also, products crucial to developing countries (that is paper products/timber) are disproportionately covered by PPM measures. In other words, if PPM favour new technologies, then the capacity gap means that the less technologically advanced will continue to lag behind.

In order to deal with the differing views on the legitimate use of PPM in the trading system, an important compromise was struck during the Tokyo Round (Table 38.1). First, PPM were divided into two types; product-related PPM (prPPM) and non-product-related PPM (nprPPM) (Organization for Economic Cooperation and Development 1994). This was done in order to reclaim some of the traditional divisions between products and processes under the GATT's concept of 'like' products. According to this distinction prPPM were subject to the disciplines of the TBT Code and its dispute settlement provisions (TBT Code, Article 14:25).

In the Uruguay Round, some Member States again tried to have both prPPM and nprPPM disciplined; this time under the binding TBT Agreement. Yet, at the end of the round, the only change was that prPPM would be covered by the TBT Agreement, not nprPPM. This means that the rights and obligations of the TBT Agreement only apply to those PPM measures that have an effect on the attributes of the final product. Or, equivalently, it applies only to PPM measures that change the end-use characteristics of the product sufficiently for it to be no longer considered a 'like' product. Accordingly, coverage includes 'product characteristics or their related processes and production methods' but only as they avoid 'consumption externalities' (TBT Agreement, Annex 1). Therefore, only consumption externalities associated with prPPM are within the scope of the TBT Agreement.

Yet, there are limits to the permissible use of prPPM-based measures that Members may enact. Under the TBT Agreement the legitimate deviations can include scientifically justified product quality impacts as well as less precise different social objectives and priorities attached to various technical measures (Organization for Economic Cooperation and Development, 1994). Consider, for example, food trade where prPPM can include, for instance, the type of veterinary practices and quality assurance systems that may be employed in a beef production system because such PPM may affect both the safety and quality of the final beef products. That is, prPPM are associated with the consumption or use stage of the product causing consumption externalities.

On the other hand, nprPPM which have no demonstrable consumption externalities are out of scope of the TBT Agreement, and are the sovereign domain of the Member government. From a trade perspective, such measures must explicitly follow the PND even if

Table 38.1   Technical PPM-based measures

Process and Production Methods (PPMs) Non-safety related	
prPPM In-Scope of the TBT Agreement Compliance requires that the technical measures meet the PND.	nprPPM Out-Scope of the TBT Agreement No legitimate use according to international trade rules.

these nprPPM have demonstrable negative production environmental externalities. That is, labour, animal welfare and environmental standards are not trade compliant unless they produce a demonstrable consumption externality. From an environmental protection perspective, the problem with the fact that nprPPM are out of scope is that the pursuit of sustainable development and the protection of biodiversity often focus on production externalities and result in pressures on domestic governments to establish environmental protection measures pertaining explicitly to nprPPM which can become regulatory market access barriers. But, in the event of a trade dispute, the TBT Agreement specifies that such market access barriers are an unjustified trade barrier. Despite the importance of the issue, the compatibility of PPM-based environmental measures with the rights and obligations of the TBT Agreement remains uncertain (Caldwell 1998). The fragmentation of PPM into various categories based on vague criteria makes it difficult to understand which environmental regulations are in compliance with international trade obligations and which are in contravention.

Consider another example associated with genetically modified (GM) agricultural crops which illustrates an additional unresolved issue that exacerbates the trade uncertainty (Isaac 2002). The issue is whether or not GM crops can even be categorized as having different PPM than conventional, non-GM crops. Consider that genetic modifications are made to the cells of the crop, which are then cultured into seeds. In the case of production-trait varieties, the GM crops are then grown in the same agronomic system as the conventional varieties. Then the crops are harvested and sold into the same processing and distribution system as non-GM varieties. Accordingly, GM crops which do not require new or different agronomic or processing systems would not be grown under process or production methods different from conventional crops and it appears there would be no difference between the nprPPM of GM crops and non-GM crops. Furthermore, as many of the approved GM varieties to date have been approved as like products or as substantially equivalent to conventional varieties, there are no differences in prPPM either and there are no consumption externalities to consider. In this case, the TBT Committee will have to decide on, first, the applicability of PPM to GM crops in the first instance, and second, on the legitimacy of the principle of substantial equivalence. Of course, the TBT Committee does not have to make this decision proactively. Instead, it could allow differences of opinions among Members to escalate from regulatory barriers, to trade tensions, followed by trade disputes brought to the WTO's dispute settlement body.

Therefore, while the TBT Agreement initially appears clear regarding technical measures based upon process and production methods, there is considerable uncertainty surrounding how such measures should be practically applied.

The TBT Agreement and labelling
Often consumer concern about particular ethical issues goes hand-in-hand with a desire for product labelling about the PPM embodied in a product to address these issues. Therefore, it is crucial to also assess how the Agreement deals with labelling.

General concern about the potential impact of product labelling upon international trade has been raised at the multilateral level since the mid-1970s, with significant attention paid to various environmental labelling or eco-labelling schemes that were emerging at the time. As the discussion on environmental labelling measures is directly applicable to all product quality assurance programmes it will be discussed in detail below.

The General Agreement on Tariffs and Trade (GATT 1947) sustained the divide between national environmental preferences and international trade agreements, through the common exemption of environmental and natural resource issues under Article XX (General Exemptions). As with PPM, the Tokyo Round of the GATT formalized the international trade discipline of labelling schemes through the TBT Code. The Code specified that Contracting Parties (CPs) must avoid discrimination and the creation of unnecessary trade barriers when setting technical measures. With the emergence of the TBT Agreement during the Uruguay Round, eco-labelling became a specified issue to reconcile with trade obligations.

In addition to the focus on PPM discussed above, the initial TBT Code negotiated in the Tokyo Round also dealt with two other relevant issues to labelling which continue to be pressing trade policy issues; the distinction between mandatory and voluntary labelling requirements and the distinction between public and private standards-making bodies.

Mandatory and voluntary labelling requirements
Whether mandatory or voluntary, all labelling requirements must fulfil a legitimate objective as disciplined under the GATT/WTO (Caldwell 1998).

With respect to mandatory labelling requirements, the TBT Code required all mandatory standards to be notified to the GATT and be based on internationally agreed standards so as not to create unnecessary barriers to trade. These would then be subject to TBT provisions.

Voluntary labelling requirements were not as straightforward. The distinction between mandatory and voluntary labelling requirements was important to eco-labelling schemes because if voluntary schemes did become *de facto* market standards, then they would be essentially mandatory labelling requirements for market access. As a result, it was argued that the voluntary schemes should be disciplined under trade principles as if they were mandatory labelling requirements. Voluntary labelling standards were subject to the 'Code of Good Practice for the Preparation, Adoption and Application of Standards'. Essentially, this Code committed Contracting Parties to make their best endeavours to ensure that voluntary requirements met the same principles and rules as those laid down for mandatory requirements.

Public and private standards-making bodies
With respect to the second issue, there was less trade discipline over the distinction between public and private standards-making bodies developing voluntary labelling criteria. Some Contracting Parties at the Uruguay Round such as Canada, India and the

US sought to make public standards-making bodies subject to TBT provisions, even if the labelling requirements were voluntary. For instance, voluntary eco-labelling schemes would have to be consistent with the TBT Agreement if they are funded by the government and if the government has authority in product selection and criteria development. This would have effectively included public European eco-labelling schemes while excluding the private Canadian TerraChoice and the US Green Seal eco-labelling schemes. Such a lack of reciprocity was unacceptable to the EU. The compromise was Article 9 which proposes a voluntary code of conduct; the 'Code of Conduct for Standards-Making Bodies' that requires Contracting Parties to ensure that both public and private bodies administering voluntary labelling schemes comply with Article 7 – the 'Code of Good Practice for the Preparation, Adoption and Application of Standards'. Further, under the Code of Conduct, standards-making bodies are to ensure that labelling criteria do not create trade barriers, are based on international criteria – such as the International Organization for Standardization (ISO) – where possible and are notified to these organizations and to outside parties in order to allow an opportunity to comment on the criteria prior to adoption.

There are three common complaints about public labelling schemes (most often raised by the US). The first is that the criteria developed by a public agency tend to focus on domestic environmental preferences that may be inappropriate for foreign producers. Second, foreign producers have little voice in a scheme that is dominated by domestic interests. Third, public standards-making bodies can become captured by the public interest of the day, rather than remaining objective and market-oriented as private standards-making bodies are supposed to.

On the other hand, there are two common concerns with private labelling schemes (most often raised by the EU). The first is a concern about the accountability of private schemes that wield discretionary power and make subjective decisions on product selection, criteria development and label award. Second, the focus on market-oriented standards may inadequately reflect the 'social' or non-market environmental concerns which public policy needs to address.

Therefore, with respect to labelling, the TBT Agreement distinguishes between mandatory and voluntary schemes according to whether or not they are administered by public or private labelling agencies. Basically, mandatory, public labelling schemes are only trade compliant if they focus on prPPM.

Conclusions

The analysis in this chapter reveals that while consumers are increasingly concerned about ethical issues such as labour, animal welfare and environmental standards domestic measures focusing on such standards will only likely be trade compliant if there is a demonstrable product-related impact from the use of such standards. Without such an impact, domestic measures are likely to be found trade incompliant.

Notes

1. Safety-related attributes deal with the safety and health measures achieved during the production and processing of, say, food products or children's toys. Food safety-related trade measures pertain to sanitary and phytosanitary issues and are beyond the scope of this chapter.
2. A formal discussion of how technical measures are dealt with in the WTO's Agreement on Technical Barriers to Trade is beyond the scope of this chapter.

3.   Essentially, this concept embeds reciprocity into the international trading system by allowing market access negotiations to occur between a limited number of countries with the expectation that the concessions negotiated will be extended to all (Finger and Winters, 2002).
4.   The relationship between the TBT and the SPS Agreements is as follows. The former is the broad, overarching agreement generally covering all technical measures (both safety and non-safety related) while the SPS Agreement is the specific agreement that disciplines the legitimate use of safety-related measures. Therefore, from a practical trade policy perspective, the general distinction is that the SPS Agreement deals with safety issues and the TBT Agreement deals with technical, non-safety issues (although there are some safety issues not covered under the SPS Agreement which necessarily fall under the purview of the TBT Agreement).
5.   The Agreement states that measures should be applied on a most-favoured nation (MFN) basis to all imported products from all contracting parties (TBT Agreement, Article 2:1 – MFN Principle of Non-Discrimination). It also states that measures should not extend to imported products treatment that is less favourable than that extended to domestically produced like products (TBT Agreement, Article 2:1 – National Treatment Principle).

References

Bureau, J. C., S. Marette and A. Schiavina (1997a), 'Trade, Labels and Consumer Information: The Case of Hormone-Treated Beef', Contributed Paper at the XXII Conference of the IAAE, IAAE, Sacramento.

Bureau, J. C., S. Marette and A. Schiavina (1997b), 'Non-Tariff Barriers and Consumers' Information: The Case of US–EC Trade Disputes on Food Products', *INRA Working Paper Series – August*, INRA, Versailles.

Caldwell, D. J. (1998), *The WTO Beef Hormone Ruling: An Analysis*, Washington, DC: Community Nutrition Institute.

Cheyne, I. (1995), 'Environmental Unilateralism and the WTO/GATT System', 24 *Georgia. Journal of International Law and Comparative Law*, 433–65.

Correa, C. M. (2000), 'Implementing National Public Health Policies in the Framework of the WTO Agreements', *Journal of World Trade*, **34**(5), 89–121.

Daly, M. and H. Kuwahara (1998), 'The Impact of the Uruguay Round on Tariff and Non-Tariff Barriers to Trade in the Quad', *The World Economy*, **21**(2), 207–34.

Ehring, L. (2002), 'De Facto Discrimination in World Trade Law National and Most-Favoured Nation Treatment or Equal Treatment?' *Journal of World Trade*, **36**(5), 921–77.

Enders, A. (1997), *Openness and the WTO*, Winnipeg: International Institute for Sustainable Development.

Fauchald, O. K. (2003), 'Flexibility and Predictability Under the World Trade Organization's Non-Discrimination Clauses', *Journal of World Trade*, **37**(3), 443–82.

Ferrantino, M. J. (1997), 'International Trade, Environmental Quality and Public Policy', *The World Economy*, **20**(1), 43–72.

Finger, J. M. and L. A. Winters (2002), 'Reciprocity in the WTO', in B. Hoekman, A. Mattoo and P. English (eds), *Development, Trade and the WTO: A Handbook*, Washington, DC: The World Bank, pp. 50–60.

Gamberale, C. and A. Mattoo (2002), 'Domestic Regulations and Liberalization of Trade in Services', in B. Hoekman, A. Mattoo and P. English (eds), *Development, Trade and the WTO: A Handbook*, Washington, DC: The World Bank, pp. 290–303.

Hagen, P. and J. B. Weiner (2000), 'The Cartagena Protocol on Biosafety: New Rules for International Trade in Living Modified Organisms', *Georgetown International Environmental Law Review*, **12**, 697–717.

Hart, M. and B. Dymond (2003), 'Special and Differential Treatment and the Doha "Development" Round', *Journal of World Trade*, **37**(2), 395–415.

Hobbs, A. L., J. E. Hobbs, G. E. Isaac and W.A. Kerr (2002), 'Ethics at the WTO: Assessing the EU Proposal on Animal Welfare', *Food Policy*, **27**, 437–54.

Hooker, N. and J. Caswell (1999), 'A Framework for Evaluating Non-Tariff Barriers to Trade Related to Sanitary and Phytosanitary Regulations', *Journal of Agricultural Economics*, **50**(2), 234–46.

Horton, L. (1997), 'Internationalization of Food and Veterinary Medicine Regulation', in R. P. Brady, R. M. Cooper and R.S. Silverman (eds), *Fundamentals of Law and Regulation*, Washington, DC: FDLI, pp. 381–484.

Howse, R. (1998), 'The Turtles Panel: Another Environmental Disaster in Geneva', *Journal of World Trade*, **32**(5), 73–100.

Howse, R. and J. Trebilcock (1999), *The Regulation of International Trade*, (2nd edn), London: Routledge.

Hufbauer, G., B. Kotschwar and J. Wilson (2002), 'Trade and Standards: A Look at Central America', *The World Economy*, **25**(7), 991–1018.

Isaac, G. E. (2002), *Agricultural Biotechnology and Transatlantic Trade: An International Political Economy Analysis of Social Regulatory Barriers*, Cambridge, MA: CAB International Publishing Inc.

Isaac, G. E. (2003a), 'The WTO and the Cartagena Protocol: International Policy Coordination or Conflict?' *Current Agriculture, Food & Resource Issues*, **4**, 152–9.

Isaac, G. E. (2003b), 'Increasing the Openness of Trade Policy: Challenges and Implications', *Journal of International Law and Trade Policy*, **4**(1), 58–74.

Isaac, G. E. and W. A. Kerr (2003), 'GMOs at the WTO: A Harvest of Trouble', *Journal of World Trade*, **37**(6), 1083–95.

Jha, V. (2002), 'Environmental Regulation and the WTO', in B. Hoekman, A. Mattoo and P. English (eds), *Development, Trade and the WTO: A Handbook*, Washington, DC: The World Bank, pp. 472–82.

Laird, S. (2002) 'Market Access Issues and the WTO: An Overview', in B. Hoekman, A. Mattoo and P. English (eds), *Development, Trade and the WTO: A Handbook*, Washington, DC: The World Bank, pp. 97–104.

Mahe, L. P. (1996), 'Environment and Quality Standards in the WTO: New Protectionism in Agricultural Trade? A European Perspective', Conference Paper at the Eighth Annual Congress of European Agricultural Economists, 3–7 September, Edinburgh, Scotland.

Majone, G. (1990), *Deregulation vs. Reregulation: Regulatory Reform in Europe and the United States*, London: Pinter Publishers.

Marceau, G. and J. P. Trachtman (2002), 'The Technical Barriers to Trade Agreement, the Sanitary and Phyto-Sanitary Measures Agreement and the General Agreement on Tariffs and Trade: A Map of the World Trade Organization Law of Domestic Regulation of Goods', *Journal of World Trade*, **36**(5), 811–81.

Marvoidis, P. and T. Cottier (2000), *Regulatory Barriers and the Principle of Non- Discrimination*, Ann Arbor, MI: University of Michigan Press.

Organization for Economic Cooperation and Development (1994), *Synthesis Report: Trade and Environment, The PPM Issue*, OECD Working Paper Series, Paris.

Perdikis, N., W. A. Kerr, and J. E. Hobbs (2001), 'Reforming the WTO to Defuse Potential Trade Conflicts in Genetically Modified Goods', *The World Economy*, **24**(3), 379–98.

Phillips, P. W. B. and G. E. Isaac (2001), 'Regulating International Trade in Knowledge-Based Products', in P. W. B. Phillips and G. G. Khachatourians (eds), *The Biotechnology Revolution in Global Agriculture: Invention, Innovation and Investment in the Canola Sector*, Cambridge, MA: CAB International Publishing Inc., pp. 243–70.

Phillips, P. W. B. and W. A. Kerr (2000), 'Alternative Paradigms: The WTO Versus the Biosafety Protocol for Trade in Genetically Modified Organisms', *Journal of World Trade*, **34**(4), 63–76.

Regan, D. H. (2002), 'Regulatory Purpose and "Like Products" in Article III:4 of the GATT (With Additional Remarks on Article III:2)', *Journal of World Trade*, **36**(3), 443–78.

Regan, D. H. (2003), 'Further Thoughts on the Role of Regulatory Purpose Under Article III of the GATT', *Journal of World Trade*, **37**(4), 737–60.

Roberts, D., T. Josling and D. Orden (1999), 'A Framework for Analyzing Technical Trade Barriers in Agricultural Markets', Market and Economics Division, Economic Research Service, US Department of Agriculture, Technical Bulletin No. 1876.

Roessler, F. (2003), 'Beyond the Ostensible: A Tribute to Professor Robert Hudec's Insights on the Determination of Likeness of Products Under the National Treatment Provisions of the General Agreement on Tariffs and Trade', *Journal of World Trade*, **37**(4), 771–81.

Schoenbaum, T. J. (1997), 'International Trade and Protection of the Environment: The Continuing Search for Reconciliation', *American Journal of International Law*, **91**, 268–313.

Sinclair, I. (1973), *The Vienna Convention on the Law of Treaties* (1st edn), Manchester: Manchester University Press.

Spracker, S. M. and D. C. Lundsgaard (1993), 'Dolphins and Tuna: Renewed Attention on the Future of Free Trade and Protection of the Environment', *Columbia Journal of Environmental Law*, **18**, 385–418.

Waincymer, J. (2001), 'Settlement of Disputes Within the World Trade Organization: A Guide to the Jurispredence', *The World Economy*, **24**(9), 1247–78.

Wilson, J. (2002), 'Standards, Regulation and Trade: WTO Rules and Developing Country Concerns', in B. Hoekman, A. Mattoo and P. English (eds), *Development, Trade and the WTO: A Handbook*, Washington, DC: The World Bank, pp. 428–38.

World Trade Organization (1999), *Trade and the Environment: Special Studies 4*, Geneva: WTO.

Zampetti, A. B. (2000), 'Mutual Recognition in the Transatlantic Context: Some Reflections on Future Negotiations', in P. Marvoidis and T. Cottier (eds), *Regulatory Barriers and the Principle of Non-Discrimination*, Ann Arbor, MI: University of Michigan Press.

39 Trade and the environment: what do we know?
Brian R. Copeland

Introduction

Is globalization bad for the environment?[1] This issue attracts heated debate, much rhetoric and sharply divergent views. Anti-globalization protesters in Seattle dressed up in turtle suits to protest what they viewed as interference by the World Trade Organization (WTO) with the rights of countries to restrict trade for environmental reasons. The popular media points to examples such as the shipbreaking industry[2] in which weak environmental standards appear to be a major factor in inducing rich countries to shift their environmental problems to poor countries. And there is much concern that forests and fish stocks are depleted more rapidly when export markets are available.

On the other hand, the pro-free trade lobby argues that free trade and a clean environment are not incompatible. WTO rules simply require that governments not discriminate against foreign-produced goods, and leave countries free to implement tough environmental standards. Moreover by increasing real incomes, trade gives countries more resources to allocate to protecting the environment. And globalization promotes both the diffusion of new environmentally friendly technology, and the diffusion of ideas and environmental lobby groups across borders.

This debate has stimulated a great deal of research in the past few years, and in this chapter I review what we know about how trade affects the environment, how we know this, and what we still need to know.[3] Although some of the debate stems from different views about the trade-off between environmental quality and income, there are also important disagreements about the facts. The debate is not about whether or not we should have globalization, but rather about the rules and institutional structures under which globalization occurs. Hopefully, better evidence about how trade affects the environment can lead to a more informed debate about the direction in which these rules should evolve.

Linkages between market integration and the environment

There are several ways in which globalization can affect the environment. Here I briefly outline some of the channels that have received the most attention from those who are concerned about the possible adverse effects of trade on the environment.

- *Growth* One of the major arguments in favor of freer trade and capital mobility is that it will increase growth and consumption. But if growth is bad for the environment, then by promoting growth trade can be bad for the environment.
- *Competitiveness* If we trade with countries that have weaker environmental policies than we do, then this gives foreign firms a competitive advantage. Freer trade exacerbates this effect.
- *Race to the bottom* Trade-induced concerns over competitiveness may make it politically difficult for governments to tighten up environmental policy. As well,

governments may not enforce environmental regulations to help shield firms from the pressures of foreign competition. Hence globalization may lead to a competition among governments which results in downward pressure on environmental standards.

- *Pollution havens*   Polluting industry may concentrate in poor countries with weak environmental regulation. This is related to concerns over competitiveness and race to the bottom. But there are also issues of environmental justice – low income people may be exposed to disproportionately large amounts of pollution; and concerns about global environmental quality – trade may shift the most polluting activities to countries that are least able to control them, and consequently reduce average global environmental quality. Finally, by shifting polluting production away from the high income people who consume the output, there will be less pressure to innovate and find more environmentally friendly ways to produce.
- *Sovereignty*   Global trading rules reduce national sovereignty by placing restrictions on governments' ability to regulate – the successful US challenge to the European ban on the sale of beef from cattle treated with artificial growth hormones is an example.

Are these valid concerns? Since we cannot run experiments to compare a free trade world with a world with high trade barriers, we have to rely on the accumulated evidence across countries and over time as the stringency of environmental policy and openness to trade has varied. Although the concerns listed above touch on a wide variety of issues, evidence on three main questions can go a long way toward shedding some light on all of them.

First, is growth in fact bad for the environment? Second, do differences in environmental policy affect trade and investment flows? This lies at the root of concerns over competitiveness, 'race to the bottom', and pollution havens. Finally, how does environmental policy respond to domestic and international pressure? Environmental quality depends not just on market outcomes, but also on how responsive and pro-active governments are in redressing market failures.

Growth and the environment

Economists use a combination of theory and empirical evidence to try to understand how the world works. Theory helps us ask the right questions, know what to look for, and avoid attributing too much credence to simple correlations in the data. Empirical evidence is used both to test theories and to highlight anomalies in the data that cannot be explained by existing theories.

The study of the relation between growth and the environment began with some empirical evidence. Grossman and Krueger (1993), in a study of the potential effects of NAFTA on the environment, used data on air quality in a sample of cities from 42 different countries over 12 years. They found an inverse-U shaped relation between air quality and per capita income: pollution first rose as income rose, but once countries were sufficiently rich, then pollution fell. One interpretation of this result was that growth is bad for the environment in poor countries, but good for the environment in rich countries. However, subsequent research has shown that the relation between growth and income is far more complex than this.

This work attracted a lot of attention, and has been frequently cited. It stimulated many similar studies for different measures of environmental quality, different sets of countries, and different time periods. The results are mixed and it is clear that there is no simple consistent relationship for all types of environmental quality. Perhaps the strongest indication of this is a paper by Harbaugh *et al.* (2002) who use updated data covering the same countries and pollutants as Grossman and Krueger and find that the shape of the relation between pollution and income is very sensitive to which countries are in the sample and the time period. Stern and Common (2001) obtain similar results. Both of these papers suggest that there does not exist a stable inverse-U shaped relation between pollution and income.

At this point, theory becomes helpful in moving forward. One approach that has been fruitful is to decompose variations in pollution across time and communities into scale, composition and technique effects.[4] It is clear that growth has an inherent tendency to increase environmental damage because it increases the scale of economic activity. Two things can potentially offset or reverse this tendency: changes in the composition of economic activity, and changes in production techniques that reduce environmental damage per unit of output.

Growth can change the composition of economic activity: for example, richer countries may shift away from pollution intensive manufacturing and toward cleaner service industries. However, once we realize that growth may come from different channels (such as for example, the exploitation of natural resources, increases in education levels of workers, or foreign investment); then one can see that the changes in the composition of economic activity accompanying growth will vary across countries. Consequently, it seems a bit much to expect a simple predictable relation between growth and pollution. This is consistent with the Harbaugh *et al.* (2002) result – a model relying mainly on income as an explanatory variable is likely to be mis-specified.

The second major channel which can offset the scale effect of growth is changes in production techniques that reduce the pollution intensity of production. If richer countries have more stringent environmental policy, then they will use cleaner production techniques, and this can offset the effects of a larger scale of production. However, a focus on policy as a possible explanation for an improvement in environmental quality in richer countries also leads us to expect heterogeneity in the relation between pollution and income both across countries and pollutants – countries with different forms of government may well have different policy responses to environmental problems.

A focus on scale, composition, and technique (or policy) effects suggests that rather than looking for a simple relationship between pollution and income, we instead study how growth and globalization affect the composition and techniques of production and whether these effects vary across countries and time. Antweiler *et al.* (2001) have tried to measure each of the scale, composition and policy effects separately. They confirm that increases in scale do lead to more pollution; and that, controlling for scale and composition of the economy, increases in per capita income lead to reductions in pollution, although the strength of this latter effect varies with government type.

Several other types of study have provided more evidence that policy tightens up as per capita income rises. Hilton and Levinson (1998) show that the lead content of gasoline declines as per capita income rises, a result that is most likely due to more stringent regulatory policy in high income countries. Many studies have found that individual willingness to pay for environmental quality (such as clean air and water) rises with income (Kriström and Riera 1996; Hokby and Soderqvist 2002). If governments respond to consumer demand, this would suggest that governments would have an incentive to tighten up environmental policy as income rises. Finally, there are studies which look directly at the stringency of environmental policy. Dasgupta *et al.* (2001) develop an index of environmental policy stringency for 31 countries and find that stringency increases with per capita income. Pearce and Palmer (2001) use data on public expenditure on environmental protection in OECD countries and find that it is strongly positively related to income.

The most consistent and robust result coming out of this literature is that there is an income effect that tends to lead to an improvement in environmental quality, and that this income effect most likely works via an improvement in policy; if all else is held equal. That is, there is a force that works to improve the environment as countries grow. But there are other forces (such as increase in scale, and capital accumulation) that lead to more pollution. Which effect is stronger depends on the source of growth, the type of pollution, and the country's political system. Without knowing the relative strength of these opposing forces we cannot simply conclude that environmental quality will improve once income reaches a certain level. But we have a better understanding now of what we need to measure in specific cases to make a prediction.

How is this relevant to helping us understand the effects of trade on the environment? First, the above work confirms that economic growth does indeed lead to a deterioration in environmental quality for many countries. There are opposing forces, but these kick in at different income levels for different countries and different pollutants. On the other hand, many countries are poor and want to grow. They will grow whether or not they are open to trade. The issue for these countries is not whether growth is bad for the environment, but whether or not growth in an open economy is better or worse for the environment than growth in a closed economy. Is there some reason why we should expect trade-induced growth to be systematically biased against the environment in certain types of countries? This suggests that in looking for the effects of globalization on the environment, we should compare countries with similar income levels, but different levels of openness.

A second major finding is that growth does lead to an increase in the demand for environmental quality and on average seems to lead to an improvement in environmental policy. So the effects of trade on income need not all be bad for the environment. Put another way, we may get misleading predictions about the long-run effects of trade on the environment if we do not take into account the potential beneficial effects of higher income on policy.

Does environmental policy affect trade flows?

Perhaps the key piece of evidence needed to clarify issues in the debate over trade and the environment is whether or not differences in environmental policy affect trade flows. The pollution haven hypothesis is that trade will shift polluting industry to poor countries because of their weak environmental policy. The concerns about competitiveness are that weak environmental policy gives foreign firms an unfair advantage. The race to the bottom hypothesis is that governments respond to competitiveness concerns by weakening environmental policy in an explicit attempt to affect trade flows. And whether or not trade-induced growth has different environmental effects than other sources of growth is going to be influenced by whether or not differences in environmental policy affect trade flows.

Although the question of how environmental policy affects trade flows seems straightforward, it has been surprisingly difficult to answer. Work on this issue started in the 1970s, but work in the field is probably much more active now than at any time in the past.

Progress in this area has been difficult for a number of reasons. First, we need good data on the stringency of environmental policy across jurisdictions. In many countries, environmental regulations are not easily quantified, and so such data are difficult to obtain. For this reason, much of what we know on this issue comes from studies of differences in environmental policy across states in the US. This is not ideal when trying to extrapolate to globalization. Second, environmental control costs are not a large part of total costs in most industries (typically less than 3 percent of costs). This means that differences in environmental policy can get swamped in the data by other differences in costs across jurisdictions. And finally, environmental policy is something that changes over time; and in particular may change in response to trade and investment flows. This is known as the endogeneity problem, and it can create serious difficulties for statistical analysis of the data.

Research in the area has come in two waves. Up to about 1997, there was almost universal consensus among economists that differences in environmental policy had no significant effect on trade flows. Jaffe *et al.* (1995) is a good survey of this work. A variety of studies looked at the role of abatement costs and other measures of the stringency of environmental policy in affecting trade flows, plant location, and foreign investment flows. In virtually all cases, this work was unable to find any statistically significant effect of environmental policy. In some cases, the evidence seemed to suggest that jurisdictions with more stringent environmental policy were in fact more likely to attract investment in polluting industries.

This was a puzzle, because standard economic theory would suggest that more stringent regulation should raise costs and hurt competitiveness. One explanation was that environmental costs are just too low to matter; another was offered by Porter and van de Linde (1995) who suggested that stricter environmental policy may in fact make firms more competitive by forcing them to look for innovative ways of doing things. However, the most convincing resolution of the puzzle has emerged from more recent work which takes into account the fact that environmental policy is endogenous; that is, it responds to the seriousness of environmental problems, the trade regime, and political pressure.

Arik Levinson (1999) studied hazardous waste trade within the US. He first used the methods of previous work in this area, and found that hazardous waste was more likely to flow to states with high taxes or charges on the disposal and processing of such waste. That is, stringent environmental regulations seemed to be associated with more imports of toxic waste, rather than less, as theory would suggest. However, he then recognized that states vary in their capacity and ability to process such waste. So in the absence of any regulation at all, some states would attract more hazardous waste than others. These states face more pressure on their environment and therefore have more of an incentive to tighten up regulations. Once he controlled for this, his statistical results were reversed: all else equal, more stringent environmental policy deters hazardous waste imports into a state. That is, states that are attractive places for toxic waste disposal on average have higher disposal taxes; but if they raise these taxes, hazardous waste flows into their state fall.

Since then, a number of other studies have found similar results. Becker and Henderson (2000) used a panel of county-level US data on where new manufacturing plants chose to locate. Previous studies using state-level data had found that differences in environmental policy at the state level did not seem to have a significant effect on plant location. However, using non-compliance with the Clean Air Act as an indicator of stringent environmental policy,[5] they find that more stringent environmental policy at the county level has a significant and sometimes large negative effect on the chances that a plant will choose to locate in that county. This was an important study both because it was able to control for unobserved differences across locations (which was the key to Levinson's (1999) hazardous waste trade study), but also because it showed that using aggregate data (such as state level data) may make it difficult to measure some important forces. Several other studies (Kahn 1997; Greenstone 2002; List *et al.* 2002) have confirmed the Becker–Henderson results on the Clean Air Act.

Several papers have used these new techniques to investigate international trade and investment. Keller and Levinson (2002) find that abatement costs have a statistically significant negative effect on foreign investment in US states. Ederington and Minier (2003) use cross-sectional time-series data on net imports in US manufacturing from 1978 to 1992. When they treat pollution policy (abatement costs) as endogenous and responsive to political pressure, they find that more stringent pollution policy leads to more imports; that is, stringent environmental policy reduces international competitiveness. Levinson and Taylor (2004) also use data on US imports and find a large and significant positive effect of abatement costs on net imports; again supportive of the hypothesis that more stringent environmental policy reduces competitiveness.

There is therefore a growing body of recent work that provides evidence that environmental policy affects trade and investment flows within the US, and that it affects US imports. These studies use techniques that allow the researcher to take into account unobserved differences between locations (such as other factors that affect competitiveness). Currently, because of a lack of cross-country, time-series data on the stringency of environmental policy, there is very little work of this type on trade between rich and poor countries. However, one might conjecture that if differences in environmental policy matter for the location of production within the US, they are also likely to matter between countries as well, particularly since differences in environmental policy are much larger in an international context.

We may therefore tentatively conclude that differences in environmental policy do affect trade and investment flows. What are the implications of this?

First, it means that more stringent environmental policy does likely reduce competitiveness. This in itself is not necessarily a problem. Differences in labour costs also affect competitiveness, but this is one of the major motives for trade. The US and Canada trade with China and Mexico, which have much lower wages. In principle, differences in environmental policy are no different from differences in wages as a potential motive for trade. The stringency of environmental standards varies across countries in response to differences in pressures on the environment, differences in climate and other natural conditions, and (perhaps more controversially) differences in income. This is just one of many sources of legitimate cost differences that affect trade patterns.

However, if differences in labour costs cause labour intensive industries to concentrate in poor countries, this helps workers in poor countries. In contrast, if differences in pollution policy cause pollution intensive industry to concentrate in poor countries, this will bring pollution-caused health problems to workers in poor countries and damage the global environment. That is, if environmental policy does affect trade flows, we have to take the pollution haven hypothesis seriously. Moreover, environmental policy differs from labour costs in that the latter is mainly determined by markets, while the former is mainly determined by government policy. This means that environmental standards are more subject to political manipulation than are labour costs. If environmental policy does affect competitiveness, we have to take the race to the bottom hypothesis seriously. In the next two sections, I consider each of these possibilities.

Pollution haven hypothesis
The pollution haven hypothesis is that trade liberalization will shift polluting industry to poor countries with weak environmental policy. It is important to emphasize that this means a lot more than that environmental policy affects trade flows. What it requires to be correct is that differences in environmental policy are the most important cause of trade flows.

An analogy to labor markets is again useful. Mexican wages are lower than American wages. However, this has not meant that all American manufacturing industry has shifted to Mexico. The reason is that labor costs are one component of costs that have to be balanced against other components, such as productivity differences, capital costs, access to skilled labor, and so on Similarly, just because we have evidence that differences in environmental policy are one of the factors that affect competitiveness, that does not mean that it is the dominant factor determining the pattern of trade.

There have been very few studies that explicitly test the pollution haven hypothesis. There is some evidence that the pollution intensity of exports from poor countries has been rising over time, and the pollution intensity of exports from the US has been falling. However, this is also consistent with economic growth in poor countries: if rich countries had a head start in industrializing, then they would initially be producing more pollution intensive manufacturing. As poorer countries catch up, they will begin producing these types of goods as well, and they would have done this with or without trade. Hence these trends are suggestive but do not address the issue of causation.

Antweiler *et al.* (2001) use data on sulfur dioxide pollution in cities to try to address this issue directly. They control for scale and capital abundance, and try to determine whether trade has shifted the composition of production toward or away from pollution-intensive production in a sample of rich and poor countries. Their results are illustrated in Figure 39.1, which plots the estimated effect of increases in openness to trade on sulfur dioxide pollution as a function of per capita income (controlling for scale, capita abundance, and other factors, such as climate). If the pollution haven hypothesis is correct, the relationship should be downward sloping: trade would shift production toward polluting industries in poor countries, and do the reverse in rich countries. In fact, they find the reverse: the slope is positive, suggesting that higher income countries have a comparative advantage in SO_2-intensive industries, so that trade liberalization would shift SO_2-intensive polluting industry to richer countries. This is consistent with results from Grossman and Krueger's (1993) study of NAFTA which drew upon simulations of the effects of trade liberalization on trade flows and concluded that NAFTA would, at the margin, shift pollution-intensive industrial production to the US. It is also consistent with

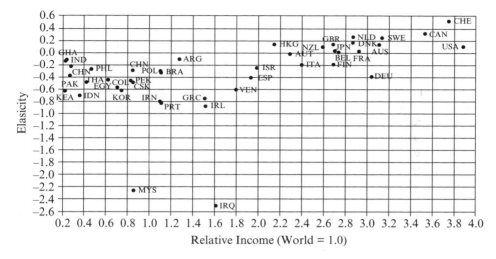

Note: The vertical axis measures the percent increase in SO₂ pollution resulting from a 1 percent increase in openness, controlling for scale, income, and capital abundance. Each dot corresponds to a different country.

Source: Figure 2.1 Antweiler *et al.* (2001) p. 896.

Figure 39.1   Increase in SO₂ pollution compared to increase in openness

the existing pattern of trade, in which pollution intensive industry is heavily concentrated in high income countries. A likely explanation of this result is that SO₂-intensive industry is capital intensive, and rich countries are capital abundant. If capital costs are higher than pollution control costs, then capital abundance effects swamp pollution control cost effects in determining trade patterns. Rich countries export SO₂-intensive production in spite of their stricter environmental policy because of their capital abundance.

These results apply only to one type of pollution, and it is likely that there are other cases where factor abundance and pollution regulation effects reinforce each other. The shipbreaking example is a likely possibility: low labor costs combine with weak environmental regulation to shift that industry to low income countries.

Ederington *et al.* (2004) provide an alternative test of the pollution haven hypothesis. They first look at changes in the pollution content of US imports and exports from 1972 to 1994. They look at 14 different pollutants in 459 different industries. Holding emission intensities constant[6] (at 1987 levels) they calculate the amount of various types of pollutants that was generated during the production of US manufacturing imports and exports. They find that US imports have become cleaner over time, and that US exports have become dirtier relative to US imports. This holds also when they focus on imports from non-OECD countries: contrary to the pollution haven hypothesis, the data suggest that imports from developing countries have been shifting toward cleaner goods.

Next, they test the pollution haven hypothesis econometrically by examining how variations in abatement costs across industries and time affect US net imports. If the pollution haven hypothesis were correct, we would expect that tariff reductions would increase US imports more in high abatement cost industries (because trade would induce production in these industries to shift out of the US). In fact, they find the opposite: imports in polluting industries are less responsive to tariff reductions than are other industries. They interpret this finding as reflecting a US comparative advantage in pollution intensive industries. That is, their results are consistent with Antweiler *et al.* (2001): US capital abundance and technological capabilities give it a comparative advantage in polluting industries despite its more stringent environmental policy.

This is an issue for which there is much scope for more research. However, most of the available evidence at this point suggests that for most industries, pollution control costs are not the major determinant of trade patterns, suggesting that concerns about pollution havens are overstated.

Race to the bottom

Environmental regulations typically raise production costs, so one would expect that governments would always face pressure from affected firms to make environmental policy less stringent. Since there is evidence that environmental policy affects international competitiveness, we would expect that this pressure could increase as countries become more open to trade and capital flows. However, there is also pressure from environmental and health groups in favour of more stringent environmental regulation, and this imposes costs on governments that weaken environmental policy. Moreover, governments have many other ways available to help firms that are lobbying for protection. Subsidies, tax breaks, and other forms of regulatory relief are other options available that may be less costly politically. Hence the competitiveness argument suggests that governments may be responsive to firms threatened by foreign competition,[7] but it is not obvious that weaker environmental policy will be the result.

To determine whether governments do in fact weaken environmental policy in response to trade competition, we need to measure government behavior directly. So far, there are very few studies that do this. Eliste and Fredriksson (2002) investigate agricultural trade liberalization and find some evidence that governments have weakened environmental regulations affecting agriculture after trade has been liberalized. Ederington and Minier (2003) investigate the relationship between import penetration and the stringency of environmental policy in the US and find some evidence that environmental policy is weakened in response to import competition.

There is thus some limited evidence that suggests that although we may not expect a literal race to the bottom; the presence of increased international competitive pressure may play some role in affecting environmental policy. Other pieces of casual evidence support this – several European countries had some form of carbon tax in the 1990s, but in many cases there were exemptions for exporting industries for reasons of competitiveness.

The possibility that environmental policy may be affected by international competitive pressure does not mean that the solution is to restrict trade. However, it does have important implications for the design of trade agreements, suggesting that in some cases, some coordination across countries in the setting of environmental standards may be needed. This is the approach that is taken within the European Union, and within national federations, such as the US and Canada for some types of environmental policy. One might conjecture that as economies become more deeply integrated via globalization or via regional free trade arrangements, there will be greater pressure for some form of coordination of environmental policies.

Is free trade bad for the environment?

We have reviewed the evidence on the various channels through which trade can affect the environment. There is some evidence that environmental policy affects trade flows, but little evidence in support the pollution haven hypothesis. There is some preliminary evidence that environmental policy may be responsive to the trade regime, but there is also evidence that increases in income per capita (which is likely to result from trade liberalization) lead to more stringent environmental policy. What is the net effect of trade on the environment?

There are two ways to approach this issue. One is to ask whether there is any evidence to suggest that trade and globalization is systematically related to increased environmental degradation, either globally or within specific countries. The other is to try to determine whether trade has exacerbated specific environmental problems in specific countries. A problem with the second approach is that trade is likely to stimulate some types of polluting activities and reduce others as output patterns within a country respond to the trade regime. For our purposes, it is of more interest to know the net effect on environmental outcomes.

There is still relatively little direct evidence on the effects of trade on environmental outcomes. The reason for this is that it is very difficult to isolate the effects of trade from the effects of other changes in the economy. For example, if we wanted to measure the contribution of trade to increased pollution in China over the past 20 years, we would need to try to isolate the effects of trade from the effects of a switch to a more market-driven economy and the effects of rapid growth within China. These are the more obvious changes in China. As well, there are numerous other changes that may not be readily observable to the investigator, but which affect environmental degradation and whose timing is similar to that of changes in the trade regime. This raises the danger that one may falsely attribute changes in pollution to changes in the trade regime when in fact they are due to something else.

There have been several studies which use a panel of cross-country data and ask whether or not various measures of environmental quality are systematically related to openness to trade, when other factors (such as income) are controlled for. Grossman and Krueger (1993) is an early study of this type, and Frankel and Rose (2005) is a recent example of this approach. The studies typically find that openness to trade either has no significant effect on environmental quality, or that it is slightly beneficial. That is, these studies suggest that while there is heterogeneity across countries and time in environmental outcomes, this variation is not due to trade per se but to other factors.

A weakness of this approach is that it looks for the average effect of trade on the environment, whereas if there were pollution haven effects, one could imagine the environment getting better in rich countries and worse in poor countries. These studies would still find that on average across countries there was not much effect. Antweiler *et al.* (2001) allow for the effects of trade on the environment to vary with country type, and in particular ask whether certain types of countries (such as those which are poor or capital abundant) are more likely to experience greater pollution from trade than other types of countries. They use data on only sulfur dioxide pollution. They find evidence that the pure effect of trade (controlling for scale, capital abundance and income) is to marginally shift sulfur-dioxide intensive production to richer countries. Since the rich countries have stricter environmental policy than poor countries, trade on average has a very small beneficial effect in reducing sulfur dioxide pollution on average. Moreover, because the trade-shifting effect is very small relative to income effects, the net effect is to reduce pollution for most countries in the sample. There are two important caveats to this result. First, it applies to only one type of pollution, and so we still need to do more work on other types of environmental problems. And second, Antweiler *et al.* find fairly strong evidence that capital accumulation is associated with increased sulfur dioxide pollution, even when the income-induced policy effect is taken into account. This raises the possibility that capital mobility may have very different effects on environmental outcomes than trade; however, more work needs to be done, since capital flows not just from rich to poor countries but also from poor to rich countries.

Conclusion

There is no evidence that trade has been a major source of environmental degradation. Much of the deterioration of environmental quality in developing countries is due to growth and capital accumulation, and not trade. It is likely that trade has stimulated some of this growth, and so trade may be indirectly implicated. However, poor countries want to grow, and so the relevant question is whether more open economies are more polluted than more closed economies, for a given level of income. The evidence suggests not.

It is also difficult to find support for the pollution haven hypothesis. There is a growing body of evidence that suggest that differences in environmental policy do affect competitiveness; however, environmental policy is just one of many sources of competitiveness, and most evidence suggests that other factors, such as productivity and labor costs, are a much more important determinant of trade and investment patterns than environmental policy. This is why most of the world's industrial pollution emission still comes from high income countries.

The evidence that environmental policy does affect competitiveness suggests that some of the concerns about the effects of liberalized trade on the political process determining the stringency of environmental policy may be justified. There are only a very small number of studies that directly try to determine whether the stringency of environmental policy is adversely affected by openness to trade. These studies have found some evidence that it is. There is also much evidence that the stringency of environmental policy increases with income and so the net effect of globalization on the stringency of policy is not at this point known. However, this recent work may have some implications for the design of trade agreements, suggesting that groups of countries which become deeply integrated will face pressure to develop institutions that lead to some coordination of environmental policy.

Notes

1.   An earlier version of this paper was prepared for and presented at the conference on 'Globalization and Free Trade: Who Wins? Who Loses?' sponsored by the Newkirk Center for Science and Society at the University of California, Irvine in October 2004. The author is particularly indebted to Joe DiMento and Carol McAusland for their encouragement and comments on this paper, and to Scott Taylor for helping to shape my thoughts on many of these issues throughout several years of collaboration on work in this field.
2.   See Langewiesche (2000).
3.   Most of my discussion in this chapter will focus on domestic pollution. For a non-technical discussion of other important environmental problems, such as renewable resource depletion and global pollution, see Copeland and Gulati (2004). For a more technical treatment of some of the issues discussed in this paper,

see Copeland and Taylor (2003, 2004). For another useful non-technical perspective from an economist on trade and the environment, see Frankel (2003).

4. Grossman and Krueger (1993) discuss this approach and attempt to measure each effect in the context of NAFTA; Copeland and Taylor (1994) develop a theoretical framework; and Antweiler *et al.* (2001) show how to estimate each effect empirically using a common data set.

5. Countries with air quality that did not meet EPA standards were required to implement a plan to improve air quality; typically this meant tighter emission regulations. particularly for new plants.

6. This means that they are measuring the effects of changes in the scale and composition of production and trade in manufactured goods over their time period.

7. Gawande (1999) provides evidence that governments respond to tariff reductions by increasing the use of non-tariff barriers to trade.

References

Antweiler, W., B. R. Copeland and M. S. Taylor (2001), 'Is Free Trade Good for the Environment?' *American Economic Review*, **91**(4), 877–90.

Becker, R. and V. Henderson (2000), 'Effects of Air Quality Regulations on Polluting Industries,' *Journal of Political Economy*, **108**(2), 379–421.

Copeland, B. R. and S. Gulati (2004), 'Trade and the Environment in Developing Economies,' Discussion Paper, Initiative for Policy Dialogue, Columbia University, in R. Lopez and M. A. Toman (eds), *Economic Development and Environmental Sustainability: New Policy Options*, New York: Oxford University Press.

Copeland, B. R. and M. S. Taylor (1994), 'North–South Trade and the Environment,' *Quarterly Journal of Economics*, **109**, 755–87.

Copeland, B. R. and M. S. Taylor (2003), *Trade and the Environment: Theory and Evidence*, Princeton, NJ: Princeton University Press.

Copeland, B. R. and M. S. Taylor (2004), 'Trade, Growth and The Environment,' *Journal of Economic Literature*, **42**(1), 7–71.

Dasgupta, S., A. Mody, S. Roy and D. Wheeler (2001), 'Environmental Regulation and Development: A Cross-Country Empirical Analysis,' *Oxford Development Studies*, **29**(2), 173–87.

Ederington, W. J and J. Minier (2003), 'Is Environmental Policy a Secondary Trade Barrier? An Empirical Analysis,' *Canadian Journal of Economics*, **36**, 137–54.

Ederington, W. J, A. Levinson and J. Minier (2004), 'Trade Liberalization and Pollution Havens,' *Advances in Economic Analysis and Policy*, **4**(2), Article 6, Berkeley, CA: Berkeley Electronic Press.

Eliste, P. and P. G. Fredriksson (2002),'Environmental Regulations, Transfers and Trade: Theory and Evidence,' *Journal of Environmental Economics and Management*, **43**(2), 234–50.

Frankel, J. A. (2003), 'The Environment and Globalization,' NBER Working Paper 10090.

Frankel, J. A. and A. K. Rose (2005), 'Is Trade Good or Bad for the Environment? Sorting out the Causality,' *Review of Economics and Statistics*, **87**(1), 85–91.

Gawande, K. (1999), 'Trade Barriers as Outcomes from Two-stage Games: Evidence,' *Canadian Journal of Economics*, **32**(4), 1028–56.

Greenstone, M. (2002), 'The Impacts of Environmental Regulations on Industrial Activity: Evidence from the 1970 and the 1977 Clean Air Act Amendments and the Census of Manufactures,' *Journal of Political Economy*, **110**, 1175–219.

Grossman, Gene M. and Alan B. Krueger (1993), 'Environmental Impacts of a North American Free Trade Agreement,' in Peter M. Garber (ed.), *The Mexico–US Free Trade Agreement*, Cambridge, MA and London: MIT Press, pp. 13–56.

Harbaugh, W., A. Levinson and D. Wilson (2002), ' Re-examining Empirical Evidence for an Environmental Kuznets Curve,' *Review of Economics and Statistics*, **84**, 541–51.

Hilton, H. and A. Levinson (1998), 'Factoring the Environmental Kuznets Curve: Evidence from Automotive Lead Emissions,' *Journal of Environmental Economics and Management*, **35**, 126–41.

Hokby, S. and T. Soderqvist (2003), 'Elasticities of Demand and Willingness to Pay for Environmental Services in Sweden,' *Environmental and Resource Economics*, **26**, 361–83

Kahn, Matthew (1997), 'Particulate Pollution Trends in the United States,' *Regional Science and Urban Economics*, **27**(1), 87–107.

Kriström, B. and P. Riera (1996), 'Is the Income Elasticity of Environmental Improvements Less Than One?' *Environmental and Resource Economics*, **7**, 45–55.

Jaffe, A., S. Peterson, P. Portney and R. Stavins (1995), 'Environmental Regulation and the Competitiveness of US Manufacturing: What Does the Evidence Tell Us?' *The Journal of Economic Literature*, **33**, 132–63.

Keller, W. and A. Levinson (2002), 'Pollution Abatement Costs and Foreign Direct Investment Inflows to US States,' *Review of Economics and Statistics*, **84**, 691–703.

Langewiesche, W. (2000), 'The Shipbreakers,' *The Atlantic Monthly*, **286**(2), 31–49.

Levinson, A. (1999), 'State Taxes and Interstate Hazardous Waste Shipments,' *American Economic Review*, **89**, 666–77.

Levinson, A. and M. S. Taylor (2004), 'Trade and the Environment: Unmasking the Pollution Haven Effect,' NBER Working Paper No. 10629.

List, J. A., W. W. McHone, D. L. Millimet and P. G. Fredriksson (2003), 'Effects of Environmental Regulations on Manufacturing Plant Births: Evidence from a Propensity Score Matching Estimator,' *Review of Economics and Statistics*, **85**(4), 944–52.

Pearce, D. W. and C. Palmer (2001), 'Public Spending and Environmental Protection: A Cross-country Policy Analysis,' *Journal for Fiscal Studies*, **22**(4), 403–56.

Porter, Michael E. and Claas van de Linde (1995), 'Toward a New Conception of the Environment-Competitiveness Relationship,' *Journal of Economic Perspectives*, **9**(4), 97–118.

Stern, David I. and Michael S. Common (2001), 'Is There an Environmental Kuznets Curve for Sulfur?,' *Journal of Environmental Economics and Management*, **41**(2), 162–78.

40 Trade agreements and Multilateral Environmental Agreements
Ken Belcher

Introduction

The impact of trade on the environment has become an increasingly important issue in recent years. While there is no conclusive evidence that trade in and of itself necessarily harms the environment, in fact some more recent empirical research indicates that freer trade may be good for the environment (for example Antweiler *et al.* 2001; Grossman and Krueger 1995). However, there is also a body of research that shows that the increased specialization of the economy, in response to trade opportunities, may be environmentally degrading if the expanding industry is more environmentally damaging, and that the increased scale of production in response to trade may result in greater usage of resources and increased waste emissions (for example Rock 1996). It should be noted that there is also evidence that trade may improve environmental conditions with specialization in environmentally improving or benign activities and changing social preferences, with higher income, that increases the demand for environmental improvement and the justification for environmental policies (Grossman and Krueger 1995). Interaction of economic growth and the environment was summarized by Arrow *et al.* (1995):

> Economic growth is not a panacea for environmental quality; indeed it is not even the main issue. What matters is the content of growth – the composition of inputs and outputs. This content is determined by, among other things, the economic institutions within which human activities are conducted. These institutions need to be designed so that they provide the right incentives for protecting the resilience of ecological systems. Such measures will not only promote greater efficiency in the allocation of environmental resources at all income levels, but they would also assure a sustainable scale of economic activity within the ecological life-support system.

The high degree of uncertainty associated with identifying and/or quantifying the environmental impacts of economic growth, development and trade has inspired a number of institutional responses. Specifically, Multilateral Environmental Agreements (MEA) have been created among groups of nations to address concerns over environmental degradation at a supranational level.

This chapter will discuss the interactions between the rules set out in the WTO agreement and the MEAs. Specifically the next section will explain the motivation behind developing MEAs using a simple economic model. Following this there will be a discussion of existing MEAs including their role and goals and an examination of trade measures included. The following section will explore the interaction between trade agreements and MEAs including areas of potential conflict, resolution and synergies. The last section will discuss future considerations in the interaction between trade and MEAs.

Economic development, trade and environmental damage
The fact that economic activity can negatively impact the local and global environment is well known and has received increasing attention in the last quarter of the twentieth century. The genesis of the disciplines of resource and environmental economics, and more recently ecological economics, was driven by concerns over this issue. The body of research that forms the foundation of the resource, environmental and ecological economic disciplines focuses almost exclusively on this broad issue. While the majority of the resource/environmental economics literature has not explicitly evaluated the impact of liberalized trade policies on environmental systems, the insight into the causes of environmental degradation provided by this work is important.

The economic model that is central to the evaluation of the environmental impact of economic activity highlights the conditions where the market forces of supply and demand fail to allocate resources in a way that is optimal from society's perspective. A simple graphical model can be used to depict a market failure associated with, for example, the emission of a substance that degrades some aspect of the global environment, such as greenhouse gases (GHGs) that contribute to climate change (Figure 40.1). For the purpose of this model it is assumed that there is some non-zero level of GHG emissions that is socially optimal. In this model GHG emissions provide benefits through the activities that, for example, burn fossil fuels to provide energy. The optimal quantity of emission is given by the point where the marginal benefit of emissions (demand) is just equal to the marginal cost imposed by that level of emissions. In this model, the private optimum GHG emission level will also be optimal for society if all costs are captured, including the costs imposed by a changing climate (for example coastal flooding, extreme weather events). However, the public good characteristics of the global climate, and the associated climate control services, leads to external costs in the form of environmental externalities which are not incorporated in economic prices and decision making such that consumers and producers do not take into account the full cost of their actions that emit GHGs, as represented by the divergence between private and social marginal costs

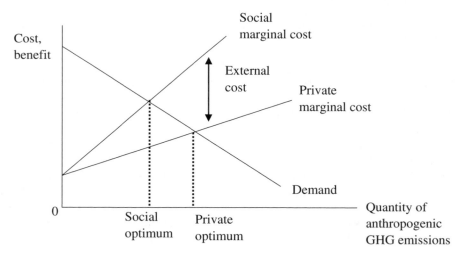

Figure 40.1   Market failure in the market for GHG emissions

(private marginal cost + external cost = social marginal cost) (Figure 40.1). The failure of the market to capture the environmental costs of climate change results in too many resources being invested in activities that emit GHGs and too few resources invested in emission abatement, resulting in levels of GHG emissions (private optimum in Figure 40.1) that are not socially optimal (social optimum in Figure 40.1). A wide range of environmental problems, including other forms of pollution, and water and land allocation, can be described using similar models. While these market failures are often due to ineffective institutions at the national level (for example environmental taxation, regulation) it has been argued that trade can act to magnify unsustainable patterns of economic activity thereby exacerbating environmental problems such as pollution and resource depletion (Brack 1997). MEAs represent an institutional response to correct the market failure that is at the heart of the environmental damage.

Multilateral Environmental Agreements

MEAs have been defined as agreements among governments that cooperatively address shared environmental problems by identifying cooperative solutions, creating mechanisms to equitably share benefits and burdens and to limit the use of unilateral measures (Stillwell and Tarasofsky 2001). MEAs have been identified a preferred institutional mechanism to deal with transboundary environmental problems. For example, Principle 12 of the Rio Declaration (United Nations 1992) clearly states that:

> Unilateral actions to deal with environmental challenges outside the jurisdiction of the importing country should be avoided. Environmental measures addressing transboundary or global environmental problems should, as far as possible, be based on an international consensus.

The Members of the WTO have also endorsed and supported the idea that environmental problems of a transboundary or global nature are best addressed by governments using multilateral solutions based on international cooperation and consensus and that due respect be afforded to both WTO agreements and MEAs (Sampson 2000).

The earliest multilateral treaty related to the environment was developed in 1868 and the total number has increased to over 500 international environmental treaties and other agreements, of which 323 are regional (UNEP 2001). At present, over 200 MEAs exist and there is continuing activity in the development of new MEAs to address ongoing and newly developing environmental problems. These MEAs can range from relatively small groups of signatory countries, to agreements involving over 180 countries. Global MEAs have been developed to address a wide range of environmental concerns or clusters (UNEP 2001) including the following agreements and appropriate protocols:

- Atmospheric protection
  - 1985 Vienna Convention for the Protection of the Ozone Layer – 1987 Montreal Protocol on Substances that Deplete the Ozone Layer
  - 1992 UN Framework Convention on Climate Change – 1997 Kyoto Protocol
- Biodiversity and wildlife
  - 1946 International Convention for the Regulation of Whaling
  - 1971 Ramsar Convention on Wetlands of International Importance
  - 1973 Convention on International Trade in Endangered Species (CITES)
  - 1979 Bonn Convention on the Conservation of Migratory Species

- 1992 UN Convention on Biological Diversity – 2001 Cartagena Protocol on Biosafety
- Marine environment
    - 1972 London Convention on the Prevention of Marine Pollution by Dumping Wastes and other Matter
    - The 1973 Convention for the Prevention of Pollution from Ships – 1978 Marpol Protocol
    - 1982 UN Convention on the Law of the Sea
    - 1995 Agreement on Conservation and Management of Straddling Fish Stocks and Highly Migratory Fish Stocks
- Chemicals and Hazardous Wastes
    - 1989 Basel Convention on the Control of Transboundary Movements of Hazardous Wastes and their Disposal
    - 1998 Rotterdam Convention on the Prior Informed Consent Procedure for Certain Hazardous Chemicals and Pesticides in International Trade
    - 2001 Stockholm Convention on Persistent Organic Pollutants. (Brack and Gray 2003)

There are also a number of more regional agreements addressing region specific concerns.

MEAs have proven to be a very dynamic, rapidly evolving body of international law as jurisdictions attempt to shape effective, efficient and equitable responses to accelerating, and potentially irreversible, ecological damage (OECD 1994). Overall, this collection of agreements provides a fairly broad framework dealing with existing transboundary environmental issues. However, some subjects are more effectively covered than others with such issues as forestry, environmental impact of ocean fisheries and coastal zone management being identified as having weak or insufficient coverage by existing MEAs (Brack and Gray 2003; UNEP 2001). These areas of weak coverage notwithstanding, it seems evident that a significant proportion of regional and global economic activity may be influenced by MEAs in some way.

MEAs and trade

Existing MEAs include general to very specific objectives with respect to the environmental issue being addressed. Further, the objectives and priorities of the collection of MEAs are very wide ranging as influenced by the different stage of implementation of the many agreements. In a review of 41 MEAs UNEP (2001) identified the following cross-cutting priorities: (a) strengthening of the capacity of Parties or member states to meet their obligations or responsibilities under these agreements; (b) enhancing membership of governments in the MEA; (c) public education and awareness; (d) strengthening scientific basis for decision-making; and (e) strengthening international partnerships. In order to meet these objectives and priorities each agreement incorporates a set of mechanisms, guidelines and rules that provide guidance in delivery, and in some cases enforcement of actions. While the menu of tools used by the MEAs varies, approximately 30 of the MEAs have been identified as incorporating some measures to regulate or restrain trade in target substances or products (WTO 2003).

In the trade policy context, trade measures are defined as any policy instrument that attach requirements, conditions or restrictions on imported or exported products or services themselves, or the process of their importation or exportation, and can range from trade bans to product standards, from notification procedures to labeling requirements (OECD 1999). More specifically, the policies and measures included in MEAs that may impact international trade include: (a) reporting requirement – the extent of trade in a specific product must be monitored and reported; (b) labeling requirement – traded products must be labeled in some way to identify the product or process characteristics; (c) requirement for movement documents and/or notification of consent – trade in products cannot proceed without documentation indicating consent of the involved states; (d) targeted trade bans – banned trade in specified products with particular states (generally non-complying parties or non-parties); (e) general trade bans – trade in specified products with any state is not permitted and often accompanied by production and consumption bans within the applying state; and (f) market transformation measures – taxes, charges, subsidies and other fiscal and non-fiscal measures such as government procurement applied to products to increase market share for desired products and reduce it for non-desired products to comply with the MEA requirements (Brack and Gray 2003).

The broad range of MEA trade measures presented in the previous paragraph can be designated as either specific – the measure is explicitly described in the MEA and is a mandatory obligation of the agreement, or non-specific – the measure is not explicitly described in the agreement but may be applied by parties to comply with their obligations or fulfilling MEA objectives. Therefore, whether specific or non-specific, trade measures have been deemed to have a role in helping MEA parties to meet the objectives and priorities of the international agreement. For example, the OECD (1999) argues that 'even if trade is not the sole cause of the broader environmental issues at stake, the international community can address limited aspects of the problems by bringing environmental considerations to bear on one of the points at which domestic-based issues have an international aspect, namely when trade occurs'.

The role of trade measures in MEAs
While it is fairly well understood that certain MEAs do contain trade measures, it is worthwhile examining the role that these trade measures play in enabling MEA parties to meet the agreement's priorities and objectives. One of the more common roles of trade measures within an MEA is to provide a means of monitoring and controlling trade (including complete exclusion in some cases) in products where the uncontrolled trade would lead to, or contribute to, environmental damage. This type of trade measure is incorporated in a number of MEAs. For example, CITES prohibits trade in listed endangered species in the absence of export permits or import licenses, while the Basel Convention requires prior notification and consent from import, export and transit states for the shipment of hazardous waste (WTO 2003). Brack and Gray (2003) also highlight the fact that the closer regulation of trade and enhanced tracking and verification procedures is a popular policy response to the growing problem of 'international environmental crime' whereby agents evade environmental laws and regulations involving cross-boundary movements of goods and substances.

A second common role of trade measures within MEAs is to provide a means for the party to comply with the requirements of the MEA such that controls on trade are required in order to achieve other objectives of the agreement (Brack and Gray 2003). For example, the Montreal Protocol requires parties to control consumption and production of ozone depleting substances, where production is defined as 'production plus imports minus exports'. Therefore, parties must impose some control over trade, including voluntary agreements, product labeling, taxes or import restrictions or bans, if they are to satisfy their control obligations (Brack and Gray 2003). In addition, Brack *et al.* (1999) concluded that the objectives and requirements of the Kyoto Protocol suggest an important role for this type of trade measure if the agreement enters into force. While this category of trade measures is considered non-specific, they may prove to be an increasingly important part of the debate on MEA trade measures as new MEAs are developed and current MEAs evolve to meet changing pressures.

A third common role of trade measures within MEAs is to provide a means of enforcing the MEA by forbidding trade with non-parties or parties that do not comply with the MEA. This application of trade measures is to back up the assumption that compliance with the MEA is costly, a cost which some countries (non-parties or non-complying parties) will try to avoid. Therefore, the trade restrictions, usually trade bans, are aimed at preventing these countries or industries from gaining a competitive advantage in trade with states controlled by the MEA (the problem of environmental leakage arising from less than universal participation) and thereby maximize the participation in the MEA (Brack 1996). This category of trade measures represents the most drastic interference with international trade. An example of this category of trade measure is present in CITES which states that trade with non-parties is not permitted in the absence of documentation equivalent to a CITES permit. Where countries have a record of non-compliance, CITES recommends parties take stricter domestic measures than those provided by the treaty including complete prohibition of trade against the offending country. As of late 2000, CITES trade bans have been threatened on an estimated 37 countries of which 17 have been subject to general CITES or species-specific trade bans (Brack and Gray 2003). It is interesting to note that in almost all of these cases the offending country has come back into compliance or acceded to the Convention. This observation seems to suggest that this type of measure is an effective tool for the MEA. A more detailed discussion of effectiveness is provided in the following section.

MEA trade measure effectiveness
An examination of trade measures found in MEAs should include an evaluation of the effectiveness of these trade measures in helping the parties meet the objectives of the MEA. However, any such evaluation of effectiveness of trade measures must consider legal, economic, political and scientific aspects and can encompass broad cost/benefit analysis to very specific measurement of scientific factors or legislative implementation (OECD 1999). In addition, effectiveness and/or the ability to measure this will be determined by the specific characteristics of the MEA and the environmental issue that it targets. As a result, it would be difficult or impossible to generalize about trade measure effectiveness in MEAs. Such a specific analysis of effectiveness is beyond the scope of this chapter.

The OECD (1999) reviewed the effectiveness of trade measures in CITES, the Montreal Protocol and the Basel Convention, and concluded that trade measures can be an appropriate and effective policy measure to use in MEAs for example: (a) when the international community agrees to collectively tackle and manage international trade as a part of the environmental problem; (b) when trade controls are required to make regulatory systems comprehensive in their coverage; (c) to discourage free-riding which can often be a barrier to effective international co-operation; and (d) to ensure compliance with the MEA. The study also cautioned that, to be effective, trade measures should be carefully designed and targeted to the environmental objective and should consider all environmental and economic ramifications, consider the technical and institutional capacity of all countries, ensure adequate flexibility of trade measures as MEAs evolve and should base non-equal treatment of countries on clear environment-related criteria. Members of the WTO, including the United States and Europe, have stated that in some cases, trade measures were the most effective tools available to achieve an MEA's goals, but should be determined on a case by case basis (WTO 1997).

Although trade measures in MEAs have, to some extent, helped MEA parties meet their objectives, there is a strong argument that trade restrictions are usually a suboptimal method for correcting market failures (Leger *et al.* 1999). Trade measures in MEAs, including trade barriers, are argued to be attractive means for firms and nations to protect themselves from international economic competition but defended on the basis of addressing environmental damage. Protectionist vested interests have recently begun to argue that unfair foreign competition arises due to less stringent environmental regulations and/or enforcement of those regulations (Kerr 2002). An approach that is considered superior to trade measures to address market failures that result in environmental damage is the development of effective domestic policy (Belcher *et al.* 2003).

Interaction of MEAs and trade rules

An assessment of the areas of interaction, including conflict and resolution, between MEA rules and WTO rules are necessarily case specific and as a result are beyond the scope of this chapter. However, there is a literature that details some of these specific areas of conflict and interaction within a range of existing MEAs (for example Brack and Gray 2003; WTO 2003; UNEP 2001; OECD 1999). This section will highlight some of the issues relating to areas of potential conflict, resolution and synergies with respect to MEAs and the trade rules administered by the WTO.

Areas of conflict

The potential for conflict between MEA trade measures and the rules for trade overseen by the WTO has been a central part of the trade and environment debate for the last decade. However, the potential for a conflict occurs only where a party to the treaties cannot comply with the obligations under both treaties simultaneously. In other words, a conflict does not exist unless one treaty requires a particular course of action that is either prohibited in the other agreement, or the latter agreement requires the opposite course of action (Brack and Gray 2003). It is useful, in this discussion, to highlight those WTO principles that are most likely to be compromised by trade activities adopted to meet MEA objectives:

- *GATT Article 1*   General Most Favored Nation Treatment – requires that GATT signatories must not discriminate between trading partners in the trade of like products through the granting of most favored nation (MFN) status. This may be particularly important from an environmental perspective where two products are considered 'like' even though one may be produced using more environmentally damaging practices than the other. The criteria for determining when products are 'like' products have been subject to extensive deliberation and adjudication in past GATT/WTO dispute settlement cases (OECD 1999). Therefore, a conflict could arise if a country were to deny another WTO member MFN status in implementing its obligations under an MEA.

- *GATT Article III*   National Treatment – requires that imported and domestic 'like products' must be treated in the same way with respect to internal regulations and taxes. As an example, regulations and taxes have been used by parties to help meet the consumption and production phase-out commitments of the Montreal Protocol. If these regulations or taxes were applied differently to imported compared to domestic products, this could be considered a violation of Article III. However, this has not yet occurred (OECD 1999).
- *GATT Article XI*   General Elimination of Quantitative Restrictions – requires that no prohibitions or restrictions, other than duties, taxes or other charges (for example no export or import bans) shall be applied to imported or exported products. A number of MEAs recommend or even require import and/or export bans (for example CITES, Montreal Protocol) which may violate Article XI.
- *GATT Article XIII*   Non-discriminatory Administration of Quantitative Restrictions – requires that 'like' products coming from, or going to, all countries be treated in the same way with respect to import and export licenses, prohibitions and quotas. It seems that similar MFN (non-discriminatory) issues could arise under this Article as in Article I.

The above Articles represent areas of the GATT/WTO where measures implemented by a MEA member in order to meet their MEA commitments may be determined to be in conflict with WTO obligations. In contrast, the following Article appears to accommodate trade restrictions in the pursuit of environmental protection under certain circumstances. This Article is important in that it may allow countries to adopt MEA measures that are inconsistent with the above Articles, and others.

- *GATT Article XX*   General Exceptions – the clauses that are of particular interest in MEA/Trade conflicts are: paragraph (b) allows countries to pursue measures deemed 'necessary to protect human, animal or plant life or health'; and paragraph (g) permits measures relating to conservation or exhaustible natural resources. The *chapeau* to Article XX specifies limits, the extent to which such measures can be applied such that the measures must not result in unjustified or arbitrary discrimination, or be a disguised restriction on international trade.

Despite the potential role of Article XX in disputes involving MEA commitments, there is significant confusion concerning the interpretation and uncertainty in the application of its specific terms such as when is a trade restrictive regulation necessary (Belcher *et al.* 2003). For example, there is disagreement among WTO members over whether Article XX can be used to permit the use of trade measures to deal with extrajurisdictional environmental challenges (WTO 1997). Nonetheless, it seems that Article XX will serve an important role in the resolution of a dispute that arises between WTO rules and MEA rules.

Dispute resolution

At the time of writing there has not yet been a dispute involving an MEA trade measure in conflict with a WTO commitment. Therefore, any analysis of how such a dispute would be resolved would have to be purely speculative. However, Brack and Gray (2003) provide an in depth analysis of the important considerations in the resolution of such disputes. The following section will highlight the relevant parts of this analysis.

Given that international law governs the WTO agreements and their interaction with MEAs, and that MEAs are recognized as international treaties and therefore form part of international law, there appears to be considerable scope for an Appellate Body to consider MEAs in its interpretation of WTO agreements, including Article XX. It is worthwhile to note that in 1998 the Appellate Body decided that the interpretation of Article XX is to be read in light of the 'contemporary concerns of the community of nations about the protection and conservation of the environment'. This decision appears to make Article XX particularly relevant to prevent disputes involving MEAs. Brack and Gray (2003) argue that in interpreting Article XX 'it seems likely that there would be a concerted attempt to find coherence between MEA and WTO obligations and determine whether MEAs and the WTO agreements could be interpreted in a manner that avoids reading that one agreement requires what another prohibits'. As a result, by avoiding a ruling that one agreement is in conflict with another, the focus of the dispute analysis can be on the particular measure taken by the WTO member, rather than the treaty on which it is based. Therefore, these authors feel that when possible dispute decisions will be avoided.

Despite the evidence and analysis that disputes involving MEA trade measures and WTO commitments will be avoided, there will likely be circumstances where this will not work. Brack and Gray (2003) argue that the measure taken pursuant to an MEA could be deemed to be a justified measure under Article XX. As noted earlier, multilateral action has been designated through international agreement as the preferred approach to deal with transboundary environmental issues. The existence of the MEA, or negotiations leading up to an agreement, could help to provide the 'necessity' of the exception claimed under Article XX(b), whether the measure is 'related to' the objective sought in the trade measure under Article XX(g), and – as a demonstration of good faith to find a multilateral solution – that is not 'arbitrary under the *chapeau* to Article XX' (Brack and Gray 2003).

With respect to the actual process of dispute settlement, both MEAs and the WTO include mechanisms for settling disputes. However, as written into the agreement, WTO dispute settlement is compulsory and as such may be viewed as more effective than the mechanisms in the MEA. The dispute settlement mechanisms contained in MEAs include negotiation, mediation, conciliation and arbitration. However, there is no instance in which these MEA mechanisms have ever been used. Brack and Gray (2003) state that it is difficult to conceive of a bilateral dispute arising within most MEAs and if such a dispute did arise over a trade measure it seems likely that parties may prefer to refer it to the WTO's relatively tougher dispute resolution system. However, the MEAs may have an important role in such disputes settlement processes by providing information to the WTO and providing expert participation in the WTO process. This could help broaden the information available to the WTO dispute settlement mechanism and break down its institutional isolation from non-trade concerns (Brack and Gray 2003).

Discussions at the Doha Ministerial Conference addressed the relationship between WTO rules and MEAs. It was agreed that negotiations to clarify the relationship between WTO rules and MEAs which contain specific trade obligations would commence. However, it was stated that the outcome of the negotiations would be limited to conflicts between WTO Members who are parties to an MEA (WTO 2004). In essence, the WTO Members agreed to clarify the legal relationship between WTO rules and MEAs, rather than leaving the matter to the WTO's dispute settlement body to resolve individual cases. Specifically, with respect to MEAs the Members agreed to negotiate: (a) information exchange – develop procedures for regular information exchange between secretariats of MEAs and the WTO and (b) observer status – develop criteria for observer status being granted to MEAs (at present the process is blocked for political reasons) (WTO 2002). However, Brack and Gray (2003) argue that the discussion has been limited to a narrow subset of the wider debate in that it would be difficult to conceive of an issue arising from the MEAs now in force that would be taken to the WTO and not be dealt with within the MEA framework. There appears to be more uncertainty over non-specific trade measures and over the party–non-party relationships, but these are not addressed in the Doha mandate. As such, these authors suggest that, while it was hoped the Doha conference would have stimulated some resolution to the MEA–WTO debate, there appears to be little sign of any conclusions emerging.

Proposed resolutions

A number of proposals have been put forward to develop ways in which the relationship between the WTO and MEAs could be refined in order to avoid conflicts that may arise when MEA objectives and methods are considered at cross-purposes with WTO objectives. At the heart of most of these proposals is improved cooperation or greater synergy between MEA agreements and the WTO. For example Brack and Gray (2003) proposed the negotiation of a new WTO agreement on MEAs, similar in status to other WTO agreements. Development of this agreement would avoid amending existing rules (for example broadening Article XX), and could create a very clear set of rules that would apply only to MEA trade measures. The agreement would cover, for example: (a) the definition of an MEA; (b) the definition of trade measures, and the treatment of different categories of measures, possibly exempting these measures from dispute; (c) definition of non-specific and specific measures for the particular MEA; and (d) mechanisms for settling disputes between MEA parties.

Another mechanism to improve synergy is through increased information exchange between MEA secretariats and the WTO, as specified in the Doha Declaration. In fact it has been argued that simple information exchange is not enough and mechanisms should be put in place to facilitate exchanging advice since the design of MEAs and WTO agreements will be made stronger with a better understanding of the other's operation framework (Brack and Gray 2003). This approach would help the development of MEAs and the WTO to ensure that measures used, including trade measures, are consistent. A common proposal to facilitate this increased interaction is through the granting of observer status to MEA secretariats on relevant WTO bodies as a means to develop a more open and transparent trading system. As discussed earlier, the process for granting of observer status has been blocked for political reasons. This change would also ensure that the WTO panels will be better able to make use of the expertise of MEA secretariats and experts.

In closing, it seems that any developments in the area of resolution between MEAs and the WTO will be slow in coming with apparent disagreement over the necessity of such negotiations. For example, in 2000 Switzerland stimulated discussion in this area by calling for a WTO decision to prevent unnecessary conflicts between the WTO and trade measures in MEA through mutual supportiveness whereby the WTO and MEAs would focus on their primary competence. This call was supported by a number of Members, including Canada, Europe, Hungary, Iceland, Japan and Norway. However, other Members, including Australia, New Zealand and the United States, felt that the WTO already provides a sufficient framework to facilitate this mutual supportiveness. Further, Hong Kong, China, India, Brazil, Malaysia and Pakistan, among others, said that concerns in this area should not be exaggerated with only 10 percent of the MEAs containing trade measures and there not being a challenge to date. These members felt that there was no need to clarify WTO rules in this regard and that trade measures are just part of a carefully balanced package of instruments in MEAs (WTO 2000).

References

Antweiler, W., B. R. Copeland and M. S. Taylor, (2001), 'Is Free Trade Good for the Environment?' *The American Economic Review*, **91**(4), 877–908.

Arrow, K., B. Bolin, R. Costanza, P. Dasgupta, C. Folke, C. S. Holling, B-O. Jansson, S. Levin, K.-G. Mäler, C. Perrings and D. Pimentel (1995), 'Economic Growth, Carrying Capacity, and the Environment', *Science*, **268**, 520–21.

Belcher, K., A. L. Hobbs and W. A. Kerr (2003), 'The WTO and Environmental Sustainability: Is There a Conflict?' *International Journal of Environment and Sustainable Development*, **2**(1), 2–18.

Brack, D. (1996), *International Trade and the Montreal Protocol*, Royal Institute of International Affairs, London: Earthscan Publications Ltd.

Brack, D. (1997), 'The Trade and Environment Debate: Guide to the Issues', in D. Brack (ed.) *Trade and Environment: Conflict or Compatibility?* Proceedings of the The Royal Institute of International Affairs conference, London, April.

Brack, D. and K. Gray (2003), *Multilateral Environmental Agreements and the WTO: Report September 2003*, The Royal Institute of International Affairs – Sustainable Development Programme, International Institute for Sustainable Development.

Brack, D., M. Grubb and C. Windram, (1999), *International Trade and Climate Change Policies*, Royal Institute of International Affairs, London: Earthscan Publications Ltd.

Grossman, G. M. and A. B. Krueger (1995), 'Economic Growth and the Environment', *Quarterly Journal of Economics*, **110**(2), 353–77.

Kerr, W. A. (2002), 'Who Should Make the Rules of Trade? The Complex Issue of Multilateral Environmental Agreements', *The Estey Centre Journal of International Law and Trade Policy*, **3**(2), 163–75, www.esteyjournal.com.

Leger, L. A., J. D. Gaisford and W. A. Kerr (1999), 'Labour Market Adjustments to International Trade Shocks', in S. Bhagwan Dahiya (ed.) *The Current State of Economic Science*, Vol. 4, Rohtak: Spellbound Publications PVT Ltd, 2011–34.

Organisation for Economic Co-operation and Development (1994), *Trade and Environment: Processes and Production Methods*, Paris: OECD Publications Service.

Organisation for Economic Co-operation and Development, (1999), *Trade Measures in Multilateral Environmental Agreements*, Paris: OECD Publications Service.

Rock, M. (1996), 'Pollution Intensity of GDP and Trade Policy: Can the World Bank be Wrong?' *World Development*, **24**: 471–79.

Sampson, G. P. (2000), *Trade, Environment, and the WTO: The Post-Seattle Agenda*, Policy Essay No. 27, Overseas Development Council, Baltimore, MA: Johns Hopkins University Press.

Stillwell, M and R. Tarasofsky, (2001), 'Towards Coherent Environmental and Economic Governance: Legal and Practical Approaches to MEA–WTO Linkages', a WWF–CIEL Discussion Paper, October.

United Nations (1992), *Report of the United Nations Conference on Environment and Development. Annex I: Rio Declaration on Environment and Development. Principle 12*, A/CONF.151/26 (Vol. I), 12 August.

United Nations Environment Programme (2001), *International Environment Governance: Multilateral Environmental Agreements (MEAs)*, UNEP/IGM/1/INF/3, 6 April.

World Trade Organization (1997), *Trade and Environment News Bulletin*, TE/021 – 19 December, http://www.wto.org/english/tratop_e/envir_e/te021_e.htm accessed October 2004.

World Trade Organization (2000), *Trade and Environment News Bulletin.* TE/033 – 10 July 2000, http://www.wto.org/english/tratop_e/envir_e/te033_e.htm accessed October 2004.

World Trade Organization (2002), *The Doha Declaration Explained: Trade and Environment*, http://www.wto.org/english/tratop_e/dda_e/dohaexplained_e.html#environment accessed October 2004.

World Trade Organization (2003), *Matrix on Trade Measures Pursuant to Selected Multilateral Environmental Agreements*, Committee on Trade and Environment Special Session, WT/CTE/W/160.Rev.2, TN/TE/S/5, April.

World Trade Organization (2004), *Trade and Environment at the WTO: Background Document*, April 2004, http://www.wto.org/english/tratop_e/envir_e/envir_backgrnd_e/contents_e.htm accessed October 2004.

PART VI

TRADE POLICY AND DEVELOPMENT

41 Import substitution industrialization
James B. Gerber

Origins of import substitution industrialization

Import substitution industrialization (ISI) is an economic development strategy that was in wide use from approximately the end of World War II through the mid-1980s. At its zenith in the 1960s, it was adopted by developing countries in Africa, Asia, and especially Latin America. ISI was characterized by over valued exchange rates, high levels of protectionism, and extensive government interventions into production, all of which was justified by the assumption that market failures would limit industrial development in the world's poorer regions. Macroeconomic problems associated with the Third World Debt Crisis of the 1980s caused many nations to reject ISI policies, although it remains a major component of development policy in a number of countries, Uzbekistan for example.

In an early critique of the performance of ISI policies, Little, Scitovsky and Scott defined it as follows:

> Industries have been set up to produce goods that were previously imported, and these goods have mainly been sold in the home market. Governments have ensured the profitability of these industries by protecting them against the competing imports through tariffs and controls. (Little *et al.*, 1970, 1)

Although ISI is usually considered to have begun at the end of World War II, many countries adopted similar economic strategies prior to then as a way to cope with the loss of export markets and the unavailability of manufactured imports during the two world wars and the worldwide interwar depression (Thorp 1992). The first empirical justification and theoretical expression of ISI as an economic development strategy dates from the more-or-less simultaneous work of Hans Singer (United Nations 1949) and Raul Prebisch (1950). Singer and Prebisch both wrote about the problems of developing countries, and although their work was equally important to the intellectual development of ISI, Prebisch is often given credit since Singer's 1949 work was published by the United Nations without attribution (Toye and Toye 2003). As the Executive Secretary (1948–1962) of the UN's Economic Commission for Latin America, Prebisch was able to disseminate his work widely and directly influenced postwar development strategies throughout Latin America, and indirectly in Asia and Africa.

The fundamental reasons for ISI

In its most basic expression, ISI policy asserts that the terms of trade (the ratio of export and import prices) for primary commodity producing countries has a long run tendency to decline. The reasons given differed between Singer and Prebisch, and Prebisch himself seems to have emphasized different elements over the course of his life. For Singer, the key was that developed economies experience productivity gains in manufacturing as higher incomes, while productivity gains in primary commodity production show up as lower commodity prices. To the extent that industrial economies do not produce raw materials, and that developing countries export them, the asymmetry in the effects of productivity gains is also an asymmetry in the effect on developed and developing countries. Singer (1948, 1950) argued that the basic cause of this difference was monopoly power and strong labor unions in industrial nations.

Singer's ideas were consistent with Prebisch's emphasis on the asymmetric power relations between countries in the 'Center' and the 'Periphery,' but Prebisch also added the effects of the business cycle. In his view (Prebisch 1950), prices (and wages) rise during economic expansions, but are sticky downwards during slumps, particularly in the Center where unions protect workers. Prebisch argued that rising primary product prices during economic booms lead to strong contractions in industrial production, and cause severe price declines for primary products. Hence, industrialized nations drain resources from developing countries regardless of their unionization or the relative bargaining power of labor. Much later, Prebisch (1984) seems to have dropped this explanation and resorted to the more frequently encountered argument first advanced by Kindleberger (1943), that Engel's Law supports the idea of a falling terms of trade for primary commodities.

The position taken by Singer and Prebisch regarding the tendency of primary product prices to decline is notable for standing classical theory on its head. According to Malthus and other nineteenth century classical economists, primary commodities should become increasingly scarce as population growth outstrips the ability of farmers and other producers to keep up.

Given that agricultural land, minerals and forest reserves are finite, classical economists thought that the problem for society would be an ever-increasing price for commodities such as foodstuffs, until a famine or some other calamity checked the demand. Kindelberger's use of Engel's Law, as well as the arguments given by Prebisch and Singer for a decline in commodity prices, were a break with this intellectual history since they argued that it is manufactured goods, not primary commodities, that become relatively more expensive.

The consequences of a long run decline in the terms of trade for primary products is that exporters of coffee, sugar, bananas, tin, copper and so forth, will be required to produce increasingly larger amounts of their commodities in order to obtain the same quantity of imported manufactured goods. That is, if developing countries rely on their traditional exports of raw materials as the primary means for fostering economic growth and development, they will run into a growing shortage of foreign exchange and growing barriers to the purchase of imported goods. The latter are essential given that imports are the means by which developing countries obtain new technology. In other words, traditional export dependencies will limit the access of developing countries to new technologies, and make industrial development all but impossible.

The argument that industrialization cannot be financed through the export of primary commodities rests on a belief that: (a) the terms of trade have a long run tendency to decline for primary commodity producers; (b) foreign exchange shortages will result; and (c) the best way to address this problem is with an activist, state-sponsored development strategy designed to block certain imports and support the growth of import-competing industries. Point (a) remains contentious today, while point (b) follows logically if (a) is an accurate reading of the historical record.[1] Point (c) is perhaps the most complex of the ideas since it implicitly makes a number of assumptions about the quality of institutions, the relationship between imports and economic growth, and the ability of planners to target the industries that have a large impact on economic development without simultaneously creating unintended negative consequences elsewhere in the economy.

Did the terms of trade decline?
Looking first at the validity of the Singer–Prebisch Hypothesis about the terms of trade, there does not appear to be a strong consensus in either direction. The data marshaled by Singer and used by Prebisch, covered the years from 1876 to 1948. It shows a clear downward trend in the terms of trade for primary commodities up to 1938, with a partial recovery thereafter. In 1948, the last year of this analysis, the terms of trade were still about 30 percent below their 1876 level (United Nations 1949). Since the original work by Singer and Prebisch, a large body of research has used more advanced statistical techniques to derive more reliable measures of long run trends in primary commodity prices, but without arriving at a consensus. In 1988, Grilli and Yang published an influential study showing a 0.6 percent per year decline from 1900 to 1986. While their statistical series was adopted by many researchers, not all of them agreed with their interpretation. For example, Bleaney and Greenaway (1993) found that while primary commodity prices probably declined from 1900 to 1991, the trend was very slight, and included a long period of stability from 1925 to 1980. Further, Bleaney and Greenaway argue that there was a high degree of variability between different commodity categories, making an overall generalization difficult, and perhaps explaining the failure of economists to reach a consensus.

Hadass and Williamson (2003) take an original approach by pointing out that Singer's data is for commodity prices in the United Kingdom, and that imports and exports are measured asymmetrically since the former include transport and insurance costs (CIF prices), while the latter do not (FOB prices). The use of UK prices is problematic since those prices are not the same as country-specific prices earned by exporters or paid by importers. Probably the biggest problem with the data is that given the worldwide decline in transport costs over the last decades of the nineteenth century and first decades of the twentieth century, CIF import prices fell everywhere and they fell independently of the movement of commodity prices. Consequently, an observed increase in the UK's terms of trade does not imply the opposite for its trading partners or its raw material suppliers. Hadass and Williams find that all countries experienced increases, not decreases, in their terms of trade, 1870 to 1914, which were driven by falling transport costs.

Other impulses to ISI
Technical justifications for ISI based on a questionable belief in the long run tendency for the terms of trade to decline are, in some respects, irrelevant. At the end of World War II, most countries were on the path toward economic policies involving much higher levels of government intervention. Industrial economies adopted Keynesian fiscal policies in order to tame the business cycle, while economic planners in developing countries took responsibility for directing their national economic development. The later tendency was reinforced by several independent factors in Latin America, the region which might be credited or blamed with having done the most to originate and employ ISI policies,.

First, Prebisch offered a set of reasons for state intervention in support of industrial development based on his use of the Center–Periphery model of international economic relations. In this model, the Center, represented by the most industrialized economies of the world, organizes an international economic order for the purpose of benefiting its economic interests. This view grew out of Prebisch's and Singer's research in the late 1940s and early 1950s, which sought to understand whether the former colonial powers would duplicate their economic relationships with their former colonies without resorting to direct political control. Prebisch (1984) argued that the arrangement of market relations would cause former colonies to continue supplying raw materials, that technological penetration would be too slow to significantly raise living standards, and that whatever technology passed from the Center to the Periphery would exclusively remain in the export sector.

A second factor leading to the adoption of ISI policies grew out of Latin America's historical experience. The region emerged at the end of World War II with large foreign exchange reserves that had been earned through wartime exports of raw materials. The absence of imported consumer and industrial goods during the war created a natural form of import substitution, or 'import swallowing' (Hirschman 1968; Thorp 1992) and constituted a set of infant industries that were as yet unable to compete against producers in industrial nations. Not only did this justify some level of import barrier, but it also identified ISI with the much older infant industry arguments for protection.

A third factor leading to ISI policies was the impact of the United States' focus on Europe, where the reconstruction needs and the potential security threat were greater than in Latin America. The Eurocentric focus of US policy caused concern in Latin America and led directly to the creation of the Economic Commission for Latin America,[2] as a kind of parallel organization to the UN's European Commission. ECLA gave Prebisch a prestigious venue which he used to spread his ideas and influence development thinking.

The policy and tools of ISI
The assumption that markets will not lead to industrialization is key to ISI. In many respects, the presumed reason for the market's failure did not matter. Market failures linked ISI to the older and widely accepted infant industry argument for protection and gave a green light to state policies that were designed to support manufacturing through various interventions.

ISI was proposed as a series of well-defined, highly sequential and tightly staged efforts (Hirschman 1968). In stage one, countries were expected to concentrate on consumer nondurables such as textiles, apparel, food processing and furniture. In most cases, developing countries are suited to produce these items, and there is less need for protection. Nevertheless, the fact that they may have had a comparative advantage did not stop countries from implementing protectionist trade policies. Stage two was intended to add intermediate goods and consumer and producer durables to the country's industrial portfolio. Goods such as petrochemicals, machinery, autos and appliances tend to be much more capital intensive, and to rely on scale economies for their efficient production. The capital requirements of these industries, together with their scale and human skill requirements, put developing countries at a disadvantage, particularly if the domestic market is small. The importance of scale economies depends on the specific product, but in small economies the lack of scale caused domestic resource costs to be above world levels (Balassa 1980). This led directly to internationally uncompetitive industries and a need for protection.

Multiple policies were employed to protect the home market by import substituting countries. The policy maker's tool box included tariffs, quantitative restrictions – often in the form of import licenses – multiple exchange rates, and various forms of direct industrial subsidies. The latter included loans at subsidized rates, tax concessions and favorable foreign exchange rates. Ultimately, many governments engaged in direct production through nationalization of existing industries, or the development of new industries that were nationally owned. Steel, airlines, telephone networks and a variety of other industries were placed under national ownership. In some cases, for example telephone and utility networks, the logic of natural monopolies under the technologies of the 1950s and 1960s, justified nationalization, or some form of national regulation. In others, for example steel, the presumed importance of the industry and its hoped-for spillovers caused governments to take direct control in order to ensure production.

Obstacles to import substituting industrialization
The consensus among economists is that the barriers to industrializing through import substitution are large and overcoming them is difficult, if not impossible. There are a number of reasons for this view, but four stand out. These are the difficulty of actively managing a system of tariff and quotas so that they provide the desired incentives, the absence of economies of scale when production is directed exclusively or almost exclusively toward the domestic market, the problem of public choice and government failure, and the general issue of widespread distortions in the price system.

Given that most developing countries have a comparative advantage in one or more lines of production that are singled out for development in ISI's first stage, it is not surprising that the most serious obstacles to implementation occur in the second stage, when countries attempt to develop more sophisticated, capital and skill intensive, production lines. One current of analysis, represented by Balassa (1980), points toward the lack of economies of scale, and the fact that high rates of protection necessitate a careful attention to inter-industry relationships. Tariffs on intermediate inputs will harm final goods producers that use those inputs, and if economic planners are not careful, they create unintended negative impacts on industries using imported inputs. Balassa (1980: 9–10), for example, cites cases in Argentina and Hungary where high tariffs killed export industries that used imported goods. Similarly, tariffs can delay investment in a desired industry (for example, aluminum) by providing strong investment incentives to a protected industry (for example, steel).

The lack of careful attention to inter-industry relations also meant that final goods producers often received higher than intended rates of protection. The effective rate of protection exceeds the nominal rate if the value added in the home country is only a small share of the total value of the final good, and intermediate goods enter the home market either tariff free or at low rates of protection. In that case, the full weight of the tariff falls on the share of the value added in the home country. Little *et al.* (1970: 174) estimate, for example, that effective rates of protection in India and Pakistan exceeded 200 percent and were over 100 percent in Argentina and Brazil.

An additional problem of the administration of the trade regime is examined by Bhagwati and Krueger (1973). They focus on the specific use of quantitative controls, and the tendency for controls to reduce competition while creating over-capacity. The problem relates to the allocation schemes for import licenses, which are usually based on the import shares of firms, plus some adjustment for new entrants. This mechanism encourages over-capacity, however, since it leads to a proportional expansion of all firms in an industry. In addition, it reduces the amount of direct competition between firms, and leaves the industry with the same firms. As a result, there is less winnowing out of uncompetitive firms.

The second problem, a lack of economies of scale, can theoretically be overcome in a couple of ways. Hirschman (1968) points to the possibilities for regional trade agreements and the potential to use intermediate inputs in multiple ways. Latin American countries, in particular, attempted to expand their national markets through the formation of trade zones such as the Central American Common Market (1961), the Andean Pact (1969) and the Caribbean Common Market (1973). These agreements proved to be of little value, however, until they were reorganized in the 1990s in a climate of greater openness, as developing countries in the 1960s were unwilling to grant their trade partners significant market access. Hence, few agreements led to significant and effective reductions in trade barriers and the resulting lack of economies of scale was serious.

A further problem is related to the quality of institutions and the ability of government bureaucracies to make decisions for technical reasons rather than political ones. ISI policies give governments valuable commodities in the form of import licenses, access to foreign exchange, loans at favorable interest rates, tax subsidies and the potential to use the government budget to support specific lines of production. Predictably, the opportunity to obtain direct and indirect forms of government support leads to rent seeking by the economic agents who will potentially benefit. Weak or unskilled bureaucracies, clientelism, crony capitalism, outright corruption, or other institutional pathologies, intensify the problems as they make it impossible for governments to respond effectively to pressure from the private sector, and lead to poor allocation decisions.

Even when bureaucracies were free from favoritism or corruption, there remained the problem of information gaps in the knowledge needed for making intelligent investment decisions. The lack of expert staff and the need to also provide more basic services such as schools and health care, along with basic infrastructure such as safe drinking water, roads, and ports, were significant challenges to governments. If the more sophisticated demands of industrialization stretched their capacities for planning and resource allocation, some of the basic functions of government were carried out poorly.

The issue of institutional quality mattered greatly, as it determined whether resources would be allocated relatively efficiently or whether domestic price distortions would accumulate over time. Taylor (1998) shows that price distortions, measured by black market premia on foreign exchange, the cost of capital, and currency depreciations, were all greater in inward-looking countries, 1950–1980, and that they explain a significant part of the poor growth record when inward looking Latin America is compared to outward oriented East Asia. The inability of governments to consistently make decisions based on their merit also meant that even when government planners lost their faith in ISI policies, they were unable to dismantle them, and as the enthusiasm for ISI began to wane in the late 1960s, distortions continued to accumulate through the 1970s and 1980s (Taylor 1998: 19). Long after it became apparent that ISI policies were under-achieving, Latin American governments continued to support individual firms and their owners who had successfully captured ISI policies, much to detriment of broader social interests.

The performance of ISI

The overall growth record of ISI countries is not impressive. While many observers point to the high rates of economic growth achieved by Latin America, in particular, during the

1950s and 1960s, and the subsequently low rates of growth after the reorientation of economic policy in the 1980s and 1990s, comparisons of Latin America to other regions are far less favorable. Given that nearly all the world's countries grew faster from 1950 to 1973, and more slowly thereafter, it is better to compare a cross-section of countries at a given point in time rather than a time series which involves shifts in the global economic climate. For example, Brazil's growth record from 1950 to 1973 is probably the best of any ISI country, perhaps because its size is sufficient to negate the problem of scale economies encountered with inward oriented development policies. At 3.8 percent per year growth in per capita GDP from 1950 to 1973, it would be considered a huge success if it achieved the same rate in 2005. According to Maddison (1995: 62–3), Western and Southern Europe, and much of non-ISI Asia grew faster, while most other ISI countries grew far slower. Inward oriented India saw its GDP per capita grow 1.6 percent per year over the same period, while six other large Latin American economies managed only 2.1 percent per year.

In addition to its mediocre growth record, the legacy of ISI included a number of other characteristics that were detrimental over the long run. First, at its best, ISI neglected the development of agriculture, and at its worst, it actively discouraged agricultural investment. By raising the return to investment in manufactured import competing substitutes, it turned the internal terms of trade against exports, particularly primary commodity exports. Balassa (1980: 11) argues that this led to a decline in the export shares of cereals, meat, oilseeds and nonferrous metals, and benefited the US and other developed market economies which were able to supply those goods.

The lack of investment and neglect of agriculture had several additional negative effects. It created an urban bias in development policy which favored urban dwellers over rural, and exacerbated the movement of people from rural areas to urban centers. In Latin America, urbanization rates are far higher than any other developing region and nearly as high as those in developed countries. The rapid growth of urban centers after World War II posed a serious challenge to the ability of countries to supply housing, utilities and other urban infrastructure, and contributed to problems of inequality which were also worsened by the inattention to the rural sector.

Furthermore, the pressure on key urban centers was increased by the incentives to produce for the domestic market. Using a trade model with economies of scale in production and transportation costs, Krugman and Livas Elizondo (1995) show that the growth of mega-cities in developing countries is partly a result of inward oriented policies. Economies of scale imply that firms will produce in only a few places, while transportation costs force those places to be next to the market. When production incentives favor the domestic market, it is often the capital city or other major urban center that benefits. Mexico's history illustrates this point, both with respect to the growth of Mexico City which captured a disproportionate share of Mexican economic activity, and the subsequent growth of the northern border region, next to the US market, as ISI policies were dismantled.

The slowdown in primary commodity exports and the lack of manufactured exports that occurred under ISI policies led to foreign exchange shortages and balance of payments problems. This is ironic given that one of Prebisch's arguments in favor of ISI was that it would overcome foreign exchange shortages caused by a fall in the terms of trade. As foreign exchange became scarce, imports became harder to get as well, with well-known negative effects on economic growth. Cardoso and Fishlow (1992), for example, show that imports mattered significantly to the rate of growth of Latin American countries during the period between 1950 and 1980, while exports mattered even more, and increasingly so over the period.

The end of ISI

Critics of import substitution industrialization were not hard to find, even from its earliest days. For example, both Viner (1952) and Haberler (1959) criticized the heavy use of import controls as early as the 1950s, and Little *et al.* (1970) provided numerous empirical examples of ISI failures while summarizing a growing literature critical of inward oriented strategies. In the 1970s, the National Bureau of Economic Research commissioned a multi-volume series, called 'A Special Conference Series on Foreign Trade Regimes and Economic Development'. This series ran to 11 volumes, including nine volumes of country case studies and summary volumes by Bhagwati (1978) and Krueger (1978). The overwhelming conclusion is that ISI regimes are barriers to economic development, not promoters.

Nevertheless, whether out of inertia or entrenched political interest, many ISI countries continued to follow the same strategy through the 1970s and into the 1980s. Given that several East Asian examples of successful outward oriented policies were visible, it is hard to make the case that the ISI countries did not have available an alternative policy. As the 1970s wore on, the slowdown in world economic growth and the increase in oil prices generated macroeconomic imbalances that were difficult to resist, particularly in countries that increasingly were dependent on central government expenditures to maintain positive rates of economic growth.

The break with ISI policies does not have a specific date, but for lack of a more apt historical marker, 19 August 1982, will serve. That is the date on which Mexico notified the world that it could not service its foreign debt, and the Third World Debt Crisis took off. It would not be accurate to blame the debt crisis on ISI policies since many countries followed those policies for decades without accumulating large debts, and because poor management of the macroeconomy suffices to explain the crisis. When the crisis hit, however, 30 plus years of ISI policies left most countries vulnerable and unable to respond adequately until they made major structural changes in their economies. Large debts and weak export sectors led to nearly a decade of stagnation and recession in many countries, and ultimately created a crisis large enough to force a re-examination of development policy. When that happened, the outward oriented models of the high growth East Asian Tigers offered alternatives.

Notes

1. The emphasis on foreign exchange shortages is one of Prebisch's main contributions to development economics, and plays a role in his thinking that is very similar to the role of savings in the work of a number of other economists.
2. The Economic Commission for Latin America (ECLA, or CEPAL by its Spanish acronym) later added the Caribbean to its interest area and changed its name to the Economic Commission for Latin America and the Caribbean (ECLAC). ECLA was created in 1948, largely at the instigation of the Chilean Hernán Santa Cruz.

References

Balassa, B. (1980), 'The Process of Industrial Development and Alternative Development Strategies', *Essays in International Finance*, **141**, Princeton, NJ: International Finance Section, Department of Economics, Princeton University.

Bhagwati, J. (1978), *Foreign Trade Regimes and Economic Development: Anatomy and Consequences of Exchange Control Regimes*, A Special Conference Series on Foreign Trade Regimes and Economic Development, Volume XI, New York: National Bureau of Economic Research.

Bhagwati, J. and Krueger, A. O. (1973), 'Exchange Control, Liberalization, and Economic Development', *American Economic Review*, **63**(2), 419–27.

Bleaney, M. and Greenaway, D. (1993), 'Long-run Trends in the Relative Price of Primary Commodities and in the Terms of Trade of Developing Countries', *Oxford Economic Papers*, **45**(3), 349–63.

Cardoso, E. and Fishlow, A. (1992), 'Latin American Economic Development: 1950–1980', *Journal of Latin American Studies*, 24, Quincentenary Supplement: The Colonial and Post Colonial Experience. Five Centuries of Spanish and Portuguese America, 197–218.

Grilli, E. R. and Yang, M. C. (1988), 'Primary Commodity Prices, Manufactured Goods Prices, and the Terms of Trade of Developing Countries: What the Long Run Shows', *World Bank Economic Review*, **2**, 1–48.

Haberler, G. (1959), *International Trade and Economic Development*, Cairo: National Bank of Egypt.

Hadass, Y. S. and Williamson, J. G. (2003), 'Terms-of-trade Shocks and Economic Performance, 1870–1940: Prebisch and Singer Revisited', *Economic Development and Cultural Change*, **51**(3), 629–56.

Hirschman, A. O. (1968), 'The Political Economy of Import Substitution', *Quarterly Journal of Economics*, **82**, 1–32.

Kindleberger, C. (1943), 'Planning for Foreign Investment', *American Economic Review*, **33**, 347–54.

Krueger, A. O. (1978), *Foreign Trade Regimes and Economic Development: Liberalization Attempts and Consequences*, A Special Conference Series on Foreign Trade Regimes and Economic Development, Volume X, New York: National Bureau of Economic Research.

Krugman, P. and Livas Elizondo, R. (1995), 'Trade Policy and the Third World Metropolis', *Journal of Development Economics*. **49**, 137–50.

Little, I., Scitovsky, T. and Scott, M. (1970), *Trade and Industry in Some Developing Countries*, Oxford: Oxford University Press.

Maddison, A. (1995), *Monitoring the World Economy, 1820–1992*, Paris: OECD Development Centre.

Prebisch, R. (1950), *The Economic Development of Latin America and Its Principal Problems*, UN Doc. E/CN.12/89/Rev.1. Lake Success, NY: United Nations.

Prebisch, R. (1984), 'Five Stages of my Thinking on Development', in G. M. Meier and D. Seers (eds) *Pioneers in Development*, New York: Oxford University Press, pp. 175–91.

Singer, H. (1948), 'The Terms of Trade Controversy and the Evolution of Soft Financing: Early Years in the UN', in G. M. Meier and D. Seers (eds) *Pioneers in Development*, New York: Oxford University Press, pp. 275–303.

Singer, H. (1950), 'The Distribution of Gains Between Investing and Borrowing Countries', *American Economic Review*, **40**(2), 473–85.

Taylor, A. M. (1998), 'On the Costs of Inward-looking Development: Price Distortions, Growth, and Divergence in Latin America', *The Journal of Economic History*, **58**(1), 1–28.

Thorp, R. (1992), 'A Reappraisal of the Origins of Import-substituting Industrialisation 1930–1950', *Journal of Latin American Studies*, **24**. Quincentenary Supplement: The Colonial and Post Colonial Experience. Five Centuries of Spanish and Portuguese America, 181–95.

Toye, J. and Toye, R. (2003), 'The Origins and Interpretation of the Prebisch–Singer Thesis', *History of Political Economy*, **35**(3), 437–67.

United Nations. (1949), *Post-war Price Relations in Trade between Under-developed and Industrialized Countries*, UN Doc. E/CN.1/Sub.3/W.5, Lake Success, NY: UN Department of Economic Affairs.

Viner, J. (1952), *International Trade and Economic Development*, Glencoe, IL: Free Press.

42 Export promotion policies
James B. Gerber

Export promotion is an economic development strategy emphasizing the exploitation of a country's actual or potential comparative advantage through production for foreign markets. It is often contrasted with import substitution industrialization (ISI) policy since it is 'outward looking' while ISI is 'inward looking'. Modern forms of export promotion first came to prominence in the 1960s when several East Asian countries turned away from ISI strategies and began to promote manufactured exports (Bruton 1998). The success of these Asian export economies, known variously as the Little Dragons or Four Tigers,[1] called into question the idea of export pessimism, the belief that low and middle income developing economies could not compete with manufactured goods in developed country markets. By the mid-to-late 1980s, export promotion had completely replaced ISI as orthodoxy.

In addition to the demonstration effect of East Asian export economies, several other factors stood behind the success of export promotion as a policy idea. Prominent among them were the loss of confidence in interventionist, state-led management of the economy, as exemplified by the Thatcher and Reagan reforms in the United Kingdom and the United States, and the failure of traditional import substitution industrialization policies to address the worsening economic conditions of Latin America stemming from the debt crisis of the 1980s. A third major factor that contributed to developing country adoption of export promotion is the communication and transportation revolution of the last decades of the twentieth century. Technological changes in transport and communications enabled firms to locate more production abroad and increased the opportunities for developing countries to participate in production processes spanning several nations. All of these changes supported the ideas of pursuing comparative advantage and exports as engines of growth.

Export promotion in historical context

The identification of export promotion policy as a development strategy is relatively new, although the idea of export promotion itself is very old. Book IV of Adam Smith's *The Wealth of Nations* is, in part, a discussion of export promotion within the framework of a closed mercantilist economy.[2] Smith notes that mercantilists encourage exports through a variety of policy measures, 'sometimes by drawbacks, sometimes by bounties, sometimes by advantageous treaties of commerce with foreign states, and sometimes by the establishment of colonies in distant countries' (1776 [2000]: 479). He speaks favorably of drawbacks, as they re-establish 'the natural balance of industry, the natural division and distribution of labour . . .' (539). In modern terminology, drawbacks offset the production and consumption distortions caused by domestic taxes and import tariffs.[3] Export bounties, on the other hand, force 'some part of the industry of the country . . . not only into a channel that is less advantageous, but into one that is actually disadvantageous; the trade which cannot be carried on but by means of a bounty being necessarily a losing trade' (552).

In *The Wealth of Nations,* Smith reasons that if the purpose of the bounty is to raise or maintain production, then nations are better off if they use a production bounty rather than an export bounty. Production bounties, he points out, are more direct and tend to lower the domestic price of the good, while export bounties raise the domestic price. He goes on to point out that merchants and manufacturers prefer export bounties precisely for these reasons: they remove surpluses from the domestic economy and push up domestic prices.

In several ways, Smith's discussion is still useful, not least because the mechanisms he describes are still in use. For example, drawbacks are used to encourage exports in a variety of ways, including export processing zones (EPZs) such as Mexico's maquiladora sector or China's special economic zones. Export processing zones are a widely used development strategy to encourage foreign direct and domestic investment by offering special tax incentives (drawbacks) when goods are exported. EPZs have a mixed record of achievement in practice, as they are often implemented with a variety of supplementary policy objectives beyond export promotion, including regional development, employment generation, and local sourcing. Moran (2002: Chapter 2) surveys EPZs and characterizes the elements of successful and unsuccessful cases.

Bounties, called export subsidies in modern terminology, are also widely used to encourage industrial development and have become part of a wide ranging debate over the efficacy of industrial policy. The central ideas in this debate focus on whether or not nations can effectively promote specific industries, whether or not export promotion can be used to unlock development, and whether or not this was an essential component of East Asian export success. In recent years, export subsidies have become somewhat more problematic as an official development policy, as the Uruguay Round of the General Agreement on Tariffs and Trade officially limits their use in manufacturing (but not agriculture).

National welfare, trade policy, and subsidies

Export promotion should not be confused with a more liberal or open trading system. This is an obvious point, but one worth making since there is a tendency to justify trade liberalization by citing its effects on exports. Export growth (or decline) can occur in a variety of trade policy environments, including slow or rapid liberalization, as well as relatively closed or open economies. For example, Corden (1997: 256–7) identifies several scenarios under which import protection may turn a domestically produced product into an export, and Adam Smith's *Wealth of Nations* can be read as an argument against a policy of export promotion in an otherwise closed economy. Furthermore, rapid liberalization of closed economies has sometimes led to a loss of exports in the short run, as the transition period for the economies of Central Europe painfully demonstrated.

The welfare effects of export promotion are therefore not to be confused with the welfare effects of trade liberalization. In general, export promotion, for example with subsidies, are a second best policy unless there are external benefits associated with exporting. For example, these could be beneficial exchange rate adjustments resulting from a change in trade flows (Corden 1997). Smith's observation that production subsidies are more efficient than export subsidies is consistent with contemporary analysis of the welfare effects of export subsidies. If externalities exist, they are likely to be associated with production and not exporting. Hence, a policy that goes directly to the source of the divergence between social and private benefits is more efficient than one that encourages production indirectly by encouraging exports.

Export subsidies and production subsidies are both considered unfair competition and subject to countervailing duties by importing countries. The irony is that both types of subsidies benefit the importing country because it obtains the good at a lower price. In the absence of external benefits from production or exporting, the subsidies harm the exporting country because they use domestic resources to push production beyond the socially optimal level and reduce the prices paid by foreign consumers. Most importing countries reject this bargain, however, and impose countervailing duties to raise the domestic price of the imported good. Countervailing duties can offset the effects of the subsidy, but still leave a transfer from the exporting country to the importing one which takes shape in the form of duties paid on imports.[4]

When externalities exist, then subsidies may be a first best policy as a means of capturing the external benefits of production. It is often argued, for example, that certain industries are strategic for economic or political security and that market incentives do not take this into account. Therefore a subsidy is warranted as a means to correct the market failure. This assumes, however, that the size of the external benefit can be more or less measured so that the optimum size of the subsidy can be determined. Furthermore, it assumes that administrative costs are insignificant or small, and that such a subsidy will not encourage wasteful rent-seeking by other interests.

A more unusual case for subsidies came to the attention of economic theorists in the mid-1980s under the rubric of strategic trade policy (Brander and Spencer 1985). The core of this argument is dependent on the presence of large economies of scale extending over the entire range of global demand. As a consequence, one firm can meet the entire world's demand at the lowest possible cost. The industry that is most often discussed in these terms is production of commercial jet airliners, where two firms dominate at the upper end (Boeing and Airbus) and two firms dominate in the middle range of 30–60 passenger jets (Bombadier and Embraer).[5] While one firm alone can be highly profitable, under certain conditions, a new firm like Airbus is able to enter the market and cause both itself and Boeing to sustain losses due to the splitting of the market in two. If Airbus is subsidized, and Boeing is not, then Airbus can sustain the losses while Boeing may not be able to. Further, if Boeing perceives that Airbus will stay in the market, its loss-minimizing strategy will be to leave the market and stop production. The end result is that strategic subsidies to Airbus might enable it to capture the entire market, both domestic and export.

The moral of this story is that subsidies can be used strategically to capture export markets. It does seen naive, however, from a political economy perspective, as the ongoing trade disputes between Airbus (a European consortium) and Boeing (US) and between Bombadier (Canada) and Embraer (Brazil) testify. Furthermore, the situation in practice is complicated by the fact that export promotion through the use of subsidies is regulated by the World Trade Organization's General Agreement on Tariffs and Trade (GATT-1994). Subsidies are considered unfair when used for the promotion of one nation's exports at the expense of another nation's domestic industry. More specifically, the GATT-1994 identified three types of subsidies: prohibited, actionable and non-actionable. The first includes any subsidy that is contingent on export performance; the second includes any subsidy which adversely impacts another country's domestic industry; and the third category 'could either be non-specific subsidies, or specific subsidies involving assistance to industrial research and pre-competitive development activity, assistance to disadvantaged regions, or certain type of assistance for adapting existing facilities to new environmental requirements imposed by law and/or regulations' (WTO, n.d.). In essence, export promotion through basic research, non-product-specific technology development, regional development, infrastructure construction, or environmental protection, are permitted. (Agriculture is not included the general regulations.) Hence, there is a fairly large space for policy to act, and active debates continue over the legality or illegality of a subsidy under the GATT rules.

Export promotion and economic growth

One characteristic of the rapid-growth East Asian economies has been the rapid growth of their exports. More generally, the World Bank (1993: 123) attributes their high growth rates to a 'supportive macroeconomic climate' and 'suitable microeconomic incentives'. The latter varied greatly but included export promotion components such as duty exemptions for exporters, investment incentives, low interest export loans, open door policies for skilled professionals and technologists, fiscal incentives for research and development activities, export requirements, export processing zones, and infrastructure investment, among others. Most, if not all of these, can be classified under the categories of bounties and drawbacks, as discussed by Smith (1776 [2000]: 533–60).

While the most fundamental purpose of exports may be broadly understood as enabling imports, several other benefits are often cited as deriving from exports. It is argued that they make macroeconomic management easier, they serve as a useful yardstick for measuring success, and, perhaps most critically but somewhat controversially, they raise productivity (Pack 1997; Noland and Pack 2003). Macroeconomic management is made easier in several respects. For one, foreign markets constitute a more stable source of demand than production for a nation's own domestic market which is limited by the rate of growth of the national economy and is subject to the national business cycle. Exports can grow more rapidly since there is a larger market and they are not affected in the same way by cyclical variation in national demand. Second, exports are thought to provide greater flexibility to macroeconomic policy when there are external shocks that redirect production from internal demand to external demand. In general, it is easier and more reliable to create a shift in the relative prices of tradable and non-tradable goods than to cause an export response by firms accustomed to inward oriented policies. The slow export response by inward-looking Latin American firms during the debt crisis of the 1980s, and the relative rapid response by outward-looking East Asian firms during the financial crisis of 1997–1998 are cases in point. In other words, exports may reduce macroeconomic volatility. Third, exports reduce the foreign exchange constraint on growth, if it exists. This essentially reiterates that point that the purpose of exports is to enable imports.

In addition to facilitating management of the macroeconomy, exports in the East Asian case probably accelerated the structural transformation of economies. This meant a faster growth of manufacturing and higher productivity growth rates (Pack 1997). It is logical, however, to question the direction of causation for this claim. Do exports cause productivity growth, or does high productivity growth cause exports? Girma *et al.* (2004) perform a microeconomic analysis of matched UK firms and arrive at the result that firms self-select into exporting (have higher productivity to start), but that they subsequently continue to increase their productivity once they enter export markets. There are probably two reasons for this. The first is the presence of scale economies as production for a world market invites techniques that may not be cost effective when production is for the national market. Second, it is believed that there may be stronger learning effects when firms compete against international rivals.

The East Asian case
The World Bank's *The East Asian Miracle: Economic Growth and Public Policy* (1993) offers an interesting and readable introduction to the debates surrounding high East Asian growth rates and the role of exports and economic policy. The Bank's analysis was partly a response to activist government interpretations of the East Asian experience (Wade 1990) and spawned a variety of responses (Fishlow *et. al.* 1994; Stiglitz 1996) and counter-responses (Noland and Pack 2003) addressing the role of export promotion and industrial policy as development strategies. While there continue to be important points of disagreement about the role and capacity of governments to promote development, several points of consensus or near-consensus also emerged. First, it was understood that significant modern export promotion strategies emerged in the 1960s, first in Taiwan and South Korea, where export promotion was in response to the distortions and low growth that had resulted from following import substitution policies. Westphal (1990) provides background on the Korean case, while Fei *et al.* (1979) examine Taiwan.

Most analysts also agree that for export promotion to succeed as a pro-development strategy, it must include institutional development along with human and physical capital investments. Bruton's (1998) contrasting of ISI with export promotion shows that the success of the latter is dependent on a number of factors, including entrepreneurship, institutions, infrastructure, human capital and perhaps most critically, a system for learning-by-doing. Exporting alone, he and most others argue, is inadequate for creating development.

The Republic of Korea is an important case study since it has closed the income gap between itself and the high income industrial world at a very rapid pace and because most observers give at least part of the credit to its successful export promotion policies. In 1960, before its shift from inward to outward looking policies, Korea's GDP per capita was about 11.7 percent of the US level. By 2000 it had reached 41.9 percent of the US and continued to grow at rates several percentage points above the average for high income OECD countries (Heston *et al.* 2002; World Bank 2005). Between 1960 and 2000, Korea's exports and imports rose from 3 and 12 percent of GDP, respectively, to 41 and 38 percent (World Bank 2005). Westphal (1990) shows that South Korea's economy took off when a set of economic reforms were instituted in the early 1960s, based on infant industry protection and export promotion, with the latter formulated within a 'neutral' set of resource allocation incentives so that drawbacks and bounties offset the effects on export industries of policies that were implemented for reasons other than export promotion, such as infant industry development.[6] Korea's export success was achieved by 'insulating export activity from the otherwise adverse consequences of policies motivated by other concerns' (Westphal 1990: 44). Korea, like the other Asian Tigers, offered a variety of supports for exports, including access to credit through the publicly owned banking sector, drawbacks on import and domestic taxes, preferential interest rates, and preferential access to import licenses.[7]

What comes next?

By the first decade of the twenty-first century, export promotion policies had become a more-or-less standard component of development strategies across the globe as well as a primary mechanism for international economic integration. Consequently, it is worth thinking about the long run, as an increasing share of the world's population tries to export its way to prosperity. For example, China's 1.3 billion people are quickly joining the international economy, followed by India's 1.1 billion, and in both cases, merchandise and service exports are a primary vehicle for their international economic integration.[8] The amazing growth record of China, in particular, raises a number of questions about the capacity of the world economy to absorb their surplus and must lead one to wonder about the future of international commercial relations as many more countries adopt similar export promotion strategies. Between 1980 and 2000, China's share of world merchandise exports rose from under 1 percent to almost 4 percent (World Bank 2005). This is still a small share of the world total for a country with 20 percent of the world population, and India's impact on the world economy has so far been smaller,[9] but both cases raise questions about the viability of widespread adoption of export promotion strategies.

China's 2001 succession into the World Trade Organization portends an increasing acceptance of its presence on the world stage, albeit with many conditions, and in spite of disputes over trade imbalances, currency values, intellectual property rights and other issues. Perhaps most important is the recognition that the combined Chinese and Indian populations of 2.4 billion in 2006 are not solely engaged in export activities, but also represent enormous markets for both domestic and foreign producers. Ultimately, the extent to which one views these changes as an opportunity or a threat depends on one's attitude toward international economic integration. Exports are integrating India, China and other developing countries into the world economy and that fact alone will create changes that will force many workers, firms, and even nations to adapt. Ultimately, however, the successful development of poor countries must be seen as a positive change in world history, and as a consequence, the most serious issue may not be the impact of successful export promotion policies on world trade balances, but rather the effects of economic development on the world's natural environment.

Notes

1. These terms were widely used to refer to Hong Kong, Taiwan, Singapore and the Republic of Korea. Another often used term is High Performance Asian Economies, first presented by the World Bank in its 1993 study, *The East Asian Miracle*. The Bank used the term as shorthand to refer to the rapidly growing economies of East Asia. The standard list includes the four tigers plus Japan, Thailand, Malaysia and Indonesia. Obviously, China fits into this group as well, although the Bank did not include it in its analysis.
2. 'Of Systems of Political Economy.'
3. Drawbacks can be either taxes on home production that are returned when the good is exported, or import taxes that are returned when the foreign goods are re-exported.
4. The countervailing duty returns the imported good to its higher, non-subsidized, price. The same number of imports enter the country, but with the countervailing duty there is a wedge between the price paid by consumers and the price received by producers. The difference between the price received by exporters and the price paid by consumers is the size of the subsidy. This is paid by the exporting nation in the form of a price reduction and accrues to the government of the importing country.
5. Software or other products with high fixed costs may also qualify.
6. Corden (1997: 20–21) shows the connection between 'protection' and 'promotion'. The former occurs when countries impose tariffs or other import limiting measures, while the latter refers to a case in which a domestic good is both protected and offered export subsidies. The distinction is important because, in

the words of Corden, '*Protection* creates a home-market bias, *promotion* avoids it' (p. 20; emphasis in the original).

7.   Westphal (1990) also argues that Korean industrial policies were essential to its success in the export arena, but that the political and institutional conditions that favored successful policymaking would be difficult to duplicate elsewhere. This is the essential point of disagreement between many interpretations of East Asian experiences.

8.   Population figures are from the US Census Bureau, International Data Base. Available: http://www.census.gov/cgi-bin/ipc/agggen. The emphasis here is on exports, not trade liberalization. Nothing is implied about the commercial policies of either country, other than the fact that both are attempting (successfully) to increase their presence in goods and services export markets.

9.   Over the same period, 1980 to 2000, India's share of world merchandise exports rose from 0.4 percent to 0.65 percent (World Bank 2005).

References

Brander, J. A. and B. J. Spencer (1985), 'Export Subsidies and International Market Share Rivalry,' *Journal of International Economics*, **16**, 83–100.

Bruton, H. J. (1998), 'A Reconsideration of Import Substitution,' *Journal of Economic Literature*, **36**(2), 903–36.

Corden, M. (1997), *Trade Policy and Economic Welfare*, (2nd edn), New York: Oxford University Press.

Fei, J. C., G. Ranis and S. Kuo (1979), *Growth with Equity*, New York: Oxford University Press.

Fishlow, A., C. Gwin, S. Haggard, D. Rodrik and R. Wade (1994), *Miracle or Design? Lessons from the East Asian Experience*, Policy Essay No. 11, Washington, DC: Overseas Development Council.

Girma, S., D. Greenaway and R. Kneller (2004), 'Does Exporting Increase Productivity? A Microeconometric Analysis of Matched Firms,' *Review of International Economics*, **12**(5), 855–66.

Heston, A., R. Summers and B. Aten (2002), *Penn World Table Version 6.1*, Philadelphia, PA: Center for International Comparisons at the University of Pennsylvania (CICUP).

Moran, T. H. (2002), *Beyond Sweatshops: Foreign Direct Investment and Globalization in Developing Countries*, Washington, DC: Brookings Institution Press.

Noland, M. and H. Pack (2003), *Industrial Policy in an Era of Globalization: Lessons from Asia*, Washington, DC: Institute for International Economics.

Pack, H. (1997), 'The Role of Exports in Asian Development,' in N. Birdsall and F. Jaspersen (eds) *Pathways to Growth: Comparing East Asia and Latin America*, Washington, DC: Inter-American Development Bank, pp. 227–63.

Smith, Adam (1776 [2000]), *The Wealth of Nations*, New York: The Modern Library.

Stiglitz, J. (1996), 'Some Lessons from the East Asian Miracle,' *The World Bank Research Observer*, **11**(2), 151–77.

Wade, R. (1990), *Governing the Market: Economic Theory and the Role of Government in East Asian Industrialization*, Princeton, NJ: Princeton University Press.

Westphal, L. E. (1990), 'Industrial Policy in an Export Propelled Economy: Lessons from South Korea's Experience,' *The Journal of Economic Perspectives*, **4**(3), 41–59.

The World Bank (1993), *The East Asian Miracle: Economic Growth and Public Policy*, New York: Oxford University Press.

The World Bank (2005), *WDI Online*, available: http://web.worldbank.org/WBSITE/EXTERNAL/DATASTATISTICS/0,,contentMDK:20398986~menuPK:64133163~pagePK:64133150~piPK:64133175~theSitePK:239419,00.html.

The World Trade Organization (n.d.), 'Agreement on Subsidies and Countervailing Measures,' *A Summary of the Final Act of the Uruguay Round*, available: http://www.wto.org/english/docs_e/legal_e/ursum_e.htm#top. Accessed January 4, 2006.

43 The generalized system of preferences and special and differential treatment for developing countries in the GATT and WTO

Robert Read

The Generalized System of Preferences (GSP) and the concept of Special and Differential (S&D) treatment for the exports of developing countries were incorporated into the GATT as a result of the Kennedy and Tokyo Rounds of trade negotiations. Prior to this, however, some industrialized economies granted preferential market access to the exports of specific developing countries on a selective bilateral basis. These preferences were generally asymmetric in that they did not require the developing country beneficiaries to make reciprocal trade concessions. The GSP was adopted on a voluntary basis by many industrialized economies as a result of the Kennedy Round but the implementation of the GSP and S&D treatment only became a legal obligation for the wealthiest GATT Member countries at the conclusion of the Tokyo Round in 1979.

This chapter provides a critical overview of the GSP and S&D treatment for the exports of developing countries. The first section outlines the original GATT provisions for developing countries. This is followed by a brief discussion of the origins of the GSP and S&D in the formation of UNCTAD and their incorporation into the GATT Kennedy and Tokyo Round trade negotiations. The key GATT articles dealing with the GSP and the obligations of S&D treatment are then summarized. The modifications and amendments made as a result of the Uruguay Round are then outlined. The final section provides a critique of the GSP and S&D treatment with respect to their impact upon the trade and growth of developing countries.

The GATT 1947 and the developing countries: GATT Article XVIII

The need for greater flexibility in trade policies dealing with developing countries was considered in several articles of the draft Havana Treaty of the ITO. Only one article subsequently remained in the GATT 1947 text, Article XVIII, Governmental Assistance to Economic Development. This Article was intended to encourage the full participation of developing countries in the global trade system although very few of them were GATT Members at the time. The Article recognized that multilateral trade liberalization has the potential to stimulate growth and development but that certain exceptions (derogations) from the GATT principles might be necessary to ensure the achievement of these objectives.

> [I]t may be necessary . . . in order to implement programmes and policies of economic development designed to raise the general standard of living of their people, to take protective or other measures affecting imports, and that such measures are justified in so far as they facilitate the attainment of the objectives of this Agreement. (WTO 1999)

Revisions made to Article XVIII in 1954–1955 explicitly identified two specific types of permissible trade measures that could be used by developing countries.

The first was 'infant industry' protection:

(a)   to maintain sufficient flexibility in their tariff structure to be able to grant the tariff protection required for the establishment of a particular industry. (WTO 1999)

and the second, emergency balance of payment measures:

(b)   to apply quantitative restrictions for balance of payment purposes in a manner which takes full account of the continued high level of demand for imports likely to be generated in their programmes of economic development. (WTO 1999)

These derogations were dealt with in Sections A and B of the Article respectively. The text however, also recognized that

[T]here may be circumstances where no measure consistent with those provisions is practicable to permit . . . [a developing country] . . . to grant the governmental assistance required to promote the establishment of particular industries with a view to raising the general standard of living of its people. (WTO 1999)

The procedures under which these additional trade measures for developmental purposes were sanctioned by the GATT were dealt with in Section C of the Article. In Section D, similar procedures were set for the use of such measures by more advanced countries.

It is important to consider the underlying implications of the derogations granted to developing countries in GATT Article XVIII. The prevailing philosophy of economic development was that infant industry protection and emergency balance of payments measures were designed to restrict imports by developing countries, albeit on a temporary basis, rather than promote their trade. The implicit reasoning was that industrialization should precede trade expansion; an argument that was not fully compatible with the GATT view that multilateral trade liberalization would itself stimulate growth and development. Emergency balance of payments measures were intended to enable developing countries to prioritize essential imports, including capital goods, in the event of foreign exchange crises caused by commodity price downturns. This highlights contemporary concerns about the declining commodity terms of trade of developing countries. Industrialization therefore offered the means for developing countries to overcome their dependence upon primary commodity exports through the broad application of infant industry protection – the 'infant economy' argument. Much of this new industrial growth was import substituting, that is it was designed to replace imports with local output in the domestic market and therefore reduce overall trade. The GATT derogations therefore sanctioned the expansion of industrial activity in developing countries via policies that were explicitly 'anti-trade'.

Tariff preferences could also be granted to developing countries under GATT Article I, Most Favoured Nation. This permitted the metropolitan powers to maintain existing preferences for their former colonies subject to the proviso that the margin of preference granted did not exceed that prevailing in 1947. The granting of preferences to additional developing countries or any increase in the margin of preference required an Article I waiver. For example, the trade and aid framework of the 1963 Yaoundé Convention between the newly formed European Union and its Members' former colonies relied upon such a waiver.

Balassa (1982) describes the treatment of developing countries in the GATT as a 'Faustian bargain'. They could restrict imports but their industrialization, based upon export-led growth, was severely impeded by trade barriers in the leading industrialized economies. These barriers targeted processed primary commodities, both minerals and agricultural products, and simple manufactures, such as textiles and clothing. Nevertheless, the impact of Article XVIII was limited by the relatively marginal role of developing countries in the GATT during this period since much of the trade of developing countries was accounted for by trade between the colonial powers and their colonies.

UNCTAD and the GATT Kennedy and Tokyo Rounds
The emergence of many former colonies as newly independent states during the 1950s and early 1960s raised the profile of the developing countries in international affairs and paved the way for their greater participation in international organizations. The political bargaining power of the developing countries also increased as they flexed their new-found independence. The increasing number of developing country members of GATT led to demands for greater recognition of their special problems in the multilateral rules on trade, including improved access to the markets of the leading industrialized countries.

The UN conference on trade and development
A key turning point in the relationship between the GATT and the developing countries came in 1964 with the first UN Conference on Trade and Development (UNCTAD I). This led to the formation of UNCTAD as an alternative multilateral forum to address the special situation of developing countries.

The principal demand of UNCTAD I was for the introduction of a general system of unilateral tariff preferences by the industrialized economies on exports of interest to the developing countries. This position was supported by the EU as an extension of its own Yaoundé Convention but strongly opposed by Sweden and the United States, among others. The grounds for opposition was that such concessions contravened the fundamental GATT principal of non-discrimination embodied in Article I, Most Favoured Nation (MFN), that all GATT member countries are treated equally in trade matters. The outcome was stalemate in spite of concerns that the developing countries might withdraw from the GATT and instead pursue their trade objectives under the auspices of UNCTAD.

The issue of special trade preferences for developing countries was again high on the agenda at the second UNCTAD conference, UNCTAD II, in 1968. This time, there was no concerted opposition to these proposals. The outcome was that the industrialized economies agreed to grant unilateral trade preferences to the developing countries that were both below MFN bound tariff rates and non-reciprocal. This meant that these preferences also contravened the fundamental GATT principal of reciprocity, whereby members agree to make broadly equivalent tariff reductions simultaneously. The UNCTAD II agreement is known as the Generalized System of Preferences (GSP) and Special and Differential treatment for developing countries.

The GATT Kennedy Round and the developing countries
The special trade arrangements for the developing countries agreed at UNCTAD II was referred back to the GATT Kennedy Round negotiations and incorporated under three

new Articles contained in Part IV of the GATT on Trade and Development. The GSP however, became operational in 1971 only after the conclusion of the Kennedy Round trade negotiations. The obligations of Part IV, the GSP, therefore remained non-binding on GATT members until the completion of the Tokyo Round.

The GSP was operationalized within the GATT by the 1971 Protocol on Trade Negotiations Among Developing Countries, the Geneva Protocol. This agreed a general extension of the existing Article I ('grandfather') waiver for trade preferences for former colonies for an initial period of ten years. Under the new GATT waiver all developing countries benefited from the GSP framework but it allowed the industrialized countries to determine both the magnitude and applicability of their trade preferences. The GSP also included provisions on trade between developing countries, the Global System of Trade Preferences (GSTP). This was based upon the principles of reciprocity and MFN but applied specifically to developing countries under an Article XXV waiver.

The EU was the first to incorporate the GSP and S&D treatment of all developing countries into its external trade policy in 1971. The GATT waiver, however, enabled the EU to discriminate between different groups of developing countries and so maintain larger tariff preferences for signatories of the Yaoundé Convention and, after 1975, the Lomé Convention. Because the implementation of Part IV was not binding on GATT members, many industrialized countries were much slower to grant preferences; for example, the United States did so only after it passed the 1974 Trade Act.

The GATT Tokyo Round and the developing countries
The GSP and S&D were formally incorporated into the GATT (Part IV) as part of the Tokyo Round negotiations in 1979 through the adoption of a Framework Agreement including an Enabling Clause, Differential and More Favourable Treatment, Reciprocity and Fuller Participation of Developing Countries. This Enabling Clause made the adoption of the GSP binding upon all GATT Members and extended the Article I waiver indefinitely. The Clause also codified the use of trade measures to protect the balance of payments through changes to GATT Articles XII and XVIII, so rendering most of Article XVIII effectively redundant. It also relaxed the conditions governing the formation of regional trade agreements between developing countries in Article XXIV. In return, the concept of graduation was introduced whereby the most successful developing countries would eventually lose their preferential status. There was, however, no agreement on a specific definition or threshold for graduation.

The GSP and Special and Differential Treatment for developing countries
Part IV of the GATT, Trade and Development, comprises three Articles (XXXVI to XXXVIII) that detail its objectives and the respective obligations of industrialized and developing GATT members.

The principles and objectives of the GSP
GATT Article XXXVI sets out the special position of developing countries in substantially greater detail than was the case in Article XVIII. It recognizes: the urgent need for growth in developing countries; their problems of export price and earnings instability; the wide gap in their living standards; the need for action to promote development; the need for rules on international trade; and the scope for special measures within the GATT.

The remainder of the Article is concerned with the means by which developing countries may achieve these objectives. Many merely reiterate Article XVIII in terms of the participation of the developing countries in global trade, their reliance upon primary commodity exports, their need for diversification as well as financial assistance and international support.

Three Paragraphs however, reflect a fundamental shift in the institutional thinking underlying the key issues facing developing countries. Paragraph 2 states that:

> There is a need for a rapid and sustained expansion of the export earnings of the less-developed contracting parties. (WTO 1999)

This is an important change in emphasis from Article XVIII in that it explicitly advocates development through export-led growth as opposed to import-substituting industrialization. It recognizes the limits to inward-looking growth and also the early growth success of the East Asian economies, particularly Japan, based upon exports. More importantly, it represents a revival of emphasis by the GATT upon the beneficial role of trade in growth and economic development rather than the need for protection.

Paragraph 4 also extends the discussion of the dependence of developing countries upon primary products to emphasize both the role of exports and market access:

> Given the . . . dependence . . . [on] . . . a limited range of primary products, there is need to provide . . . more favourable and acceptable conditions of access to world markets for these products (and) to stabilize and improve conditions of world markets . . . thus permitting an expansion of world trade and demand and . . . steady growth of . . . real export earnings. (WTO 1999)

The term 'primary products' was subsequently clarified in Ad Article XXXVI.4 to include agricultural products. The market access of agricultural exports by developing countries is discussed briefly below. The inclusion of measures to stabilize and manage world commodity prices and markets foreshadows the plethora of international commodity agreements that were a particular feature of the 1970s. These were based upon increasing co-operation between developing countries, backed by the 'Group of 77', and the emergence of the New International Economic Order.

The discussion of improved preferential export access for developing countries to the markets of the industrialized countries is extended to manufactures in Paragraph 5 and again highlights the renewed emphasis of Part IV of the GATT upon export-led growth.

> There is . . . need for increased access . . . to markets under favourable conditions for processed and manufactured products currently or potentially of particular export interest. (WTO 1999)

Finally, the non-reciprocal terms of the GSP are outlined in Paragraph 8:

> The developed contracting parties do not expect reciprocity for commitments made by them in trade negotiations to reduce or remove tariffs and other barriers to the trade of less-developed contracting parties. (WTO 1999)

This is supplemented in Ad Article XXXVI.8 by:

> [They are not] expected . . . to make contributions [to trade negotiations] which are inconsistent with their individual development, financial and trade needs. (WTO 1999)

The commitments of the industrialized economies under the GSP

GATT Article XXXVII sets out the commitments and undertakings to the GSP on the part of the industrialized economies that are to be given effect 'to the fullest extent possible'. Paragraph 1 details the trade concessions that are expected of the industrialized economies along with a commitment not to introduce new trade measures that adversely affect developing countries. The key elements of this Paragraph are:

(a)   accord high priority to the reduction and elimination of barriers to products of currently or potentially of particular export interest . . . including customs duties and other restrictions which differentiate unreasonably between such products in their primary and processed forms;

(b)   refrain from introducing, or increasing the incidence of, customs duties or non-tariff import barriers on products currently or potentially of particular export interest;

(c)   (i) refrain from imposing new fiscal measures, and (ii) in any adjustments of fiscal policy accord high priority to the reduction and elimination of fiscal measures . . . which hamper, significantly the growth of consumption of primary products, in raw or processed form, wholly or mainly produced . . . [by] . . . less-developed contracting parties, and which are applied specifically to those products. (WTO 1999)

These commitments appear to be straightforward in terms of undertakings by the industrialized countries to reduce existing tariff and non-tariff barriers while refraining from introducing new ones. Two points, however, are of interest. The differentiation between raw and processed products mentioned in Paragraph 1(a) refers explicitly to tariff escalation in the trade policies of industrialized economies. This issue is discussed at greater length below. Second, the latter part of Paragraph 1(c) includes measures such as specific excise taxes; for example, that on coffee in Germany which still exists. The second Paragraph outlines the means of redress for developing countries where industrialized economies do not adhere to the provisions of Paragraph 1.

Paragraph 3 then outlines several additional obligations on the part of the industrialized economies:

(a)   [to] make every effort, in cases where a government directly or indirectly determines the resale price of products wholly or mainly produced in the territories of less-developed contracting parties, to maintain trade margins at equitable levels;

(b)   [to] give active consideration to the adoption of other measures designed to provide greater scope for the development of imports from less-developed contracting parties and collaborate in appropriate international action to this end;

This is extended in Ad Article XVIII(b):

[Such as] steps to promote domestic structural changes, to encourage the consumption of particular products, or to introduce measures of trade promotion.

(c)   [to] have special regard to the trade interests of less-developed contracting parties when considering the application of other measures . . . to meet particular problems and explore . . . constructive remedies before applying such measures where they would affect [their] essential interests. (WTO 1999)

The implication of Paragraph 3 is that S&D treatment extends beyond matters directly related to trade and incorporates 'non-trade' concerns that impinge on domestic policy issues in the industrialized economies. Paragraph 3(a) clearly applies to the use of price controls but can also be interpreted as applying to the activities of state-owned firms, including state monopolies. The reference to structural change in Paragraph 3(b) includes the particularly sensitive issue of the protection of declining industries, especially those in which developing countries might be expected to have a potential comparative advantage. This again raises the issue of tariff escalation, dealt with below. The final Paragraph refers primarily to the use of emergency safeguard measures by the industrialized economies that might have adverse effects upon developing countries.

Paragraph 4 deals with trade between developing countries and requires that actions permitted under Part IV do not damage unduly the trade interests of other developing countries. Paragraph 5 provides for the use of the standard GATT dispute settlement procedures, since superseded by the WTO Dispute Settlement Understanding, in the event of disagreement over the implementation of the commitments in Article XXXVII.

GATT joint action

The final Article of Part IV of the GATT, Article XXVIII, sets out proposals for improved collaboration and joint action between GATT members to achieve the objectives specified in Article XXXVI. These proposals include: action to improve market access for primary products and stabilize their prices at remunerative and equitable levels; promoting institutional collaboration; providing financial and policy assistance; and harmonizing national commercial and technical regulations.

The GATT Uruguay Round, the developing countries and the WTO

The participation of developing countries, both individually and as a group, was much more significant in the Uruguay Round negotiations than in any of the previous GATT trade rounds. Their role was crucial in the successful conclusion to the Round because the component Uruguay Round Agreements were all part of a single undertaking; that is that every agreement was accepted by all parties. This was in marked contrast to the multi-track outcomes of the GATT Tokyo Round where each country decided which undertakings to accept – 'GATT à la carte'. The developing countries made use of their improved bargaining power to influence the design of several key Agreements in return for concessions on others.

S&D treatment for developing countries remains embedded in the Uruguay Round Agreements. It is important to note, however, that S&D treatment under these Agreements is not binding on the industrialized economies whereas the Agreements themselves are binding on the developing countries. Several countries have since proposed that this S&D treatment be made binding. The developing countries still enjoy more favourable treatment, particularly with respect to the timetables for the implementation of these Agreements, notably for the General Agreement on Trade in Services (GATS).

Special additional concessions were made in the Uruguay Round for the least developed countries over and above those for developing countries. These are set out in the Ministerial Decision on Measures in Favour of Least-Developed Countries which recognizes their special problems and reaffirms the provisions of the 1979 Geneva Protocol. The Decision states that:

> [T]he least-developed countries, and for so long as they remain in that category . . . will only be required to undertake commitments and concessions to the extent consistent with their individual development, financial and trade needs, or their administrative and institutional capabilities. (WTO 1999)

The additional concessions are detailed in Paragraph 2 of the Decision:

  (i)   Expeditious implementation of all special and differential measures taken in favour of least-developed countries . . . shall be ensured.

  (ii)   MFN concessions on tariff and non-tariff measures agreed in the Uruguay Round on products of export interest to the least-developed countries may be implemented autonomously, in advance and without staging. Consideration shall be given to further improve GSP and other schemes for products of particular export interest.

 (iii)   The rules . . . and transitional provisions in the Uruguay Round should be applied in a flexible and supportive manner for the least-developed countries.

 (iv)   In the application of import relief measures and other measures [referred to in GATT] Article XXXVII . . . special consideration shall be given to the export interests of least-developed countries.

  (v)   Least-developed countries shall be accorded substantially increased technical assistance in the development, strengthening and diversification of their production and export bases including those of services as well as in trade promotion, to enable them to maximize the benefits from liberalized access to markets. (WTO 1999)

The GSP remains an integral part of the WTO obligations of the industrialized countries through Part IV of the GATT 1994. Its scope, however, is now more circumscribed in that each of the Uruguay Round Agreements incorporates separate provisions, albeit non-binding, for S&D treatment. The most explicit innovation of the Uruguay Round in this context was the introduction of additional concessions relating to the situation of the least developed countries in the special Ministerial Decision outlined above. The distinction between developing and least developed countries, however, remains ambiguous apart from a per capita income threshold of $1000 specified in the Agreement on Subsidies and Countervailing Measures. The general issue of graduation is discussed further in the next section.

A critique of the Generalized System of Preferences and S&D Treatment
That there is undeniable merit in granting preferential treatment to the trade of the developing countries is implicitly accepted here. It is important to recognize, however, that the framework that has evolved under the auspices of the GATT and WTO is not necessarily an optimal or even efficient economic system of trade preferences. It is useful therefore to consider critically the underlying structures of these preferences and their impact upon the patterns of trade by the developing countries.

GATT Article XVIII and the developing countries
The original GATT Article XVIII was designed specifically to deal with the special problems of the developing countries. The Article was all that remained of the more comprehensive framework contained in the Havana Treaty of the ITO. It can be argued that the developing countries had very little input into the terms of the original GATT concessions. The 1954–1955 revisions, however, reflect the prevailing structuralist view of economic development as espoused by Raùl Prebisch (1950) and Hans Singer (1950), among others. Article XVIII provided derogations from the GATT principles that permitted developing countries to use selective import controls to promote diversification away from primary commodities through infant industry or, in many cases, infant economy protection.

Article XVIII can therefore be seen to have had an anti-trade impact to the extent that it advocated growth and development based upon import-substituting industrialization. The measures outlined in the Article to protect the balance of payments and infant industries were intended to be temporary although no time limits were defined. These import controls remained in place in many developing countries almost indefinitely.

The impact of the GSP and S&D on trade flows between developing and industrialized countries

The GSP and S&D treatment were incorporated into the GATT, informally in 1971 and formally in 1979, in response to growing demands from the developing countries for preferential access to the markets of the leading industrialized economies. This pressure was the result of the success rather than the failure of the import-substituting growth strategies being pursued. In spite of the limits to growth through import substitution, this strategy resulted in the emergence of several dynamic export industries in which developing countries possessed a comparative advantage. These activities included processed agricultural products and minerals together with labour-intensive manufactures such as textiles, clothing and footwear. The problem, however, was that developing country exports of these products were either denied access to the markets of the industrialized economies or were subject to substantial tariff and non-tariff barriers, hence their demands for preferential market access. The GSP and S&D treatment were introduced only after the developing countries threatened to breakaway from the GATT after having formed UNCTAD.

There is a consensus concerning the positive trade effects of the GSP on trade and growth in the empirical literature although the magnitude of these effects varies between studies. The impact upon individual developing countries, however, is dependent upon the short- and long-run price responsiveness of their export sectors. The most comprehensive study by Karsenty and Laird (1987) found that the GSP significantly increased imports by the industrialized economies. Much of this gain, however, was accounted for by newly industrializing countries – Hong Kong, Korea and Taiwan. The trade creating effects of the GSP were limited by the industrialized economies protecting domestic output while trade diversion was correlated with protectionist sentiments. Other studies emphasize the impact of the GSP on the trade structure of developing countries with the emergence of 'new' exports, such as seasonal agricultural products, canned tuna and light manufactures (Stevens and Weston 1984; McQueen and Read 1987).

Several important additional issues can be identified with respect to the discussion of the effectiveness of the GSP and its impact upon the trade and growth of developing countries.

Non-binding preferences

The GSP commitment to treat developing countries more favourably than MFN, as set out in Part IV of the GATT, became binding on the industrialized economies at the conclusion of the Tokyo Round in 1979. The specific preferential trade concessions that were granted however, were not binding. The industrialized economies therefore remained free to determine the magnitude and scope of their own GSP schemes and modify them arbitrarily without fear of sanction by the GATT in the event of import surges or other threats to sensitive domestic sectors. The United States generally set its GSP tariff preferences at zero but those of the EU were often non-zero so as to maintain a margin of preference for the ACP (Lomé) countries. Many GSP schemes, such as that of the United States, also set import ceilings for individual developing countries beyond which MFN tariff rates applied, that is tariff quotas. The 1974 Trade Act also enables the United States to use the GSP as a bargaining counter if developing countries do not provide 'reasonable' reciprocal market access and/or protect intellectual property rights.

Part IV of the GATT introduced a derogation from the MFN principle that provided for the preferential treatment of developing countries under the GSP. The fundamental problem was that no bounds were defined for GSP preferences such that the GATT thereby permitted the uncontrolled use of trade policies by the industrialized economies. Developing countries therefore had no guarantee of long-term access to particular export markets such that any preferential benefits were effectively regarded as windfall gains (Pomfret 1997). The Uruguay Round Agreements also provide for the non-binding preferential treatment of developing countries.

Discrimination between developing countries

Some of the shortcomings of the GSP have been avoided by the requirement of non-discrimination between developing countries under the WTO. This has necessitated greater accountability in the use of preferential trade policies by the industrialized economies. The special trade preferences granted by the EU to the ACP developing countries over and above the GSP were permitted by the Lomé Waiver. The potential to discriminate between developing countries, however, was tested in the WTO banana dispute, which required that any treatment under such waivers must be WTO-consistent. The Lomé Convention, and its waiver, has since been superseded by the Cotonou Agreement and regional economic partnership arrangements (REPAs) between the EU and groups of ACP countries. These are covered by GATT Article XXIV on regional trade arrangements as well as Paragraph 4 of Article XXXVII on south–south trade.

Graduation issues

This refers to the setting of appropriate thresholds beyond which preferential status for least developed and developing countries no longer applies, generally according to per capita income levels. The GATT made no attempt to identify individual countries that were deemed eligible under Article XVIII and Part IV and this ambiguity was carried over into the Uruguay Round Agreements. Instead, the preferential trade system continues to rely upon self-selection whereby countries declare themselves to be developing. There is, however, a general consensus among the industrialized economies that the WTO provisions apply to 48 least-developed countries as defined by the UN. The GATT also provided scope for the industrialized countries themselves to select the countries to which they would grant GSP benefits. In practice, graduation has generally been confined to the most outstanding performers from East Asia and agreed bilaterally.

The failure of the GATT to define the specific eligibility of developing countries gave the industrialized economies considerable leeway in their trade policies. Given that the GSP commitments were non-binding, this exposed the system of trade preferences to domestic political influence. Graduation under the US Trade Act was automatic according to a defined per capita income formula but could also be applied simply on the basis of export success – thereby penalizing those developing countries that made effective use of the GSP.

The sectoral scope of the application of the GSP

The products eligible for trade preferences under the terms of the GSP were also limited by the pattern of protectionism in the industrialized economies. This was especially notable in 'sensitive' sectors such as agriculture and relatively labour-intensive manufactures; goods in which the developing countries might be expected to possess a comparative advantage. These sectors were either excluded from the GSP or subject to high-tariff and non-tariff barriers in spite of their critical export importance to developing countries.

Agriculture has long been a sensitive issue in both the GATT and WTO. Trade reform has lagged well behind that of manufactures because of the extent of domestic support to farmers, particularly in the EU, Japan and the United States. The first comprehensive multilateral agreement on trade in agriculture, the Agreement on Agriculture, was negotiated as part of the Uruguay Round. This was agreed only after considerable pressure from the Cairns Group of agricultural exporting countries, most of which are developing, and the cross-linking of agriculture with other negotiations on other issues such as trade in services.

Trade in textiles and clothing was governed by the Multi-Fibre Arrangement (MFA), a separate agreement from the GATT which imposed quantitative restraints (quotas and VERs), primarily on exports from developing countries. This is a key growth sector for developing countries because of its relative labour-intensity but the MFA was used to protect increasingly inefficient firms in the industrialized economies from import competition. Under the Agreement on Textiles and Clothing, the MFA was phased out at the end of 2004.

The growth of labour-intensive manufactured exports from developing countries, such as electronic consumer goods, has also been constrained by anti-dumping actions and countervailing duties to offset their cost advantage in industrialized economy markets.

Tariff escalation in the industrialized economics

This refers to the pattern of increasing protection at successive stages in the value chain within a particular sector such that processed goods face higher trade barriers than their component raw materials. The apparently gentle escalation of many nominal tariffs in the industrialized economies, however, gives rise to significant escalation in the extent of effective protection. Tariff escalation therefore inhibits the emergence of export-oriented processing activities in developing countries that embody higher domestic value added, regardless of underlying comparative advantage. Under the GSP and Lomé, effective protection resulting from tariff escalation is estimated to range between three and nine times the nominal tariffs (Trebilcock and Howse 1999). In its strongest form, tariff escalation could confine developing countries to being exporters of primary commodities almost indefinitely. The developing countries have consistently pressed for action to deal with this issue although little progress has been made. The main factor in the declining impact of tariff escalation has been multilateral trade liberalization which has resulted in across-the-board reductions in tariffs.

Restrictive Rules of Origin

Rules of Origin refer to the imposition of minimum thresholds for the local value added embodied in any good for it to constitute an export originating from a specific country. Their primary function is to prevent discriminatory trade barriers being circumvented by routeing exports via a preferred third country; for example, to enforce country-specific

MFA quotas. By raising the value added threshold, however, Rules of Origin have been used by the industrialized countries – often in conjunction with tariff escalation – to limit import penetration by developing countries, particularly of export-platform manufactures. Complex Rules of Origin also impose a high administrative burden on developing country exporters to prove their value added.

The asymmetric benefits of the GSP
Trade preferences may be important in promoting growth in developing countries through trade but they are by no means sufficient. The effectiveness of the GSP must be considered with respect to the extent to which individual developing countries have been able to take full advantage of the opportunities for preferential market access. Karsenty and Laird (1987) find that the benefits of S&D treatment have largely been for textiles and other manufactures exported by the leading NICs, notably Hong Kong, Korea and Taiwan. These are the developing countries best placed to take advantage of the GSP and least in need of such preferential treatment. Most developing countries, however, and the least developed ones in particular, have not benefited greatly from the GSP because market access is not the source of their poor export performance. Rather, it is caused by the standard constraints of development resulting from low levels of investment, technology, productivity and market knowledge along with inelasticities in the supply of exports.

Trade liberalization and GSP margins of preferences
The margin of preference enjoyed by the developing countries under the GSP has been significantly eroded by the substantial reduction in MFN bound tariff rates as a direct consequence of multilateral trade liberalization. This has reduced the value of S&D under the GSP and, in some cases, has provided a justification for developing country opposition to further trade liberalization. Karsenty and Laird (1987) find that further multilateral tariff liberalization, with a corresponding cut in the margin of GSP preferences, would lead to substantial additional gains for developing countries. These gains, however, would primarily accrue to the NICs. The least developed countries would be the principal losers because the negative impact of their reduced margins of preference would outweigh the benefits of improved market access owing to inelasticities in their supply response.

Concluding comments
In spite of the shortcomings of the GSP, S&D treatment still retains the support of most developing countries since no other multilateral preferential trade arrangement of its type exists. The international trading system has made significant progress in recognizing the special position of the developing countries, and that of the least developed in particular. The 'anti-trade' provisions of the original GATT Article XVIII were superseded by the trade-supportive GATT Part IV after a stand-off with the industrialized countries. The Uruguay Round Agreements administered by the WTO all incorporate specific non-binding provisions for the least developed countries, supported by the binding Ministerial Decision on Measures in Favour of Least-Developed Countries. That the markets of the industrialized economies are accessible to exports from developing countries is a necessary but insufficient condition for their growth. Economic development is a broader and more complex undertaking and additional non-trade measures are therefore required to overcome domestic supply constraints, particularly in the case of the least developed countries.

Developments in S&D in the Doha Development Round
The debate on the role of S&D within the WTO Agreements has intensified during the Doha Round negotiations. The developing countries made 88 specific proposals relating to S&D, raising the possibility of a new agreement on the issue. Most of these proposals revolved around market access, derogations, aid to relieve supply side constraints and technical and financial assistance. Some of these issues were resolved in early 2003 while discussions of others have been referred to the appropriate Doha negotiating fora. Progress, however, has stalled in the wake of the Cancún WTO Ministerial Meeting in September 2003 although this has possibly made a new agreement more likely.

Further reading on the GSP, trade and the developing countries
There are several general sources that place the GSP in the context of global trade system, including *The Political Economy of the World Trading System* (Hoekman and Kostecki 2001) and *The Regulation of International Trade* (Trebilcock and Howse 1999). Two recent volumes focus specifically upon trade by the developing countries; *Developing Countries and the Multilateral Trading System: From GATT to the Uruguay Round and the Future* (Srinivasan 1998) and *Developing Countries in the World Trading System: the Uruguay Round and Beyond* (Adhikari and Athukorala 2002). *The European Community and the Developing Countries* (Grilli 1993), focuses exclusively on the EU's preferential trade policy. Chapter 15 of *The Economics of Regional Trading Arrangements* (Pomfret 1997) provides a brief review of the empirical literature on the impact of the GSP, including the major study by Karsenty and Laird (1987).

References
Adhikari, R. and Athukorala, P. (eds) (2002), *Developing Countries in the World Trading System: the Uruguay Round and Beyond*, Cheltenham, UK and Northampton, MA, USA: Edward Elgar.
Balassa, B. (1982), *Development Strategies in Semi-industrial Economies*, Baltimore: Johns Hopkins.
Grilli, E. R. (1993), *The European Community and the Developing Countries*, Cambridge: Cambridge University Press.
Hoekman, B. M. and Kostecki, M. M. (2001), *The Political Economy of the World Trading System* (2nd edn), Oxford: Oxford University Press.
Karsenty, G. and Laird, S. (1987), 'The GSP: a Quantitative Assessment of the Direct Trade Effects and Policy Options', *Weltwirtschaftliches Archiv*, **123**, 262–96.
McQueen, M. and Read, R. (1987), 'Prospects for ACP Exports to the Enlarged Community', in C. Stevens and J. V. van Themaat (eds), *Europe and the International Division of Labour: New Patterns of Trade and Investment with Developing Countries, The EEC & the Third World, A Survey 6,* London: Hodder & Stoughton, pp. 88–108.
Pomfret, R. (1997), *The Economics of Regional Trading Arrangements*, Oxford: Oxford University Press.
Prebisch, R. (1950), *The Economic Development of Latin America and Its Principal Problems*, UN Doc. E/CN.12/89/Rev.1. Lake Success, NY: United Nations.
Singer, H. (1950), 'The Distribution of Gains Between Investing and Borrowing Countries', *American Economic Review*, **40**(2), 473–85.
Srinivasan, T. N. (1998), *Developing Countries and the Multilateral Trading System: From GATT to the Uruguay Round and the Future*, London: HarperCollins.
Stevens, C. and Weston, A. (1984), 'Trade Diversification: Has Lomé Helped?', in C. Stevens (ed.), *Renegotiating Lomé, The EEC and the Third World: A Survey 4*, London: Hodder & Stoughton, pp. 25–52.
Trebilcock, M. J. and Howse, R. (1999), *The Regulation of International Trade* (2nd edn), London: Routledge.
WTO (1999), *The Legal Texts: the Results of the Uruguay Round of Multilateral Trade Negotiations*, Cambridge: Cambridge University Press.

44 International commodity agreements
Christopher L. Gilbert

Introduction

The term 'international commodity agreement' (henceforth ICA) refers to a treaty-agreement between governments of both producing and consuming countries to regulate the terms of international trade in a specified commodity. There have only been five ICAs which have had 'economic' (that is interventionist) clauses:[1] the International Cocoa Agreement (ICCA), the International Coffee Agreement (ICOA), the International Natural Rubber Agreement (INRA), the International Sugar Agreement (ISA) and the International Tin Agreement (ITA).

In the second section of this chapter, I look at the growth of the ICA movement up to the end of the 1970s. The third section summarizes the main features of the five ICAs. The fourth section looks at problems associated with the agreement price range. The fifth section is devoted to the decline of the ICAs through the 1980s and 1990s. The sixth section attempts to evaluate the success of the agreements, while the seventh section is devoted to the claim that the ICOA, the most successful of the five agreements, functioned as an internationally sanctioned cartel. The final section contains a brief summary.

Genesis

Primary commodity markets have been subjected to governmental intervention at least as far back as the 1930s. At the end of the Second World War, there was a widespread expectation that low prices and excess capacity might return. The unratified 1948 Havana Charter, which would have set up the International Trade Organization as the third pillar of Bretton Woods, included measures aimed at the alleviation of situations of 'burdensome surplus' (Rowe 1965). It was envisaged that this would be accomplished primarily through supply regulation – typically export controls. In the absence of the institutional structures which the Havana Charter aimed to create, interested governments negotiated free-standing agreements of which the 1954 ISA and ITA were the first. Both relied primarily on supply management – the ISA entirely so, while the ITA also utilized a buffer stock, the initial purpose of which was seen as supporting the price over the period in which export restrictions took effect – see Fox (1974). These two agreements continued an interventionist tradition inherited from interwar colonial administrations.

The situation was somewhat different by 1962 when first the ICOA was negotiated. At that time, coffee was predominantly a Latin American commodity (Brazil and Colombia were the largest exporters), although production was already expanding in Africa. The *Instituto Brasileiro do Cafe* (the IBC) was responsible for Brazilian coffee policy and had favoured supply management for many decades, but the Colombians had resisted this, preferring to expand production under unfettered conditions. However, as coffee consolidated in Colombia, political power shifted towards the coffee-growing regions (Bates, 1997). The United States was, and remains, the single largest coffee consuming nation, and the crucial element which resulted in the ICOA, which was modelled on the ISA as a pure export control agreement, was the willingness of the US government to agree to export controls. This was the period immediately following the socialist revolution in Cuba, and it is often supposed that the US saw the advantage of higher coffee prices for Latin American exporters as outweighing the disadvantages arising from a controlled market. Bates (1997) argues that the highly concentrated and imperfectly competitive US coffee roasting industry was more concerned with reliability and security of supply than with price and may have seen agreement to controls as an acceptable price for governmental goodwill. Gilbert (2004a) suggests an alternative explanation which we take up later in the chapter.

While coffee is predominantly a Latin American commodity, cocoa is predominantly West African, although there is significant production for export in south-east Asia (Latin America now produces almost entirely for domestic consumption). Many of the West African cocoa producers are also coffee producers, and West African cocoa had inherited a tradition of state-controlled marketing from the British and French colonial administrations. In this context, it was natural that the cocoa producers would seek an agreement similar to that negotiated in coffee. However the US government declined to join the 1972 ICCA. The ICCA differed from the ICOA in that its primary instrument was the buffer stock, with export controls playing a supplementary role.

With the 1964 foundation of the United Nations Conference on Trade and Development (UNCTAD), ICAs moved into a more political environment. Existing ICAs came under the auspices of UNCTAD, which also sought, from 1976, to stimulate the negotiation of new agreements as part of the Integrated Programme for Commodities (IPC) in connection with the so-called New International Economic Order (NIEO). The NIEO was intended to set up what its proponents viewed as a more equitable system of trading relations between the developed and the developing world. The IPC was endorsed by the United Nations General Assembly in 1974. Its most explicit statement is in UNCTAD Resolution 93(IV) which sought the stabilization of commodity prices around levels which would be 'remunerative and just to producers and equitable to consumers' (UNCTAD, 1976). UNCTAD produced a list of ten 'core' commodities in which it hoped to see ICAs[2] but developed country governments argued for a commodity-by-commodity approach to negotiations. These negotiations took place in Geneva over the following years.

Brown (1980) gives an account of the UNCTAD negotiations. Although the rhetoric of the negotiations related to the variability of commodity prices, with buffer stock intervention now the favoured instrument, developed countries remained suspicious that the main intention of the producer country governments related to the level rather than the variability of prices. The INRA was the only new agreement to emerge from this long process.

Features

Table 44.1 summarizes the general features of the five ICAs. The principal instruments used by ICAs have been supply management and buffer stock intervention. Supply management presupposes the ability of government to control either production or exports. Where production is in the hands of large private companies, such controls are likely to be resisted. Instead, where production is undertaken by smallholders, as is typically the case in cocoa, coffee and sugar, governments were frequently able to control marketing

Table 44.1   Summary features of international commodity agreements (ICAs)

	Cocoa (ICCA)	Coffee (ICOA)	Natural rubber (INRA)	Sugar (ISA)	Tin (ITA)
First agreement	1981	1962	1980	1954	1956
Breakdown or lapse of intervention	suspended 1988	suspended 1989	terminated 1999	lapsed 1983	collapsed 1985
US membership	no	yes	yes	yes	mixed[a]
Buffer stock	yes	no	yes	no	yes
Export controls	supplementary[b]	yes	no	yes	yes

Notes:
  [a] The US was a member of the first five ITAs, but not of the sixth ITA which collapsed in 1985.
  [b] The first two ICCAs made provision for export controls but these were never employed. The fourth ICCA provided for producing member countries to 'withhold' supplies in the event that the buffer stock reached its maximum level. This provision was never implemented. The fifth ICCA, which came into effect in 1993, no longer provided for a buffer stock but did allow the possibility of 'production management'. This provision was never implemented.

through monopsony–monopoly marketing boards (a feature of many ex-British colonies) or *caisses de stabilisation* (standard in many ex-French colonies). However, both smuggling and problems in controlling re-exports undermined export controls. Effective buffer stock stabilization supposes storability together with a relatively competitive (international) market structure (since otherwise large producers could act strategically with respect to the buffer stock). Both forms of intervention are made more difficult to the extent that the commodity lacks homogeneity.[3]

As noted, the ICOAs and ISAs operated entirely through export controls – coffee and sugar are smallholder crops and governments do not have the power to set production levels. The ITAs employed both export controls and a buffer stock with the emphasis within the successive ITAs shifting from supply controls towards increased reliance on buffer stock stabilization. The ICCA was conceived as relying on a buffer stock but with the possibility of supply controls held in reserve, while the INRA relied entirely on its buffer stock.

Trends and cycles

Commodity agreements typically functioned on the basis of price targets. The ITA buffer stock operated with a price band of ±15 per cent around a central price. The ICCA had a dual band system with an outer ±17.3 per cent band and a permissive inner band of ±14.5 per cent, within which the buffer stock manager was prohibited from operating. In practice the cocoa buffer stock manager seldom had the resources to do anything. The INRA used an even more complicated triple band system with buffer stock intervention defined in terms of the two inner bands (a permissive ±15 per cent band and a wider ±20 per cent band at which point the buffer stock manager was obliged to operate) with the objective of keeping the price within the outer (+28 per cent, −25 per cent) band – see Gilbert (1987, 1996). While ICOAs did not use a buffer stock, export controls were triggered if a 15 day moving average of a price index (the ICO Composite Indicator Price) fell beneath a trigger level, and were lifted once it rose above a higher trigger. In practice, the definition of the bands was less important than the identification of the central price (in coffee, the trigger prices) about which they were defined, and the procedures for updating these prices.

Any stabilization exercise relies on the ability of the stabilization authority to separate cycle from trend: the authority aims to reduce or eliminate the cyclical variation but cannot aim to beat the trend since this would require indefinitely large resources – either physical (in the case of a positive trend) or financial (negative trend). From a statistical standpoint, it matters whether the trend in a commodity price is deterministic or stochastic. Equivalently, one may ask what proportion of any price change should be considered as permanent and what proportion transitory. If the trend is completely deterministic, any movement about that trend is transient. If instead the trend is completely stochastic, the current price provides the best forecast for the future and the authority cannot beat the market. Using long time series, the data favour the stochastic view, but once one allows the deterministic trend to have a time-varying slope (the so-called 'smooth trend') the two models fit equally well (Gilbert 2004b). What emerges is that commodity price trends are variable and difficult to predict.

It is tempting to argue that because commodity price volatility is large relative to drift, concerns about long-run declines in price trends are less important than concerns over the implications of increasing price volatility – see Deaton (1999) and Cashin and McDermott (2002). The ICA experience suggests that this view is wrong.

It is well known and widely accepted that primary commodity prices generally follow a negative trend relative to the prices of manufactures – see Prebisch (1962, originally 1950), Singer (1950) and Grilli and Yang (1988). Through the 1960s and 1970s, this declining real trend was hidden by nominal inflation with the result that nominal dollar price targets[4] were generally conservative and updating tended to be positive and *ad hoc*. This is evident in the cocoa agreements where the stabilization range in the first two agreements through the 1970s was always beneath the actual market price (Gilbert 1987).

With US dollar inflation reduced to low levels through the early 1980s and 1990s, a declining real trend translated directly into a declining nominal trend, and this implied that stabilization price targets were typically too high. The third cocoa agreement saw the price below the stabilization range almost all the time, but with the ICCA lacking the funds to intervene. Except from the INRA (see below), the ICAs lacked formal procedures for downward revision, probably because this problem had simply not been anticipated. Coffee provides an example – with the dollar prices of other commodities falling sharply through the mid- and late 1980s, the ICOA succeeded in holding the nominal dollar price at historical levels. Once intervention broke down, and stocks held back by exporters were released, the price collapse was dramatic.

The single exception to this story was the INRA, the newest and in certain respected the best designed ICA. The INRA's contained semi-automatic procedures for both upward and downward revision of its price bands. The result was that the stabilization range followed the market price with the result that the agreement smoothed rather than stabilized prices.

Decline

Pressure for advance towards the NIEO resulted in the commodities debate becoming increasingly politicized through the latter half of the 1970s and into the 1980s. Within that context, policy discussion of commodity agreements became increasingly informed by welfare economics. The 1981 publication of David Newbery's and Joseph Stiglitz's book *The Theory of Commodity Price Stabilization* (Newbery and Stiglitz 1981) was particularly important. Newbery and Stiglitz argued that, in the absence of a complete set of forward and contingent markets, there is no reason to suppose that the competitive allocation is even constrained Paretian.[5] However, they also recognized that this observation has limited implications. In particular, there is in general no reason to suppose that private sector storage is inadequate, which is the premise of public buffer stock stabilization. Furthermore, buffer stock stabilization is expensive, both in terms of the opportunity cost of funds employed and because public stocks displace private stocks (Miranda and Helmberger 1988).

Developed country governments saw price stabilization as a costly diversion of funds from more pressing development objectives. Further, they suspected that many of the producing countries wished to substitute a socialist-style 'planned' commodity economy which would be inefficient and might result in an unfavourable shift in the terms of trade. Industry groups saw the continuing UNCTAD negotiations as driven by political rather than commercial concerns. Reinforced by the welfare economics arguments, consumer governments in effect filibustered the UNCTAD negotiation process.

From this point onwards, the ICA movement went into reverse. The ISAs had never managed to overcome the problems caused by the USA's 1962 decision to deny access to Cuba, then the largest sugar-exporting country, to the US market, and by the substantial growth in sugar production in the European Union. The fourth ISA terminated in 1984 and was replaced by an agreement which did not contain market intervention clauses (Gilbert 1987). The ICCA does remain in existence and does, in principle, allow the possibility of market intervention through unspecified production management measures, but no longer through the buffer stock. However, the ICCAs have never had either the finance or the country coverage to be able to have more than a small effect of the cocoa market (Gilbert 1987, 1996). Effectively, therefore, the active ICAs consisted of the ITA, the ICOA and the INRA. The ITA broke down spectacularly on United Nations Day (24 October) 1985 – see Anderson and Gilbert (1988) – and the ICOA effectively abandoned supply management ambitions on (US) Independence Day (4 July) 1989. This left the INRA to stagger on until 1999, a year prior to the formal ending of the third INRA, when first Malaysia (13 October 1999) and then Sri Lanka and Thailand gave notice of withdrawal from the agreement. These actions were in part motivated by the perception that, because of adjustment of the price bands, the INRA offered too little stabilization. This effectively terminated the agreement and hence also the ICA movement.

There is no single reason for the breakdown or lapse of the commodity agreements. The cocoa and sugar agreements lapsed because they were ineffective. The tin agreement collapsed because it was attempting to hold the price at too high a level with too little finance to do this.[6] This was the single case which corresponds to the widespread view that ICAs attempt to stand Canute-like against the incoming market tide, but it is important also to recall that the ITA was effective for the first 25 years of its existence. More interesting are the cases of coffee and natural rubber where the agreements lapsed rather than collapsed. In rubber, this was because producing country governments saw little benefit from continued price smoothing, while in coffee the agreements lost support from consumers and to some extent also from producers – see below.

These changes in support took place in the context in which the markets for tropical export commodities were being liberalized and in which domestic stabilization agencies – marketing boards and *caisses de stabilisation* – were being dismantled or forced to accept reduced powers – see Akiyama *et al.* (2001). The private sector was becoming more important and government involvement in agriculture was diminishing. Governments had both less power than previously to control supplies, and also a diminished willingness to do so. Increasingly, the ICAs appeared anachronistic and international meetings, in which diplomats deployed non-commercial arguments about price and export levels, seemed irrelevant to the need to compete in free and competitive markets.

ICA Effectiveness

The extent to which ICAs have (a) raised and (b) stabilized prices remains controversial. Evaluations have typically relied on counterfactual simulation of econometric models, for example Smith and Schink (1976) on tin, and Palm and Vogelvang (1981) on coffee. Exercises of this sort are subject to qualification with regard to the extent that the models employed in the simulations adequately reflect market behaviour. These worries are underlined by the 'Lucas problem' that stockholding and other strategies will adapt to the policies followed by the stabilization authority (Miranda and Helmberger 1988).

Gilbert (1996, 2004b) reports the results of a cruder evaluation procedure and this is updated in Table 44.2. The table gives the annual price averages for cocoa, coffee, natural rubber, sugar and tin over the five years following cessation of intervention. In each case, prices are measured relative to the IMF Commodity Price Index (non-fuel commodities), with the ratio normalized to 100 in the 12-month period before intervention ceased or was abandoned. The indices in Table 44.2 should therefore be seen as indices relative to the general level of non-energy commodity prices. Except in the case of natural rubber, the ending of intervention was associated over the following two years with prices around 40 per cent lower than in the final year of control. Despite subsequent recovery in coffee and sugar, on average prices remained 30 per cent lower over the next three years, and much of this difference persisted over the following five years.

Table 44.2   Post-ICA price changes

Year	Cocoa	Coffee	Natural Rubber	Sugar	Tin	Average
− 1	100.0	100.0	100.0	100.0	100.0	100.0
0	62.5	65.1	101.3	60.2	55.7	69.0
1	52.3	68.6	91.3	56.7	51.1	64.0
2	59.6	62.3	110.6	82.3	43.7	71.7
3	60.4	56.7	148.1	99.6	54.4	80.4
4	53.9	80.8	162.7	138.6	41.9	87.8
Average 5–9	64.7	117.2	n.a.	121.0	39.8	85.7[a]

Note:
[a] Excludes natural rubber.

Taken at face value, the figures in Table 44.2 suggest that ICAs raised commodity prices by a substantial amount. However, this conclusion is too simple. The five ICA commodities considered in Table 44.2 fall into three groups.

- In cocoa and sugar, the agreements lapsed at least in part because over-supply made it impossible to maintain prices at historic levels. For these two commodities, the price falls were caused by this over-supply and not by the ending of control. It is difficult to claim that this over-supply was caused by the ICAs themselves.
- In coffee and tin, by contrast, it is plausible to argue that the price falls are attributable to the ending of controls. In particular, both agreements saw the release of stocks which had been held off the market, by producers in the ICOA and by the buffer stock in the ITA. It is generally believed in the respective industries that the scale of this stock release took prices below long run production costs. It is plausible that both agreements did raise prices above production costs, but the 40–50 per cent figures in Table 44.2 probably overestimate this.
- The INRA was effective only by being ineffective. It is therefore unsurprising that the end of the agreement had little effect on rubber prices.

Did the ICAs also stabilize prices? The answer to this question is complicated by the fact that commodity prices should be less variable when supply is plentiful – see Williams and Wright (1991), Deaton and Laroque (1992) and Brunetti and Gilbert (1995) – and the end of controls increased availability at least in the cases of coffee and tin. Looking at the three-year period immediately following the lapse or collapse of controls in relation to the three-year period immediately preceding this, the coefficient of variation of monthly coffee prices fell from 23.6 per cent to 10.7 per cent, while the coefficients of variation for cocoa and tin rose from 6.9 per cent to 14.3 per cent and from 8.3 per cent to 14.3 per cent respectively. Coffee moved from a regime of high but volatile prices to one of stable depressed prices,[7] and the rise in the coefficients of variation for cocoa and tin is entirely attributable to lower average prices – the price standard deviations are almost identical before and after the end of stabilization. Rubber price volatility has reflected changes in market tightness – prices became less volatile in the weak market conditions at the time of the ending of the agreement but volatility has subsequently increased dramatically as the markets for all industrially-consumed raw materials have become very tight.

Even if ICAs did generate benefits to exporting countries, we need to ask who were the beneficiaries within the countries. There is some evidence, particularly from the coffee agreements, that benefits were diverted to elites (Bohman *et al.*, 1996). Export controls always create rents, partly because export quotas can be allocated to friends or political allies, and also because the administration of controls generates employment and therefore a vested interest in the continuation of controls. One reason Brazil lost interest in coffee market control was the perception that the major beneficiary was the controlling IBC bureaucracy (Gilbert 1996).

Evaluation of the overall 'success' of the ICAs is problematic on account of the confusion over their objectives. The rhetoric of the agreements, at least over the final decades of the century, stressed reduction in price variability, but here the effects appear to have been at best marginal. By contrast, producer governments have always seen ICAs as a means of raising prices, or at least of avoiding low prices, and on this criterion, the agreements – in particular the ICOA and the ITA – do appear to have enjoyed some success. However, the success (up to 1980) of the tin agreement reflects a very particular market situation in which the US General Services Administration released surplus strategic stocks, accumulated in the Korean War period, in tight market situations, and the ITA buffer stock held up prices in weak market conditions – see Fox (1974) and Gilbert (1987). If any success is to be attributed to the ICA movement, we must look for this in the coffee agreements.

The coffee agreement as a cartel
Law (1975) described ICAs as internationally sanctioned cartels. The claim is only interesting in relation to the ICOA, since the other agreements were either ineffective (ICCA, ISA), weak (INRA) or operated in special conditions (ITA).

A cartel is a cooperative arrangement between producers (here producer governments) to restrict supplies and thereby raise prices. In Chamberlin's (1929, 1933) classic model, oligopolistic producers of a homogeneous product, recognizing their interdependence, either explicitly or tacitly agree to restrict supply and produce the monopoly output. The ICOA had this power and frequently resorted to it.

In common with other primary commodities, coffee is priced against terminal market prices. During the periods in which the ICAs were operative, the important terminal markets for coffee were the (New York) Coffee, Sugar and Cocoa Exchange (CSCE), now part of the New York Board of Trade, which traded a mild arabica contract, and the London Commodity Exchange (LCE), now part of Euronext-LIFFE, which traded a robusta contract. Exporters typically enter contracts, either for delivery at a negotiated (known) premium or discount against the 'unknown' terminal market price at (or around) the date of delivery. Terminal market prices are determined by the balance of aggregate supply and demand at the time, and by expectations of the future balance. It follows from that, the coffee markets should be viewed as a case of Cournot competition in which producers make quantity (export) decisions and the resulting terminal market prices clear the resulting aggregate demand and supply.

Cooperation is an alternative to competition. Cooperative equilibrium supported by the threat of retaliation, is a Nash equilibrium in a repeated game (Tirole 1988). Producers have an incentive to cooperate without the support of an ICA and such cooperation results in a straightforward producer cartel. The Organization of Petroleum Exporting Countries (OPEC) is the most familiar example of a commodity cartel. Producer cartels experience problems with both detection and enforcement. Countries may export in excess of quota, typically through delivery to terminal markets. Excess exports will generally be detectable retrospectively from the import statistics of consuming countries, and the commodity trade will often have strong suspicions as to where material is coming from at the actual time. However, even if excess exports are detected, the only available threat of retaliation – flooding the market as a form of tit-for-tat punishment – will generally lack credibility. The major historical instance (oil in 1985) was not notably successful.

Gilbert (2004a) argues that, by operating within the framework of an ICA, producers may hope to attain superior detection and enforcement and to thereby reduce free riding. Detection is improved through the obligation on all producing members of the agreement to report accurate statistics on a timely basis. Enforcement is improved by the involvement of consumers in limiting imports. These considerations suggest that an ICA has the potential to be more effective than the corresponding producer cartel. They are sufficient to demonstrate why those producers who favour a producer cartel to competition may further prefer an ICA to the cartel.

The more interesting question is why consuming country governments should agree to join ICAs. In fact, many consumer country governments have chosen not to join many potential ICAs, which is one reason why relatively few ICAs have actually been operative. It is sometimes suggested that ICAs yield other benefits, such as price stability, which consumers may value, or ICAs may be seen as non-transparent mechanisms for transferring resources to developing countries. Such benefits are likely to be small – either ICAs do not reduce price variability, or consumers do not value any such reduction,[8] or both of these; and if developed country governments wish to transfer resources to developing countries, they prefer more transparent and targeted mechanisms. In that case, and in the absence of other compelling political arguments, consumer governments prefer lower to higher commodity prices. This suggests that they should be expected to oppose any form of cartel, and if ICAs are more effective than unilateral producer cartels, they will disfavour ICAs more than producer cartels. On this narrow logic, it will never have been rational for a consumer government to join an ICA.

This argument is too simple. If consumer governments are offered the choice between an ICA, a producer cartel and a Cournot-competitive outcome, they will certainly prefer the competitive outcome. However, in market situations in which producers can credibly threaten a unilateral producer cartel, the effective choice may be between the producer cartel and an ICA. In such cases, consumer governments may prefer to operate within the framework of an ICA, where they can influence outcomes, to being obliged to live with a producer cartel, which they cannot influence. In particular, they can force moderation of the cartel prices as their price for the improved detection and enforcement technology.

Gilbert (2004a) formalizes this intuition and argues that it provides a good explanation of why consumer country governments, including that of the United States, supported coffee agreements in the 1970s and 1980s. He advances two classes of evidence for this claim.

- Under the ICOAs, coffee could only be imported into consuming member countries if accompanied by a licence issued by the International Coffee Organization (ICO) which guaranteed that it was within quota. These import restrictions were enforced by the consumer government customs authorities on behalf of the ICO. Consumer government membership of the ICOAs therefore provided an improved detection and enforcement technology for the cartel. This was the incentive for the producer governments to accept an ICA rather than a unilateral producer cartel with inferior quota enforcement.
- A sequence of incidents, both prior to the first ICOA and during a period in the late 1970s during which export controls were suspended, demonstrated the willingness of the producing countries in general, and Brazil in particular, to resort to unilateral export controls if controls could not be agreed within an ICA framework. The most notorious of these incidents was the manipulation of the 1979 CSCE coffee futures contract described in Greenstone (1981). This willingness to act independently of consumer governments provided the incentive for the latter to agree to cooperate within the framework of the ICOA and thereby obtain more moderate prices.

Gilbert (2004a) shows that, under certain parameter configurations, both consumers and the large producers can gain from cooperation, at the expense of high cost marginal producers who free ride on the producer cartel but are forced to restrict output under the agreement by virtue of the consumer country import controls. This situation changed by the late 1980s as the growth in coffee consumption in Brazil, by then the second largest consumer, after the United States, as well as the largest producer, undermined its interest in maintaining high coffee prices, and through the perception that much of the benefit of high prices was being absorbed by the IBC. Once Brazil was no longer able to credibly threaten a cartel, the United States and other consumer country governments no longer had an interest in cooperation.

This approach can also throw light on the US decision not to join the 1981 ICCA. A simple view is that this decision reflects the perceived lack of strategic importance of West Africa at that time, or the fact that cocoa grinders and chocolate manufacturers[9] were generally not disposed towards controls. An alternative view, suggested by Gilbert's (2004a) model, is that the decision rather reflects the inability of the cocoa exporters to credibly threaten a universal cartel, despite a number of attempts by Côte d'Ivoire, the largest producer, to manipulate prices by withholding supplies. Crucially, those efforts lacked any support from other major producers, in particular Ghana and Indonesia.

Summary

International commodity agreements were conceived as part of a programme based on a perceived need to regulate competitive markets in order to avoid prolonged periods of low prices resulting from chronic excess supply. They operated through a combination of supply management (export controls) and public sector (buffer stock) storage. Interventions were mandated either to keep the market price within a predefined price band, or once the price hit pre-defined trigger prices. Except in the natural rubber agreement, there were no clear procedures for updating these price ranges or triggers over time, and this deficiency caused major problems during the deflationary 1980s.

Commodity agreements broke down or lapsed in the 1980s and 1990s, in part because of failure to adapt to the deflationary climate, in part because consumer governments took fright at what they saw as an excessively interventionist approach adopted by UNCTAD in the negotiations for the New International Economic Order, and in part because of a general shift towards free market policies in the developed as well as the developing countries. The last active agreement expired in 1999.

It is a mistake to argue that international commodity agreements can never be effective, or that they are bound to break down under the tidal onslaught of market developments. At the same time, more agreements have been ineffective than have been effective, and some agreements have broken down by attempting to hold prices too high. Others have been abandoned because either producer governments, consumer governments or both have no longer seen controls as worthwhile.

Evaluation of the success of intervention begs the question of the criteria by which success is to be judged. On any basis the cocoa and sugar agreements were too weak to achieve any of their objectives. By contrast, the coffee agreement does appear to have both raised and stabilized the coffee price over its period of activity, and the same is broadly true of the tin agreement up to 1980, although particular features of the tin industry suggest that one should not generalize on that basis. The rubber agreement was less ambitious and probably smoothed rather than stabilized prices. Overall, therefore, it is only in coffee that the commodity agreement movement can claim a major success. However, closer examination of the coffee experience indicates that its success was based on a credible threat of a unilateral producer cartel, rather than the benevolent cooperation for the good of all as part of a new international order.

Notes

1. There is also a large number of 'study group' style agreements whose functions are information collection and dissemination, market promotion and, in certain cases, the fostering of research and development. The Lead and Zinc Study Group provides a prominent example.
2. Cocoa, coffee, copper, cotton, jute, rubber, sisal (later extended to all hard fibres), sugar, tea and tin.
3. No commodity is completely homogeneous. However, only in coffee was heterogeneity an important factor in the operation of the agreements. There are two broad types of coffee – arabica and robusta. Arabica, which is grown on volcanic mountain slopes in Latin America and east Africa, is more expensive to produce but has superior flavour. It commands a variable premium over robusta coffees which can be grown at lower altitudes in a much wider range of countries. Most retail coffee is blended and includes both arabica and robusta in varying proportions. Arabica and robusta beans are themselves far from homogeneous with the best arabicas, and a few highly rated robustas, selling at high premiums to the rest of the market. By contrast, cocoa butter (the main cocoa intermediate product), latex rubber, refined sugar and tin metal vary only within narrow limits – one seldom finds, for example, sugar or chocolate sold by origin.
4. The ICOA, ICCA and ISA used US dollar price ranges. The ITA moved from a sterling price range to a price range defined in terms of the Malaysian dollar while the INRA used a curious average of the Malaysian and Singapore dollar – see Gilbert (1987). In practice, the Malaysian and Singapore dollars moved closely with the US dollar over the relevant period.
5. That is Paretian relative to the markets that do exist.
6. The International Tin Council (ITC) made a complicated set of Enron-style forward transactions to increase its leverage. This resulted in its bearing an exposure to the tin price which vastly exceeded the ITA limit on its tin holdings – hence the default once the price fell. However, these dubiously legal derivative transactions were not the fundamental cause of breakdown. Anderson and Gilbert (1988) argue that they may have prolonged the exercise by several months, but the basic problem was that of too high a support level and too little finance. The tin breakdown also serves to warn of the dangers in Massell's (1969) suggestion that it may be more efficient for a stabilization agency to support the forward price than to hold physical inventory.
7. This conclusion is sensitive to the choice of window. In the final eight (calendar) years during which the ICOA controls were in effect (1981–1988), monthly nominal coffee volatility, measured as the standard deviation of logarithmic monthly average prices, was 14.8 per cent while in the eight post-intervention years (1990–1997), it doubled to 37.0 per cent. However, this rise in volatility mainly reflects the impact of the 1994 Brazilian frosts. The sugar price remained highly variable before and after the lapse of the ISA, probably reflecting the residual nature of the free market in sugar at that time.
8. Households are well diversified across commodities and therefore suffer little from the price variability of any particular commodity (Gilbert 1985). Furthermore, to the extent that commodity price movements originate from supply shocks, consumers will actually benefit from the intertemporal substitution possibilities that variability introduces (Waugh 1944; Massell 1969).
9. Cocoa beans are ground (processed) to produce cocoa butter and cocoa powder. Cocoa butter is the intermediate product in chocolate manufacture. Cocoa grinding is subject to increasing returns to scale and is highly concentrated both in Europe and North America. Increasing returns are not evident in chocolate production and that industry is less concentrated.

References

Akiyama, T., J. Baffes, D. Larson and P. Varangis (eds) (2001), *Commodity Market Reforms: Lessons from Two Decades*, Washington, DC: World Bank.
Anderson, R. W. and C. L. Gilbert (1988), 'Commodity Agreements and Commodity Markets: Lessons From Tin', *Economic Journal*, **98**, 1–15.
Bates, R. H. (1997), *Open-Economy Politics: The Political Economy of the World Coffee Trade*, Princeton, NJ: Princeton University Press.
Bohman, M., L. Jarvis and R. Barichello (1996), 'Rent Seeking and International Commodity Agreements: the Case of Coffee', *Economic Development and Cultural Change*, **44**, 379–404.

Brown, C. P. (1980), *The Political and Social Economy of Commodity Control*, London: Macmillan.
Brunetti, C. and C. L. Gilbert (1995), 'Metals Price Volatility, 1972–95,' *Resources Policy*, **21**, 237–54.
Cashin, P. and C. J. McDermott (2002), 'The Long Run Behavior of Commodity Prices: Small Trends and Big Variability,' *Staff Papers*, International Monetary Fund, **49**, 175–99.
Chamberlin, E. (1929), 'Duopoly: Value where Sellers are Few,' *Quarterly Journal of Economics*, **43**, 63–100.
Chamberlin, E. (1933), *The Theory of Monopolistic Competition*, Cambridge, MA: Harvard University Press.
Deaton, A. (1999), 'Commodity Prices and Growth in Africa,' *Journal of Economic Perspectives*, **13**, 23–40.
Deaton, A. S. and G. Laroque (1992), 'On the Behaviour of Commodity Prices,' *Review of Economic Studies*, **59**, 1–23.
Fox, W. (1974), *Tin: The Working of a Commodity Agreement*, London: Mining Journal Books.
Gilbert, C. L. (1985), 'The Impact of Exchange Rates and Developing Country Debt on Commodity Prices,' *Economic Journal*, **99**, 773–84.
Gilbert, C. L. (1987), 'International Commodity Agreements: Design and Performance,' *World Development*, **15**, 591–616.
Gilbert, C. L. (1996), 'International Commodity Agreements: An Obituary Notice,' *World Development*, **24**, 1–19.
Gilbert, C. L. (2004a), 'International Commodity Agreements as Internationally Sanctioned Cartels,' in P. Z. Grossman (ed.), *How Cartels Endure and How They Fail*, Cheltenham, UK and Northampton, MA, USA: Edward Elgar.
Gilbert, C. L. (2004b), 'Trends and Volatility in Agricultural Commodity Prices,' revised version of a paper given at the Symposium on State of Research and Future Directions in Agricultural Commodity Markets and Trade, held at the FAO, Rome, 16–17 December 2003.
Greenstone, W. M. (1981), 'The Coffee Cartel: Manipulation in the Public Interest,' *Journal of Futures Markets*, **1**, 3–16.
Grilli, E. R. and M. C. Yang (1988), 'Primary Commodity Prices, Manufactured Good Prices and the Terms of Trade of Developing Countries: What the Long Run Shows,' *World Bank Economic Review*, **2**, 1–47.
Law, A. D. (1975), *International Commodity Agreements,* Lexington, MA: D. C. Heath.
Massell, B. F. (1969), 'Price Stabilization and Welfare,' *Quarterly Journal of Economics*, **83**, 284–98.
Miranda, M. J. and P. G. Helmberger (1988), 'The Effects of Commodity Price Stabilization Programs,' *American Economic Review*, **78**, 46–58.
Newbery, D. M. G. and J. E. Stiglitz (1981), *The Theory of Commodity Price Stabilization*, Oxford, Oxford University Press.
Palm, F. C. and B. Vogelvang (1981), 'The Effectiveness of the World Coffee Agreement: a Simulation Study using a Quarterly Model of the World Coffee Market,' in W. C. Labys and J.-B. Lesourd (eds), *International Commodity Market Models*, London: Chapman and Hall.
Prebisch, R. (1962), 'The Economic Development of Latin America and its Principal Problems,' *Economic Bulletin for Latin America*, **7**, 1–22 (initially published (1950) as a separate document by the United Nations).
Rowe, J. W. F. (1965), *Primary Commodities in International Trade*, Cambridge: Cambridge University Press.
Singer, H. (1950), 'The Distribution of Gains Between Investing and Borrowing Countries,' *American Economic Review, Papers and Proceedings*, **40**, 473–85.
Smith, G. W. and G. R. Schink (1976), 'The International Tin Agreement: A Reassessment,' *Economic Journal*, **86**, 715–28.
Tirole, J. (1988), *The Theory of Industrial Organization*, Cambridge, MA: MIT Press.
UNCTAD (1976), *The Integrated Programme for Commodities Resolution 93(IV)*, Geneva: United Nations.
Waugh, F. V. (1944), 'Does the Consumer Benefit from Price Instability?,' *Quarterly Journal of Economics*, **58**, 602–14.
Williams, J. C. and B. D. Wright (1991), *Storage and Commodity Markets*, Cambridge: Cambridge University Press.

45 International trade and wages
Eugene Beaulieu

Introduction

This chapter presents an overview of how international trade affects labor markets and surveys the recent literature on trade and wages. In the early 1990s researchers observed an increased wage differential between skilled and unskilled workers in the US coinciding with an expansion in American trade. These two developments led to a lively debate over the impact that trade had on wages and labor markets. A conclusion, which developed fairly early in the debate, was that technological change had more to do with increased wage inequality than international trade. This line of thinking seemed to be supported by the emerging evidence that wage inequality was increasing in both developed and developing countries. A standard proposition in international trade theory known as the Stolper–Samuelson Theorem predicts that wage inequality should increase due to trade in skill-abundant developed countries but should decline in skill-scarce developing countries. The theoretical and empirical literature has evolved and there are several recent theoretical explanations of how international trade may increase wage inequality in both developed and developing countries. Meanwhile, technological change continues to be an important part of the story. Although the chapter provides some discussion of trade and wages around the world, the focus is primarily on North American countries.

Edward Leamer and James Levinsohn (1995: 1341) have remarked:

> The first message is: 'Don't take trade theory too seriously'. In practice this means 'Estimate, don't test'. . . . Our second piece of advice points in the opposite direction: 'Don't treat the theory too casually'. In practice this means: 'Work hard to make a clear and close link between the theory and the data'.

This advice appears particularly relevant for the debate on trade and wages. By the early 1990s the coincident phenomena of increased wage inequality and increased trade seemed to be causally related. The early explanations in this literature were from labor economists who showed an empirical relationship between increased trade and rising wage inequality in America. This notion also seemed to mesh with economic theory, at least as long as the focus remained on the US. According to the Stolper–Samuelson Theorem, increased trade between the relatively skill-abundant US and the relatively skill-scarce rest of the world should increase wage inequality in the US.

Perhaps ironically, it was the international trade economists who led the charge against the idea that trade was causing increased wage inequality in the US. Trade economists seemed to be arguing that researchers were guilty of not paying enough attention to theory. Few of the empirical papers showing the link between trade and wages provided a proper theoretical foundation. However, some trade economists then became guilty of taking trade theory too seriously by arguing that increased wage inequality in poor labor-abundant and skill-scarce countries implied that trade was not the culprit in increasing wage inequality in these countries because this was contrary to the Stolper–Samuelson Theorem.

This error of taking theory too seriously led Wolfgang Stolper to write a letter to *The Economist* (11–17 January 1997) magazine arguing that the Stolper–Samuelson Theorem should not be asked to do more than was intended. He points out that the theorem is based on a static model but that real economies are evolutionary. Indeed, the literature evolved and both empirical and theoretical evidence revealed that there are several channels through which international trade may be contributing to increased demand for skilled workers.

This chapter takes the reader through the evolution of trade and labor markets from the 1990s to the present day and provides a survey of the literature on trade and wages over this time. It documents the evolution of the literature over this period. Most of the empirical evidence reviewed is related to the three North American economies.

The start of the modern literature on trade and wages

The initial literature on international trade and labor markets grew out of the desire to understand the relationship between two observed facts: an increased earnings differential (measured in a number of different ways) between skilled and unskilled workers in many industrialized economies and an increase in trade with less-developed countries. The rapid growth of literature examining this issue resulted in an excellent survey of the early literature at the time by Burtless (1995) as well as several symposia addressing the issue including: one published by *The World Economy* (1992); a second held by the Federal Reserve Bank of New York (1995); and a third published in *The Journal of Economic Perspectives* (Summer 1995).

The initial research was by labor economists focusing on the US labor market. An important and widely cited paper in the early literature was by Revenga (1992). Revenga focused exclusively on explaining observed declines in manufacturing employment and real wage stagnation in the 1980s, rather than the distributional issue of wage inequality. She used time series data and found that increased import penetration had significant effects on both employment and wages.

There were two important early empirical results that led scholars to look at the impact of international trade on wage differentials between skilled and unskilled workers. The first basic result was that the wage premium between skilled and unskilled workers increased in the 1980s. The second basic result was that the increased premium was driven by increases in demand. Bound and Johnson (1992), Murphy and Welch (1991) and Berman *et al.* (1994) all found that there were large increases in the education-wage premium (the difference between wages of skilled workers and unskilled workers) in the US.[1] Murphy and Welch (1991) found that although the wage differential between university and high school collapsed during the 1970s, this trend was reversed during the 1980s.

Bound and Johnson (1992) argued that two stylized facts characterized changes in the US labor market in the 1980s. First, the average real wage stagnated, and second, there was a dramatic change in the wage structure. The wage structure changed such that the average wage of a university graduate relative to a high school graduate increased by over 15 percent. They also found that the average wage of experienced workers, particularly among low skilled groups, increased relative to new entrants, and the average wage of women increased relative to men.

Murphy and Welch (1991) decompose changes in wage differentials among groups categorized by education, gender, experience and race. Their work focused on whether demand for labor was stable over the period of increasing wage differentials by looking at whether changes in wage premiums occurred between or within groups. The authors point out that if demand were constant we would expect to see wages fall in the ranges of the wage structure where populations of workers expanded most rapidly. For example, the increase in average education should lead to a narrowing wage differential between those with different levels of education. They found that stable demand in the 1970s as the educational wage differentials narrowed and age-based differentials widened. In the 1980s the education–wage differentials expanded and age–wage differentials for high school graduates continued to expand even though average age increased. The authors therefore maintain that the skill composition of demand must have shifted in a manner favorable to the most skilled.

Bound and Johnson (1992) consider several alternative explanations for the observed labor market changes. They also argue that the increased wage premium was from the demand side not the supply side. The wage premium did not increase due to relative supply changes, they argue, because in a neoclassical labor market a supply change creates a negative correlation between wages and employment. However, they found that labor types with the highest relative wage increases in the 1980s also had the largest increase in relative supply. The authors consider other plausible culprits such as immigration, product demand shifts, changes in labor quality, technological change and outsourcing. They found little role for immigration, changing levels of union penetration and/or legislation such as minimum wage laws or changes in labor quality. They agree that changes in product demand, caused by changes in domestic tastes or changes in the degree of foreign penetration, were an important contributing factor.

Bound and Johnson (1992) were probably the first labor economists to examine the impact that the foreign outsourcing of production jobs had on the US labor market. They found several effects of foreign outsourcing. Outsourcing contributed to: higher returns to skill, because non-production jobs are kept at home; increased returns to experience, especially among production workers because foreign outsourcing creates seniority-based layoffs; and increased returns for women because clerical jobs are less likely to be outsourced. They also found a role for technological change in the changing wage structure. In particular, technological change biased towards skill and experience groups may have also contributed to the structural changes seen in the 1980s.

Berman *et al.* (1994) was an early attempt to explain the factors that caused the observed trends of a higher wage premium and the higher proportion of non-production workers employed within US manufacturing. Their work helped to tip the consensus to a view that technological change was the main cause contributing to an increased wage premium. They found that about two-thirds of the shift in manufacturing employment from production to non-production workers was accounted for by within-industry shifts as opposed to between-industry shifts. Within-industry shifts refers to skill upgrading in a specific industry, while between-industry refers to the reallocation of production away from industries with a high share of production workers in their workforce to those industries with low shares. This implies that international trade may not be the central factor for two-thirds of the increased wage premium because trade is more likely to affect the labor market between industries. They found that much of the skill upgrading that drove the changing proportion of non-production workers was positively correlated with investment in computers and to research and development (R&D) expenditures, implying a predominant role for production labor-saving technological change in explaining the shift in demand toward skilled labor and as a cause of the skill upgrading itself.

The early literature on trade and wages focused on the United States but some work was also done on Canada and other industrialized economies. However, the increased wage premium during the 1980s appeared to be largely an American phenomenon. Freeman and Needels (1993) compared the labor market performance of Canada and the US. They found that the earnings gap increased much less in Canada than in the United States. They argued that one possible explanation for a more modest increase in Canada was the greater expansion in the relative number of college educated workers (supply) in that country. They speculated that other factors such as unionization, trade, growth of real output and technological change may in part account for the differences between the two countries.

Taking theory seriously
There was a substantial backlash against the empirical trade and wages literature by those arguing that there was very little attempt to include theoretical underpinnings in the literature on trade and wages. There may be a correlation between the increased wage inequality and expanding international trade, but to prove causation there must be a theoretical connection.

In fact, in this early literature there is a clear dichotomy between theoretical and empirical discourses. There were a number of criticisms of the empirical literature. Even within the empirical literature, the consensus that was emerging was that skilled-biased technological change was the most important factor with some role for international trade affecting the wage premium. What was the theoretical connection?

A formal theoretical relationship between trade and wages was first established by Stolper and Samuelson in 1941 in their article 'Protection and Real Wages' in the *Review of Economic Studies*. This result – now known as the Stolper–Samuelson Theorem (SST) – has been frequently cited from the outset of the recent literature on trade and wages. The SST implies that the reduction in trade barriers will increase the real return to the factor that is relatively abundant in the country, and decrease the real return to the relatively scarce factor. Since developed countries, like the United States, are abundant in skilled labor and the developing countries in unskilled labor, the SST seems to provide a prima facie plausible explanation for the observed trends. That is, increased trade between the skill-abundant United States and skill-scarce other countries, would increase wage inequality in the United States.

However, the empirical evidence was not consistent with the SST. There are two important problems that the SST has in explaining wage inequality. First, although there is convincing empirical evidence that increased trade volumes are associated with increased wage inequality, the SST connects output prices to factor prices and is silent on the relationship between trade volumes and wages. There is no evidence that changes in goods prices increased wage inequality. Second, a number of studies began to emerge to show that international trade increased wage inequality in both skill-abundant and skill-scarce countries.

Deardorff and Hakura (1994) provided an important first lesson concerning the theoretical and empirical link between trade and factor prices. Since the volume of trade and the level of wages are simultaneously determined in general equilibrium trade models, it is incorrect to examine the effect of one upon the other. There is not a causal link between trade (volumes) and wages (factor prices) but a relationship that must hold under certain conditions. It is important to ask the proper question. The best approach to the question: 'How does trade affect wages?' is to answer the question: 'How does a decrease in tariff rates affect wages?' In this case, commercial policy can legitimately be treated as exogenous.

There were other critics of the conventional story on trade and wages at the time. In a widely cited article with the provocative title, 'International Trade and American Wages in the 1980s: Giant Sucking Sound or Small Hiccup?' Lawrence and Slaughter (1993) argued that if trade were the cause of higher wage premiums, then the SST implied that two intermediate steps must hold. There must be: first, an increase in the relative prices of skill-intensive goods and, second, a decline in the ratio of skilled to less-skilled workers employed in all industries. They present empirical evidence contrary to both of these hypotheses. Slaughter (2000) provides an overview of the literature that examines the role of product prices in determining wages and finds that there is little evidence of a rise in the relative price of goods intensive in skilled workers. Bound and Johnson (1992) and Berman *et al.* (1994) present detailed industry level studies and show that the ratio of skilled to less-skilled workers had risen in almost all industries over the period under investigation. Krugman (2000) argues that this was due to a shift toward skilled workers within sectors despite a rise in the skill premium.

As the literature progressed, another difficulty with the SST explanation was that studies were beginning to find increased wage inequality in poor countries as well. This literature is described in more detail in the next section of this chapter. However, what evolved was a new theoretical literature making a link between trade and wages that did not rely on the SST and tried to capture some of the well established empirical results.

One of the earliest and most interesting theoretical connections between trade and wages was posited by Bhagwati and Dehejia (1994). They developed a theory based on globalization and wages. The theory is consistent with the fact that most US trade is intra-industry trade with similarly high-skill-endowed economies – not skill scarce countries. The proposed explanation that they put forward has come to be known in the literature as the Bhagwati–Dehejia hypothesis (BDH).[2]

The BDH is based on the observation that trade liberalization has made many industries 'footloose' such that small shifts in costs can cause comparative advantage to shift suddenly from one country to another. Consequently, comparative advantage has become 'kaleidoscopic' where one country may have comparative advantage in *X* and another in *Y* one day, and the next day this may suddenly be reversed. This in turn leads to increased labor turnover. The added turnover means that mobile workers could be accumulating fewer skills causing a reduction or stagnation in the real wages of the affected workers. However, it is assumed the less-educated will be affected more. These factors as a whole provide a trade-depended explanation for the observed wage differential between educated and less-educated labor. There is some empirical support for the BDH for Canada in Beaulieu *et al.* (2004b)

Before considering other possible theoretical connections between trade and wages it is worth looking at trade and wage inequality in other countries. As mentioned, the SST explanation suffered when it became clear that wage inequality was increasing across a wide spectrum of other countries with different development levels.

Rising wage inequality everywhere

The Canada–US Free Trade Agreement

One of the first papers to take the Deardorff–Hakura critique seriously was Gaston and Trefler (1997), who focused on the labor market consequences of tariff changes dictated by a free trade agreement. They compared the labor market patterns across the tradables-sector industries for Canada and the US between 1988 and 1993. The key insights from this comparison were that: (a) the average tariff decline was 3.6 percent in Canada and 2.2 percent in the US; (b) the high tariff industries in Canada experienced a 6.1 percent decline, whereas the low tariff industries experienced only a 1.2 percent decline; (c) manufacturing sector employment declined in both countries over this period, though much more in Canada (19 percent) than in the US (8.3 percent); (d) the Canadian employment declined proportionately more in high-tariff industries (24.2 percent) than in low-tariff industries (14.8 percent); (e) there was only small changes in average earnings, with no discernible difference between high- and low-tariff industries.

However, Gaston and Trefler (1997) did not look at the impact on skilled and unskilled workers. Were skilled workers affected by the CUSTA differently than unskilled workers? Real wages in Canada did not change very much with the initial implementation of the CUSTA in the late 1980s. Moreover, there was little change in the structure of wages in Canada. Education-based measures of skill reveal similarly small increases in the wage ratio of skilled to less-skilled workers. Beaulieu (2000) found that wages and relative wages between skilled and unskilled workers in Canada changed very little from 1986 to 1990.

Although there was very little wage movement in Canada to be explained by the CUSTA, Beaulieu (2000) examined the issue of how employment and wages reacted to the tariff changes. Like Gaston and Trefler (1997), Beaulieu finds that tariff reductions did not have a large impact on the average earnings in the manufacturing sector, but also finds that Canadian tariff reductions did reduce employment, and the reduction was felt disproportionately among less skilled workers.

Mexico

Mexico was one of the first developing countries to be examined within the trade and wages literature. Cragg and Epalbaum (1996) were the first to examine the role of industry-specific and occupation-specific effects in explaining growing wage dispersion in Mexico. They found that industry-specific effects explain little of the growing wage dispersion, while portable (occupational) skills that are associated with a particular task explain almost half of the dispersion growth. Moreover, they found that workers in the highest paid occupations, such as managers and professionals, experienced the largest wage growth. This is consistent with other transitional economies, where in times of liberalization, the occupational types that are most required are also the ones with the most restricted supply. From this, the authors conclude that rising wages in occupations that require more sophisticated task-specific skills are evidence that the demand for skills increased rapidly in Mexico. They also found that the Mexican economy became more skill-intensive and that this effect was larger in the tradables sector. Finally, the authors maintain that trade has a differential effect across industries. Manufacturing industries that see large declines in protection have declining industry returns, while industries that stand to gain from freer trade see increases in wages and employment. Their conclusion is that import competition played a role in the fall in demand for less skilled workers in low-skill-intensive industries.

Robertson (1997) examined inter-industry wage differentials (IIWDs) in the US and Mexico from 1987 to 1993, in an attempt to determine whether they are stable across time and across the two countries. He found that differentials were stable over time in the US but not in Mexico. He took the theory seriously and directly examined whether changes in product prices affected the pattern of differentials. He found that in Mexico a 10 percent increase in output prices led to an increase in the wage differential of 0.8 percent.

Robertson (2000) examined the general consensus that trade liberalization in Mexico increased the demand for skilled workers and therefore wage inequality. At first glance this is puzzling from a Stolper–Samuelson perspective given that Mexico is abundant in unskilled labor relative to the US. Robertson found that this is not incongruent with the Stolper–Samuelson theorem given that Mexico was protecting its abundant factor, unskilled labor, prior to the free trade agreement rather than its scare factor, skilled labor. Still, evidence on trade and wages from other developing countries also cast doubt on the SST explanation.

Other developing countries
Robbins (1996) examined trade and wage data from the following nine developing countries: Argentina, Chile, Costa Rica, Colombia, Malaysia, Mexico, the Philippines, Chinese Taipei and Uruguay. He found evidence that trade liberalization was accompanied by rising relative wages and labor demand for skilled versus unskilled labor. Specifically he found that the wage gap grew in Chile, Columbia, Costa Rica and Argentina, but it fell in Malaysia and the Philippines. The relative supply of skilled labor grew very rapidly in all nine of these countries, and except in Chinese Taipei, the supply shifts had large negative effects upon relative wages. Based on this finding, he argued that to identify relative demand shifts for these countries, which may be subsequently related to trade liberalization, the impact of relative supply on relative wages needs to be netted out. He found that trade liberalization led not to falling, but rising relative wages for skilled labor. These findings are contrary to the Stolper–Samuelson model.

However, recently the evidence has become more mixed. Das (2002) found that wage inequality increased in Mexico and Chile but decreased in the Philippines, Singapore and Taiwan. Consequently, theoretical explanations of trade and wages may want to allow wage inequality to increase in some skill-scarce countries – but not in all. There may be some role for factor endowments – but this is not the entire story. Zhu and Trefler (2001) examined Gini coefficients from 29 developing and newly industrialized countries and found that wage gaps increased in 16 countries, decreased in 12 countries, and did not change in one country. Once again, the evidence indicates that wage inequality has increased in some, but not all developing countries. The two most often cited causes of this labor market phenomenon are trade liberalization and skill-biased technological change.

Indirect evidence
Before discussing the more recent literature on alternative explanations for the impact of trade on wages – there is some indirect evidence on trade and wages from a political

economy approach. Magee (1980) was the first to use political data to empirically examine aspects related to trade and wages. However his focus was on whether labor and capital groups adopt opposite positions on trade liberalization. His question was about whether factors of production are mobile between sectors – or not. With perfectly mobile factors, all members of a factor group will gain from trade liberalization or all members will lose, and each interest group within the factor group will lobby on the same side of the trade bill regardless of industry. If factors are immobile across industries, however, the inputs in different industries are separate factors of production. Thus, we would expect to see labor (or capital) groups in some industries favoring trade liberalization and those in other industries opposing it.

A more recent literature builds on Magee's work and examines trade policy preferences from survey data. Recent research by O'Rourke and Sinnott (2001), Beaulieu *et al.* (2001), Baker (2005) and Mayda and Rodrik (2005) find that skilled workers are more likely to support free trade than unskilled workers in almost all of the countries in their sample. All four papers examine preferences in 24 high-income and transitional economies. However, the notable exception from this result is the Philippines. It is the only country where unskilled workers are more supportive of trade liberalization than skilled workers. The Philippines is the poorest country in the sample of countries. Mayda and Rodrik (2005) interpret these results as being consistent with the SST whereas Beaulieu *et al.* (2004) question this view arguing that skilled workers in the other low-skill-abundant countries are more supportive of trade liberalization than unskilled workers. That is, although the result from the Philippines is consistent with SST, the SST would predict that unskilled workers would be more likely to support free trade in other unskilled-abundant countries in the sample such as Bulgaria, Latvia and Hungary. The difficulty in sorting out this issue hinges on the fact that that the Philippines is the poorest country in the sample.

Baker (2005) and Mayda and Rodrik (2005) add additional variation in country endowments by analyzing individual survey data on trade policy preferences from the 1995–1997 World Values Survey (WVS). This survey measures trade attitudes in 43 countries ranging in per capita income from US$832 in Nigeria to US$27 395 in the US using purchasing power parity currency conversions. The 43 countries include 16 that were below the worldwide median per-capita income of US$4000. Even in this dataset with expanded coverage Baker (2005) and Mayda and Rodrik (2005) obtain results similar to findings based on the more limited 24 countries. That is, they find that skill is a critical determinant of trade preferences and skilled workers in almost all countries are more likely than unskilled workers to support free trade. As before this positive correlation between individual skill level and trade preferences is stronger in countries abundant in high-skilled workers than it is in low-skill-abundant countries. However, skilled workers in both skilled-labour- and unskilled-labour-abundant countries are more likely to support free trade. Remarkably, only in the case of Nigeria, the most unskilled-abundant country in the sample, are unskilled workers more likely to support free trade. The problem for a strict Stolper–Samuelson interpretation of these results is that, as Baker (2005) elegantly puts it, unskilled workers are not more supportive of free trade than skilled workers even in 'unskilled-labour powerhouses' such as Bangladesh, Pakistan, India and China.

The evidence from individual survey data on trade policy preferences across countries is consistent with the evidence from labor market studies. The labor market studies reveal that wage inequality has increased in both skill-abundant and skill-scarce countries. Several studies have linked trade, at least in part, to increased wage inequality in both developed and developing countries. Preferences on trade policy reflect the possibility that international trade is increasing demand for skilled workers in both skill-abundant and skill-scarce countries.

These important and perhaps surprising empirical results suggest that the mechanism through which international trade affects labor markets is not likely to be the Stolper–Samuelson Theorem. The most recent phase of the literature on trade and wages is motivated by the desire to reconcile the theory with the empirical results.

Alternative trade-related explanations

Based on the empirical evidence, several trade-liberalization explanations of increased wage inequality have emerged that are not subject to the pitfalls of the SST. A number of papers have developed theoretical models in which trade expansion increases wage inequality in all the countries involved. Some of the papers focus on understanding that wage inequality might increase due to trade between similarly endowed countries. Others examine how trade between skill-abundant and skill-scarce countries can yield increases in wage inequality in both countries. Others still focus on trade and wages in models where intra-industry trade is an important feature. Yet other papers focus on how wage inequality within industries can increase due to international trade.

Dinopoulos and Segerstrom (1999) and Sener (2001) present a dynamic framework with two rich countries to show that a reduction in tariffs leads to higher wage inequality in developed countries. Feenstra and Hanson (1996) and Sachs and Shatz (1998) use a North–South (rich–poor) country model to show that international trade can increase wage inequality in both developed and developing countries when intermediate inputs are traded. The important innovation of Feenstra and Hanson (1996) is that they incorporate trade in intermediate inputs into their general equilibrium trade model which allows them to return to the issue of outsourcing. Their model focuses on final goods and intermediate goods trade between the skill-abundant 'North' and the skill-scarce 'South'. There are three goods in their model and two of them are intermediate inputs. The North imports an intermediate good that is intensive in the use of unskilled labour. A drop in the price of an imported intermediate good will decrease the relative price of the factor intensively used in producing that good. In this case, therefore, it decreases the relative wage of unskilled workers. Since technological change in the South will lower the price of the North's imported intermediate input, the relative wage of unskilled workers is driven down in the North. Demand for skilled workers in the South also increases due to the technological improvement. Consequently, wage inequality will increase in both the North and the South based on trade in intermediate goods.

Beaulieu *et al.* (2004a) present a simple static model that blends a standard Heckscher–Ohlin–Samuelson analysis of inter-industry trade with a technology-driven Ricardian model of intra-industry trade involving varieties of skill-intensive high-tech goods.[3] Trade barriers, in the form of tariffs, act as impediments to intra-industry trade. Within the high-tech sector, comparative advantage is based on international differences in adoption lags for new technology styled after Krugman (1985). They provide an explanation of how trade liberalization can potentially generate growing wage inequality in an explicitly North–South context rather than the North–North framework widely used in the literature.

Increased wage inequality in both the North and South can occur based on trade in final, rather than intermediate, goods. This is in contrast to the North–South models of Feenstra and Hanson (1996) and also Sachs and Shatz (1998).

Zhu and Trefler (2001) argue that rising wage inequality is common and is correlated with export growth in developing and new industrial countries. They develop a theoretical model of North–South trade where the South's technology can partially catch up to that of the North. Their model includes both Ricardian technology and Heckscher–Ohlin endowments based on comparative advantage where they incorporate a Dornbusch et al. (1980) continuum of goods based on factor intensity differences across product varieties. They focus on how technological convergence or 'Southern catch-up' rather than trade liberalization affects wage differentials between skilled and unskilled labor. In this model, Southern catch-up creates a correlation between export expansion and rising wage inequality in both the North and the South. The catch-up also induces changes in trade patterns and skill upgrading in both the North and the South.

Thus, the most recent literature on trade and wages finds theoretical and empirical support for the notion that international trade is possibly contributing to increased demand for skilled workers. However, for both empirical and theoretical reasons, the mechanism is not likely to be based on inter-industry trade between differently endowed economies. While there may be some role for inter-industry trade, the new mechanisms emphasize intra-industry trade and trade in intermediate goods.

Conclusion

The literature on trade and wages has evolved considerably over the past decade. The early literature was empirical in nature and initially focused on the United States. The theoretical and empirical literatures have built on each other and important critiques of the empirical literature spawned new currents in the theoretical literature. The recent literature has focused on providing theoretical explanations for the empirical analysis showing that international trade is affecting labor markets in both the North and the South. Trade patterns based on inter-industry comparative advantage between different countries and trade patterns based on intra-industry trade between similar countries are affecting labor markets around the world. As trade continues to expand, the issue of wage inequality is likely to remain central. No doubt, as the literature continues to expand and evolve, the debate will remain heated.

Notes

1. Some of this work examined the wage premium for those with university education versus those with high school. Other work looked at the wage premium between non-production and production workers.
2. See, for example, Feenstra and Hanson (1996).
3. Dinopoulos *et al.* (1999) develop a North–North model of intra-industry trade and wage inequality.

References

Baker, Andy (2005), 'Who Wants to Globalize? Consumer Tastes and Labor Markets in a Theory of Trade Policy Beliefs,' *American Journal of Political Science*, **49**(4), 925–39.
Beaulieu, E. (2000), 'The Canada–U.S. Free Trade Agreement and Labour Market Adjustment in Canada,' *Canadian Journal of Economics*, **33**(2), 540–63.
Beaulieu, E., M. Benarroch and J. Gaisford (2001), 'Intra-Industry Trade Liberalization: Why Skilled Workers in Most Countries Resist Protectionism,' Economic Research Papers – Loughborough University Department of Economics, 01/12.

Beaulieu, Eugene, Michael Benarroch and James Gaisford (2004a), 'Trade Barriers and Wage Inequality in a North–South Model with Technology Driven Intra-Industry Trade,' *Journal of Development Economics*, **75**(1), 113–36.

Beaulieu, Eugene, Vivek Dehejia and Omar Zakhilwal (2004b), 'International Trade, Labour Turnover, and the Wage Premium: Testing the Bhagwati–Dehejia Hypothesis for Canada,' CESIFO Working Paper No. 1149, March.

Berman, E., J. Bound and Z. Griliches (1994), 'Changes in the Demand for Skilled Labor within US Manufacturing: Evidence from the Annual Survey Of Manufactures,' *Quarterly Journal of Economics*, **109**(2), 367–97.

Bhagwati, Jagdish and V. H. Dehejia (1994), 'Free Trade and Wages of the Unskilled – is Marx Striking Again?' in J. Bhagwati and M.H. Kosters (eds), *Trade and Wages: Leveling Wages Down?*, Washington, DC: AEI Press, pp. 36–75.

Bound, J. and G. Johnson (1992), 'Changes in the Structure of Wages in the 1980s: An Evaluation of Alternative Explanation,' *American Economic Review*, **82**(3), 371–92.

Burtless, G. (1995), 'International Trade and the Rise in Earnings Inequality,' *Journal of Economic Literature*, **33**, 800–816.

Cragg, Michael, C. and Mario Epelbaum (1996) 'Why has Wage Dispersion Grown in Mexico? Is it the Incidence of Reforms or the Growing Demand for Skills?' *Journal of Development Economics*, **51**, 99–116

Das, S. P. (2002), 'Foreign Direct Investment and the Relative Wage in a Developing Country,' *Journal of Development Economics*, **67**, 55–77.

Deardorff, A.V. and D. S. Hakura (1994), 'Trade and Wages – What are the Questions?' in J. Bhagwati and M. H. Kosters (eds), *Trade and Wages: Leveling Wages Down?* Washington, DC: American Enterprise Institute, pp. 76–104.

Dinopoulos, E., C. Syropoulos and B. Xu (1999), 'Intra-industry Trade and Wage Inequality,' Mimeo, University of Florida.

Dinopoulos, E. and Paul Segerstrom (1999), 'A Schumpeterian Model of Protection and Relative Wages,' *American Economic Review*, **89**, 450–72.

Dornbusch, Rudiger, Stanley Fischer and Paul A. Samuelson (1980), 'Heckscher–Ohlin Trade Theory with a Continuum of Goods,' *Quarterly Journal of Economics*, **95**(2), 203–24.

Economist (1997), 'Letter to the Editor by Wolfgang Stolper', 11–17 January, 4.

Feenstra, R. C. and G. H. Hanson (1996), 'Foreign Investment, Outsourcing and Relative Wages,' in R. C. Feenstra, G. M. Grossman and D.A. Irwin (eds), *The Political Economy of Trade Policy: Papers in Honour of Jagdish Bhagwati*, Cambridge MA: MIT Press, pp. 89–127.

Freeman, R. B. and Karen Needels (1991), 'Skill Differentials in Canada in an Era of Rising Labor Market Inequality,' NBER Working Paper, No. 3827.

Gaston, Noel and Daniel Trefler (1997), 'The Labour Market Consequences of the Canada–US Free Trade Agreement,' *Canadian Journal of Economics*, **30**(1), 18–42.

Krugman, P. R. (1985), 'A "Technology Gap" Model of International Trade,' in K. Jungenfelt and D. Hague (eds), *Structural Adjustment in Advanced Economies*, London: Macmillan Press, London, pp. 35–49.

Krugman, P. R. (2000), 'And Now for Something Completely Different: An Alternative Model of Trade, Education, and Inequality,' in Robert C. Feenstra (ed.), *The Impact of International Trade on Wages*, National Bureau of Economic Research, Chicago, IL: The University of Chicago Press, pp. 15–36.

Lawrence, Robert Z. and Matthew J. Slaughter (1993), 'International Trade and American Wages in the 1980s: Giant Sucking Sound or Small Hiccup?' in *Brookings Papers: Microeconomics*, **2**, 161–226.

Leamer, Edward, E. and James Levinsohn (1995), 'International Trade Theory: The Evidence,' in Gene M. Grossman and Kenneth Rogoff (eds), *Handbook of International Economics: Volume III*, Amsterdam: Elsevier, pp. 1339–90.

Magee, Stephen, P. (1980), 'Three Simple Tests of the Stolper–Samuelson Theorem,' in Peter Oppenheimer (ed.), *Issues in International Economics*, Stockfield, England: Oriel Press. Reprinted in Alan V. Deardorff and Robert M. Stern (eds) (1994), *The Stolper–Samuelson Theorem: A Golden Jubilee*, Ann Arbor, MI: The University of Michigan Press, pp. 185–204.

Mayda, Anna Maria and Dani Rodrik (2005), 'Why are Some People (and Countries) More Protectionist than Others?' *European Economic Review*, **49**, 1393–430.

Murphy, Kevin, M. and Finis Welch (1991), 'The Role of International Trade in Wage Differentials,' in Marvin Kosters (ed.), *Workers and their Wages*, Washington, DC: The AEI Press, pp. 39–76.

O'Rourke, Kevin and Richard Sinnott (2001), 'What Determines Attitudes Toward Protection? Some Cross-Country Evidence,' in Susan M. Collins (ed.), *Brookings Trade Forum*, Washington, DC: The Brookings Institute.

Revenga, Ana (1992), 'Exporting Jobs? The Impact of Import Competition on Employment and Wages in US Manufacturing,' *Quarterly Journal of Economics*, **107**(1), 255–84.

Robbins, D. (1996), 'Evidence on Trade and Wages in the Developing World,' OECD Development Centre Technical Paper, No. 119, December.

Robertson, Raymond (1997), 'Inter-industry Wage Differentials Across Time, Borders, and Trade Regimes: Evidence from the US and Mexico,' Syracuse University, mimeo.

Robertson, Raymond (2000), 'Trade Liberalization and Wage Inequality: Lessons from the Mexican Experience,' *World Economy*, **23**(6), 827–49.

Sachs, J. D. and H. J. Shatz (1998), 'International Trade and Wage Inequality in the United States: Some New Results,' in S. M. Collins (ed.), *Imports, Exports, and the American Worker*, Washington, DC: Brookings Institution Press, pp. 215–40.

Sener, F. (2001), 'Schumpeterian Unemployment, Trade and Wages,' *Journal of International Economics*, **54**, 119–48.

Slaughter, M. J. (2000), 'What are the Results of Product Price Studies and What Can We Learn from Their Differences,' NBER Working Paper No. 6591.

Stolper, W. F. and P. A. Samuelson (1941), 'Protection and Real Wages,' *The Review of Economic Studies* **9**, 58–73.

Zhu, S. C. and D. Trefler (2001), 'Ginis in General Equilibrium: Trade, Technology and Southern Inequality,' National Bureau of Economic Research Working Paper No. 8446.

PART VII

TRADE POLICY: ENFORCEMENT AND COERCION

46 Dispute settlement, compensation and retaliation under the WTO

Robert Read

One of the key outcomes of the General Agreement on Tariffs and Trade (GATT) Uruguay Round negotiations was the creation of more effective system for dealing with international trade disputes, the World Trade Organization's (WTO) Dispute Settlement Understanding (DSU). This entered into force on 1 January 1995. The DSU succeeded the original GATT system for dispute settlement which had become increasingly unable to resolve major trade conflicts between its Member countries. This chapter outlines the structure and operation of the WTO trade dispute settlement system, particularly with respect to the implementation of dispute panel findings and the issues of compensation and retaliation. The first section provides an overview of the objectives of the DSU in the context of the shortcomings of the previous GATT dispute settlement system. The next section summarizes the key articles and procedures of the DSU. This is followed by a discussion of the DSU framework for the suspension of concessions, compensation and retaliation supported by illustrative examples from recent cases. The final section offers a brief critique of the key issues that have arisen in the first decade or so of the operation of the DSU.

The origins of the WTO dispute settlement system

Prior to the introduction of the DSU, the GATT system of dispute settlement had been functioning more or less successfully for almost 50 years in spite of its evident shortcomings. The new WTO DSU was the outcome of a thorough overhaul of the GATT system although it mirrored much of the original GATT legal framework and retained the accumulated body of case law and precedent.

The GATT dispute settlement system

The GATT system of dispute settlement was founded upon two principal articles: Consultation (Article XXII) and Nullification or Impairment, that is compensation (Article XXIII). The operation of the dispute system from 1947 led to the incremental evolution of procedures and case law based upon accumulated legal interpretation and precedent. The linchpin of the GATT system for settling trade disputes was the principle of consensus which required all parties to a dispute to accept the outcome of any investigation. Any findings only became binding if a panel report was accepted by consensus. Defendants in a case could therefore veto this ratification procedure and so avoid complying with the findings.

The consensus requirement was one of several weaknesses of the system leading to growing frustration about its failure to resolve trade conflicts among GATT Members. The principal shortcomings of the GATT system were: a lack of clear objectives and procedures; ambiguity about the role of consensus, leading to adverse decisions being blocked; a lack of time constraints, leading to delays and uncertainty; and frequent delays in and partial non-compliance (Read 2005). The survival of the GATT system for almost 50 years owes much to its members' commitment to multilateralism and their realization that persistent flouting of the trade rules and conflict served to undermine the long-term benefits of a relatively liberal global trade regime.

The GATT system was, to some extent, a victim of its own success in that it was originally intended to regulate the trade of just 23 countries. Its rules were simply not designed to deal with the massive growth of world trade in the latter half of the twentieth century. This was partly fuelled by trade liberalization under the GATT Kennedy and Tokyo Rounds, a rapidly growing membership (there are now 147 WTO Members) and the increasing volume and complexity of trade conflicts. All of these developments placed increasing stresses and strains on an imperfect dispute settlement system. By the start of the Uruguay Round negotiations in 1986, the general view among GATT Members was that the system for the settlement of trade disputes needed to be reformed.

It is important to note that some 88 per cent of all GATT trade dispute cases 1948–1989 were resolved through full or partial compliance. This compliance rate, however, did fall to 81 per cent post-1980 – a period covering more than half the total number of cases (Hudec *et al.* 1993). The actual performance of the GATT dispute settlement system can thus be regarded as having been reasonably successful; a view reinforced by the incorporation of its basic legal framework into its successor, the WTO Dispute Settlement Understanding.

The WTO dispute settle system
The DSU superseded the GATT system from 1 January 1995 and is regarded as being one of the central achievements of the Uruguay Round negotiations. The desire for the reform of the GATT dispute settlement system was made very apparent in the Punte del Este Declaration at the commencement of the Uruguay Round:

> To assure prompt and effective resolution of disputes to the benefit of all contracting parties, negotiations shall aim to improve and strengthen the rules and procedures of the dispute settlement process, while recognizing the contribution that would be made by more effective and enforceable GATT rules and disciplines. Negotiations shall include the development of adequate arrangements for overseeing and monitoring of the procedures that would facilitate compliance with adopted recommendations. (GATT 1986)

There was, however, no clear consensus as to how any new system for settling trade disputes should be constructed. The United States sought the creation of a rule-oriented approach ('automaticity'), along the lines of the NAFTA system, with a defined timetable for dispute resolution and the potential for cross-retaliation. In contrast, the primary objective of most other members of the OECD, along with many developing countries, was a system that would constrain unilateral action by the United States. The final outcome of the negotiations was the DSU which dealt with many of the perceived weaknesses of the GATT system as well as, at least partially, satisfying the differing objectives of its leading members.

The new negative consensus requirement means that the implementation of panel findings can no longer be blocked by respondents, so triggering the right of plaintiffs to retaliate. Automaticity is a pivotal element of the DSU, which includes a clearly stipulated timetable for the dispute settlement procedures and limited potential for cross-retaliation between sectors. Unilateral action is constrained by the requirements that Members abide by the rules and procedures of the DSU and that their national laws comply with their obligations under the WTO.

The introduction of the DSU must also be viewed as having been a necessary condition for the successful implementation of the range of revised and new trade rules, known collectively as the Uruguay Round Agreements. The more substantial legal framework of the DSU is capable of enforcing the complex rules of these agreements but this would not have been possible under the previous GATT system.

The key articles and operating procedures of the WTO dispute settlement system

The DSU is an integral part of the Uruguay Agreements, running to 27 Articles and four Appendices. This section outlines the principal operating procedures of the WTO dispute settlement system with respect to the key articles of the DSU.

The grounds for a complaint under the WTO DSU

GATT Article XXIII, Nullification or Impairment, stood at the centre of the GATT dispute settlement system and its paragraphs continue to define the conditions under which violation of the WTO rules permit Members to seek redress and their means of so doing. There are three specific circumstances identified in GATT Article XXIII under which WTO Members are permitted to make a complaint under the DSU. The standard case is where a Member country violates the WTO rules and thereby adversely affects other Members. The second is 'non-violation' where harm is caused even though there is no specific violation of a GATT provision. Finally, there is a 'catch-all' provision. The scope of the application of the article covers all of the component multilateral agreements of the WTO. This means that any Member country may seek redress with respect to any violation of the WTO rules by another. There is no requirement to demonstrate that a violation has resulted in injury since all Members are legally obliged to conform to the WTO rules.

The WTO complaints procedure

The primary objective of the WTO DSU system is to settle trade disputes between Members by means of bilateral consultations and mediation in the first instance. Recourse to the establishment of a formal dispute panel is intended as a last resort when all other avenues of conciliation have been exhausted. Further, the provisions permit third parties, including other Member countries and the WTO Secretariat, to mediate in a dispute and take part in the consultations. Any agreed solution, however, must be consistent with the WTO Agreements. It is only after the failure of the consultation and/or mediation process that a plaintiff may have recourse to the formal dispute provisions. Third parties with a 'substantial trade interest' in a dispute may also engage in the consultation process, subject to the agreement of the respondent.

The specific guidelines and timetable for consultations to take place are provided in Article 4 of the DSU. Consultations are a mandatory condition for a subsequent request to be made to establish a dispute panel. A respondent has a 10-day limit within which to reply to a request for consultations, a maximum of 30 days to enter into consultations and a minimum of 60 days to engage in the consultations. If a Member does not meet one or more of these deadlines, a plaintiff may request the establishment of a panel immediately.

In practice, many parties to disputes often take considerably longer over consultations that the minimum of 60 days (WTO 2004).

Many trade disputes never go further than the consultation stage, particularly given that WTO Members are under an obligation to resolve their disputes by this means. The parties to a dispute may also make use arbitration as an alternative method, subject to mutual agreement.

The establishment of a WTO dispute panel

In the event that a trade dispute is not resolved through consultations, a plaintiff can then proceed to a formal request for the establishment of a dispute panel no earlier than 60 days after the request for consultations. Such a request is submitted in writing to the Chair of the Dispute Settlement Body (DSB) and sets out briefly and clearly the grounds for a complaint. This request forms the legal basis for a complaint and its contents define the scope and extent of the remit of a dispute panel investigation and adjudication. The formal request document is then circulated to all WTO Members, so as to inform the respondent together with any interested third parties, and included on the agenda for the next meeting of the DSB. The first time that a request is presented to the DSB, a plaintiff has the right to block a panel being set up. Under the negative consensus requirement introduced in the Uruguay Round, any such request is automatically accepted at a second DSB meeting.

Where there is more than one plaintiff in a case or where several Members file similar complaints, Article 9.1 provides for the establishment of a single panel 'whenever feasible'. Co-plaintiffs, however, may request the publication of separate reports.

Any third party country with 'substantial interest' in a trade dispute also has a right to make submissions to and be heard by a panel, even if they were not involved in the consultation process. Participation in panel procedures as a third party requires the DSB to be notified, in practice within 10 days of the establishment of a panel. In the event of nullification or impairment of their benefits, third parties may also have recourse to the DSU.

The functions and procedures of WTO dispute panels

The functions and procedures of WTO dispute panels are laid out in Articles 7, 8 and 11 to 15 of the DSU. Their primary function is to assist the DSB by making an objective assessment of the facts and conformity with the relevant WTO agreements. Their Terms of Reference are to examine the facts of a trade dispute with respect to the complaint as laid out by the plaintiff in the request for the panel's establishment. Panels are thus required to investigate the evidence in the context of the relevant provisions of the WTO agreements cited by the parties of a dispute. They then make recommendations or rulings to the DSB with regard to the relevant WTO agreements.

The composition of WTO dispute panels is set out in Article 8 of the DSU. A panel normally has three members but may, in certain cases, have five. The panellists are nominated by the WTO Secretariat from an indicative list that includes the nominees of Member countries. Panellists are required to possess expertise appropriate to a case but may not be citizens of parties or third parties to a dispute.

The procedures for dispute panels are set out in Appendix 3 of the DSU, including a proposed timetable for panel deliberations (shown in WTO 2004). This timetable is, to some extent, flexible dependent upon the complexity and evidential needs of particular cases. In general, most dispute cases take between nine and 12 months from the establishment of a panel to the publication of its report. Dispute panels have the power to seek information and technical advice from any appropriate individual or body and evidence may also be requested from an Expert Review Group. All Panel deliberations are confidential and non-attributable.

Panel procedures normally begin with the receipt of (often lengthy) written submissions by the plaintiff and respondent, which are then exchanged. Any third parties may then make their own submissions. These tend to be shorter commentaries on specific aspects of a case (WTO 2004). This is followed by a closed oral hearing involving all of the parties after which the parties exchange written rebuttals to each other's legal arguments. A second closed oral hearing is then held, during which the parties' arguments and rebuttals are presented. Where expert evidence, usually of a scientific nature, is required, additional sets of oral hearings may be held. A panel then drafts the 'descriptive' section of its report outlining the arguments of each party and summarizing all of the factual and legal arguments which is circulated to the parties for comments and corrections. This is followed by the circulation of the Interim Review, which contains the description of the case along with a panel's findings and conclusions regarding the legal validity of the complaint. Again, the parties are permitted to make comments, request corrections and ask a panel to review specific points. These amendments and elaborations are then incorporated to produce a Final Panel Report which is circulated to all WTO Members and published.

The adoption of panel reports

A Final Panel Report – and therefore its recommendations – has no standing until it is adopted at a meeting of the DSB. Under the negative consensus requirement, however, Final Reports are automatically adopted and their rulings become binding if they are placed on the agenda and submitted to the DSB. A victorious plaintiff may therefore choose not to add a Report to the DSB agenda, in which case it will not be adopted. This contrasts with the potential of losing respondents in trade dispute cases to use a veto under the GATT dispute settlement system which enabled them to block the implementation of panel rulings indefinitely. Once a Panel Report is adopted by the DSB, its recommendations become binding on the parties to a dispute.

The role and function of the WTO Appellate Body

A party (but not a third party) to a dispute has 60 days after the publication of a Final report to lodge an appeal. In this case the Report is not submitted to the DSB until the appeal process is completed. Although respondents and plaintiffs may appeal against the findings of a dispute panel with respect to the case in question, it is not unusual for parties to request clarification or reinterpretation of particular legal points with respect to their broader implications for future cases. The Appellate Body has the power to modify or reverse the findings and recommendations of a Panel Report following procedural rules that have been amended periodically since 1996.

The Appellate Body has seven members, three of whom (the division) are selected to preside over an appeal by rotation. An appellant has ten days to submit its legal arguments concerning the relevant point(s) of law in a Panel Report, followed later by an oral hearing. The collegiality of the Appellate Body is sustained by sanctioning deliberations between the division and its remaining four members to ensure jurisprudential consistency and coherence. The objective of the Appellate Body is to resolve dispute cases and this may also require it to complete the legal analysis of a case by examining other claims not dealt with by the original panel. After drafting, the Appellate Body Report is circulated to all WTO Members and published. It is also submitted to the DSB for adoption and the parties to a dispute must accept its recommendations unconditionally in the absence of a negative consensus.

The implementation of WTO panel decisions

Once a Final or Appellate Body Report has been adopted by the DSB, its recommendations and rulings become binding on the parties to a dispute and the losing respondent is required to bring its trade regime into compliance with the WTO rules. This normally means the disputed measures that were the subject of the original dispute and found to be inconsistent with the WTO are withdrawn. Under Article 21, Surveillance of Implementation, losing respondents have 30 days after the adoption of a Report to inform the DSB of their intentions regarding the implementation of Panel or Appellate Body recommendations. While the onus is on 'prompt compliance . . . to ensure effective resolution of disputes', compliance is required to be 'within a reasonable time', normally not exceeding 15 months. The DSB is responsible for the surveillance of the implementation of adopted recommendations and rulings.

In the event that there is dissatisfaction or disagreement concerning a respondent's compliance with the recommendations and rulings of the DSB, a plaintiff has further recourse to the dispute settlement procedures and a new Panel Report (Article 21.5). Actions under this article are not uncommon and have been used by both plaintiffs and respondents to establish whether any regulatory changes that have been made are WTO-compatible.

Other means of WTO dispute settlement: arbitration and mutually agreed solutions

The use of dispute panel procedures is the most well known means of resolving trade disputes between WTO Members, primarily because of the publicity generated by high profile cases, such as the recent EU–US banana and steel disputes. The principal alternative to a dispute panel is arbitration, the procedures for which are outlined in Article 25 of the DSU. The use of arbitration is by mutual agreement between the parties to a dispute. The outcome of arbitration must be WTO-compatible and is binding on the parties. Any award for nullification or impairment is subject to the same Articles on compensation and the suspension of concessions as a dispute that follows panel procedures.

Parties to a trade dispute may, at any time, side-step the formal dispute settlement process in favour of securing a mutually agreed solution. This is normally a bilateral agreement negotiated between the parties to a dispute. The DSU procedures actively promote negotiation and conciliation to avoid conflict, such that mutually agreed solutions to disputes are encouraged subject to their satisfying the need for consistency with the WTO rules. If such a solution is WTO-incompatible, the original respondent could be vulnerable to a dispute action by adversely affected third parties.

The compensation, suspension of concessions and retaliation provisions of the WTO

The power of the DSB and therefore a Dispute Panel to authorize the suspension of trade concessions by a plaintiff to a respondent where there is harm (nullification or impairment) is established in Paragraph 2 of Article XXIII of GATT 1994. This paragraph effectively binds Members of the WTO to accepting the rulings of the DSB and also, where appropriate, for the DSB to permit sanctions against countries found to be acting contrary to the WTO rules.

The nature of compensation, the suspension of concessions and retaliation
Compensation and the suspension of concessions, that is of Most-Favoured Nation (MFN) treatment, to a WTO Member are intended to be temporary measures. They are only implemented if the recommendations and rulings of the DSB are not acted upon within a reasonable time period. Where compensation and the suspension of concessions are sanctioned by the DSB, a respondent has the alternative option of withdrawing from the WTO and its associated treaty obligations within 60 days.

Neither compensation nor the suspension of concessions however, can be applied retrospectively. This means that there is no recompense for any harm caused by an illegal trade measure prior to and during the implementation of dispute procedures.

Where nullification or impairment is ruled to have occurred, a respondent may choose either compensation or the suspension of concessions as the form of restitution. Compensation normally takes the form of tariff reductions and is purely voluntary since the suspension of concessions is the default means of restitution. Any compensation must satisfy the requirement that it is compatible with the provisions of the WTO. Compensation is rarely used, however, because most tariff reductions are not consistent with the requirement of MFN treatment (WTO 2004).

The suspension of concessions is more complex. In the first instance, the general principle is to suspend concessions in the same sector as the violation occurred – that is within goods, services and trade-related intellectual property rights (TRIPs) respectively. If this is not practicable, then concessions are suspended in other sectors covered by the same agreement – that is all of the WTO Agreements covering trade in goods, the General Agreement on Trade in Services (GATS) and TRIPs respectively – and only then between agreements. These provisions are particularly important for smaller developing countries where the adverse impact of the suspension of equivalent concessions within a sector or an agreement may be quite substantial (WTO 2004).

In requesting the suspension of concessions, a Member is required to take into account the trade and its importance to them in the relevant sector or under the relevant agreement along with the broader economic consequences of suspension. The suspension of concessions must be temporary and may only remain in place until a WTO-inconsistent measure is removed, any harm ceases or there is a mutually agreed solution.

The grounds for compensation, the suspension of concessions and retaliation
The grounds for compensation, the suspension of concessions and retaliation are dealt with under Article 22 of the DSU. In the event of an illegal measure not being brought into compliance and no satisfactory compensation being agreed between the parties to a dispute, a plaintiff may request authorisation to suspend concessions to a respondent, This may be requested 20 days after the expiry of the 'reasonable period of time'.

The principal objective of compensation or the suspension of concessions is to induce Member countries to comply with the WTO rules. This punitive action results in a tangible loss by a respondent through the removal of its preferential access to the market of a plaintiff. This is incurred through reduced earnings by exports and exporters in those sectors targeted by the plaintiff's suspension of concessions. A plaintiff may gain from increased tariff revenue but its consumers will face higher prices such that neither side is better off as a result of permitted retaliation.

In some cases, a respondent may choose not to withdraw an illegal trade measure, whether for logistical or other reasons. Instead, the provision of compensation is permitted as 'a temporary measure pending the withdrawal of the measure that is inconsistent'. In the dispute over beef produced with growth hormones brought by Canada and the United States, the EU has refused to remove its import restrictions in spite of their being found to be illegal by a WTO panel. Instead, the EU has willingly accepted retaliation on the grounds that its import restrictions are justified by health fears over the long-term effects on consumers.

An important procedural dispute arose in the second WTO banana case between the EU and the United States over the relative primacy and sequencing of compliance and compensation (Articles 21 and 22 of the DSU). The United States wished to retaliate immediately while the EU argued that this could only be done if its new trade measures for bananas were found not to comply with the WTO rules. This matter was eventually referred to the WTO General Council for clarification. An arbitration panel, however, ruled that an Article 21.5 ruling was not a prerequisite for action under Article 22.6. This decision has never been adopted since neither the EU nor the United States desired this legal precedent to become established in WTO case law because of its broader implications for dispute settlement.

The magnitude of compensation, the suspension of concessions and retaliation
The magnitude of any compensation or suspension of concessions is required to be equivalent to the level of harm (nullification or impairment) that is caused by any illegal measure. The DSB authorizes the suspension of concessions automatically under the negative consensus rule unless the respondent objects, in which case the matter is referred to arbitration, normally to the original panel.

An objection can be lodged against the suspension of concessions by a respondent on two grounds: that the proposed level of suspension is greater than the nullification or impairment incurred; or that the procedures contained in Article 22 have not been adhered to. If a dispute over compensation is referred to arbitration, then concessions cannot be suspended in the meantime. The only concern of the arbitrator is whether suspension of concessions is equivalent to the nullification or impairment and has been carried out in accord with the procedures in the article. The arbitrator's decision is final and there is no recourse to a second arbitration.

In the beef hormone dispute, arbitration established that the annual value of trade affected by these measures was C$11.3 million for Canada and $116.8 million for the United States. This represents only a small fraction of the total value of the transatlantic beef trade. In the banana dispute, the initial claim for the suspension of concessions by the United States was for $520 million but this was reduced to $191.4 million after arbitration. In the same dispute, the Arbitration Panel awarded Ecuador sanctions worth $201.6 million, substantially greater than the annual value of its imports from the EU. In the case of the recent steel dispute, the EU estimated that the lost value of its trade concessions as a result of US restrictions on steel imports was some $3 billion (€2.407 billion) per annum.

Retaliatory lists of products for the suspension of concessions
The procedure for implementing the suspension of concessions includes the drawing up and publication of a retaliatory list of products to be targeted by a plaintiff. A respondent may object to the list if there is dispute over the value of the harm or that the products covered do not conform to the sectoral requirements.

Retaliation by Canada and the United States in the beef hormones dispute specifically targeted key EU agricultural exports, particularly from France, with the US retaliatory tariffs set at 100 per cent. In addition, the United States has also threatened to escalate its retaliation by 'carouseling', that is rotating the products on its retaliatory list every 180 days. This would increase the uncertainty faced by EU exporters to the United States. Carouseling is not illegal under the WTO rules but its use would be expected to result in legal action by the EU. In the banana dispute, the United States made it known that its retaliatory targets included exports of luxury cashmere products from Scotland. In the recent steel dispute, the EU proposed a 'short' retaliatory list worth some $390 million and a 'long' list worth $625 million. In addition to targeting imports of US steel products, these lists targeted sensitive exports from politically key marginal states in the 2004 US Presidential Election.

Further reading on the DSU and WTO trade disputes
The best source of information about the WTO DSU is *A Handbook on the WTO Dispute Settlement System* (2004). This provides a full discussion of the procedures and operation of the DSU, the interpretation of its articles and recent developments. A comparative overview of the performance of the GATT and WTO dispute settlement systems can be found in 'Trade Dispute Settlement Mechanisms: the WTO Dispute Settlement Understanding in the Wake of the GATT' (Read 2005). More general analyses of the WTO, including the DSU, can be found in *The Political Economy of the World Trading System* (Hoekman and Kostecki 2001) and *The Regulation of International Trade* (Trebilcock and Howse 1999).

Up to date documentation for every case dealt with under the DSU is available on the WTO website at http://www.wto.org/english/tratop_e/dispu_e/dispu_e.htm#disputes. Information and documentation about WTO trade disputes involving the EU can be found on its website at http://trade-info.cec.eu.int/wtodispute/search.cfm. Details and publications relating to investigations by the US International Trade Commission (USITC) can be found at http://www.usitc.gov/webinv.htm. In depth discussions of several recent trade disputes, including bananas, beef hormones and steel can be found in *The WTO and the Regulation of International Trade: Recent Trade Disputes Between the European Union and the United States* (Perdikis and Read 2005). The banana and beef hormones cases are also discussed in *Transatlantic Economic Disputes: the EU, the US and the WTO* (Petersmann and Pollack 2003).

A critique of the WTO system of trade dispute settlement
Almost all of the 300-plus trade disputes that have arisen since the inception of the DSU have been resolved in accord with WTO disciplines. The number of completed cases is now sufficient for several critical issues of concern to be identified relating the operation and application of the WTO dispute settlement system.

The willingness of the world's strongest and most influential economies to adhere to an agreed set of multilateral trade rules must be seen as a positive indication of not only the health of the global economy but also of the effectiveness of the DSU and international economic relations in general. This view is supported by the leading role played by the DSU in resolving recent major trade disputes between the EU and the United States in bananas and steel. Nevertheless, questions still remain concerning the scope of the WTO trade rules and the effectiveness of the DSU.

Bias in the use and outcomes of the DSU

The WTO dispute settlement system has been accused of being biased against developing countries in that it favours the leading industrialized countries. The EU and the United States, in particular, are seen as having created and using the DSU to achieve their own objectives by virtue of their international economic and political leverage, greater resources and retaliatory power. The DSU, however, is a more effective system for settling disputes because the dependence of the GATT system on positive consensus was vulnerable to pressure.

Empirical analyses of WTO dispute cases indicate that the industrialized countries have been the primary complainants and respondents although the NICs are now making increasing use of it. The EU and the United States, however, have been the most frequent litigants; trade disputes between them account for 40 per cent of all complaints from 1995 to 2002. None of the least-developed countries were involved in any cases at all. Normalizing according to the share of global trade suggests that there is little evidence of systematic bias in the use of the DSU. Even if there is no bias in the use of the DSU, the leverage and resources of the industrialized countries may mean that they are more likely to win dispute cases.

The high success rate of the DSU suggests that it has been more effective in resolving trade disputes than the GATT system. This issue is complicated by the fact that many disputes do not result in formal complaints and not all complaints result in panel reports. There is some evidence to indicate that WTO Members with greater economic and political leverage are more likely to achieve a mutually agreed settlement – resolving or dropping complaints prior to the issuing of a panel report – while weaker Members rely more upon the judicial process of the DSU. The empirical literature on the performance of the GATT and DSU systems is reviewed in Read (2005).

The function and composition of WTO panels

Some concern has been expressed about the function and composition of WTO Panels, particularly the reliance of the DSU procedures on part-time non-professional panellists. The greater effectiveness of the DSU has meant the rapid growth of both the volume and complexity of dispute cases. Doubts have arisen about the competence of part-time panellists, given the rules-based legal foundations of the dispute settlement procedures and the heavy workload. As a consequence, the EU has proposed that the WTO should create a permanent or standing body of qualified and experienced panellists.

Automaticity

There is a concern, arising partly as a consequence of the misgivings about panellists, that panels and the WTO Appellate Body are exceeding the scope of their remit. That is, that they are interpreting some of the WTO Agreements in a manner that affects the rights of Members, positively or negatively, without their consent.

The transparency of the panel and appellate systems
A further concern relating partly to automaticity and the functions of panels and the Appellate Body is that their procedures lack transparency. Because evidence and written submissions to panels are generally confidential until the publication of Panel Reports, the WTO system has been accused of excessive secrecy. Greater transparency is unlikely to have an adverse impact upon the system although it is opposed by many developing countries.

The implementation of panel recommendations and sequencing
There is some debate about the relative primacy of Articles 21.5 and 22.6 of the DSU, highlighted by the WTO banana case. The former provides for referral back to a panel where there is disagreement about compliance with a ruling while the latter provides for automatic retaliation in such a case. The DSU currently provides no indication of which Article should take precedence although logic suggests that the suspension of concessions should await a decision on the consistency of a revised measure.

The participation of developing countries in the DSU
Although the DSU Articles pay special attention to the needs of developing countries, their participation continues to be constrained by a lack of financial and intellectual resources necessary to fight dispute cases, whether as plaintiffs or respondents. The failure of least-developed countries to use the system at all gives some cause for concern. While this reflects the small number of least-developed Members of the WTO and their small share of global trade, their vulnerability to retaliatory action means that positive evidence is needed to demonstrate that they are not failing to make appropriate use of the DSU.

National sovereignty and the democratic deficit
The WTO dispute settlement system raises important issues relating to the competing demands of its Member countries' obligations under international agreements and their domestic democratic mandates. Popular disquiet with the WTO, among other international agreements, is by no means confined to the anti-globalization movement. There is a growing feeling in many Member countries, both developed and developing, that the WTO is 'usurping' the democratic process by enforcing externally imposed rules on sovereign states.

In the past, the recourse of national governments to international agreements has been seen as a means to sidestep domestic constituencies opposed to trade liberalization. A democratic deficit has emerged, however, between policy-makers convinced of the long-term beneficial effects of such commitments and national electorates, some part of which remain sceptical of such benefits. The WTO rules do impose constraints upon the exercise of its powers designed specifically to preserve the sovereignty of the nation state. Nevertheless, national governments may be faced with a crisis of credibility in the face of substantial domestic opposition to the obligations required by the WTO among others. At its mildest, this might lead to the adoption of a policy of non-compliance while possible outright rejection of the WTO could mean a reversion to unilateralism with its attendant problems.

Critical current factors in this apparent deficit relate to national concerns about the interfaces between the international trade rules and environment and consumer food health and safety issues – so-called process and product method (PPM) issues. The perceived strict interpretation of the rules on trade by the WTO to the neglect of broader issues of great concern to consumers has engendered further scepticism over and above those related to trade liberalization. Although the consideration of PPM issues at the WTO remains incomplete, incremental progress in the interpretation and establishment of appropriate legal grounds for trade restrictions on environmental and health grounds has been made in several recent dispute cases. Any fundamental reform of the WTO, however, remains in the hands of its Members.

Acknowledgements

The author is grateful for critical supportive comments made by William A. Kerr and Nick Perdikis.

References

GATT (1986), *Ministerial Declaration*, Punta del Este, Geneva: GATT.
Hoekman, B. M. and M. M. Kostecki (2001), *The Political Economy of the World Trading System* (2nd edn), Oxford: Oxford University Press.
Hudec, R., Kennedy, D. and Sgarbossa, M. (1993), 'A Statistical Profile of GATT Dispute Settlement Cases, 1948–1989', *Minnesota Journal of Global Trade*, **2**(1), 1–25.
Perdikis, N. and Read, R. (eds) (2005), *The WTO and the Regulation of International Trade: Recent Trade Disputes Between the European Union and the United States*, Cheltenham, UK and Northampton, MA, USA: Edward Elgar.
Petersmann, E.-U. and Pollack, M. A. (2003), *Transatlantic Economic Disputes: the EU, the US and the WTO*, Oxford: Oxford University Press.
Read, R. (2005), 'Trade Dispute Settlement Mechanisms: the WTO Dispute Settlement Understanding in the Wake of the GATT', in N. Perdikis and R. Read (eds), *The WTO and the Regulation of International Trade: Recent Trade Disputes Between the European Union and the United States*, Cheltenham, UK and Northampton, MA, USA: Edward Elgar, pp. 41–67.
Trebilcock, M. J. and R. Howse (1999), *The Regulation of International Trade* (2nd edn), London: Routledge.
WTO (2004), *A Handbook on the WTO Dispute Settlement System*, Cambridge: Cambridge University Press.

47 Economic sanctions for foreign policy purposes: a survey of the twentieth century
Gary Hufbauer and Barbara Oegg

Introduction

On 22 May 2003 the United Nations Security Council unanimously passed Resolution 1483 formally ending more than over a decade of comprehensive sanctions against Iraq. For most of the 1990s, the Iraqi sanctions regime, the most comprehensive sanctions apart from the two World Wars, dominated the debate about the use and effectiveness of economic sanctions, about their humanitarian impact, and about the legitimacy and morality of this 'deadly weapon'.

Economic sanctions have long been at the core of international relations. The first documented incidents of sanctions for political ends date to ancient Greece – the best-known episode being the Megarian decree (432 BC), which banned all trade between Megara and the Athenian Empire. Throughout the history of economic sanctions, from ancient Greece through the nineteenth century, sanctions almost always foreshadowed or accompanied warfare.

The idea that economic sanctions might be an alternative to the use of force only received attention after the First World War, largely owing to President Woodrow Wilson's advocacy. Subsequently economic sanctions were incorporated as an enforcement tool in each of the two collective security systems established in the twentieth century – the League of Nations and the United Nations. Economic sanctions imposed by the League of Nations succeeded in a few small episodes, but they failed miserably in the one big case – the attempt to pry Italy out of Ethiopia in 1935. The failure of the League sanctions against Italy in 1935–1936 ultimately led to the demise of the League. Despite this disappointing episode, an increasing number of sanctions have been launched in the decades after the Second World War.

Use and effectiveness in the twentieth century
Trends in the use of sanctions

Economic sanctions are the deliberate, government-inspired withdrawal, or threat of withdrawal, of customary trade and financial relations with a target country in an effort to change that country's policies. We emphasize two phrases in this definition: 'threat of withdrawal' and 'customary'. Threats can be as important and sometimes more effective than actual denial. 'Customary' includes not only the normal flow of private trade and finance, but also the normal flow of military supplies and government finance. For example, the United States is not obligated to sell F-16s or provide Export–Import Bank finance to any particular country, but if the United States stalls or cancels a transaction for political reasons, that constitutes a sanction.[1]

Total embargoes, such as the UN sanctions against Iraq or US unilateral sanctions against Cuba and North Korea, are rare. Most sanctions are much less drastic. Trade bans frequently affect only one or a few goods. Australia, for example, cut off shipments of uranium to France from 1983 to 1986 because of France's refusal to halt testing of nuclear weapons in the South Pacific.

Financial sanctions typically involve the suspension of official development aid, concessionary lending or export credit guarantees. The ultimate form of financial control – freezing a target country's foreign assets – has been primarily used in time of war. In the 1990 Middle East crisis, for instance, the US government and its allies froze Kuwait's assets to prevent Saddam Hussein from plundering them.

While economic sanctions have preceded or accompanied war for most of modern history, the motives behind the use of sanctions have changed since the First World War. Economic sanctions during wartime were primarily focused on reducing a target's capabilities. In modern times, the core motives shifted to changing a target state's behavior, deterring others, demonstrating resolve to allies and domestic constituencies, or simply sending a message of disapproval in response to objectionable behavior. When military action would be too expensive and diplomatic protest too mild, world leaders increasingly resorted to sanctions. Over recent decades economic sanctions have also been used for an ever broader array of foreign policy objectives. They have been utilized to combat weapons proliferation, to support nuclear disarmament, to stop drug trafficking, to fight terrorism, to end civil wars, and to promote democracy and human rights. No country in the world has so often employed economic sanctions in pursuit of multiple foreign policy goals as the United States.

Changes in use in the 1990s
While the United States remains the most frequent user of economic sanctions in absolute terms, the frequency of new unilateral US initiatives declined in the 1990s. Some high profile unilateral ventures such as Cuba were inherited from previous decades, but the majority of new US sanctions in the 1990s were undertaken in conjunction with other senders (see Figure 47.1). Less than a quarter of the cases initiated in the 1990s were purely unilateral ventures. By contrast, in the 1970s, the United State was involved in 31 sanctions episodes and three-quarters of them were unilateral initiatives.

One factor in the decline of US unilateral adventures was the collapse of the Soviet Union: the end of the superpower rivalry allowed for much greater cooperation of major powers under the United Nations framework. The UN has played a much bigger role in international disputes in the 1990s than in any previous era. The new activism of the UN is reflected in the fact that the Security Council imposed mandatory sanctions 13 times[2] in response to instances of civil strife, regional aggression or grave violations of human rights. This record compares to just twice – against South Africa and Rhodesia – in previous decades. In many cases, these sanctions are imposed in response to threats that are no longer of paramount concern to either the United States or its Western allies. Unwilling to commit substantial financial resources or military troops, the United States and its Western allies have resorted to UN sanctions in the face of pressure to 'do something'. Meanwhile, the theaters of action have little or no concern to China and Russia, both permanent members of the Security Council. The UN arms embargoes imposed on Rwanda (1994) and Ethiopia and Eritrea (2000) illustrate these points.

In addition to the increase in institutionally endorsed sanctions, the 1990s also saw the emergence of new sender countries. The Soviet Union or its allies were targets of Western

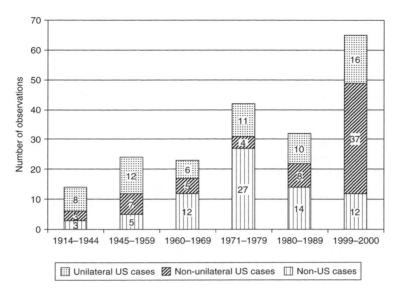

Source: Preliminary results, Hufbauer *et al.* (forthcoming).

Figure 47.1   Trends in the use of US economic sanctions

sanctions 12 times during the 1970s and 1980s. With the end of the Cold War Western sanctions against the Former Soviet Union (FSU) and East bloc countries sharply diminished. At the same time, Russia itself initiated six sanction episodes against the newly independent states of the former Soviet Union in an effort to secure political rights for Russian minorities and better economic terms from its newly independent neighbors (Drezner 1999).

The European Union as well has become a much more active user of economic sanctions over the last decade (Hufbauer and Oegg 2003a). An important element in the rise of EU sanction initiatives is the development of a Common Foreign and Security Policy and increased coordination of the Union's foreign policy during the 1990s. Moreover, the Common Commercial Policy of the European Union means that restrictions on external commercial relations require implementation by common institutions (Anthony 2002). Another factor is that, compared to previous decades, new cases targeting Latin American countries declined in the 1990s as that region moved toward democratic governance. Instead new sanction initiatives were concentrated in Africa, in response to the rise of ethnic strife, regional conflict and the atrocious behavior of oppressive regimes. This shift in geographical focus – from the US backyard to a region with historically closer ties to Europe – is another factor in the decline in unilateral US sanctions and in the emergence of the EU as sender of economic sanctions.

Effectiveness of foreign policy sanctions
Defining success
Public controversy over the use of economic sanctions was relatively quiet in the 1950s, 1960s and 1970s. But the proliferation of sanctions in the late 1980s and 1990s (and in

particular UN sanctions against Iraq) generated intense debate among policy makers, corporations and scholars. Much of the debate and research has centered on the question whether economic sanctions are effective tools in shaping a target country's policies. Advocates of economic sanctions regard them as an important middle-of-the-road policy between diplomatic protest and military force. Opponents, on the other hand, stress that economic sanctions are generally ineffective in achieving policy changes abroad, and that the costs of sanctions, both to the sender and the civilian population in the target country, are seldom worth the benefits derived.

Assessments of sanction effectiveness vary as widely as definitions of economic sanctions themselves. Each scholar and practitioner tends to have his or her own idiosyncratic litmus tests for identifying the foreign policy success or failure of economic sanctions. Depending on what goals sanctions are measured against, assessments can diverge sharply. Some scholars emphasize the signaling purposes of sanctions, such as deterring future wrongdoing, demonstrating resolve both to allies and domestic constituencies, and preserving of international norms. Measured against these symbolic goals, economic sanctions that fail to change a specific target country's policy may nevertheless succeed – for example, by deterring similar behavior by other countries. Others argue that unless sanctions alone achieve the stated foreign policy goal, by default they have failed. Under this interpretation, a sanctions episode that was accompanied or followed by the use of force would be considered a failure. Similarly, if foreign policy goals are only partially achieved through the imposition of sanctions, under this sort of strict test the sanctions may be considered a failure.[3]

Effectiveness in achieving goals should be distinguished from effectiveness in interrupting customary economic relations. Sanctions can be very effective in interrupting relations yet fall short of their foreign policy goals; this was true in both Iraq (1990–2003) and Haiti (1991–1994). By contrast, limited sanctions feebly enforced – such as UN sanctions against Libya (1992–1999) to secure the extradition of alleged terrorists and to extract compensation – can nevertheless achieve their goals.

Our own evaluation of the success of an economic sanctions episode has two parts, both judgmental: policy result, which evaluates the extent to which the stated foreign policy goal of the sender country has in fact been achieved and the sanctions contribution, which evaluates the contributions made by sanctions to a positive outcome.[4] Outcomes are judged in terms of changes in a target country's policies, military or economic capabilities, or changes in its regime. We do not attempt to measure collateral outcomes, such as giving satisfaction to domestic constituencies or deterring other countries.

Effectiveness of foreign policy sanctions, 1919–2000
Preliminary results of our research for the third edition of *Economic Sanctions Reconsidered* (Hufbauer *et al.* forthcoming) suggest that the effectiveness of economic sanctions in achieving their stated foreign policy goals has steadily declined since the early post-Second World War decades (see Table 47.1). Between 1945 and 1969, sanctions contributed to a positive policy outcome in 43 percent of the cases studied. By the 1990s the success rate, by our evaluation, had dropped to 35 percent.

The decline in effectiveness is even more pronounced when it comes to US sanction initiatives, both unilateral and multilateral. As Table 47.1 shows, US sanctions were successful over 50 percent of the time in the early post-war period (1949–1969). Since then

Table 47.1   Use and effectiveness of economic sanctions as a foreign policy tool

	Total number of observations	Number of successes	Success as a percentage of the total (%)
All cases			
1914–1944	14	7	50
1945–1969	47	20	43
1970–1979	42	14	33
1980–1989	32	8	25
1990–2000	65	23	35
Total	200	72	36
All cases involving the United States			
1945–1969	29	16	55
1970–1979	31	9	29
1980–1989	22	3	14
1990–2000	49	16	33
Unilateral US Sanctions			
1945–1969	17	12	71
1970–1979	27	6	22
1980–1989	14	1	7
1990–2000	12	2	17

Source: Preliminary results, Hufbauer *et al.* (forthcoming).

the success rate of US cases has dropped to much lower levels. Between 1970 and 2000, the United States succeeded in roughly one-quarter of all its cases. US unilateral sanctions fared particularly poorly. Between 1945 and 1969, US unilateral sanctions achieved their goal in more than 70 percent of the cases; after 1970 the success rate dropped below 20 percent. Broadly speaking, the drop in foreign policy effectiveness was not a continuous slide, but rather a steep decline to a lower plateau.

While the European Union increasingly used its economic power as leverage for political purposes in the 1990s, these attempts to influence third countries have thus far had only limited success. In only 10 out of 34 cases identified did EU economic sanctions contribute to a successful policy outcome. A success rate of 30 percent is about equivalent to the success rate of US sanction initiatives in the 1990s. This result is not surprising since in most EU initiatives the sanctions were imposed in cooperation with other countries and in particular with the United States. Of the 34 observations identified for the 1990s, only in two instances – against Turkey (1995) and Algeria (1992–1994) – did the EU impose unilateral sanctions (Hufbauer and Oegg 2003a).

Expectations of more successful interventions by the United Nations have also not been fulfilled. With the exception of UN sanctions imposed against Libya (1992–1999) in response to the terrorist attack on Pan Am flight 103 and possibly those imposed against Yugoslavia (1991–2001) over the civil war in Bosnia, UN sanctions failed to achieve their objectives. In fact the decade long comprehensive sanctions regime against Iraq (1991–2001) and subsequent revelations about corruption within the UN Oil-For-Food program generated considerable political backlash against economic sanctions.

A common explanation for the drop in both the effectiveness of sanctions generally, and unilateral sanctions in particular, is globalization. Compared to the 1950s and 1960s, target countries found it much easier to tap into world trade and capital markets for alternative goods and finance in the 1970s, 1980s and 1990s. It has become nearly impossible for the United States, acting alone, to deny a target country access to vital markets and finance. At least the cooperation of other OECD countries is required. These global forces probably contributed as well to the shift from unilateral actions towards multilateral initiatives.

Costs of economic sanctions
Costs to the sender country
While the success of a sanctions episode is often elusive, the costs of sanctions to the sender country are not. The intent of trade sanctions is of course to reduce trade, both exports and imports. Financial sanctions and asset freezes also reduce trade. An empirical study (Hufbauer and Oegg 2003b) by the Institute for International Economics (IIE) measured the impact of economic sanctions on bilateral merchandise trade flows. The study found that extensive sanctions[5] have a large depressing effect on trade. US bilateral merchandise trade with target countries was between $11.5 billion to $25 billion lower in 1999 than is would have been without sanctions. Limited and moderate sanctions on the other hand seemed to have had very little or no impact on trade flows between the United States and the sanctioned countries.

When sized against the vast US economy, or even total trade, sanctions seem to exert a small economic impact. The reductions of bilateral trade due to extensive sanctions amount to around 0.7 percent to 1.8 percent of total US merchandise trade. However, the costs of sanctions in the sender country are never spread evenly; typically the costs are concentrated on a very few firms and communities that trade or invest in the targeted country. The US trade embargo against Libya (1978–2004), for example, primarily affected the US oil service industry. Given that industry's geographic concentration, Texas was comparatively more burdened. By the same token, the US embargo on Cuba (1960–) arguably has a much larger impact on Florida than on other states. Some domestic firms and communities may experience severe dislocation in the wake of sanctions that are aimed at foreign countries. In addition, our estimates only take into account changes in merchandise trade and not trade in services; they may therefore underestimate the total cost of economic sanctions.

We have not empirically measured the economic impact of UN and EU sanctions on the trade of sender countries. However, with the exception of comprehensive embargos on Iraq and Yugoslavia, most economic sanctions imposed by the UN and the EU are limited in nature. Since limited and moderate US sanctions had little or no effect on US bilateral trade flows, we assume the most UN and EU sanctions likewise had a relatively minor impact.

In addition to the immediate impact on bilateral trade, the adverse effects may linger long after sanctions have been lifted because firms come to be regarded as 'unreliable suppliers'. Countries may avoid buying from sender county's suppliers out of fear that one day they too might be caught up in a sanctions episode. Capital equipment exports lost today may mean lower exports in the future, because markets are lost for replacement parts and follow-up technologies. We found little empirical evidence to support this argument.

Costs to the target country

The economic impact of sanctions on the target country is largely determined by the severity of sanctions and the extent of the target country's trade and investment links with the sender country or coalition. Research by the IIE indicates that sanctions tend to be more effective as a diplomatic weapon against friends than foes. Countries with substantial trade, investment and financial relations, and close political ties with the sender, are thus more vulnerable to sanctions. But close trade, investment and financial ties with the target country also raise the economic and political costs of imposing sanctions to the sender country. This link makes the imposition of sanctions less likely (or, when imposed, less severe) against traditional partners. The United Kingdom, for example, was never enthusiastic about placing sanctions on Southern Rhodesia or South Africa; Russia was lukewarm about participating in the sanctions against Serbia; and China has never imposed sanctions on Pakistan or North Korea.

Any evaluation of the impact of sanctions on a target country must consider how easy it is for the target country to replace goods and capital. For example, unilateral US sanctions against Iran and Libya for their support of international terrorism in the 1980s imposed only modest costs on the respective countries. Iran and Libya found alternative buyers for their oil exports, and alternative suppliers of capital goods.

In terms of the economic costs of sanctions to target countries, the comprehensive UN sanctions regime against Iraq is a clear outlier. The costs of the UN embargo to the Iraqi economy may have exceeded $10 billion annually, even if the offsetting costs of the oil-for-food program are taken into account. Excluding Iraq, our research shows that, on average, the annual costs of economic sanctions to the target country economies were typically around $200 million (with a substantial variance). In fact, the majority of cases involve only minor economic sanctions with annual costs well below $100 million.

When related to target country's GNP, the impact of a majority of economic sanctions is relatively minor. In over 50 percent of the sanctions episodes we analyzed, annual economic costs did not exceed 1 per cent of GDP. Only in a few severe cases, Iraq being one of them, did costs as a percentage of GNP reach two-digit percentage levels. Similarly, per capita costs are relatively modest in the majority of cases, with annual costs often below $2 per person. Iraq again stands out with an annual per capita cost of around $800. In other words, the costs of sanctions often do not exceed the economic costs of a moderate recession.

However, the most vulnerable groups in society may bear the largest burden of sanctions. As UN sanctions against Iraq exemplify, target regimes are often skilled in using economic scarcity to solidify their control over the population. In many cases, political elites in the target country control the profitable black markets and smuggling activities created by trade embargoes, while the citizens are deprived of basic items. Child mortality rates in Iraq reportedly doubled in the 1990s.

Can sanctions be made 'smarter'?

Lessons learned from the proliferation of economic sanctions in the early 1990s sparked sanction reform efforts both within the United States as well as internationally at the UN level.

Mainly in response to UN sanctions against Iraq, scholars and human rights groups have sounded an alarm about the humanitarian effects of economic sanctions and their impact on third countries. These groups have raised serious questions regarding the legal and ethical basis for UN sanction activities. As the collateral damage from the 'blunt weapon' of comprehensive trade embargoes becomes less acceptable, more specific and creative sanctions are being invented in an effort to address these concerns. The goal is to better target economic sanctions on those responsible for the objectionable behavior.

'Targeted sanctions' or 'smart sanctions', like 'smart bombs', are meant to focus their impact on the leaders and political elites responsible for the objectionable behavior in question, while sparing powerless civilians. Growing emphasis on the individual accountability of those in power for the unlawful acts of states (highlighted by the Pinochet case and the Bosnian war crimes trials), has made the concept of targeted sanctions all the more attractive.

Targeted sanctions, such as arms embargoes, travel bans and asset freezes, are a relatively new concept. An IIE survey of sanctions cases in the twentieth century shows that in only 20 cases (out of 200) were targeted measures imposed outside the framework of comprehensive embargoes. Even in these 20 cases, targeted sanctions were almost always accompanied by selective export restrictions or aid suspensions.

Record of arms embargoes and travel bans
Arms embargoes are targeted in the sense that their purpose is to deny military and political leaders access to weapons and related military equipment. In addition, arms embargoes help to identify and stigmatize those who violate international norms. Embargoes of sensitive materiel and equipment – for example, plutonium, centrifuges and special timing devices – may have slowed the acquisition of nuclear bombs by India, Pakistan and Iran. But the effectiveness of arms embargoes in ending conflicts remains elusive. Weak enforcement, poor monitoring, and dire conditions in bordering countries all work to undermine the effectiveness of arms embargoes. The UN system has no standing military force to enforce the embargoes, and UN resolutions are often deliberately vague, leaving wide room for diverging interpretation by member states.

Trafficking in small arms is a high profit enterprise, and the profits are even greater following the imposition of an embargo. The market for illicit arms is almost as lucrative as the market for illegal drugs, and the chances of being caught are far less. The money is especially good when the targeted group controls valuable natural resources, exemplified by the control exercised by the National Union for the Total Independence of Angola (UNITA) over Angolan diamonds. UNITA used its profits from the diamond trade to finance weapons purchases. In reaction, the UN Security Council imposed an embargo on uncertified diamond exports from Angola (1993–2002). However, these sanctions were only weakly enforced until 2000. Implementation of sanctions was considerably tightened with the creation of the UN Panel of Experts and Monitoring Mechanism and may, in the end, have contributed to the weakening of UNITA's military capacity and therefore the military victory of the Angolan Armed Forces.

Travel or aviation bans can be divided into two categories: restrictions on all air travel to and from a target country, and restrictions on the travel of targeted individuals, groups or entities. In the case of restrictions on air travel to and from a target country, or areas under the control of targeted groups (such as UNITA), the assumption is that the flight ban will affect people in power substantially more than the general population. Travel bans and visa restrictions against individuals not only avoid the cost of imposing a trade embargo, but are also useful in denying legitimacy to political leaders, military officials and their supporters. Yet the assumption that flight bans exert minimal humanitarian impact may not always hold. The 1999 UN ban on all international flights by the Afghan national airline has practically grounded an airline that relied on the United Arab Emirates for maintenance. At the time, international aid agencies operating in Kabul criticized the ban. They claimed that the ban hampered their relief work and, due to the dependence of the postal service on the airline, cut off poor Afghans from money sent by relatives abroad (Constable 1999). Although it is difficult to draw general conclusions, this example calls attention to the difficulty of crafting truly 'smart sanctions'.

An interesting case study of smart sanctions that actually contributed to a successful policy outcome was the European Union 'blacklist' of Serbian President Milosevic's supporters. The 600 individuals on the blacklist were prohibited from traveling in Europe and their assets in European banks were frozen. While Milosevic and his supporters benefited from the Serbian trade embargo by controlling the black market, they did mind their personal international isolation. Cut off from their companies and bank accounts abroad, they found that conducting business became more difficult (*New York Times*, 10 February 2000 and *Financial Times*, 15 February 2000). These targeted sanctions probably contributed to the ultimate fall of President Milosevic.

Financial sanctions: What have we learned?
Financial sanctions, such as asset freezes, limiting access to financial markets, restricting economic assistance, or prohibiting new investment, have received considerable attention from practitioners and scholars. In the last few years, the Swiss government has led an international effort to study the complexities associated with asset freezes and other financial sanctions. While travel bans and arms embargoes are mostly symbolic, financial sanctions can potentially harm the targeted group, company or individual, thus increasing the likelihood of success. Empirical evidence based on our research supports this argument. Historically, financial sanctions have been more successful in achieving their foreign policy goals than, for example, trade sanctions alone.

Financial sanctions are attractive for a variety of reasons. Technical expertise, developed in international anti-money-laundering efforts for identifying and tracking financial assets, can prove useful for the implementation of targeted financial sanctions. Furthermore, the United States has substantial experience in administering financial sanctions. The US Treasury Department Office of Foreign Assets Control (OFAC) has continuously administered some form of asset freeze or other financial control since 1940. In recent years, OFAC has implemented UN-mandated freezes on foreign assets of specifically designated individuals, state-owned companies, and governments in connection with sanctions against Haiti, Serbia-Montenegro, the Bosnian Serbs, and the Angolan rebel faction UNITA. Unilateral US initiatives include the creation of a 'Specially Designated Narcotics Traffickers' (SDNT) program that identifies Colombia's drug cartels and denies them access to the US financial system and commerce with US firms. This program seems to have succeeded in hitting its targets. According to reports from OFAC, nearly a third of the businesses identified by the program between 1996 and 1999 have gone into liquidation. These companies had a combined net worth of more than $45 million and combined annual income of over $200 million (Newcomb 1998). Other effects, such as the cost to companies and individuals denied access to the US financial and commercial systems, are real but not yet quantified.

Following the attack on 11 September 2001, law enforcement focused sharply on the financial trails of terrorist networks. Existing legislation that prohibited financial transactions with terrorist organizations and 'Specially Designated Terrorists' was broadened to expand the class of targeted groups and provide authority to block US assets, and deny access to US markets to foreign banks refusing to cooperate with US investigations. Despite the substantial experience of the OFAC in administering financial sanctions, its pre-September 11 efforts to stop the money flow to terrorist organizations were not particularly successful. Dramatically improved international cooperation from individual countries, as well as at the UN level, in the wake of September 11 may have made the biggest difference in tracking down terrorist assets so far.

Conclusions

Targeted sanctions operate on a level of intervention and discrimination in the internal affairs of states that was unknown in previous decades. Their effective implementation requires a tremendous amount of detailed knowledge about the country, person and groups targeted. Identification of funds belonging to the individuals, governments and companies targeted can be difficult. Even when funds can be identified, secrecy and speed are critical to preventing targets from moving assets to numbered accounts in offshore banking centers. In many instances, countries lack the financial resources and administrative capacities to adequately monitor and enforce targeted measures making them mere symbolic gestures. However, as support for broader sanctions wanes, we are likely to see sender countries resorting to this new 'brand' of economic punishment more frequently.

Notes

1.   Other scholars and practitioners apply a much more restrictive definition of economic sanctions. See, for example, the article authored by Senator Jesse Helms in *Foreign Affairs* (January/February 1999).
2.   Iraq (1990), former Yugoslavia (1991), Liberia (1992), Libya (1992), Angola (1993), Haiti (1993), Rwanda (1994), Sudan (1996), Sierra Leone (1997), Federal Republic of Yugoslavia/Kosovo (1998), Afghanistan (1999) and Ethiopia and Eritrea (2000).
3.   See for example: Pape (1997).
4.   Policy result is scaled from 1 [failed] to 4 [success], and the sanctions contribution also scaled from 1 [negative] to 4[significant]. We multiply the two elements to derive a 'success score' that ranges in value from 1 to 16. We consider a 'success score' of nine and higher a success. Thus, a score of nine means that sanctions made a modest contribution to the goals sought by the sender country and that the goal was in part realized; a score of 16 means that sanctions made a significant contribution to a successful outcome.
5.   Because economic sanctions can take a wide variety of forms we divided cases into three categories. Extensive sanctions are comprehensive trade and financial embargoes such as those against Iraq or Cuba. Limited sanctions are minor aid cuts or travel sanctions, while broader trade and financial sanctions like asset freezes and investment bans are moderate sanctions.

References

Anthony, Ian. (2002), 'Sanctions Applied by the European Union and the United Nations,' *SIPRI Yearbook 2002: Armaments, Disarmament and International Security*, Stockholm: Oxford University Press, pp. 203–28.

Constable, Pamela (1999), 'Flights of Frustration,' *Washington Post*, 6 December 1999, A17.

Crossette, Barbara (1999), 'A Delay in the Security Council Blocks Relief Aid for Afghanistan,' *New York Times*, 16 December, A10.

Drezner, Daniel (1999), *The Sanctions Paradox: Economic Statecraft and International Relations*, Cambridge Studies in International Relations, no. 65, Cambridge: Cambridge University Press.

Hufbauer, Gary and Barbara Oegg (2003a), 'The European Union as Emerging Sender of Economic Sanctions,' *Aussenwirtschaft*, **58**, 547–71.

Hufbauer, Gary Clyde and Barbara Oegg (2003b), 'The Impact of Economic Sanctions on US Trade: Andrew Rose's Gravity Model,' Policy Brief 03-4, Washington, DC: Institute for International Economics.

Hufbauer, Gary Clyde, Jeffrey J. Schott, Kimberly Ann Elliott and Barbara Oegg (forthcoming), *Economic Sanctions Reconsidered* (3rd edn), Washington, DC: Institute for International Economics.

New York Times (2000), 'US Supports Tightening of Sanctions on Belgrade', Jane Perlez, 10 February, A12.

Newcomb, Richard R. (1998), 'Targeting Financial Sanctions', paper presented at the First Interlaken Seminar on Targeting United Nations Financial Sanctions, 17–19 March, available at: www.smartsanctions.ch.

Norman, Peter (2000), 'Serbian Sanctions Air Travel Eased, But Visa Ban Extended to More of Milosevic's Cronies', *The Financial Times*, 15 February.

Pape, Robert A. (1997), 'Why Economic Sanctions Do not Work,' *International Security*, **22**(2), 90–136.

Further readings on sanctions

Carter, Barry E. (1988), *International Economic Sanctions: Improving the Haphazard US Legal Regime*, Cambridge: Cambridge University Press.

Center for Strategic and International Studies (1999), 'Altering US Sanctions Policy', Final Report of the CSIC Project on Unilateral Economic Sanctions, Washington: CSIS, February.

Cortright, David and George A. Lopez (eds) (1995), *Economic Sanctions: Panacea or Peacebuilding in a Post-Cold War World?* Boulder, CO: Westview Press.

Cortright, David and George A. Lopez (2000), *The Sanctions Decade: Assessing UN Strategies in the 1990s*, Boulder, CO: Lynne Rienner Publishers.

Doxey, Margaret P. (1980), *Economic Sanctions and International Enforcement* (2nd edn), New York: Oxford University Press, for Royal Institute of International Affairs.

Drezner, Daniel W. (1999), *The Sanctions Paradox: Economic Statecraft and International Relations*, Cambridge Studies in International Relations, no. 65, Cambridge: Cambridge University Press.

de Jonge Oudraat, Chantal (2000), 'Making Sanctions Work,' *Survival*, **42**(3) 105–27.

Elliott, Kimberly Ann and Gary Clyde Hufbauer (1999), 'Same Song, Same Refrain? Economic Sanctions in the 1990's,' *American Economic Review*, **89**(2), 403–8.

Haass, Richard N. (1998), *Economic Sanctions and American Diplomacy*, New York: Council on Foreign Relations.

Hufbauer, Gary Clyde, Jeffrey J. Schott and Kimberly Ann Elliott (forthcoming), *Economic Sanctions Reconsidered* (3rd edn), Washington: Institute for International Economics.

Malloy, Michael P. (1990), *Economic Sanctions and US Trade*, Boston: Little, Brown.

Preeg, Ernest H. (1999), *Feeling Good or Doing Good with Sanctions: Unilateral Economic Sanctions and the US National Interest*, Washington: Center for Strategic and International Studies.

Rodman, Kenneth A. (2001), *Sanctions Beyond Borders: Multinational Corporations, Extraterritoriality, and US Economic Statecraft*, Lanham, MD: Rowman & Littlefield.

US Library of Congress (1988), *US Economic Sanctions Imposed Against Specific Foreign Countries: 1979 to the Present*, CRS Report for Congress 88-612 F, rvd. 9 September, Washington, DC: Congressional Research Service.

Weiss, Thomas G., David Cortright, George A. Lopez and Larry Minear (eds) (1997), *Political Gain and Civilian Pain*, Lanham, MD: Rowman & Littlefield Publishers.

48 Trade related aspects of intellectual property: enforcement issues
William A. Kerr

Introduction

In trade policy, the imposition of retaliatory tariffs has been the accepted method of sanctioning countries that are judged to have not lived up to their multilateral commitments. This sanctioning provision was enshrined in the 1947 General Agreement on Tariffs and Trade (GATT 1947) although it was seldom called upon largely because the Contracting Parties tended to abide by their commitments. If there was an accusation of 'nullification of benefits', the consensus-based dispute resolution system, which required the agreement of the country accused of not living up to its multilateral commitments, usually meant that Panel recommendations were not accepted. Effectively, this meant that retaliatory tariffs could not be imposed.

The use of tariffs as a punishing mechanism in trade was also well understood in the pre-GATT 1947 era where tit-for-tat ramping up of tariff levels was a hallmark of bilateral 'trade wars'. The lose–lose outcome of tit-for-tat retaliations, however, was well understood by economists and trade policy makers. Thus, while it was understood that some form of enforcement mechanism was required in multilateral trade agreements, it was important that it did not lead to a destructive cycle of ever increasing tariffs. Thus, accepted retaliation became a central principle of the GATT 1947 (Kerr and Perdikis 1995). Accepted retaliation meant that a country that could not comply with the judgment of a GATT panel would accept retaliation from the Contracting Party(ies) that the panel ruled in favour of; and would not re-retaliate. Even if seldom used, the idea of retaliation was deemed a necessary threat to give credibility to the multilateral system of trade rules and to induce countries to participate.

The imposition of retaliatory tariffs on countries that would not comply with a panel ruling was, however, strictly proscribed. The value of trade lost due to the imposition of retaliatory tariffs was not to exceed the value of the benefits that had been nullified by the actions of the country ruled against by the GATT panel. The aggrieved country was allowed to choose the goods upon which it would impose retaliatory tariffs and the levels of those tariffs. Typically, the products chosen for retaliatory tariffs were those considered sensitive in the offending country so that the maximum lobbying pressure would be applied on the offending government to alter its original policy (Kerr and Hobbs 2005). Once the country complied with the panel, the retaliatory tariffs would be withdrawn.

Of course, the entire retaliatory exercise was counterproductive to the aims of the multilateral trading system. The original restriction on trade that brought forth the complaint remains in place and trade is further restricted by the retaliatory tariffs. The industry that has had its benefits nullified is not better off. Given that 'innocent bystander' industries can be targeted for retaliatory tariffs, the risks associated with investing in production for export increased. Despite these counterproductive aspects of retaliation, the system was carried over into the GATT 1994 and enshrined in the World Trade Organization (WTO).

The acceptance of retaliation can be viewed as a crucial linchpin of the multilateral system from a political perspective – it limits the sovereignty granted to multilateral trade institutions. It means that a country can choose to ignore its already agreed commitments in the GATT/WTO if the domestic political cost of compliance is deemed to be too high. Hence, trade commitments may be ignored, but not without cost. The cost is the loss of exports by the producers of products selected for retaliatory tariffs and the political fall-out that follows from it. Domestic politicians are choosing one domestic political constituency over another. The most high profile WTO dispute where acceptance of retaliation was chosen over compliance is the case of a European ban on importation of beef produced using growth hormones.[1] The US and Canada, where the use of growth hormones in beef production is legal and widespread, initiated a WTO dispute over the EU ban. The Panel found in favour of the US and Canada and ordered the EU to bring its import regulations into compliance with its WTO commitments. Given the contentious nature of growth hormones among some European Union consumers, the European Commission chose not to comply with the Panel and the US and Canada imposed retaliatory sanctions. The European Union did not remove its ban on the import of beef produced using hormones once the retaliatory tariffs were put in place. Thus, the efficacy of retaliatory tariffs is called into question.

In international relations, the use of restrictions on trade is not confined to purely trade matters. Trade restrictions, in the form of sanctions, are also recognized as one of the mechanisms available to countries attempting to induce other countries to change their behaviour. Trade sanctions lie along a continuum that has diplomacy (termed moral suasion by economists) at one extreme and military force at the other. By imposing trade sanctions, it is hoped that the economic costs suffered by the country engaging in the behaviour judged unacceptable by its trading partners will be sufficient to induce it to alter its behaviour. Trade sanctions have been applied by the United Nations against a number of countries – Apartheid era South Africa, Iraq, Serbia, and so on – and unilaterally – by the US against Cuba. Under the United Nations, the ability to apply sanctions is limited to the Security Council. The efficacy of trade sanctions applied for political reasons in inducing a change of behaviour in the targeted country is mixed at best. In some cases, the use of military force has been required to induce a change of behaviour – implying that the cost of sanctions was not sufficient inducement. The way that trade sanctions are applied might be improved to enhance their efficacy[2] but it is likely that they will only be effective in a limited set of circumstances. The ability to apply trade sanctions has also been included in a number of multilateral environmental agreements (MEAs) but these remain largely untested because MEAs have not been endowed with binding dispute settlement mechanisms (Kerr and Hall 2004).[3] As we will see below, the use of trade sanctions to induce a change of behaviour by Member States was enshrined in the WTO when it was established in 1994. The behaviour change envisioned was enforcement of foreign intellectual property rights. As a result, the efficacy of trade sanctions in inducing compliance has become an important issue in trade policy. Other interests would also like to acquire the ability to punish foreign government that engage in activities they do not agree with such as lax or poorly enforced environmental regulations, labour standards, animal welfare standards, and so on (Kerr 2001; Gordon *et al.* 2001)

Trade sanctions and intellectual property in the WTO
The proportion of the value of goods comprised of intellectual property increased dramatically over the last 20 years of the twentieth century and this trend has continued into the twenty-first century. While computer programs are the most visible manifestation of the increasing importance of intellectual property – not only in the computers used directly by individuals but also through their inclusion in a wide range of consumer goods such as automobiles and capital goods such as robots – intellectual property is increasingly important in such diverse fields as nanotechnology and modern biotechnology. Intellectual property, and particularly the generation of future intellectual property, are cornerstones of the 'knowledge economy' around which most developed countries have planned their future growth.

The protection of intellectual property lies at the heart of the knowledge economy strategy of developed countries as it provides the incentive for private sector investment in innovative activities. Increased investments in innovative activity has meant, however, that product life cycles have been shortened – because new or improved models or substitute products come along much more quickly. As a result, to increase the probability that an investment in innovative activities has a positive return, access to the widest possible markets is required – including access to markets in developing countries (Boyd *et al.* 2003).

As developing countries produce little intellectual property, they have little incentive to protect it. Protecting the intellectual property of foreign firms is not perceived as a good use of their scarce resources. Further, developing countries observe that they suffer the losses associated with the monopoly granted innovators without gaining any of the long term benefits. This complaint is particularly acute in pharmaceuticals where the large numbers of poor people may not be able to afford monopoly prices for drugs and in agriculture where impoverished farmers may not be able to access inputs sold at monopoly prices.

Prior to 1994 and the establishment of the WTO, the international management of intellectual property was co-ordinated under the World Intellectual Property Organization (WIPO). A plethora of previous agreements on patents, copyright, trademarks and so on. was administered by the WIPO. The WIPO was a plurilateral organization without compulsory membership and, as a result, many developing countries did not belong. Further, the WIPO had no binding dispute settlement system and no enforcement mechanism. This was a frustrating organizational structure for firms based in developed countries seeking to expand the markets where protection for intellectual property was provided. It seemed particularly unlikely that the WIPO could be reformed to provide it with a strong enforcement mechanism – developing countries had no incentive to agree.

At the negotiations that established the scope of the GATT's Uruguay Round it was agreed that the protection of intellectual property would be brought under the umbrella of the multilateral trading system. In fact, the GATT was replaced by the WTO which was specifically designed to provide an enforcement mechanism for the international protection of intellectual property. The GATT's already existing right to impose trade sanctions was central to the enforcement intellectual property rights internationally.

The WTO was given responsibility for administering three agreements: (a) a revised GATT agreement, GATT 1994; (b) a new agreement on trade in services, the General Agreement on Trade in Services (GATS); and (c) the Agreement on Trade Related Aspects of Intellectual Property (TRIPS). The WTO was also given a new binding disputes settlement mechanism that was to be applied to all three agreements. The centrepiece of the dispute settlement mechanism was cross-agreement retaliation whereby a failure to live up to commitments in one WTO agreement could be sanctioned through actions taken under another agreement. Specifically, a failure to provide protection for the intellectual property of foreign firms under the terms of the TRIPS could be punished by the imposition of trade barriers on imports of goods from the offending country under the GATT 1994.[4] The TRIPS was made mandatory for WTO members – so that a country could not obtain the benefits arising for trade in goods and services under the GATT and GATS unless it agreed to protect foreign intellectual property under the TRIPS. Thus the weaknesses of the WIPO – lack of compulsory membership and the absence of an enforcement mechanism – were corrected in the WTO.[5] This was, however, a major departure in the development of international trade policy institutions. In effect, the World Trade Organization was given the role of being the adjudicator of the international protection of foreign intellectual property and indirectly the multilateral international property policeman – although the direct sanctioning power lies with the individual Member States through their ability to apply WTO authorized retaliatory trade sanctions. The WTO was essentially captured by those with an interest in increasing the international protection of intellectual property. There is little doubt that the WTO was chosen as the institution to undertake this role due to the GATT already having been granted the power to allow the imposition of trade sanctions. Given that other interests would like the ability to impose trade sanctions on countries that do not share their social policy view, the cross-agreement retaliation function of the WTO regarding the protection of foreign intellectual property warrants careful scrutiny.

While far from happy with having to accept the TRIPS, developing countries agreed because they were promised increased market access for their agricultural products and textiles under the GATT 1994.[6] TRIPS commitments require all members of the WTO to put in place a domestic legal regime to protect intellectual property that conforms to international standards (for example 20-year protection for patents),[7] grants 'national treatment' for foreign intellectual property, provides for judicial penalties for those who engage in piracy and to make resources available for enforcement. The latter provision, however, is vague and as yet untested in a WTO dispute. Developing and least developed countries were granted longer implementation periods than developed countries; otherwise all countries are expected to provide similar degrees of protection for foreign intellectual property.

If a Member State believes that another Member State is not protecting the intellectual property of its firms it can bring a complaint to the WTO dispute mechanism. If its allegation is supported by a WTO Panel and the offending country does not alter its domestic intellectual property regime in the ways suggested by the Panel, the aggrieved party can be authorized to retaliate through the withdrawal of TRIPS protection or across agreements through the imposition of trade sanctions under the GATT.[8] Given that most developing countries produce little intellectual property, direct retaliation through the TRIPS is unlikely to be effective and the imposition of trade sanctions via cross-agreement retaliation is the likely result.

The efficacy of cross-agreement retaliation for failure to protect foreign intellectual property under TRIPS

The elaborate restructuring of multilateral trade institutions, in large part to provide a means to sanction countries that fail to protect foreign intellectual property, is premised on the assumption that the threat of the imposition of trade sanctions will be sufficient to induce countries to live up to their TRIPS commitments. In an extensive search of the literature, Yampoin and Kerr (1996) found no indication that the question of the efficacy of trade sanctions had been formally assessed prior to the end of the Uruguay Round. Thus, cross-agreement retaliation appears to have been a 'leap of faith' among advocate Member States during the Uruguay Round negotiations. The question has received little attention since the WTO came into being.

The efficacy of trade sanctions in providing an incentive to enforce foreign intellectual property rights was examined using a static model by Yampoin and Kerr (1998). As there is little information on the enforcement costs associated with the protection of intellectual property, particularly in developing countries, they assumed a best case for enforcement – zero cost to the developing country. Even under this optimistic assumption, it was found that under only a limited set of market conditions would the costs that trade sanctions impose on the country exceed the benefits of allowing firms to engage in piracy. Only if the pirate industry was small would trade sanctions provide sufficient incentive to enforce intellectual property rights by shutting down pirate industries. Of course, if the pirate industry was small, it would be difficult for firms to convince their governments to mount a TRIPS challenge at the WTO. As the size of the pirate industry increases, the probability of trade sanctions being effective declines – which is when firms owning intellectual property would most desire its protection. Yampoin and Kerr (1998) also found that to establish the appropriate value of the sanctions to be applied requires the construction of a counterfactual argument based on assumptions that can always be challenged.

Gaisford *et al.* (2002) investigate the efficacy of trade sanctions using game theory. They develops a model of an enforcement game between a developing country's government and a foreign holder of intellectual property rights to examine the efficacy of the WTO's TRIPS agreement for the protection of intellectual property. The conclusion is that the TRIPS is unlikely to provide sufficient protection and, thus, will lead to sub-optimal levels of investment in innovative activities. Some key findings of their analysis were that the presence of the trade penalty for infractions of intellectual property rights under the WTO will, under some circumstances, have no impact on the enforcement of these rights in developing countries. This could occur, for example, if the effectiveness of enforcement was particularly low. Lower penalties and smaller probabilities of penalty also increase the likelihood of completely ineffective enforcement. Further, as the magnitude of the trade penalty increases, eventually the level of enforcement will begin to rise. Thus, at some point, the penalty will become large enough to encourage positive enforcement. Finally, the trade penalty may have to be infinite to completely eliminate pirate production at least on some markets. Since this is not a reasonable expectation, some pirate production can be expected to persist on such markets even if highly punitive penalties are introduced. They conclude that the current penalty mechanism may not be effective under all circumstances and, as a result, the TRIPS may simply result in trade distortions that are completely unrelated to the original intellectual property violation. They suggest that this calls into question the efficacy of linking trade penalties to the protection of intellectual property.

Beyond the conclusions from theoretical investigations, intellectual property piracy in developing countries does not appear to have been significantly deterred by the threat of cross-agreement retaliation through the WTO. Intellectual property piracy is continuing unabated and is likely increasing.[9] Developed countries appear reluctant to bring TRIPS violations forward to the WTO disputes system. Given the limited theoretical evidence available to date, it may be wiser to leave the threat untested.

Conclusion

Trade sanctions have had a limited role in trade policy, although they have had a well recognized role in international political relations. Trade sanctions are imposed in the hope of altering the behaviour of governments, not in the aid of trade policy objectives – although the mechanisms such as border taxes and import prohibitions may be used for both purposes. A major change in the development of trade policy occurred during the Uruguay Round when the structure of the WTO was negotiated. The multilateral trading system was redesigned so that it could be used to sanction governments for non-trade reasons – specifically the failure of governments to protect foreign intellectual property. Other interests may also wish to use trade sanctions to change the behaviour of governments.

The question of the efficacy of trade sanctions as an enforcement mechanism is central to this (and other possible) expansion in the scope of trade policy. The question, however, has been little studied. The limited evidence to date suggests that the applications of trade sanctions in cases where governments fail to protect intellectual property are unlikely to be effective. As a result, the question of trade sanctions in trade policy probably deserves more attention than it has thus far received.

While a strong case can be made on global welfare grounds for the international protection of intellectual property, accomplishing that goal will probably require that a means for sharing the benefits of innovation with developing countries be found – the proverbial carrot (Boyd *et al.* 2003). The evidence thus far suggests that the 'stick' of WTO sanctioned retaliation through barriers to trade in goods is unlikely to lead to the result desired by those that produce intellectual property or the governments that have premised their future relative prosperity on the knowledge economy.

Notes

1. See Kerr and Hobbs (2005) for an analysis of the beef hormone case.
2. See Kerr and Gaisford (1994) for a discussion of how the efficacy of trade sanctions put in place for political reasons could be enhanced.
3. Along with the right to sanction members, some MEAs also have the right to sanction non-members. As yet, this power has not been formally challenged but sanctioning non-members of voluntary international organizations has the potential to be an important issue in international law. See Isaac and Kerr (2003) and Hobbs *et al.* (2005) for a discussion of this issue in the context of trade in the products of biotechnology
4. Interestingly, countries have begun to withdraw the protection of intellectual property under the TRIPS when other countries fail to comply with panel decisions regarding practices under the GATT 1994. This tactic has been used or threatened by developing countries that could not credibly punish large developed economies by imposing barriers on trade in goods. This form of cross-agreement retaliation was not likely anticipated by those that designed the WTO.
5. The WIPO retains its role in administering previous agreements regarding intellectual property and in developing international standards in new areas of intellectual property protection.
6. These expected benefits, to a considerable degree, failed to materialize as developed countries limited market access for agricultural products through 'dirty tariffication' and the use of contingent protection measures and bilateral arrangements to offset the dismantling of the import quotas of the Multifiber Agreement. Developing country dissatisfaction with what they perceive as the Uruguay Round having been reneged on has been manifest in the difficult and acrimonious negotiations over 'implementation issues' in the Doha Round (Kerr 2005).

7.   See Gaisford and Richardson (2000) for a discussion of internationally standardized protection for intellectual property.
8.   It would also be possible to withdraw commitments to open services markets under the GATS.
9.   See for example USTR (2003). Loppacher and Kerr (2004) provide a discussion of enforcement in one major developing country that has recently accepted TRIPS commitments – China.

References

Boyd, S.L., W.A. Kerr and N. Perdikis (2003), 'Agricultural Biotechnology Innovations versus Intellectual Property Rights – Are Developing Countries at the Mercy of Multinationals?' *The Journal of World Intellectual Property*, **6**(2), 211–32.

Gaisford, J. D. and R. S. Richardson (2000), 'The TRIPS Disagreement: Should GATT Traditions Have Been Abandoned?' *Estey Centre Journal of International Law and Trade Policy*, **1**(2), 137–69, www.esteyjournal.com.

Gaisford, J. D., R. Tarvydas, J. E. Hobbs and W. A. Kerr (2002), 'Biotechnology Piracy: Rethinking the International Protection of Intellectual Property,' *Canadian Journal of Agricultural Economics*, **50**(1), 1–14.

Gordon, D. V., R. Hannesson and W. A. Kerr (2001), 'Of Fish and Whales: The Credibility of Threats in International Trade Disputes,' *Journal of Policy Modeling*, **23**(1), 83–98.

Hobbs, A. L., J. E. Hobbs and W. A. Kerr (2005), 'The Biosafety Protocol: Multilateral Agreement on Protecting the Environment or Protectionist Club?' *Journal of World Trade*, **39**(2), 281–300.

Isaac, G. E. and W. A. Kerr (2003), 'GMO's at the WTO – A Harvest of Trouble,' *Journal of World Trade*, **37**(6), 1083–95.

Kerr, W. A. (2005), *Agriculture: A Key to the WTO Doha Development Agenda*, proceedings of an Asian Development Bank High Level Meeting on WTO Key Doha Round Issues, Osaka, Japan, 3–5 August, http://www.adb.org/Documents/Events/2005/High-Level-Meeting-on-WTO/paper-kerr.pdf.

Kerr, W. A. (2001), 'The World Trade Organization and the Environment,' in H. J. Michelman, J. Rude, J. Stabler and G. Storey (eds), *Globalization and Agricultural Trade Policy*, Boulder, CO: Lynne Rienner, pp. 53–65.

Kerr, W. A. and J. D. Gaisford (1994), 'A Note on Increasing the Effectiveness of Sanctions,' *Journal of World Trade*, **28**(6), 169–76.

Kerr, W. A. and S. L. Hall (2004), 'Multilateral Environmental Agreements and Agriculture: Commitments, Cooperation and Conflicts,' *Current Agriculture, Food and Resource Issues*, **5**, 39–52.

Kerr, W. A. and J. E. Hobbs (2005), 'Consumers, Cows and Carousels: Why the Dispute Over Beef Hormones is Far More Important than Its Commercial Value,' in N. Perdikis and R. Read (eds), *The WTO and the Regulation of International Trade*, Cheltenham, UK and Northampton, MA, USA: Edward Elgar, pp. 191–214.

Kerr, W. A. and N. Perdikis (1995), *The Economics of International Business*, London: Chapman and Hall.

Loppacher, L. J. and W. A. Kerr (2004), 'Integrating China's Biotechnology Industry into Global Knowledge Creation – Intellectual Property is the Key,' *Journal of World Intellectual Property*, **7**(4), 549–62.

United States Trade Representative (USTR) (2003), *2003 Special 301 Report*, available online at http://www.ustr.gov/reports/2003/special301–306.htm.

Yampoin, R. and W. A. Kerr (1996), *Suppressing the New Pirates: Protection of Intellectual Property Rights in Asia – A Challenge for the World Trade Organization*, EPRI Report No. 96-01, Excellence in the Pacific Research Institute, University of Lethbridge, Lethbridge.

Yampoin, R. and W. A. Kerr (1998), 'Can Trade Measures Induce Compliance With Trips?' *Journal of the Asia Pacific Economy*, **3**(2), 165–82.

Index